W9-CGN-621

AMERICAN GOVERNMENT

Strategy and Choice

PETER H. ARANSON
Emory University

WINTHROP PUBLISHERS
Cambridge, Massachusetts

Library of Congress Cataloging in Publication Data

Aranson, Peter H.
American Government.

Includes indexes.
1. United States—Politics and government.
2. Political science—Decision making. I. Title.
JK274.A78 320.973 80-28356
ISBN 0-87626-023-7

For DONNA LYNN,
HANNAH FREDA,
and
ELI SAMUEL

17 Dunster Street, Cambridge, Massachusetts 02138

10 9 8 7 6 5 4 3 2 1

Contents

Preface

My goal in writing this book was to provide the reader with a comprehensive view of the substance of American politics and government using elementary rational choice theory throughout. (Rational choice theory is also called positive political theory, formal theory, deductive theory, public choice theory, game theory, decision theory, and somewhat inaccurately, empirical theory and the economic approach to politics.)

This goal posed three challenges. First, while political scientists have been "doing" rational choice theory for a quarter of a century (and economists, for much longer), this approach has not yet widely penetrated the political science curriculum. Some students seem unprepared for the rigor of economics in politics and government courses. While the text does not sacrifice rigor, it does hold the use of symbols to a minimum. Furthermore, the mathematics involved is at the level of students who have completed one year of high school algebra. Finally, all analytical concepts and operations are accompanied by common sense examples drawn from hypothetical or real political and governmental situations.

The second challenge concerned the limited extent to which rational choice theory had been applied to the entire range of political and governmental decision making. The progress of a science enjoys its own logic, unencumbered by pedagogical concerns. Positive political theory initially concentrated on various aspects of elections and coalitions, with only limited (but nevertheless significant) attention to bureaucratic, judicial, and interest-group decision making. Such limitations were very much in mind when I began to write this book. At first, I thought I would have to construct theory as I went along, and indeed in many places, such as in the discussion of franchise extension, I have done so. But in the intervening years since I began this work, political scientists have applied their new and powerful analytical tools of public choice theory to an ever expanding set of phenomena. Certain phenomena remain to be explored using these tools—for example, procedural rules such as the Supreme Court's "rule of four" are likely candidates for analysis. But today the author of a text such as this one is less concerned with failing to explain a particular phenomenon and more concerned with failing to have included a recent scholarly contribution about that phenomenon, so rapid is the development in this field of political science.

The third challenge follows from the first two. Explaining new analytical concepts takes space, yet I was determined not to compromise the text's coverage of the substance of American politics and government. To my surprise, this challenge evaporated, as I *should* have expected. Good theory promotes parsimonious explanation and allows substance to be organized and presented efficiently. Accordingly, this text covers traditional substantive concerns as completely as most other texts. But the organization is somewhat different. For example, franchise extension, mentioned earlier, now appears in the chapter about the link between elections and public policy (Chapter 8), rather than in its place in a traditional text at the beginning. Furthermore, rational choice theory compels a far greater attention here to candidate decision making, bureaucracy, and litigation than one finds in other texts.

As a natural outgrowth of its theoretical perspective, the book is also cumulative in the material covered. One cannot read chapters at random, as one would an encyclopedia, for a grasp of the material in any one chapter depends on understanding the preceding chapters. In this respect the text is more like a science text than is the traditional American government book.

The specific intellectual debts I have incurred in writing this book are well documented in its footnotes, but certain people deserve special mention. Ferdinand K. Levy, former Dean of the Georgia Institute of Technology College of Management, and Henry G. Manne, Director of the Law and Economics Center of Emory University, contributed to this book by the kind of intellectual environment and support they provided me at their respective institutions. While neither is a political scientist, each fully understood the importance of this text and warmly encouraged its progress and completion.

Several people read the manuscript and suggested substantial improvements. These include John Aldrich, Paul Aranson, Robert Craig, James Enelow, Melvin Hinich, Samuel Krislov, William Mitchell, Morris Ogul, Peter Ordeshook, David Saffell, and Robert Salisbury.

My secretary, Mrs. David (Gillian) Lisle skillfully typed the final draft of the manuscript and efficiently coordinated the many other tasks associated with completing a project of this magnitude.

James J. Murray III, President and Political Science Editor of Winthrop Publishers, Inc., showed unusual patience, persistence, and faith in the text and kept the project on track at several critical points. Robert Duchacek and

Herbert Nolan, also of Winthrop, diligently and painstakingly directed the book's production.

Finally, the dedication expresses my deepest appreciation for the love, kindness, and support my wife Donna has always given me and as well records our wish that this book might help to make a better world for our children.

P. H. A.

Atlanta, Georgia

Part I

Theory

Since the establishment of the Constitution of the United States in 1788, the size of the public sector in America has grown at a faster rate than the size of the private sector. As a consequence, politics and government now figure importantly in the life of every American, and if past trends continue, each of us can expect politics and government to become even more important in the future.

The public sector in the United States is made up of several government organizations (legislatures, bureaus, courts, and cabinets) at the federal, state, and local level. Each organization produces various goods and services, in different quantities (levels), at different prices (costs), and of different quality. Calling the "products" of these organizations "goods and services" does not mean that government and politics only concern economic problems. Of course, the quantities, qualities, and prices of these goods and services are sometimes easy to measure in economic terms. For instance, we can try to calculate the cost of sending a letter by mail. But at other times, it is more difficult to calculate the quantity, quality, or price of a publicly supplied good or service. For example, even experts find it difficult to measure our level of national defense; nor can we easily calculate the costs and benefits of public actions concerning emotional issues, such as equal rights for women, abortion, prayer in the schools, busing to achieve racial integration, and freedom of the press.

This book's central goal is to provide the reader with the tools needed to explain past actions taken in the public sector and to predict future ones. These explanations and predictions rest on the fundamental postulate that people's actions follow explicitly or implicitly from their decisions. Hence, this book helps the reader to explain and predict actions taken in the public sector by explaining and predicting the decisions of those who make up the public sector: citizens, voters, activists, candidates, senators and representatives, presidents and vice-presidents, bureaucrats, and judges.

This book is divided into four parts. Part I, entitled "Theory," provides the tools necessary to understand how people make decisions in general and political and governmental decisions in particular. Part II, entitled "Elections," first explains the rules under which Americans conduct their elections and then analyzes the decisions of those who participate in them: citizens, activists, and candidates. Part III, entitled "Institutions," examines decision making by members of Congress, the president, bureaucrats, and judges. Part IV, entitled "The Coming Agenda," analyzes the effects of adopting several proposals to reform American politics and government.

Chapter 1 begins by distinguishing between collective actions, which are political and governmental actions resting on a coercive sanction, and private actions, which are largely voluntary. The chapter then describes the nature, extent, and growth of collective action in the United States. Collective actions result from decisions, and a reasonable way to explain and predict decisions is to assume that people's choices reflect the efficient pursuit of their goals. This assumption is called the *postulate of rational choice.* In explaining and predicting political and governmental decision making in the United States, this book relies on the postulate of rational choice.

The term "rational" as used here is a technical term, which implies nothing about the "correctness" of a decision or the "sanity" of the decision maker. Nor must people explicitly calculate the effects of each decision they make. The postulate of rational choice requires only that they act *as if* they do. Finally, though they are "rational," decision makers may care passionately about what they are doing. This book's gentle reader will certainly understand that politics and government engage the deepest and sometimes the most violent aspects of human nature.

Chapter 2 describes elements of the theory of human choice. When we apply this theory to explain and predict private action, we call it *economics.* When we apply it to explain and predict political and governmental decisions, we call it *political science.* Chapter 2 first describes the components and conditions of every decision-making situation. Then, the chapter illustrates how to explain and predict decisions that people make under three different conditions: certainty, risk, and uncertainty. While this discussion of decision making is necessarily abstract, each example of a decision is drawn from American politics and government.

Chapter 3 uses the decision theory that Chapter 2 describes to explain and predict the first and most fundamental decision in politics and government: the decision to place some area of human action in the private sector or in the public sector. If there has been no collective action, then the first decision to make some action collective is tantamount to creating a government. Chapter 3 then describes the desirable and undesirable consequences of both private choice and collective choice. Of course, to explain and predict whether someone would choose to make some action private or collective requires that we find out how that person evaluates the relative desirable and undesirable consequences of private and collective choice. Chapter 3 provides some tools to make such judgments.

Because we concentrate on people's preferences and decisions, we are able to identify three major problems in representative democracies such as the United States. (These problems are undoubtedly present in dictatorships and in other forms of government.) The first problem, which Chapter 2 introduces, is an incoherence in collective decision making: no apparent relationship may exist between the preferences and decisions of the citizens on the one hand and collective action (public policy) on the other. Stated differently, the citizens' actions in voting for particular public policies or candidates in elections cannot be aggregated or summarized or distilled in a way that would instruct candidates or officeholders which public policies to adopt. Stated yet another way, decision making in representative democracies, through voting in electoral and legislative processes, creates no public policy equilibrium. One effect of this problem is that candidates will not know which public policy positions will win elections. Consequently, they may not make these positions plain in their campaigns.

The second major problem, which Chapter 3 introduces, is the lack of a relationship between theoretical reasons for collective action and actual reasons for collective action. For example, according to the theory of collective action to which most economists and political scientists would subscribe, the president and the members of Congress should choose missile systems, military base locations, and naval vessel designs using criteria that measure national defense benefits for the entire nation. However, both in theory and in practice, government decision makers ordinarily choose among national defense alternatives according to the likelihood of winning election or reelection in particular states or districts and gaining the support of various interest groups. In sum, "private" benefits (for states, districts, and interest groups) motivate collective decisions where a consideration of "public" benefits should prevail.

The third problem, which Chapter 7 introduces, is collective action in the presence of intense minorities. These are groups of voters who judge candidates according to their positions on a single issue, while ignoring their positions on all other issues. The presence of intense minorities leads candidates and officeholders to withdraw from public policy position taking, and public policy positions are again made ambiguous if they are discussed at all. Theoretically desirable policies also may not be identifiable in the presence of intense minorities, since no one knows whether to satisfy the intense minority or the relatively more apathetic majority.

These three problems are endemic to representative democracy and have no apparent solutions in collective choice. However, these problems arise in different contexts, and proposals for change and reform will affect the frequency and severity with which they occur. Hence, the consideration of these problems occurs throughout this book.

1

The Study of American Politics and Government

This book is about politics and government in the United States. Here, *politics* and *government* refer to human actions involving **public choice,** public decision making, sometimes called collective choice or nonmarket decision making. Other human actions involve **private choice,** private decision making. Politics and government thus make up the domain of **collective action,** while other human events make up the domain of **private action.**

PRIVATE ACTION, COLLECTIVE ACTION, AND PUBLIC POLICY

Private action. Private action occurs without force or the threat of force—that is, without physical coercion.[1] If people act privately, then both their actions and the actions of those with whom they interact are voluntary. People engage in particular forms of private action because they prefer to, not

[1] Brainwashing raises a problem under this definition of private action. The study of brainwashing is more in the realm of the psychologist than of the political scientist. (For example, I do not know what the correct verdict in the Patricia Hearst case would be. Hearst, granddaughter of newspaper magnate William Randolph Hearst, was kidnapped by an underground group calling itself the Symbionese Liberation Army (SLA) on February 4, 1974 and was found by the FBI on September 18, 1975. Following her abduction, she participated in a bank robbery and made propaganda tapes for the SLA. At her trial for bank robbery, she pleaded innocent on the grounds that she had been brainwashed. She was released through executive (presidential)

because others threaten them with force. Most marketplace actions (producing, buying, and selling, for example) are private, although there are important exceptions.

Collective action. Collective action occurs with force or the threat of force. If people engage in particular forms of collective action, then either someone forces their actions, or they force someone else's actions, or the force is reciprocal. Political and governmental actions are collective because they occur simultaneously with force or the threat of force.[2]

Few human actions are either purely private or purely collective. For example, marriage seems to be private: it is a voluntary agreement of consenting persons. But if these persons are too young, if there are more than two of them, if they are of the same sex, or if they try to end the agreement without a judge's permission, then they will learn just how collective marriage can be. Economic exchange in the marketplace provides a second example of how private and collective actions are interrelated. While exchange itself is voluntary, it rests on laws about property and the conditions under which rights to use it may be bought and sold. Chapter 3 shows that if a correct set of laws about property is adopted, exchanges become more efficient and everyone's welfare increases. Otherwise, welfare declines. Thus, particular forms of collective action not only set the terms of private action, but also affect the relative desirability of private action.

Public policy. The fundamental political problem in any nation is to determine which actions shall be private and which collective. A subsidiary problem is how to make a particular action collective. For example, shall

---

clemency on February 1, 1979.) If brainwashing works, and if it is forcibly applied or if opposing points of view are forcibly eliminated, then brainwashing itself and actions taken as a consequence of brainwashing certainly are collective actions, not private ones.

[2] The presence of force may be explicit or implied. People might voluntarily undertake a collective action, but at some point force will be the response to dissent or disobedience:"[T]he authority of governors, directly or indirectly, rests in all cases ultimately on *force*. Government, in its last analysis, is organized force." Woodrow Wilson, *The State: Elements of Historical and Practical Politics,* rev. ed. (New York: Heath, 1898), p. 572. Criminals and government agents both use force. However, beyond moral judgments, what distinguishes collective actions from crime is that the agents of government claim, and usually nearly succeed in achieving, monopoly control of the use of force. Its use by others is outlawed except in very limited circumstances (involving parents' control of children, private security guards' protection of private persons and property, and athletes' participation in contact sports). Criminals seldom claim such monopoly control, although organized criminals do claim and often enforce monopoly control over markets for particular goods and services (which the agents of government usually have outlawed). These include markets for certain drugs, prostitution, loans at high interest rates, and gambling. A political revolution is an attempt by those not in government to gain monopoly control of the use of force for themselves. Therefore, it is not by accident that revolutionaries and their adversaries in government often call each other criminals.

American railroads be entirely private? Should private railroads enjoy the right of eminent domain (that is, the right to take private lands for public or private use without the owners' consent)? Or, if the president and members of Congress make the provision of railroad transportation collective, shall they do so partially, by regulation and subsidy, or completely, by government takeover? Such questions can be asked about nearly every human action. The pattern of collective action in a nation is called its **public policy.**

THE EXTENT OF COLLECTIVE ACTION IN THE UNITED STATES

The central concern of this book is collective action in the United States, and therefore it is useful to try to assess how extensive such action has become. Several measures of collective action are available. No single measure is sufficient, and all measures have certain drawbacks. Nevertheless, each measure illustrates a different aspect of collective action. Here we identify the costs and regulations imposed by collective action to emphasize its compulsory nature. We will identify and analyze the benefits of collective action in later chapters, and particularly in Chapter 3.

Government expenditures and related measures. By most measures, collective action in the United States is extensive and growing. Government expenditures provide one such important measure because most of the money to finance them comes from a nation's inhabitants. These expenditures can be financed in many ways from several sources of revenues. Taxes on individual incomes, corporate incomes, sales transactions, property, production, and wealth support most government expenditures; goods or services for which a fee is charged, such as government publications, Social Security, mail delivery, and gasoline taxes to pay for public roads, support others. Imported goods can be taxed, and government expenditures can also be financed by issuing public debt and printing (and otherwise creating) more money. Citizens must pay for this debt with future taxes or inflation (or both).

Citizens eventually pay for all revenues that support government expenditures. Taxes are an obvious and direct form of payment. When goods or services are publicly provided, private-sector providers are usually put out of business or placed at a competitive disadvantage because they lack government subsidies. Thus, would-be producers, as well as consumers who would benefit from competition among producers, are indirectly taxed. Subsidies in support of services provided by government also are almost always paid for by general tax revenues. Tariffs, another source of revenues, raise the price of imported goods by taxing them, and of domestic goods by protecting their manufacturers against the price competition of foreign firms. Similarly, government debt competes with private borrowers, sometimes crowding them out of credit markets. The money printed and otherwise created to pay government debt dilutes the value of money that citizens presently hold. The resulting inflation is equivalent to a tax.

Government expenditures and the direct and indirect taxes that finance them enjoy the sanction of law. Observance of law ultimately rests on force, and therefore each dollar of government expenditures is a dollar that elected and appointed officials remove from private, voluntary action and transfer to collective, coercive action. Hence, one measure of collective action is the ratio of government expenditures to the sum of all expenditures, both public and private.

"Gross national product (GNP) is the total national output of goods and services valued at market prices" and is made up of four categories: consumer purchases of goods and services; purchases of goods and services by all levels of government; gross private domestic investment; and net exports of goods and services.[3] The annual sum of these expenditures measures GNP. Partly because of inflation, partly because of productivity increases, and partly because of population growth, GNP expanded from $21.6 billion in 1902 to about $2.456 trillion in 1979. By this reckoning, GNP in 1979 was nearly 114 times its 1902 level. Expenditures for all levels of government—federal, state, county, and local—increased from $1.7 billion in 1902 to $796.2 billion in 1979. Hence, government expenditures in 1979 were over 468 times their 1902 levels. In 1902, government expenditures represented 7.9 percent of GNP, but in 1974, they represented 32.4 percent of the GNP. Figure 1.1 shows the trend of this increase.

Compound annual growth rates—calculated just like compound interest on savings accounts—provide another comparison between private- and public-sector growth rates. Between 1901 and 1974, the compound annual growth rate in federal taxes was 9.54 percent; in prices, 2.69 percent; and in real (inflation-adjusted) GNP, 3.17 percent; between 1899 and 1974, the compound annual growth rate in the total labor force (those employed or seeking employment) was 1.62 percent, and in public employment, 3.46 percent.[4]

Centralization. Using gross expenditure levels to measure the extent of collective action might seem misleading because a dollar spent by a local government might have a different effect from a dollar spent by the federal government. Some scholars argue that less coercion accompanies collective action by local governments than by the federal government. Citizens have more control over a local government, and they can "vote with their feet"—

---

[3] *Statistical Abstract of the United States, 1978* (Washington, D.C.: Government Printing Office, 1978), p. 437. Net exports of goods and services means the value of exports minus the value of imports. If the value of imports exceeds the value of exports, the nation has a balance-of-payments deficit.

[4] Compound growth rates are reported in Allan H. Meltzer and Scott F. Richard, "Why Government Grows (and Grows) in a Democracy," *The Public Interest,* 52 (Summer 1978), pp. 111–118.

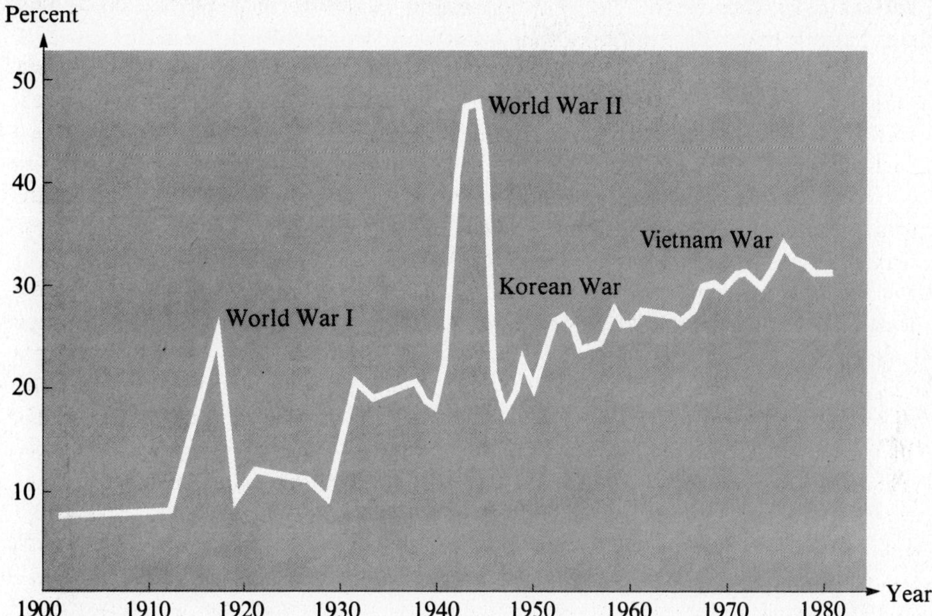

Figure 1.1 Government expenditures as a percentage of gross national product, 1938–1978 and selected years 1902–1936.

Sources: Data for 1938–1978 are from the *Economic Report of the President* (Washington, D.C.: Government Printing Office, 1979); data for 1902–1936 are from *Historical Statistics of the United States: Colonial Times to 1970* (Washington, D.C.: Government Printing Office, 1973).

that is, if public policy in one town meets with their disfavor, they can always move to another town (which costs less than moving to another country). This escape mechanism, it is believed, sets limits on how much coercion any one citizen might have to endure and induces city councilors and state legislators to temper their claims on the citizen.[5] Only a small number of citizens must move to have an impact. Local governments thus compete for residents and businesses in the same way that private firms compete for customers.

Because such differences between local and central governments are possible, it seems reasonable to inquire, Which level of government does what? Furthermore, are there discernible trends in the division of activities between state and federal governments? Partial answers are provided by a rating of seventeen government functions according to which level of government performs each function.[6] These functions include such activities as

[5] Charles M. Tiebout, "A Pure Theory of Local Expenditures," *Journal of Political Economy,* 64 (October 1956), pp. 416–424. The comparative advantages and disadvantages of local collective action are discussed in Chapters 4 and 13.

[6] William H. Riker, *Federalism: Origin, Operation, Significance* (Boston: Little, Brown, 1964), pp. 82–83. Comparisons of state and federal government expenditures

the conduct of foreign affairs and national defense, the provision of education, and the regulation of transportation and communication. Of the seventeen functions, since 1790 thirteen (76.5 percent) have become more centralized, three (17.6 percent) have remained unchanged, and only one (5.9 percent) has become less centralized. Table 1.1 shows the complete set of ratings.

Despite the subjective assignment of these ratings, there seems little doubt that the federal government has assumed an ever greater number of tasks. State governments too probably do more now than in earlier years, but the federal government exercises relatively more control. As a result, people today have less control over collective choice and public policy, either by

Table 1.1 The Degree of Centralization in the United States by Substantive Functions and at Points in Time

Functions	ca. 1790	ca. 1850	ca. 1910	ca. 1964	ca. 1979*
1. External Affairs	4	1	1	1	1
2. Public Safety	5	4	4	4	4
3. Property Rights	5	5	4	4	4
4. Civic Rights	5	5	5	3	2
5. Morality	5	5	5	5	5
6. Patriotism	3	3	3	3	3
7. Money and Credit	3	4	3	1	1
8. Transportation and Communication	4	4	2	2	2
9. Utilities	5	5	5	4	4
10. Production and Distribution	5	5	4	2	2
11. Economic Development	3	4	3	2	2
12. Resources	—	—	2	2	2
13. Education	—	5	5	4	4
14. Indigency	5	5	5	2	2
15. Recreation	—	4	4	3	3
16. Health	—	—	4	3	2
17. Knowledge	1	1	1	2	2
Average	4.1	4.0	3.5	2.8	2.6

Rating system: 1, performed exclusively or almost exclusively by the federal government. 2, performed predominantly by the federal government, although the state governments play a significant secondary role. 3, performed by federal and state governments in about equal proportions. 4, performed predominantly by state governments, although the federal government plays a significant secondary role. 5, performed exclusively or almost exclusively by the state governments. —, the functions were not recognized to exist at the time.

* Supplied by Professor Riker, 1979.

Source: William H. Riker, *Federalism: Origin, Operation, Significance* (Boston: Little, Brown, 1964), p. 83.

voting or by moving, than they did in years gone by. The costs and obligations imposed on the citizen by state and local law may appear less ominous or less distant from citizens' preferences than those imposed by federal law. But the domain of federal action has grown substantially since colonial times, and thus the citizen's ability to escape compliance or reduce the burden of compliance has simultaneously declined.

Regulation. Measures of government expenditures, employment, and tendencies to centralization might fail to include the full extent of collective action because federal, state, and local bureaucrats (at small cost as reflected in their bureaus' budgets) make and enforce rules and regulations that severely limit the domain of private action.[7] Complying with these rules and regulations also imposes substantial costs on private-sector producers and consumers, and sometimes on citizens in their personal lives.

For example, consider the things that the agents of government forbid you to do. In the industries of communications, you may not form a telephone or telegraph company or a radio or television station without government (Federal Communications Commission) approval. If the area in which you want to operate already has a telephone company or the regulators decide there are too many radio or television stations, you may not set up shop at all. Newspaper companies are limited in the number of radio and television stations they may own. The content and balance of broadcasts is partially regulated, as is political "fairness" toward competing candidates in election campaigns. Even the delightful anarchy of citizens band radio does not escape attempts at federal regulation, not to mention the more orderly but still hectic activity on amateur radio frequencies. Of course, under no conditions can you legally deliver first-class mail.[8]

In the industries of interstate transportation, while the regulatory process has been in a state of change since 1978, you still may not form a railroad, bus line, trucking firm, or airline without government (Civil Aeronautics Board or Interstate Commerce Commission) approval.[9] If you seek this per-

---

are not very revealing, because growth rates differ over different periods and because many state and local expenditures are paid for by federal funds from programs such as Federal Revenue Sharing.

[7] Here, the term *bureaucrat* denotes an unelected, nonjudicial government employee. See Chapter 11.

[8] See *Brennan v. U.S. Postal Service,* 47 L.W. 3476 (1979). Important legal actions are often mentioned in this book. They are referenced by naming the plaintiff (the party bringing the action, or lawsuit) first, the letter *v.* meaning *versus* second, and the defendant third. Then a volume number is followed by letters identifying the book or periodical in which the justice's or justices' opinions appear. In this case, the plaintiff is *Brennan,* the defendant is the *U.S. Postal Service,* and the periodical is *Law Week,* volume 47, beginning on page 3476. This is the case of a Rochester, New York, firm that for a few years delivered local first-class mail. A federal circuit court of appeals ruled the firm's actions illegal, and the Supreme Court refused to review the circuit court's decision.

[9] Airline deregulation and interstate trucking and bus line deregulation began in

mission, your would-be competitors will almost certainly lobby the members of the appropriate federal regulatory agency to see that your application is denied. If it is approved, then under certain conditions you must not operate on routes or at times for which you lack permission; usually, the price you charge is also partially regulated. Of course, in nearly every state and municipality you need a special license to drive a taxicab, a private automobile, or a motorcycle or moped, which you must not operate without wearing a helmet. Even privately supplied public bus-stop benches must be licensed and can be summarily hauled away for incorrect placement.

In the industries of personal services, you cannot practice law, medicine, pharmacology, radiology, psychology, physical therapy, veterinary medicine, accountancy, barbering, real-estate or insurance selling, or primary and secondary school teaching without licensing or certification. In Connecticut, state law requires the licensing of hypertrichologists (hair removers), while in California, the state legislators from time to time have considered bills to license astrologers.

In the area of personal action, in many states you must not smoke or possess marijuana, hashish, or peyote. You must not produce, own, rent, or sell movies or literature that by "community standards" are considered pornographic.[10] You must not engage in many forms of commerce on Sunday. You must not go naked in public (and occasionally not even in private). You must not engage in any of a spate of sexual practices with members of your own or the opposite sex (even by mutual consent), and, as noted earlier, you must not form marriage agreements with entire classes of human beings. You must not attempt suicide or agree with someone else to end your life. And you must not advocate the violent overthrow of the government.

In the field of commerce generally, you must not operate a business in an area that your community's zoning board members deem inappropriate. You must not agree with competitors to set prices, product lines, supplies, or business territories by mutual consent. On the other hand, you must do one or more of these things if the rules of a federal regulatory agency require it. You must not trade in the stock of your own company if you have information that is not yet public. You cannot operate most businesses without a license. You must not act or speak against unionization if you are an employer whose employees are voting on union representation. Nor in many states may you work for a unionized company for more than sixty days without joining the union. Naturally, you may not operate a bank, insurance company, hospital, or power plant without government approval.

Now, consider the things government agents insist that you do. You must pay your taxes, even if you are the president. In most states, except in

---

1978. Some regulations remain, but the regulatory agencies are now giving these businesses a freer hand to decide what fares to charge and which routes to service.

[10] The "community standards" doctrine for judging a book or movie to be pornographic was developed in *Miller v. California*, 413 U.S. 15 (1973). "U.S." refers to *United States Reports*, which publishes Supreme Court opinions.

special circumstances, you must go to school until you reach a specified age, and to go to school you must be vaccinated against several diseases. You must have a Social Security number to do most work or to have a bank account, and you must contribute part of your earnings to the Social Security fund. If you are an eighteen- or nineteen-year-old male, you are now required to register with the Selective Service System, and at the agreement of the president, a majority of the members of Congress, and the members of your draft board, you may have to join the armed forces and perhaps fight and die.

These *do's* and *don'ts* are collective because government personnel stand ready to enforce each command with the physical force of the police. Measuring the extent of such regulations seems difficult because there appears to be no meaningful way to count them. However, some measures do suggest just how extensive these regulations have become and the rate at which their presence has grown. One such measure is the increase in the number of federal regulatory agencies. As Figure 1.2 shows, before 1900 there were only six regulatory agencies; today there are more than fifty. The greatest numbers of regulatory agencies were added in the 1930s and 1970s.

The decisions of these regulatory agencies and their proposed and adopted rules and regulations and those of other federal bureaus are published in the *Federal Register.* One very rough indication of the growth of agency and bureau activities is the number of pages in the *Federal Register.* Figure 1.3 depicts the growth of the *Federal Register* from 1937 to 1980. The budgets of regulatory agencies have also expanded, especially in recent years. From 1974 to 1977, while United States population increased by 2 percent, GNP by 34 percent, and federal expenditures by 49 percent, direct federal regulatory expenditures grew by 55 percent. The increase in federal regulatory expenditures from 1974 to 1979 was expected to be 115 percent.[11]

Emphasizing the collective-coercive aspect of regulations, one very important measure of regulatory activities is the level of the obligatory costs of compliance they impose on private citizens. How the full costs of regulations might be computed is one of the most intensively researched subjects in law, political science, and economics today. As Chapters 3, 11, and 12 note, many scholars believe that regulations often reduce private-sector competition, innovation, and efficiency. Moreover, one set of computations of the private-sector costs of complying with federal regulations suggests that every dollar in a regulatory agency's budget represents a compliance cost for the private sector of twenty dollars. Therefore, the $4.8 billion projected combined budgets of regulatory agencies for 1979 might cost producers and consumers an additional $100 billion.[12]

Curiously, certain aspects of regulation seem to have declined in recent

[11] Data and projections are from Murray L. Weidenbaum, "The Impacts of Federal Regulation: A Study Prepared for the Joint Economic Subcommittee on Economic Growth and Stabilization of the United States Congress," Working Paper 52, Washington University Center for the Study of American Business, St. Louis, 1978.

[12] Weidenbaum, "The Impacts of Federal Regulation," p. 5.

years. Airline and trucking deregulation has occurred to some extent, and the relaxation of some banking regulations appears likely. But nowhere has deregulation been so noticeable as in laws concerning personal morals. Statutes against marijuana possession have been made substantially more lenient in many states. Pornography, as well as literature that some judge to be pornographic, today seems less an object of prosecution than it once was, and personal practices such as homosexual relationships are less and less a concern of government action. Indeed, calls for regulation of those who would discriminate against homosexuals are becoming more common.

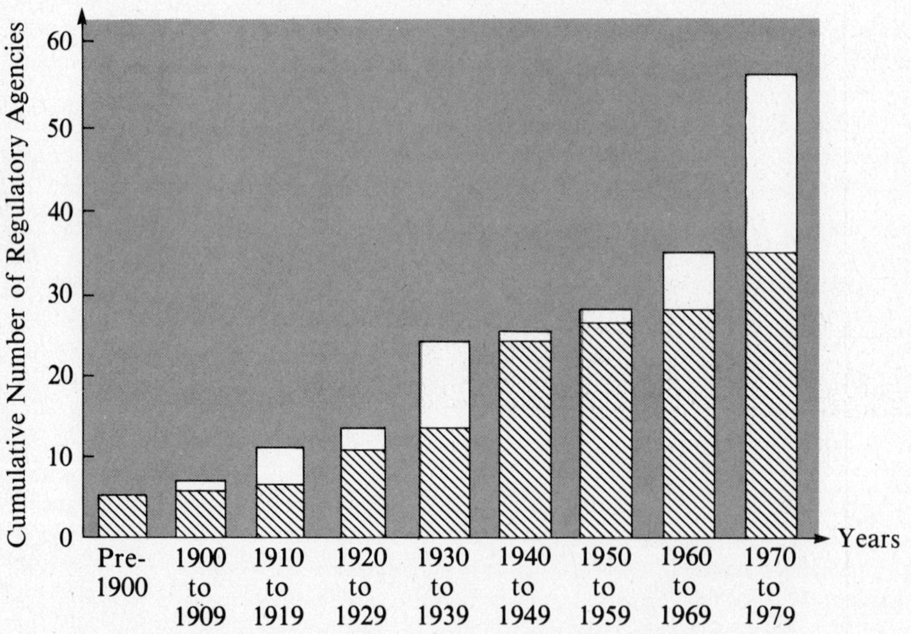

Figure 1.2 Growth chart of federal regulatory agencies. [The shaded area represents the number of agencies carried over from previous decades; the unshaded area represents the number of agencies added in the decade specified.]

Source: Ronald J. Penoyer, *Directory of Federal Regulatory Agencies,* 2nd ed. (St. Louis: Washington University, Center for the Study of American Business, 1980), p. 2.

federal register

Friday
September 5, 1980

Highlights

TWICE-A-WEEK PUBLICATION SCHEDULE

For a change in the schedules of "Agency Publication on Assigned Days of the Week", see the note appearing under the table in the Reader Aids section of this issue.

58801 **Convention for the Safety of Life at Sea** Executive Order

58803 **Natural Gas Supply Emergencies** Executive Order

58805, 58807 **Executive Schedule** Executive Orders amending levels IV and V

58820 **Campaign Funds** FEC announces effective date of 9–5–80 for final rule relating to public financing of Presidential General Election Campaigns

58935 **Grant Programs—Education** ED announces acceptance of applications for grants in the program of Research Grants on Teaching and Learning; apply by 1–27–81

58970 **Medical Devices** HHS/FDA considers establishing uniform standards for electromedical devices; comments, data and information by 11–4–80

CONTINUED INSIDE

This is the front page from the *Federal Register* of September 5, 1980. The highlights reported include executive orders of the president, the announcement of a rule-making deadline by the Federal Election Commission, the announcement of available grants by the Department of Education, and the announcement of Food and Drug Administration consideration of standards for devices such as cardiac pacemakers. This issue of the *Federal Register* is representative of the materials usually published in it.

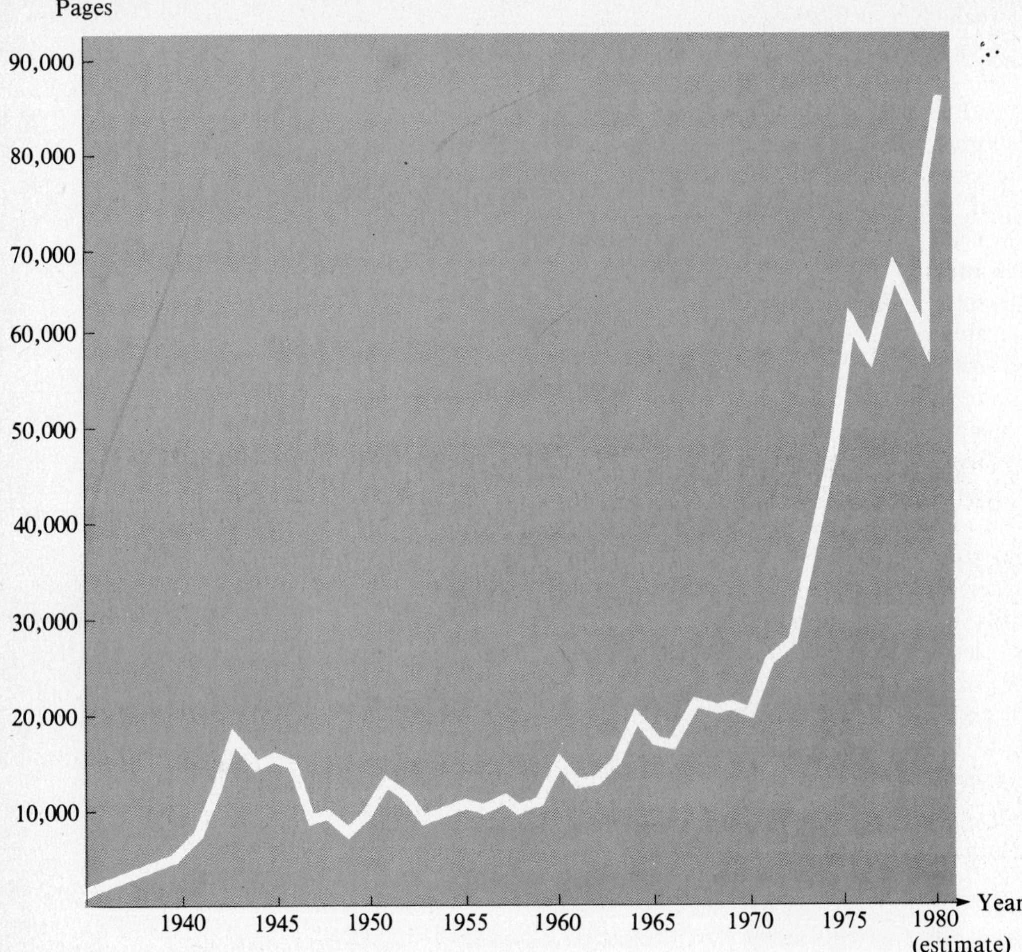

Figure 1.3 Number of pages in the *Federal Register,* 1937–1980.

THE GOALS OF THIS BOOK

This book's central goal is to provide the tools to explain past public policy decisions in the United States and to predict future ones—for example, the regulatory *do's* and *don'ts* just listed. Why do people choose to make certain actions collective, and in what form do they make those actions collective? Or, why are some actions left private? To explain and predict such decisions is to understand politics and government in the United States.

However, public policy is the result of individual actions that are many and varied and closely interrelated. To appreciate this complexity, consider a highly simplified view of public policy making in the United States. The process begins with citizens who vote or who abstain from voting for presidential, House, and Senate candidates. Before citizens vote, activists—those who do more than vote but less than run for office—nominate candidates, contribute money and other resources, and staff campaigns. Those who are elected then bargain over legislation, some of which they pass into law, formal public policy. Bureaucrats take this law and execute it. Judges rule on the appropriateness (for example, the constitutionality) of public policy, adjudicate disputes that occur because of it, and interpret it to apply to specific instances. With their decisions, judges sometimes even make law by themselves. Participants in this public-policy-making process continually revise their own actions to reflect what they expect other participants to do.

All of these actions—voting, nominating, contributing, bargaining, legislating, administering, and adjudicating—occur within a framework of pre-existing rules that specify more or less perfectly who has the legal right to act: to vote, to pass or enforce laws, and to abrogate them. These pre-existing rules, which in this country consist of the Constitution and the judicial decisions that interpret it, also specify the procedures that people must use to make public policy. But these rules too result from human actions. Therefore, to explain and to predict public policy in the United States—to understand collective action—we must first explain and predict human action generally.

METHODOLOGICAL INDIVIDUALISM

Those who study politics and government bring to their work two very different approaches for explaining and predicting collective action. The first approach holds that the fundamental unit of analysis should be the group, or **collectivity**. The second approach, which is the one used here, holds that the fundamental unit of analysis should be the individual human being. This approach is called **methodological individualism,** which should not be confused with philosophical individualism, or even rugged individualism.

The action of collectivities. A collectivity is a number of individual human beings who share some characteristic. Examples are all males (the male sex); all females (the female sex); members of a family (the Smiths); citizens of a town (the Bostonians), state (the Texans), or nation (the Russians); members of the Senate and of the House of Representatives; employees of a bureau, of the armed forces, or of a corporation; and members of an economic or social class (the proletariat). Those who rest their understanding of politics and government on the actions of such collectivities believe that in explaining and predicting collective action, the unit of analysis must be a group or groups. Groups, then—the actions of which must be understood—become the objects of study.

This **organic concept of politics** is defective because naming a collection of persons cannot breathe life into the name itself. Such terms as Middle America, the silent majority, the middle class, the proletariat, the Aryan race, the military-industrial complex, the Mafia, the Catholic Church, the Congress, the Supreme Court, the nation, the Democratic party, the Republican party, the public, General Motors, the Pentagon, the Justice Department, the American Medical Association, the Black Muslims, and even the Establishment, society, and the system are merely names. To give these names life beyond a shorthand usage, to reify them, is to commit the **organic fallacy:** the attribution of individual human qualities to collections of human beings. It is sloppy. It is mythical. And, as will be argued later in this chapter and in Chapters 2 and 3, it has no place in a political science.

A portion of President Dwight D. Eisenhower's farewell address provides a good example of the organic fallacy used in political discourse.

> In the councils of government, we must guard against the acquisition of unwarranted influence, whether sought or unsought, by the military-industrial complex. The potential for the disastrous rise of misplaced power exists and will persist.
>
> We must never let the weight of this combination endanger our liberties or democratic processes. We should take nothing for granted. Only an alert and knowledgeable citizenry can compel the proper meshing of the huge industrial and military machinery of defense with our peaceful methods and goals, so that security and liberty may prosper together.[13]

This treatment of groups of individual human beings as living organisms leads to a dead end because groups, *as groups,* do nothing! The military-industrial complex cannot pick up a telephone, dial a number, and order two pizzas, one with anchovies and one with mushrooms. It cannot choose to go to war. It cannot decide to "endanger our liberties or democratic processes." Any warring or endangering that occurs must be the result of individual actions, and they must be studied and understood as such. In sum, groups do not live, cannot choose, and are unable to act apart from the lives, choices, and actions of the individual members who make them up.[14]

---

[13] "Farewell Radio and Television Address to the American People," January 17, 1961, from *Public Papers of the Presidents of the United States, Dwight D. Eisenhower, January 1, 1960–January 20, 1961* (Washington, D.C.: Office of the Federal Register, 1961), p. 1038.

[14] It is vitally important to distinguish between shorthand usages and organic fallacies. Sentences such as "The audience applauded wildly," or "The mob stormed the Bastille," seem proper, since naming each member of the audience of mob is nigh on impossible. There even may be important dynamic processes that lead the members of audiences to applaud wildly and the members of mobs to storm prisons,

The actions of individual human beings. This book studies the distinct actions of individual human beings, not groups, to explain and predict (understand) political and governmental events in the United States. Such actions, taken one by one, produce all of the events that make American public policy what it is. This methodological individualism holds that the ability to explain and predict the actions of individual human beings implies the ability to aggregate those actions to understand the actions that collections (groups) of human beings might take. Therefore, to explain and predict *individual* human actions in politics and government *is* to understand *collective* actions.

ACTION, CHOICE, AND GOALS

Since public policy is the result of individual actions, understanding public policy requires a science that explains and predicts those individual actions. That science, which Chapter 2 develops more fully, requires two postulates, as well as a description of the properties of human goals.

Actions and decisions. The first postulate is that people act *as if* they choose their actions. That is, actions follow explicitly or implicitly from decisions. This postulate thus holds that a science capable of explaining and predicting decisions also can explain and predict actions. Plainly, many human actions appear to be automatic, not controlled by conscious decisions. However, the ***as if* provision** removes the requirement that actions must follow only conscious decisions.[15]

The chain of public policy causation now extends as follows: Public policy results from the distinct actions of individual human beings; the distinct actions of individual human beings result from their individual decisions. Accordingly, explaining and predicting public policy requires the explanation and prediction of individual choice, which in turn requires the construction of a theory of choice, a **decision theory.** This theory, when it is applied to political and governmental (public) choice, becomes a **political science.**

---

actions that no one person in the audience or mob would take alone. However, all of these actions must be understood on the basis of individual actions, and they remain incomprehensible on the basis of a fictious group aliveness.

[15] The *as if* provision often appears in this book. It implies nothing mystical. For example, suppose a sentence reads "She saw the oncoming car and applied the brakes quickly," while another reads "She saw the oncoming car and decided to apply the brakes quickly." A different way to write both sentences is "She saw the oncoming car and acted *as if* she decided to apply the brakes quickly." This third sentence is implied by the other two sentences. The *as if* provision is a metaphor similar to those used in other sciences, such as physics and chemistry. For example, both of these sciences assume that matter acts *as if* it is made up of certain elementary particles, none of which is directly observable. The test of such metaphors is the power of the explanations and predictions they generate.

(When decision theory is applied to certain kinds of private choices—those made in the marketplace—it becomes an **economic science,** or economics.)

Decisions and goals. A science of decision making requires a second postulate to motivate it. This postulate goes by the technical name of the assumption of **rational choice.** By postulating that the people they study are rational, decision theorists assume absolutely nothing about their subjects' psychological makeup or their states of mind at the time decisions are made. The assumption of rational choice postulates only that people act *as if* they have goals that they pursue efficiently. People—rational decision makers—may even make mistakes, which are themselves often predictable. Mistakes are commonly the result of someone's rational decision not to pay the cost of becoming better informed or of making more accurate calculations. In its broadest sense, the assumption of rational choice implies that people do not make decisions at random. Rational choice is purposive choice: the efficient pursuit of goals. However, as shall become evident in Chapter 2, the different conditions under which people make decisions can lead to different rules under which they efficiently pursue their goals.

Goals. Explanations and predictions of decisions also depend mightily upon the decision maker's purpose, or **goal;** decision making without a goal is random, unexplainable, unpredictable, and in some sense unthinkable. Therefore, before explaining or predicting someone's decisions, an observer must actually know or assume something about that person's goals. If these goals (and some other conditions) are known, then decision theory explains that person's past actions and predicts his or her future ones. A thorough grasp of the meaning of the term *goal,* then, is central to understanding decision theory. Seven properties of goals are important to the study of both public and private choice: (1) **methodological individualism,** individual human beings have goals, and a group does not; (2) **complexity,** one person can have many goals; (3) **scarcity,** often, a person can achieve one goal only at the expense of achieving another; (4) **ordering,** people can order their goals; (5) **variety,** different people have different goals; (6) **conflict,** often, if one person achieves his goal, another person cannot; (7) **subjectiveness,** goals are personal; no scientific basis exists for claiming that one person's goals are better than another's.

Methodological individualism. That individual human beings have goals and groups do not partially derives from the discussion of the organic fallacy. Our analysis of the property of variety will also show that the concept of a group goal may be logically inconsistent with the concept of an individual person's goal. As noted earlier, a group of people is not a living entity. It cannot think. It cannot decide. It cannot act. And, it cannot hold a goal. These are things that people do individually, even if they claim group membership. To talk about America's goals, the Republican party's goals, the goals of the

Catholic Church, the black community's goals, or the goals of organized labor may provide a convenient journalistic shorthand, but scientifically the words remain meaningless. A group can have no goal apart from those goals that individual members of the group might pursue.[16]

Complexity. Most problems of explaining and predicting decisions occur because one person simultaneously holds several goals. It often becomes useful to assume that a person holds a single goal: the candidate wants to win the election; the Supreme Court justice wants to embody his beliefs in the law; and the secretary of state wants peace with honor. But the candidate also wants to maintain independence; the Supreme Court justice also wants the future agreement of his fellow justices; and the secretary of state also wants to maintain military preparedness. Few acts or decisions stem from a single-minded purpose, for people hold sets of goals that can become extraordinarily complex.

Scarcity. A person can often achieve one goal only at the expense of achieving another. This reflects the scarcity of the things people want and their limited resources for getting them. Natural resources are scarce, and human mortality limits the natural resource of productive time. Everything desirable has a cost, and if a person buys more of one thing he must buy less of another. This property of goals is best expressed by the acronym **TANSTAAFL:** *there ain't no such thing as a free lunch.*[17] The members of Congress cannot enact laws that help to create both an infinite supply of energy and a perfectly clean environment, or, for that matter, an unlimited supply of both guns and butter. You can never simultaneously achieve all of your goals. Human mortality itself prevents complete bliss. Your wants and those of others seem insatiable, but your means are limited.

Three political examples illustrate this property of goals. First, you may believe it wrong that millionaires and well-funded labor leaders can finance election campaigns, and you fear that a few people might buy a candidate, perhaps even a president. To achieve your goal of fair elections, you lobby for government financing of all federal campaigns and for the outlawing of all varieties of private political contributions. Alas, you also hold dear the goal of freedom of the press, guaranteed by the First Amendment to the Constitution. After a few years you become wealthy. Believing strongly that a particular candidate is an especially decent human being, you publish your own

---

[16] This argument in no way implies that we cannot characterize the members of a group by using statistical techniques. As will be noted in Chapter 5 and elsewhere, such characterizations can prove to be extremely useful. Of course, they should not be used to conceal individual differences or to reintroduce organic fallacies.

[17] I cannot find the origin of TANSTAAFL. The earliest usage I know of is in Robert Heinlein, *The Moon is a Harsh Mistress* (New York: Putnam's, 1966). See also Edwin Dolan, *TANSTAAFL: The Economic Strategy for Environmental Crisis* (New York: Holt, Rinehart, and Winston, 1971).

UNITED STATES ENVIRONMENTAL PROTECTION AGENCY

WASHINGTON, D. C. 20460

THE ADMINISTRATOR

Honorable Ray Marshall
Secretary of Labor
Washington, D. C. 20210

Dear Mr. Secretary:

In accordance with our interagency agreement of 1971, I am submitting the 1980 first quarter report of the Economic Dislocation Early Warning System.

During the quarter, EPA identified two environmentally related plant closures that resulted in the loss of 105 jobs (Attachment A) and one plant that is threatening to close, involving 25 workers (Attachment B).

I am also revising information regarding the layoff by Kaiser Steel Corporation I reported last quarter. The report stated that Kaiser shut down several facilities, resulting in 400 environmentally related job losses. A more recent investigation, however, shows that only the closure of two open-hearth furnaces, involving about 125 workers, was related in part to environmental regulations. Kaiser's other layoffs result more directly from strong import competition.

Attachment C summarizes cumulative data on economic dislocations reported since 1971. EPA now has identified 167 plants that claimed environmentally related actual or threatened job losses, of which actual closings or curtailments by 141 plants dislocated approximately 25,311 workers. (This number also reflects the revised figure for Kaiser's layoffs.) During the nine-year period, a much larger number of plants reported threatened closings, but more than half of those plants eventually resolved their compliance problems and remained in operation.

The dislocations continue to be dominant in the following four industries: primary metals, chemicals, paper, and food processing. These industries claim 69 percent of the actual jobs lost and 89 percent of the threatened jobs.

EPA believes that the Early Warning System reports the vast majority of environmentally related plant closings affecting 25 employees or more. The Early Warning System statistics do not include plant closings affecting fewer than 25 persons.

Our regional offices are continuing to report actual and potential dislocations directly to the Department of Labor regional offices as soon as they learn of these situations. We also report potential dislocations to the Economic Development Administration regional offices, and those affecting small businesses to the Small Business Administration regional offices for possible loan assistance. Your staff should direct any inquiries concerning this report to Bob Cronon at 287-0708 in EPA's Economic Analysis Division.

Sincerely yours,

/s/ Barabara Blum Acting

Douglas M. Costle

Attachments

This letter, from Environmental Protection Agency (EPA) Administrator Douglas M. Costle to Secretary of Labor Ray Marshall, reports the loss of certain jobs in the first quarter of 1980, which were directly attributable to EPA regulations. Most economists who study environmental problems would agree that such reports are inaccurate, because secondary effects on employment and job losses in small businesses are not included. Nevertheless, this letter emphasizes the problem of scarcity: the price of cleaner air may be fewer jobs—TANSTAAFL.

editorials in your own newspaper, which you bought to help your candidate's cause. As the federal marshals haul you off to jail for violating the Fair Campaign Practices Act, for which you successfully lobbied, and as you loudly protest about your lost constitutional right to a free press, just remember one thing—*TANSTAAFL: there ain't no such thing as a free lunch.*[18]

Second, you may find it deplorable that some people earn low salaries. Your goal is a living wage for every American, and you join with others who believe as you do to lobby for a doubling of the minimum wage. The president and a majority of the members of Congress recognize your concern as well as your votes: they pass the measure. But you also hold dear the goal of jobs for everyone who wants to work. However, labor is a factor of production just like any other service or commodity. Your law doubles the cost of some labor and substantially increases the cost of other labor. Since a dollar now buys less labor, some employers go out of business, some stop or reduce hiring of new workers, some lay off employees, and some automate. Before your political success, many people had jobs, although at a lower rate of pay. Now work is no longer available, and your intended beneficiaries begin to visit the unemployment office to collect the unemployment payments your taxes support (if *you* still have a job). Particularly hard hit are black teenagers without job skills or employment records, whose economic futures depend heavily on their first few years of work.[19] As unemployment rates grow and as many become poorer and go on welfare, just remember one thing—*TANSTAAFL: there ain't no such thing as a free lunch.*

Third, you may think it unjust that those who own the means of production can charge whatever they please for their goods and services. (They can charge whatever they please, but they may not be able to get their price.) Inflation seems to be out of control. To achieve your goal of stable prices, you join with others who believe as you do and lobby for the imposition and

---

[18] Campaign contribution and expenditure laws and regulations have been changing since 1974, when in response to Watergate-related activities the members of Congress passed a comprehensive Federal Election Campaign Act, PL 93-443. ("PL" means public law; the number 93 refers to the Ninety-third Congress.) The justices of the Supreme Court found certain sections of that act unconstitutional in *Buckley v. Valeo,* 424 U.S. 1 (1975). The members of the Federal Election Commission now interpret and enforce the law. Because of the rapid state of change in campaign contribution laws, the scenario reported here is more nearly imagined than real. However, a similar problem emerged in the 1980 presidential election when several political action committees claimed the right to raise and spend money independently on behalf of Ronald Reagan's presidential campaign. This practice effectively circumvented federal limitations placed on spending by Reagan campaign committees. For a discussion of campaign contributions, see Chapters 6 and 13 and the references cited therein.

[19] For a review of the effect of minimum wage laws on unemployment among black adolescents, see Walter E. Williams, "Government Sanctioned Restraints That Reduce Economic Opportunities for Minorities," *Policy Review,* 2 (Fall 1977), pp. 7–30, and Finis Welch, *Minimum Wages: Issues and Evidence* (Washington, D.C.: American Enterprise Institute, 1978).

maintenance of wage, rent, and price controls. Since there appear to be more buyers than sellers, the persuasion of a perceived plurality gets the president and a majority of the members of Congress to act. But you also hold dear the goal that there should be enough goods and services to supply buyers' wants. Since prices cannot rise, your law makes the housing industry unprofitable, so fewer new apartments are built, some landlords fail to maintain older units, and other owners actually abandon their buildings. (These events have occurred under New York City's rent-control law and wherever else rents are controlled.) Condominium conversions of rental housing to get around rent controls also severely threaten the availability of rental apartments for retirees and others on relatively fixed incomes. Your law limits the fees physicians can charge for their services, so they play more golf. Ranchers stop investing in raising cattle. Oil wildcatters stop their exploratory drilling. Automobile manufacturers use cardboard paneling on vehicle interiors. Tree farmers refuse to harvest trees until price controls are removed. Coal miners refuse to mine coal. Before wage, rent, and price controls, consumers had the choice to buy or not to buy a service or a commodity at the going market price, which you considered unfair. Now consumers have stable prices on unavailable goods. As shortages become rampant, as black markets flourish, as industries slow or stop production and lay off workers, and as the economy takes a nose dive, just remember one thing—*TANSTAAFL: there ain't no such thing as a free lunch.*[20]

Finally, you may look at these three examples and conclude that *the system* itself is evil. Accordingly, you might decide to agitate for a revolution to replace the present form of government and economy with another. When you call for your own particular version of utopia, as so many before you have done, just remember one thing—*TANSTAAFL: there ain't no such thing as a free lunch.*

The point of these examples is neither that these are bad goals nor that some goals are necessarily better than others. Fair elections, freedom of the press, high salaries, full employment, low prices, no shortages—all of these are desirable, and there may be other ways to get them than the methods used today. However, the point is that goals *are* goals precisely because someone has not yet achieved them. Why not? Because people have limits. Some of these limits mean that there are goals human beings might never achieve (for example, immortality, perfect health, and perfect happiness). Other limits mean that a person must give up the achievement of some goals to achieve others.

Ordering. That people hold many goals may seem to be a serious problem, because the achievement of some goals does conflict with the achievement of others. Which of two mutually exclusive goals will someone try to

[20] Black markets are illegal exchanges of commodities and services that circumvent a government restriction or tax on exchange or production. These markets seem to be an inevitable result of price controls, sales taxation, or prohibitions.

achieve? To answer this question we must assume that people act as if they can order their goals. And, to understand goal ordering, it is helpful to introduce the concept of an **outcome,** which is more general than the concept of a goal.

The extent to which people achieve their goals results from what they do, what others do, and natural occurrences such as sunshine, disease, floods, and earthquakes. Therefore, goal achievement or non-achievement is a composite result of many possible events, some of which people control completely, some of which they control partially, and some of which they do not control at all. The results of these events are called outcomes. Some of these outcomes are identical to the achievement of a desired goal, in which case an outcome *is* a goal. Other outcomes may not be goals, and the decision maker might even wish to avoid their occurrence. However, it does not matter whether an outcome is a goal, because all unrealized goals are potential outcomes. So if people can order outcomes, they can also order their goals.

Rational choice is impossible without goals, and to have goals, a person must be able to distinguish between outcomes and therefore between goals. Ordering means that people act as if they can compare two outcomes and state a preference between them. For example, someone could say about the two outcomes "having a Republican president" and "having a Democratic president" that one of three sentences holds true: (1) I prefer having a Republican president to having a Democratic president; (2) I prefer having a Democratic president to having a Republican president; and (3) I am indifferent as between having a Democratic president and having a Republican president.

Because rational choice requires goals and because the existence of conflicting goals requires the ability to state a preference or to express indifference, the ability to prefer is a requirement of rational choice, and consequently it is also a requirement of decision theory. Stated formally, people act *as if* they have a **preference** (or indifference) **ordering** over any pair of *outcomes.* This property is called the **axiom of connectedness.** A corollary of this axiom is that people act *as if* they have a preference or indifference ordering over any pair of *goals.* They either prefer to achieve one goal rather than another or they are indifferent as between which of the two they achieve.

The axiom of connectedness says only that someone can order any two outcomes. What happens if more than two outcomes are possible? The answer lies in the **axiom of transitivity.** Suppose an election has three possible outcomes: (1) the Republican candidate wins; (2) the Democrat wins; and (3) the Socialist wins. If a citizen prefers the Republican to the Democrat and the Democrat to the Socialist, then by the axiom of transitivity, the citizen must prefer the Republican to the Socialist. If so, he has a **transitive preference ordering.** If someone's preference orderings over all outcomes, including goals, are both connected and transitive, then he or she has a **complete preference ordering** and can distinguish among many goals or other outcomes.

The achievement of a goal, however, is almost never an either-or proposition. A business executive wants a profit, not a loss, and a candidate wants to win an election, not to lose one. But the executive actually wants to maximize profits and prefers a smaller loss to a larger one, while the candidate similarly might prefer a larger majority to a smaller one. Stated somewhat imprecisely, there are measurable *levels* of goal achievement or non-achievement, such as wealth, unemployment, inflation, economic growth, welfare payments, environmental quality, energy costs, racial integration, war, peace, and happiness. Someone may set a particular level of one of these things as a goal. However, goals and outcomes usually are quantitative rather than qualitative measures of possible future conditions. They mean more-or-less rather than either-or.

The likelihood that a goal or outcome might occur is also seldom certain. People rarely know exactly which particular outcome(s) will result as a consequence of their actions. Situations do exist in which a particular action leads invariably to the occurrence of a particular outcome and only that outcome, but these situations seem rare in politics and government. Probability may be involved, and probabilities can vary with the action someone chooses. Often, even probabilities may be unknown or meaningless.

Different probabilities can affect a person's choices. For example, as Chapter 5 notes, some voters in the 1968 presidential election preferred George Wallace to Richard Nixon and Richard Nixon to Hubert Humphrey, but even so they voted for Nixon. Voting for Wallace appeared to them to be risky. They believed he had little or no chance of winning. The odds were that a vote for Wallace would be wasted, leaving Humphrey, their least preferred candidate, with a higher probability of defeating Nixon, their second choice, than Humphrey might have had if they voted for Nixon. Therefore, following this reasoning, they voted for Nixon. Following a similar logic, in the 1980 presidential election, Jimmy Carter tried with some success to convince the supporters of independent candidate John Anderson, who had little chance to win, that a vote for Anderson was a vote for the Republican candidate, Ronald Reagan; therefore Anderson supporters should vote for Carter, their second choice, rather than risk throwing their vote away by voting for Anderson, their first choice. These two examples show that in situations where risk or uncertainty is present, a simple preference ordering may not be sufficient for explaining and predicting decisions.

Variety. Different people hold different goals. Political examples abound. Some prefer Democrats and others Republicans. Some prefer capitalism and others communism. Some prefer monarchy and others democracy. Some prefer government to supply more guns, and others, more butter. The variety of individual preferences often leads to an identifiable incoherence in decisions made by collective choice. This incoherence, which is discussed in nearly every chapter of this book, not only represents a central problem for those who study democratic governments, but also emphasizes the internal contradiction of organic interpretations of collective action. To provide an example of this incoherence, let us suppose that, in violation of methodological individualism, a group can have a goal; it can order its preferences over outcomes. This assumption can lead to the paradox that either an individual human being has a transitive preference ordering or a group has a transitive preference ordering, but a transitive preference ordering for both is impossible. This is precisely the inconsistency hinted at earlier, in the discussion of methodological individualism.

Suppose the delegates to the Democratic National Convention of the year 2000 must nominate a presidential candidate from among three contenders unimaginatively named Washington, Adams, and Jefferson. The convention delegates are unpledged (that is, they can vote as they wish), and a nomination requires a majority vote. Of 3000 delegetes, 1000 prefer Washington to Adams and Adams to Jefferson (call this preference ordering A); another 1000 prefer Adams to Jefferson and Jefferson to Washington (preference ordering B); and the remaining 1000 prefer Jefferson to Washington and Washington to Adams (preference ordering C). All individual preference orderings, as summarized in Table 1.2, are transitive.

What is the Party's Goal, the Will of the Majority, the Group's Interest, the Group's Preference Ordering, or, for that matter, the Public Good? First, notice that the 2000 delegates with preference orderings A and B will vote for Adams over Jefferson, which means that the group's preference ordering, as a majority vote of 2000 to 1000 would reveal, is that *the Convention prefers Adams to Jefferson.* Only delegetes with ordering C would vote for Jefferson over Adams. Second, notice that the 2000 delegates with preference orderings A and C will vote for Washington over Adams, which means that the group's preference ordering, as a majority vote of 2000 to 1000 would again reveal, is that *the Convention prefers Washington to Adams.* Only delegates with ordering B would vote for Adams over Washington. This appears to provide a complete preference ordering for the Convention: *the Convention prefers Washington to Adams and Adams to Jefferson.* Such an ordering of outcomes is necessary for explaining and predicting choice and action. Hence, it is possible to treat the group, the Convention, as if it is an individual decision maker—or is it? Rational choice requires an ordering over outcomes that is both connected *and* transitive.

Now, notice that the 2000 delegates with preference orderings B and C would vote for Jefferson over Washington, which means that the group's preference ordering, as a majority vote of 2000 to 1000 once more would reveal, is that *the Convention prefers Jefferson to Washington.* Only delegates with preference ordering A would vote for Washington over Jefferson. The Convention's complete preference ordering now becomes: *the Convention prefers Washington to Adams, Adams to Jefferson, and Jefferson to Washington.* That is, as revealed by a majority vote, the group has an **intransitive preference ordering.** Consequently, given the information at hand, it is not possible to explain or predict what the group, as a group, chooses to do.[21]

[21] Certain information about institutional arrangements, such as who controls the Convention agenda (the order of voting), might help in predicting who the winning candidate might be. But if the agenda controllers themselves are elected, then

Table 1.2 Preference orderings in hypothetical Democratic National Convention

	First Choice	Second Choice	Third Choice
Preference ordering A	Washington	Adams	Jefferson
Preference ordering B	Adams	Jefferson	Washington
Preference ordering C	Jefferson	Washington	Adams

This example demonstrates that transitivity, and thus also rational choice, is an attribute of individual human beings and not of groups. Organic views and methodological individualism are therefore antithetical. After all, what is the rational choice for the Convention to make? No one knows, although one can speculate about what the rational decision for an individual convention delegate might be. Because different persons hold different preference orderings over outcomes, the "preference orderings of groups," if such can be said to exist, often will be intransitive, making group rationality, and sometimes predictability of group decisions, logically impossible.

Conflict. Especially with collective action, if one person achieves his goal, often another cannot. Some scholars call this book's approach to politics and government a conflict model because it emphasizes the problem of incompatible goals. However, people might agree completely about which goals to pursue and still disagree about who should pay the cost of achieving them. Even if they were all to agree that they should cooperate and share this cost, they may end up doing nothing, with each trying to be a free rider on everyone else's efforts. Since this is roughly one-half of what politics and government are about, the model used here, rather than being a conflict model, is as much about the resolution of cooperation—conflict over who should support mutually beneficial collective actions—as it is about the resolution of conflicts over goals. This problem of cooperation and free riders, like the problem of the incoherence of group action, remains a central theme throughout this book.

Conflict is also a logical extension of scarcity, which limits the amount of a valued good or service that any person might have. The extension of scarcity from one person to many seems clear. For instance, the Saudi Arabians produce just so much oil in any one year. If Americans consume a barrel of Saudi oil, neither the Russians nor the Europeans nor the Japanese can consume that same barrel. Either a Democrat is president or a Republican is president. The United States is either at war or at peace, and either 10 or 15 percent of GNP is spent on national defense. Abortion is either legal or illegal. A favorite election candidate either wins or loses. These examples imply that

---

an intransitive ordering is likely to occur again, in the voting process that chooses them. Discussions of agenda control are provided in Chapters 7, 8, and 9.

since one person's preferences can differ from another's, a limit to goal achievement often means that if some have their way, others will not. This is the stuff of politics, government, and public policy precisely because collective action often enforces by coercion a particular outcome among many possible but mutually exclusive outcomes.

Subjectiveness. Goals and preferences are personal, and no scientific basis exists for claiming that one person's goals and preferences are better than another's. The subjectivity of goals and preferences is fundamental; its importance rests on the distinction between science and ethics. Ignoring this distinction causes much confusion about rational choice, because some people mistakenly interpret our usage of the term *rational* to mean reasonable, or good, or moral.

While a scientist's activities *as a scientist* provide no way to order the philosophical or ethical quality of different human goals and preferences, two kinds of judgments about someone's goals and preferences remain possible. First, we can explore the logical implications of two (or more) goals to see if their achievement is consistent with each other. For example, an economist can demonstrate that achieving the goals of full employment and a high minimum wage may be mutually exclusive, and a political scientist can show that the goal of carrying on trade and friendly diplomatic relations with the communist Chinese can sour our hopes for better relations with their present adversaries, the Soviets. But if someone prefers higher salaries to full employment or better relations with the Chinese at the expense of cooler relations with the Russians, then the scientist, as a scientist, cannot argue that such preferences are wrong or defective.

Second, the scientist can explore the efficiency of particular actions and decisions for meeting desired goals. For example, suppose someone wants to become president of the United States. Political scientists can analyze how efficiently the would-be candidate pursues this goal, but they cannot say that the goal itself is better or worse than another goal, such as becoming a knacker.

That scientists cannot scientifically judge the ethical content of goals and preferences does not mean that they are themselves devoid of personal goals and values. (Indeed, a person without goals or values is monstrous to conceive of.) I hold my goals and values very strongly, but they are personal and are based on my own philosophical positions. Even if you believe that your goals can be arrived at and defended objectively, that knowledge would not be useful to you for explaining and predicting the goal orderings and decisions of others. Political scientists, when they act as scientists, do not legislate preferences; they merely observe and analyze them.

QUESTIONS FOR DISCUSSION AND REVIEW

1. Are the costs of collective action more readily measurable than the benefits? Are there exceptions? How will elected officeholders and bureaucrats try to manipulate the measurability and perceptions of the costs and benefits of collective action? How might one measure the benefits of incurring an additional public expenditure (cost) of $10 billion for national defense? How might one measure the benefits of spending an additional $100 million on preventing the sale of heroin? On finding a cure for cancer?
2. How would one account for the overall growth of government expenditures and regulation in the United States? Is the aggregate size of the public sector—the extent of collective action—itself the result of a conscious decision, or is it the product of many other decisions about separate public policies?
3. Why is there no meaningful way to count government regulations? How might regulations be weighted relative to one another? Why are representatives of regulated industries (both executives and union leaders) often the most outspoken opponents of deregulation?
4. Why are groups commonly treated as unitary, living entities in newspaper editorials, political discourse, and debate? Are such usages always objectionable? Is reference to "the system" an organic fallacy?
5. Are "rational mistakes" really mistakes? Can rational error ever be avoided? Would avoiding rational error be rational?
6. Why is decision making without a goal unthinkable? Would the decision to make a decision with no goal in mind be possible?
7. Would a political scientist enjoy an advantage over an opponent who is not a political scientist in running for public office? Would the political scientist enjoy an advantage over someone who is not a political scientist in providing a moral defense for determining what the goals of collective action ought to be?

NEW CONCEPTS AND TERMS

New concepts and terms appear in bold face in the chapter and are defined in the glossary which appears as Appendix A at the end of the book.

as if provision
axiom of connectedness
axiom of transitivity
collective action
collectivity
complete preference ordering
complexity
conflict
decision theory
economic science

goals
intransitive preference ordering
methodological individualism
ordering
organic concept of politics
organic fallacy
outcome
political science
preference ordering
private action
private choice
public choice
public policy
rational choice
scarcity
subjectiveness
TANSTAAFL
transitive preference ordering
variety

2

Elements of Decision Theory

Chapter 1 states that this book's central goal is to provide the tools to explain and predict public policy decisions in the United States. These decisions result from political and governmental (collective) actions. But collective actions result from the actions of individual human beings. As Chapter 1 points out, here we assume that people act as if their actions result from their decisions. Hence, to explain and predict collective action, and thus American public policy, we must explain and predict the decisions that individual human beings (mostly Americans) make. These explanations and predictions in turn are based on elements of a theory that this chapter provides, a theory of human choice.

COMPONENTS AND CONDITIONS OF DECISION MAKING

Chapter 1 also postulates that people act as if they are rational, efficient goal seekers, and begins to construct a decision theory by describing seven properties of goals. Now the discussion must turn to the problem of actually explaining and predicting human choice, tasks that require us first to identify the components of a decision and then to examine the conditions under which decisions are made.

The Components of a Decision

The three principal components in any formal decision situation are outcomes, alternatives, and states of nature.[1] Chapter 1 briefly describes what an outcome is. Here it is necessary to add only one thing to that description. When decision makers contemplate the outcomes that might occur as a consequence of their decisions and the decisions of others, they need not be omniscient. Outcomes about which they are unaware might well be possible, and they might be wrong about the outcomes they believe *are* possible.

An **alternative** is the action a decision maker chooses. The fundamental problem for decision theory is to explain decision makers' past choices of alternatives and to predict their future ones. We ordinarily consider a person's alternatives at any time as a related set. For example, the delegates to the hypothetical Democratic National Convention mentioned in Chapter 1 have four alternatives: to abstain, to vote for Washington, to vote for Adams, and to vote for Jefferson. Normally, we simplify matters by using symbols to represent alternatives. For instance, the alternatives might be written: a_O, abstain; a_W, vote for Washington; a_A, vote for Adams; and a_J, vote for Jefferson. We also refer to the convention delegate's set of alternatives, $\{a\}$, and write this set out fully, $\{a\} = \{a_O, a_W, a_A, a_J\}$. As with outcomes, so with alternatives: decision makers do not choose alternatives about which they are unaware.

The **state of nature** provides the connection between alternatives and outcomes. Suppose—to use a nonpolitical example—that you are trying to decide between two mutually exclusive alternatives: a_1, to go on a picnic, and a_2, to stay home and work. There are two possible states of nature: S_1, it is sunny, and S_2, it rains. Finally, there are four possible outcomes. To simplify matters, let O_{11} be the outcome associated with a_1 and S_1. O_{11}, then, occurs if you go on a picnic and it is sunny. The four outcomes become: O_{11}, you have a sunny picnic; O_{12}, you have a rainy picnic; O_{21}, you have a sunny work day; and O_{22}, you have a rainy work day. Table 2.1 shows the form of the relationships among alternatives, outcomes, and states of nature. There are two alternatives, two states of nature, and four outcomes in this decision problem. Generally, if there are m alternatives and n states of nature, then there are m times n outcomes.

The Conditions of Decision Making

The conditions under which people decide vary according to their beliefs about which state of nature to associate with each alternative. There are three ways to characterize decision-making conditions: decision making under

[1] The word *formal* emphasizes the *as if* nature of these components. Decision makers need not actually identify such components and then go through the calculations described in this chapter and elsewhere in this book. As Chapter 1 notes, they only must act *as if* they do.

Table 2.1 The picnic decision problem

Alternatives	States of Nature S_1, it is sunny	 S_2, it rains
a_1, to go on a picnic	O_{11} (sunny picnic)	O_{12} (rainy picnic)
a_2, to stay home and work	O_{21} (sunny work day)	O_{22} (rainy work day)

Table 2.2 School superintendent election decision problem

Alternatives	S_1, two votes for Adams	States of Nature S_2, one vote for Adams, one vote for Baker	S_3, two votes for Baker
a_1, to vote for Adams	Adams wins	Adams wins	Baker wins
a_2, to vote for Baker	Adams wins	Baker wins	Baker wins

conditions of certainty, decision making under conditions of risk, and decision making under conditions of uncertainty.[2] Each of these conditions provides a different assumption about the decision maker's beliefs concerning the relationship among alternatives, states of nature, and outcomes.

Decision making under conditions of certainty. Conceptually, the simplest form of choice is **decision making under conditions of certainty.** To illustrate this condition, suppose you are one of three school-board members who must choose a new school superintendent by majority rule. Two candidates, Adams and Baker, apply for the job. Your two alternatives are a_1, to vote for Adams, or a_2, to vote for Baker. There are three possible states of nature: S_1, both of your fellow board members vote for Adams; S_2, one votes for Adams and the other for Baker; and S_3, both vote for Baker. Majority rule means that whichever candidate gets two or three votes wins. Hence, if the other members both vote for the same candidate, that candidate wins regardless of how you vote. Table 2.2 summarizes this decision problem.

Decision making under conditions of certainty occurs if you know exactly which state of nature prevails. If S_1 prevails, Adams wins with or without your vote; if S_3 prevails, Baker wins with or without your vote; if S_2 prevails, your vote completely controls the election outcome. In this example, you are certain about the prevailing state of nature, how your fellow board

[2] See R. Duncan Luce and Howard Raiffa, *Games and Decisions: Introduction and Critical Survey* (New York: Wiley, 1957), pp. 12–15.

members vote. Therefore, you know precisely which outcome will occur for each alternative you choose.

Decision making under conditions of risk. The election in Table 2.2 becomes a problem of **decision making under conditions of risk** if you do not know which state of nature prevails but you do have some subjective estimate of the probability that each state of nature prevails. For example, suppose one board member promises to vote for Adams while the other promises to flip a fair coin. Since Baker no longer can get two votes without your vote, the probability that S_3 prevails is zero. But the probability that S_1 prevails is one-half (50 percent), as is the probability that S_2 prevails. In decision making under conditions of certainty, you know exactly what your vote accomplishes. In risky choice conditions such as this one, you know only with some probability what your vote accomplishes. Risky choice, then, introduces the notion of probability.

Decision making under conditions of uncertainty. To illustrate **decision making under conditions of uncertainty,** consider the school-superintendent election from the candidate's viewpoint. Suppose that people in your community are sharply divided over school desegregation. Schools are now highly segregated, and the next school superintendent has three public policy choices: (1) to leave things as they are and permit segregation to continue; (2) to institute an open schools policy, allowing parents to send their children to whichever school they want; and (3) to use forced busing to achieve racial integration. The school-board members, who elect the superintendent, have their own preferences on the issue. Member A prefers forced busing to open schools and open schools to the status quo. Member B prefers open schools to the status quo and the status quo to forced busing. You, member C, prefer the status quo to forced busing and forced busing to open schools. All preferences, as summarized in Table 2.3, are connected and transitive.

Suppose each candidate submits in writing the plan he or she expects to adopt. If both candidates submit the same plan, each school-board member flips a coin to decide how to vote. Although one candidate will win, the coin toss is random, and therefore the election outcome is analytically equivalent to a tie. However, if the candidates submit different plans, then the members vote their preferences. For example, if Adams proposes forced busing while Baker proposes open schools, then members A and C vote for Adams, member B votes for Baker, and Adams beats Baker by a two-to-one vote.

Each candidate now has three alternatives: to propose forced busing, to propose open schools, or to propose the status quo. For reasons noted later in this chapter, these alternatives are different from those found in decision making under conditions of certainty or risk, because the alternative one candidate chooses is the prevailing state of nature for the other candidate's decision. As we shall see, probability is not meaningful in these situations. Such situations are called **games of strategy,** and each participant's alterna-

Table 2.3 Board member public policy preferences on school integration

	First Choice	Second Choice	Third Choice
Member A	forced busing	open schools	status quo
Member B	open schools	status quo	forced busing
Member C	status quo	forced busing	open schools

Table 2.4 Candidates' strategies and outcomes in superintendent election game

		Baker's Strategies	
Adams's Strategies	Forced busing	Open Schools	Status Quo
Forced busing	tie	Adams wins	Baker wins
Open schools	Baker wins	tie	Adams wins
Status quo	Adams wins	Baker wins	tie

tives are called **strategies.**[3] The problem is to predict the strategies the candidates will adopt as well as to predict which candidate might win.

To complete the example, suppose that the two candidates are indifferent as among the three proposals because each wants only to become superintendent of schools.[4] Table 2.4 summarizes the election outcome as a function of each candidate's strategies. Notice that whichever strategy Adams chooses, Baker can defeat it. If Adams advocates forced busing, Baker can win by advocating the status quo; if Adams advocates the status quo, Baker can win by advocating open schools; and if Adams advocates open schools, Baker can win by advocating forced busing. In any case, the first candidate to announce a position loses the election.[5]

[3] Games of strategy occur when another person controls the prevailing state of nature. Examples include bargaining, election contests, and war. Games of chance involve only risky choice, such as in roulette and bingo. Games of skill, such as golf, involve little formal interaction with others. Most games, such as poker, tennis, and football, involve all three elements of strategy, chance, and skill.

[4] One should not be misled into believing that conscience is an advantage in such an election. A candidate who seeks only to win has a distinct advantage over one who wants to espouse the right or moral policy. In elections such as this one, a candidate who only advocates policies to get elected usually defeats an opponent who only advocates policies he believes in, as long as the candidate without policy preferences knows what policy his opponent's beliefs dictate. The implications of this finding for democratic elections are worrisome. In any case, lack of sincerity is difficult to identify and seldom is itself an issue. Candidates who are caught shifting their positions can always claim they are only trying to represent the voters' preferences more accurately.

[5] The candidate's announcement of a position may be a clear implication of belief or conscience (see footnote 4), or it may result from policy announcements made

This situation is an example of decision making under conditions of uncertainty because control of the prevailing state of nature is in the hands of an intelligent opponent.[6] Indeed, the state of nature *is* the opponent's strategy. Therefore, it is not clear either how a person can be certain about which state of nature prevails—which strategy will be chosen by his or her opponent—or how that person might estimate the probability that each state of nature prevails. A decision maker's inability to assign meaningful probabilities to different states of nature is the hallmark of decision making under conditions of uncertainty. By contrast, those who decide under conditions of risk act as if they know or believe they know the relevant probabilities.

UNDERSTANDING DECISION MAKING UNDER CONDITIONS OF CERTAINTY

Decision making under conditions of certainty is the simplest form to explain and predict. There is no chance or risky element and no uncertainty. Each state of nature either occurs or it does not occur, and the decision maker knows precisely which state of nature prevails.[7] For example, in the election shown in Table 2.2, you know precisely which outcome occurs as the result of choosing each alternative. For instance, if S_2 prevails with certainty—if Adams and Baker each have one vote—then your vote decides the election. If you choose a_1, to vote for Adams, then the outcome is a victory for Adams; if you choose a_2, to vote for Baker, then the outcome is a victory for Baker.[8] By the properties of human goals listed in Chapter 1, in particular the property of

---

in previous election campaigns or from policies advocated while in office. Notice that the pattern of preference orderings among school-board members is identical to the pattern of preference orderings among convention delegates in Table 1.2. The policies of status quo, open schools, and forced busing have merely been substituted for candidates Washington, Adams, and Jefferson, respectively.

[6] In the two preceding examples, the prevailing states of nature were also chosen by intelligent human beings. However, in the case of decision making under conditions of certainty, we *assumed* that the choices made by the intelligent human beings were already known, and thus certainty prevailed. We also assumed that probabilities could meaningfully be estimated in the case of decision making under conditions of risk, because one person had revealed that his choices would be made by a randomized process, flipping a fair coin. Ordinarily, risky choice situations will entail the use of a process that generates probabilities whose exact value or relative magnitude are known.

[7] This highly abstract discussion of decision making under conditions of certainty greatly simplifies some very complex theory. Mathematical programming, and linear programming in particular, is one principal tool used to analyze such decisions. The solutions to many problems of decision making under conditions of certainty are so complex that they can only be approximated.

[8] This description of outcomes is imprecise but it will suffice here. The exact outcome would be that Adams (or Baker) wins by a vote of two to one; the immediate outcome is the division of the vote and not the name of the winner.

ordering, you can order goals and other outcomes. Thus, if S_2 does prevail and if you prefer the election of Adams to the electon of Baker, then we predict that you will vote for Adams.

UNDERSTANDING DECISION MAKING UNDER CONDITIONS OF RISK

Decision theory began in the 1700s as an attempt by mathematicians and philosophers to help European aristocrats improve their gambling skills. These scholars may not have realized that their efforts would exert such a great effect on twentieth-century social science. It is appropriate to examine choice, and especially risky choice, from a gambler's viewpoint, since games of chance are the easiest situations to represent with decision theory.

Maximizing Expected Value

Simple calculations. One way to begin the discussion of risky choice is with a calculation of what is called **expected value.** Suppose you are asked to remove a slip of paper from a hat; if you remove a red slip, you receive $10, while if you remove a white slip, you receive nothing. You know that six red slips and four white slips are in the hat. That is, there are ten slips of paper; you have a 60 percent chance of removing a red slip (and of getting $10) and a 40 percent chance of removing a white slip (and of getting nothing). Stated differently, the probability of getting $10 is 0.6, while the probability of getting nothing is 0.4. The expected value of this draw is 0.6($10) + 0.4($0) = $6. If there were seven red slips and three white slips, the expected value would become 0.7($10) + 0.3($0) = $7. If a white slip were worth $5 and there were four red slips and six white slips, the expected value of the draw would become 0.4($10) + 0.6($5) = $7. If there were seven red slips and three white slips, the expected value would be 0.7($10) + 0.3($5) = $8.50.

Generally, if each outcome has a countable, objective external value—for example, numbers of dollars, potatoes, shoelaces, or intercontinental ballistic missiles—then it is simple to calculate expected value by multiplying each outcome's number by its associated probability of occurring and summing the resulting numbers. Symbolically, in some particular gamble, if O_i is the ith of m outcomes, and if P_i is the probability that the ith outcome occurs, then the gamble's expected value, EV, becomes

$$EV = P_1O_1 + P_2O_2 + \ldots + P_iO_i + \ldots + P_mO_m.$$

An initial proposition about decision making under conditions of risk is that people choose alternatives that maximize their expected value. For instance, suppose there are two hats, each containing slips of paper. A draw from the first hat has an expected value of EV^1, and from the second, EV^2. If

EV^1 is greater than EV^2, then we would predict that someone who maximizes expected value will choose to draw from the first hat rather than from the second. Put differently, if a_1 is the alternative "draw from the first hat," while a_2 is the alternative "draw from the second hat," and if EV^1 is greater than EV^2, we would predict that decision makers who act as if they maximize expected value will choose a_1 over a_2.

A problem with expected value. It is often useful to assume that under conditions of risk, people choose the alternative with which they associate the greater (or greatest) expected value. However, a problem emerges with expected value, which leads to the invention of another concept, **expected utility.** To illustrate this problem, suppose you have two possible gambles. Gamble *1*, which is hardly a gamble at all, would give you $1 million with certainty. Gamble *2* would give you $10 million with a probability of 0.11 (11 percent) and nothing with a probability of 0.89 (89 percent).[9] Write on a slip of paper the gamble in which you would prefer to participate.

The expected value of gamble *1* is

$$EV^1 = 1.0(\$1,000,000) = \$1,000,000,$$

while the expected value of gamble *2* is

$$EV^2 = 0.11(\$10,000,000) + 0.89(\$0) = \$1,100,000.$$

Plainly, EV^2 is greater than EV^1. Yet most (not all) people would choose to participate in gamble *1* rather than gamble *2*, and it is more than likely that you are one of those people (check your slip of paper).

Very well, you probably fail to maximize expected value under conditions of risk: you maximize something else, which is called expected utility. Predictions about your choice between the two gambles might have been wrong because they assumed that you evaluate an outcome such as money strictly according to its value alone. How would you evaluate an outcome involving a particular amount of money? The answer to this question depends on the answers to three other questions. First, how much money, or amount of the outcome, is involved? Second, how much money, or amount of the outcome, do you already have? Third, what other factors influence your evaluation? The preceding example suggests that you act as if you calculate not simply the external, objective value of an outcome—an amount of money, for example. Rather, you have a personal evaluation of the value of an outcome, and that personal evaluation differs from the value itself.

---

[9] This example is suggested by Maurice Allais, "Le comportement de l'homme rationnel devant le risque: Critique des postulates et axioms de l'école americaine," *Econometrica,* 21 (October 1953), pp. 503–546. See also Karl Henrik Borch, *The Economics of Uncertainty* (Princeton, N. J.: Princeton University Press, 1968), Chapter 6.

Utility

This is another way of saying that you have a **utility** for an amount of money. Utility is neither externally determined nor objective, nor necessarily related to the usefulness of the outcome to the decision maker. Utility has a technical definition.

Value and utility. **Value,** as just noted, is an external, objective standard that counts (enumerates) the number of units in an outcome. Utility is a decision maker's personal, comparative evaluation of different outcomes. For example, you may ask what a person's utility for a prize with a value of $10 is. Or you may ask simply what that person's utility for $10, or for friendship, or for health, or for any other conceivable outcome, is. There is absolutely no requirement that utility must be for money or even for a countable outcome. People act as if they have utility for anything, including the election of candidates and the decisions in Supreme Court cases.

To see the difference between value and utility, consider Figure 2.1. The horizontal axis measures an outcome's value—say, dollars won in a gamble—while the vertical axis measures a person's utility for the outcome. A unit of utility is a **utile.** Notice that in Figure 2.1, the gain of a unit of value—a dollar, for example—results in the gain of a unit of utility, a utile. This relationship holds true no matter how much of the outcome a person gets and no matter how much of the outcome a person already has.

If we recall the previous example of the two gambles, this figure has a natural interpretation. First, as the value of the outcome increases, utility increases. For example, the outcomes in the two gambles are $0, $1 million,

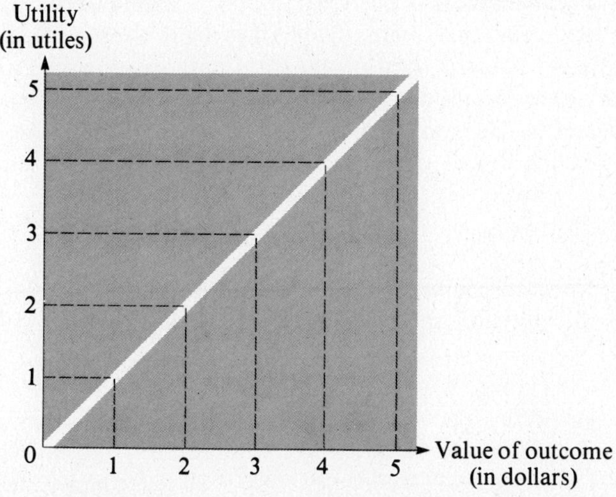

Figure 2.1 Relationship between value of outcome (in dollars) and utility of outcome—I.

and \$10 million. Let $U(O_1)$ represent someone's utility for outcome 1. The relationship in the figure says that if O_2 (outcome 2) is greater than O_1 (for example, if there is more money in O_2 than in O_1), then a decision maker's utility for O_2, $U(O_2)$, is greater than $U(O_1)$. Referring back to the two gambles, this means that $U(\$10{,}000{,}000)$ is greater than $U(\$1{,}000{,}000)$, which in turn is greater than $U(\$0)$.

Second, notice that in Figure 2.1, utility is independent of the amount of money someone already has. Thus, if a person has \$1000 and gets another dollar, he gains as much utility as he would if he had \$1 and then got another dollar. One way to say this symbolically is

$$U(\$2) - U(\$1) = U(\$1001) - U(\$1000).$$

In sum, the relationship between an outcome and a person's utility for that outcome in Figure 2.1 is an identity: the outcome's size—the amount of money—equals the number of utiles a person receives from it.

However, there is no reason why this identity should hold true. For example, consider Figure 2.2, in which value is no longer the same as utility. Similarly, $U(\$5) - U(\$4)$ is less than $U(\$4) - U(\$3)$; $U(\$4) - U(\$3)$ is less than $U(\$3) - U(\$2)$; $U(\$3) - U(\$2)$ is less than $U(\$2) - U(\$1)$; and $U(\$2) - U(\$1)$ is less than $U(\$1) - U(\$0)$. In both Figure 2.1 and Figure 2.2, utility increases with dollars received, but the relationship between money and utility in Figure 2.2 differs from the one in Figure 2.1 in an important way. In Figure 2.2, an increase from \$0 to \$1 produces a larger utility difference than does an increase from \$1 to \$2. This decline in added, marginal, utility continues, so the more money one either has or contemplates having, the less utility one gains from each additional dollar.

This is a reasonable property of utility. It implies that if you have no money and saw your last meal three days ago, then your utility for an additional dollar is greater than if you have millions of dollars.[10] This property, which economists call **diminishing marginal utility,** explains the inability of an expected value maximizing framework to predict your choice in the preceding gambles. Recall that expected value, *EV*, has the equation

$$EV = P_1O_1 + P_2O_2 + \ldots + P_iO_i + \ldots + P_mO_m.$$

To calculate expected utility, *EU,* rather than expected value, simply replace each O_i with the decision maker's utility for each O_i, $U(O_i)$. That is,

$$EU = P_1U(O_1) + P_2U(O_2) + \ldots + P_iU(O_i) + \ldots + P_mU(O_m).$$

[10] This properly does not imply that a rich person has a smaller utility for an additional dollar than a poor person has. It does imply that as a particular person has more and more money, his or her utility for each additional dollar grows smaller and smaller. The reason for this restriction on the interpretation of utility, which is discussed momentarily, is that utility is not interpersonally comparable.

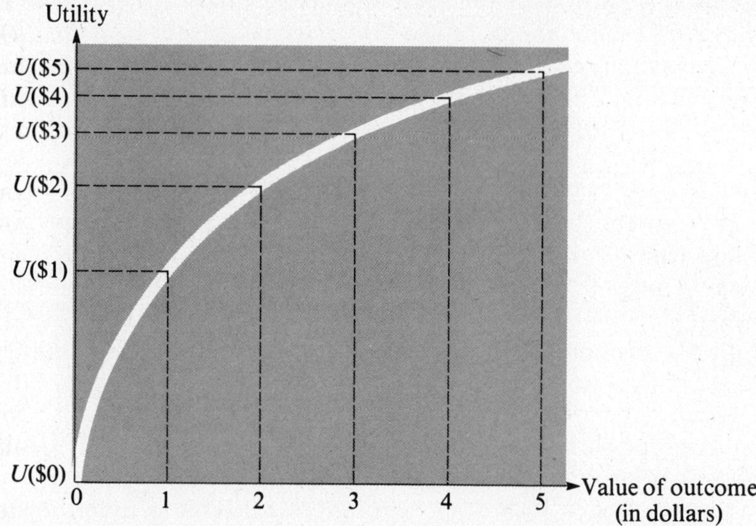

Figure 2.2 Relationship between value of outcome (in dollars) and utility of outcome—II.

Decision makers faced with risky choice act as if they choose alternatives that maximize their expected utility. To calculate expected utility for the preceding gamble, see that EV^1 becomes EU^1, and EV^2 becomes EU^2. Thus,

$$EU^1 = (1.0)U(\$1{,}000{,}000),$$

and

$$EU^2 = (0.11)U(\$10{,}000{,}000) + (0.89)U(\$0).$$

EU^1 may be greater than EU^2 even though EV^2 is greater than EV^1. This reversal occurs because your utility for $10 million is not necessarily ten times your utility for $1 million; chances are it is quite a bit less than that. Thus, you may quite reasonably have chosen gamble *1* over gamble *2*.

Calculating utility. The determination of a person's utility for an outcome begins with an arbitrary assignment of numbers. For a particular set of outcomes, we usually let someone's utility for his most preferred outcome in that set be equal to one and for his least preferred outcome be equal to zero. For example, in the previous gambles it is reasonable to suppose that you prefer $10 million to $1 million and $1 million to $0. Therefore, following the one-zero assignment to your most and least preferred outcomes, $U(\$10{,}000{,}000) = 1.00$, while $U(\$0) = 0.00$.

Now, consider the intermediate outcome, $1 million. If 1.00 and 0.00

are respectively your utilities for the most and least preferred outcomes, then your utility for \$1 million must be less than one and greater than zero. Denote this intermediate utility with the letter u, so that $U(\$1{,}000{,}000) = u$. Recall that your expected utility for gamble *1* is $EU^1 = U(\$1{,}000{,}000)$, which now becomes $EU^1 = u$. Similarly, your expected utility for gamble *2* is

$$EU^2 = (0.11)U(\$10{,}000{,}000) + (0.89)U(\$0).$$

Substituting 1.00 for $U(\$10{,}000{,}000)$ and 0.00 for $U(\$0)$, this expected utility becomes $EU^2 = 0.11$. If you chose gamble *1* over gamble *2*, then EU^1 was greater than EU^2, which means that u is greater than 0.11. Put differently, your utility for \$1 million with certainty (u) is greater than your utility for a gamble whose expected value is \$1.1 million. This conclusion seems most reasonable.

The concept of utility finds extensive use throughout this book, and therefore it is helpful to be able to calculate utility and to know how it can be employed. Here we describe one method of calculating utility, using the preceding example of two gambles.[11] Recall that a hypothetical player's expected utility for the first gamble is u, and for the second gamble, 0.11. Thus, if the player chooses the first gamble over the second, then EU^1 must exceed EU^2, which means u is greater than 0.11. If the player chooses the second gamble over the first, then EU^2 exceeds EU^1, which means u is less than 0.11. Indifference, an inability to state a preference as between the two gambles, means that u equals 0.11.

An ability to calculate u is obviously crucial to a broad application of utility. In the example of the two gambles, we cannot make a prediction unless we can measure u, at least hypothetically. To show how u might be calculated, suppose the player actually prefers gamble *1* to gamble *2*. Of course, this means that u is greater than 0.11. But how much greater? Suppose we improve the odds, so that a player choosing gamble *2* would have a 12 percent chance of getting \$10 million. EU^2 would become

$$\begin{aligned} EU^2 &= (0.12)U(\$10{,}000{,}000) + (0.88)U(\$0) \\ &= (0.12)(1) + (0.88)(0) = 0.12. \end{aligned}$$

Which gamble will the player now choose? If he chooses gamble *1*, this means that u exceeds 0.12. If the player is indifferent, u equals 0.12. If he chooses gamble *2*, u is greater than 0.11 but less than 0.12.

The odds in gamble *2* can be adjusted until the player is indifferent as between the two gambles. At that point—called the **indifference point**—$EU^2 = EU^1$, and u, as it turns out, equals the probability associated with the most preferred outcome (in this case \$10 million).

This example rests on a general method for finding utilities experimen-

---

[11] See Luce and Raiffa, *Games and Decisions*, pp. 29–31.

tally. Three outcomes are arrayed. The most preferred outcome is assigned a utility, $U(O_1)$, of 1.0; the least preferred, $U(O_3)$, 0.0; and the middle choice, $U(O_2)$, u. Then the player is offered a gamble involving his or her most and least preferred outcomes against the certainty of the middle choice. Probabilities are adjusted until indifference is reached, at which point the probability associated with the most preferred outcome equals u. Stated formally, if P and $(1 - P)$ are the probabilities in the gamble, at indifference $U(O_2) = PU(O_1) + (1 - P)U(O_3)$. But $U(O_2)$ equals u, $U(O_1)$ equals 1.0, and $U(O_3)$ equals 0.0. Thus, $u = P(1.0) + (1 - P)(0.0) = P$. Using this method, we can calculate utilities for *any* three outcomes, whether they are monetary or highly subjective and intangible. If there are more than three outcomes, we can run repeated experiments to find the different middle-outcome utilities.

Interpersonal Comparisons of Utility

The concept of utility is central to all of decision theory. Therefore, before we consider decision making under conditions of uncertainty, it is important to discuss separately the concept's most significant limitation. Simply put, decision theory provides no basis for making **interpersonal comparisons of utility.**

A hypothetical example. To see what an interpersonal comparison of utility is and why it is unjustified, consider a hypothetical situation, the American presidential election in the year 2000. Three candidates appear on the ballot: a communist, a fascist, and an anarchist. Person A prefers the communist to the fascist and the fascist to the anarchist. By transitivity, A prefers the communist to the anarchist. B's preference ordering is the reverse of A's, so B prefers the anarchist to the fascist and the fascist to the communist. By transitivity, B prefers the anarchist to the communist.

Suppose A and B hold the following utilities for the election of the candidates:

	Person A	**Person B**
utility for communist	1.00	0.00
utility for fascist	0.83	0.47
utility for anarchist	0.00	1.00

Recall that each person's utility for the most preferred candidate is arbitrarily fixed at 1.00, for the least preferred candidate at 0.00, and for the intermediate candidate at u, which is less than or equal to 1.00 and greater than or equal to 0.00.

Person A's utility for the fascist's election is 0.83, while B's utility for the same outcome is 0.47. Can these two utilities be compared, and if so, is it acceptable to conclude that A has a higher utility for the fascist's election than

B has? Absolutely not. Recall that choosing 1.00 and 0.00 as someone's utility for his or her most and least preferred outcomes respectively is entirely arbitrary, merely a mathematical convenience. It would be just as easy to set B's utility for the anarchist's election equal to 10.00 and for the fascist's election equal to 4.70, in which case B's utilities for the election of each candidate would become as follows:

	Person B
utility for communist	0.00
utility for fascist	4.70
utility for anarchist	10.00

B's new utility for the fascist's election, 4.70, is greater than 0.83, A's original utility for the same outcome. Can we conclude that B now has a higher utility for the fascist's election than A has? Absolutely not.

It is not even possible to say that A's utility for the communist's election (1.00) is greater than B's utility for the same outcome (0.00). Why not? Suppose two other candidates, a Republican and a Democrat, enter the hypothetical election, while the fascist and the anarchist quit the race. One might then find the following utility numbers, perhaps because A and B prefer the election of either major party candidate to the election of the communist:

	Person A	**Person B**
utility for Republican	0.76	1.00
utility for Democrat	1.00	0.90
utility for communist	0.00	0.00

Can we conclude that now A and B have the same utility for the communist's election? Again, absolutely not. The number 0.00 merely indicates that among these three outcomes, both A and B least wish the communist to be elected.

Utilities are highly individualistic, subjective numbers representing a person's relative evaluation of more than one outcome. The social scientist normalizes someone's utility by setting the utility for a most preferred outcome in a particular set equal to one, and for a least preferred outcome equal to zero. This is the scientist's calculation, not the person's. It is a convenience: multiply a number, x, by 1.00 and the result is x; multiply a number, x, by 0.00 and the result is 0.00. The utility numbers remain relative and express only one person's utilities for some specified set of outcomes.

There is no way in the real world to compare the utility that two persons have for the same or different outcomes; though some observers may utter a comparison, it has no meaning. Consequently, should someone say, "I love my country more than (or as much as, or even less than) you do," you may counter that scientists have no way to verify such claims, especially if love reflects utility or vice versa. There might be various ways to verify other statements, such as "I would die to defend my country against a military attack." However, even if one person offers to die while another does not, it remains impossible to compare utilities, for to do so would entail a comparison of utilities for death. All such comparisons are meaningless.

Ethical claims and interpersonal comparisons of utility. People often do make interpersonal comparisons of utility for literary, ethical, and advocacy purposes. For example, what should the election outcome be if A and B were the only voters? One ethical view would require us to add the utilities for each outcome and designate the outcome with the greatest summed utility as the ethical, or moral, outcome. The original utilities and their sums for the hypothetical election in the year 2000 would be thus:

	Person A	**Person B**	**Summed Utilities**
utility for communist	1.00	0.00	1.00
utility for fascist	0.83	0.47	1.30
utility for anarchist	0.00	1.00	1.00

Choosing by summed utilities, the fascist wins. Yet the sum of utilities conveys no meaning, because the individual utilities are not comparable. Nor is this a practical scheme for doing things; if A and B know how the choice is selected, then each will have an incentive to report his or her utilities inaccurately.

Ethical claims and the redistribution of wealth. As Chapter 3 points out, a substantial amount of collective action in the United States is aimed at redistributing wealth and income. Private action continuously redistributes wealth and income, but redistributions made by collective action ordinarily seek to overcome the wealth and income distributions created by market forces. Several arguments are advanced for and against redistributions by collective action. One argument against them is that tastes differ, and that because of their superior education, childhood training, interests, and perhaps even genetic superiority, rich people can appreciate the things that money can buy better than poor people can. Rich people drink fine wines and listen to Beethoven symphonies on sophisticated audio equipment, while poor people drink beer and watch sports on television. These patterns, it is argued, would persist regardless of wealth. Therefore, to take money from the rich and give it to the poor would be foolish, because poor people cannot appreciate the better things that money can buy as much as rich people can. We might even consider taxing the poor to support the superior tastes of those rich people who become temporarily embarrassed by financial reverses.

Nonsense? Of course, although some public policies in the United States and elsewhere, such as state support of colleges and universities, tend to redistribute wealth from lower-income citizens to their wealthier neighbors.[12] Yet several problems undermine a taste-related argument for redistributions from poor to rich. For example, even if the tastes of rich and poor are as this argument supposes, a wealth redistribution from rich to poor would allow less wealthy citizens to buy more beer and better television sets. But the argument goes wrong theoretically principally because it contains an explicit interpersonal comparison of utilities. A rich person's utility for fine wines and recordings of classical symphonies is compared to a poor person's utility for such symbols of affluence as well as for beer and for viewing the World Series. Because interpersonal comparisons of utility are impossible, the argument remains unconvincing.

One argument offered in favor of the opposite political redistribution of wealth, from rich to poor, holds that utility curves look like the one in Figure 2.2—that is, an additional dollar produces a smaller increase in utility if one has $1000 than if one has $10. Therefore, a millionaire deprived of a dollar loses less utility than the pauper who receives it gains.[13] But this argument also presupposes that two people have equivalent utilities for money, which is merely another interpersonal comparison of utilities. A rich and a poor person's utilities for money can no more be compared than can their respective utilities for the finer things of life. Hence, to say that a rich person does not miss the money lost to government redistributions as much as a poor person gains from such redistributions is again nonsense. Indeed, if we were to follow the logic of an interpersonal comparison of utilities, and if a millionaire's utility curve bends upward (unlike the one in Figure 2.2, which bends downward), then the millionaire must be given all of the poor person's money, for such a curve would indicate that the millionaire, like Uncle Scrooge, receives more and more utility with each additional dollar.

Although one may attempt to compare utilities among different persons and arrive at some ethical policy or redistribution, decision theory provides no basis for such comparisons. Furthermore, we cannot judge the relative goodness of different persons' competing goals by comparing the utilities of those who hold them, for both utilities and goals are relative, personal, and subjective. Fortunately, interpersonal comparisons of utility are absolutely not required for explaining and predicting most private and public decisions. We can also make many—but not all—evaluative judgments about decisions, public policies, and governmental processes, as becomes evident in this chapter and in Chapter 3, without drawing such comparisons.

---

[12] See W. Lee Hansen and Burton A. Weisbrod, *Benefits, Cost, and Finance of Public Higher Education* (Chicago: Markham, 1969), and Hansen, "Income Distribution Effects of Higher Education," *American Economic Review,* 60 (May 1970), pp. 335–340.

[13] Walter Blum and Harry Kalven, Jr., *The Uneasy Case for Progressive Taxation* (Chicago: University of Chicago Press, 1953).

DECISION MAKING UNDER CONDITIONS OF UNCERTAINTY: THE THEORY OF GAMES

This chapter earlier described an example of decision making under conditions of uncertainty in which two rival candidates for school superintendent compete for election, with school-board members as voters. The example shows that in decision making under conditions of uncertainty, one does not know which state of nature might prevail for each alternative chosen. Indeed, it is impossible or meaningless to assign probabilities to the occurrence of each state of nature, because for an important class of decisions made under uncertainty, other decision makers, by their choices of strategies, also choose the states of nature that might prevail.

The Best Man: An Example of Dirty Politics

A second example vividly demonstrates the problem of decision making under conditions of uncertainty and also provides the structure for an important class of situations that reemerges throughout this book. The example comes from a loose rendering of Gore Vidal's play *The Best Man.*[14]

In the play, two rivals compete for their political party's presidential nomination. One candidate, a secretary of state in a former administration, is liberal, witty, articulate, charming, and very much the intellectual-politican in the mold of the late Adlai E. Stevenson II. Although the secretary's apparent strength is his great intellect, both he and his foe know that he once suffered a nervous breakdown that required his hospitalization. The secretary's foe, a young, vigorous senator, is action-oriented rather than contemplative, homespun rather than scholarly, conservative rather than liberal, and an old-fashioned proponent of traditional morality rather than a progressive advocate of new ideas. Although the senator's alleged strengths are his embodiment of traditional American virtues and the *machismo* he exudes, both he and his foe know that a former army colleague of the senator has alleged that while in the service they shared a homosexual relationship.

Each candidate has two strategies; he can keep silent about his rival's alleged past, or he can reveal it to the delegates at the party's nominating convention. Without prejudging the morality of the problem, we shall call the first strategy, that of keeping silent, "fight clean," and the second strategy, that of revealing the foe's past, "fight dirty." The problem is to construct a theory that explains and predicts each candidate's strategy choice. The delegates might vote at any moment.

Suppose both candidates decide to fight clean. Vidal implies that they

---

[14] Gore Vidal, *The Best Man* (Boston: Little, Brown, 1960). I take great liberties with Vidal's ideas. However, with some modifications, this discussion abstracts a good part of the situation in the play.

have an equal chance of being nominated, that no other candidate has a real chance, and that these two candidates despise each other. Consequently, if both candidates use their respective fight-clean strategies, the outcomes are these:

Candidate	Strategy	Payoff (outcome)
the secretary	fight clean	probability of winning nomination is one-half; probability that senator wins nomination is one-half
the senator	fight clean	probability of winning nomination is one-half; probability that secretary wins nomination is one-half

There are two outcomes, or payoffs, for this pair of strategies and for all other pairs, because in such games there can be different payoffs for each of the decision makers. Also, notice that such games require two decisions—one by each player—to determine an outcome pair.

If both candidates fight dirty, the realistic political implication is each candidate's political oblivion. The only positive satisfaction each receives is that his hated foe is also destroyed. Consequently, if both candidates use their respective fight-dirty strategies, then the payoffs become these:

Candidate	Strategy	Payoff (outcome)
the secretary	fight dirty	political oblivion for self and senator
the senator	fight dirty	political oblivion for self and secretary

If the secretary fights dirty while the senator fights clean, then the senator is consigned to political oblivion and the secretary wins the nomination. Following our previous format, the payoffs now become these:

Candidate	Strategy	Payoff (outcome)
the secretary	fight dirty	nomination victory, senator's political oblivion
the senator	fight clean	political oblivion, secretary nominated

If, on the other hand, the secretary fights clean while the senator fights dirty, then the payoffs are reversed, with the secretary consigned to political oblivion and the senator winning the nomination.

Table 2.5 summarizes each candidate's strategies and the associated payoffs. The entries in each cell list the secretary's payoffs above the senator's. To predict each candidate's strategy choice requires that we have a knowledge of his preference ordering over the possible payoffs. One quite reasonable ordering inferred from Vidal's play is that nomination victory and political oblivion for hated foe is preferred to probability of self and foe's nomination

Table 2.5 Strategies and payoffs in *The Best Man*

		Senator's Strategies	
		fight clean	fight dirty
Secretary's Strategies	fight clean	probability of self and foe's nomination is one-half probability of self and foe's nomination is one-half	political oblivion for self, hated foe nominated nomination victory, political oblivion for hated foe
	fight dirty	nomination victory, political oblivion for hated foe political oblivion for self, hated foe nominated	political oblivion for self, political oblivion for hated foe political oblivion for self, political oblivion for hated foe

Table 2.6 Abstract representation of *The Best Man*

		Senator's Strategies	
		fight clean	fight dirty
Secretary's Strategies	fight clean	+5, +5	−6, +10
	fight dirty	+10, −6	−3, −3

each equaling one-half, which is preferred to political oblivion for self and hated foe, which in turn is preferred to political oblivion for self and hated foe nominated.

To simplify the discussion, utility numbers (utiles) can be used to represent the candidates' payoffs. Any numbers that preserve the preference ordering just given are acceptable. Thus, let the utility for a nomination victory with one's foe in political oblivion be +10, for equal probability (one-half) of self and foe's nomination be +5, for self and foe's political oblivion be −3, and for foe's nomination and self's political oblivion be −6. Table 2.6 records these assignments, with the secretary's payoff placed first in each cell and the senator's payoff second.

What happens, theoretically? Which strategies will the secretary and the senator choose? Clearly, this is *not* a case of decision making under conditions of risk or certainty. The "Nature" that determines the prevailing state of nature no longer remains a passive universe but becomes an active human being, an intelligent opponent who partially controls the payoffs. This is a classic example of decision making under conditions of uncertainty.

To predict each candidate's decision, consider the payoffs from the secretary's point of view. If the senator fights clean, then the secretary gets +5 utiles from fighting clean and +10 from fighting dirty. On the other hand, if the senator fights dirty, then the secretary gets −6 from fighting clean and −3 from fighting dirty. Since +10 is a larger number than +5, and since −3 is a larger number than −6, the secretary would prefer to fight dirty: he will give the convention delegates his information concerning the senator's alleged homosexual activity.

Now consider the payoffs from the senator's point of view. If the secretary fights clean, then the senator gets +5 from fighting clean and +10 from fighting dirty. On the other hand, if the secretary fights dirty, then the senator gets −6 from fighting clean and −3 from fighting dirty. Since again +10 is a larger number than +5, and since −3 is a larger number than −6, the senator would prefer to fight dirty no matter what the secretary does. Hence, the senator will fight dirty: he will give the convention delegates the information concerning the secretary's nervous breakdown. Since each candidate prefers fighting dirty to fighting clean, the two destroy each other.[15]

Introduction to the Theory of Games

Game theory. The preceding case, in technical language, is a game. That part of decision theory that explains and predicts the candidates' strategic choices is called **game theory,** or sometimes the theory of games. Like algebra and geometry, game theory is a subfield of mathematics. The mathematician's interest in game theory concerns abstract mathematical structures. By contrast, the political scientist's interest is to translate the components of such abstract structures so that by analogy they model real political or governmental situations—for example, the dirty-politics problem. Therefore, a mathematical game is an abstract representation of a real situation. If a political scientist can solve the game, much as one solves an equation for an unknown in algebra, then the game's solution explains and predicts what decision makers in the real world of politics and government might do in the situation the game represents.

The structure of a game. There are two principal ways to distinguish among games. One way is by number of players, particularly between games with two players and games with more than two players. The first are called **two-person games,** and the second, ***n*-person games.** This distinction is important because in *n*-person games, some players might form **coalitions.** Coalitions of many players occur in the two houses of Congress, among the justices of the Supreme Court, among the members of different branches of

[15] Vidal's plot is not fanciful; similar situations actually happen. Sometimes people find a way out of such situations, but to escape they must have other strategies besides those listed here. However, suppose one candidate has a deep moral aversion to fighting dirty, while the other has no such reluctance. The candidate with the moral aversion loses to the one without it. Earlier this chapter offered the example of the school-superintendent election, in which honest candidates, who espouse what they believe, consistently lose to unscrupulous ones. *The Best Man* provides another instance in which one might worry about the character of some who win elections.

government, during elections among people who belong to identifiable groups in the population, and among government leaders of different nations in matters of international relations. Since coalitions are not possible in two-person games, we study such games differently.

A second way to distinguish among games is by the theoretical possibility of communication between or among the players. In the two games examined earlier, between two candidates for school superintendent and between two candidates for a party's presidential nomination, information about an opponent's strategy is useful. In the first game, if one school superintendent candidate knows his opponent's strategy (to advocate the status quo, open schools, or forced busing), then the knowledgeable candidate can win. In the second game, the ability to communicate is important because without it the candidates seem unlikely to avoid mutual political destruction.

Communication may be complete or partial, but it is necessary, though not sufficient, for cooperation. Accordingly, a game in which the players cannot communicate is called a **non-cooperative game,** and one in which they can communicate is called a **cooperative game.** These terms do not mean that if people can communicate, they will be cooperative. People communicate and cooperate only if it is desirable individually for them to do so. The terms *non-cooperative* and *cooperative* only indicate the possibility or impossibility of communication between or among players.[16]

Two-Person Non-Cooperative Games

Two-person zero-sum games. Consider the game represented in Table 2.7. This game models a situation in which the players' interests are strictly opposed. For instance, suppose player A chooses a_3, while B chooses b_1. Player A receives 6 utiles and B, −6. Whatever one player wins, the other loses. Hence, this game represents pure conflict. The sum of the payoffs to the two players associated with any pair of strategies is always zero, so this game is called a **zero-sum game.**

---

[16] A common belief is that if people would communicate, they would get along. Applied to international relations, this belief appears to support the creation and maintenance of such agencies of communication as the United Nations as well as such practices as cultural and student exchanges. Applied to interpersonal relationships, this belief supports the usefulness of encounter groups and confrontation sessions. Actually, the belief that communication is conducive to good will and peace is sometimes without merit. Someone may believe that a new neighbor is a benign, friendly chap until he starts talking: "No, you may not borrow my rake! Why don't you paint your house before the street becomes a slum? And tell your creepy hippie kid to keep his hands off my daughter!" Although communication sometimes promotes cooperation and perhaps even good will, the opposite result can also occur. Indeed, by communicating, two people may learn for the first time that their goals are conflicting. On the other hand, two enemies may learn by communicating that they really have nothing to fight about. Therefore, without additional information we can utter few general sentences about the relationship between communication and harmony.

Table 2.7 Two-person zero-sum game

		B's Strategies		
		b_1	b_2	b_3
	a_1	9, −9	3, −3	4, −4
A's Strategies	a_2	11, −11	8, −8	12, −12
	a_3	6, −6	5, −5	7, −7

To understand how such games are played, consider the game in Table 2.7 from A's point of view. Suppose A chooses a_1. Of course, A's payoff partly depends on the strategy B chooses. If B chooses b_1, then A gets +9; if B chooses b_2, then A gets +3; and if B chooses b_3, then A gets +4.

A player's **security level** from playing a particular strategy is the worst possible payoff—the minimum payoff—that he or she might receive from choosing it. For example, if A chooses a_1, then A's possible payoffs are in a row: +9, +3, +4. A's security level from playing a_1 is the row minimum, +3, which occurs if B chooses b_2. A's security level from choosing a_2, the row minimum of +11, +8, and +12, is +8, which occurs if B chooses b_2. And, A's security level from choosing a_3, the row minimum of +6, +5, and +7, is +5, which also occurs if B chooses b_2.

A now has a security level, a row minimum, for each strategy: +3 from a_1; +8 from a_2; and +5 from a_3. Observe that +8 is the maximum of the row minima. Stated differently, +8 is A's maximum security level. By choosing a_2, A can guarantee himself at least +8 no matter what B does. Since a_2 guarantees A at least this *maxi*mum amount of the row *min*ima, a_2 is called A's **maximin strategy.**

Considering the same game from B's point of view, suppose B chooses b_1. If A chooses a_1, then B gets −9; if A chooses a_2, then B gets −11; and, if A chooses a_3, then B gets −6. B's security level from choosing b_1 is −11, which occurs if A chooses a_2. This payoff is the column maximum (loss). Similarly, B's security level from choosing b_2 is the column maximum (loss) of −3, −8, and −5, or −8, which occurs if A chooses a_2. B's security level from choosing b_3, the column maximum (loss) of −4, −12, and −7, is −12, which also occurs if A chooses a_2.

B now has a security level, a column maximum (loss), for each strategy: −11 from b_1; −8 from b_2; and −12 from b_3. Observe that −8 is the minimum of the column maxima (of loss). Stated differently, −8 is B's maximum security level. By choosing b_2, B can be guaranteed a loss of not more than −8 no matter what A does. Since b_2 guarantees B at least this *mini*mum amount of the column *max*ima (of losses), b_2 is called B's **minimax strategy.**

Plainly, if A chooses his maximin strategy, a_2, then B has no incentive to choose a strategy other than his minimax strategy, b_2. Similarly, if B chooses his minimax strategy, b_2, then A has no incentive to choose a strategy other than his maximin strategy, a_2. This is a unique condition. The set of strategies

Table 2.8 Two-person zero-sum game without pure equilibrium strategies

		B's Strategies	
		b_1	b_2
A's Strategies	a_1	2, −2	5, −5
	a_2	4, −4	3, −3

$\{a_2, b_2\}$ is called an **equilibrium strategy pair** (sometimes it is just called an equilibrium pair) because if one player chooses his best strategy, the one that guarantees him the greatest security level, then the other player must do the same. Hence, A's maximin strategy, a_2, and B's minimax strategy, b_2, are both **equilibrium strategies.** Generally, an equilibrium strategy is the strategy that works best if a player's opponent is also at his equilibrium strategy.

For a large class of two-person zero-sum games, explaining past strategy choices and predicting future ones is simple: we need only identify the players' maximin and minimax strategies respectively and name the equilibrium strategy pair. The game's outcome consists of the payoff to each player associated with that equilibrium pair. (Indeed, the analysis of such games proves extremely useful in Chapter 7 for the study of campaign strategies in elections.) However, consider the two-person zero-sum game in Table 2.8.

A's security level from choosing a_1 is +2, and from a_2, +3. So his maximin strategy seems to be a_2. Similarly, B's security level from choosing b_1 is −4, and from b_2, −5. So his minimax strategy seems to be b_1. But is $\{a_2, b_1\}$ an equilibrium pair? Suppose A does choose a_2 while B chooses b_1. A gets +4 and B gets −4. However, B can do better by leaving b_1, his apparent minimax strategy, and adopting b_2. This gives A, +3 and B, −3. Hence, $\{a_2, b_1\}$ is *not* an equilibrium pair. Anticipating B's desire to choose b_2, A decides to choose a_1, in which case A gets +5 and B gets −5. But B is aware of A's cleverness and decides to play b_1 instead of b_2, in which case A gets only +2 while B gets −2. Quite logically, A now shifts from a_1 to a_2, so A and B arrive where they began, and the entire cycle starts over again. In sum, A and B can find no equilibrium.

This inability to find equilibria is a problem that lies in the requirement that A and B must choose what are known as **pure strategies.** An alternative would be to allow them to choose **mixed strategies.** For example, B might flip a coin and choose b_1 if heads appears or b_2 if tails appears. Or, B might use a spinner—a simplified roulette wheel—to make a choice. Half of the circle would be marked b_1 and the other half, b_2. Both players would spin their respective dials and announce their strategies simultaneously.

The logic of such mixed strategies and the procedure for calculating them is beyond an introductory text. However, mixed strategies involve playing each pure strategy with a known probability (not necessarily one-half). Chapters 3, 7, and 8 show that many elections are really games without pure strategy equilibria. And, the lack of pure strategy equilibria in elections turns out to be a major problem for collective choice. The underlying preference orderings in Tables 1.2 and 2.3 are of the sort that can produce election games without pure strategy equilibria. Candidates react to the absence of pure strategy equilibria in predictable ways, which Chapter 7 discusses in detail.

Communication. Zero-sum games have symmetric payoffs: one player's payoff is the mirror image of the other's. Because of this symmetry, pure or mixed equilibrium strategies are relatively easy to identify. However, in **nonzero-sum games**—those in which the payoffs associated with each set of strategies do not add to zero—payoffs are not mirror images of each other, and solutions to such games may be difficult to define.

The two games recorded in Table 2.9 illustrate some of the problems of finding solutions to nonzero-sum games in general and particularly to those games without communication. Game One requires little knowledge to specify each player's correct decision. A and B adopt the strategy pair $\{a_1, b_1\}$ and receive 20 utiles each. Whether or not they can communicate seems irrelevant. However, in Game Two the non-cooperative aspect becomes more important. A and B cannot necessarily find a way to arrive at a correct strategy pair, either $\{a_1, b_1\}$ or $\{a_2, b_2\}$. If each chooses a mixed strategy—say, of playing each strategy 50 percent of the time—they do less well than if they get together. Of course, if A and B play this game several times, then the experience of earlier plays provides a kind of communication; eventually the players might adopt either $\{a_1, b_1\}$ or $\{a_2, b_2\}$. But in the first few plays of the game, some (0, 0) outcomes are bound to occur.[17] For two-person zero-sum games, communication is irrelevant, because the players' interests are strictly opposed and there is nothing to bargain about.

The prisoners' dilemma. The interplay between communication and the nonzero-sum element is emphasized in a game between two thieves who hold up a liquor store while each is on parole for an earlier offense. The store clerk cannot positively identify either thief, but each thief is arrested after the robbery and placed in an isolated cell. The two thieves cannot communicate with each other. The district attorney says to Thief A, "We caught you with a gun in violation of your parole. For this you must serve out the remainder of your term from the last conviction: one year. However, we have reason to believe you were near Triple-A Liquor Store when it was held up last night. We suspect an acquaintance of yours, Thief B, of the crime. If you will

[17] The players in these games might tacitly coordinate their strategies. For instance, A and B might go directly to $\{a_1, b_1\}$ and stay there. This is much like deciding on where to meet someone who is looking for you when you have not previously agreed about a meeting place; most people would go to the most prominent landmark in the area. See Thomas C. Schelling, *The Strategy of Conflict* (New York: Oxford University Press, 1963), p. 54, *passim.*

Table 2.9 The effects of communication

Game One (B's Strategies)

A's Strategies	b_1	b_2
a_1	20, 20	0, 0
a_2	0, 0	0, 0

Game Two (B's Strategies)

A's Strategies	b_1	b_2
a_1	20, 20	0, 0
a_2	0, 0	20, 20

Table 2.10 The prisoners' dilemma

Thief A's Strategies	*Thief* B's *Strategies*: do not rat, b_1	rat, b_2
do not rat, a_1	1 year for Thief A 1 year for Thief B	11 years for Thief A freedom for Thief B
rat, a_2	freedom for Thief A 11 years for Thief B	10 years for Thief A 10 years for Thief B

Table 2.11 Prisoners' dilemma in utiles

Thief A's *Strategies*	*Thief* B's *Strategies*: do not rat, b_1	rat, b_2
do not rat, a_1	$-1, -1$	$-11, 0$
rat, a_2	$0, -11$	$-10, -10$

identify B as the robber, we will drop the violation-of-parole charge against you." Naturally, the district attorney tells Thief B the same thing.

Table 2.10 summarizes this game, which is called the **prisoners' dilemma.** Each prisoner has two strategies: rat on partner and do not rat on partner. If neither rats, $\{a_1, b_1\}$ is chosen, and each receives a one-year term for violation of parole. If A rats but B does not, A goes free while B gets ten years for armed robbery and one year for violation of parole. If both thieves rat, then good to his word the district attorney drops the parole violation charge but sends them both up for ten years on the armed robbery charge.

Without sacrificing any generality, suppose each thief loses one utile for each year in jail. Table 2.11 summarizes these utilities. Although the players' decisions in the non-cooperative form of the prisoners' dilemma can be predicted, there is little satisfaction in this notion of a solution. While $\{a_2, b_2\}$ maximizes the players' respective security levels, another strategy pair, $\{a_1, b_1\}$, does better for each of them. The problem is that the thieves cannot communicate. Of course, communication will only partly solve their problem, for if the thieves do not trust each other, each will have a clear incentive to chisel on any agreement not to testify.

Now look again at the game between the secretary and the senator in Table 2.6. Although the utility numbers in that game differ from those of the prisoners' dilemma, the games are equivalent because they preserve the same order of utility for each player. Thus, as far as the payoffs are concerned, fighting dirty is like ratting and fighting clean is like not ratting. The similarity between these two games is important. Each represents a distinctly different social situation. Yet, if each game's substance is abstracted away, leaving only strategies and utilities, there remains a common explanation for the players' decisions. Therefore, whenever someone characterizes a social situation as a two-person non-cooperative prisoners' dilemma, you know exactly what decisions and outcomes to expect.

Chicken. The game of **chicken** is well known to students of the 1950s. In this game, two drivers propel their automobiles at each other down a narrow road, and whoever swerves first to avoid a collision is chicken. Each player has two strategies: swerve and do not swerve. Utilities for the payoff structure in chicken are listed in Table 2.12.

Recall that in the non-cooperative prisoners' dilemma, there is some reason to believe that the players will adopt $\{a_2, b_2\}$. Here, no such reasoning applies. This game, which is fundamentally unstable, appears to have no pure strategy equilibrium. Though we might wish to predict a strategy choice, a finding of instability remains important because it identifies an indeterminacy and randomness in social life.

Two-Person Cooperative Games

The cooperative prisoners' dilemma. How should players in a prisoners' dilemma proceed if they can communicate—if the game is cooperative? The answer to this question depends on whether the players trust each other or not and on whether agreements can be enforced or not. If mutual trust prevails, the players can agree to choose $\{a_1, b_1\}$, and the game is straightforward. However, in many political and governmental situations, the degree of trust necessary to get to $\{a_1, b_1\}$ is lacking. Therefore, people find ways of enforcing a mutual agreement to choose $\{a_1, b_1\}$, and this enforcement often makes up the stuff of politics and government.

Criminals who are members of organized crime groups and who have been charged with criminal offenses provide real examples of prisoners' dilemmas. Secrecy is important to members of a criminal organization, especially if one of their number faces prosecution. It is often in an indicted criminal's interest to trade organization secrets or testimony for a lighter sentence or no sentence at all. Even though this trade might lead to the imprisonment of many fellow organization members, it remains attractive for defendants who would otherwise face long prison terms. To enforce a

Table 2.12 The game of chicken

		B's *Strategies* swerve, b_1	B's *Strategies* do not swerve, b_2
A's *Strategies*	swerve, a_1	0, 0	−10, 20
	do not swerve, a_2	20, −10	−30, −30

cooperative solution, organization leaders invoke *omertà,* the law of silence: they reward defendants who refrain from cooperating with prosecutors and kill those who turn state's evidence. Because of *omertà,* it is often difficult to convict members of criminal organizations.

Enforcing strategic choices beneficial to the members of an organization is not exclusive to criminal groups, however. Most government regulations of the private sector, as Chapters 3 and 11 point out, are supposedly designed to solve a game resembling an n-person prisoners' dilemma. For example, people sometimes will pollute the environment or not pay taxes because it is in their individual interests to do so. Such actions result in less-than-desirable outcomes for everyone, including the polluter and the tax evader. Government regulations and other collective actions are supposed to be designed to enforce the desired strategy choice by requiring reduced pollution emissions and compelling compliance with the tax code.

The cooperative game of chicken. The cooperative game of chicken shows the difference between *cooperative* meaning "going along" and *cooperative* meaning, technically, "the ability to communicate." In cooperative chicken, the second meaning applies. Players of chicken try to communicate their commitment to a no-swerve strategy. The game's payoff structure makes it evident that if player A can convince B that he will not swerve, then B must swerve. As Chapter 10 points out, cooperative chicken provides a useful analogue for several international confrontations, such as the one that occurred between the United States and the Soviet Union in the Cuban missile crisis of 1962. The president's problem in such cases is to convince his international adversary of his intention not to swerve, not to back down.

Cooperative games and bargaining. Communication, the defining aspect of cooperative games, makes bargaining possible. Bargaining occurs constantly in politics and government, as well as in the private sector; consequently, we consider it here under the topic of cooperative games.

What is a good bargain? For market decisions—private choice—the answer is deceptively simple: ordinarily, a good bargain is any bargain that occurs. Why? Recall that private choice occurs in the absence of coercion. Thus, suppose you make a bargain with an automobile dealer to buy an automobile for $8000. You must prefer the automobile to the $8000, and the dealer must prefer the $8000 to the automobile, or else you would not have made the bargain. Hence, by trading, both of your utilities have increased. Chapter 3 analyzes such private-sector bargains at some length. By contrast, political decisions—collective choices—imply the presence of coercion, so we are less certain about what a good bargain is in public choice than in market choice.[18]

To develop some notions of goodness, we must consider bargains abstractly.[19] First, what does *good* mean? It does not mean that the bargain has the blessings of someone other than the parties to it. Nor does it mean that the bargainers necessarily like the outcome. It means that each party to the bargain individually believes that it has improved his or her lot compared to what it would have been without the bargain.

Consider Figure 2.3, which depicts all of the outcomes of an arbitrary two-person game. The horizontal axis measures player A's utility, U, while the vertical axis measures player B's utility, V. The letters U^* and V^* denote the utility outcomes of a good bargain. In the two-dimensional representation of Figure 2.3, a good bargain is a point with coordinates (U^*, V^*). What properties should it have?

First, the bargain must be feasible, which means that the pair of utilities, (U^*, V^*), must be a possible outcome. Hence, the outcome must fall within the gray area denoted by the letter R and including the area's boundaries. The term usually applied to bargains the terms of which are known by at least one party to be infeasible is **fraud,** because one bargainer seeks to convince the other to accept an impossible outcome. The letter R denotes all feasible bargains. In sum, the utilities associated with a good bargain must coincide with a point in R.

Now consider the points U_0 and V_0, which arbitrarily represent each bargainer's utility before the bargain or in the absence of a bargain. Since people do not make bargains from which they expect to be worse off, the second property of a good bargain is that each bargainer must expect to be either better off or no worse off after the bargain. That is, U^* must be greater than or equal to U_0, and V^* must be greater than or equal to V_0. No one expects to lose because of the bargain. Referring to Figure 2.3, this condition means that A rejects any bargain yielding less utility than U_0. Hence, a good bargain is restricted to the area to the right of the line connecting U_0 and a (including the line itself). B rejects any bargain yielding less utility than V_0. So, a good bargain is also restricted to the area above the line connecting V_0 and f (including the line itself).

Bargaining requires implicit or explicit communication between the

---

[18] Those who make political and governmental bargains usually expect to be better off because of the bargains. But often in politics and government, a bargain between A and B places obligations on C, who had little or no say in the negotiations. As Chapter 3 points out, this lack of consent can also be a problem in the private sector, but it is commonly an intended consequence of decisions taken in the public sector.

[19] For a generalized discussion of bargaining, see Luce and Raiffa, *Games and Decisions,* pp. 124–137.

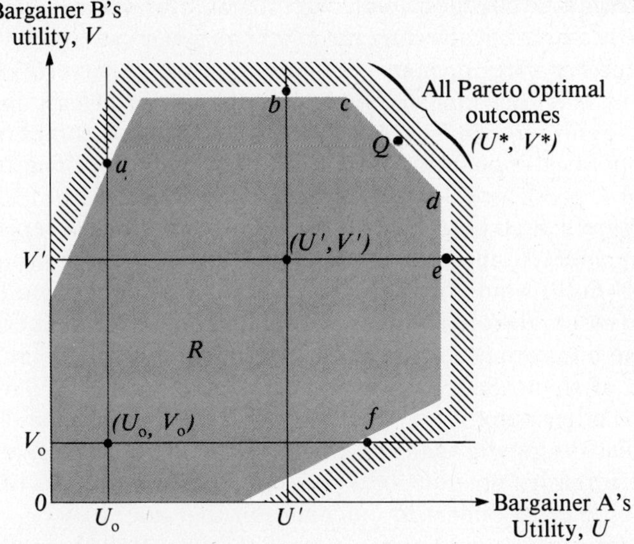

Figure 2.3 Outcomes of two-person bargain.

Source: Suggested by R. Duncan Luce and Howard Raiffa, *Games and Decisions: Introduction and Critical Survey* (New York: Wiley, 1957), p. 136, Figure 10.

players. But one of the bargainers may break off communication at any time and proceed to treat the situation like a non-cooperative game, perhaps by using a minimax strategy. Both bargainers enjoy this threat capacity, and neither would accept a cooperative, bargained outcome with less utility than he could get by playing the game non-cooperatively. Suppose (U', V') is the non-cooperative solution to the game. The third property of a good bargain is that each bargainer must expect to do better or no worse cooperatively than non-cooperatively. That is, U^* must be greater than or equal to U', and V^* must be greater than or equal to V'. Hence, bargaining, communication, must pay for the players to continue discussions. Referring again to Figure 2.3, we find that this third property of a good bargain means that A rejects any bargain yielding less utility than U', and B rejects any bargain yielding less utility than V'. So a good bargain must fall within the area to the right of the line connecting U' and *b* and above the line connecting V' and *e* (including the lines themselves).

The first three properties of a good bargain limit bargained outcomes to those that for the players are feasible, no worse than the status quo, and no worse than the non-cooperative solution. Now consider again the point (U', V') in Figure 2.3, and notice that A can get a better bargain at point *e* without affecting B's utility. If the bargainers move from (U', V') to *e*, they can also improve B's utility by moving from *e* to *d* without diminishing A's utility. Similarly, from (U', V') the bargainers can move to *b* and from *b* to *c*. These movements indicate changes in outcomes that improve at least one bargainer's utility while at worse not affecting the other bargainer's utility. The bargainers jointly prefer outcomes such as *c* and *d* to outcomes such as (U', V'). Indeed, once at *c* or *d*, it is impossible to move without harming at least one bargainer. Such points represent what are called Pareto optimal outcomes (named after the Italian political economist Vilfredo Pareto). **Pareto optimality** is the final property of a good bargain.

In Figure 2.3, all points on the line connecting *c* and *d* represent Pareto optimal outcomes. If an outcome falls elsewhere in *R*, at least one bargainer (and usually both) would be better off with a point on the line connecting *c* and *d*, at no cost to the other bargainer. Similarly, if the bargainers go to some point on the line connecting *c* and *d*, a move to any other point on that line harms one of them. Stated formally, for (U^*, V^*) to be a Pareto optimal outcome, no other point (U, V) can exist that is feasible (in *R*) and that has the property that *U* is greater than or equal to U^* and *V* is greater than or equal to V^*. Put differently, no outcomes that are not on the line *cd* are jointly preferred by the bargainers to outcomes on that line.

What point along the line connecting *c* and *d* will the bargainers choose? Without more information, we cannot say. The actual point the bargainers choose on the Pareto optimal line is probably a function of their bargaining skills. Some argue that this outcome should maximize the product of the two utilities, U^* times V^*. This outcome would lie halfway down the line connecting *c* and *d*, at the point labeled *Q*. But choosing a point by this criterion amounts to choosing one of a number of Pareto optimal outcomes. Although this criterion requires no explicit interpersonal comparison of utilities, it does require a knowledge of each bargainer's utilities that is more nearly precise than what is commonly available.

In most social and political situations, especially those involving large numbers of people, a Pareto optimal outcome or public policy cannot always be identified. Often, too many imponderables remain for us to declare with confidence that some outcome is indeed Pareto optimal. Nevertheless, in such situations the Pareto optimality criterion is helpful in distinguishing between two or more outcomes. We can refer to outcomes being **Pareto preferred** rather than being Pareto optimal: when we compare two outcomes, we say that the first is Pareto preferred to the second if the first but not the second would be Pareto optimal provided these two outcomes were the only ones feasible. For instance, in Figure 2.3, (U', V') is Pareto preferred to (U_0, V_0) because both bargainers are better off with (U', V'). Similarly, *b* is Pareto preferred to (U', V') because with it B is better off without making A worse off. Generally, public policy (or outcome) *X* is Pareto preferred to policy *Y* if at least one person is better off with *X* than with *Y*, while no one is worse off. Of course, Pareto optimal outcomes are also Pareto preferred, though the opposite does not necessarily hold true. The Pareto preferred condition is thus weaker than the Pareto optimal condition, but it will find use throughout this book.

N-Person Games

Many basic ideas about politics and government come from studying risky choice and two-person game theory. However, public choice commonly includes situations with more than two persons, which require a theory of n-person games for making explanations and predictions. N-person game theory is more complex than two-person game theory, but in this book we use only a few central concepts from n-person game theory.

Coalitions. The essential feature of n-person games, especially n-person cooperative games, is the possibility of coalitions. Usually a coalition is a number of people who join together, explicitly or implicitly, to coordinate strategies and thus to achieve some goal they hold in common. For example, American political parties are really coalitions whose members seek to elect a common slate of officeholders. Similarly, in foreign relations, the leaders of NATO countries and of Warsaw Pact nations represent two more or less stable coalitions. But coalitions do not need formal labels or organization titles. For many years, as Chapter 9 recalls, southern Democrats and northern Republicans in the Congress maintained a conservative coalition against the proposed legislation of President Franklin D. Roosevelt's New Deal. The notion of a coalition follows from the idea of people coordinating their strategies to win something (for example, they might agree to vote together in a certain way).

A simple three-person game. The most direct way to introduce n-person game theory as it applies to politics and government is with a simple three-person game. Suppose three members of the House of Representatives, A, B, and C, form a committee to decide how to allocate highway funds to their respective states. Also, suppose that the taxpayers in each state contribute $10 million, so that $30 million is available for distribution. Finally, assume that the members of the House will accept whatever recommendation a majority of the members of the committee decide to make.

Without further information, most people would argue that a reasonable distribution of the funds would give each state an amount equivalent to what the taxpayers of that state have paid in. Since each state's taxpayers have contributed $10 million, each state should therefore receive back $10 million in highway funds. Suppose that (a, b, c) represents the amount of money, in millions of dollars, that each state is to receive as a result of the vote in the committee. The preceding argument suggests an allocation of (10, 10, 10).

However, majority rule makes several other kinds of allocations possible. In particular, if A and B form a coalition, the allocation might be (15, 15, 0); if A and C form a coalition, it might be (15, 0, 15); and if B and C form a coalition, it might be (0, 15, 15). There is no way of knowing in advance which of these three coalitions might form. Hence, in situations such as these we can expect a fundamental instability and a lack of uniqueness in explanations and predictions of payoffs and coalitions.

The size principle. One attempt to find uniqueness in explaining and predicting coalitions and payoffs, or at least to limit considerably the set of possible coalitions and payoffs, is the **size principle.**[20] This principle states that for certain classes of n-person zero-sum games, only **minimum winning coalitions** form. To understand the logic of the size principle, suppose there is a legislature of 101 senators, one from each of 101 states. The taxpayers of each state contribute $1 to the treasury, and the senators vote by majority rule on how to allocate the funds to the states. If a coalition of all of the 101 senators, a **grand coalition,** forms and votes to give each state its original $1, the net monetary benefit to each state is zero.[21] However, a coalition of 100 senators might vote to give nothing to the remaining senator's state and spread the extra dollar around among their own states. The losing senator would be in a coalition by himself, and the payoff to the senator's state becomes minus $1; assuming equal division, the 100 other states receive a net monetary benefit of one cent each from the payoff of $1 to their coalition. (Net benefits are arrived at by subtracting each state's original contribution of $1.) The winning coalition would probably continue to expel members until only 51 remained. At that size, the coalition would continue to win, and since the winners win what the losers lose, the winnings to the coalition would be maximized at $50. Again assuming equal division, this would amount to a net benefit of $50 divided by 51 states—practically $1—for each state in the winning coalition. The minimum winning coalition has the greatest payoff and therefore is most likely to form.

The game of dividing $30 million among three congressional districts can be turned into a zero-sum game by subtracting the tax share of each district from its payoff. For example, if A and B form a coalition, the payoff configuration might be (15, 15, 0). Subtracting $10 million from each entry yields a payoff configuration of (5, 5, −10). The sum of these payoffs is zero, and thus we expect a minimum winning coalition of only two members.[22]

The preceding examples assume that states are equally weighted in the Congress, so we cannot say which states might become members of the winning coalition and which members of the losing coalition. However, if the states are unequally weighted, then more accurate predictions about coalition membership are possible. For example, if states A, B, and C have six, ten, and fifteen representatives (legislative votes) respectively, and if state con-

[20] William H. Riker, *The Theory of Political Coalitions* (New Haven, Conn.: Yale University Press, 1962).

[21] Technically, each state would receive less than nothing. Its taxpayers would have to pay a cost to maintain the senators at their place of business and an additional cost to collect and disburse the money. If all legislative action were of this nature, not having a Senate would be Pareto preferred to having one.

[22] If payoffs in a game always add up to the same constant (other than zero), the game is called a **constant-sum game,** a special case of a nonzero-sum game. By subtracting out this constant from each player's payoffs, the game can be converted into a zero-sum game. Therefore, it should come as no surprise that constant-sum games are played like zero-sum games.

gressional delegations vote as blocs, then under majority rule, the size principle would predict the formation of a coalition of A and B.

Whether or not states are equally weighted, a hypothesis derived from the size principle predicts that large, overweighted coalitions are less stable than small, minimum winning ones. Larger coalitions have less to distribute to members to ensure their loyalty. Evidence indicates that winning coalitions in American state legislatures become more and more stable as they approach minimum winning size. Stability here means that the coalition lasts longer and survives further tests of voting or of other political activities. Grand coalitions, coalitions of the whole, are least stable of all.[23]

This result is pessimistic. It implies that in zero-sum-like social or political situations—or in constant-sum conditions when the size of "the pie" is fixed—stable unity, or harmony, lies beyond human capacity. There is nothing perverse about such an implication. Changing this situation, in which a small majority exploits a large minority, would require a departure either from the zero-sum condition itself or from the perception of the situation as zero sum. Different social and political problems can be interpreted according to whether they are zero-sum-like. However, zero-sum games come very close to representing many racial, religious, ethnic, ideological, and international conflicts. In such situations, people often perceive no gains from bargaining in a market setting of private action. Hence, they turn to collective action to enforce their wishes. Majority rule then creates differences in the net costs and benefits members of the majority and minority coalitions experience as a consequence of collective action.

QUESTIONS FOR DISCUSSION AND REVIEW

1. Is the decision to vote for one of the candidates or to abstain from voting in a presidential election made under conditions of certainty, risk, or uncertainty, or under some combination of these conditions? What are the relevant alternatives, outcomes, probabilities, and states of nature? Are all probabilities meaningful? Would your answers to these questions change in any way if abstention were severely punished by law?
2. Suppose the situation depicted in Table 2.2 is a case of decision making under conditions of certainty, because you are sure that both of your fellow school–board members will vote for Adams. Why might you then vote for Adams, even if you prefer Baker to Adams?

[23] Riker, *The Theory of Political Coalitions,* pp. 54–76. See also David B. Meltz, "Legislative Party Cohesion: A Model of the Bargaining Process in State Legislatures," *Journal of Politics,* 25 (August 1973), pp. 647–681. Chapter 7 applies the size principle to a recent series of presidential elections.

Does your answer pose a problem for making rational decisions, or for explaining and predicting decisions using the postulate of rational choice, or for both or neither?

3. Two friends walking down the street suddenly spot a frog. Tom says to Dick, "I'll pay you $10 if you eat that frog." Dick agrees, eats the frog, and collects $10 from Tom. Not long after, they spot another frog, and Dick says to Tom, "I'll return your $10 if you eat that frog." Tom agrees, eats the frog, and gets his $10 back. Suddenly Tom and Dick look at each other and ask simultaneously, "What have we done?" How would you answer their question? (This problem is attributed to Professor Amos Katz of Virginia Polytechnic Institute and State University.)
4. In the movie *Little Big Man,* General Custer asks an Indian scout if hostile Indians are waiting to attack his troops in valley *X* or valley *Y*. Custer suspects the scout is disloyal. The scout is aware of Custer's suspicions, and Custer knows the scout is aware of them. If the scout says, "They wait in valley *X*" Custer might proceed into valley *Y* or he might reason that the scout is lying and proceed into valley *X* or he might go through a he-thinks-that-I-think-that-he-thinks routine and proceed into valley *X* . . . or *Y* . . . or *X* . . . . What kind of game is this? What is Custer's best strategy? What is the scout's best strategy? Does a pure strategy equilibrium pair exist?
5. Suppose interpersonal comparisons of utility were both possible and meaningful. Under what circumstances would public policies recommended by such comparisons be the same as public policies recommended by the Pareto optimality standard? Under what circumstances would they be different? Do elected officeholders ever use either standard in enacting public policy? Should they? Would a decision made by unanimous consent be equivalent to one made by using either standard?
6. Speaking in very general terms, what kind of games can be used to represent private choice? What kind can be used to represent public choice? Explain your answers. What importance do your answers hold in choosing between private- and public-choice mechanisms?
7. Should political and social unrest be most expected while an economy is expanding or while it is standing still or contracting? Would answers to this question based on the size principle accord with observations based on real experiences?

NEW CONCEPTS AND TERMS

alternative
chicken
coalition
constant-sum game

cooperative game
decision making under conditions of certainty
decision making under conditions of risk
decision making under conditions of uncertainty
diminishing marginal utility
equilibrium strategy
equilibrium strategy pair
expected utility
expected value
fraud
game theory
games of strategy
grand coalition
indifference point
interpersonal comparison of utilities
maximin strategy
minimax strategy
minimum winning coalition
mixed strategies
non-cooperative game
nonzero-sum game
n-person game
Pareto optimality
Pareto preferred
prisoners' dilemma
pure strategies
security level
size principle
state of nature
strategy
two-person game
utile
utility
value
zero-sum game

3

Elements of Public Policy

Chapter 1 describes the extent of collective action in the United States and discusses certain aspects of goals. Chapter 2 introduces elements of decision theory used throughout this book. Now this chapter turns to the first and most important decision of politics and government: whether to make some set of human actions private or collective. This decision usually is complex and includes a host of other decisions.

Suppose some activity is now private. A decision to make it collective simultaneously includes decisions about five things:

The decision to take collective action. First, people must decide whether to make the activity collective or not. In the absence of any other public-sector activity, a decision to undertake the first collective action is equivalent to a decision to create a government, a public sector. In the presence of some public-sector activity, a decision to undertake a new form of collective action usually implies an expansion of the public sector. In either case, a decision to make some formerly private action collective or to expand the public sector where there has been no private activity entails a move from private, voluntary decision making about that activity to some formal, coercive structure, complete with laws and regulations.[1]

---

[1] Suppose people decide upon collective action where no private action has been. Manned space exploration is a good example. Why would this decision entail a move away from private, voluntary decision making about some activity toward some formal, coercive structure? If no one in the private sector had already undertaken a particular

The form of collective action. Second, people must decide upon the proper or desirable manner or substance of collective action. What will the new law or regulation do, and how will it do it? For example, consider the many conceivable forms of collective action concerning the once private activities of manufacturing and selling alcoholic beverages: socialize all or part of these activities, allowing government agents to manufacture or sell alcohol, with or without continued private manufacture or sale; license only some people to manufacture or sell alcohol; subsidize liquor manufacturers or retailers; tax the sale of alcohol; place tariffs or quotas on the importation of alcohol; ration alcohol; relive the "noble experiment" and enact prohibition again; regulate the manufacture and sale of alcohol with laws concerning price, purity, proof, and cleanliness; or, regulate the sale of alcohol by not allowing minors to purchase it. Naturally, a governmentally established system of property rights that defines and protects ownership of alcohol as well as of all other privately owned goods represents a fundamental collective action that is often overlooked. What is true for alcohol also holds true for all other human activities, from postal service to prostitution to police protection; only human imagination and scarcity limit the form collective action might take.

The legislators of collective action. Third, people must choose the proper legislators of collective action. That is, they must decide which group of people at what level of government should be vested with the legal authority to say that from now on a particular human activity remains private or becomes collective. In representative democracies such as the United States, the national legislators of collective action ordinarily are the members of Congress and the president. At the state and local level, the legislators of collective action are the state legislators, governors, mayors, and city councilors. But the justices of the Supreme Court and regulatory agency commissioners and other bureaucrats sometimes make these decisions themselves, and citizens occasionally vote directly in referendum elections on proposed collective actions. To decide who is the legislator of collective action is to decide who will decide whether and in what form an activity becomes private or collective.

In places without governments or with governments less stable than those of most Western democracies, decisions about collective action are the stuff of domestic violence, civil war, and revolution. Violent conflict often prevails precisely because there is little or no agreement about who the proper, or legitimate, legislators of collective action should be. However, even in stable political orders, disputes arise over who should be designated by laws, customs, and constitutions as the proper legislators of collective action. For

---

action, that means that no one would undertake it voluntarily. Everyone privately decided not to do it. Therefore, collective action in the absence of earlier private action would require a coercive decision procedure to get people to do (or pay for) what they had privately decided not to do in the absence of that procedure.

example, a common disagreement in the United States concerns the rights of state and local officials to make public policy, especially when that policy conflicts with the preferences and goals of federal officeholders. Conflict between national and state and local leaders has emerged in the past concerning the civil rights of blacks, and conflict between the same leaders reemerges today concerning environmental quality and nationally mandated affirmative action policies. Clearly, the designation of the legislators of collective action is important for defining the rights of federal officeholders and of those at other levels of government, for whoever holds the right to legislate enjoys an enhanced ability to pursue his or her own public policy goals.

The collective action decision rule. Fourth, people must choose an appropriate collective action decision rule. This rule specifies the number or percentage of people who must agree to a collective action before it is adopted. For example, to place the domestic production and sale of energy under government ownership would require the approval of a *majority* of those voting on the energy nationalization bill in the House of Representatives and in the Senate; such a public policy would also require the president's agreement, and that of a majority of those Supreme Court justices voting if a constitutional challenge were brought against the nationalization law. If the president vetoed the bill, then at least *two-thirds of a quorum* of each house of Congress would have to vote for it to make it law. (Chapter 9 describes more fully how a bill becomes a law.)

As a second example, consider a decision to have a national religion. The collective action decision rule in the preceding example is, roughly, a *majority* vote of a quorum in both houses of Congress and the president's agreement, or a *two-thirds* vote of a quorum in both houses of Congress with the president's veto. But the decision rule for making a decision to adopt a national religion would be different, because the First Amendment to the Constitution reads in part: "Congress shall make no law respecting an establishment of religion. . . ." Consequently, the adoption of a national religion would require an amendment to the Constitution, and approval for that (by one method) requires an agreement of *two-thirds* of the members of each house of Congress and a majority vote of legislators in *three-fourths* of the state legislatures. Article 5 of the Constitution specifies the amendment process.

The American jury system provides a third example of a collective action decision rule. For a defendant to be found guilty of a capital offense and of most other criminal offenses requires in most places the *unanimous* vote of a twelve-member jury. By contrast, the expenditure of trivial amounts of public funds for personal transportation requires only one person to push a button in a city-hall elevator. In sum, collective action decision rules vary greatly. Chapters 4, 9, and 12 discuss reasons for these variations.

The executors and enforcers of collective action. Finally, people must decide who shall execute and enforce collective actions and how they shall do so. For example, in 1934 the members of Congress passed and President Franklin D. Roosevelt signed the Federal Communications Act. The terms of that law specify that the president will nominate and with the advice and consent of the Senate will apoint seven members to a Federal Communications Commission. Within statutory guidelines set by the 1934 act, these commissioners must regulate interstate electromagnetic communications "as the public convenience, interest, or necessity requires. . . ." For radio frequency communications and other forms of interstate electromagnetic communications such as telephone and telegraph service, the commissioners are the executors and enforcers of collective action. In practice, the commissioners act like a little legislature in regulating communication services, and they adjucicate disputes among contenders for commercial broadcast licenses. Therefore, they are really lawmakers and judges as well as executors and enforcers of collective action.

Interrelationships. Interactions among these five decisions make choices to initiate collective action far more complex than they might otherwise seem and generate some of the toughest problems of politics and government. For example, suppose citizens want to make air pollution control collective—something that has already partially been done. This decision depends mightily on how the other collective action decisions are resolved. For instance, if the executors and enforcers of collective action in each state are the members of small commissions chosen by a state-wide political process, then commission members might compete for industries to locate within their respective states by adopting relatively weak pollution regulations. However, the members of a national pollution control commission, chosen by a national political process, imposing regulations on all states simultaneously, might adopt regulations that are harsher than optimal in states with minor pollution problems and more lenient than optimal in states with severe pollution problems. Therefore, citizens may prefer collective action if one set of regulators controls it, but may not prefer it if another set does so. These preferences ultimately depend on whether citizens would prefer the kind of collective action, regulation, they expect each set of commissioners to enforce. In our example, the law initiating collective action might also provide for taxing polluters according to the kind and amount of pollutants they emit, for prohibiting all pollution or some pollution, for fines on pollution, or for subsidies to clean up industrial waste. These are variations on the form of collective action, and citizens' preferences for collective action can vary according to which form is proposed.

In sum, collective action itself conveys little meaning without a knowledge of who would legislate it, what form it might take, the appropriate decision rules, and the identity of executors and enforcers. This chapter's major concern is with the initial and most important choice, the decision to take or not to take collective action itself.

PRIVATE CHOICE

Why would people prefer or decide to use private action or collective action? Alternatively, why would people prefer or decide to make future decisions about some activity by using a private-choice mechanism such as a market or a public-choice mechanism such as an election or a legislative or bureaucratic system? At the most abstract level, if people prefer the outcomes of one mechanism over those of another, then they prefer to use the mechanism with which they associate the preferred outcomes. For example, if citizens prefer—have a higher utility for—how a market would allocate, say, petroleum resources to how federal bureaucrats would do so, then they would prefer to make decisions about petroleum in a marketplace rather than in a federal bureau. That is, they would decide to make future decisions about petroleum with a private-choice mechanism rather than with a public one. Thus, to explain and to predict a preference for a particular decision mechanism, we must first understand what kinds of outcomes private- and collective-choice mechanisms actually create.

A Simple Market

We begin a comparison of public- and private-choice mechanisms by analyzing a simple market. To avoid complications discussed later in this chapter, suppose that collective action with regard to this market is limited to protecting citizens' property rights to the goods and services they exchange and to enforcing contracts (voluntary agreements). Hence, there is minimal coercion, and the market may fairly be said to represent a private, noncoercive decision mechanism: a system for deciding how to allocate scarce resources among competing claimants.

Defining a market. Markets provide good examples of private-choice mechanisms because most people are familiar with them and because a discussion of them brings into focus some important characteristics of human interactions. Simply defined, a market minimally consists of two persons, two goods, and the opportunity for exchange. This definition is fundamental to an understanding of private-choice procedures, so it is useful to analyze it.

First, to describe markets as minimally consisting of two persons seems to oversimplify reality, because markets commonly are made up of huge corporations, labor unions, and millions of buyers and sellers. However, this view misses the essential character of markets. No matter how many people are involved, a market is no more than a series of bilateral (two-person) exchanges. A market's size and complexity consists less in the number of persons who take part in it than in the numbers and patterns of bilateral exchanges. In a complex market, such as the one for automobiles, there are laborers, union and corporate officials, stockholders, middle management, shop foremen, advertising agents, television crews, retailers, customers, bank loan officers, and even Ralph Nader and Environmental Protection Agency and National Highway Traffic Safety Administration personnel. At each step in the automobile production and consumption processes, though, from the mining of iron ore to the kicking of tires in the used-car lot, this giant marketplace consists of millions of smaller markets, each with a single two-person exchange.

Now, consider the two goods in any market. A **good** is anything that produces a change in at least one person's utility with a change in the amount of the good produced or consumed. This definition has several important properties. First, the term *good* carries with it no moral or ethical meaning. A good is merely a commodity, a service, or a state of the world about which a person can utter a preference compared to some other commodity, service, or state of the world. Therefore, peace is a good for a gentle person because gentle people prefer—have a higher utility for—more peace to less, and a change in the amount of peace would produce a change in a gentle person's utility.

Second, everyone need not experience a utility change with a change in the amount of a good produced or consumed, but the utility change must hold true for at least one person. For example, some people are totally indifferent to the numbers of surviving whales, wild polar bears, snail darters, and furbish louseworts. For others, the possible extinction of whales, polar bears, and other creatures and plant life has become a burning national issue. If at least one person gets more utility from the existence of one more polar bear, then the polar bear—or, more precisely, the number of polar bears in existence—is a good.

Third, a person's utility need not increase with increased levels of production or consumption of a commodity, service, or state of the world for it to be called a good. Utility might decline. For example, air pollution, sometimes called a *bad,* is a good. At least one person's utility changes with a change in the amount of air pollution produced (and consumed by inhaling). Sometimes one person's utility can even increase while another's declines with a change in the amount of a good produced or consumed. An excellent example of this phenomenon, discussed later in this chapter and elsewhere in this book, is the production of abortions. At least in the abstract, zero population growth advocates might lose utility from every new child born. Hence, their utility would increase with each additional abortion. But many devout Catholics, as well as others, view abortion as murder. Hence, their utility would diminish with each additional abortion.

Fourth, the reason for two goods is obvious. Suppose that person A has fifty pencils and nothing else of value to B, while B has twenty pencils and nothing else of value to A. A and B get additional utility from each additional pencil they own, but there is no basis for exchange, for A and B have nothing to offer each other. But if A has many pencils and no paper while B has no pencils and reams of paper, then an exchange becomes possible.

The final characteristic of a market is the opportunity for exchange. Barriers to exchange involve technological problems of transportation and communication, as well as government prohibitions and restrictions. Some of the greatest developments in early exploration grew out of the desire to open up new exchange opportunities—new markets. The history of these markets shows that language differences seldom remain a barrier when two persons get together to barter. However, an actual exchange need not occur for it to be said that a market has existed. People may decide that it is in their best interest not to trade, in which case the market outcome is the status quo.

How markets work. While it is beyond this book's scope to explain fully how markets work, we can describe a simple bilateral exchange, which is the fundamental activity in any market. Consider again persons A and B, contemplating the exchange of paper and pencils. To simplify matters, suppose A's utilities for pencils and paper are equivalent, so that if A has, say, three pencils and three sheets of paper, then getting another pencil would produce as much additional (marginal) utility as getting another sheet of paper would produce. Also, suppose A's utility for a unit of pencils or paper can be represented by these numbers: 0 units (pencils or sheets of paper), 0 utiles; 1 unit, 400 utiles; 2 units, 600 utiles; 3 units, 700 utiles; 4 units, 750 utiles. Such numbers illustrate the notion of diminishing marginal utility discussed in Chapter 2. An increase from 0 to 1 unit adds 400 utiles; from 1 unit to 2 units, 200 utiles; from 2 units to 3 units, 100 utiles; and from 3 units to 4 units, 50 utiles.

To see how to use this information, suppose A has one pencil and two sheets of paper. He then has 400 utiles from the pencil and 600 utiles from the sheets of paper, for a total utility of 400 plus 600, or 1000 utiles.[2] (This calculation assumes that the number of pencils A has does not affect his utility for paper, and vice versa.) Now, suppose B's utilities for pencils and paper can be represented by the same numbers as A's are. (This assumption is merely a convenience and implies no interpersonal comparison of utilities.)

To get the market started, suppose A shows up at the trading place owning four sheets of paper and no pencils, while B shows up with no paper and four pencils. Therefore, each has an initial utility of 750 utiles. A begins by giving B one sheet of paper in exchange for one pencil. Person A now has three sheets of paper (700 utiles) and one pencil (400 utiles) for a total of 1100 utiles. B's new endowment of paper and pencils is the reverse of A's, and B's new utility is also 1100 utiles. That is, A and B each experience an increase of 350 utiles from the exchange. But this does not end the trading sequence, as A can give up another sheet of paper and get another pencil from B. A now has

[2] Recall from Chapter 2 that it is customary to set A's utility from the most preferred outcome equal to 1.0, and from the least preferred outcome equal to 0.0. Here, though, A has 1000 utiles. It is simple to alter this result by letting 1000 equal 1.0, in which case 600 utiles would become 0.60, and so forth. This simple transformation in no way affects the calculations.

two sheets of paper (600 utiles) and two pencils (600 utiles), for a total of 1200 utiles. B's holding of paper and pencils is the same as A's. Beginning with 750 utiles, each has gained a grand total of 450 additional utiles from the sequence of exchange.

Market Optimality

A and B exchange goods up to the point at which neither can gain from further bargaining, unless it is at the expense of the other person. Neither A nor B has actually produced more pencils or paper, yet by trading from initial endowments, both increase their utilities. This is a remarkable property of market exchange and a principal reason for its constant use in human action. Each person bargains voluntarily, without coercion. Neither would trade if it were not in his or her interest to do so. The exchange must be mutually agreeable. Thus, in terms of voting, an abstract market operates on the principle of unanimous consent: each person whose utility might be affected by the exchange must consent to its result. Hence, the final outcome of any trade is that neither party expects to be worse off after the exchange than before it, or else he or she would not consent to it.

Recall the second property of a good bargain from Chapter 2: the outcome is equal to or better than the outcome of the status quo for each bargainer. That is, each bargainer must expect to be either better off or no worse off after the bargain than before it. Otherwise, he or she would not make the exchange. Clearly, the exchange of pencils and paper satisfies this property of a good bargain.

In most market (private) exchange, there is little or no difference between this property and the third property of a good bargain: for each bargainer the outcome of a good bargain is equal to or better than the outcome of the non-cooperative solution. This equivalence occurs because the utility from the status quo outcome is the same as the utility from not bargaining, and not bargaining is the act of not communicating, which defines a non-cooperative game. Thus, this hypothetical market exchange of paper and pencils also meets the third property.[3]

The first property of a good bargain is that it is feasible: the exchange must be possible. The pencil-and-paper exchange meets this condition because the sum of each person's endowments both before and after the exchange equals the total amount of available resources. Before the exchange, A

---

[3] The equivalence of the non-cooperative and status quo outcomes depends upon bargaining being relatively costless. However, often it is not; see Gordon Tullock, *Private Wants, Public Means: An Economic Analysis of the Desirable Scope of Government* (New York: Basic Books, 1970), pp. 55–70. Bargaining is probably inexpensive, as are the associated costs of search and information, in ordinary markets for goods such as paper and pencils. To the extent that these costs are negligible, the non-cooperative outcome and the status quo outcome are equivalent. Bargaining may not be so inexpensive in markets for goods such as homes, automobiles, and jobs. In these markets,

has no pencils and four sheets of paper, while B has no paper and four pencils. After the exchange, A and B each have two pencils and two sheets of paper. At no time does the number of pencils or sheets of paper exceed four. Therefore, the hypothetical market meets the first property of a good bargain: the bargain's outcome is feasible.

Finally, the exchange is Pareto optimal. At the completion of the trading sequence, a further trade cannot be made without harming at least one bargainer, or both. Since the agreement must be voluntary, either A or B or both will not consent to such a move. In sum, these hypothetical markets result in good bargains.

The pencil-and-paper example refers to a single market exchange in which no production of additional physical resources occurs. Exchanges in such markets are shown to be Pareto optimal. In most exchanges, the two items traded are money and some other good or service. When people buy an automobile or a loaf of bread or a nickel bag of marijuana, they *must* prefer the good or service they receive to the money they pay for it, and sellers must prefer the money they receive to retaining ownership of the good or service (forgone leisure) they sell. Whether one speaks of money and mousetraps or paper and pencils, then, in private (market) choice, a resource flows—is allocated—to its most highly valued use. For example, before the exchange, A values an additional pencil more than a forgone piece of paper, B values an additional piece of paper more than a forgone pencil, and the market process "sends" paper and pencils in the correct direction based on this valuation by A and B. That is, market choice is allocatively optimal.

The same property of optimality characterizes an entire economy of bilateral exchanges including exchanges of goods and services used to create other goods and services: production is optimal. People sell resources to the highest bidder they can find, and buyers sell their money to the highest bidder of the desired resource. Through this process, the entire economy constantly moves to Pareto preferred resource allocations.

Market Ethics

The scope of market exchange. Since a good is anything that produces a change in at least one person's utility with a change in the amount of the good produced or consumed, the preceding discussion describes most real exchanges. Yet there are unusual markets for illicit drugs, pornography, and prostitution; there is a market for crime and a market for justice. There is

---

people actually specialize in becoming sources of information and agents for buyers and sellers. If the agent's payment is contingent upon the completion of a sale, then the non-cooperative and status quo outcomes remain equivalent. However, a difference occurs between these outcomes if bargaining or information becomes costly or if bargaining or information services cannot be bought. In that case, the decision to communicate adds a cost to the status quo, so that the status quo and non-cooperative outcomes might diverge.

even a market for marriage, in which the parties make explicit or implicit agreements. (Most marriages that get into trouble do so because of a disagreement over the terms of the exchange or a desire by one or both parties to renegotiate.) In sum, the analysis of market exchange, of private choice, goes far beyond matters of money. The broad definition of the term *good* ensures this generality.

Exchange as symmetric and impersonal. Brand names aside, the names of the persons in a market mean nothing.[4] The analysis of market exchange holds for any two persons, without names or other labels of race, religion, political belief, or any other identifying characteristics. Markets tend to be impersonal. Most people overlook the importance of this impersonality because they think less about two abstract persons than about the labels under which people operate in exchange: landlords and tenants, creditors (sometimes loan sharks) and debtors, employers and employees (bosses and workers), pushers and junkies, hookers and johns, doctors and patients, merchants and customers, entertainers and audiences, teachers and students, and, of course, buyers and sellers. Some of these terms often take on emotional colorations, even though the positions of the two persons in most exchanges are symmetric. Manifestly, every buyer is a seller and every seller is a buyer. For example, a buyer of labor is an employer. Normally, the employer is also a seller of money, while employees are sellers of labor whose currency of exchange, their labor—leisure forgone—buys money.

Exploitation. As the next part of this chapter shows, markets sometimes create real problems. But people do not always fully grasp or appreciate what market exchange accomplishes. The market begins with two persons, two goods, and the opportunity for exchange. By characterizing this circumstance as a market, a private-choice mechanism, we immediately assume that neither person, nor anyone else, shall use or threaten to use physical coercion. Hence, whatever people do or agree to do they must do voluntarily. This is the essential quality of private choice, and this quality guarantees that market exchange results in a good bargain.

People sometimes refer to market exchanges as involving the exploitation of one person by another. By *exploitation* they mean the second dictionary definition: "to make unethical use of for one's own advantage or profit; turn selfishly or unfairly to one's own account."[5] But to say that one person exploits

[4] For a clear statement of the economic function of brand names, see Armen Alchian and William R. Allen, *Exchange and Production: Competition, Coordination, and Control* (Belmont, Calif.: Wadsworth, 1977), pp. 294–295. As Chapter 5 points out, in public choice a candidate's political party or party identification shares certain characteristics with a product's brand name.

[5] *Webster's New World Dictionary of the American Language* (New York: World, 1962), p. 513.

another in private exchange is either to be wrong or to say that the exchange was fraudulent or not private to begin with. Again, the fundamental property of a market is voluntary, unanimous agreement. If people voluntarily agree to bargains, then there can be no exploitation. They must expect to be better off after their bargains than before them, or they would not agree to the terms. Exploitation can occur only with force, the threat of force, or fraud.

UNDESIRABLE CONSEQUENCES OF PRIVATE CHOICE

After reading this complimentary description of simple markets, one might wonder why anyone would prefer or choose collective-decision mechanisms over private ones. However, there are certain instances in which the use of a coercive mechanism through collective action is said to improve upon the allocations and decisions of private-choice procedures. Sometimes people prefer to make an activity collective because they want to force others—and perhaps themselves—to do what they would not otherwise agree to do voluntarily. At other times people might show a preference for public choice if the inherent unanimity of the market is violated because people are harmed against their will. Pollution damage, which a person does not agree to accept and for which there is no compensation, is a good example of how the unanimity condition might be violated. Also, people sometimes want particular goods to be available, but for various reasons it is difficult or impossible to establish a market in those goods. National defense is an example.

Collective Goods

One very general reason for preferring collective decision making and collective action to strictly private choice concerns the marketplace production of less-than-optimal quantities of some goods and more-than-optimal quantities of others. Consider the example of a steamship company whose vessels all too often ground on a reef near their home port. After one or two disasters, company executives contemplate building a lighthouse to warn their captains of the navigational hazard. The company and all other steamship companies and small-boat owners would benefit from the light, so each person's utility would increase. Therefore, the lighthouse—more precisely, the light itself—is a good.

But this particular good has two properties that distinguish it from goods such as paper and pencils. First, the lighthouse has a property called **jointness of supply.** This means that if one person uses a given amount of the good, then no one else's opportunity to use the good diminishes. In this case, everyone benefits from the lighthouse, and one person's benefit from the warning beam does not diminish because another person also sees—buys or consumes—its rays.[6] Contrast this property of jointness of supply with the characteristics of paper and pencils. If a third person wants a sheet of paper that A has already bargained away to B, the newcomer cannot buy that sheet of paper from A, nor can B simultaneously keep that sheet of paper and let someone else buy it.

The second property of the lighthouse is **jointness of consumption.** This means that if one person supplies the good, everyone else has the opportunity to consume it, whether or not they helped to pay for it. Suppose the steamship company wants to collect fees from those to whom the lighthouse affords protection. Because the company does not own the ocean, it is not clear how it would make such collections. Consequently, even though others benefit from the light, they need not pay for it. A price system—a market—for lighthouse services seems difficult to establish without some kind of external intervention. Contrast this property of jointness of consumption with the characteristics of paper and pencils. Without force or fraud, no one gets either good without paying for it. But the lighthouse beam cannot easily be withheld from those who do not pay for it. Jointly supplied or consumed goods are sometimes called **collective goods** or **public goods,** while goods such as paper and pencils are called **private goods.**[7]

Collective goods that display positive externalities. Suppose the lighthouse beam bothers no one, and everyone either benefits from it or is indifferent to its presence. The steamship company that builds and operates the lighthouse gets some utility from its operation, but so do others. However, this additional utility to others is external to the utility of the firm whose executives decide to pay for the lighthouse. This external utility the lighthouse supplies is called an **externality.** (Be careful to keep separate the good itself and the externality, which is the external utility people have for the good.) Since this good adds to people's utilities, the good's external utility is called a **positive externality,** or sometimes an **external economy.** Hence, the lighthouse is a collective good that displays a positive externality.

The problem with public goods that display positive externalities is that sometimes people fail to produce them or produce suboptimal amounts of them. The lighthouse problem is an appropriate example. Suppose two steamship firms, *1* and *2,* use a particularly treacherous harbor, and that each company expects to lose $\$B$ in wrecks until a new harbor is completed. (B thus

---

[6] However, a well-lit harbor might be more congested and therefore present more navigational hazards than a poorly lit one. The benefits of a lighthouse would be overestimated if this congestion were not taken into account.

[7] Some goods may be jointly consumed only because the law makes them so. A bridge without a tollgate is a jointly consumed public good. Put a gate across it, collect tolls for its use, and it becomes a private good. With little traffic, the bridge is also a jointly produced good. However, crowding eventually might reduce the utility gained from using the bridge, so it is only jointly produced within reasonable technological limits of traffic flow.

represents each firm's benefits from preventing wrecks.) The cost of a lighthouse, which would prevent all wrecks, is $C. Assume that $C exceeds $B, so that for each firm the cost of the lighthouse is greater than its benefits, the costs of prevented shipwrecks. But suppose $B exceeds $C/2, so that joint production of the lighthouse, with the two firms sharing costs equally, would be profitable. Table 3.1 shows the resulting two-person game.

Plainly, if *1*'s managers expect *2*'s managers to pay for the lighthouse, then *1* will not contribute to its construction, since B is greater than $B - C/2$. If *1*'s managers expect *2*'s managers not to contribute, then *1* again will not contribute, since $B - C$ is less than zero. Thus, no matter what *2*'s managers decide to do, *1*'s managers will decide not to contribute. The game in Table 3.1 is clearly a prisoners' dilemma.

Two things produce the failure to construct the lighthouse, to provide the public good. The first is jointness of consumption. If it were technologically feasible to withhold the lighthouse beam from those who fail to pay for it, they would receive nothing instead of B. The second is that the cost of the lighthouse, C, exceeds the benefits, B, for any given contributor. A public good for which B is greater than C might well be privately supplied.[8]

The problem of supplying public goods is also called the **free-rider problem.** *Ceteris paribus* (everything else being equal), people sometimes fail to contribute to the supply of a collective good that displays a positive externality. This phenomenon occurs even though each person wants the collective good. No one individually is willing to pay for it; everyone hopes that everyone else will pay for it, and no one does—hence, no good! Therefore, the market fails to reach a theoretically possible allocation that everyone would otherwise prefer. If producing a public good is feasible by public choice

Table 3.1 The Lighthouse Problem Game

		Company 2's Strategies	
		contribute	do not contribute
Company 1's Strategies	contribute	$\left(B - \frac{C}{2}, B - \frac{C}{2}\right)$	$(B - C, B)$
	do not contribute	$(B, B - C)$	$(0, 0)$

[8] The public-goods problem is often misunderstood. Some believe that collective goods almost never get produced in private choice, market situations, especially if many people want these goods. However, although a good is collective, its private production need not be impossible. But if a good *is* collective, if no one individually can afford it, and if the entire cost of the good exceeds any one person's benefit from consuming it, then no one will produce it. Incidentally, notice that if B exceeds C, the game in Table 3.1 becomes a game of *chicken,* in which case it is impossible to predict whether or not the good will be produced.

but not by private choice, then the private-choice mechanism fails to reach a Pareto preferred allocation of resources. Some people may thus prefer the outcomes of public choice to and choose them over those of private choice. For example, in the lighthouse problem, collective action to coerce contributions can make both firms better off without making either worse off. Therefore, the agents of government are called upon to force a contribution from the steamship firms in their own interests.[9] People in similar situations might actually prefer being coerced to remaining uncoerced, especially if they understand the free-rider problem.

Collective goods that display negative externalities. Collective goods that display **negative externalities** are sometimes called **public bads.** Pollution is an example. The operation of automobiles, steel mills, electric power plants, and municipal garbage disposal systems, and even the presence of pine forests, add pollutants to the air. By virtue of the supply of pollution, everyone in the relevant geographical area must consume dirty air, and no one's consumption of such air reduces anyone else's consumption of it. Therefore, dirty air produced by human beings is a collective good because it shows jointness of supply and jointness of consumption. The problem that sometimes emerges with collective goods that display positive externalities is to get people to supply them. By contrast, the problem that sometimes emerges with collective goods that display negative externalities is to get people not to supply them, which is equivalent to supplying the condition that would prevail in their absence.

A game between two automobile drivers shows this problem most clearly.[10] Say that the installation of an antipollution device on one of their automobiles costs $75, while it produces $50 in clean-air benefits for each driver (because of jointness of supply). A device on both automobiles therefore produces an aggregate of $100 in clean-air benefits for each driver. Thus, if both drivers install a device, each receives a net benefit of $25 ($100 minus $75).

Table 3.2 shows the associated two-person game growing out of this situation. Again, the game is a prisoners' dilemma; neither driver installs the device, and pollution continues unabated. The jointness of the benefits from reducing pollution creates this result. Clearly, (25, 25) is better for the drivers than (0, 0). However, they are not likely to arrive at the (25, 25) outcome with

[9] This finding in no way implies that the agents of government must build and maintain lighthouses. They must only see to it that *1* and *2* contribute funds to whoever builds and operates the lighthouse. Indeed, private ownership with collectively enforced user fees rather than general taxes has been argued to be a superior way to solve the lighthouse problem. For an account of such developments, see Ronald H. Coase, "The Lighthouse in Economics," *Journal of Law and Economics,* 17 (October 1974), pp. 357–376.

[10] A version of this game is developed in William H. Riker and Peter C. Ordeshook, *An Introduction to Positive Political Theory* (Englewood Cliffs, N. J.: Prentice-Hall, 1973), p. 250–252.

Table 3.2 Air Pollution Device Game

		Person B's *Strategies*	
		install device	do not install device
Person A's *Strategies*	install device	25, 25	−25, 50
	do not install device	50, −25	0, 0

ordinary private-choice procedures. Stated differently, by not installing a device, each driver imposes a cost of $50 on everyone else. This cost arises from the public bad of air pollution. The public choice problem is to coerce polluters to incorporate such **external costs** (the opposite of external economies) into their own decision processes—to make them bear the costs they impose on others. Again, people might call upon a coercive decision process, or collective action, to produce this result, for without collective action it would be difficult to construct a market-like result that would "charge" polluters for using the ambient air as a sink.

The symmetry of positive and negative externalities. The terms *positive* and *negative* indicate whether someone's utility increases or decreases with the amount of a public good produced. But these are two sides of the same coin. The pollution problem is to get drivers to stop supplying a collective good, air pollution, which displays a negative externality. We could just as easily say that the problem is to get drivers to begin supplying a collective good, clean air, which displays a positive externality. The lighthouse problem is to get firms to begin supplying a collective good, contributing to the lighthouse, which displays a positive externality. One could just as easily say that the problem is to get firms to stop supplying a collective good, a dark harbor, which displays a negative externality.

Whenever there is a potential collective good that displays a positive externality, there is always a corresponding potential collective good that displays a negative externality and vice versa. This is apparent with both the lighthouse problem and the pollution problem. Reducing your car's exhaust helps a neighbor, and increasing your car's exhaust harms a neighbor. Contributing to the lighthouse helps another ship's crew, and not contributing harms the crew. If people do not supply the public good, then they supply the public bad; and if they supply the public good, then they do not supply the public bad.

Collective goods, voluntary action, and the state. People are often unwilling voluntarily to supply public goods or to refrain from supplying public bads. However, voluntary action is the keystone of private choice. Therefore, when their fellows fail to go along, those who wish to produce one public good or to suppress the production of another may prefer to use a coercive procedure such as a political decision mechanism, rather than a voluntary one such as a market. That is, people who want a public good produced or a public bad suppressed may turn away from private choice and toward government to force themselves and others to take the appropriate action.

The degree of coercion required to produce a public good or suppress the production of a public bad can vary according to circumstances and private motivations. Military service provides a good example. The public good in question is national defense. Of course, no one soldier wins a war or protects a nation. The good of national defense comes about from the combined contributions of all soldiers and taxpayers, and no one person alone can afford to supply it. Yet some join the armed forces without being drafted. For many, military service provides a higher income and a greater degree of social mobility than might be available in civilian life; others join because of sentiments of duty and patriotism. School teachers, clerics, and parents sometimes teach such values. To the extent that they are not taught, a draft becomes more likely in future crises that are deemed to require full military mobilization. Sentiments such as patriotism explain why some people provide collective goods without the threat of coercion: they share values that impel them to "do their duty," they get utility by acting in a way they regard as just, and they would find it emotionally painful to act otherwise. Hence, people do contribute voluntarily to the supply of collective goods; but whether for money or advancement, or out of a sense of duty, they make such contributions for private, personal reasons.

At different times people's attitudes toward military service as well as toward the draft have changed. One reason for such changes is that the collective good in question often is not merely national defense but national defense against a particular enemy. Fighting Imperial Japan and Nazi Germany in World War II was popular. Fighting the Viet Cong and the North Vietnamese in the 1960s and 1970s eventually became much less so. The renewed draft registration in response to Soviet aggression in Afghanistan received mixed reactions, especially when people contemplated the possibility of drafting women. Probably the immediacy and credibility of each threat makes some difference. Put differently, people believe that government ought to supply some collective goods—for instance, the thwarting of a particular case of military aggression—and ought not to supply others. Just as some people choose not to produce or consume certain private goods because costs exceed benefits, so too some people choose not to produce or consume certain public goods for similar reasons. Nor does it always pay to eliminate all public bads. Many argue that the production and consumption of alcohol, cigarettes, and marijuana create negative externalities. However, the costs of suppressing the production and consumption of these goods may be too high, although some might disagree about how high is too high. Reflecting that disagreement, public policy in some states (but not in others) now bans smoking in many public places. New York City even has a "noise pollution"

SELECTIVE SERVICE SYSTEM
Registration Form
READ PRIVACY ACT STATEMENT ON REVERSE
PLEASE PRINT CLEARLY

—DO NOT WRITE IN THE ABOVE SPACE—

1 DATE OF BIRTH
Name of Month ____ Day ____ Year ____

2 SEX
☐ MALE
☐ FEMALE

3 SOCIAL SECURITY NUMBER
___ ___ ___ | ___ ___ | ___ ___ ___ ___

4 PRINT FULL NAME
Last ____ First ____ Middle ____

5 CURRENT MAILING ADDRESS
Number and Street ____ City ____ State or Foreign Country ____ Zip Code ____

6 PERMANENT RESIDENCE
Number and Street ____ City ____ State or Foreign Country ____ Zip Code ____

7 CURRENT PHONE NUMBER
Area Code ____ Number ____

8 ☐ Check here if we may give your name, address and telephone number to Armed Forces recruiters.

9 I AFFIRM THE FOREGOING STATEMENTS ARE TRUE
Today's Date ____ Signature of Registrant ____

Postal Date Stamp & Clerk Initials
☐ ID
☐ NO ID
☐ OTHER

SSS Form 1 (Feb 80) ☐ (Previous Editions Will Not Be Used) OMB Approval 194-R0002

HOW TO COMPLETE THIS FORM

- Read the Privacy Act Statement.
- Print all entries except your signature clearly in ink.
- Do not sign or date the form until asked to do so.
- Complete Blocks 1 thru 8 and take your form to the clerk.
- Print your date of birth in Block 1. Use a three letter abbreviation for the month and numerals for the day and year (Example: OCT 29 1960).
- Check the correct box in Block 2.
- Print your Social Security Number in Block 3.
- Print your full legal name in Block 4 in the order listed.
- Print your current mailing address in Block 5.
- Print your permanent residence address in Block 6, include ZIP code. If it is the same as your current mailing address (Block 5), leave this block blank.
- Print your telephone number in Block 7.
- Check the box in Block 8 if we may furnish the listed information to Armed Forces Recruiters.
- When you have completed your form to this point, recheck it and take it to the clerk.

PRIVACY ACT STATEMENT

The Military Selective Service Act, Selective Service Regulations, and the President's Proclamation on Registration require that you provide the indicated information, including your Social Security Account Number.

The principal purpose of the required information is to establish your registration with the Selective Service System. This information may be furnished to the following agencies for the purposes stated:

Department of Defense—for exchange of information concerning registration, classification, enlistment, examination and induction of individuals, availability of Standby Reservists, and if Block 8 is checked, identification of prospects for recruiting.

Alternate service employers—for exchange of information with employers regarding a registrant who is a conscientious objector for the purpose of placement and supervision of performance of alternate service in lieu of induction into military service.

Department of Justice—for review and processing of suspected violations of the Military Selective Service Act, or for perjury, and for defense of a civil action arising from administrative processing under such Act.

Federal Bureau of Investigation—for location of an individual when suspected of violation of the Military Selective Service Act.

Immigration and Naturalization Service—to provide information for use in determining an individual's eligibility for re-entry into the United States.

Department of State—for determination of an alien's eligibility for possible entry into the United States and United States citizenship.

Office of Veterans' Reemployment Rights, United States Department of Labor—to assist veterans in need of information concerning reemployment rights.

General Public—Registrant's Name, Selective Service Number, Date of Birth and Classification, Military Selective Service Act Section 6, 50 U.S.C. App. 456.

Your failure to provide the required information may violate the Military Selective Service Act. Conviction of such violation may result in imprisonment for not more than five years or a fine of not more than $10,000 or both imprisonment and fine.

Following the Soviet invasion of Afghanistan, President Carter reactivated draft registration. Eighteen- and nineteen-year old men were required to fill out this form. The conscription of young men is one way to compel the provision of a collective good, in this case national defense.

ordinance forbidding people to carry blaring portable radios. New York City's "dog pollution" law is also famous. Plainly, what constitutes a public bad is a political issue.

A similar debate occurs concerning the pollution problem. The costs and benefits of reducing pollution are seriously argued. Some say that air and water pollution create major degradations of health and well-being, and they call for stringent controls. Others believe that stringent domestic pollution controls would lead many firms to locate in countries whose political leaders are less sensitive about pollution. As a consequence, many workers might lose their jobs, and the economy could be seriously harmed. While the problems of pollution are more complex than this summary implies, TANSTAAFL is nevertheless a reasonable description of the trade-offs involved. Private, personal differences in the costs and benefits expected from cleaner air and water thus explain some of the differences in preferences for pollution-control policies.

There are three other reasons beyond cost and benefit considerations why the existence of a public good or a public bad does not automatically call for corrective government action. First, political scientists and economists cannot tell people when making a human action collective is or is not justified; they can only explain and predict preferences for a given decision procedure and the likely consequences of the procedure that is actually adopted. The concepts of collective goods and externalities aid in these tasks. But ours is a scientific undertaking and in no way provides the cloth from which one can cut a pattern of moral justification. Second, even if one believes that these considerations and others discussed later in this chapter do provide a justification for government action, the argument remains incomplete. Supplying collective goods may be problematical for private choice, but what are the problems of public choice? As this and other chapters point out, the externalities associated with private choice may seem tolerable when compared to the problems of collective choice. Third, there is no collective good of which one can say unambiguously that its externalities are all positive or all negative. A clear example is abortion, the medical termination of pregnancy.

There are several choice mechanisms for making decisions about abortion. At one end of the spectrum, people can make such decisions in a market largely, though not completely, unregulated by government. That is, a woman gives a physician money, in exchange for which the physician aborts the woman's pregnancy, and no one intervenes. At the other end of the spectrum, a law can make the buying and selling of all abortions illegal. There seem to be many intermediate positions, but two are principal: first, the law may permit abortions on demand during the first three (or six) months of pregnancy; second, the law may permit an abortion only to save a woman's life or preserve her health. These positions can be placed somewhat arbitrarily along a line, as in Figure 3.1.

Why would someone prefer a private-choice mechanism (position Z), or a collective-choice mechanism that coercively limits private choice (positions

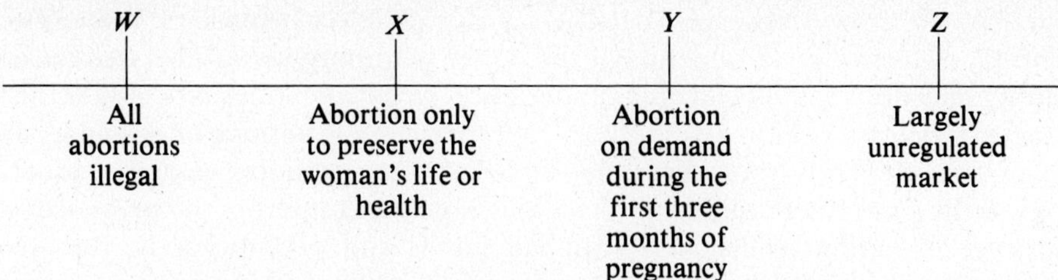

Figure 3.1 Structure of positions on abortion issue.

W, X, or *Y*) on the abortion issue? First, consider a devout Catholic who believes that abortion is murder. (Of course, many non-Catholics hold the same view, and some Catholics do not.) For such a person, the supply of abortions to anyone is tantamount to the supply of the collective bads of murder and immorality. Many Catholics prefer to live in what they regard as a moral community, and certainly do not want to expose their children to this practice. Thus, in terms of the positions on the issue, the devout Catholic prefers *W* to *X*, *X* to *Y*, and *Y* to *Z*. Notice also that public protection and acceptance for any position other than *W* coercively imposes a negative externality on devout Catholics.

Second, consider a non-Catholic member of Zero Population Growth, Incorporated, a person who holds the Malthusian view that the Earth cannot support its growing human population. The ZPG member loses utility with the birth of each additional child beyond the replacement rate, and therefore each additional child beyond the replacement rate is a collective good that displays a negative externality. Consequently, for the ZPG advocate, the buying and selling of abortions represents the supply of a collective good, a stable population.

Here is a single act: the supply of abortions. For some, the supply of this good reduces utility, displays a negative externality. For others, its supply increases utility, displays a positive externality. Directly or indirectly, most collective goods can share this ambiguity about whether the attendant externality is positive or negative. Thus, the presence of goods that are collective in no sense provides an a priori justification for government action to alter the pattern of externalities, for that action can harm people as well as help them.[11]

[11] One might argue that abortions harm no one, either because the destroyed fetus is not a person or because no one other than the patient and physician enters into the exchange; therefore, those who oppose abortions suffer only imaginary harm. I do not know whether or not a fetus is a person (nor have I settled in my own mind what the correct public policy on this issue might be, or even whether such a policy exists). However, in the realm of utility and of methodological individualism, there is no such thing as imaginary harm. Harm, a loss of utility, is subjective. It is what a person perceives as harm, and not what someone else defines it to be. By contrast, it would seem that goods such as air pollution are inalterably public bads. However, their *over-suppression* could indirectly impose negative externalities on many.

As Chapter 5 observes, whether or not people get more or less utility from a collective good depends on how they get utility itself. The sources of utility may derive from learning, experience, or genetic inheritance. Whether the externality a person attaches to a collective good is positive or negative, or even zero, depends upon that person's beliefs. Accordingly, we define **ideology** as the pattern of utilities, externalities, a person gets from the presence or absence of various collectively supplied public and private goods. Because measures of externalities also are measures of utilities, there is no scientific way to sum them or otherwise to aggregate them. Hence, one cannot make interpersonal comparisons of utility to decide what is the best policy.

The Distribution of Resources

A second reason why someone might prefer outcomes of a collective-choice mechanism to those of a private-choice mechanism concerns the distribution of resources, which refers to how much of each good each person has. In the example of two persons exchanging paper and pencils, if A has all four pencils and all four sheets of paper, no basis for exchange exists. But if A and B are on a desert island, if the commodities involved are water and bananas rather than paper and pencils, and if A has all of the commodities and refuses to part with any of them, then B might find this arrangement less than satisfactory and perhaps even fatal. Moreover, what actually happens in a marketplace depends at least partly on the distribution of resources before exchanges occur. That is, people's initial endowments of resources can affect their final endowments after all exchanges are made.

Most demands for the collective, coercive, redistribution of resources, of course, have little to do with preventing the starvation that theoretically might come from the rigors of private choice. On the contrary, those who make these demands include middle-income families who want wealthier and poorer persons to pay for their children's educations by supporting state universities, business people and union members who want the redistributions of wealth implicitly created by tariffs, bureaucrats who want higher salaries for themselves and their staffs, and sick people who want healthy people to share their otherwise higher costs of health insurance. These demands aside, we can describe several theoretical reasons that people prefer a political, nonmarket **resource redistribution** to the redistributions that occur as a result of private choice.

The desire for equality. First is a desire for equality. Poor people seldom want equality and usually only want more goods than they presently have. However, even those with great wealth sometimes want everyone in the nation, and perhaps the world, to become equal in material goods. This desire has become a common ideology, but not one without problems. For instance, suppose that *equality* means that everyone should have exactly the same amount of every good—money, land, food, and medical care, for example.

Furthermore, imagine that everyone is suddenly made equal in the goods and services they own. People will quickly become unequal again, merely because tastes and preferences differ. The diabetic would exchange much of what he owns for an adequate supply of insulin; the classical-music lover would exchange his beer for a Beethoven symphony recording; the sports-car enthusiast would go hungry to get a new Jaguar; and the scholar would give up his ration of dog food for another book. Because goods are scarce, because people prefer different combinations of them, and because even tastes for risk differ, any redistribution toward equality by a collective, coercive decision process is bound to fail. People will enter into market exchange at the most rudimentary level to thwart egalitarian aims.

Inequality also reappears because some of the resources that people own, such as physical and mental skills, beautiful voices, and lovely and handsome faces and bodies, are inalienable. Others value these inalienable resources differently and consequently pay for their derivative products in different amounts. More important, tastes for leisure differ, so that even if everyone began with equal material and natural endowments, those who preferred to consume more leisure than others would end up with fewer material possessions.

Maintaining an equality of resources is impossible, then, as long as people hold different preferences and can talk to each other and trade. The ownership of equal resources also does not imply equal utilities. Can equal utility be produced? No. There is no way to compare utilities interpersonally. Thus, both material and utility equality seem impossible.[12]

Minimum resource guarantee. Collective-choice redistributions to achieve complete material equality fail to command widespread popular support in the United States. Even communist nations have not taken steps to ensure complete equality. Most people believe that guarantees of complete equality might retard production, since taxes and subsidies would diminish incentives to produce, thus making everyone worse off. Therefore, even those who favor public-choice redistributions toward equality recognize the serious limitations of such a policy.[13] A more popular policy calls for limited redistributions to prevent people from falling below some minimum economic level. One view suggests that if people were writing a constitution behind a *veil*

---

[12] It is important to distinguish between equality of opportunity and equality of result. We can characterize a social arrangement according to how much equality of both opportunity and result it provides different persons. Are educational opportunities equal? How would one know? Most people in the United States favor some variant of equality of opportunity. Fewer persons (but a growing number) have come to favor equality of result, meaning more nearly equal division of the national product, independent of individual effort, productivity, and taste. They believe equality of opportunity is either impossible or will not bring about equality of result under present circumstances.

[13] For a statement of the problem, see Arthur M. Okun, *Equality and Efficiency: The Big Tradeoff* (Washington, D. C.: Brookings Institution, 1975).

of ignorance concerning their economic position in a future society to be governed by that constitution, they would have the constitution guarantee at least a subsistence level to everyone.[14] The preference for this policy follows a minimax-like reasoning: one would wish to ensure that the worst possible outcome provides for survival. However, such a policy would not guarantee equality in a modern, technologically advanced economy.

Aesthetics and altruism. Beyond redistribution to ensure equality or subsistence, some wish to advance equality of result for aesthetic and altruistic reasons. The aesthetic preference for resource redistribution grows out of a distaste for the ugly physical manifestations of poverty, such as slums. The altruistic preference for resource redistribution rests on the premise that such redistributions follow from moral or religious imperatives.

Resource redistribution as insurance. Preferences for collective resource redistributions also follow from a desire to avoid violence. Because the relief of poverty is often involved, extortion may be a harsh word to use, but it correctly describes the process of political redistribution of resources under the threat of violence. Typically, some people make a claim for more goods and services than they now receive in the marketplace, and they threaten to riot, burn, and loot unless their demands are satisfied. Potential victims prefer to write a check to pay off (in taxes) those who threaten them than to assume the implied risks of violence. The politically imposed tax and subsequent redistribution thus buy the equivalent of riot insurance.

More is better than less. Most commonly, people use the coercive sanction of government to redistribute resources simply because they expect to receive more utility than they now receive from private-choice procedures. The egalitarian expects more utility from a world of equals than from one of unequals. The aesthete or altruist expects more utility from a world without poverty than from one with poverty. The person fearing violence expects to lose less utility from taxes paid for redistributions than from flying bricks and bullets and gutted buildings. The resulting redistributions all involve the principle that people get more valued resources—for example, equality, domestic tranquility, and relief from ugliness—than they are willing or able to pay for through private, voluntary means. Though markets and other private-choice mechanisms do redistribute resources, some prefer the results of non-market redistributions.

Nevertheless, as noted earlier, most collective, coercive redistributions seem far more mundane than these examples. Tariffs protect domestic procedures against foreign competition at the expense of foreign producers and domestic consumers. Farm subsidies and agricultural marketing orders limit

---

[14] A similar view is expressed in John Rawls, *A Theory of Justice* (Cambridge, Mass.: Harvard University Press, 1971).

farm production and increase the cost of food; the farmer benefits and the consumer loses. Regulatory agencies often control prices and entry into various businesses; such controls indirectly subsidize existing producers and impose additional costs on consumers, who would benefit from increased competition if deregulation occurred.

One major recurring problem this book addresses concerns the form of popular demands for collective action and the resulting shape of public policy. The description of reasons why people would prefer the outcomes of public choice to those of private choice includes the existence of theoretical problems such as supplying public goods, suppressing public bads, redistributing resources, regulating monopolies, and defining property rights. But people very often use public choice to get purely private goods at collective cost.

Even when the desire to correct one of the theoretical problems is involved, private interests come into play, for the collective-choice solution to many of these problems requires the accumulation and expenditure of substantial resources in which many have private interests. For example, building an aircraft carrier that contributes to supplying the public good of national defense requires huge amounts of private-sector resources: labor, steel, sophisticated electronic equipment, a shipyard, and hundreds of thousands of prefabricated units. Many of these resources are produced in identifiable congressional districts. Just as the private sector cannot by itself provide a good such as national defense because of its nondivisible characteristic of jointness, for the same reason the private sector cannot generate the political demand for creating an *optimal level* of national defense; that too is a public good. Hence, political demands for aircraft carriers are driven by private interests in defense construction contracts. The public policy result is largely redistributive, with little or no regard to an optimal public policy, theoretically defined.[15] As Chapters 6, 7, 9, 11, and 13 point out, there are few imaginable public policies that do not suffer from this dynamic.

The mechanics of redistribution. In a general sense, resource redistributions occur simultaneously with any change in public policy. The redistribution may be in tangible goods, such as commodities and services, or in intangible goods, such as perceived moral climates or symbolic actions. People have different resources and utilities after government actions than before them. Market choice also results in redistributions. The difference between private and collective redistributions is that the first, in the absence of externalities, are voluntarily and unanimous, while the second remain coercive and seldom

---

[15] Peter H. Aranson and Peter C. Ordeshook, "The Political Bases of Public Sector Growth in a Representative Democracy," paper prepared for delivery at the annual convention of the American Political Science Association, Washington, D. C., September 1978; Aranson and Ordeshook, "A Prolegomenon to a Theory of the Failure of Representative Democracy," in Richard D. Auster and Barbara Sears, eds., *American Re-evolution: Papers and Proceedings* (Tucson: University of Arizona Department of Economics, 1977), pp. 23–46.

are unanimous. Put differently, political resource redistribution requires for its adoption something less than unanimous consent.

A brief example demonstrates the logic and mechanics of collective-choice redistributions. Suppose a city has one hundred citizens, who make collective decisions by majority vote; forty rich citizens have $1000 each, while sixty poor ones have $500 each, for a total of $70,000 in the community. Someone makes a motion to confiscate $300 from each rich citizen and give the money to each poor citizen. The motion passes by a vote of sixty to forty. Suppose the numbers are reversed: there are sixty rich citizens and forty poor ones. The rich citizens might vote to confiscate all of the poor citizens' money. Although such tendencies are constantly at work, there are obvious sources of inertia in any nation (constitutional restraints, for example) that lessen their effects.

Resource redistributions as collective goods. We can now join this discussion with the preceding analysis of public goods and bads. Collective-choice resource redistributions are collective goods. For those who favor government resource redistributions, they are collective goods that display positive externalities, and their absence is a collective good that displays a negative externality. For those who oppose government resource redistributions, they are collective goods that display negative externalities, and their absence is a collective good that displays a positive externality. (One person might also favor some collective-choice redistributions and oppose others.) Resource redistributions exhibit both jointness of supply and jointness of consumption.

Consider the reasons why people want collective resource redistributions. Egalitarians prefer material equality for all citizens. The closer people become in possessions, the more utility an egalitarian receives. An individual egalitarian could calculate the average wealth in the nation and give away all of his possessions until he reaches the average position. But this would accomplish little, for his wealth is limited. The egalitarian regrets that others seem unwilling to contribute to the attainment of equality, and sometimes he is willing to use government coercion to overcome what he regards as a public bad. Even a nation of many willing egalitarians may not achieve equality, because if one egalitarian decides to supply it, all other egalitarians gain utility from the move toward equality by his largesse, with no generosity on their part. Hence, a free-rider problem might emerge, provided that egalitarians also receive utility by enjoying some wealth of their own. Aesthetes and altruists want resource redistributions to reduce the ugliness of poverty (a good similar to pollution) or to further an altruistic goal, but no single altruist or aesthete can relieve everyone's material suffering. The failure of others to join the altruist or aesthete is a collective goods problem identical to the egalitarian's—the problem of a collective good not supplied. So, too, the absence of minimum resources guarantees is a public bad for those who want them.

The redistribution process to arrest the threat of extortion, as noted, is often poverty-related. But a public poverty program represents a resource redistribution not only to those who are poor, but also to those who fear violence perpetrated by the poor. Government supply of "extortion" payments thus simultaneously supplies a good that displays a positive externality for the potential victims and a negative externality, tax payments, for all others.

Those who seek a resource redistribution merely to be wealthier may be unable or unwilling to secure additional wealth in the marketplace. Others are unwilling to give away their resources voluntarily. Therefore, those who think they can do better with it prefer redistribution by a collective-choice procedure to redistribution by a private-choice procedure; those who benefit receive a positive externality, while those who lose receive a negative externality.

Monopoly

Monopolies represent another potential problem of private choice. A **monopoly** occurs if one producer alone markets a good for which there are no close substitutes. A monopoly can be sustained only if potential competitors cannot enter the marketplace. One bar to entry occurs if, at its optimal size, a single firm would supply a particular good or service to an entire market (electric power is a good example). Monopolies arising because of the production efficiencies of size are known as natural monopolies. Compared to markets with many producers, natural monopolies supply fewer units of the goods and services they sell and market them at a higher price. A dead-weight economic loss is said to result.

Monopolists prefer to maintain their monopoly positions, but their customers prefer to get more goods and services at a lower price. Private decision procedures provide few direct means for getting owners and managers of natural monopolies voluntarily to give away part of their businesses or to grant at least some control of the monopoly to others. Therefore, consumers might prefer to turn to a collective-choice mechanism to alleviate perceived problems of monopoly.[16] In the United States, the usual procedure for controlling natural monopolies is to establish regulatory agencies to set their price schedules and quality and quantity of service. European states commonly nationalize such monopolies.

Public-choice antimonopoly solutions are resource redistributions. The

---

[16] The appropriate public policy toward natural monopolies is not at all a settled issue. Evidence suggests that price regulation has little or no effect on prices. See George J. Stigler and Claire Friedland, "What Can Regulators Regulate? The Case of Electricity," *Journal of Law and Economics,* 5 (October 1962), pp. 1–16. Some have argued that the natural-monopoly problem can be solved without price regulation. Under one scheme, would-be producers would bid for ownership or control of the monopolized resource. The bid would reflect both price and terms of service. See Harold Demsetz, "Why Regulate Utilities?" *Journal of Law and Economics,* 11 (April 1968), pp. 55–65.

resource in question is the control of industrial capacity. Shareholders of the monopoly prefer to maintain control, while some consumers may prefer to take it away. Therefore, the monopoly problem is a resource redistribution problem, and thus also a public goods problem.[17]

Sometimes the resource redistribution is explicit. When natural monopolies are not involved, antitrust laws and regulations allow private suits by competitors against business practices defined by law to be monopolistic or predatory. Government suits attack price fixing and related practices. Successful private plaintiffs can collect triple damages. When the government is named as the plaintiff, the United States attorney can seek a breakup of the accused firm as well as the imprisonment of its executives if a criminal conspiracy is proved. The economics of both private and public antitrust suits are very much disputed, but many scholars agree that plaintiffs in private suits have a private interest in hindering the defendants, who are usually their competitors. These defendants are almost always more successful firms. Thus, such actions also involve explicit redistributions from a stronger competitor to a weaker one.

Property Rights

The collective goods problem and its special cases of resource redistribution and monopoly are really part of a larger public-choice problem, the problem of defining **property rights.** The term *property right* has no ideological or moral content; rather, it denotes the legal ability to own title to a particular resource and the conditions under which the property can be used and its title transferred to others. The problem of creating an optimal arrangement of property rights is the first problem of government, and we can subsume all other problems under it. At the beginning of this chapter's discussion of markets, we assumed that property rights were defined and enforced. But suppose you have something I want. I can offer you something in exchange for it. I can try to get it elsewhere. Or I can try to take it from you forcibly or otherwise without your consent: I can steal it. Without the collectively supplied protection of government—property rights—what is to prevent me from doing so? Only your efforts at self-defense. The British philosopher Thomas Hobbes characterized the condition of people without government, without property rights, as being wretched.

[17] The public goods aspect of the monopoly problem also involves problems of correctly pricing goods such as electricity. Within the limits of generating capacity, the more total kilowatt hours of electricity all customers purchase, the cheaper on average each kilowatt hour becomes. Hence, an increase in my consumption level lowers your cost, and vice versa. The externality is evident. See Abba P. Lerner, "Conflicting Principles of Public Utility Price Regulation," *Journal of Law and Economics,* 7 (October 1964), pp. 61–70. Others argue that stretching the collective goods problem to include questions about monopoly is inappropriate. See James M. Buchanan, *The Bases of Collective Action* (New York: General Learning Press, 1971).

> Whatsoever therefore is consequent to a time of Warre, where every man is Enemy to every man; the same is consequent to the time, wherein men live without other security, than what their own strength, and their own invention shall furnish them withall. In such condition, there is no place for Industry; because the fruit thereof is uncertain: and consequently no Culture of the Earth; no Navigation, nor use of the commodities that may be imported by Sea; no commodious Building; no Instruments of moving, and removing such things as require much force; no Knowledge of the face of Earth; no account of Time; no Arts; no Letters; no Society; and which is worst of all, continuall feare, and danger of violent death; and the life of man, solitary, poore, nasty, brutish, and short.[18]

This famous quotation relates directly to the problems of government, public choice, and property rights. Hobbes argued that without government, no civil rights to property and no ownership exist. If you build a house of wood, nothing but your own strength (and my honesty) can stop me from tearing it to pieces to get firewood or from moving in and calling it my own. If you collect wood to build a fire, I may take the wood to build a house or to fuel my own fire.[19] You may hire your own private police force or army, but I may offer them a higher price to turn against you. In sum, no one protects ownership and enforces agreements. Contracts are meaningless and may be breached whenever it is advantageous to do so.

Without a mechanism to protect property rights, fewer houses would be built, because the expected utility from using a house in the future is reduced, while the cost of house building at least remains unchanged. Less firewood would be collected for the same reason. People would also have to spend resources for protecting their own property—more than they would spend to pay taxes in support of police, who specialize in such activities and are therefore more efficient at them.[20] Thus, everyone would produce and consume less of everything, including leisure. By contrast, a correct property rights system increases production and leisure and adds to the expected utility of all resources to their users and owners.

Most people view property rights as concerning material things; however, recent developments in the study of law and economics interpret property rights to include nearly every right that people regard as a civil right or a civil liberty. For example, the right of a free press is a clear property right to

---

[18] Thomas Hobbes, *Leviathan, Or the Matter, Forme and Power of a Commonwealth, Ecclesiasticall and Civill.* Edited with an introduction by C. B. Macpherson (Baltimore: Penguin, 1968), p. 186.

[19] This problem is discussed explicitly in Tullock, *Private Wants, Public Means,* Chapter 2.

[20] The state of "Warre" Hobbes referred to can also occur if police are used by some to oppress others. The creation of a public coercive agency does not automatically guarantee that property is secure. The level of protection may be inadequate, greater than optimal, or merely a facade for legalized oppression.

use a productive resource. Supreme Court cases have addressed the problem of how extensively that right can be exercised and whether and to what extent news personnel are protected against charges of libel and against subpoenas of reporters' confidential information.[21] The right to due process in a criminal trial, including a jury of one's peers and a speedy trial, is also a property right to which the courts have given considerable attention.[22] The condition that a person cannot be deprived of life, liberty, or property without due process of law is also a property right. Property, then, is all things people value to which rights can be defined and granted.

A simple example shows the relationship between property rights and the problems of collective goods and bads. Suppose a rancher and a farmer live side by side. The rancher's cattle roam over the farmer's land, destroying crops. In this hypothetical two-person society, the damaged crops are a clear instance of a collective good that displays a negative externality, the farmer's lost utility.[23]

The farmer can claim all cattle on his land, shoot the rancher, build a fence, or do nothing. But the farmer can also offer to pay the rancher to contain his cattle. The rancher can ignore the farmer, accept the money, shoot the farmer, or build a fence. However, in the absence of a collectively enforceable definition of property rights, there is little stability to the problem, and the neighbors might just as well kill each other—which sometimes happened in the range wars of the American West.

---

[21] On the libel question, see *Wolston v. Readers Digest Association,* 99 S. Ct. 2701 (1979); *Herbert v. Lando,* 99 S. Ct. 1635 (1979); *New York Times v. Sullivan,* 376 U. S. 254 (1963); and *Curtis Publishing Co. v. Butts,* 388 U. S. 130 (1966). On immunity from subpoena of reporters' notes and records, see *New York Times v. Jascalevich,* 98 S. Ct. 3058 (1978), application for stay denied; and *New York Times v. Jascalevich,* 98 S. Ct. 3060 (1978), application for stay denied. See also *Zurcher v. Stanford Daily News,* 98 S. Ct. 970 (1978) and *Warden v. Hayden,* 387 U.S. 294 (1967), on whether a newspaper office is immune from a surprise search by police. See *Gannet Co. v. DePasquale,* 99 S. Ct. 2898 (1979) and *Richmond Newspapers, Inc. v. Virginia,* 48 L.W. 5008 (1980) on whether the public, including the press, can be excluded from a judicial proceeding on a criminal matter.

[22] See *Duren v. Missouri,* 99 S. Ct. 664 (1979); *Burch v. Louisiana,* 99 S. Ct. 1623 (1979); and *Kentucky v. Whorton,* 99 S. Ct. 2088 (1979).

[23] This example derives from one of the most creative works in economic and political theories of collective goods. See Ronald Coase, "The Problem of Social Cost," *Journal of Law and Economics,* 3 (October 1960), pp. 1–44. Much of Coase's argument is omitted here, and other parts of it are restated. Coase shows that the initial assignment of property rights does not matter in a world without transactions—for example, bargaining—costs. The result remains Pareto optimal even in the presence of externalities. Coase also shows that the result is technologically efficient, since resources flow to their most highly valued economic use. An insightful extension of Coase's argument, showing the connections among collective goods, property rights, and law and public policy, is provided in Harold Demsetz, "The Exchange and Enforcement of Property Rights," *Journal of Law and Economics,* 7 (October 1964), pp. 11–26. See also Demsetz, "Toward A Theory of Property Rights," *American Economic Review,* 57 (May 1967), pp. 347–369.

Nevertheless, suppose the law, public policy, establishes a property right in the rancher's favor, to let his cattle wander. The farmer can now offer the rancher money to restrain his cattle. If the farmer's offer is less than the farmer's loss from wandering cattle and more than the rancher's cost of restraint, then a market exchange solves the externality problem. Indeed, the resulting bargain is Pareto optimal. However, if the law establishes a property right in the farmer's interest, then the rancher can pay the farmer to let the cattle wander, or he can restrain his cattle. Again, a private agreement settles the problem, and the resulting bargain is Pareto optimal. Even if the two make no bargain, the allocation based on a prior property right that can be bought and sold remains Pareto optimal.

Today, a problem similar to that caused by the wandering cattle exists with air and water pollution. No one has a clear property right or title to air or water. The agents of government have partially failed to define such rights. If you owned the air above your land or the water along your banks, then polluters would have to pay you to pollute that air or water, or else not pollute at all. However, if polluters held the property right to dispose of wastes in the air or water, then you would have to pay them to refrain from polluting or to reduce their pollution, or else accept dirty air or water. Clearly, such ownership, if feasible, would solve the pollution problem. But in this instance, the transactions and bargaining costs for each citizen to exchange rights to pollute and rights to clean air and water with every other citizen, unlike those faced by the farmer and the rancher, would be too high.[24] Hence, government personnel in effect claim certain property rights to air and water and then proceed to adopt pollution policies.

The monopoly problem is also one of property rights. In the case of natural monopolies such as electric power companies, government regulatory commissioners deprive a company's stockholders and managers of the right to set prices and to make certain decisions about service. In the case of other firms, owners' rights to acquire additional companies, or even to keep the ones they already own, can be limited if competitors or antitrust attorneys in the Justice Department and the Federal Trade Commission bring successful legal actions.

The agents of government sometimes change a system of property rights itself. For example, the deregulation of airline routes begun in 1978 deprived airlines of more or less exclusive property rights to those routes they formerly owned by virtue of government-controlled entry. Of course, a change in property rights during a term of ownership is itself a collective good that displays a positive externality for those who want the change and a negative externality for those who do not. Changes in the structure of property rights

---

[24] There is also an apparent free-rider problem. If I pay a factory not to pollute, then you receive the benefit of my transaction although you have not paid for it. Thus, we can ordinarily expect bargains between polluters and those who oppose pollution to be undersupplied.

also create resource redistributions as a consequence of the collective goods and bads allocated.

UNDESIRABLE CONSEQUENCES OF COLLECTIVE CHOICE

One might have concluded from our initial description of market exchange that outcomes of private choice appear superior to those of collective choice. However, private choice has now been found to have problems that public choice might alleviate. Thus, one might conclude that outcomes of public choice appear superior to those of private choice. But public choice also has its disadvantages. Here, we introduce five basic problems of collective choice mechanisms: the cost of abandoning market advantages; the production by collective action of public goods *and* bads; nonmarket discrimination; the generation of monopolies; and Arrow's paradox, with its associated problem of incoherence. Later chapters more fully discuss other problems with public choice, which seem to derive from the political process itself.

Lost Market Advantages

Signals from prices. I took a midwinter vacation trip from Atlanta to the Florida Keys during the 1973–1974 energy crisis. After flying to Miami, I rented a car with one-quarter of a tank of gas. No service stations in Miami seemed to have gas—I entered a three-mile-long line at one station and waited two hours, but the station ran out of gas three cars before my turn came. Heading south on a hope and a prayer, I finally found an open station with gasoline (three out of four in Miami were closed). To my surprise, when I arrived in the Keys, I found that all of the local service stations had more gas than they could sell, had no customers, and were turning away gas deliveries because their tanks were full.

What happened? During that period, Federal Energy Office personnel decided that oil dealers were not to be allowed to allocate gasoline themselves. Instead, they tried to do the allocating. The results were shortages here and abundances there. To his credit, FEO Director William E. Simon did not try too hard to supplant market allocations of gasoline, and he resisted congressional demands to try harder, for further government efforts would have made the sitution much worse. Shortages in the summer of 1979 mirrored the crisis five years earlier, and the Department of Energy itself reported that government allocations made a minor inconvenience caused by the revolution in Iran much worse than it needed to be.

This argument is valid not in spite of oil-company and gas-station-owner greed but because of it. If a commodity is in short supply in one place, its price rises. If the price rises sufficiently, people no longer sell the commodity where it is abundant and cheap, but send it to where it is scarce and expensive. The private-choice mechanism, the market, gives producers and sellers price signals to which they respond by moving commodities to where they can command the highest price. This response tends to even out shortages and surpluses over different areas of the country, and it also sends resources to the area in which they are most highly valued economically.

The signaling capacity of price, controlled by supply and demand, does far more than even out regional price and supply variations, however. In the short run—the period of time less than that which is necessary to add productive capacity, such as refineries—a sudden increase in demand or drop in supply results in a higher price. This higher price signals (provides an incentive for) producers to bring more of the commodity to market and simultaneously signals (provides an incentive for) consumers to use less of the commodity by switching to substitutes or by limiting consumption. Soon the market reaches a new equilibrium, and the amount of the commodity demanded continues to equal the amount of the commodity supplied. There are neither shortages, as evidenced by long lines at filling stations, nor surpluses.

In the long run—the period of time longer than that which is necessary to add productive capacity—greater profits from higher prices signal (provide an incentive for) new competitors to come into an industry and signal (provide an incentive for) existing producers to expand productive capacity. The resulting long-run increase in supply then drives real prices down. Sometimes this long-run signaling function of price seems poorly understood. For example, on June 6, 1978, California voters overwhelmingly passed Proposition 13, an amendment to the state constitution. The amendment immediately reduced local property taxes by 57 percent. Most voters expected an immediate reduction in rents on apartments and houses. However, rents did not fall immediately even though landlords received large reductions in their property taxes. Of course, this was to be expected, since there were no short-run changes in the amount of rental units supplied or demanded. But in the long run, lower taxes mean higher profits, which will draw more resources into building more apartments and other rental dwellings. Relative to other prices rents will fall, but not for a year or two. As expected, those who failed to understand this delay, including many proponents of Proposition 13, called for rent controls, which would defeat one desirable long-run effect of the tax reduction by stopping all or most additional building generated by greater profits.

Political signals. By contrast, public-choice mechanisms have no such signaling capability. Because of their jointness of supply and consumption, it is nearly impossible to establish prices, and therefore price signals, for public goods. Hence, signals (incentives) for government officials take the form of votes or bureaucratic imperatives. As Chapters 6, 7, 9, and 11 point out, these signals usually have little to do with an optimal allocation of resources. More important, public-choice mechanisms commonly fail to signal which government agencies are efficient and which are not. In private choice, a firm that cannot keep pace with its competition goes out of business. Those who produce efficiently are rewarded, and those who do not are punished. The imperative of business is to maximize profits by giving consumers what they want; the alternative is to go broke.

What is the bureaucrat's or politician's imperative? What kinds of signals do these people receive? Later chapters identify the most likely goals of public-sector "producers" and show how these goals affect the public and private goods that governments produce. Here, though, we merely observe that bureaucrats sometimes try to maximize the size of their budgets and that politicians try to maximize their chances for election and reelection. The efficient pursuit of *these* goals often leads to the adoption of public policies that perpetuate the lifespans of inefficient bureaus and that help to elect politicians whose legislative decisions sometimes seem to make no economic sense at all.

Collective Action and Public Policy

The second major undesirable consequence of collective choice partly explains why public-choice procedures sometimes lose the benefits of private ones. All collective actions produce public goods and bads; hence, any collective action aimed at correcting a collective goods problem or the related problems of redistribution, monopoly, and property rights also creates new public goods and bads.

Enforced consumption. Suppose that some public good, such as lighthouse services or national defense, is underproduced, and therefore people abandon private-choice procedures and go to public choice. But collective goods can only be supplied at a given level at a given time. Unlike shoes, breakfast cereals, and automobiles, which come in different shapes, sizes, colors, and prices, particular collective goods such as national defense or lighthouses can be supplied at only one level, and everyone must consume them at that level. For example, the defense budget might account for 10 percent or 15 percent of GNP. It cannot be both. Either we are at war or we are not at war; we cannot be both. If someone buys us an army or engages us in a war, or enacts or fails to enact a particular energy policy, then we consume the results, like it or not.

Consider again the abortion issue and the possible public policies on that issue. The policy that is adopted becomes a collective good because people must consume its results, no matter what policy is adopted and whether they like it or not. That is, the public policy decision on abortion is fixed, and the government monopoly on coercion enforces this public choice. Terrible conflict can thus result from the adoption, or even non-adoption, of any public policy precisely because it creates a public good that some see as a bad. In the case of abortion policy, conflict seems inevitable no matter which policy the agents of government adopt. People hold intense preferences on such issues, and this is a central problem, which is discussed in Chapters 7 and 13.

Public goods and plural societies. Even if people agree on the collective production of a public good, they may disagree on how it should be distributed. Public goods are often partly divisible because they benefit some people more than others, and herein lies a problem that can be particularly severe in plural societies, because it creates racial conflict.[25] For example, consider a hypothetical American city in which the population is 51 percent white and 49 percent black. Because of discrimination and wealth differences, black residents live in the southern part of the city while white residents live in the north. There is little or no neighborhood integration. Figure 3.2 illustrates this neighborhood racial configuration.

Suppose city council members are voting on where to put a new fire station. The city council is elected at large and, like the city itself, is 51 percent white and 49 percent black. While the fire station will serve everyone, its important characteristic is its closeness to a particular neighborhood. The black city council members, representing the southern part of the city, vote for Location *Z*, and the white city council members, representing the northern part of the city, vote for *X*. Probably no one votes for *Y*, although *Y* would be the market location in the absence of any other fire stations. It is also the location that minimizes the distance from the station to the average home. But *X* wins by a majority vote of 51 percent.

The fire station is a collective good for several reasons.[26] White residents consume its protection because it is in their neighborhood. Black residents

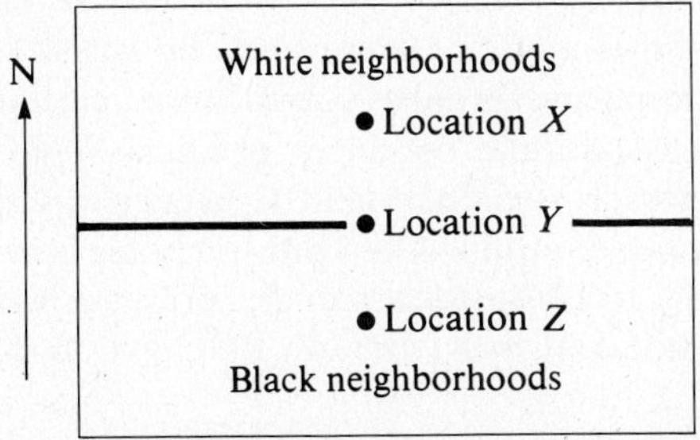

Figure 3.2 Fire station location in hypothetical biracial city.

[25] Alvin Rabushka and Kenneth A. Shepsle, *Politics in Plural Societies: A Theory of Democratic Instability* (Columbus, Ohio: Merrill, 1972).

[26] Fire protection can be privately supplied—indeed, it is so in some American communities. However, it becomes a public good when laws are enacted to make it available to everyone, no matter how large or small their contribution to its supply, or when buildings are close enough together that protecting or not protecting one building affects the safety of others.

lose most of its potential protection because of its distance from their homes. But everyone must pay taxes to build and maintain the new fire station, no matter what level of protection he or she receives from it. Such taxes are a public bad. Furthermore, several years of such political decisions about various public services for which black citizens pay taxes but from which they gain few benefits provide the stuff of which race riots are made.

Optimal supply and prices. Finally, recall that public goods are jointly produced and consumed. Even those who contribute nothing to their supply cannot be prevented from using them, and adding more users in no way reduces the supply available to everyone else. As noted earlier, it remains unclear how a market might be created for producing, buying, and selling such goods, with optimal prices reflecting the amounts of the goods supplied and demanded. Since people know they will have the goods to consume anyway, they are unlikely to reveal truthfully how much they would be willing to pay for them. Private markets provide such revelations by actual choices. But in political markets for public goods—and for all related public policies concerning monopolies, redistributions, and property rights—one cannot meaningfully identify optimal prices and levels of supply.[27]

Nonmarket Discrimination

The least-understood difference between private- and collective-choice procedures lies in the degree to which each creates conditions underlying discrimination. *Discrimination* means "distinguishing among persons or goods according to some characteristic." People discriminate when they buy one product, read one book, or vote for one candidate rather than another. One form of discrimination is among persons on the basis of race, religion, age, sex, sexual or affectional preferences, physical or mental disability, or other characteristics, such as national origin or political beliefs. It is obvious that discrimination can worsen racial conficit. However, discrimination problems often become even more complex when public choice is involved. Considering the previous example, black residents might not care whether a firehouse is in a white neighborhood, if only they do not have to pay for it.

The effects of government regulation. With private-choice procedures, profits come to represent the principal criterion by which actions are judged. For instance, an employer might prefer hiring whites to hiring blacks, or vice versa; but if discriminatory hiring becomes unprofitable for any reason, then this would-be discriminator must change his or her ways or suffer.

The mechanism by which regulation creates employment discrimination

---

[27] See Mancur Olson, Jr., "Evaluating Performance in the Public Sector," paper prepared for delivery at the annual meeting of the Public Choice Society, Pittsburgh, Pennsylvania, May 1972; and Paul A. Samuelson, "The Pure Theory of Public Expenditure," *Review of Economics and Statistics,* 36 (1954), pp. 387–390.

rests on the notion that an employer has a large supply of workers he or she can hire for each new job opening. Some of these workers may be "preferred" and others "non-preferred" in the eyes of the prejudiced employer (for example, gentiles may be "preferred" and Jews, "non-preferred"). To get a job, each "non-preferred" person must offer to work at a wage discount to compensate for the employer's loss of utility from working with a "non-preferred" person. The employer then converts the wage discount into a higher level of profits.[28]

However, government regulation of many firms—for example, gas and electric power companies and transportation and telephone companies—removes profitability as a standard of action. Generally, members of federal and state regulatory commissions fix the prices of such firms by using a standard that calls for a "reasonable rate of return" on investment, which means a guaranteed profit as well as a limit to profits. Large but otherwise competitive corporations, whose managers sometimes are believed to hold down profits purposely in fear of antitrust prosecution, are also affected by a kind of regulation: the fear of such legal action.

If business executives are prevented by regulation or fear of legal action from fully maximizing profits, they sometimes turn to nonmonetary benefits, such as having "preferred" colleagues at work. Under these circumstances, "non-preferred" persons cannot compensate prejudiced employers by offering to work at a lower wage rate, for government regulation or the threat of antitrust litigation has placed a cap on profits. Therefore, the prejudiced employer has no way to convert the lower wage rate a "non-preferred" worker might offer into a higher profit. Accordingly, these prejudiced employers hire fewer "non-preferred" workers.

One study reports a finding to this effect for Jews and gentiles in industry.[29] The study takes a random sample of 352 Harvard MBA graduates, 128 of whom are Jews and 224 of whom are gentiles, and divides the sample according to whether a graduate found a job in a regulated or concentrated industry (such as transportation, communications, public utilities, finance, insurance, and real estate) or in an unregulated or competitive industry (such as agriculture, forestry, fisheries, mining, manufacturing, wholesale and retail trade, business services, amusement, recreation, and professional services). Table 3.3 reports the results.

Unregulated industries were found to hire a much larger percentage of

---

[28] This argument is explored at great length in Cotton Mather Lindsay, *Equal Pay for Comparable Work: An Economic Analysis of a New Antidiscrimination Doctrine* (Coral Gables, Fla.: Law and Economics Center Occasional Paper, 1980), and in Armen Alchian and Reuben A. Kessel, "Competition, Monopoly, and the Pursuit of Pecuniary Gain," in *Aspects of Labor Economics,* 157 (National Bureau of Economic Research, 1962). An excellent review of this article and a spelling out of the underlying argument is in Harold Demsetz, "Minorities in the Market Place," *North Carolina Law Review,* 43 (February 1965), pp. 271–297.

[29] Alchian and Kessel, "Competition, Monopoly, and the Pursuit of Pecuniary Gain."

Table 3.3 Employment of Jewish and Gentile Harvard MBA's in Different Industries

	Percent Jews Employed	Percent Gentiles Employed
Regulated industries and monopolies	18	82
Unregulated industries and nonmonopolies	41	59
Entire sample	36	64

Source: Armen Alchian and Reuben A. Kessel, "Competition, Monopoly, and the Pursuit of Pecuniary Gain," in *Aspects of Labor Economics,* 157 (National Bureau of Economic Research, 1962), as quoted in Harold Demsetz, "Minorities in the Market Place," *North Carolina Law Review,* 43 (February 1965), pp. 271–297.

Jews (41 percent) than do regulated industries (18 percent), supporting the view that one effect of government regulation is discrimination in hiring. If profit maximizing were to become a more important motive in regulated and concentrated industries, then hiring practices might change. Of course, what is true for Jews might also hold true for blacks, women, and others who experience employment discrimination. To the extent that government regulation reduces profit incentives, the substitution of nonpecuniary payments, as this discussion reveals, might be expected. The effects of this shift must be counted as a cost of collective action.

The effects on civil liberties. Collective decision procedures also can affect the exercise of civil liberties. The First Amendment to the Constitution provides that "Congress shall make no law respecting an establishment of religion, or prohibiting the free exercise thereof; or abridging the freedom of speech or the press; or the right of the people peaceably to assemble, and to petition the government for a redress of grievances." This is a clear restriction on government prerogatives, yet people often urge government personnel to violate the First Amendment because they dislike what someone else says, writes, or believes. If the members of Congress or of some other legislature want to violate the First Amendment, either in letter or in spirit, then individual citizens occasionally have very limited protection to which they can turn.

A private-choice mechanism such as an unregulated market often gives harassed citizens just such a protection against those who would persecute them for their unpopular views. One example of this kind of protection is suggested in the case of those screen writers who during the late 1940s came under the scrutiny of various congressional committees investigating an alleged communist influence in the movie industry.[30] In response to congressional threats, the Motion Picture Academy, as well as the movie industry

[30] Milton Friedman, *Capitalism and Freedom* (Chicago: University of Chicago Press, 1962), pp. 19–21.

generally, blacklisted suspected communists and others. A *Time* magazine report tells the whole story and then some:

> The Oscar-awarding ritual is Hollywood's biggest pitch for dignity, but two years ago dignity suffered. When one Robert Rich was announced as top writer for *The Brave One,* he never stepped forward. Robert Rich was a pseudonym, masking one of about 150 writers . . . blacklisted by the industry since 1947 as suspected Communists or fellow travelers. The case was particularly embarrassing because the Motion Picture Academy had barred any Communist or Fifth Amendment pleader from Oscar competition. Last week both the Communist rule and the mystery of Rich's identity were suddenly rescripted. Rich turned out to be Dalton (*Johnny Got His Gun*) Trumbo, one of the original "Hollywood Ten" writers who refused to testify at the 1947 hearings on Communism in the movie industry. Said producer Frank King, who had stoutly insisted that Robert Rich was "a young guy in Spain with a beard: We have an obligation to our stockholders to buy the best script we can. Trumbo brought us *The Brave One* and we bought it. . . ."
>
> In effect it was the formal end of the Hollywood blacklist. For barred writers, the informal end came long ago. At least 15% of current Hollywood films are reportedly written by blacklist members. Said producer King, "There are more ghosts in Hollywood than in Forest Lawn [a plush Hollywood cemetery]. Every company in town has used the work of blacklisted people. We're just the first to confirm what everybody knows."[31]

Trumbo's past or present political views are irrelevant to this discussion. However, some accused him of undermining a private-choice mechanism, the market. That, surely, is an implication of communism. Moreover, Trumbo's accusers used a public-choice mechanism—congressional investigations—to hurt him. But a private-choice mechanism, based on producer and stockholder profit maximization, allowed Trumbo to continue to write for a living. We are also reminded:

> From 1933 to the outbreak of World War II, Winston Churchill was not permitted to talk over the British radio, which was, of course, a government monopoly administered by the British Broadcasting Corporation. Here was a leading citizen of his country, a Member of Parliament, a former cabinet minister, a man who was desperately trying by every device possible to persuade his countrymen to take steps to ward off the menace of Hitler's Germany. He was not permitted to talk over the radio to the British people because the BBC was a government monopoly and his position was too "controversial."[32]

---

[31] "Blacklist Fadeout," *Time,* January 26, 1959, p. 77. As quoted in Friedman, *Capitalism and Freedom,* pp. 19–20. Reprinted by permission from *Time,* The Weekly News Magazine; copyright Time Inc. 1959.

[32] Friedman, *Capitalism and Freedom,* p. 19.

In sum, if people decide about more and more things with collective-choice procedures, many civil rights may be endangered, and economic and other forms of discrimination against the members of racial, religious, or political groups may worsen. For example, it may be that if most businesses in the Soviet Union were privately owned, few Soviet Jews would lose their jobs upon applying for exit visas. Today the opposite holds true.

Government and Monopolies

The fourth problem with public-choice procedures is that they often produce monopoly or monopoly-like conditions. Earlier, this chapter cites the regulation and control of monopolies as one reason why people prefer to use a public-choice mechanism. But there are two problems with the way in which collective action handles monopolies. First, government itself is a monopoly; its agents claim a monopoly on the use of force and on the right to supply several goods and services, such as the delivery of first-class mail, police protection, courts, and military defense.[33] Thus, the very procedure used to control or regulate private monopolies itself creates more monopolies, with all of the attendant problems.

Second, public-choice procedures often create private-sector monopolies and cartels or reduce competition in the private sector. For example, manufacturers and union leaders frequently lobby for governmentally administered tariffs and trade quotas to limit foreign competition. The resulting monopoly position given to domestic manufacturers allows them to charge more, which means that the tariff creates an indirect tax on consumers. Regulatory commissions, which often have the explicit aim of creating monopolies, provide another example of the same problem. Public utility regulatory commissions in transportation (airlines, railroads, buses, and interstate trucking) and domestic services (power, water, and telephones) have often ruled competition to be illegal. For similar reasons, licensing in several professions creates monopoly-like situations. Since members of licensed professions serve on licensing boards and control entry into their own trades, the result is often fewer producers, and consequently higher prices charged for services, than might otherwise be true.

Many government regulatory policies also make it difficult for new firms to form and compete. Securities and Exchange Commission regulations create very large expenses for new firms whose owners want to sell shares in their corporations to raise venture capital for building and expansion. Older and larger firms are often thereby effectively protected from competition. Government regulations concerning product and worker safety also dispropor-

---

[33] While private police forces, detectives, and protection agencies do coexist with government police, the public-sector suppliers of these services are paid for by coercively imposed taxation, and the control that government police exercise over private-sector suppliers of police services ordinarily is assured by law.

tionately disadvantage smaller competitors. The tax code itself sometimes works to the disadvantage of newly established firms. A reduction in competition, increased prices, and reduced output of goods and services thus accompany many regulatory actions, whether such consequences are intended or unintended.

The Problem of the Public Interest

The final problem of collective choice that this chapter examines concerns the existence and definition of the public interest. It also concerns the coherence of decisions made by collective-choice procedures, a matter referred to in Chapters 1 and 2. Both private- and public-choice mechanisms have their respective benefits and costs, which a person might compare to form a preference for using a variant of one procedure or the other. However, it is usually not possible to say that the choice of a decision procedure in general, and of a collective-choice procedure in particular, serves the public good, or the public interest, or the general welfare. There are several reasons why this is so, some of which we have already mentioned.

First, if people contemplate and successfully impose the use of a public-choice mechanism, then (except in prisoners' dilemma situations) someone almost always must lose. Those who oppose the collective action—usually those whom it forces to do something against their will—are the losers. Thus, the decision to make some human action collective often is part of a zero-sum-like game or a game in which there is some degree of conflict of interest. It is sometimes argued that the public interest compels collective action, but this disembodied interest could only be defined by comparing the added utility of the winners with the forgone utility of the losers, in which case this notion of a public interest rests on an organic fallacy. Calling the collectivity "the public" changes nothing.[34]

Second, it is not clear exactly what the notion of a transcendent interest

---

[34] It is important to distinguish between public policy decisions and constitutional decisions. First, consider a public policy decision. For example, suppose that as a result of several congressional, presidential, and military decisions, you must die in battle "to provide for the common defense." As a result of your death, every other citizen seems marginally safer. But no one can claim that your death served the public interest, because such a claim would require an interpersonal comparison of utility (unless you were not included as a member of the public). However, at the constitutional level, and before an actual war is at hand, you might be asked to consent to a scheme allowing political and military leaders to conscript you and others into the armed forces, which might eventually lead to your death in battle. You understand that this arrangement actually increases your chances of surviving a war, and may even increase the chances of peace, because it provides for the collective good of national defense. Indeed, such a scheme might command nearly unanimous consent, in which case it would probably approach as close to Pareto optimality as any public policy arrangement can. But we continue to make no claims about the public interest, and once the constitutional question is settled, substantial disagreements will occur about particular wars, strategies, tactics, and orders not to retreat.

in publicness, which somehow guides the decisions of human beings, would add to our ability to explain and predict others' decisions about public policy. For the social scientist, the notion of a public interest is simply not useful. This does not mean that the political use of the concept "the public interest" is uninteresting. Citizens do refer to the public interest when advocating a political or economic policy; the term is propagandistic. Nevertheless, beyond its use for emotional appeal, it does not help to explain and predict human action.

Third, and most important, suppose that one could define what the public interest is. The ability to do so does not mean that the public interest exists. As a nonsense example, suppose the public interest is defined as the political view of a barber in a town in which the barber shaves all men who do not shave themselves. Since the barber is a man who shaves himself, he cannot get a shave from a barber, and so forth. No such town and no such barber can exist, and using such a definition, no public interest could exist.

On the existence of the public interest. An entire line of inquiry has been generated by asking if such a thing as the public interest can indeed exist.[35] This inquiry does not ask what the public interest is or whether the public interest exists. Rather, it supposes that a decision—a public- or private-choice—procedure is like a machine, that individual preferences go into the machine like raw materials, and that the machine's product is some decision. Some reasonable criteria are proposed for judging the decision, the machine's product, and then it is proved that a machine simultaneously satisfying all of these criteria cannot logically exist. Of course, if one agrees that a procedure must meet these criteria to produce decisions in the public interest, then the public interest cannot exist, because no procedure (machine) could produce it. Five conditions (criteria) have been offered for such a machine, and we discuss the meanings of these conditions here.[36]

Condition 1: Universal Admissibility of Individual Orderings. The first condition, the **universal admissibility of individual orderings,** concerns the input of raw materials to the collective-choice machine. These inputs are the citizens' preference orderings. Condition 1 holds that among the outcomes for which citizens state a preference, a given preference ordering should not be excluded. For example, suppose there are three proposals to be voted on concerning Social Security payments: proposal *X*, to increase payments; *Y*, to leave payments unchanged; and *Z*, to decrease payments. Each citizen might have one of six logically possible preference orderings: (1) *X* is preferred to *Y*, and *Y* is preferred to *Z*; (2) *X* is preferred to *Z*, and *Z* is preferred to *Y*; (3) *Y* is

[35] Kenneth J. Arrow, *Social Choice and Individual Values,* 2nd ed. (New York: Wiley, 1963).

[36] Arrow, *Social Choice and Individual Values.* The titles for these conditions are taken from Riker and Ordeshook, *An Introduction to Positive Political Theory,* Chapter 4. My discussion, except for that of condition 1 and 3, follows theirs closely.

preferred to *X,* and *X* is preferred to *Z;* (4) *Y* is preferred to *Z,* and *Z* is preferred to *X;* (5) *Z* is preferred to *X,* and *X* is preferred to *Y;* and (6) *Z* is preferred to *Y,* and *Y* is preferred to *X.* Condition 1 says that the decision procedure should not prohibit a particular preference ordering as raw material input into the collective-choice mechanism. For example, one might think that to prefer a payment increase to a payment decrease and a payment decrease to no change in payments makes no sense. But the vote of someone who holds such a preference cannot be excluded. One implication of condition 1 is that even those with unusual preferences are guaranteed the right to participate in making a public choice.

Condition 2: Non-perversity, or Positive Association of Individual and Social Values. The second condition, **non-perversity,** is quite simple. Using the Social Security example, suppose that the collective-choice mechanism yields a decision that the public policy should be *X,* an increase in Social Security payments, rather than *Y* or *Z.* Someone calls for a new vote on the motion. Jones preferred *Z* to *Y* and *Y* to *X* in the original vote, but now prefers *X* to *Y* and *Y* to *Z.* Jones votes accordingly in the new balloting. If no one else changes his or her vote or if any change that does occur is in favor of *X,* then the second condition requires that *X,* the original winner, continues to be the social, collective choice, the outcome of the public-choice mechanism. Stated differently, *X* moved higher in Jones's preference ordering. This should not cause *X* to decline in the aggregate ordering that the public-choice procedure reveals.

Condition 3: Independence from Irrelevant Alternatives. Suppose that a congressional committee of three members, A, B, and C, is voting on the three Social Security proposals. Representatives A and B prefer *X* to *Y* and *Y* to *Z,* while C prefers *Z* to *Y* and *Y* to *X.* Clearly, motion *X* wins by a majority vote. However, suppose the committee members use a rating system known as a **Borda count** to decide the matter. Using this system, each member would score one point for his or her most preferred motion, two points for a second choice, and three points for a third choice. Using A, B, and C's preference orderings as just stated, the numbers resulting from a Borda count are listed in Table 3.4 under *Vote 1.* The motion with the lowest number of points wins; hence *X,* with five points, remains the committee decision.

At this point, member C says he has changed his mind and asks his colleagues for the courtesy of a new vote. They comply with this request, but keep their preferences as before. C, however, now ranks *Y* above *Z,* producing the configuration under *Vote 2* in Table 3.4.

No member's preference ordering as between *X* and *Y* has changed, but now motion *Y* ties motion *X* in the Borda count. Obviously, something is amiss. That something is the location of the irrelevant alternative, *Z,* which scores third in both systems. We call *Z* an irrelevant alternative because it should not affect the pairwise vote or comparison between *X* and *Y.* The results of a Borda count voting scheme, as this example shows, obviously do not exhibit **independence from irrelevant alternatives.**

Table 3.4 Borda Counts on Hypothetical Congressional Social Security Vote

		Vote 1		
Motion	Points from A	Points from B	Points from C	Total Points
X	1	1	3	5
Y	2	2	2	6
Z	3	3	1	7
		Vote 2		
Motion	Points from A	Points from B	Points from C	Total Points
X	1	1	3	5
Y	2	2	1	5
Z	3	3	2	8

Condition 4: Citizens' Sovereignty. The fourth condition, **citizens' sovereignty,** requires that there must be some way to get a particular motion out of the decision process as a winner. For the Social Security example, this means that some collection of individual preferences exists that would yield each of the motions as a winner. Suppose that there is no way to get *X*, an increase in payments, as a winner in some voting system, even if it was a unanimous first choice. If this occurs, the citizens have no sovereignty, and the collective choice is said to be imposed.

Condition 5: Non-dictatorship. The fifth condition, **non-dictatorship,** requires that there must be no person whose preferred outcome is the social choice no matter what all other persons' preferred outcomes might be. Suppose that in a state of one-hundred persons, all but one person prefer *X* to any other motion. If that one person's preference, say *Y*, becomes the collective choice, then that person is a dictator. Put differently, a person is a dictator if the collective choice is *Y* when he or she prefers *Y* to *X*, regardless of everyone else's preferences. Condition 5 requires that this cannot be true.

When these five conditions are stated in symbolic terms, a most disturbing mathematical impossibility theorem can be proved: there cannot exist a decision mechanism that produces a connected and transitive public choice and simultaneously satisfies all five conditions.[37] That is, suppose reasonable people agree that any social decision procedure that seeks to identify or enact the public interest must render connected and transitive preference orderings over possible outcomes and satisfy all five conditions. No such mechanism

[37] Another way to state this theorem is that any decision procedure that satisfies conditions 1, 2, and 3 and produces connected and transitive collective preference orderings over outcomes must result in outcomes that are either imposed (which violates condition 4) or dictatorial (which violates condition 5).

exists! If such a mechanism is required to identify or enact the public interest, then the public interest does not exist.

The paradox of voting. This is **Arrow's paradox,** named after the economist who developed this line of inquiry, Kenneth J. Arrow. The classic applied example of Arrow's paradox manifests itself in a paradox of voting, the **cyclical majority** problem. This cycle occurs if each voter's preferences are connected and transitive but the collective-choice procedure yields an intransitive preference. Thus, the connection between intransitive aggregated preferences and Arrow's impossibility theorem is that certain collections of transitive individual preferences, when aggregated by a social-choice procedure, yield an intransitive public choice. One such collection of transitive individual preferences is used to prove Arrow's theorem.

Chapter 1 included an example, concerning 3000 delegates to a presidential nominating convention, showing how intransitive public choices arise from such a collection of transitive individual preferences. The convention delegates had three kinds of preference orderings: 1000 preferred Washington to Adams and Adams to Jefferson; 1000 preferred Adams to Jefferson and Jefferson to Washington; and 1000 preferred Jefferson to Washington and Washington to Adams. The election (collective-choice) procedure revealed the social preference to be: *The Convention preferred Washington to Adams, Adams to Jefferson, and Jefferson to Washington.* Chapter 2 provided a second example, concerning three school-board members whose collective preference on the school integration issue was also intransitive. By voting for a school superintendent, these board members revealed a collective preference for forced busing over open schools, open schools over the segregated status quo, and the segregated status quo over forced busing.

In both examples, a social decision—a public interest—did not exist. Arrow's paradox finds intransitivities, and therefore incoherence, in the outcomes of choice procedures. This incoherence makes it impossible to define a public interest. Furthermore, as Chapter 7 points out, such intransitivities lead election candidates to mask their intentions, and as Chapters 8 and 9 report, intransitivities in collective-choice bodies such as the Congress can lead to the manipulation of agendas to produce almost any public choice.

Private and collective choice as paradox generators. Arrow does not restrict his attention to collective-choice mechanisms; indeed, his findings apply as well to private decision procedures such as markets. However, the nature of private-choice mechanisms makes it most unlikely that a cycle will occur with their use, for markets violate the first condition, universal admissibility, in a not objectionable way. A cyclical majority requires particular configurations of individual preferences. While these configurations may be very common, they are much more likely to occur in political situations than in market choice. For instance, consider the example of preferences for changes in Social Security payments used in the discussion of conditions 1 through 5.

Two preference orderings seemed to make no sense: the first had a voter preferring an increase, *X*, to a decrease, *Z*, and a decrease to no change, *Y*; the second had a voter preferring a decrease to an increase and an increase to no change. These individual orderings make no sense because most people in an economic capacity prefer more of something to less, or vice versa—but not both. With *X* preferred to *Z* preferred to *Y*, more is preferred to less, which in turn is preferred to no change. In economic exchanges, one of the other four orderings and not one of these two bizarre orderings, should hold. Hence, as a practical matter, condition 1 is modestly violated by market exchange (the theorem still holds, however).

Now consider a strictly political issue, the Vietnam War. During President Lyndon B. Johnson's administration, three very general policy positions were prevalent: *X*, to escalate the war (the hawk position); *Y*, to keep things as they were (Johnson's position); and *Z*, to disengage immediately (the dove position). Six possible preference orderings also held. A classic hawk would have preferred *X* to *Y* and *Y* to *Z*. A classic dove would have preferred *Z* to *Y* and *Y* to *X*. Johnson's supporters might have preferred either *Y* to *Z* and *Z* to *X*, or *Y* to *X* and *X* to *Z*.

These four individual preference orderings could not be aggregated to yield an intransitive public choice; a group of citizens with these orderings could not get into a voting cycle. But a citizen could reasonably have had one of two other preference orderings: he might have preferred either *X* to *Z* and *Z* to *Y*, or *Z* to *X* and *X* to *Y*. These are akin to the individual orderings that we found not to be sensible in the Social Security example. Here, though, they make sense. The person who prefers *X* to *Z* and *Z* to *Y* says, "Escalate the war or get out—do not continue as is"; the person who prefers *Z* to *X* to *Y* says, "Get out or escalate the war—do not continue as is." With these two reasonable possibilities combined with some of the other four preference orderings, a cyclical majority again becomes possible. For example, if one-third of the voters prefers *X* to *Y* and *Y* to *Z*, one-third prefers *Y* to *Z* and *Z* to *X*, and one-third prefers *Z* to *X* and *X* to *Y*, then a voting cycle occurs. Cycles can only be ruled out by carefully limiting the individual preference orderings admitted into the public-choice mechanism. Unusual preference orderings can be admitted and cycles avoided only if some more common orderings are *not* permitted.

As noted earlier, markets, and private-choice mechanisms generally, avoid the paradox because they violate condition 1. Most people share a common preference concerning private goods: more is better than less. Hence, "unreasonable" patterns are extraordinarily rare. If you are like me, then $1000 is better than $100 and $100 is better than $10. If you are unusual, then $10 is better than $100 and $100 is better than $1000. I have never met someone for whom $1000 is better than $10 and $10 is better than $100, or for whom $10 is better than $1000 and $1000 is better than $100. In principle, private-choice procedures do not avoid the Arrow problem, as the theorem is general. However, in practice, private-choice procedures do not share the preference patterns that make voting cycles possible. Human nature seems to preclude this occurrence.

QUESTIONS FOR DISCUSSION AND REVIEW

1. Why is it difficult to find the correct quantity to produce and price to charge for a public good? Would these problems sometimes be solved by allowing several producers to compete in a market for public goods? Does a positive answer to this question explain federalism as well as the presence of many local governments in a metropolitan area? Or is such an arrangement merely accidental? Are there limits to the ability of competing jurisdictions to solve the price and supply problems of public goods (and bads)? If so, what determines these limits?
2. What considerations would be important in deciding whether to nationalize the petroleum industry in the United States? In deciding whether to make the U.S. Postal Service private? In deciding whether to institute national health insurance?
3. Do real political decisions to take collective action reflect any of the theoretical considerations offered in this chapter? Which ones? Can you provide some examples of political decisions that bear no relationship to the considerations offered here?
4. Is love a collective good? Should its supply be regulated by government? Why? Why not?
5. Could the five conditions of Arrow's theorem be written in a constitution? Would it be desirable to do so? What would be the terms of each condition in everyday language? Does the present Constitution of the United States contain any of these conditions? Which ones? Do any of these conditions require Pareto optimality?
6. As political decisions about public-sector activities become more complex, is it more or less likely that a particular decision will be incoherent (have no pure equilibrium)? Why? Why not?
7. Of the various games described in Chapter 2, in which would players do "better" using private choice; in which, public choice? Explain each answer. Are answers to this question unambiguous?

NEW CONCEPTS AND TERMS

Arrow's paradox	citizens' sovereignty
Borda count	collective (public) good

cyclical majority
external cost
external economy
externality
free-rider problem
good
ideology
independence from irrelevant alternatives
jointness of consumption
jointness of supply
monopoly
negative externality
non-dictatorship
non-perversity (positive association of individual and social values)
positive externality
private good
property rights
public bads
resource redistribution
universal admissibility of individual orderings

Part II

Elections

We now turn to elections in the United States. Elections, which are the fundamental process Americans use to make collective decisions, take the individual preferences and decisions of citizens, voters, activists, and candidates, and aggregate these preferences and decisions into a collective choice. The actual choice selected, be it the election of a particular candidate or the adoption of a particular public policy, is very much the product of the rules under which an election is conducted.

Chapter 4 describes and interprets the rules of different American elections and emphasizes the effects that these rules have on election outcomes. We find that majority rule is a special case of election rules (collective action decision rules) that might require different numbers of citizens to consent before a collective decision is made. Next, the chapter examines the characteristics of different election systems and distinguishes between direct and indirect elections and between elections in proportional representation and single-member district systems. We then consider the problems of apportionment and the gerrymander. Chapter 4 also describes the rules of American national elections, those controlling elections to the House of Representatives and to the Senate as well as to the presidency and vice-presidency. We partially interpret these rules as resulting from bargains among the participants at the Constitutional Convention. Chapter 4 then looks at nomination procedures and specially those used to nominate presidential candidates. Finally, we consider the importance of election and nomination rules in the workings of a representative democracy. Particular election rules are themselves the result of rational decision making, and therefore people choose these rules to serve their self-interest. Hence, as much conflict can arise over the selection of election rules as over the outcomes of the elections those rules are to govern.

Chapter 5 considers the decisions of the first and fundamental participant in elections, the citizen. We begin by building a theoretical view of how citizens evaluate public policy. Using this evaluation, citizens then form opinions about candidates, but those opinions also include considerations of issues beyond public policy, such as candidate characteristics, party identification, and group membership. Chapter 5 then shows how to represent the preferences of an entire electorate. Finally, the chapter presents a theory that explains and predicts whether citizens will vote or abstain.

Chapter 6 considers activists, those who do more than vote in elections but less than run for office. Of course, the consideration of activists' decisions extends beyond their participation in elections, for they also lobby and take part in judicial and bureaucratic processes to satisfy their public policy demands. We first examine group action and develop a theoretical view of problems of forming and maintaining active and successful political organizations. Then, we analyze the public policy demands of interest groups, showing that these demands very often generate the major problem of public action to satisfy interest group members' private interests. Chapter 6 next considers activist organizations according to whether they are interest groups or political parties and whether their members are amateurs or professionals. Then, we explore party and interest group activity in primary and general elections, with special emphasis on "political money." Chapter 6 concludes by considering the "iron law of oligarchy," which some believe undermines the democratic nature of governments in large republics.

Chapter 7 stands at the heart of Part II, for it explains and predicts how election candidates respond to the public policy demands that citizens and activists press upon them. We first explore candidates' election strategies and then examine their election goals. Next, we develop a theoretical view of candidates' decision making in response to pure public policy demands. We show how elections as a method of collective choice can be incoherent, as well as how they resolve or fail to resolve the problem of intense minorities. Chapter 7 then ties candidates' decision making very closely to public policy questions in both simple elections (without activists) and complex elections (with activists). The chapter concludes by considering the effects that demands for private benefits might have on the electoral process in the United States.

Chapter 8 provides a bridge between the electoral process described in Chapters 4 through 7 and the institutions of government described in Chapters 9 through 12. Our goal in Chapter 8 is to see how electoral considerations affect lawmakers' actions in the institutions of government. First, we show that the way in which election district lines are drawn clearly affects the public policy adopted in a representative body such as the House of Representatives or the Senate. But the matter does not end there, for lawmakers not only draw their own district boundaries but also control the franchise, the right to vote. We can expect legislators to make decisions affecting these two sets of activities in their self-interest. Chapter 8 then examines the preferences elected officials hold concerning future elections, public policy, the institutions in which they serve, and other personal matters. We then show that the rules and procedures used in a legislature can affect the public policy that legislators eventually choose. Hence, two legislatures drawn from identical constituencies might adopt different public policies because different procedural rules are used in each legislature. Finally, we explore some normative questions about representation, such as how representatives *should* act depending upon whom they seek to represent and how.

4

Elections in the United States

Elections are the fundamental collective-choice procedure used in the United States. Americans elect members of the House of Representatives, senators, presidents, and governors and other state and local officials, who then try to shape public policy. This chapter examines the rules and procedures of popular elections in the United States—those involving citizens voting for various referenda or for candidates for public office.

ELECTIONS AS COLLECTIVE-CHOICE MECHANISMS

Chapter 3 describes the conditions under which someone might prefer private or collective action. To convert a preference for collective action into public policy requires a mechanism for choosing the legislators of collective action, who then make subsequent public choices.[1] In the United States, this mechanism is usually a popular election. The choice of an election, rather than a procedure such as a dictatorship or a hereditary monarchy, to select the legislators of collective action, is itself a decision, and therefore the theory of human choice should help to explain and predict its outcome.

Different elections also use different collective action **decision rules.**

[1] Such a mechanism would also be required to convert a preference for private action into public policy if the action in question was presently collective.

These rules concern who can vote, how many votes each person can cast, how votes are counted, the form of the ballot, and whether or not balloting is done in secret, as well as several other matters. To show how such rules might be chosen, we consider by way of example one very important collective action decision rule, which concerns the number or percentage of votes needed to win an election. The common practice, or decision rule, in the United States is to use majority rule. But why not require a two-thirds rule, or a three-fourths rule? Here we explore the logical origins of this collective action decision rule to show that we can interpret the selection of one rule rather than another as the product of rational decisions. This exploration, which is really a case study about one particular kind of electoral decision rule, demonstrates that such rules (and probably most others concerning elections) affect the kind of public policy eventually adopted and thus help to determine the eventual distribution of public and private costs and benefits. Because rules affect outcomes, people can and do invest considerable resources to manipulate the choice of electoral decision rules to their advantage.

External costs and collective action decision rules. Suppose n persons make up an electorate, and, to simplify matters, assume they all vote in each election. If the collective action decision rule requires all n persons to agree to an action or choice, then the rule is called *unanimous consent.* If the rule requires at least $(n/2) + 1$ persons (if n is an even number) or $(n + 1)/2$ persons (if n is an odd number) to agree, then the rule is called *majority rule.* If the rule requires at least two persons to agree, provided no one else is affected by their decision, then the rule is usually called a market agreement.

A rational choice theory has been developed that explains and predicts preferences for different collective action decision rules.[2] The theory begins by observing that all public choices impose costs on someone. Then, it asks a simple question: What is the relationship between the **external costs** (externalities) a person might experience as a result of the decisions to be made, on the one hand, and the collective action decision rule used to make each decision, on the other hand? If the decision rule calls for unanimous consent—all n persons—then people will individually reject any public policy that imposes an external cost (an externality) on them, unless they are fully compensated for bearing it. So, with unanimous consent, the *net* cost any person experiences from collective action must be no less than zero. But if the decision rule requires only one person to take an action or make a decision, then the external cost can be enormous. Generally, the more votes the decision rule requires for an action or public policy to be approved, the lower are the external costs that the action or policy can impose on any given person. That is because if a greater number of people are required by law to be members of a winning coalition—a coalition large enough to make a

[2] James M. Buchanan and Gordon Tullock, *The Calculus of Consent: Logical Foundations of Constitutional Democracy* (Ann Arbor: University of Michigan Press, 1962). This section greatly depends on their work.

decision—the probability that any one person must be a member of that coalition (must have his or her consent secured by the coalition's leaders) is increased. Figure 4.1 shows a hypothetical representative relationship between the decision rule and external costs. Notice that the external cost *falls* as the number of people whose consent is required to take an action—adopt a public policy—increases from one to *n*.

Decision costs and the collective action decision rule. The theory next inquires about the relationship between the decision rule and the **decision costs** associated with making a public choice. A decision cost includes the (perhaps compensating) payments one person must make to others to get them to agree to a desired action or policy. For voters and legislators, such payments usually take the form of policy concessions, political support, and sometimes cash. If the decision rule calls for unanimous consent, then decision costs can be very great, since everyone's vote must be secured. However, if the rule requires only one or a few persons to consent to the collective choice, then decision costs might be very low. Generally, the more votes the rule requires for the approval of an action or public policy, the higher is the decision cost that the action or policy can impose on someone who must pay to get others to consent to it, to vote with him. Figure 4.2 shows a representative relationship between the decision rule and the decision cost. Notice that the decision cost *rises* as the number of people whose consent is required to take an action—make a collective choice—increases from one to *n*.

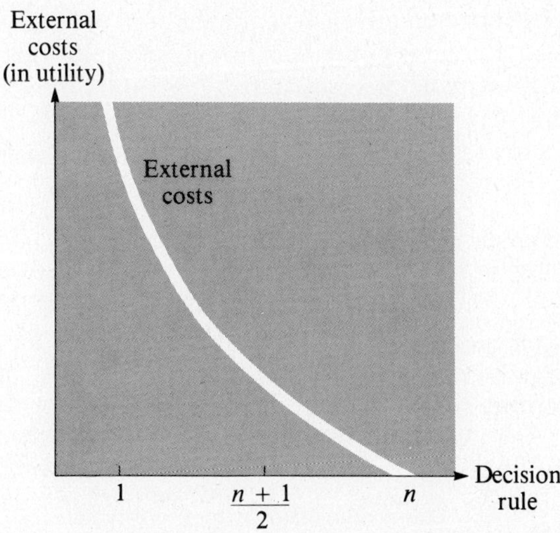

Figure 4.1 The relationship between the decision rule and external costs.
Source: Adapted from James M. Buchanan and Gordon Tullock, *The Calculus of Consent* (Ann Arbor: University of Michigan Press, 1962), p. 65.

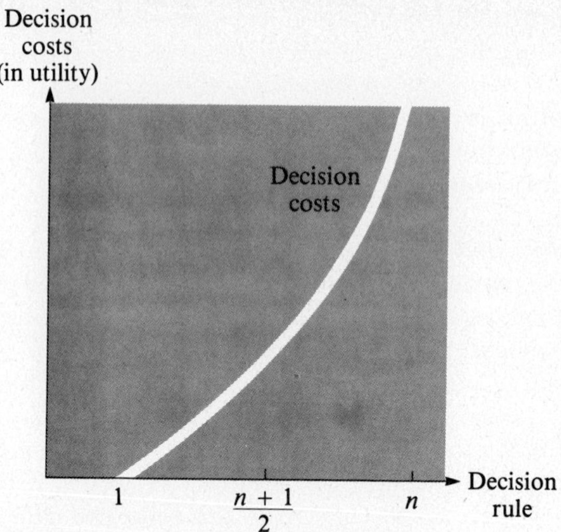

Figure 4.2 The relationship between the decision rule and decision costs.
Source: Adapted from James M. Buchanan and Gordon Tullock, *The Calculus of Consent* (Ann Arbor: University of Michigan Press, 1962), p. 70.

Minimum cost decision rules. Figures 4.1 and 4.2 illustrate one person's external cost and decision cost associated with a particular decision. These figures show both costs as functions of the decision rule. The decision rule actually preferred will minimize the sum of decision costs and external costs. Figure 4.3 shows a representative curve for the sum of the two costs depicted in Figures 4.1 and 4.2. This curve is constructed arbitrarily, so that a minimum occurs at majority rule. Because in this case minimum total costs occur at majority rule, this decision rule would be preferred.[3]

Figure 4.4 shows how perceived differences in external costs can affect

[3] Once an election is decided upon as a public-choice mechanism, it seems reasonable to require at least a majority to win. Otherwise, two or more minority coalitions, neither of which is decisive, can claim victory. But majority rule can also be shown to be preferred on grounds of maximizing expected utility. Suppose you are writing a constitution in complete ignorance of what issues will be decided by the public-choice procedures the constitution's terms will require. Should a majority rule, or should a minority rule? Let P be the probability that you are in the majority on any given vote and $1 - P$ be the probability that you are in the minority. U_A is your utility from being on the winning side and U_B from being on the losing side. Your expected utility from majority rule is $PU_A + (1 - P)U_B$. Your expected utility from minority rule becomes $PU_B + (1 - P)U_A$. You prefer majority to minority rule if $PU_A + (1 - P)U_B$ is greater than $PU_B + (1 - P)U_A$. The inequality holds if P exceeds one-half. But it is true necessarily that P exceeds one-half, for without further information you expect to be in the majority more than one-half of the time. For a similar analysis, see Douglas W. Rae, "Decision-Rules and Individual Values in Constitutional Choice," *American Political Science Review,* 63 (March 1969), pp. 40–56.

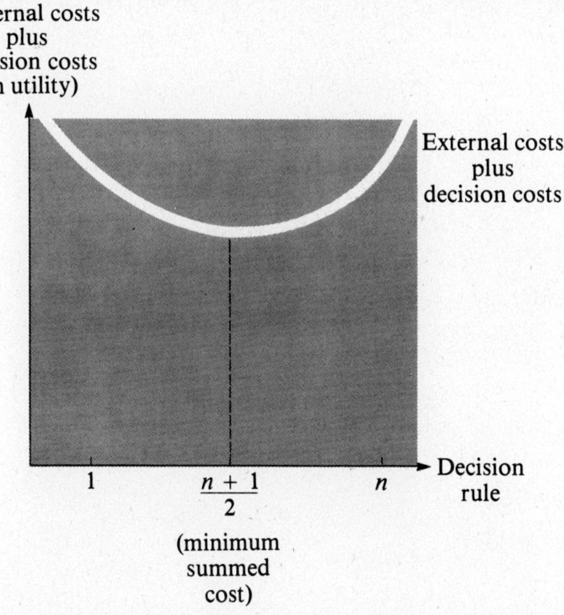

Figure 4.3 The relationship between the decision rule and the sum of external costs and decision costs.

Source: Adapted from James M. Buchanan and Gordon Tullock, *The Calculus of Consent* (Ann Arbor: University of Michigan Press, 1962), p. 71.

preferences for decision rules. The curves in Figure 4.4 are constructed so that the points of minimum summed costs fall where the external cost curves and the common decision cost curve intersect. Differences in perceived external costs, as represented in the figure, explain why people adopt or prefer to adopt different collective action decision rules. For example, suppose several different actions all have the same decision cost curve. In Figure 4.4, this is the curve running upward from left to right and labeled "decision cost." But in this figure we have allowed external costs to vary, depending upon the kind of decision under consideration.

For example, EC_4 might represent the external cost curve associated with convicting someone of a capital offense. The external cost is extremely high, but minimized at n. Even though the decision cost is also high, reflecting the problems of achieving unanimity, the law requires the unanimous consent of a twelve-person jury. EC_3 might depict the external cost curve associated with establishing a state religion or with making other fundamental constitutional changes. Such actions would require the approval of two-thirds of a quorum in each house of the Congress and a majority vote in three-fourths of the state legislatures or state conventions called by Congress to vote on ratification. (Figure 4.4 shows only the two-thirds rule.) EC_2 might represent the external cost curve associated with electing a particular member of the House of

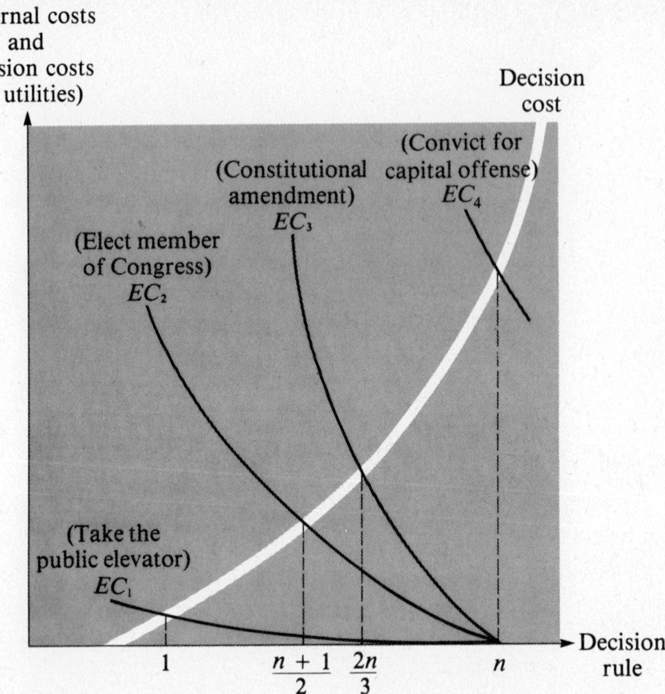

Figure 4.4 External cost variations for several collective actions.

Representatives; the collective action decision rule requires the approval of a majority of those voting in the congressional district. Finally, EC_1 might be the external cost curve associated with letting individual citizens spend public funds for electricity by allowing them to decide to ride a public elevator to the top floor of city hall. Since external costs are very low, majority rule would not be required. In pure private choice, with no externalities—no external costs—this theory would predict that the number of people required to consent to an action will be limited to the parties to the exchange. They are the only ones affected by it. Of course, as external costs grow (for example, from air pollution), the consent of more and more people will be preferred to sanction or limit the activity creating the costs.

This representation of external costs and decision costs explains how someone might evaluate existing and proposed provisions for collective action decision rules, whether those rules are part of a constitution or merely bylaws of some organization. Naturally, people differ in how they evaluate external costs and decision costs. Because an alteration in a decision rule shifts these costs, such a change itself is a collective good whose externality depends upon personal evaluation. That is why some people favor certain public-choice decision rule changes, sometimes called reforms, while others oppose them.

CHARACTERISTICS OF ELECTIONS

Elections as collective-choice mechanisms vary considerably in the rules and conditions under which they are conducted. The preceding discussion analyzes by way of example one very important variation, the number or percentage of people required to consent to a collective action. Here we describe other rules and general characteristics of elections and summarize their effects.

Elements of Elections

An **election** minimally consists of at least one voter who casts a vote for one of at least two motions, and a rule that aggregates the vote(s) into a collective choice. Now, let us take this definition apart.

Voters. The **voter** is the fundamental person in an election. Indeed, the voter might be the only person. It is useful to distinguish here among residents, citizens, and voters. A nation generally consists of many people, a population, the members of which are residents. Most Americans are residents of the United States, of a particular state, a county, and a city or town. They may also be residents of special districts, such as a school district, a water district, or a sewer district. Among the residents is a set of persons who meet all of the formal requirements to participate in elections—to vote. Today, these residents must be at least eighteen years old, they may have been required to register with some kind of election board (some states allow postcard or election-day registration), and they must not be disqualified because of insanity, a criminal record, or other reasons. Here we shall call these peoples **citizens.**[4] A voter is a citizen who votes. These distinctions among residents, citizens, and voters are not legal or part of common usage; they are a convenient, specialized shorthand used in this book and in most rational-choice studies of elections.

The vote. The vote is the citizen's fundamental political resource. Like the consumer in private choice, the citizen in collective choice must decide to use this resource or not to use it. But consumers ordinarily buy private goods with their dollars, while citizens attempt to buy public policy, which may involve both public and private goods, with their votes. Consumers can also use their unspent dollars elsewhere, while citizens cannot accumulate votes from election to election. Consumers must earn dollars from other consumers, but citizens presumably do not earn votes in any meaningful sense.

---

[4] In legal terms, citizens are usually native-born or naturalized through the legal process. In our specialized usage, they must be citizens at least in the legal sense, and usually they meet the additional requirements for registering to vote.

SAMPLE FORM

DO NOT WRITE ABOVE THIS LINE - NO ESCRIBA SOBRE ESTA LINEA | PRECINCT NO. | REGISTRATION NO

LAST NAME - APELLIDO	FIRST - NOMBRE	MIDDLE - SEGUNDO	PARTY - PARTIDO	SEX - SEXO	RACE - RAZA

RESIDENT ADDRESS - DIRECCION RESIDENCIAL	APT. - APTO.	CITY - CIUDAD	ZIP - ZONA POSTAL	MUN. CODE

MAILING ADDRESS - DIRECCION POSTAL	CITY - CIUDAD	ZIP - ZONA POSTAL	HOME TEL./TEL. CASA	OFFICE TEL./TEL. OFICINA

DATE OF BIRTH FECHA DE NACIMIENTO	PLACE OF BIRTH LUGAR DE NACIMIENTO	IF FOREIGN BORN, ARE YOU A NATURALIZED U.S. CITIZEN? YES ☐ NO ☐ IF NO, EXPLAIN BELOW. SI NACIO EN EL EXTRANJERO, ¿ES CIUDADANO NATURALIZADO DE EE. UU.? SI ☐ NO ☐ ¡SI NO EXPLIQUE!

SOCIAL SECURITY NO. (OPTIONAL) SEGURO SOCIAL NO. (OPCIONAL)	REGISTRATION DATE FECHA DE INSCRIPCION	FELONY CONVICTION? / ¿DELITO GRAVE?	REQUIRES ASSISTANCE / NECESITA AYUDA
		IF YES, ATTACH AFFIDAVIT	PHYSICALLY DISABLED INCAPACITADO ☐ BLIND CIEGO ☐ ILLITERATE ANALFABETA ☐

Oath: I do solemnly swear (or affirm) that I will protect and defend the Constitution of the United States and the Constitution of the State of Florida, and that I am qualified to register as an elector under the Constitution and laws of the State of Florida.
That I have ☐ never previously registered to vote in any other jurisdiction ☐ been registered under the name of ______________ at ______________ and request that my prior registration be cancelled, and that all of the information on this form is true.

Juramento: Juro (o afirmo) solemnemente que protegeré y defenderé la Constitución de Estados Unidos y la Constitución del Estado de la Florida, y que estoy habilitado para inscribirme como elector según la Constitución y las leyes del Estado de la Florida.
Que nunca ☐ he estado inscripto anteriormente para votar en otra jurisdicción ☐ que he estado inscripto con el nombre de ______________ en ______________ y, solicito que sea cancelada mi inscripción previa, y que toda la información en este formulario es verdadera.

DEPUTY SUPERVISOR OF ELECTIONS / SUPERVISOR ADJUNTO DE ELECCIONES

METROPOLITAN DADE COUNTY, FLORIDA

THIS REGISTRATION IS MADE IN ACCORDANCE WITH THE LAWS OF THE STATE OF FLORIDA
ESTA INSCRIPCION SE LLEVA A EFECTO DE CONFORMIDAD CON LAS LEYES DEL ESTADO DE LA FLORIDA

SIGNATURE OF VOTER / FIRMA DEL ELECTOR

LETTER OF PARTY
AFILIACION DE PARTIDO

This voter registration form is typical of those used in most jurisdictions. It requires the resident to supply information about matters affecting his or her legal qualification to vote. The form simultaneously registers the citizen in a political party, if desired.

Elections differ according to the number of votes each citizen has, the possibility of negative and "no preference" votes, the possibility of splitting one's votes among several motions or candidates, and the presence or absence of laws and other inducements that encourage or require citizens to vote or encourage them to abstain. In most elections each citizen has one and only one vote to cast in each election contest each time an election occurs. Votes are not transferable; they cannot be explicitly bought and sold.[5] Nor can the citizen abstain in a congressional election contest and use the forgone vote in a senatorial election contest, or give or sell the vote to someone else to cast.

Motions. The **motion** is the object of the citizen's vote, the thing for or against which he or she might vote. Some elections in the United States give citizens the option of voting for or against a particular public policy in a popular referendum. These elections concern such matters as state constitutional amendments and increases in the bonded indebtedness of state and local governments. However, most popular American elections have two motions, called candidates. For example, in the 1980 presidential election, the two motions were (1) Jimmy Carter should be president and Walter F. Mondale should be vice-president, and (2) Ronald W. Reagan should be president and George Bush should be vice-president. (This listing ignores minority-party candidates and the presence and effects of the electoral college, which are discussed later in this chapter.) Most people think the motions, or candidates, in presidential elections mean more than simply who should take office. However, these other considerations only enter into the citizen's evaluation of each motion, which then affects his or her voting decision. Therefore, such considerations remain apart from the formal motions in and of themselves.

Election rules. The election decision rule (for example, majority rule) takes the votes that have been cast, and aggregates or combines them to declare the winning motion, if there is one. Most American elections use some variant of plurality rule: the motion (usually candidate) with more votes than any other wins the election. For instance, suppose two candidates are running for a United States Senate seat from a given state. Let V_r be the number of votes for the Republican candidate and V_d the number for the Democrat. The Republican's plurality, Pl_r, is defined as $Pl_r = V_r - V_d$. If Pl_r is greater than zero, then the Republican wins; if Pl_r equals zero, then the election is a tie; and if Pl_r is less than zero, then the Democrat wins. Notice that $Pl_r = -Pl_d$, and $Pl_r + Pl_d = 0$. Therefore, if candidates try to maximize their plurality security

[5] For hypothetical elections with markets in which votes may be bought and sold, see Anthony Downs, *An Economic Theory of Democracy* (New York: Harper and Row, 1957), pp. 188–194. See also Buchanan and Tullock, *The Calculus of Consent,* pp. 272–276. Neither Downs nor Buchanan and Tullock fully examine the interesting features of a market in votes. For a discussion of real markets in votes, which occur in attempts to change the control of corporations, see Henry G. Manne, "Some Theoretical Aspects of Share Voting," *Columbia Law Review,* 64 (1964), pp. 1425–1443.

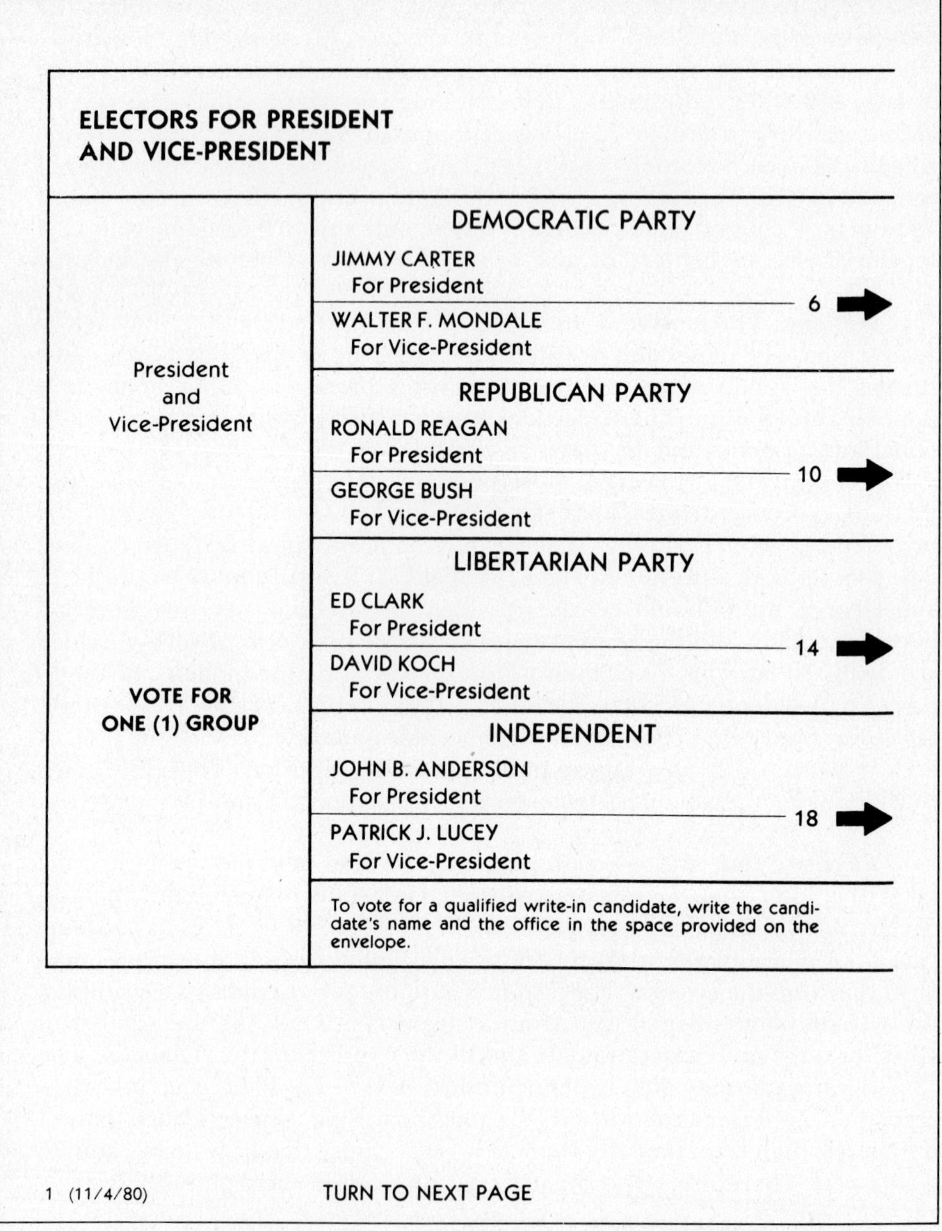

ELECTORS FOR PRESIDENT AND VICE-PRESIDENT

President and Vice-President	
	DEMOCRATIC PARTY JIMMY CARTER For President WALTER F. MONDALE For Vice-President — 6 ➡
	REPUBLICAN PARTY RONALD REAGAN For President GEORGE BUSH For Vice-President — 10 ➡
VOTE FOR ONE (1) GROUP	**LIBERTARIAN PARTY** ED CLARK For President DAVID KOCH For Vice-President — 14 ➡
	INDEPENDENT JOHN B. ANDERSON For President PATRICK J. LUCEY For Vice-President — 18 ➡
	To vote for a qualified write-in candidate, write the candidate's name and the office in the space provided on the envelope.

1 (11/4/80) TURN TO NEXT PAGE

This ballot form was used in the 1980 presidential election. It includes a listing of all candidates who qualified for a place on the Florida ballot, which resembles those used in many other jurisdictions. The ballot is employed along with a computer card on which the voter punches out chips to register a vote.

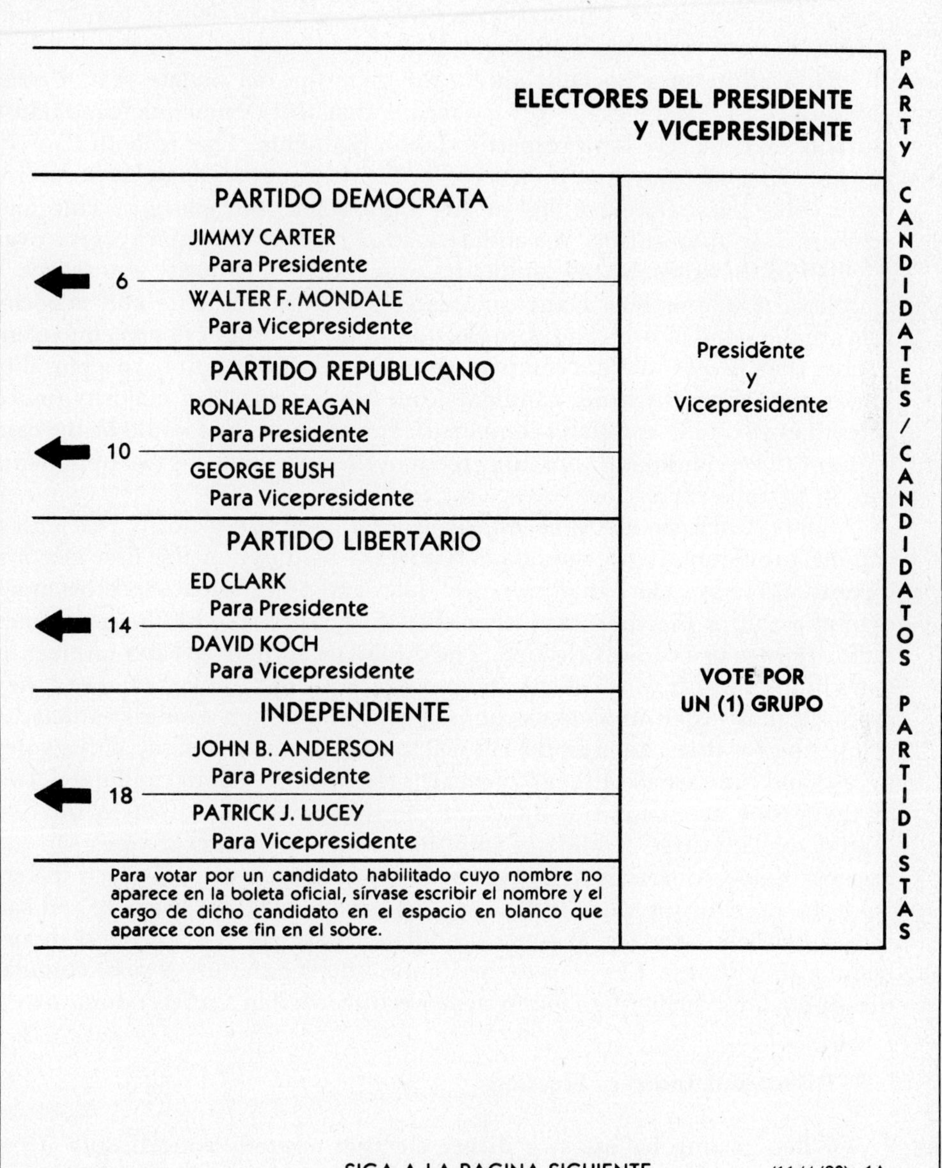

ELECTORES DEL PRESIDENTE
Y VICEPRESIDENTE

PARTY CANDIDATES / CANDIDATOS PARTIDISTAS

6	PARTIDO DEMOCRATA JIMMY CARTER Para Presidente WALTER F. MONDALE Para Vicepresidente	Presidente y Vicepresidente
10	PARTIDO REPUBLICANO RONALD REAGAN Para Presidente GEORGE BUSH Para Vicepresidente	
14	PARTIDO LIBERTARIO ED CLARK Para Presidente DAVID KOCH Para Vicepresidente	VOTE POR UN (1) GRUPO
18	INDEPENDIENTE JOHN B. ANDERSON Para Presidente PATRICK J. LUCEY Para Vicepresidente	

Para votar por un candidato habilitado cuyo nombre no aparece en la boleta oficial, sírvase escribir el nombre y el cargo de dicho candidato en el espacio en blanco que aparece con ese fin en el sobre.

SIGA A LA PAGINA SIGUIENTE (11/4/80) 1A

levels, a two-candidate, plurality-rule election becomes equivalent to a two-person zero-sum game. Chapter 7 uses this powerful analogy to explain and predict election candidates' strategic decisions.

Now suppose a Socialist enters the race for the Senate seat. Under plurality rule, a Democratic victory means that the Democratic candidate's plurality exceeds zero with respect to both opponents. That is, both $V_d - V_r$ and $V_d - V_s$ must be greater than zero: the Democratic candidate must receive more votes than either of his or her opponents. But plurality rule and majority rule may differ. A candidate who receives a majority gets over one-half of the votes. So, all candidates who receive a majority also receive a plurality, no matter how many candidates there are. Plurality and majority rule are the same in two-candidate elections; but they might not be equivalent if more than two candidates compete, since a candidate might have a plurality (more votes than any other candidate) but not necessarily a majority (more votes than all other candidates combined). For example, this would be the case if one of three candidates wins 40 percent of the vote while his two opponents win 30 percent each.

Some American elections, especially local ones, use majority rule with a run-off provision. If no candidate receives a majority in the first election (because there are more than two candidates and no candidate receives more than one-half of the votes cast), then the two candidates with the most votes must compete in a run-off election. The candidate with the greater number of votes in the run-off wins. There are many variants of plurality rule, and they are used most often in local elections. For example, ten candidates may be competing for three at-large city council seats. The voter has, say, three votes to cast, and can cast all of them (one each) for three different candidates, two of them (one each) for two different candidates, or one of them for one candidate. The three candidates with the greatest numbers of votes win the election. Some American corporations use **cumulative voting,** which differs from the previous example in that citizens have more than one vote and can use all of their votes for just one candidate or spread them around in any manner they choose. Elections to the Illinois state legislature were by cumulative voting until 1980, when that system was discarded in a referendum vote.[6]

Direct and Indirect Elections

When casting ballots in a **direct election,** citizens vote directly for a public policy motion. As just noted, direct elections in the United States are used to make collective decisions about local bond issues, state constitutional amendments, and various referenda. These elections have taken on added importance since a popular vote in California on Proposition 13 amended that

[6] Jack Sawyer and Duncan MacRae, Jr., "Game Theory and Cumulative Voting in Illinois: 1902–1954," *American Political Science Review,* 56 (December 1962), pp. 936–946.

state's constitution to limit certain state and local taxes. Before the vote, many people thought such a direct involvement in public policy to be unproductive. However, since the passage of Proposition 13, referendum elections have been held in several states concerning such problems as placing tax and spending limitations on state governments, homosexual rights, proposed bans on smoking in public places, official bilingualism, and the prohibition of nuclear power plants.

Chapter 13 examines recent trends toward a greater reliance on direct elections. Generally, a state or nation whose citizens most often use direct elections to decide matters of public policy is called a **direct democracy,** a pure democracy, or sometimes just a democracy.

When casting ballots in an **indirect election,** citizens do not vote directly for a public policy motion but for a candidate whom they would prefer to have as an officeholder to make subsequent public policy decisions for them. Hence, when they vote for a candidate to be president, senator, representative, governor, state senator or representative, judge, mayor, city councilor, board of education member, dogcatcher, health inspector, or university regent, Americans are participating in indirect elections. Generally, a state or nation whose citizens most often use indirect elections is called an **indirect democracy,** a representative democracy, or sometimes a republic.

There are substantial differences between direct and indirect elections. In direct democracies, the citizen is able to know exactly for which public policy he is voting, but he may have to vote on many issues if reliance on direct elections is extensive. In representative democracies, elected officials might not hold to campaign promises or may only make ambiguous commitments, thus generating considerable risk and uncertainty for the citizen. But the division of labor between citizens and representatives can add greatly to the time citizens have available for things other than becoming informed and voting on many public policy issues. On the other hand, citizens might be dissatisfied with their legislators' decisions and also believe that electing different representatives would not change public policy substantially. Citizens might then try direct democracy to enact particular public policies or to limit their elected representatives' discretion. Deciding whether to make public policy decisions by direct or representative democracy thus involves a tradeoff between on the one hand uncertainty and the external costs of public policy actions taken by elected representatives and on the other hand the decision costs associated with frequent popular elections to make public policy decisions directly.

Proportional Representation and Single-Member Districts

The two major systems for choosing legislators in representative democracies are the **proportional representation** (PR) **system** and the **single-member district** (SMD) **system.** The use of one system or the other leads to important

DADE COUNTY
QUESTION NO. 2

Shall the following proposal be adopted as a County Ordinance?

"Ordinance prohibiting the expenditure of County funds for the purpose of utilizing any language other than English, or promoting any culture other than that of the United States; providing for governmental meetings and publications to be in the English language; providing exception; providing severability, inclusion in the Code, and an effective date.

Be it Ordained by the People of Dade County, Florida:

Section 1. The expenditure of County funds for the purpose of utilizing any language other than English, or promoting any culture other than that of the United States, is prohibited.
Section 2. All County governmental meetings, hearings and publications shall be in the English language only.
Section 3. The provisions of this ordinance shall not apply where a translation is mandated by state or federal law.
Section 4. If any section, subsection, sentence, clause, phrase, words or provision of this ordinance is held invalid or unconstitutional, the remainder of this ordinance shall not be affected by said holding.
Section 5. It is the intention of the people of Dade County, Florida, that the provisions of this ordinance shall become and be made a part of the Code of Metropolitan Dade County, Florida.
Section 6. This ordinance shall take effect on the day after the election approving this ordinance."

FOR THE ORDINANCE	285 ➡
AGAINST THE ORDINANCE	286 ➡

11 (11/4/80) TURN TO NEXT PAGE

The laws of certain states, countries, and municipalities allow citizens to propose and vote directly on public policy motions. This proposed ordinance was one such motion voted on and passed by Dade County, Florida, citizens in the 1980 election. The ordinance overturned official bilingualism in the county, a public policy that had earlier been adopted by the county commissioners. The bilingual ballot form is ironic considering the motion's intent.

CONDADO DE DADE
PROPUESTA NUM. 2

¿Deberá adoptarse como ordenanza del Condado la propuesta siguiente?

"Ordenanza mediante la cual se prohíbe gastar fondos del Condado con el fin de utilizar un idioma que no sea el inglés o de promover una cultura que no sea la de los Estados Unidos; se estipula que las reuniones y las publicaciones gubernamentales deben llevarse a cabo y redactarse, respectivamente, en el idioma inglés; se estipulan las salvedades y la divisibilidad de derechos y obligaciones, la inclusión en el Código de estipulaciones legales así como la fecha en que entrará en vigor.

La población del condado de Dade, en el estado de la Florida, ordena que:

Apartado 1. Se prohíba gastar fondos del Condado con el fin de utilizar un idioma que no sea el inglés o de promover una cultura que no sea la de los Estados Unidos.
Apartado 2. Todas las reuniones, audiencias y publicaciones se lleven a cabo y redacten, respectivamente, en el idioma inglés, únicamente.
Apartado 3. Las estipulaciones de esta ordenanza no se apliquen en los casos en que las leyes estatales o federales ordenen que se realicen traducciones.
Apartado 4. Si se determinara que alguno de los apartados, subapartados, oraciones, cláusulas, frases, palabras o estipulaciones no fuera válido o fuera inconstitucional, el resto de esta ordenanza no sería afectado por dicho dictamen.
Apartado 5. Las estipulaciones de esta ordenanza se hagan y formen parte del Código de estipulaciones legales del Condado Metropolitano de Dade, en el estado de la Florida, por ser ésa la intención de la población de este condado.
Apartado 6. Esta ordenanza entre en vigor al día siguiente de celebrarse la elección en la que se apruebe la ordenanza."

COUNTY QUESTION / PROPUESTA DEL CONDADO

←	285	A FAVOR DE LA ORDENANZA
←	286	EN CONTRA DE LA ORDENANZA

SIGA A LA PAGINA SIGUIENTE (11/4/80) 11A

differences in election outcomes, although the effects on public policy remain unclear.

PR systems. One relatively simple PR system is used in Israel, where the Knesset, analogous to the American Congress, has 120 seats to which members are elected. In Knesset elections, each party nominates a slate of 120 names. A voter casts one vote for a slate rather than for an individual candidate. There are no districts, since all elections are nationwide.

Suppose that in a given election, three parties—A, B, and C—compete and receive votes of V_a, V_b, and V_c respectively. Let $V_a + V_b + V_c$ equal V_t. Party A's vote proportion, then, is V_a/V_t. Similarly, B's vote proportion is V_b/V_t, while C's is V_c/V_t. Party A receives a proportion of seats in the Knesset approximately equal to the vote proportion it receives in the election. Thus, for the 120-seat Knesset, S_a, party A's seat allotment is $S_a = 120V_a/V_t$. Of course, S_b and S_c are respectively $S_b = 120V_b/V_t$, and $S_c = 120V_c/V_t$.

An example should be helpful. Suppose that each party's votes are as follows: $V_a = 1000$, $V_b = 1500$, and $V_c = 2500$. The total, V_t, equals 5000 votes. Party A's vote proportion is

$$\frac{1000}{1000 + 1500 + 2500} = \frac{1000}{5000} = 0.20.$$

This proportion, 0.20, is then multiplied by 120, the number of seats in the Knesset, so $S_a = (0.20)(120) = 24$. Thus, party A receives twenty-four seats. The Israeli procedure allows the first twenty-four persons listed on the party slate to take seats in the Knesset. Party B receives thirty-six seats, and C, sixty seats.[7]

PR gives each party a legislative seat proportion roughly equal to its vote proportion. Figure 4.5 plots this relationship. PR elections differ substantially from SMD elections, which, as we shall see, tend to underrepresent minor parties and overrepresent major ones. In PR elections, a party needs only a small fraction of the votes to get a seat or two in the legislature. And, a few seats can matter. For example, suppose that parties A and B win fifty seats each while C wins one seat in a 101-seat legislature. In most PR systems, the legislators choose a government, including a prime minister and other cabinet ministers, by voting among themselves.[8] Generally, legislative voting for a government follows party lines, and any government must receive the support of over one-half of the legislators. So in this example, a government requires

[7] There are two minor variations on the pure PR scheme in Israel. First, any party receiving less than one percent of the vote receives no seats in the Knesset. Second, to make up whole seats, fractions of seats go to the larger parties at the expense of smaller parties.

[8] Americans think of a government as an institution. To Europeans, as well as to people in most other representative democracies, a government is the set of persons who have control of the institutions of the state at any particular moment. For instance,

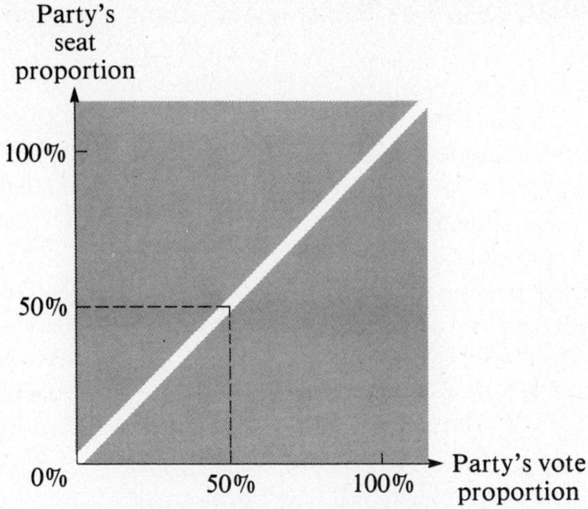

Figure 4.5 The relationship between proportion of votes and proportion of seats won in proportional representation system elections.

at least fifty-one votes of the 101-seat legislature. However, no party has fifty-one votes, and therefore a coalition government must form.

Coalition formation in this example is a three-person game. Recall from Chapter 2's discussion of *n*-person games that if payoffs are zero-sum-like or constant-sum-like, as they often are in such situations, then minimum winning coalitions tend to form. This tendency places party C in a distinctly advantageous position, even though it has only one legislative vote (seat). Party C can more easily form a minimum winning coalition with either A or B because a coalition of those two parties would be greatly overweighted and therefore unstable. Hence, the simplicity of winning only a few seats and the possible importance of such seats in forming governing coalitions give many parties an incentive to compete in PR elections. The resulting fractionalization of parties often means that no party will have enough seats to govern alone. This lack of a majority party in turn reinforces the importance of minor parties. Compared to those in SMD systems, politicians in PR systems enjoy a relatively smaller incentive to belong to a major party instead of a minor one, and therefore minor parties are easier to form.

SMD systems. With SMD systems, a nation or state is divided into a number of election districts. (Nations using PR can also be districted, with party slates running in each district.) Each district's voters usually elect one and only one representative; the collective action decision rule is either plu-

---

if "the government falls" in Great Britain, this means that the prime minister and his or her cabinet have resigned, perhaps because of a parliamentary vote of no confidence. The Queen then calls for new elections to choose a new Parliament, whose members try to choose a new prime minister and cabinet members—a new government.

rality or majority with run-off. The system's name describes it aptly: each district sends a single member to the legislature.

A simple example shows how SMD systems work. Suppose a nation with five election districts has three citizens in each district, all of whom vote. Each district's citizens choose one representative to the legislature by plurality rule, so a majority of at least two voters in a district is required to elect a representative. There are two candidates, a Republican (*r*) and a Democrat (*d*), in each district.

Suppose all fifteen citizens vote for their respective Democratic candidates. A small chart, as in Table 4.1, keeps track of the votes. Consider the first part of the table, labeled "15 Democrats, 0 Republicans." Boxes on the top line label the districts. Each box on the second line shows a combination of *d*'s or *r*'s to indicate how each citizen votes, and each box on the third line has a *d* or *r* to identify the winning candidate's party. For this case of fifteen Democratic voters and no Republican voters, all five Democratic candidates must win and become representatives. The Republican candidates win neither votes nor seats, which is exactly the result a PR system with the same national vote would produce.

Now suppose that fourteen citizens vote for Democratic candidates while

Table 4.1 Vote Distributions in Hypothetical SMD System

15 Democrats, 0 Republicans

	District 1	District 2	District 3	District 4	District 5
Votes	*d-d-d*	*d-d-d*	*d-d-d*	*d-d-d*	*d-d-d*
Representative	*d*	*d*	*d*	*d*	*d*

14 Democrats, 1 Republican

	District 1	District 2	District 3	District 4	District 5
Votes	*d-d-d*	*d-d-d*	*d-d-d*	*d-d-d*	*d-d-r*
Representative	*d*	*d*	*d*	*d*	*d*

13 Democrats, 2 Republicans—Dispersed

	District 1	District 2	District 3	District 4	District 5
Votes	*d-d-d*	*d-d-d*	*d-d-d*	*d-d-r*	*d-d-r*
Representative	*d*	*d*	*d*	*d*	*d*

13 Democrats, 2 Republicans—Concentrated

	District 1	District 2	District 3	District 4	District 5
Votes	*d-d-d*	*d-d-d*	*d-d-d*	*d-d-d*	*d-r-r*
Representative	*d*	*d*	*d*	*d*	*r*

one citizen votes for a Republican candidate. In the second part of Table 4.1, labeled "14 Democrats, 1 Republican," we have placed the Republican voter in district 5, but we could as easily have placed him in one of the other four districts. Even though the five Democratic candidates nationally receive 93⅓ percent of the votes, they must receive all of the seats, while the Republican candidates receive 6⅔ percent of the votes and no seats. Thus, at fourteen Democratic votes and one Republican vote, compared to a straight PR system, the majority party is overrepresented and the minority party underrepresented.[9]

Suppose that thirteen citizens vote for their respective Democratic candidates while two citizens vote for their respective Republican candidate *or* candidates. There are two possible patterns for this national vote. The first, labeled in Table 4.1 as "13 Democrats, 2 Republicans—Dispersed," places the two Republican voters in different districts. The Democratic candidates receive only 86⅔ percent of the votes nationally but win every seat, while the Republican candidates receive 13⅓ percent of the votes but win no seats. Thus, at thirteen Democratic votes and two Republican votes, compared to a straight PR system, the majority party is again overrepresented and the minority party underrepresented.

A pattern more favorable to the Republicans occurs if both Republican voters happen to be in the same district. This possibility is shown in Table 4.1 as "13 Democrats, 2 Republicans—Concentrated." The Democratic candidates again receive 86⅔ percent of the votes nationally but win only 80 percent of the seats, while the Republican candidates receive only 13⅓ percent of the votes but win 20 percent of the seats. This concentrated pattern in an SMD election, compared to straight PR, underrepresents the majority party and overrepresents the minority party.

Different vote divisions add to the number of different voter distribution patterns. Table 4.2 lists the vote division (number of Democratic votes and number of Republican votes), the maximum and minimum possible seat percentages the Democrats can win with each vote division, and the Democratic vote percentage. Figure 4.6 charts this relationship. Notice that with as little as 66⅔ percent of the vote, the majority party can win all of the seats, which is an impossible outcome in a PR election. Notice also in Figure 4.6 that if its candidates win more than 50 percent of the vote, the Democratic party's theoretical maximum seat percentage is quite a bit above the PR system line, while its theoretical minimum seat percentage falls only slightly below this line.

This example illustrates one of the most important characteristics of SMD elections: majority parties tend to win a greater proportion of legislative

---

[9] There is a technical problem with what to do with seat fractions. Six and two-thirds percent of five seats is one-third of a seat. If fractions of seats go to larger parties, as with the Israeli version of PR, then the Democrats would also receive all five seats in a PR system. Clearer divergences between vote and seat proportions arise in the next two paragraphs.

Table 4.2 Single-Member District System Outcomes for Hypothetical Fifteen-Voter, Five-District Election: Theoretical Seat Maxima and Minima

Votes		**Theoretical Democratic**		**Democratic Vote %**
Democrats	*Republicans*	*Seat maximum %*	*Seat minimum %*	
15	0	100	100	100
14	1	100	100	93⅓
13	2	100	80	86⅔
12	3	100	80	80
11	4	100	60	73⅓
10	5	100	60	66⅔
9	6	80	40	60
8	7	80	40	53⅓
7	8	60	20	46⅔
6	9	60	20	40
5	10	40	0	33⅓
4	11	40	0	26⅔
3	12	20	0	20
2	13	20	0	13⅓
1	14	0	0	6⅔
0	15	0	0	0

seats than the proportion of votes they won in the election, and minority parties tend to win a smaller proportion of legislative seats than the proportion of votes they won in the election. The reason is obvious. For instance, there are 435 districts from which American citizens elect members of the House of Representatives. If Democratic candidates in a particular congressional election received 51 percent of the vote nationally, and if they also won 51 percent of the vote in each district, then they would win all 435 seats in the House of Representatives. The only reason why Republicans could win any seats with only 49 percent of the vote is that Republican voters might be concentrated more heavily in some districts than in others.

Elections to the United States House of Representatives clearly exhibit this enhancement of the majority party's legislative strength and the deflation of the minority party's strength. Elections to the House are largely two-party contests between a Republican and a Democrat. Figure 4.7 shows the national Democratic vote and seat percentages since 1930, and plainly reflects the distortion of results in favor of the majority party. This pattern of distortion usually causes SMD systems to have two-party politics, compared to the multiparty politics of PR systems. If winning elections is important to candidates, it simply does not pay to run on a third-party ticket in SMD elections; but running as a third-party candidate is certainly more likely to be profitable in PR systems.

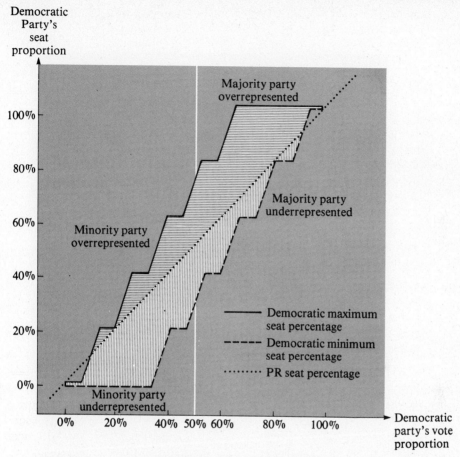

Figure 4.6 The relationship between Democratic proportion of votes and theoretical maximum and minimum seat proportions.

There is additional corroborating evidence about the comparative tendencies of these two systems:

> Elections to the city council (then called the Board of Aldermen) in New York City in 1935 were from single-member districts. Results: Democrats, 63; Republicans, 2. In 1937 the voters of New York, having reduced the number of members, decided that it would be more sporting to try a system of proportional representation. Results of a characteristic election (1945): Democrats, 14; Republicans, 3; American Labor Party, 2; Communist, 2; Liberals, 2. Those two Communists were two too many for most persons in New York, and in 1947 the city beat a retreat to the single-member district. Results of the next election (1949): Democrats, 24; Republicans, 1.[10]

---

[10] Clinton Rossiter, *Parties and Politics in America* (Ithaca, N. Y.: Cornell University Press, 1960), p. 9. For excellent general discussions of the effects of election rules

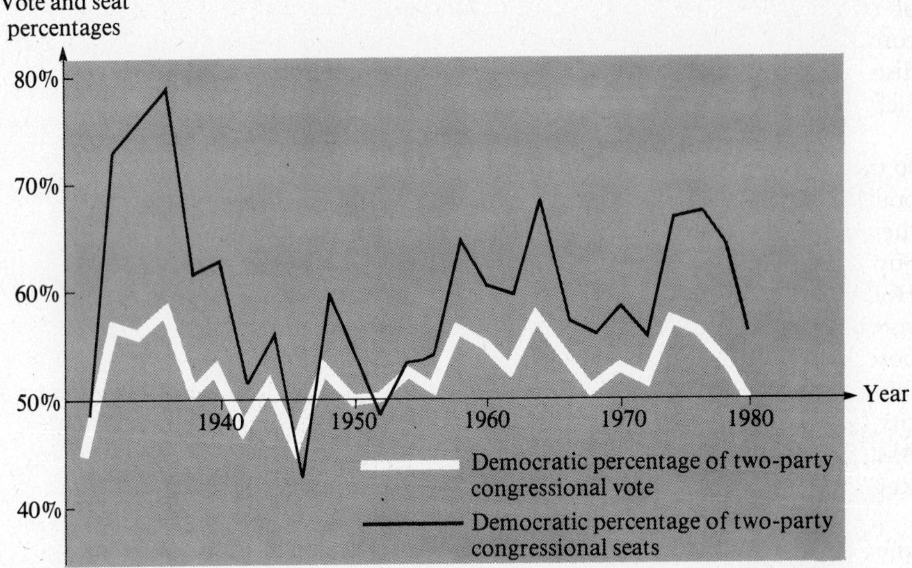

Figure 4.7 Relationship between Democratic vote and seat percentages in U.S. House of Representatives, 1930–1980.

In sum, "the single-member district may be hard on the second party but it is death on third parties."[11]

Further Problems of Elections and Representation

The preceding discussion lays bare the simple properties of direct and indirect elections and PR and SMD election systems. Two other central problems of elections and representation are the gerrymander and malapportionment, both of which have been common in American politics.

The gerrymander. The single-member district requires that someone draw the district boundaries. For House and Senate as well as for state legislature and state senate elections, this is a legal prerogative of state governments. Article 1, Section 4 of the Constitution specifies that "the Times, Places and Manner of holding Elections for Senators and Representatives shall be prescribed in each State by the Legislature thereof; but the Congress

---

on election outcomes, see Douglas W. Rae, *The Political Consequences of Electoral Laws* (New Haven, Conn.: Yale University Press, 1967), and Edward R. Tufte, "The Relationship Between Seats and Votes in Two-Party Systems," *American Political Science Review,* 67 (June 1973), pp. 540–554.

[11] Rossiter, *Parties and Politics in America,* p. 9.

may at any time by Law make or alter such Regulations, except as to the Places of chusing Senators." Thus, within the strictures of Supreme Court and congressional action, state legislators draw up congressional (and their own) district boundaries. City council members usually draw district lines for city elections.

State legislators ordinarily try to draw district lines in their own interest, so the members of the party controlling the legislature often contrive district boundaries to maximize the number of congressional or legislative districts their party can win. A hypothetical example shows how they might do so. Suppose that the citizens of a state are entitled to send five members to the House of Representatives, that the state is circular in shape, that everyone votes, and that voters are distributed uniformly over the state. Finally, suppose there is a city in the center of the state whose voters, by stereotype, are all faithful Democrats; the donut-shaped area of the rest of the state around the city is a rural area whose voters, by stereotype, are all faithful Republicans. Assume that there are as many Democrats—city dwellers—as there are Republicans—country dwellers. Figure 4.8a illustrates this configuration.

What would a "fair" districting of this state look like? Figure 4.8b shows one such scheme, which cuts the state like a pie into five wedges, all of which have an equal number of voters and an equal number of Democratic and Republican votes. With this kind of districting, party members can expect each congressional district election to be a toss-up. The expected number of seats each party can hope to win is two and one-half, which reflects the even division of voters in the state.

If the Republicans control the state legislature, they might enact a districting plan as in Figure 4.8c. (Redistricting, as with the apportionment of House seats among states, occurs every ten years if population changes require it. Population is also calculated every ten years by the national census.) This plan gives away district 1 to the Democrats by a solid 100 percent vote. Districts 2 through 5 each contain 25 percent of the Republican voters and 7.5 percent of the Democratic voters. The Republicans win by a substantial majority (five to three) in these four districts, and the state sends four Republicans and one Democrat to the House of Representatives. But if the Democrats control the state legislature, they might enact a districting plan such as the one in Figure 4.8d. This plan gives away district 5 to the Republicans by a solid 100 percent vote. Districts 1 through 4 each contain 25 percent of the Democratic voters and 7.5 percent of the Republican voters. With this plan, the Democrats now win by a substantial margin (five to three) in these four districts, and the state sends four Democrats and one Republican to the House of Representatives.

Political observers call this practice of districting for political advantage **gerrymandering,** after an early governor of Massachusetts, Elbridge Gerry. "Gerry's name connotes infamy only because . . . he helped redistrict the General Court [Massachusetts state legislature] in 1811 and 1812 in the interest of the Republican Party. One new district had a vaguely reptilian shape; and an inspired Federalist journalist coined the name from *Gerry* and

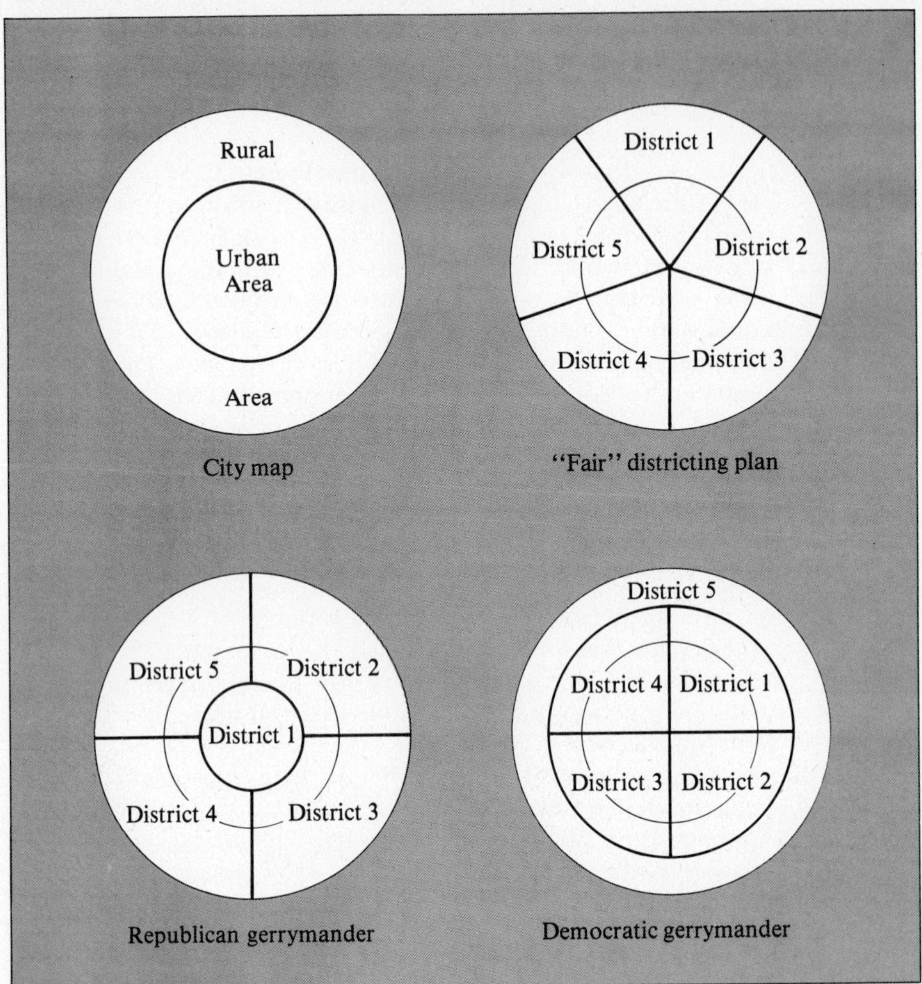

Figure 4.8 Hypothetical districting plans and the gerrymander.

salamander."[12] The reptilian shape resulted because states are not circles and people do not nicely and exclusively distribute themselves over land masses by political party membership. The political tendencies of populations are many and variegated, so shapes of apparent meaninglessness appear. For example, Figure 4.9 shows the 1950 districting of North Carolina. Districts 2 and 8 are especially interesting, and probably the result of gerrymanders. These districts became less reptilian after redistricting in 1971.

The gerrymander is ultimately an intractable problem of a district sys-

[12] William H. Riker, *Democracy in the United States*, 2nd ed., rev. (New York: Macmillan, 1965), p. 69.

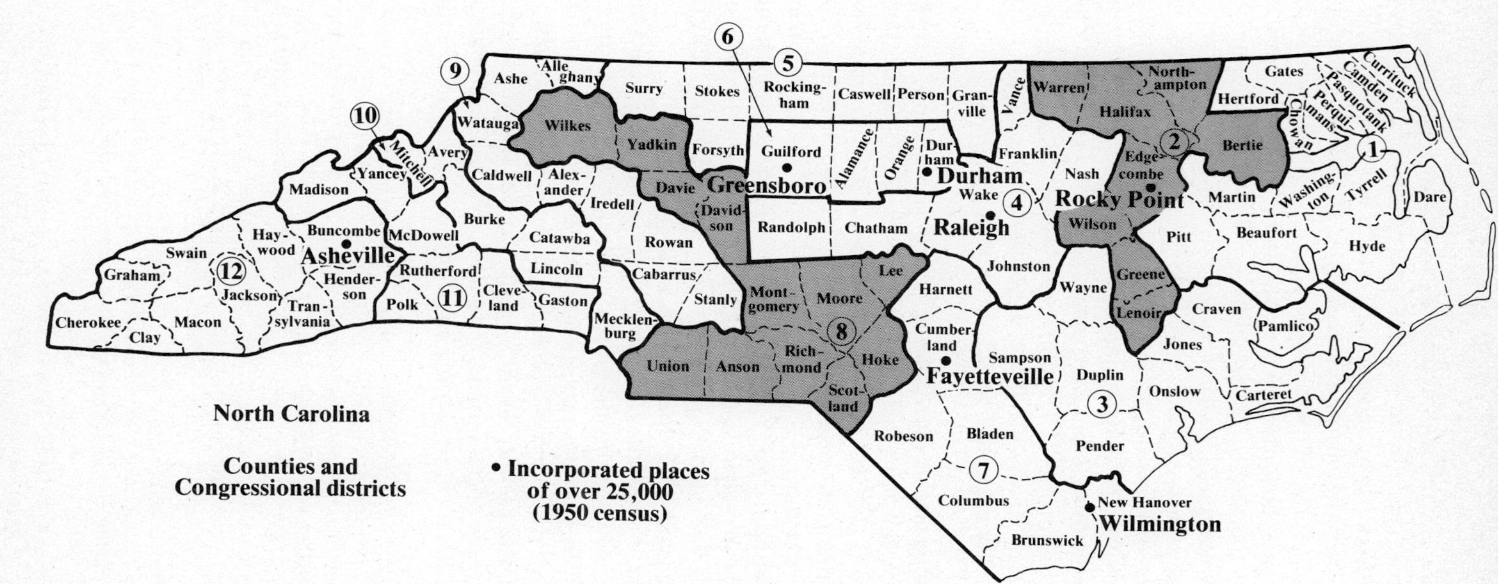

Figure 4.9 1950 congressional districts in North Carolina.

Source: This work originally appeared in *American Votes IV,* edited by Richard M. Scammon. Published in 1962 by University of Pittsburgh Press. Used by permission.

tem, as there are few court cases to instruct us and few districting standards on which people can agree.[13] Some states require districts to be contiguous and compact, while others consult additional topological properties. Occasionally, legislators turn over the districting task to nonpartisan commissions, and computer programs now help to define districts. But even if legislators use impartial consultants, how do they instruct them? Perhaps districts should be contiguous, compact, and approximately equal in population. They might add sociopolitical standards, so the resulting districts produce representatives who reflect a state's party, racial, ethnic, or economic divisions. Finally, perhaps the resulting districts ought to be as politically competitive as possible, giving neither party electoral dominance. However, it is simple to find cases in which, if a particular districting plan meets one standard, then it fails to meet one or more of the others.[14] Furthermore, any standard usually helps one party at the expense of the other, so if political districting is left to political persons, they can be expected to act in their own interests.

Malapportionment. A more tractable problem arising in district systems is legislative apportionment. Suppose a state has one million persons and a legislature of one hundred representatives elected from single-member districts. If exactly the same number of persons (10,000) lived in each district, then the state would have perfect apportionment and the districting would accord with the standard of "one man, one vote." **Malapportionment** would occur if there were grossly disparate numbers of persons in different districts. In our example, the worst malapportionment would happen if 99 districts had one person each while one district had 999,901 persons.[15]

Before 1962, malapportionment was widespread in the United States. By 1960, the largest congressional district in each state with more than one district was twice as populous as its smallest district; the Connecticut state legislature's largest district was 242 times as large as its smallest district; the figures for the Nevada senate were 223 to 1, for the Rhode Island senate, 141 to 1, and for the Georgia senate, 9 to 1.[16] This malapportionment came largely from population shifts from the farms to the cities and suburbs. Rural

---

[13] Gerrymanders whose overt purpose is to deprive minority-group members of equal legislative representation have been struck down. See *Gomillion v. Lightfoot,* 379 U.S. 249 (1960). See also *Gordon v. Lance,* 403 U.S. 1 (1971); *Whitcomb v. Chavis,* 403 U.S. 124 (1971); *Gaffney v. Cummings,* 412 U.S. 735 (1973); *White v. Regester,* 412 U.S. 753 (1973); and *United Jewish Organizations of Williamsburg v. Carey,* 430 U.S. 144 (1977).

[14] Many of the complex theoretical relationships involved in districting are explored in Richard G. Niemi and John Deegan, Jr., "A Theory of Political Districting," *American Political Science Review,* 72 (December 1978), pp. 1304–1323.

[15] See Glendon Schubert and Charles Press, "Measuring Malapportionment," *American Political Science Review,* 58 (March 1964), pp. 302–327, and Robert A. Dixon, Jr., *Democratic Representation: Reapportionment in Law and Politics* (New York: Oxford University Press, 1968).

[16] Congressional Quarterly News Service, *Congress and the Nation, 1965–1968* (Washington, D. C.: Congressional Quarterly Inc., 1969), p. 43.

legislators simply refused to reapportion themselves out of a job. Until 1962, the most recent legislative reapportionment in Alabama, Delaware, Indiana, and Vermont had occurred before 1920.[17]

While vestiges of the reapportionment problem remain today, the inequities seem far less severe than in earlier times because of several court decisions of the 1960s, which legislated serious malapportionment out of existence. In earlier reapportionment cases, such as *Colegrove v. Green,* the Supreme Court justices decided to avoid what they regarded as a political question.[18] The reapportionment breakthrough came with the 1962 Supreme Court decision in *Baker v. Carr.*[19] The Tennessee legislature had not been reapportioned since 1901, although the state constitution required a decennial reapportionment based on population. The largest district of the Tennessee legislature held 36,031 people, and the smallest, 3451—a ten-to-one difference. The figures for the Tennessee senate were 108,904 and 3727, nearly a thirty-to-one difference. A group of urban residents brought suit, and on March 26, 1962, Supreme Court Justice William J. Brennan delivered the majority's decision. He rejected the reasoning in *Colegrove*: "The mere fact that a suit seeks protection of a political right does not mean that it presents a political question. . . ." The Court's majority then held that malapportionment in Tennessee deprived the plaintiffs of their "equal protection of the laws," in violation of the Fourteenth Amendment of the Constitution.

Once the justices had rejected the reasoning in *Colegrove* and declared themselves competent to adjudicate the question of legislative apportionment, reapportionment suits flooded the courts. After all, people choose decision rules and procedures in their own interest. Apportionment is such a rule. Here was an opportunity to increase legislative voting strength through litigation, and many sought it. The case of *Wesberry v. Sanders* followed *Baker.*[20] In *Wesberry,* the justices extended what they had held for state legislatures to congressional districts themselves. Justice William O. Douglas, speaking for the majority in the case of *Gray v. Sanders* (upon which *Wesberry* was built), said, "The conception of political equality from the Declaration of Independence to Lincoln's Gettysburg Address, to the 15th, 17th, and 19th Amendments can mean only one thing—one person, one vote."[21] Justice Hugo L. Black added to this in *Wesberry*: "the command of Article 1, section 2 [of the Constitution] that the Representatives be chosen 'by the People of the several States,' means that as nearly as practicable one man's vote in a Congressional election is to be worth as much as another's."

The decade of the sixties was filled with court activity to answer ques-

---

[17] Council of State Governments, *The Book of the States, 1962–1963* (Chicago: Council of State Governments, 1963), pp. 58–62.

[18] 328 U.S. 549 (1946).

[19] 369 U.S. 186 (1962).

[20] 276 U.S. 1 (1964).

[21] 372 U.S. 368 (1963).

tions about apportionment that the *Baker* and *Wesberry* decisions had raised. For example, some argued that there is an analogy between the federal government and individual state governments. The United States Senate has two members from each state, regardless of population, while House of Representatives apportionment depends almost entirely on population. Therefore, some suggested that perhaps the state legislatures might adopt the federal system by apportioning one house of a bicameral legislature on some basis other than population. The justices rejected this analogy, asserting that both houses must be well apportioned.[22] The justices also agreed that exact district equality may be mathematically impossible, but that the population basis of apportionment must be "substantial."[23] Some states held referendum and initiative elections whose intent was to overcome the dictates of *Baker.* For instance, a large majority of voters in Colorado approved a federal system of apportionment, but the justices held that even a majority of voters could not overcome the constitutional objection: a "citizen's constitutional rights can hardly be infringed because a majority of the people choose to do so."[24]

In other cases, the justices had to address the question of how much interdistrict population variation can occur before the one-person, one-vote standard is violated. In *Swann v. Adams* they answered, "*De minimus* deviations are unavoidable, but variations of 30% among senate districts and 40% among house districts can hardly be deemed *de minimus* and none of our cases suggest that differences of that magnitude will be approved without a satisfactory explanation grounded on acceptable state policy."[25] In still other cases, the justices placed on the states the entire burden of defending variations of district populations. Hence, any state without perfectly equal districts may be considered guilty until proved innocent of violating constitutional rights.[26] Today, the one-person, one-vote doctrine extends to nearly all governmental elections.

While reapportionment problems remain, especially in local election districts, nevertheless the Supreme Court has wrought a revolution in reapportionment. For congressional elections in particular, the results have been remarkable. In the Ninety-fourth Congress (1975–1976), the smallest districts of thirty-six states were one percent or less below their state's average district size, and no district was more than 6 percent below the average. The largest districts of thirty-six states were one percent or less above their state's average district size, and no district was more than 7.3 percent above the average district size.

Most contemporary scholars and jurists believe that apportionment is a closed question. The justices interpret equal apportionment of legislative

---

[22] *Reynolds v. Sims,* 377 U.S. 533 (1964).

[23] *Reynolds v. Sims,* 377 U.S. 533 (1964).

[24] *Reynolds v. Sims,* 377 U.S. 533 (1964).

[25] 385 U.S. 440 (1967).

[26] *Kirkpatrick v. Priesler,* 394 U.S. 526 (1969); *Abate v. Mundt,* 403 U.S. 182 (1971).

districts as a constitutional requirement; each person's "share" of a legislator must be equal to every other person's share. The only remaining questions concern how much variation is tolerable, whether the courts should have acted in this area in the first place, whether the upsetting of traditional patterns was justified, and whether reapportionment has made any difference in public policy.[27] But these questions have today become largely of philosophical and historical interest only.

THE RULES OF AMERICAN NATIONAL ELECTIONS

As is commonly known, the American national government has three branches: the executive branch (president, vice-president, and much of the federal bureaucracy), the legislative branch (House of Representatives and Senate), and the judiciary (Supreme Court, courts of appeals, and other federal courts). Here, we describe the rules of national elections of representatives, senators, presidents, and vice-presidents.

Elections to the House of Representatives

Constitutional standards for elections. Article 1, Section 2 of the Constitution describes the rules for electing representatives. The Constitution requires first that voters choose representatives every two years in popular elections. Second, representatives must be twenty-five years old upon taking office and must have been citizens of the United States for at least seven years. They need not be residents of the districts that elect them (although traditionally they are so), but they must be residents of the district's state. Third, the governor must call an election to fill a vacancy in any state's congressional delegation. Finally, as noted earlier in this chapter, Article 1, Section 4 gives state legislators control over "The Times, Places, and Manner of holding Elections for Senators and Representatives," yet "the Congress may at any time by Law make or alter such Regulations, except as to the Places of chusing Senators." By Article 1, Section 5, furthermore, "Each House shall be the Judge of the Elections, Returns, and Qualifications of its own members. . . ." In sum, state governments are a first level of authority for congressional elections, and the members of each house are the final authority.

The members of Congress have sought to regulate the election process in a number of acts. In particular, the Apportionment Act of 1842 requires states to set up single-member districts. Today, some states may use at-large elections, but a 1970 law requires that only those states with one representative can do so, and they would have to do so anyway.

State apportionment of representatives. The Constitution originally specified that

[27] See Justice Felix Frankfurter's dissent in *Baker*.

> Representatives and direct Taxes shall be apportioned among the several States which may be included within this Union, according to their respective Numbers, which shall be determined by adding to the whole Number of free Persons, including those bound to Service for a Term of Years, and excluding Indians not taxed, three fifths of all other Persons. The actual Enumeration shall be made within three Years after the first Meeting of the Congress of the United States, and within every subsequent Term of Ten Years, in such a Manner as they shall by Law direct. The Number of Representatives shall not exceed one for every thirty Thousand, but each State shall have at Least one Representative. . . . (Article 1, Section 2)

The "three-fifths of all other Persons" refers to slaves, whose reduced representation resulted from a bargain between "slave" states and "free" states. The Fourteenth Amendment replaced this provision, leaving the basis for apportionment of representatives among the states largely a matter of population alone.

Before 1929, House members responded to population increases by increasing the number of seats in the House. This solution did not threaten any incumbents' seats, which would have happened if House size had remained fixed while population changes required some states (those that lagged behind average national population increases), and therefore some representatives, to lose seats. However, through following this strategy, by 1929 the House of Representatives was in danger of becoming an unwieldy legislative body, burdened by its own size. A majority of the members agreed before the 1930 census to set the 435-seat limit. Representatives today could still decide to enact some other size, but typically House leaders—whose seats are usually (though not always) safe anyway—have opposed increasing the number of seats.

Apportioning House seats by population creates a fairly linear relationship, as Figure 4.10 shows for the projected 1982 apportionment. Some distortion of pure population percentages occurs in seat percentages because small states receive one representative no matter what their population, and because of rounding errors.[28]

SMD and the election of representatives. Figure 4.7 illustrates the effect of SMD elections on the House of Representatives. The House, with nearly

---

[28] The population basis of apportionment can handle seat fractions in many ways. Generally, a population number is computed that, when divided into state populations, minimizes "remainders." The actual calculation is quite complex and can produce some bizarre results. For instance, Steven J. Brams has documented a phenomenon known as the Alabama Paradox, which occurred in 1881: if the House of Representatives had been set at 299 members, then Alabama would have had eight representatives; with a 300-member House, Alabama would have had only seven representatives. See Steven J. Brams, *Paradoxes in Politics: An Introduction to the Nonobvious in Political Science* (New York: Free Press, 1976), chapter 6.

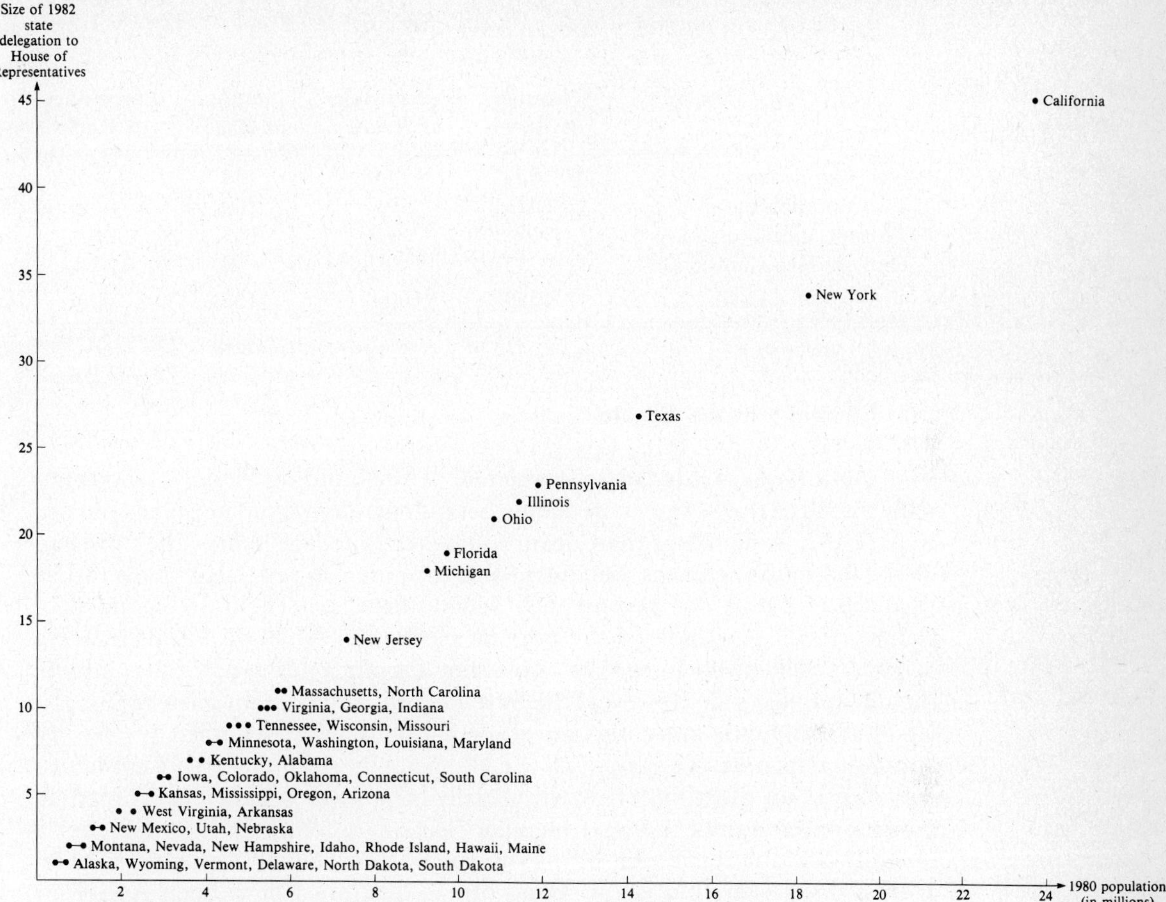

Figure 4.10 1980 population and projected number of House of Representative seats for each state following the 1982 elections.

perfect SMD constituencies, shows the expected effect of overrepresenting the majority party while underrepresenting the minority party. This effect almost always makes third-party efforts a losing proposition. Even a party whose candidates received 10 percent of the votes nationally would probably not gain a plurality in any one district; hence, as Table 4.3 shows, third-party candidacies seldom occur. Interestingly, in 1978 there were more uncontested elections (sixty-five) than three- and four-candidate elections combined (nineteen), because in some districts the presence of a popular candidate (usually an incumbent) made it unprofitable for even a second party to compete. In 1980, these patterns were considerably weakened by the Libertarian party's strong effort to break into national politics. Although this effort greatly expanded the number of three-candidate congressional races, in only twenty races did a third-party candidate receive 5 percent or more of the vote, and in no instance did a third-party candidate win.

Table 4.3 Number of Candidates in Congressional Races*

	1978		1980	
	Number of Races	**Percentage of Races**	**Number of Races**	**Percentage of Races**
One Candidate	65	14.9	34	7.8
Two Candidates	351	80.7	269	61.8
Three Candidates	16	3.7	123	28.3
Four or Five Candidates	3	0.7	9	2.1
Total	435	100.0	435	100.0

* Candidates with less than one percent of the vote are not counted.

Elections to the Senate

Constitutional standards for election. The Founding Fathers, who originally intended the Senate to be somewhat independent from popular opinion, in Article 1, Section 3 of the Constitution gave state legislatures the power to elect each state's senators. Senators were supposed to represent states rather than citizens. But the Seventeenth Amendment, passed in 1912 and proclaimed in 1913, mandated the popular election of senators. Vacancies were originally filled by having a state's governor appoint a new senator to complete the unexpired term. However, the Seventeenth Amendment gave state legislators the right to grant the governor the authority "to make temporary appointments until the people fill the vacancies by election as the Legislature may direct." In practical terms, this usually means that senators appointed by governors serve until the next biennial election, at which time voters elect a senator to fill the remainder of the unexpired term. Finally, senators must be at least thirty years old upon taking office; they must have been American citizens for at least nine years, and they must be residents of the states they represent.

The Senate, by the terms of Article 1, Section 3, is a continuous body—compared to members of the House, who face election every two years, only one-third of the senators biennially face election. The districts from which senatorial candidates run are the states themselves, and each state has two senators, regardless of its size. Thus, the Senate is intentionally malapportioned. Californians have one senator for each ten million persons, while Alaskans have one senator for each 150,000 persons.

The SMD system and the election of senators. Senate elections, like House elections, are held in single-member districts (states), so an overrepresentation of the majority party and an underrepresentation of the minority party occurs, although for some unknown reason the distortion in Senate elections is somewhat muted. As with House elections, the overrepresentation of the majority parties, along with the disadvantage to minority parties, discourages third-party candidacies for Senate seats. For example, in 1978, twenty-eight of thirty-five Senate contests were two-party affairs, while only six had three or more candidates (not counting candidates with less than one percent of the total vote). In 1980, there were twenty-one and eleven two- and three-candidate Senate races respectively, and one race had four candidates. However, in only one election did a third-party candidate receive more than 5 percent of the votes cast.

Elections to the Presidency and Vice-Presidency

Constitutional standards for elections. Procedures for electing presidents and vice-presidents are more complex than those for the House and Senate. The original constitutional provisions are listed in Article 2, Section 1. Generally, a state legislature would designate how its representatives to a national **electoral college** would be chosen. In early years, state legislators would usually choose "electors" themselves. The electors would then try to choose a president and vice-president.

Article 2, Section 1 mandated the following process. First: each state legislature would control the process of appointing electors; each state would have a number of electors equal to its number of senators (two) plus its number of representatives; and, each elector would have two votes to cast, one for each of two different candidates. Second: if one candidate had a majority vote based on the number of electors, and no other candidate had an equal number of votes, then the majority candidate became president; if two candidates had a majority vote *and* equal votes, then state delegations in the House of Representatives, each delegation casting one vote, would choose one of the tied candidates to be president. Third: if no candidate had a majority vote, then the House of Representatives, voting again as state delegations, would choose the president from among the five candidates with the greatest number of votes. Finally: whoever had the second most electoral votes would be chosen vice-president; but if a tie occurred for vice president, then the Senate would choose the vice-president from between (or among) the tied candidates.

Though complex, this arrangement worked reasonably well at first. In the elections of 1788 and 1792, George Washington received a vote from every elector, and there was sufficient division among all other candidates for Washington to receive the only majority vote. In the election of 1796, John Adams received a majority and Thomas Jefferson placed second. Hence, they became president and vice-president, respectively.

However, by 1800 two political parties had emerged, and their leaders tried to exploit presidential election rules to their advantage. Party leaders successfully sought to commit electors before the election. Federalist party electors were to vote for Adams and Pinckney, while Republican electors (who were in a majority) were to vote for Jefferson and Burr. The Federalists intended to elect Adams, president and Pinckney, vice-president, while the Republicans intended to elect Jefferson, president and Burr, vice-president. Nearly every elector followed this pattern, but there was no way to differentiate a "presidential" vote from a "vice-presidential" vote. So, both Jefferson and Burr received a majority and an equal number of votes, throwing the election into the House of Representatives. There, Federalist party members tried to reverse Republican intentions by electing Burr, president and Jefferson, vice-president. Although this ploy failed—Jefferson *was* elected president—the disagreeable possibility that it might have succeeded gave rise in 1804 to the Twelfth Amendment.

That amendment provided for distinct ballots in presidential and vice-presidential voting. The presidential candidate who has "the greatest number of votes . . . shall be President, if such number be a majority of the whole number of Electors appointed." If there is no majority candidate, then the House of Representatives, voting as state delegations with one vote for each delegation, chooses the president from among the *three* candidates with the most electoral votes. If the House fails to choose a president by March 4 (changed by the Twentieth Amendment to January 20), then the vice-president becomes acting president. Further, a vice-presidential candidate with a "majority of the whole number of Electors appointed" assumes that office. If there is no majority candidate for vice-president, then the Senate chooses a vice-president from the two candidates with the greatest number of electoral votes.

Beyond these rules, the Constitution requires presidents to be "natural born citizens" (or citizens when the Constitution was adopted). A president must be at least thirty-five years old upon taking office and must have been a resident of the United States for at least fourteen years. By the Twelfth Amendment, "no person constitutionally ineligible to the office of President shall be eligible to that of Vice-President of the United States."

The electoral college. The electoral college is a continuing source of controversy. A discussion of its potential effects on public policy must await a clearer understanding of election theory, which Chapters 7 and 8 partially provide. But the electoral college has several political properties that are important to understand here and now.

First, the Constitution allows the states to appoint their electors and specifies the number of electors to which each state is entitled, yet a state need not choose its electors by popular vote. Before the election of 1832, the legislatures in many states chose their respective electors. Between 1836 and the Civil War, however, only South Carolina failed to use a popular election, and since then all states have used popular elections to choose electors. While electors today are universally chosen in this way, there is no legal requirement that this be so. State legislators could decide at any time to remove this authority from the citizens and take it unto themselves. Of course, as a practical matter they probably would not do so, as they would most certainly be turned out of office at the next election.

Second, the Constitution does not specify the electors' constituencies. In early presidential elections, many electors were chosen from congressional districts, and electors of the same state could cast their votes for different candidates. Today, the state is a constituency unit system: whichever candidate receives a plurality of the popular vote in a state receives all of that state's electoral votes. That is, all of the "electoral college candidates" pledged to the presidential candidate become members of the electoral college for that state and usually cast their votes accordingly.

Third, however, electors are not bound to vote for a particular candidate, and they may vote differently from the way they announced before the general election. For example, Roger MacBride, a Republican elector from Virginia, decided to cast his single electoral vote in the 1972 election for John Hospers, the Libertarian party candidate, rather than for Richard Nixon. (MacBride ran for president as the Libertarian party candidate in 1976.) Although the independence of electors is occasionally challenged, judges and legislators have been unwilling to abrogate it.

Fourth, the principal source of controversy about the electoral college is its ability to produce presidents not only who have less than a majority of the popular vote (when there are three or more candidates), but also who have fewer votes than their major opponent. A hypothetical example regarding the 1972 presidential election shows how this result is possible. In that election, Richard Nixon won 60.8 percent of the popular vote and about 96.8 percent of the electoral vote to defeat George McGovern.[29]

We can move some numbers around, keeping the *total* votes cast in each state—votes for Nixon plus votes for McGovern—constant, but changing the division of the vote between them. By going through this process in a particular manner (described in a moment), McGovern's popular vote *declines* from 29,170,383 to 16,015,298, while Nixon's popular vote *increases* from 47,169,905 to 60,324,990. That is, about 14 million votes are shifted from McGovern to Nixon. But the net result of these vote changes is to *increase* McGovern's electoral votes from 17 to 270 while *reducing* Nixon's electoral votes from 521 to 268, giving McGovern the victory!

To produce these results, we take the actual number of total votes cast in every state with twelve or fewer electoral votes and divide them between Nixon and McGovern, giving McGovern just enough votes to win. We do the same with Florida, with seventeen electoral votes. This sums to 270 electoral votes, a bare majority for McGovern. Nixon is given unanimous votes in every other state. Table 4.4 summarizes these results.

This kind of pattern actually has occurred, though hardly in such an extreme form. In the election of 1876, Rutherford B. Hayes received 48.04 percent of the popular vote and a majority of the electoral vote, even though his major opponent, Tilden, received 50.99 percent of the popular vote. In the election of 1888, Benjamin Harrison received 47.86 percent of the popu-

[29] An American Independent party candidate received about 1.4 percent of the votes nationally and no electoral votes. For simplicity, his votes are eliminated from consideration and Roger MacBride's one electoral vote in Virginia is given to Nixon.

Table 4.4 Actual and Hypothetical 1972 Presidential Election

	Actual Votes				*Hypothetical Votes*			
	Popular	%	Elec-toral	%	Popular	%	Elec-toral	%
Nixon	47,169,905	61.79	521	96.84	60,324,990	79.02	268	49.81
McGovern	29,170,383	38.21	17	3.16	16,015,298	20.98	270	50.19

lar vote and a majority of the electoral vote, even though his major opponent, Cleveland, received 48.66 percent of the popular vote. Other presidents elected with a plurality but less than a *majority* of the popular vote include Polk (1844), Taylor (1848), Buchanan (1856), Lincoln (1860), Garfield (1880), Cleveland (1884 and 1892), Wilson (1912 and 1916), Truman (1948), Kennedy (1960), and Nixon (1968).

These unusual results occur first because small states have an advantage in the two extra votes they receive beyond what population alone would allow. Second, and more important, the unit rule—which gives the plurality winner in a state all of that state's electoral votes—creates obvious distortions, much as in any SMD system. With such an arrangement, the possibility remains that a minority-vote candidate can win a majority of the electoral votes. For example, Figure 4.6 shows that a party *can* receive a minority of votes nationwide in a congressional election but still win a majority of seats in the Congress. This aspect of SMD elections can occur as well with an electoral college arrangement and for similar reasons. More commonly, though, the electoral college unit rule produces an effect very much like the one ordinarily expected of a single-member district system. Figure 4.11 shows the relationship between Republican popular and electoral vote percentages of the two-party vote from 1856 to the present. Clearly, small vote deviations produce extensive shifts in electoral votes. Thus, as in most SMD elections (the states are the districts), third-party candidacies are discouraged, although they can and sometimes do have an impact on the vote division between the two major candidates, as Chapter 5 notes.

Constitutional Bargains

The preceding discussion introduces as quickly and in as condensed a form as possible the basic rules of national elections, as well as the essential properties of SMD arrangements. Yet these election rules already seem to form a crazy quilt of random institutional arrangements. We have: a popularly elected, fairly well-apportioned House of Representatives chosen every two years; a grossly malapportioned Senate, about one-third of whose members are elected every two years; and a mildly malapportioned electoral college, elected by popular vote but nevertheless capable of distorting a majority sentiment, to choose presidents and vice-presidents every four

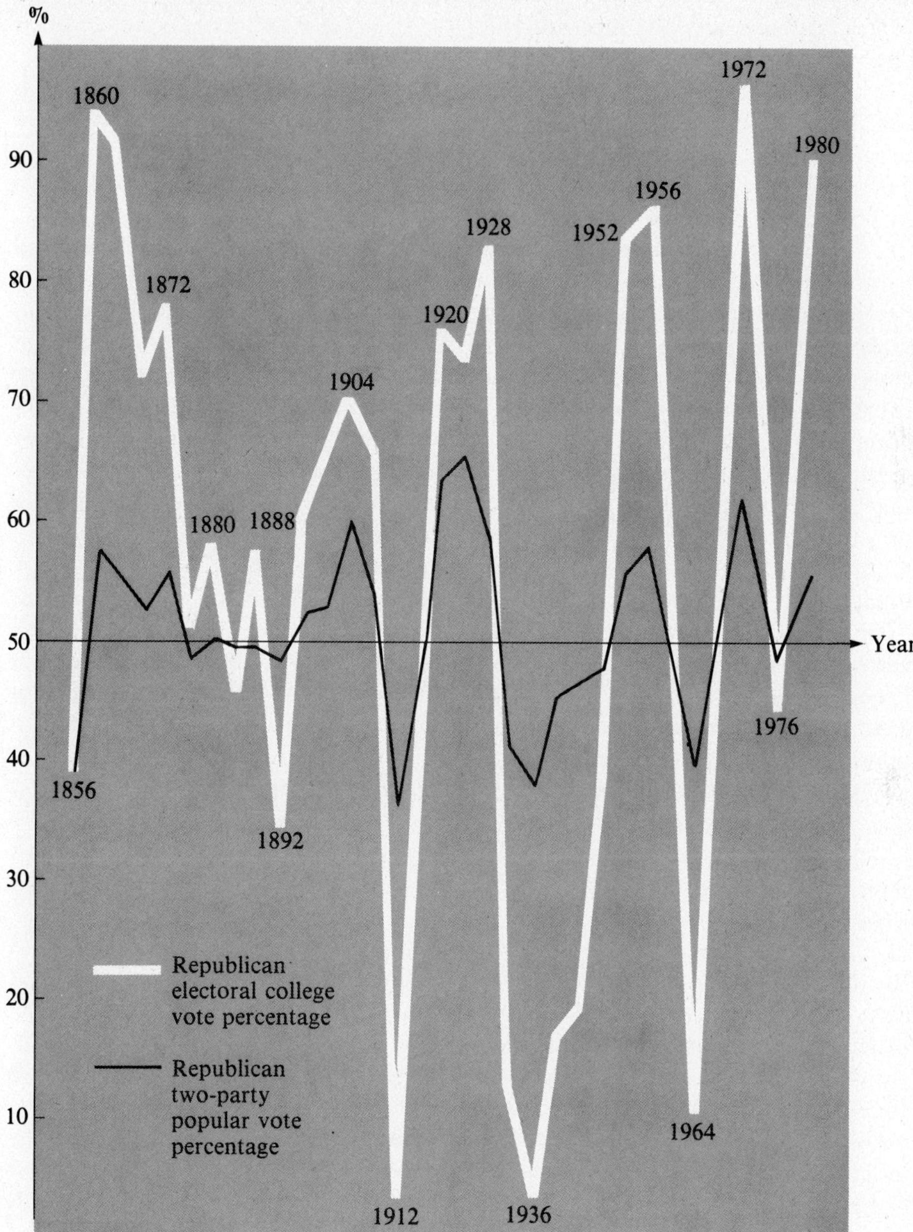

Figure 4.11 Republican percentage of popular and electoral college two-party vote, 1856–1980.

years. Such patterns of election rules seem to defy rational explanation, if not rational choice.

A long historical discussion about the origins of these election rules is not possible here, although how some of them originated can be traced in broad strokes. There are really two questions. First, why did the Founding Fathers choose these electoral arrangements? Second, why have there been so few major modifications of them?

For answers to these questions, recall the nature of human choice and bargaining. People have utilities for future outcomes that will be partially determined by rules chosen today. People act as if they are rational decision makers whether they are deciding what flavor of ice cream to buy or what candidate to vote for, or bargaining about what kind of government—what constitutional rules—to establish. The Founding Fathers were much like other people in this respect. The election and representation rules they wrote in the Constitution resulted from bargains that produced outcomes that for them probably were better than the status quo, better than the non-cooperative solution, and Pareto preferred.

The status quo was perilous. On June 21, 1788, New Hampshire became the ninth state to ratify the Constitution. (As provided in Article 7, "The Ratification of the Conventions of nine States, shall be sufficient for the Establishment of this Constitution between the States so ratifying the Same.") From November 15, 1777, to that date, governance of the former colonies went forth under the Constitution's predecessor, the Articles of Confederation, which many believed to provide an unsatisfactory set of rules. State governments remained sovereign in most matters; the Articles created no national executive, such as a president, and no national court; and while the Congress formed under the Articles could regulate foreign policy and ask state governments for money and defense, its enforcement authority was weak.

Posed against this somewhat impotent confederation was the threat of European military action, a domestic economic order upon which few could rely, the possibility of one state government exploiting the citizens of another state, and the sharp conflict between rural debtors and urban creditors. Many of the Founders were wealthy mercantilists, who thought that a strong government, a strong domestic economic order, and a prosperous nation are inextricably connected. They believed that the Articles of Confederation provided none of these. Some delegates to the Constitutional Convention, begun on May 25, 1787, opposed a strong central government, preferring instead a modest revision of the Articles. But others wanted the Articles replaced with a constitution of rules creating a much stronger central government.

For those who preferred a rigorous central government, the problem of a strong federation versus a weak confederation was profoundly one of supplying collective goods that displayed positive externalities. For example, a powerful navy could reduce piracy against American merchantmen, but the cost of such a navy was too much for any one state to bear profitably. If some states contributed to maintaining a navy, then a state that did not contribute would be a free rider and reap the benefits of protection without paying the costs. The structure of this decision problem is identical to that of building a lighthouse, described in Chapter 3 and particularly in the game represented in Table 3.1. The problem of currency was of the same ilk. One state might have a fiscally sound monetary system with a reliable, uninflated currency. However, if all other states were irresponsible about their currencies and printed money at a prodigious rate, then the residents of the responsible state would suffer, at least in the short run. Until the inflation was discovered, citizens in the irresponsible states could buy products and pay debts in the responsible state with cheapened currency. The responsible state's citizens would be disadvantaged for the opposite reasons.

A seemingly insurmountable problem was that of one state government placing tariffs on the products of another state. State governments treated each other like foreign nations, using tariffs to raise revenues and to protect their "domestic" industries. As James Madison wrote,

> The . . . want of a general power over commerce led to an exercise of the power, separately, by the States, which . . . engendered rival, conflicting and angry regulations. Besides the vain attempts to supply their respective treasuries by imports, which turned their commerce into neighboring ports . . . , the States having ports for foreign commerce, taxed and irritated the adjoining States, trading through them, as New York, Pennsylvania, Virginia, and South Carolina. Some of the States, as Connecticut, taxed imports from others, as from Massachusetts. . . .[30]

The tariff problem is a classic collective-goods problem built on a prisoners' dilemma game. Consider the following highly simplified example. Suppose a Massachusetts musket manufacturer can sell three hundred muskets per year in Massachusetts at $10 each and the same number in Virginia at that price. A Virginia musket manufacturer sells muskets in both states under identical market conditions. The governors in each state consider a $2 tariff on each musket manufactured out of state. We shall suppose that under such a tariff, the reduced sales and added transportation costs would make it unprofitable to export muskets to another state, but market conditions are such that the domestic manufacturer can expand sales in his state from three hundred to four hundred per year at a profit-maximizing price of $12.

If neither governor enacts the tariff, then each manufacturer annually sells six hundred muskets at $10 per musket, yielding each a revenue of $6000. If both governors enact the tariff, then each manufacturer sells four

[30] James Madison, *Journal of the Federal Convention,* edited by E. H. Scott (Chicago: Alfred, Scott, 1893), pp. 46–47.

hundred muskets only in his own state, at $12 per musket, yielding each a revenue of $4800. If the Massachusetts governor enacts a tariff while the Virginia governor does not, then the Massachusetts maker sells three hundred muskets in Virginia for $10 each and four hundred in Massachusetts for $12 each, yielding a total revenue of $7800. The Virginia musket maker only sells three hundred muskets at $10 each, and only in Virginia, yielding him a revenue of $3000. Of course, if the Virginia governor enacts a tariff while the Massachusetts governor does not, then the Massachusetts manufacturer receives $3000 while his Virginia competitor receives $7800. Assuming there is no interstate smuggling and no costs of tariff collection, Table 4.5 summarizes these payoffs.

This is a prisoners' dilemma game. Each governor's dominant, noncooperative strategy is to abandon free trade and enact a tariff, since his payoff is greater no matter what his counterpart in the other state does. With no strong central government to prevent them, tariff wars understandably proliferated under the Articles of Confederation, even though most people regarded them as counterproductive. Not surprisingly, the Constitution prohibited such tariffs (Article 1, Section 9). Most governors were unwilling to give up the tariff authority unilaterally. Unlike the Articles of Confederation, however, the new Constitution required every other state governor to go along. Representatives to the Constitutional Convention thus embraced a stronger national government to regulate such matters, since the status quo was not Pareto preferred.

But what kind of government might it be? This question is especially important because of differences among the preferences held by each states' citizens, on the one hand, and the nature of collective goods, on the other. Under the Articles of Confederation, the central government could not dictate public policy to any state, and there was no single policy to which states had to adhere. Thus, the collective good of national defense could not be adequately produced, nor could the collective bad of interstate tariffs be adequately suppressed. Only a stronger central government, with legislative and executive authority defined in the public policy areas, could force all

Table 4.5 Hypothetical Tariff War Between Massachusetts and Virginia Under the Articles of Confederation

		Virginia Governor's Strategies			
		Free trade		Enact state tariff	
Massachusetts Governor's Strategies	Free trade	$6000*	$6000	$3000	$7800
	Enact state tariff	$7800	$3000	$4800	$4800

* The entries in each cell are first the Massachusetts manufacturer's revenue and second the Virginia manufacturer's revenue.

states to act in the interests of their citizens. Who, though, would dominate the construction and operation of a strong central government: the "slave" states or the "free" states? the large states or the small states? Citizens in each identifiable group of states held interests opposed to those of the other group.

Delegates to the Constitutional Convention succeeded in bargaining out such differences as might be affected by constitutional provisions. The different apportionment schemes of the House and Senate followed an explicit bargain between the small states, whose delegates to the Constitutional Convention favored equal legislative votes for the states, and the large states, whose delegates favored the apportionment of legislative votes according to population alone. The three-fifths count of slaves mentioned earlier in this chapter represented an explicit compromise between "slave" states, whose delegates favored complete counting of slaves for purposes of legislative apportionment but not for purposes of taxation, and "free" states, whose delegates favored counting slaves not for purposes of legislative apportionment but only for purposes of taxation.

The delegates in both large and small states eventually agreed on a strong central government with a bicameral legislature, each house of which was to be differently apportioned, for they preferred such an arrangement to the status quo under the Articles of Confederation. A similar agreement between the "slave" and "free" state delegates on the three-fifths rule also was produced in pursuit of a strong central government. Considering the bleak alternatives, these compromises forged at the Constitutional Convention were good bargains from the delegates' point of view.[31]

The second question we asked earlier is why have there been so few major modifications in these and other constitutional electoral and governmental arrangements? (Of course, the three-fifths rule is gone.) Part of the answer is that the cost of changing to some other set of rules is too great. The amendment process itself is difficult and costly. Senators, representatives, and state officials will not voluntarily give up whatever electoral college advantages they perceive. Also, the Constitution provides "that no State, without its Consent, shall be deprived of its equal Suffrage in the Senate" (Article 5); hence, the amendment power itself is not absolute. Finally, part of the cost of amending the Constitution lies in the unpredictability of the public policy outcomes that new sets of rules might create; neither politicians nor political scientists can fully predict all of the public policy consequences that might follow proposed changes in election rules. However, for most people, political events under a known and familiar set of procedures already seem sufficiently risky.

---

[31] For a discussion of these constitutional bargains, see William H. Riker, *Federalism: Origin, Operation, Significance* (Boston: Little, Brown, 1964), pp. 12–16, 87–110.

NOMINATION PROCEDURES

An election requires a ballot, which lists opposing candidates or propositions. But where do these candidates or propositions come from? Who writes the menu from which voters choose? There must be a nomination procedure, and the most pronounced trait of these procedures in the United States is their great variation in large and small detail from state to state and from office to office. These variations occur because the Constitution never mentions political parties and nominations, and therefore it fails to regulate them directly. By contrast, general elections come under the direct control of constitutional and federal law, which accounts for their underlying uniformity. Except for some federal laws and court decisions about discrimination (noted in Chapter 8) and campaign contributions, nomination procedures are the creatures of state governments and the political parties at both the federal and state levels.

State governments enter the picture because governors and state legislators choose decision rules controlling nomination procedures as well as the rules about who can be on a primary or general election ballot. These rules understandably bear a fairly close resemblance to the preferences of those who control state governments. The political parties enter the picture because for the most part their procedures are the instrumentalities of nomination, especially of presidential candidates.

Supreme Court justices are loathe to enforce uniformity except in cases of racial discrimination. Indeed, in the 1972 presidential nomination campaign, the justices overturned a court-of-appeals decision concerning the selection of California Democratic National Convention delegates. The Court rejected judicial intervention by the court of appeals and declined to tamper with "relationships of great delicacy and essentially political in nature."[32] In such matters of nominating and party politics, if the abrogation of some fundamental constitutional right is not established, the Court has traditionally adhered to the same line of judicial restraint it once followed by a four-to-three vote in the case of *Colegrove v. Green,* concerning malapportionment. The members of Congress also seem content to consider only nomination matters concerning campaign contributions, expenditures, and "unfair" practices. Except for occasional unsuccessful attempts to impose regional or national presidential primaries, they ordinarily leave control of the fundamental procedures to state and party politics, in which they *do* participate. Therefore, nomination procedures in the United States are sometimes confusing, greatly varied, and constantly changing.

Nomination Procedure Variations

Despite variations in nomination procedures, basic patterns do emerge, the most important of which concern how easy or difficult it is to get on the

[32] *O'Brien v. Brown,* 92 S. Ct. 2718 (1972).

ballot and who controls the nomination procedure itself. Here, we review several different procedures with these characteristics in mind.

Nomination by request. The simplest nomination procedure is for would-be candidates to ask those who control the ballot to list their names on it. The leaders of small organizations sometimes follow this procedure of **nomination by request** by circulating a membership list to all members, asking those who do *not* want to run to strike their names. For those who seek nomination, the external costs of this procedure—for example, the likelihood of not being nominated—are zero, but the probability of winning is reduced in a crowded field of candidates. However, the decision costs for voters can become high. "Control" of this procedure simply means that those who regulate nominations only certify that a given candidate meets the minimum requirements to hold office. Sometimes even certification is absent.

Nomination by petition. A second nomination procedure requires that a specified number of citizens sign a petition. The actual number of signatures required to get on the ballot is sometimes a particular number set by law, such as "10,000 registered voters," and sometimes a variable number, such as "10 percent of the registered voters" or "10 percent of the number of votes cast in the last election." With **nomination by petition,** those who control the nomination not only must pass on the qualifications of the nominees, but also must certify that the citizens' petition signatures are valid. The ease or difficulty of petition procedures depends upon how many signatures are required, the cost of filing, and the signature validation rules.

Nomination by caucus. Caucus nominations were one of the first procedures used in the United States to name election candidates. The caucus was a quasi-legal group of people who bargained privately to name their party's general election candidates. Long ago, caucuses were made up of representatives, senators, governors, and professional activists. The caucus raised in the popular imagination pictures of smoke-filled rooms and bargains of questionable legitimacy. Many thought of **nomination by caucus** as the least "democratic" nomination process. (This usage of *democracy* refers to the number of persons who have a say in nomination decisions.) The old-style caucuses presumably made nomination difficult for outsiders, thus restricting access to the policy-making process. Today, the caucus is an entirely different creature used at one or more stages in some states for selecting delegates to the national presidential nominating conventions.

Nomination by convention. The convention system came into being with the 1832 nomination of Andrew Jackson. Today, both major parties use conventions every four years to nominate presidential and vice-presidential general election candidates and to write their campaign platforms. It remains unclear when the old-style caucus grows big enough to become a convention; obviously, the distinction between that kind of caucus and a convention depends on how one chooses caucus members or convention delegates. A convention of one hundred popularly elected delegates might seem more "democratic" than an old-style caucus of two hundred self-appointed "bosses." But, what if convention delegates themselves are selected by bosses, while caucus members reflect the preferences of large numbers of citizens? These speculations raise the additional, central question of how people nominate or elect the nominators when they use **nomination by convention.**

Nomination by primary election. Primary systems use elections to choose a party's nominees. **Nomination by primary** can incorporate many different rules to designate who may vote and who may run in a primary election. In a **closed primary,** voters must indicate their party identification beforehand, usually by registration, and they receive their party's primary ballot when they vote. This is the most popular method in the United States. The **open primary,** a less often used procedure, does not require voters to declare their party identification, but in the voting booth they choose the ballot of the party in whose primary contest they want to vote. The **blanket primary** is like an open primary except that each voter can vote in one party's primary for one office, say senator, and another party's primary for another office, say governor.

Many primaries generate competition among several candidates, and some states use a plurality rule for deciding the winner, while others schedule run-off elections between the top two candidates. States also vary as to who may run in a primary. Some use conventions to name a candidate or candidates to run in the primaries, and anyone whom the convention fails to nominate but who wants to get on the primary ballot must collect petitions. This is called a **challenge primary.** Sometimes all candidates must get signed petitions to get on a primary ballot. In New York, a candidate can run on the primary ballot of more than one party, a practice known as **cross-filing,** which is illegal in most states and of questionable legality in a few.

Presidential Nominations

As we have noted, the nomination of American presidential candidates of the two major parties is by national convention.[33] Delegates to the convention earn their seats by winning primaries, conventions, and caucuses in their respective states and territories, but many party officials are automat-

---

[33] The process of nomination and rational choice explanations for nomination decision making are reported in John Aldrich, *Before the Convention: Strategies and Choices in Presidential Nomination Campaigns* (Chicago: University of Chicago Press, 1980).

ically made convention delegates by virtue of holding their offices. The delegate selection mechanisms for presidential conventions are complex and constantly changing.

Democratic National Conventions. The two major parties are really large coalitions, and within each party the interests and public policy preferences of the coalition members often collide. Intraparty disagreements are important in elections, because the members of one coalition are engaged in what is very nearly a zero-sum game with the members of the other party, and sometimes even with members of their own party. From the view of n-person game theory, the members of the Democratic party today realistically constitute a coalition that is much larger than necessary to win elections.[34] This overweighted coalition is in constant danger of breaking up.

The Democratic electoral defeats in the 1968 and 1972 presidential elections were the result of the members of one group within the party taking over the convention while the members of other groups stood by, contributed nothing, or deserted. However, "taking over the convention" is far from simple. The goals of a takeover are the nomination of preferred presidential and vice-presidential candidates and the adoption of a preferred platform (a particular set of public policies). These goals are accomplished by winning state primary elections and caucuses for delegate selection. An important way in which a candidate for nomination can improve his chances for winning such victories is to change delegate selection rules and convention procedures in his favor. Three interesting examples of this strategy and its political consequences come to mind.

The first involves the decision rule controlling nomination. Before 1936, a vote of at least two-thirds of the convention delegates was required to nominate a Democratic presidential candidate. Compared to a simple majority rule, the two-thirds rule reduced everyone's likely external cost, because it was easier to forge a blocking coalition against the nomination of unacceptable candidates than it would be under majority rule. Southern convention delegates formed such coalitions to prevent the nomination of unacceptable northern liberals. However, the decision costs of this rule were quite high; for example, in 1924 the Democrats nominated John W. Davis on the hundred-and-third ballot. The bargaining that accompanies such a process commonly produces a candidate with neither enemies nor electoral appeal.

In 1936, Franklin D. Roosevelt received a unanimous vote on the first ballot. Since no one had an *immediate* interest in preserving the two-thirds rule, but everyone recognized its excessive decision costs, party leaders succeeded in amending it so that only majority rule was needed. This change made things easier for party leaders as long as they could put together a

---

[34] There are many more Democrats than Republicans, although Democrats are not a majority of *all* voters (there are large numbers of independents).

majority coalition that might win and whose members approved of their leadership and agreed with their ideologies. But southern delegates walked out of the 1948 convention and formed the Dixiecrat Party, with (now Republican Senator) Strom Thurmond as their nominee. Governor George C. Wallace deserted the party before the convention in 1968 and ran on a third-party ticket. Both defections might have been prevented had the two-thirds rule been in place, but different candidates and platforms would also surely have prevailed. Specifically, Democratic platforms and candidates' positions on civil rights legislation probably would have been different if the two-thirds rule were still in use.

The second example of how rules strategically affect convention outcomes, thus inviting manipulation, and one referred to earlier in this chapter, ended with the Supreme Court's decision in *O'Brien v. Brown.* Following the unruliness and disunity evident in their 1968 convention, the Democrats tried to adopt proportional representation in all state primary voting. Earlier, most Democratic state delegations to the national convention chosen by primary operated on a unit rule: the equivalent of the single-member district, in which the winning candidate in the state primary or convention received all of that state's national convention (delegates') votes on the first ballot at the national convention. One of the final decisions the 1968 national convention delegates took was to do away with the unit rule and adopt proportional representation: nomination candidates would henceforth receive a number of a state's pledged delegates in approximate proportion to their vote fraction in that state's primary. Of course, PR would also help challenging candidates to get convention votes.

An incident in the 1972 nomination campaign showed the powerful effects that rules exert on political outcomes. The California Democratic party chose to follow the unit rule rather than PR in allocating its first-ballot national convention votes. Most observers saw this as a clear victory for Senator Hubert Humphrey over Senator George McGovern in their contest for the nomination. McGovern seemed unlikely to win a plurality in California, and his supporters therefore challenged the California unit rule, but lost to Humphrey's supporters, who insisted on state control—and consequently the unit rule—in these matters. Both sides raised several arguments about procedural due process and justice, but justice, as these partisans perceived it, always rested with the rule favorable to their candidate's advantage. Very well—the McGovern supporters swallowed the bitter dregs, went to work, and proceeded to win a plurality in the California Democratic primary, thus capturing all of California's 151 national convention votes. Suddenly Humphrey's supporters found wisdom in the earlier arguments of the McGovern forces in favor of a PR allocation of delegates, while McGovern's followers found equal wisdom in the earlier arguments for a unit rule that Humphrey's supporters had advocated. (McGovern won the argument and the nomination, but lost the election.)

The third example of how rules strategically affect convention outcomes occurred in the 1980 Democratic National Convention. President Jimmy Carter had won a majority of the delegates before the convention, and his supporters proposed a rule to be voted on at the Convention, which would bind these delegates to him on the first ballot. Senator Edward Kennedy, his only remaining nomination opponent, preferred the rule used at the 1976 Convention, which asked delegates to "vote their conscience." Plainly, Carter might have lost and Kennedy might have won if the old rule was rejected. Of course, each side carried on the debate over the rule in terms of the demands of fairness, justice, and democracy.

In the 1980 election, Democrats had a convention of 3331 delegates. Each state receives delegates and votes as the bylaws of the national party specify, and these usually require an apportionment formula based on population, electoral votes, and Democratic voting in previous general elections. At their 1974 meeting, the Democrats adopted a new charter, which formalized the rules of subsequent national conventions and placed party authority above state laws concerning delegate selection and nomination procedures. Hence, whoever captures the national party in future years can probably dictate policy and delegate selection procedures to local party members. As evidence of the waning strength of local parties, one need only point to Jimmy Carter's ability to grasp the 1976 nomination without bargaining seriously with any strong local leaders, and his 1980 nomination victory in the face of strong opposition by congressional Democrats. This kind of independence would have been unthinkable in earlier years.

Article 2 of the Democrats' charter provides that

> The national convention shall be composed of delegates who are chosen through processes which (I) assure all Democratic voters full, timely, and equal opportunity to participate and include affirmative action programs toward that end, (II) assure that delegations fairly reflect the division of preferences expressed by those who participate in the presidential nominating process, (III) exclude the use of the unit rule at any level, (IV) do not deny participation for failure to pay a cost, fee or poll tax, (V) restrict participation to Democrats only and (VI) begin within the calendar year of the convention, provided, however, that fairly apportioned and openly selected state committees, elected no earlier than January 1*st* of the preceding midterm congressional election year, from states not having state conventions authorized to elect delegates, shall not be precluded from electing not more than 25 percent of their respective state delegations according to the standards provided in this charter and bylaws.

Provision I, along with provisions in Article 10, establishes affirmative-action programs as a goal of all state party organizations, and delegates to the 1978 party meeting in Memphis formally required that women make up one-half of the delegates to the 1980 nominating convention. Provisions II and III imply the use of PR in state primaries, a position formally and explicitly adopted at the 1978 Memphis meeting. Delegates may still be chosen in caucuses as long as an approximate proportional representation formula is in force; between 25 and 30 percent of Democratic convention delegates and about 25 percent of Republican delegates were chosen by caucuses in 1980.[35] Provision V eliminates open and blanket primaries for delegate selection, and provision VI in effect makes it formally impossible for a candidate to capture the nomination before the election year begins.

In 1980, thirty-five states used presidential primaries of one form or another. For the Democrats, twenty-three primaries were binding in their selection of delegates to the national convention; four were partially binding, allowing for the selection of some other candidates by different processes; three were advisory only; and two states combined a presidential preference vote with a delegate selection vote, but voting for each purpose was separate. Three states had Republican primaries but not Democratic ones. The eighteen states without Democratic primaries used a combination of multi-tiered caucuses and conventions to choose Democratic national convention delegates. Many of these began with local caucuses, which then sent representatives to congressional-district level caucuses. Sometimes, these were followed by an overall state-wide caucus or convention. Actual national convention delegate selection can occur at any of these levels, depending on state law and local party rules. (However, even if delegate selection is entirely by primary, all states have state party conventions to carry on other party business.) National convention delegate *candidates* were variously selected by themselves, the state parties, and by presidential candidates.

Republican National Conventions. The Republicans can afford disunity less than the Democrats. Indeed, they indulge in it most when they are certain to lose anyway, as, for example, in their 1964 convention. Nevertheless, the Republicans, like the Democrats, have tried to open up their conventions to women, blacks, and younger voters, and late in 1974 a Republican committee adopted a "positive action" policy similar to but less extensive than the Democrats' "affirmative-action" policy.

Democrats sometimes give a state a number of convention delegates different from the number of votes the state delegation receives. Republicans usually equate the two numbers. In the 1976 Republican national convention, each state received six votes, plus three votes for each representative the state had in the House. Each state with a Republican presidential victory in 1972 received four and one-half additional votes and 60 percent of its electoral vote; a state picked up another vote for having a Republican governor, one more for each Republican senator, and an additional vote if one-half or more of its representatives were Republicans. Convention votes also went to Washington, D. C., and to American territories.

This apportionment of delegates, which continued nearly unchanged in

[35] *Congressional Quarterly Weekly Report,* 37 (December 29, 1979), p. 2958.

1980, gives a minor advantage to small states, which usually form the heart of Republican strength. Considering the conservative nature of the Republican parties in small states, more liberal Republicans, such as those from Illinois, New York, and Pennsylvania, are less likely to have a wholly proportionate influence over convention decisions.

In 1980, twenty-one Republican state-wide presidential primaries were binding on delegate selection (Vermont used a combination procedure); four primaries were partially binding, with some delegates being chosen by other means; six states conducted nonbinding preference votes simultaneously with a delegate selection primary (some of these also chose some delegates by other means); and two states chose delegates without a presidential preference vote. Far fewer Republican delegates among those chosen by primaries (30.5 percent) came from PR elections than did Democratic delegates chosen by primaries (91 percent).[36]

DEMOCRACY, ELECTIONS, AND NOMINATION RULES

This chapter has described the major rules, procedures, and characteristics of American elections. We have neglected to consider several questions about these subjects here, including proposals for reform, franchise requirements, dirty politics, and campaign finance and spending. Later chapters, especially Chapter 13, take up some of these subjects after we have accumulated the tools necessary to assess the effects of election procedures on public policy. But two themes that run throughout this chapter and indeed through the book should be noted here.

First, a change in a collective-choice procedure almost invariably results in a change in the public policy that the procedure generates. Thus, changing a rule or procedure also changes the mix of private and collective action, redistributes resources, and redefines property rights. Consequently, procedural changes have public policy consequences that leave some people better off and others worse off, so preferences for procedural changes depend upon how they might affect public policy. This pattern emerges clearly in several instances. For example, legislative reapportionment and gerrymandering produce winners and losers not only of elections but also of material and intangible goods.

Second, all procedures have both costs and benefits, which people share differently. For instance, a change from SMD to PR elections might benefit minor-party candidates, and it might even help nearly everyone else by breaking up the duopoly control of national politics that the two major parties' leaders seem to take for granted. But the cost of such a change may be reflected in the instability and unpredictability of PR systems brought about

[36] *Congressional Quarterly Weekly Report,* 38 (February 2, 1980), p. 228.

by a proliferation of parties whose members seldom bear the responsibility of governing. A willingness to pay the costs of such instability depends upon how people evaluate these costs and any related benefits.

Another instance of this same theme concerns whether elections ought to be direct or indirect. Direct elections carry the benefit of people's knowing exactly what public policy they are voting on, but such elections also leave citizens with too many public policy decisions to make. Indirect elections favorably reduce the number of such decisions, but a political promise about public policy made in an indirect election often seems to be a contradiction in terms.

Finally, the attractiveness of "democratizing" or reforming rules can be offset by the lack of electoral appeal of candidates nominated under more open procedures. For example, the lore of politics holds that a nomination procedure's degree of "democracy," or "representativeness," varies directly with the number of people who participate in it. In this view, a primary seems more democratic than a convention, and a convention more democratic than an old-style caucus. But what are the consequences for public policy of democratizing the nomination process? Can a "democratic" party survive or compete successfully against a less "democratic" one? The answers to these questions may be troubling, as Chapters 6 and 7 argue. Democracy *can* be a means for choosing public policy and not an end in itself. If so, then it may be disturbing to learn (as later chapters point out) that the more democratic a party's nomination procedures become, the less likely its candidates are to be elected and its public policies to be adopted.

It is possible to write volumes about such trade-offs. People should plainly require of themselves and others a far greater understanding than they now have about how present election and nomination rules work before they advocate substitute procedures, with the optimistic expectation that future policy outcomes resulting from those procedures can be reliably predicted. As in the case of the 1972 fight over PR versus the unit rule in the California Democratic primary, arguments over and proposals for change often reflect only narrow interests in short-term electoral advantages, not long-term public policy consequences. Now, we turn to the task of generating some understanding about elections in the United States, and particularly about their public policy consequences.

QUESTIONS FOR DISCUSSION AND REVIEW

1. What are the major similarities and differences between casting votes in elections and spending money in the marketplace? What differences emerge in private and collective decisions as a result of differences between voting for candidates and buying goods and services?

2. What difference would it make if juries deciding criminal cases had six members instead of twelve? Or, if only eleven—instead of twelve—members of a twelve-member jury were needed to convict or declare a defendant innocent?
3. Compare and contrast the costs and benefits of using direct democracy and indirect democracy to decide matters of public policy. Is there a parallel between direct and indirect democracy in the private sector? Are there also parallel problems in terms of comparative costs and benefits?
4. Which election system is more "market-like," PR or SMD? Why?
5. Suppose the decision rule in a legislature required nearly unanimous consent; that is, almost all of the legislators (perhaps 90 percent of them) had to agree to pass a law; under such a rule, would malapportionment or gerrymandering of legislative districts make a difference in public policy? Why? Why not?
6. What would be the effect on public policy of giving each United States senator a number of votes in the Senate in proportion to his or her state's population? Should apportionment in the Senate be changed to one person–one vote? How might the variable-vote arrangement just mentioned in the first part of this question create public policy differences compared to those decisions made by a legislative body such as the House of Representatives?
7. What public policy effects might follow the replacement of the present presidential nomination system by a national primary or a few regional primaries all held on the same day? On different days?

NEW CONCEPTS AND TERMS

blanket primary
challenge primary
citizen
closed primary
cross-filing
cumulative voting
decision cost
decision rule
direct election
direct (pure) democracy
(democracy)
election
electoral college
external cost
gerrymander
indirect election
indirect (representative)
democracy (republic)
malapportionment
motion
nomination by caucus
nomination by convention
nomination by petition
nomination by primary
nomination by request
open primary
proportional representation
system
single-member district system
voter

5

The Citizen and Voting

Election outcomes, in a minimal sense, result directly from the number of citizens who choose to vote for each candidate or motion. The voting act itself grows out of two related decisions. First, citizens decide which candidate or motion they prefer. Second, they decide whether to vote for the preferred candidate or motion or to abstain. This chapter tries to explain and predict these two decisions and therefore the act of voting.

CITIZENS' PREFERENCES, PUBLIC POLICY, AND IDEOLOGY

Chapter 1 defines public policy as the pattern of collective action in a nation, while Chapter 3 defines ideology as the pattern of utilities (externalities) a person gets from the presence or absence of various collectively supplied public and private goods. In elections, the public and private goods involved are citizens' perceptions of what kinds of public policies they can expect candidates to enact if elected and of what kinds of backgrounds and personal qualities those candidates have. When citizens vote for a candidate or abstain, they act as if their ideologies (patterns of utilities) and their perceptions of candidates form the basis of their actions.

Primary and Instrumental Issues

It is useful to think about public policy alternatives—potential collective actions—in terms of election issues and positions on those issues. An **issue** measures some aspect of an actual or potential collective action or the result of some collective action. For instance, collective action concerning abortions, as noted in Chapter 3, might entail the election issue of a time limit on length of pregnancy, after which abortions would be illegal. Citizens act as if they hold most-preferred positions on such issues, and they receive different utilities from candidates who advocate different positions on those issues. Candidates take, or fail to take, positions on such issues. Citizens then evaluate the candidates at least partially according to the utilities they receive from the candidates' issue positions or lack of them. But issues often reflect complex combinations of public policies that measure the actual or potential achievement of goals of varying importance. To show how issues and citizens' evaluations of issues might be constructed out of complex public policies, we first distinguish between primary and instrumental issues.[1]

Primary issues. Most citizens hold nearly identical preferences about what "the good life" would be like. They usually prefer living to dying, peace to war, health to sickness, justice to injustice, riches to poverty, knowledge to ignorance, freedom to slavery, love to hate, and confidence to anxiety. Supporting this near unanimity, a 1972 survey of Americans reported that 99 percent wanted an end to all wars and a decline in domestic violence, 97 percent wanted an agreement with Russia and China to end wars, 95 percent wanted an end to unemployment and a decline in prejudice, and 93 percent wished for a life without constant tension.[2] Preferences about issues such as health, wealth, happiness, and peace exist independently of actual political events, personal expectations, real outcomes, or costs of achievement. These underlying issues are called **primary issues,** and citizens' most-preferred positions on such issues identify their prime goals.

Instrumental issues. Certain decisions and outcomes affect the degree to which prime goals are achieved. For example, two prime goals might be infinite wealth and unending leisure. The related primary issues would be the amount of wealth and leisure a person actually has. In the short run, the amount of work a person performs increases wealth but diminishes leisure; hence, a measure such as "hours worked" is an **instrumental issue** with respect to the primary issues of wealth and leisure. (The terms *primary* and *instrumental* are relative and only describe the relationship of two issues or goals, one to the other. We have not yet discovered *final* goals, in an absolute sense. For example, wealth is a primary issue in relation to hours worked, but it might in turn become an instrumental issue in relation to other measures of the quality of life, such as housing conditions or diet.)

The unemployment rate is another primary issue and can be measured

---

[1] A parallel distinction between prime and instrumental goals is offered in Robert A. Dahl and Charles E. Lindblom, *Politics, Economics, and Welfare* (New York: Harper and Row, 1953).

[2] Louis Harris, "The Harris Survey," *Minneapolis Star,* December 25, 1972, p. 2c.

on a scale from zero to 100 percent unemployment. Our prime goal might be zero unemployment, and most people, *ceteris paribus,* would prefer less unemployment to more. However, all solutions to the unemployment problem seem costly. For example, some economists believe that to lower unemployment in the short run, government spending must be increased. But increases in government spending are also believed to increase the rate of inflation, itself a primary issue. The amount of government spending thus becomes an instrumental issue with respect to the primary issues of unemployment and inflation, because a change in government spending is believed to change the unemployment and inflation rates simultaneously.[3]

To tie the matter together, suppose that citizen A holds the unemployment rate to be a primary issue, prefers a position of zero unemployment, and does not care about inflation; citizen B holds the inflation rate to be a primary issue, prefers a position of zero inflation, and does not care about unemployment. Both A and B understand the hypothesized relationship between government spending and the rates of unemployment and inflation. Hence, for both A and B, the amount of government spending is an instrumental issue. Citizen A, of course, would prefer a higher rate of government spending than would B.

Instrumental issues and public policy. Government spending affects inflation and unemployment, which in turn affect both A and B's utilities. Government spending can also be at only one level at a given time, and everyone must consume its effects. Thus, the level of government spending is a public policy, a collective action, and a collective good. For A and B in particular, higher government spending levels produce a collective good (lower unemployment rate) that displays a positive externality for A, and a collective good (higher inflation rate) that displays a negative externality for B. The externality is positive for A and negative for B because of their ideologies: the patterns of utilities (externalities) they get from the presence or absence of various collectively supplied public and private goods. As we shall see, these ideologies, or patterns of utilities, ultimately rest on citizens' preferences concerning primary issues such as inflation and unemployment.

[3] In times of reasonably stable economic conditions, annual changes in the rate of inflation were thought to be (and were measured as) inversely related to annual changes in the rate of unemployment. It is on exactly such a hypothesized relationship that this example rests. Government spending—and creation of money to pay for it—are thought to create inflation, but circulating more money also temporarily creates an increased demand for goods, which translates into an increased demand for labor: a reduction in unemployment. More recently, the validity of this hypothesized relationship has come under increasingly strong attack. The relationship breaks down in periods of higher inflation, and eventually people come to *expect* government stimulation of the economy as well as inflation. Since increased government spending and an increased demand for labor soon are fully anticipated, no new jobs are added as a result of higher levels of government spending. Hence, further stimulation only creates more inflation, with little effect on unemployment. The result has been called "stagflation."

Representations of Citizen Ideology

Basic representations. Simple lines and graphs illustrate citizens' utilities for complex issues such as those involving government spending, inflation, and unemployment. Suppose that a baker, unlike A or B, prefers zero rates of both unemployment *and* inflation. High unemployment means that people buy fewer pastries, while high inflation means that the baker's production and household costs rise while the value of his savings declines. The vertical axis on the left side of Figure 5.1 shows the baker's utility for various rates of unemployment as a function of government spending levels, which are expressed on the horizontal axis as a percentage of gross national product, GNP. The baker gains utility as the unemployment rate, measured on the right vertical axis, drops with an increase in government spending. Similarly, the vertical axis on the left side of Figure 5.2 measures the baker's utility for various rates of inflation, measured on the right vertical axis. Inflation in Figure 5.2 is stated as a function of government spending levels, which as in Figure 5.1 are again measured on the horizontal axis. The baker gains utility as the inflation rate drops with a decline in government spending.

Both Figures 5.1 and 5.2 express the baker's utilities as a function of government spending, the instrumental issue. But what is the baker's total utility for various levels of this instrumental issue? (Here we ignore questions about taxing and the exact nature of government spending.) To answer this question, we add the two utility curves together. Figure 5.3 shows the original utility curves as dotted lines; the solid white line is the result of adding them together for each level of government spending.[4] The solid line thus represents the baker's utility for various levels of government spending. The point marked Y (35 percent) is the baker's most-preferred position on this instrumental issue. To the left of Y (higher government spending) and to the right of Y (lower government spending), the baker gets less utility.

Varying most-preferred positions. Now consider a factory worker whose salary, by the terms of her labor contract, is tied to the cost of living, and who is employed by a firm whose only product is sold to the government. A decline in government spending might reduce demand for the factory's product, which means a loss of overtime pay and perhaps even unemployment for the worker. She is probably only slightly concerned with inflation relative to her greater concern for unemployment. Figure 5.4 shows this worker's utility curves. Inflation-derived utility rises very slowly with a de-

---

[4] The total utility curve in Figure 5.3 rests on an underlying assumption that someone's utilities on two separate issues can be added together. This assumption considerably simplifies the discussion, but it is unlikely that many people have such utility curves. For example, attitudes toward inflation might change at different levels of unemployment, and vice versa. However, the analysis of preferences is not materially altered if we use other, more complex utility curves.

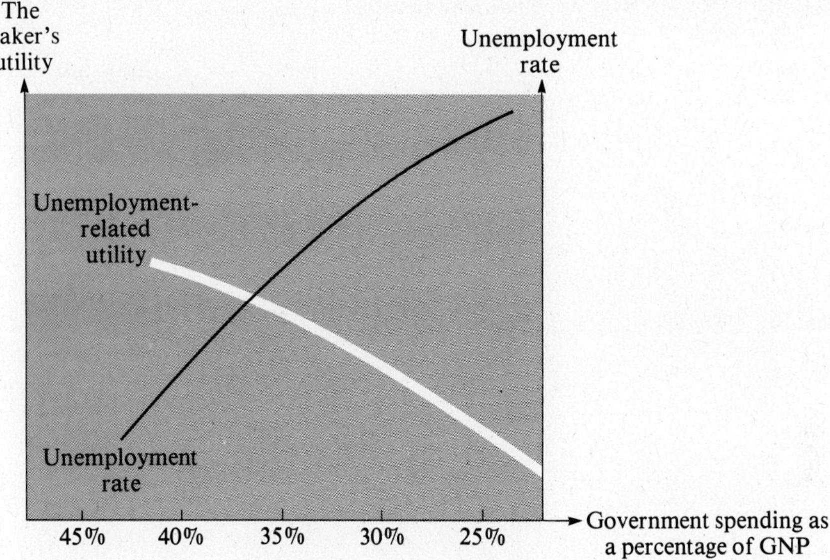

Figure 5.1 The baker's unemployment-related utility as a function of government spending.

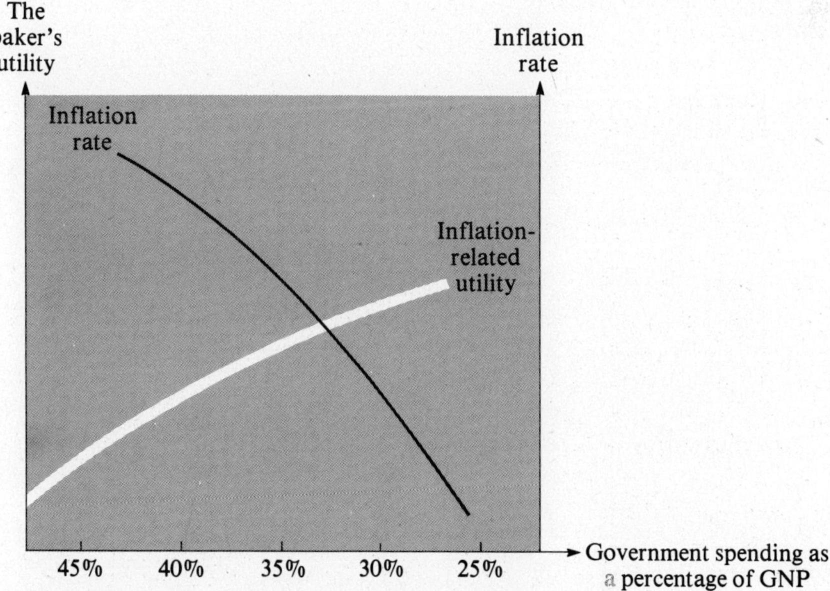

Figure 5.2 The baker's inflation-related utility as a function of government spending.

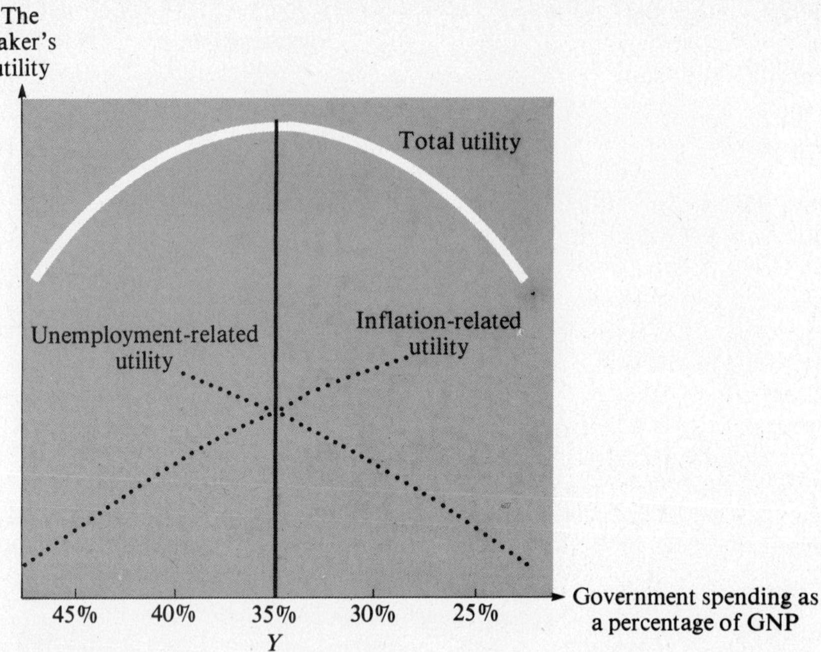

Figure 5.3 The baker's total utility as a function of government spending.

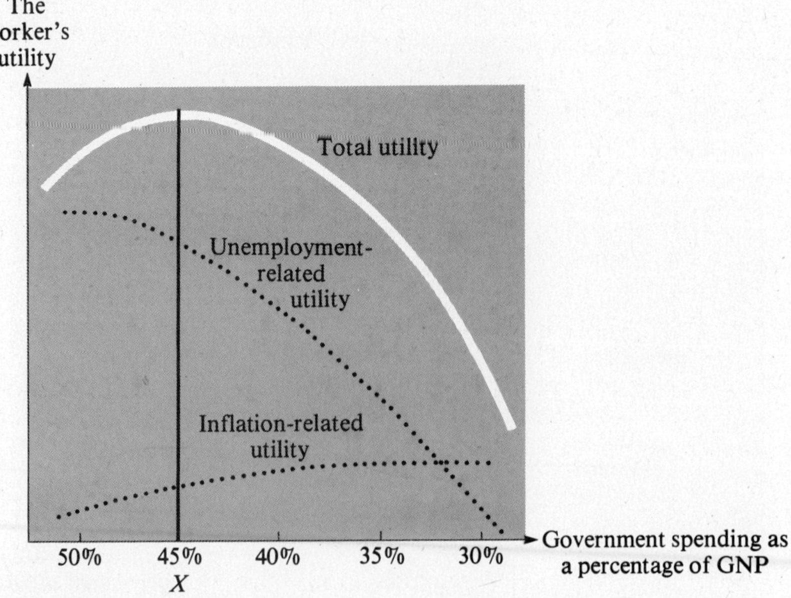

Figure 5.4 The factory worker's total utility as a function of government spending.

cline in government spending. By contrast, unemployment-derived utility falls very rapidly. Her utility over the instrumental issue of government spending, the sum of the inflation- and unemployment-derived utility curves, reaches a maximum at *X* (45 percent), which is to the left of *Y*. So the worker prefers more government spending than does the baker.

Finally, consider a retired citizen who derives income entirely from savings and a fixed pension. While disliking unemployment, the pensioner's concern about it seems slight relative to his concern for inflation. Figure 5.5 thus shows the pensioner's inflation-derived utility rising very rapidly with a decline in government spending. But, his unemployment-derived utility rises very slowly with an increase in government spending. The pensioner's utility over the instrumental issue of government spending reaches a maximum at *Z* (25 percent), which is to the right of *X* and *Y*. So the pensioner prefers less government spending than does the baker or the factory worker.

Reiteration: public policy, ideology, and collective action. Figure 5.6 brings together the utility curves of the baker, the worker, and the pensioner.[5] Government spending today, as Figure 1.1 indicates, is actually at

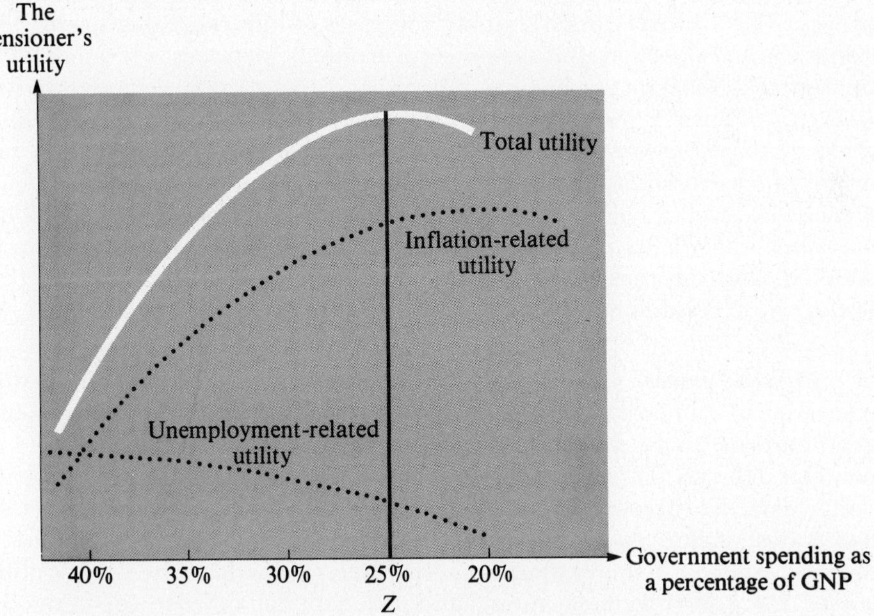

Figure 5.5 The pensioner's total utility as a function of government spending.

[5] Placing all three utility curves on the same graph is not an interpersonal comparison of utilities. Figure 5.6 only implies that one can compare each citizen's most-preferred position with those of others and that citizens lose utility as the public policy moves, to the left or to the right, away from their most-preferred positions.

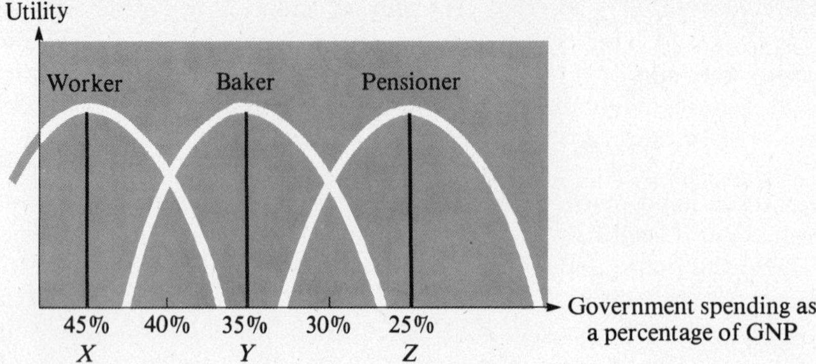

Figure 5.6 Utility curves for the baker, the factory worker, and the pensioner as a function of government spending.

about 35 percent of GNP, which is the baker's most-preferred position. Suppose that the members of Congress vote, through various measures, to increase government spending to 40 percent and that the president approves. The factory worker's utility increases, while the baker's and pensioner's utilities decline. But suppose government spending is reduced to 30 percent of GNP. The pensioner's utility now increases, while the baker's and worker's utilities decline. Clearly, changes in government spending must affect all three persons, and there is no way to change government spending in the range from 25 to 45 percent without harming at least one of them.[6] Hence, the level of government spending is a collective good: a public policy over which people have a utility; an issue for which only one position can be adopted; and the cause of conditions that all must consume whether they prefer those conditions or not.

Multiple issues. Citizens usually evaluate public policy on more than one issue or dimension. Extending the previous example, we might find another issue to be the percentage of government spending devoted to national defense. To incorporate this new issue into a graphic representation, we need a three-dimensional figure of a total utility curve. Suppose the baker most prefers that 40 percent of government spending be for national defense. Figure 5.7 shows what happens when we combine the baker's utility curves for government spending and for national defense spending: his utility curve becomes an upside-down bowl-shaped figure. Of course, while we cannot draw in more than three dimensions, it is possible to represent a citizen's utility for any number of issue dimensions mathematically.

---

[6] If government spending is more than 45 percent or less than 25 percent, a move toward *X* or *Z*, respectively, increases everyone's utility. Also notice that the Pareto optimal set of public policies falls between *X* and *Z*, including these points.

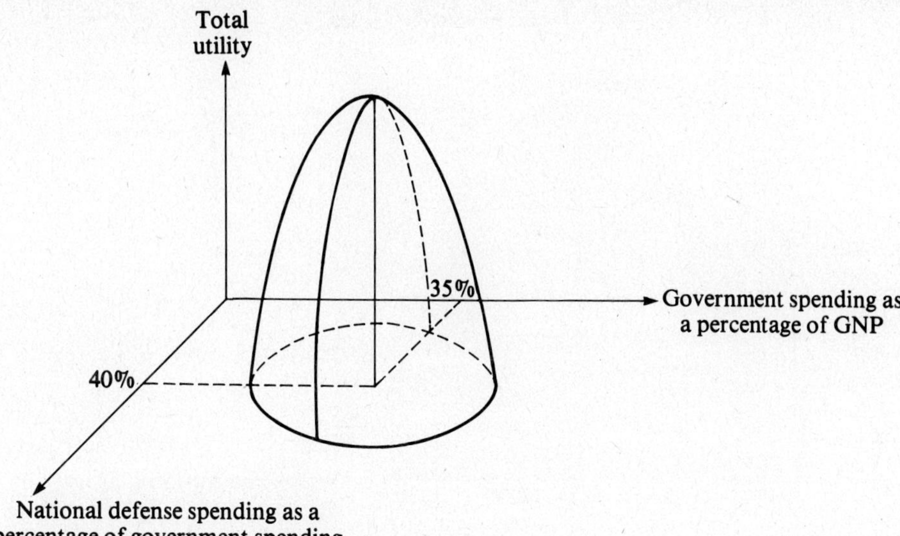

Figure 5.7 The baker's utility as a function of government spending and national defense spending.

CITIZENS' EVALUATIONS OF CANDIDATES

These graphic representations depict a citizen's utility for various positions on a set of complex instrumental issues. They also help to illustrate how citizens evaluate candidates' public policy issue positions. In Chapters 7 and 8, the same representations aid in describing candidates' election campaign decision making.

Public Policy Proposals

To illustrate citizens' evaluations of candidates, consider again the factory worker, who most prefers government spending at 45 percent of GNP. Suppose in an election campaign a Democratic candidate (*d*) proposes to increase spending from 35 to 40 percent, while the Republican candidate (*r*) proposes to diminish it to 30. Figure 5.8 reproduces the worker's utility curve from Figure 5.4. Her most-preferred position is shown at *X* (45), the Democrat's position at *d* (40), and the Republican's at *r* (30). To find the worker's utility for *d*, we draw a vertical line from *d* to a point on the utility curve and a horizontal line from that point to the vertical axis, which measures utility. There, U_d indicates the worker's utility for the Democratic candidate's position. The worker's utility for the Republican candidate's position, U_r, is similarly located. The worker associates a higher utility with the Democrat's issue position than with the Republican's.

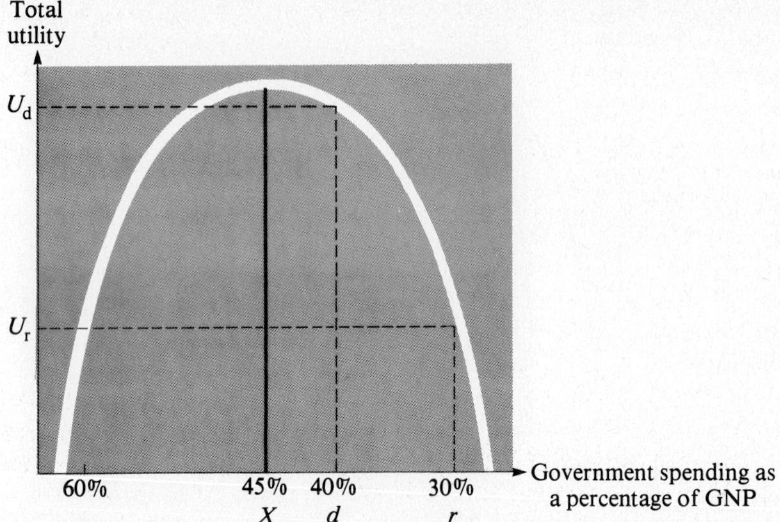

Figure 5.8 The factory worker's utility for Republican and Democratic candidates on the government spending issue.

Varying policy positions. Suppose that the Republican increases his spending proposal to 35 percent. This would raise the worker's utility for the Republican. Alternatively, if r goes to 35 but d goes to 55, then the worker would get as much utility from the Republican as from the Democrat.

To capture the *difference* in utility a citizen gets from the two candidates' positions, suppose that U_d is greater than U_r. The utility difference can be expressed with the letter B, so that $B = U_d - U_r$. Suppose the worker perceives r to be at 30 and d at 40.[7] As d increases from 40 to 45 (holding r constant), B increases. As d increases from 45 to 60, B declines and eventually equals zero when d reaches 60. If d exceeds 60, B becomes $B = U_r - U_d$, because the worker gets more utility from the Republican's position than from the Democrat's.

Varying salience. Complex elections involve more than one issue, and a citizen might weight issues differently. That is, certain issues might be more salient for the citizen than are other issues. A simple example helps to explain **issue salience.** Suppose a firm manufactures computers, which it

[7] These numbers represent the worker's *perception* of the candidates' positions. Sometimes candidates fail to take an actual position on an issue; at other times, they purposely vary their positions, telling different audiences what each wants to hear. Citizens might therefore see candidates' positions as forming lotteries over issue dimensions. These lotteries are too complicated to describe completely in an introductory text, although Chapter 7 shows how the use of such lotteries helps candidates to get elected.

sells to the Department of Health and Human Services (HHS) and to the Department of Defense (DOD). Say the firm sells twice as many computers to HHS than are sold to DOD. Assume that a change in each department's budget would be reflected by an identical change in the department's demand for computers. A 15 percent decline in DOD's budget, then, would diminish the number of computers the manufacturer sells to DOD by 15 percent. Under these assumptions, HHS's budget—welfare spending—would be twice as salient an issue for the firm's management as DOD's budget—defense spending—would be, because a one-percent decline in HHS's budget would affect the firm's revenues twice as much as would a one-percent decline in DOD's budget.

An increase in a citizen's salience for an issue is usually illustrated by making his or her utility curve on that issue steeper. To show what happens to *B* if salience changes, consider the factory worker's utility curve, *U*, for the government spending issue, as reproduced in Figure 5.9, and a new, steeper utility curve, U', reflecting a higher level of salience. With *d* at 40 and *r* at 30, an increase of salience lowers her utility for the Democrat from U_d to U'_d, and for the Republican from U_r to U'_r. But *B* increases from $B = U_d - U_r$ to $B' = U'_d - U'_r$. B' is greater than *B*, even though the worker's utility for each candidate has declined with the increase in salience. Depending on the shape of the utility curve, a salience increase usually makes *B* larger by accentuating the utility differences the citizen experiences from the candidates' positions. Put differently, clashing expenditure proposals by two candidates for village dogcatcher might seem largely irrelevant unless your dog

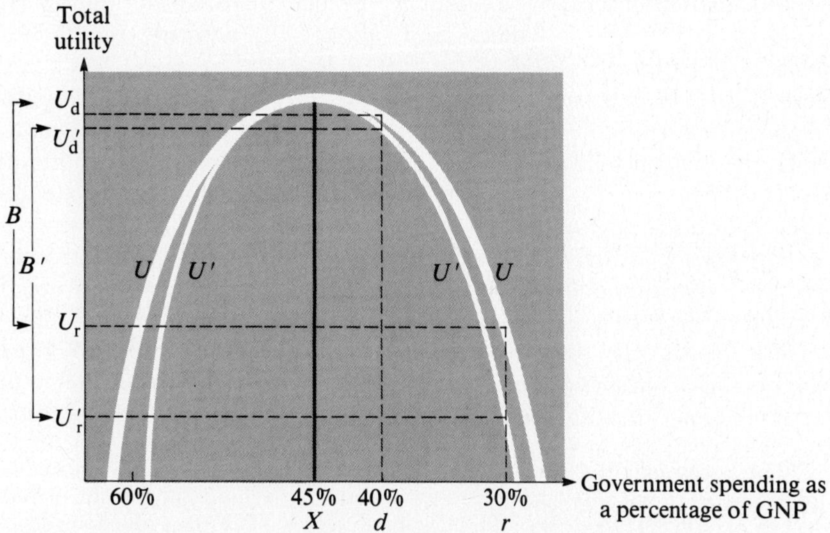

Figure 5.9 The factory worker's utility for Republican and Democratic candidates on the government spending issue: two salience patterns.

often ends up in the city pound. As Chapter 7 notes, the manipulation of issue salience represents an extremely important election strategy for candidates.

Candidate Characteristics

The preceding discussion shows how citizens might move from preferences on instrumental public policy issues to evaluations of different candidates' positions on those issues, and therefore to evaluations of the candidates themselves. However, the traditional view is that citizens seldom vote on campaign issues. They are not pictured as listening to the candidates' advocacy of issue positions, reflecting on those positions, and casting an informed vote. By contrast, they are said to judge candidates by their physical appearance, race, religion, gender, marital status, speaking ability, party identification, and media image.

For example, consider Figure 5.10, which charts citizens' perceptions of the 1960 Democratic presidential nominee, John F. Kennedy. Attitudes toward Kennedy seemed to be a function of the respondents' party identification and religion. As party identification moved from *strong Republican* to *strong Democrat,* the average perception of Kennedy became more favorable.[8] Similarly, as religion moved from *strong Protestant* to *strong Catholic,* perceptions of Kennedy again became more favorable.

Another study of the 1960 presidential election revealed that voting was strongly associated with these partisan and religious attitudes. As Figures 5.11a and 5.11b show, in 1956 the Democratic candidate, Adlai E. Stevenson, Jr., a Protestant, received about 88 percent of the vote among *strong Democrat–strong Protestant* voters and about 72 percent among *strong Democrat–strong Catholic* voters. Kennedy, a Catholic, received less than 75 percent from *strong Democrat–strong Protestants* in 1960 but almost 95 percent from *strong Democrat–strong Catholics.* In 1956, Stevenson received almost no votes from *strong Republican–strong Catholic* voters, while in 1960 Kennedy received more than 25 percent of their votes. In sum, candidate party identification and religion are strongly correlated with citizens' voting decisions. Some scholars therefore conclude that, compared to candidate characteristics, the instrumental public policy issues of a campaign seem not very important to voters.

This is an overly narrow view of issues and policies, however, because candidate characteristics *are* campaign issues. For instance, in the 1960 presidential election, a Catholic citizen might have reasoned that the traditional

[8] The assessment of a person's party identification, as well as the strength of that identification, were self-reported. Hence, a person is a "strong Republican" if he says he is. The data come from the 1960 National Election Study of the University of Michigan's Center for Political Studies as computed and reported in Donald E. Stokes, "Some Dynamic Elements of Contests for the Presidency," *American Political Science Review,* 60 (March 1966), p. 24.

exclusion of Catholics from the presidency was unjust and that Catholic children should have the opportunity to grow up to be president. On the other hand, a Protestant citizen might have reasoned that a Catholic presi-

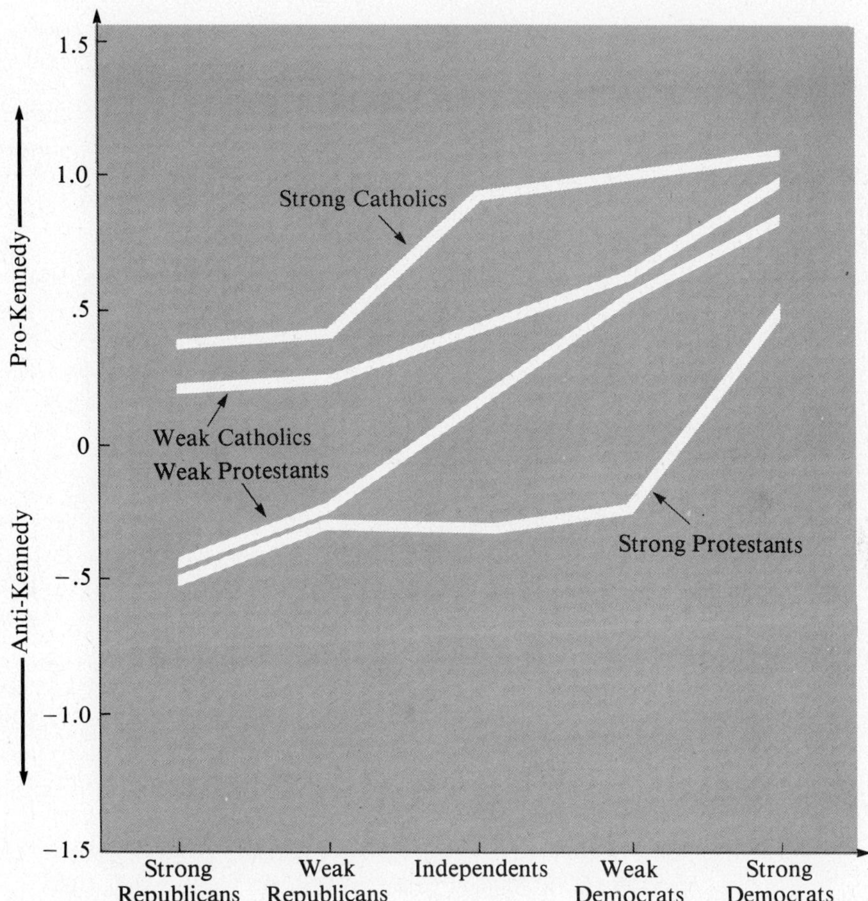

Figure 5.10 Influence of party and religious identifications on perceptions of Kennedy, 1960.

Source: Donald E. Stokes, "Some Dynamic Elements of Contests for the Presidency," *American Political Science Review,* 60 (March 1966), p. 24.

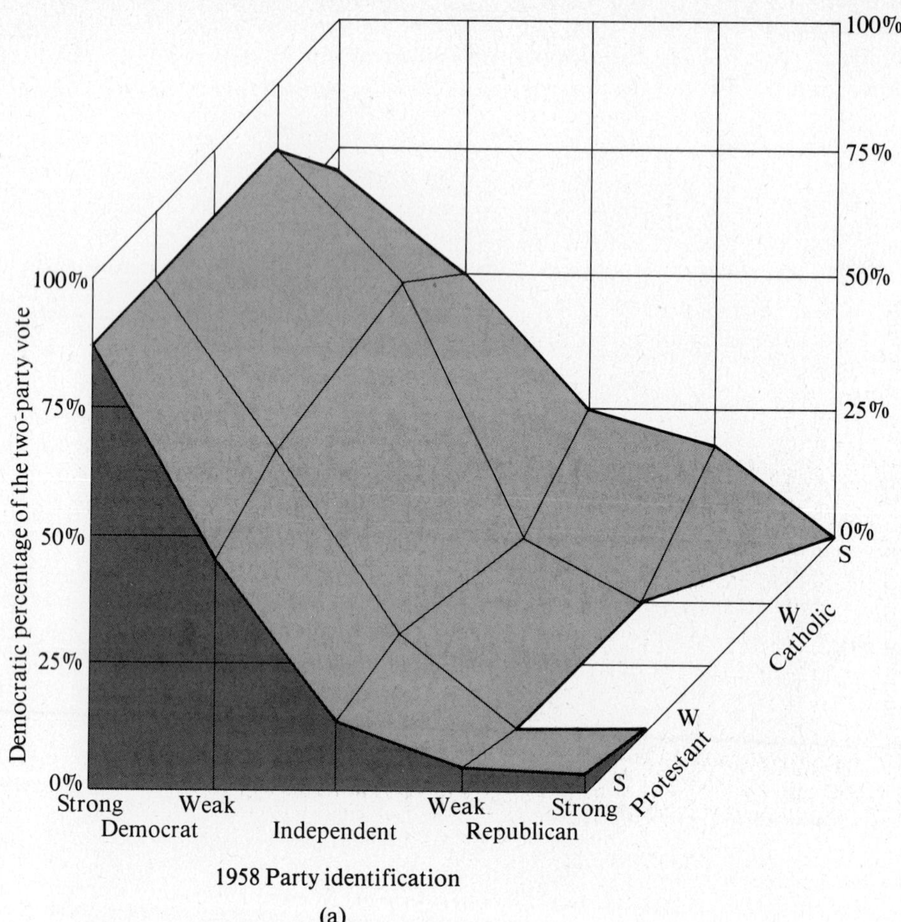

Figure 5.11 (a) 1956 presidential vote by party identification (1958) and by religious identification (1960). (b) 1960 [p. 185] presidential vote by party identification (1958) and by religious identification (1960).

Source: Philip E. Converse, "Religion and Politics: The 1960 Election," in Angus Campbell, Philip E. Converse, Warren E. Miller, and Donald E. Stokes, eds., *Elections and the Political Order* (New York: Wiley, 1966), pp. 102–103.

dent would represent a danger if United States "interests" collided with Vatican "interests," leaving the president with divided loyalties. One need not agree with or condone either view to see that a candidate's religion is a campaign issue. In a like manner, a candidate's race and sex can also become campaign issues.

These characteristics get to be issues in three ways. First, they become symbolic issues, representing subjectively desirable or undesirable changes

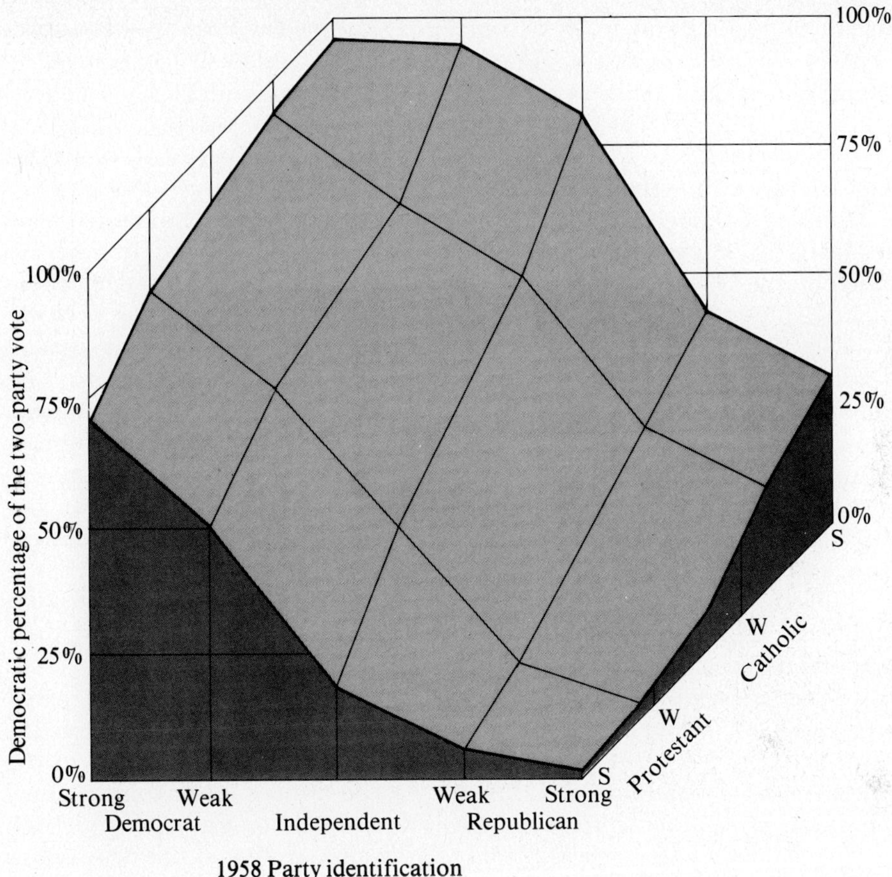

(b)

from the status quo. For example, the first black mayor or representative elected in an area holds great symbolic value for both blacks and whites. Of course, repetitions of black electoral success tend to reduce the salience of such symbolic issues. The Catholicism issue, to draw a parallel, is now relatively unimportant in presidential elections. In the next century, the same initial high salience, followed by less concern, will probably accompany the first major female, black, and Jewish presidential candidates and then presidents.

Second, personal characteristics, considered as issues, measure the citizen's perception of the candidates' abilities to carry out the duties of office. Chapter 2 discusses Gore Vidal's play *The Best Man,* which speaks directly to this problem. In the matter of candidates' personal characteristics, even the most open-minded voter comes up against some hard questions. For example, are covert homosexuals a security risk in government because someone might try to blackmail them? Do officeholders with records of psychiatric consultations represent a threat to good government because they might become psychotic at the worst possible time? Can poorly controlled alcoholics serve as fair and consistent judges of complex legislation? Do several divorces, remarriages, or extramarital affairs indicate an undesirable instability in a public official?

These questions are not hypothetical. The recent personal, family, or legal problems of Representatives Wilbur Mills (D-Arkansas), Wayne Hays (D-Ohio), and Daniel Flood (D-Pennsylvania) and Senators Thomas Eagleton (D-Missouri), Herman Talmadge (D-Georgia), and Edward Brooke (R-Massachusetts) make one sensitive to questions about personal qualifications to serve in public office. Some might continue to believe that personal characteristics and histories are "improper" matters for campaign discussions and that candidates should not strategically invoke the peccadilloes of their opponents. Yet, candidates would not use this strategy if citizens did not respond to it favorably. Therefore, the responsibility for the use of "improper" campaign strategies lies at least partially with citizens rather than entirely with candidates, just as the responsibility for the production of gas-guzzling automobiles lies at least partially with consumers rather than entirely with General Motors, Ford, and Chrysler.

Third, candidate characteristics become issues because citizens use candidates' group memberships as surrogates for information about their positions on other issues. For instance, on the issue of states' rights versus civil rights, most people do not expect black candidates to favor the states' rights position. White state officials invoked the states' rights position for many years while closing the door on black political participation. On the issue of federal funding of abortions, we can expect more congressional opposition from Catholic representatives than from non-Catholics, although the correlation between religion and congressional voting on this issue seems far from perfect.[9]

In sum, candidate characteristics *are* issues on which citizens have most-preferred positions and over which they have utility curves. Since only one person can hold a particular office at a particular time, the officeholder's characteristics also become collective goods. To put the matter differently and quite extremely, whether or not the occupant of the White House for the next four years is an avowed lesbian or perhaps an escapee from Jim Jones's People's Temple *is* a matter of collective goods and of public policy, whether one likes it or not. Those who fail to regard candidate characteristics as *real* campaign issues—issues of collective goods, ideology, and public policy—probably do not *wish* to regard these characteristics as *legitimate* issues. They believe that such matters should not be campaign issues. While this antipathy might be an acceptable ethical position, we cannot scientifically

[9] In 1977, a year with a substantial number of House votes on abortion questions, "79 out of 118 catholics [in the House] stuck with a strict anti-abortion position, while 26 took a consistently pro-choice view." Yet Robert F. Drinan, a Jesuit priest who left Congress in obedience to a Vatican order in 1980, most often voted with the pro-choice bloc. *Congressional Quarterly Weekly Report*, 36 (February 4, 1978), p. 259.

judge the validity of human goals, and therefore we cannot exile citizens who use candidate characteristics to make their voting decisions.

The Special Problem of Party Identification

The challenge of determinism. During the 1940s and 1950s, when political polling came into common use, citizens' ideologies and public policy preferences appeared to have little effect on how they voted. Many analysts believed that group membership rather than the candidates' issue positions provided the central force in voting. As one scholar noted of voting studies conducted during the 1940s and 1950s,

> the new analyses of electoral behavior . . . . can be added up to a conception of voting not as a civic decision but as an almost purely deterministic act. Given knowledge of certain characteristics of a voter—his occupation, his residence, his religion, his national origin, and perhaps certain of his attitudes—one can predict with a high probability the direction of his vote. The actions of persons are made to appear to be only predictable and automatic responses to campaign stimuli.[10]

This view stands in sharp contrast to the notion that issues somehow matter in how citizens evaluate candidates. Although most political scientists today reject this view as too crude, nevertheless the common understanding of elections remains covered with the residue of **determinism.**

The transmission of party identification. The sources of party identification and its influence on voting provide substantial evidence for the deterministic view of voting. The argument begins with the proposition that children learn their party identification from their parents. This learning occurs in much the same way that children learn religious values, cultural identification, ethical precepts, and tastes for clothes, foods, and friends.

Statistical evidence strongly suggests that children do learn from their parents to prefer one political party over another. An extensive survey completed in 1965 asked the party identification of 1669 high-school seniors and their parents. Table 5.1 shows the results. While the relationship found in this table is not perfect, it is evident that the association between parents' and child's party identification is quite strong.[11]

Party identification and voting. Having learned party identification from their parents, the deterministic argument continues, citizens receive

[10] V. O. Key, Jr. (with the assistance of Milton C. Cummings, Jr.), *The Responsible Electorate* (New York: Vintage, 1966), pp. 4–5.

[11] For an account of the acquisition of political beliefs, see M. Kent Jennings and Richard G. Niemi, *The Political Character of Adolescence* (Princeton, N. J.: Princeton University Press, 1974). This thorough study details and analyzes the 1965 survey.

the stimulus of a candidate's party label and vote accordingly. Table 5.2 shows the relationship between party identification and the percentage vote for major presidential candidates from 1952 to 1980. Again, the statistical relationship is strong. Indeed, it is one of the strongest associations known in political analysis.

Table 5.1 Student-Parent Party Identification

	Students		
	Democrat	**Independent**	**Republican**
Parents			
Democrat	66.0%	26.7%	7.3%
Independent	29.4	53.4	17.2
Republican	12.7	36.3	50.9

Source: M. Kent Jennings and Richard G. Niemi, "The Transmission of Political Values from Parent to Child," *American Political Science Review,* 62 (March 1968), p. 173. Table 5.1 collapses the party identification categories Jennings and Niemi use.

Table 5.2 Relationship Between Party Identification and Presidential Vote, 1952–1980

		Voters		
Year	**Candidates**	**Democrats**	**Independents**	**Republicans**
1952	Stevenson (D)	77%	35%	8%
	Eisenhower (R)	23	65	92
1956	Stevenson (D)	85	30	4
	Eisenhower (R)	15	70	96
1960	Kennedy (D)	84	43	5
	Nixon (R)	16	57	95
1964	Johnson (D)	87	56	20
	Goldwater (R)	13	44	80
1968	Humphrey (D)	74	31	9
	Nixon (R)	12	44	86
	Wallace (AIP)	14	25	5
1972	McGovern (D)	67	31	5
	Nixon (R)	33	69	95
1976	Carter (D)	82	38	9
	Ford (R)	18	57	91
1980	Carter (D)	69	29	8
	Reagan (R)	26	55	86
	Anderson (I)	4	14	5

Source: *The Gallup Opinion Index,* December 1976, pp. 16–17. Data for 1980 were supplied by the Gallup organization from post-election analysis of votes by demographic breakdown. Entries may not add to 100% because voting for most minor-party candidates is not included.

To sum up, with some exaggeration, the deterministic view of voting holds that people learn their political values, including their party identification, from their parents in much the same way that rats learn how to pass through a maze. After their parents program them politically, citizens respond in subsequent elections by tending to vote for the candidate whose party identification is the same as their own. There are many variants of this deterministic view, and the account offered here oversimplifies it considerably. Sometimes, race, religion, and social class seem to intervene in the voting decision, yet the deterministic view is essentially as stated.

Social determinism, rational choice, and party identification. The deterministic view of voting may seem plausible, but one study of polling data shows that an adherence to parents' party identification is rational, as is voting along party lines.[12] This study begins by supposing that the two major political parties differ on public policy matters and that there is some sensible basis for members of different groups to prefer one party over the other. Then the study presents a statistical model to predict what someone's party identification ought to be, based on such personal characteristics as income, race, and job status. Next it compares each person's predicted party identification and the actual party identification of each person's father. The purpose of this comparison is to develop a measure of *intergenerational strain.* As a rational choice perspective would predict, and as Figure 5.12 shows, the percentage of persons defecting from their father's party identification increases with intergenerational strain.

The analysis then turns to the father's party identification. Fathers may prefer one party to another for highly idiosyncratic but nevertheless rational reasons. Some of these fathers will deviate from the expected party identification, as predicted by the statistical model. However, their idiosyncratic reasons for deviant party identification may be difficult to pass along to their children, especially to those children with high educational levels and therefore independent information about political issues. Thus, the highest defection rates from paternal party identification should be among those with high education whose fathers' party identifications are statistically deviant. The lowest defection rates should be among those with high education and normal paternal party identification. As Table 5.3 shows, both predictions hold true.

Further thoughts on party identification. Party identification is like a brand name, which gives buyers—voters—information at little cost. Getting information, either about candidates or about ordinary market goods, is always costly. (Chapter 11 describes how government regulation of market products sometimes stems from a desire to provide information about these

[12] Arthur S. Goldberg, "Social Determinism and Rationality as Bases of Party Identification." *American Political Science Review,* 63 (March 1969), pp. 5–25.

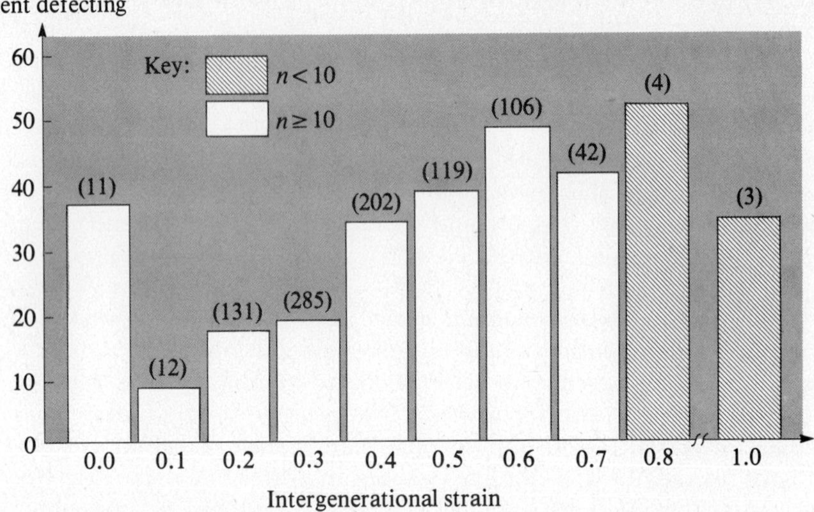

Figure 5.12 Defection from paternal party identification as a function of intergenerational strain.

Source: Arthur S. Goldberg, "Social Determinism and Rationality as Bases of Party Identification," *American Political Science Review,* 63 (March 1969) p. 9.

Table 5.3 Defection as a Function of Education and Paternal Party Identification Deviance

	Percent Defecting	
	Education	
Paternal Party Identification	High	Low
Deviant	50.0	37.9
Normal	19.7	26.2

Source: Arthur S. Goldberg, "Social Determinism and Rationality as Bases of Party Identification," *American Political Science Review,* 63 (March 1969), p. 14.

products at little cost to the consumer.) A brand name lowers information costs. Naturally, sellers might use a prestigious brand name to sell shoddy merchandise, but people usually learn quickly that the brand name now labels inferior goods.

Like a brand name, party identification reduces the citizen's cost of getting political information. That candidates are New York City Democrats or Arizona Republicans conveys so much information about their issue positions that further investments in acquiring additional information may seem unnecessary. Candidates from the same party may advocate different issue positions, and estimates of candidates' positions based on party identification also might be entirely mistaken. But the use of information surrogates such as party identification is no less rational, since the cost of getting more information may not be worth the added benefits of improved accuracy in decision making.

Knowledge and attitudes derived from parents, whether about politics or about other matters, also are useful as surrogates for independently collected information. The determinist argument holds that parents program the party identification of their children, who then respond accordingly. But learning from one's parents may be efficient. Children whose parents warn them about hot stoves, upon touching hot stoves learn not only to avoid them, but also to trust their parents' judgments on other matters. Thus, children need not learn everything from experience. The result is an incredible economy of information and learning costs.

Group Membership and Citizen Preferences

Public policies affect members of different groups differently, and therefore the members of different groups will not react in the same way to all parties and candidates. (Chapter 6 examines various forms of group participation in politics, so here we discuss group membership only as it affects voting.) Sociologists divide groups into three categories. Families and small churches are examples of **primary groups,** and we have just examined the effects of family membership on voting. Labor and professional organizations and large clubs are examples of **secondary groups.** Those people of a common age, sex, race, or income belong to **classificatory groups.** Secondary- and classificatory-group memberships are strongly associated with party identification and therefore with voting.

Secondary groups: the example of labor. The statistical importance of secondary-group membership in the voting decision is nowhere as well and as consistently documented as in the case of labor unions. Figure 5.13 shows that in all of the presidential elections between 1952 and 1980, support of the Democratic nominee by labor union members and their families exceeded that of the general population. This support is neither deterministic nor programmed, for labor-union members are no less rational than other voters. Union leaders perceive Democratic officeholders to be more favorable toward them and Republicans to be less so. AFL-CIO ratings of representatives and senators consistently show Democrats to be more pro-labor than Republicans. Democratic leaders are consistently less in favor of increasing government regulation of labor unions than are Republicans.[13]

---

[13] Herbert McClosky, Paul J. Hoffman, and Rosemary O'Hara, "Issue Conflict and Consensus Among Party Leaders and Followers," *American Political Science Review,* 54 (June 1960), p. 406, *passim.*

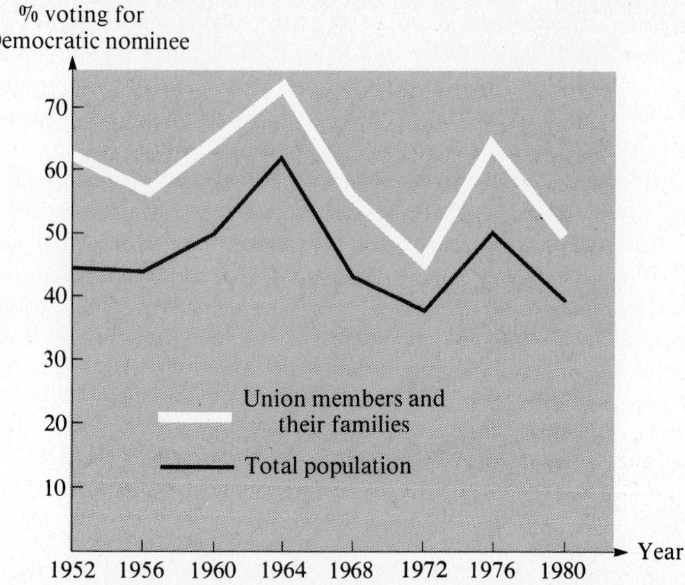

Figure 5.13 Percent of union family members and of entire voting population casting ballots for the Democratic presidential nominee, 1952–1980.

Source: Compiled from *The Gallup Opinion Index,* December 1976, pp. 16–17. Data for 1980 were supplied by the Gallup organization from post-election analysis of votes by demographic breakdown.

A 1966 survey elaborates on the same theme.[14] State AFL-CIO leaders were asked to rate their state Democratic and Republican parties' attitudes toward organized labor. As noted in Table 5.4, 62.9 percent of these labor leaders perceived their state's Democratic party as pro-labor, but only 7.7 percent perceived their state's Republican party as pro-labor. Conversely, the proportions of perceived anti-labor sentiments are 12.9 percent for the state Democratic party and 62.8 percent for the state Republican party. Not surprisingly, 69.2 percent of these labor leaders report themselves to be Democrats, 21.8 percent independents, and 3.8 percent Republicans.

Substantial reasons underlie these generalized pro-Democratic perceptions and sentiments among union leaders and members. Democrats in Congress were instrumental in enacting the Norris-LaGuardia Act (1927) and the Wagner (National Labor Relations) Act (1935), both of which gave substantial aid to union organizing activity. By contrast, Republicans were instrumental in enacting the Taft-Hartley Act (1947) and the Landrum-Griffin Act (1959), which were aimed at weeding out alleged communism and corruption in unions. The Taft-Hartley Act also provided for injunc-

[14] Data compiled by Peter H. Aranson and Melvin A. Kahn; unpublished but available from the authors.

Table 5.4 State AFL-CIO Labor Leaders' Perceptions of State Democratic and Republican Party Attitudes Toward Labor Unions, 1966

	State Democrats		*State Republicans*	
	N	**Percent**	***N***	**Percent**
Pro-labor	49	62.9	6	7.7
Neutral	18	23.1	21	26.9
Anti-labor	10	12.9	49	62.8
No Answer	1	1.3	2	2.6

tions lasting eighty days against certain strikes and gave state legislatures the right to outlaw compulsory union membership. Union leaders understandably viewed such acts as anti-union. More recently, a 1978 filibuster against a bill making it easier to organize unions was supported in the Senate by 68 percent of the Republicans voting but only 33 percent of the Democrats.

Classificatory groups: income and race. A clear association exists between race and income on the one hand and differences in party identification and voting patterns on the other. Blacks vote Democratic consistently more often than do whites, and citizens' incomes are negatively associated with the likelihood of their voting for Democrats. Table 5.5 reports both of these tendencies.

Black Democratic affiliation rests on blacks' perceptions of how the parties' historical positions and current proposals would affect them. Black citizens have fewer resources than most white citizens enjoy: black median household income (1977) is $8422, while it is $14,272 for white households; non-white infant death rates (1976) are nearly twice those of whites; life expectancy (1972) is 4.5 years less for nonwhites than for whites; and the

Table 5.5 Party Affiliation, Race, and Income, 1976

	Republicans	**Independents**	**Democrats**
Race			
Black	7%	24%	69%
White	24	33	43
Income			
$20,000 and over	31	34	35
$15,000—$19,999	22	34	44
$10,000—$14,999	19	34	47
$7000—$9999	21	30	49
$5000—$6999	18	31	51
$3000—$4999	20	27	53
Under $3000	16	23	61

Source: *The Gallup Opinion Index,* June 1976, p. 11.

black illiteracy rate (1969) is five times that of whites.[15] Democratic and Republican leaders differ substantially on several issues relating to blacks' political success and short-term economic well-being. A 1960 study of political leaders in the United States reported that of the Democratic leaders, 78.4 percent favored an increase in slum clearance and public housing, while only 40.1 percent of the Republican leaders favored such an increase; 60 percent of Democrats and 22 percent of Republicans favored a Social Security increase; 50 percent of Democrats and 15.5 percent of Republicans favored a minimum wage increase; and 43.8 percent of Democrats and 25.5 percent of Republicans favored an enforcement of integration.[16]

More recent Senate and House voting reflects these patterns. A 1978 Senate vote prohibiting the Department of Health, Education, and Welfare (HEW) "from using funds to enforce race or sex-related goals, quotas or other numerical requirements in [university] hiring and admission policies" was supported by 58 percent of the Republicans voting but only 17 percent of the Democrats.[17] A procedural motion that year to kill a House resolution of impeachment against the outspoken former United States Ambassador to the United Nations, Andrew Young—a black—was opposed by 52 percent of the Republicans voting and 6 percent of the Democrats.

These statistics account for the Democratic party identification of many black citizens. But they also account for the relationship between income and party identification, because the same self-interest that leads black citizens to identify with and vote for Democrats also leads many poor citizens to do so. Of course, not all blacks are poor, and not all poor persons care very much about integration and about outlawing discrimination. Nevertheless, economic issues concerning poverty programs and related legislation coincide with both racial and income divisions. Preferences of poor and black citizens for resource redistributions thus often seem indistinguishable. However, this pattern might change as more and more black workers begin to earn higher incomes.

Retrospective Voting

The preceding discussion offers two concepts of how citizens form opinions about candidates' issue positions. The first concept describes citizens as finding out directly where the candidates stand on each issue and then evaluating the candidates according to those directly observed issue positions. The second concept acknowledges that citizens' acquisition of

---

[15] U.S. Bureau of the Census, *Statistical Abstract of the United States: 1978,* 99th edition (Washington, D. C.: Government Printing Office, 1978).

[16] McClosky et al., "Issue Conflict and Consensus Among Party Leaders and Followers." However, recall from Chapter 1, footnote 19, that minimum wage increases adversely affect employment among minority adolescents.

[17] *Congressional Quarterly Weekly Report,* 35 (June 2, 1977), p. 1391.

information is costly. Therefore, they try to find more economical methods to learn where the candidates stand—for example, they use party identification as a surrogate for information about other attributes of the candidates, including their issue positions. The use of such information-cost-reducing devices is an important aspect of rational choice and not evidence of deterministic voting.

However, there is a certain illogic to the use of party identification as a surrogate for direct information about the candidates' issue position. First, candidates who are disadvantaged by party identification should spend resources to educate citizens about their real positions on issues. Second, and perhaps more to the point, would-be candidates should only seek nomination by the majority party. (This occurs to some extent, but is held in check by the enhanced competition for majority-party nominations.) Third, a citizen's loyalty to party identification or to a favored incumbent, along with a diminished regard for present policy positions, must rest on his or her assessment of the party or candidate's *past* record in office; a voting decision based on such an assessment is called **retrospective voting.**[18] But why should voters ignore present promises about future policies when they can often gain information about those policies and when the real test they might apply to candidates is, "What have you done for me lately?" or "What will you do for me tomorrow?"

Despite these three objections, retrospective voting is fully consistent with rational choice. First, information about candidates' positions remains costly, and for some citizens this cost may be enough to limit the amount of political information they gather. Party identification thus continues to stand as a useful and economical surrogate for information. Citizens associate the quality of their lives with the decisions of the party in office and then vote accordingly. Second, as Chapter 7 points out, candidates often intentionally

---

[18] On retrospective voting generally, see V. O. Key, Jr., *Politics, Parties & Pressure Groups* (New York: Crowell, 1964), p. 568. The phenomenon has been studied most thoroughly in Morris P. Fiorina, "An Outline for a Model of Party Choice," *American Journal of Political Science,* 21 (August 1977), pp. 601-625; Fiorina, "Economic Retrospective Voting in American Elections: A Micro-Analysis," *American Journal of Political Science,* 22 (May 1978), pp. 426–443; and Fiorina, "Short- and Long-Term Effects of Economic Conditions on Individual Voting Decisions," in Douglas Hibbs and Heino Fassbender, eds., *Contemporary Political Economy* (Amsterdam: North Holland, forthcoming). In these works, Fiorina links the retrospective voting phenomenon to changing economic conditions. On this subject see also Francisco Arcelus and Allan H. Meltzer, "The Effect of Aggregate Economic Variables on Congressional Elections," Howard S. Bloom and H. Douglas Price, "Voter Responses to Short-Run Economic Conditions: The Asymmetric Effect of Prosperity and Inflation," Saul Goodman and Gerald H. Kramer, "Comment on Arcelus and Meltzer," and Arcelus and Meltzer, "Rejoinder," all in *American Political Science Review,* 69 (December 1975), pp. 1232–1269. See also Kramer, "Short-Run Fluctuations in U. S. Voting Behavior, 1896–1964," *American Political Science Review,* 65 (March 1971), pp. 131–143, and George J. Stigler, "General Economic Conditions and National Elections," *American Economic Review, Papers and Proceedings,* 63 (May 1973), pp. 160–167.

mask their real public policy intentions. Citizens' use of party identification based on past performance is a rational response to this ambiguity that candidates often try to generate.

Third, voters face two problems of uncertainty when assessing candidates' positions. One kind of uncertainty is exactly the same as that described in game theory. A voter could try to catalogue all of the decisions elected officeholders might face until the next election. These decisions could involve the most complex trade-offs, and the voter could try to list the potentially infinite number of these trade-offs and what each opposing candidate would do in each situation. Since the candidates themselves could not possibly generate issue positions to match each imaginable contingency, the voter's only recourse is to assess how candidates and their parties have performed in the past. This retrospective assessment would rationally fill in the gaps in the voter's knowledge about precisely those issues on which the candidate has not taken—and perhaps could not take—a position.

Another kind of uncertainty voters face is deeper than the uncertainty just described. In the preceding case of a game-theoretic form of uncertainty, we assumed the citizen to be capable of listing every *possible* strategy set—potential public policies—a candidate might choose from once in office. These strategy sets made up the possible states of nature for the citizen's own voting decision. But the citizen found it impossible to assign probabilities to these states of nature because he did not know, even probabilistically, the exact policy each candidate would choose.

Sometimes, however, citizens cannot even specify a set of potential public policies (states of nature) because their ability to predict the future is limited. This second kind of uncertainty represents a total lack of knowledge about some aspects of the future. For example, who could have predicted in 1960 that President John F. Kennedy would face the Bay of Pigs debacle in Cuba, or later the Cuban missile crisis? Most Americans, for another example, had never heard of an ayatollah when Jimmy Carter first ran for the presidency in 1976. The seemingly paradoxical property of this kind of uncertainty is that voters appear to know about the future that they cannot know everything about the future. A healthy regard by citizens for the predictive power of past performance is therefore rationally reflected in retrospective voting.

Chapter 7 provides a full consideration of candidates' strategic decisions in elections. However, it should be apparent that candidates respond to the expectation that citizens will vote retrospectively. For example, during the 1980 presidential campaign, Ronald Reagan concentrated almost exclusively on the Carter administration's record in office. He referred constantly to the high rates of inflation and unemployment that prevailed during his opponent's term in office. He catalogued the list of perceived foreign policy failures of the Carter administration, and he consistently asked voters to compare their well-being and expectations from four years earlier with those at the time of the campaign. Reagan's message was clear: voters could expect the problems of the preceding four years to intensify and extend indefinitely into the future if they reelected Jimmy Carter.

Retrospective voting was also very much in Jimmy Carter's mind during the campaign. He developed a list of several previous international incidents during which Ronald Reagan had proposed a military solution. Carter called Reagan's views on foreign policy and nuclear non-proliferation "irresponsible," "disturbing," and "dangerous." He obviously implied that Reagan's earlier positions on foreign affairs promised a heightened future probability of American involvement in foreign conflicts and possibly nuclear war itself if Reagan were elected president. Carter also emphasized Reagan's 1960s opposition to Medicare and his long-standing questions about the Social Security system's actuarial soundness. While the 1980 presidential campaign did find occasional mention of each candidate's proposals for the next four years, by and large appeals to retrospective voting were what remained with the citizen.

AGGREGATE REPRESENTATIONS OF CITIZEN PREFERENCES

The preceding discussion illustrates individual citizens' utilities for various packages of collective actions and shows how citizens evaluate candidates and their positions. Now we examine a method for summarizing the individual preferences of an entire electorate.

Theoretical Aggregations

Most preferred positions. Figure 5.6 shows the utility curves for three citizens—a factory worker, a baker, and a pensioner—on the issue of government spending as a percentage of GNP. A citizen's most-preferred position is the issue position that gives him a maximum amount of utility on the issue. The most-preferred position for the worker is *X*, at 45 percent; for the baker, *Y*, at 35; and for the pensioner, *Z*, at 25. Sometimes the citizen's most-preferred position is called his **bliss point,** or simply his preference.

Preference distributions. Table 5.6 helps to show how citizens' bliss points are distributed over an issue dimension. As stated, one citizen, the worker, most prefers 45; a second citizen most prefers 35; and a third, 25. Put differently, 33⅓ percent of the citizens prefer government spending as a percentage of GNP at 45, 35, and 25 percent, respectively. This information is summarized in Table 5.6 under the entry "Simple Distribution." Figure 5.14 graphs this relationship. The horizontal axis represents the issue dimension or issue space—the various possible positions of bliss points on the issue. The vertical axis represents the proportion of citizens who most prefer each position. The entire figure, which is called a **preference distribution,** shows the location of bliss points.

Table 5.6 Simple Preference Distributions on a Single Issue

Simple Distribution

	Issue Position		
	45%	35%	25%
Number of citizens preferring position	1	1	1
Proportion of citizens preferring position	33⅓%	33⅓%	33⅓%

Unimodal Distribution

	Issue Position						
	50%	45%	40%	35%	30%	25%	20%
Number of citizens preferring position	5	15	30	50	30	15	5
Proportion of citizens preferring position	3⅓%	10%	20%	33⅓%	20%	10%	3⅓%

Bimodal Distribution

	Issue Position						
	50%	45%	40%	35%	30%	25%	20%
Number of citizens preferring position	15	35	20	10	20	35	15
Proportion of citizens preferring position	10%	23⅓%	13⅓%	6⅔	13⅓%	23⅓%	10%

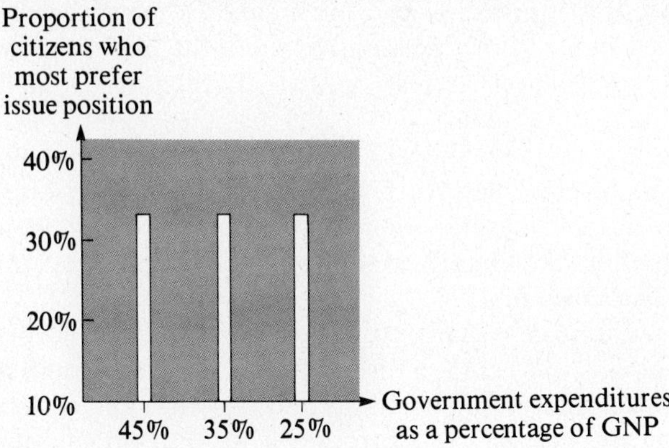

Figure 5.14 Simple preference distribution.

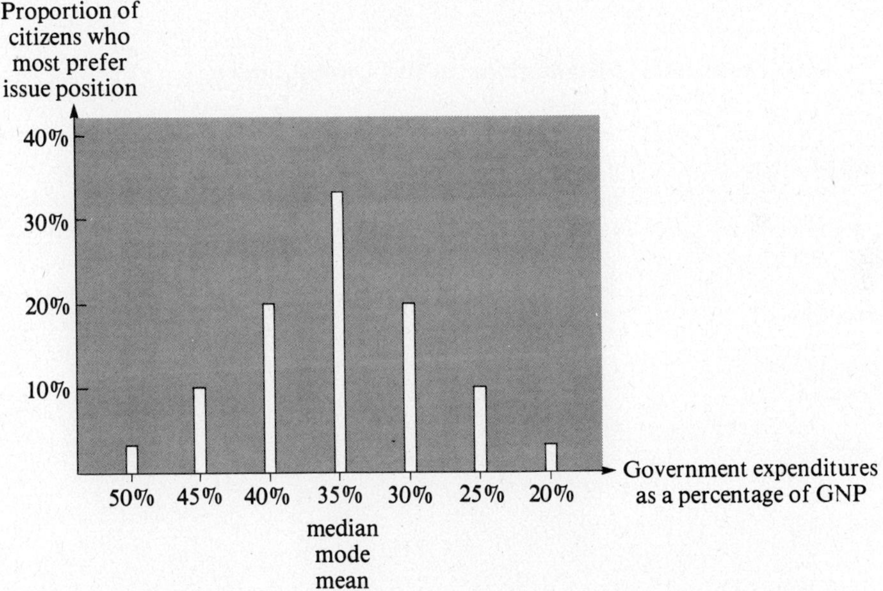

Figure 5.15 Symmetric unimodal preference distribution.

Suppose a more extensive poll on the government spending issue finds that people prefer positions other than 45, 35, and 25 percent. For example, a poll of 150 persons might reveal the data reported in Table 5.6 under the entry "Unimodal Distribution." Figure 5.15 shows this preference distribution. The issue position at 35 percent is the **mode:** more citizens prefer it than prefer positions to either side of it. Because this distribution has only one mode, it is called a **unimodal preference distribution.** The mode is also the **median:** as many citizens prefer positions to the left of 35 as prefer positions to the right of it. Thirty-five is also the **mean:** the "average" preference. The distribution in Figure 5.15 is **symmetric** about the median: there are as many citizens at 40 as at 30, at 45 as at 25, and at 50 as at 20. In sum, the distribution is symmetric and unimodal.

Suppose the poll reveals the data reported in Table 5.6 under the entry "Bimodal Distribution." Figure 5.16 illustrates this distribution. It has the same median and mean as the one in Figure 5.15, and it is also symmetric. But it has two modes, at 45 and at 25, so it is called a symmetric **bimodal preference distribution.**

There are infinitely many issue positions between 50 percent (government spending as a percentage of GNP) and 45, between 45 and 40, and so forth. If there are many issue positions and very many citizens, then instead of using straight vertical bars to represent a proportion of citizens, a smooth curve over the entire issue space can be used as a reasonable approximation. Figures 5.17 and 5.18 illustrate two such idealized curves, corresponding respectively to the symmetric unimodal and symmetric bimodal distributions.

Real Preference Distributions in the United States

Chapters 7 and 8 make extensive use of idealized preference distributions to illustrate some of the fundamental forces that operate in any election. The symmetric unimodal and bimodal preference distributions in political science are analogous to ideal gasses in chemistry and physics. Their useful-

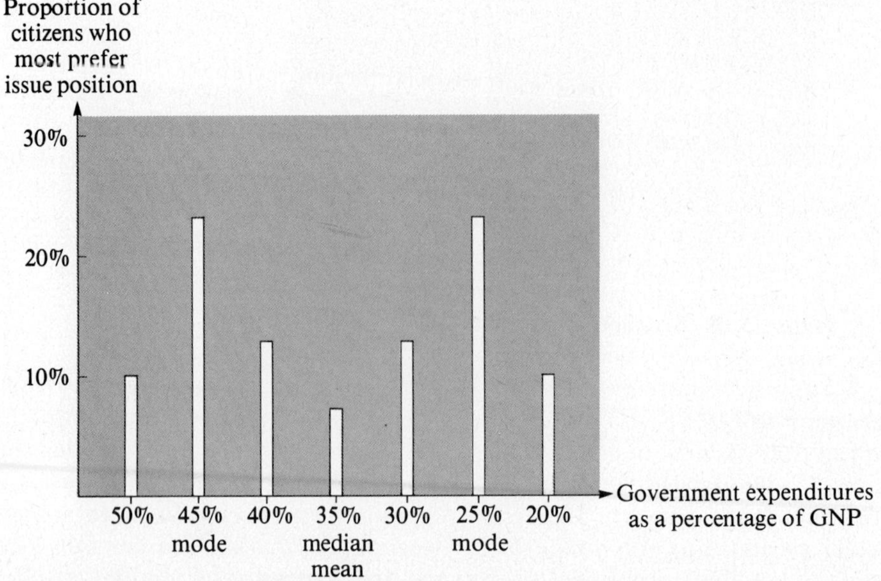

Figure 5.16 Symmetric bimodal preference distribution.

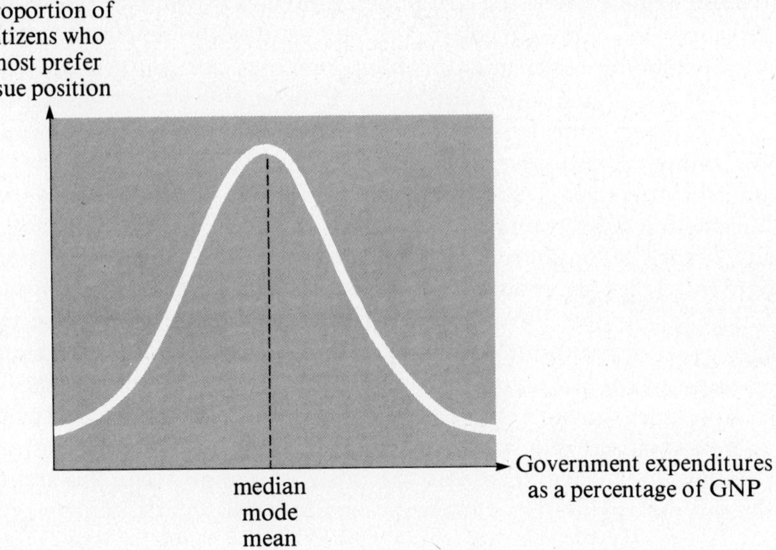

Figure 5.17 Continuous symmetric unimodal preference distribution.

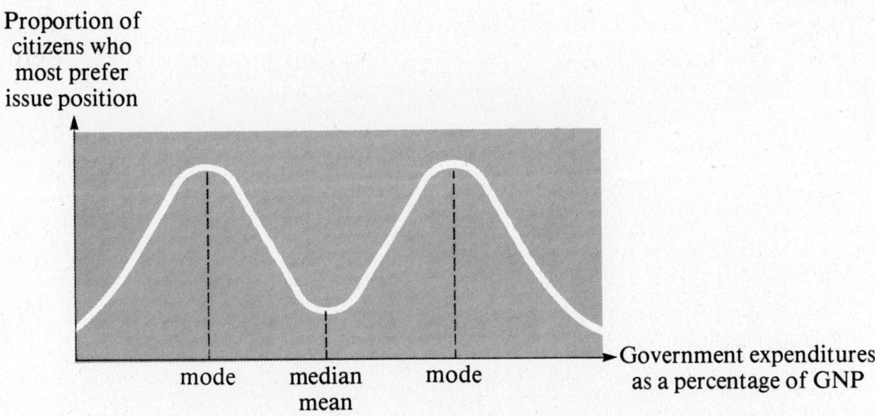

Figure 5.18 Continuous symmetric bimodal preference distribution.

ness is not in their correspondence to reality but in the understanding they generate.

In recent years, researchers at the University of Michigan's Center for Political Studies have asked a national adult sample some questions to reveal preference distributions for actual issues, some of which we review here. In all of the following cases, those who did not respond or who answered "don't know" are not counted in the percentages.

Women's rights. Bars to full equality for women are created by both legal and private restrictions. Removing these restrictions benefits women who cannot do what the restrictions prohibit, but may also reduce the utility of those whom the restrictions protect or of those who otherwise approve of them. Of course, some may view a full role for women in every part of business, industry, and government as a mixed blessing, but sex discrimination is under increasing attack. Figure 5.19 shows that in 1978 a trimodal distribution described preferences on the issue of equality for women. A plurality occurs at position *1*, and positions *1* and *2* together make up a majority. In 1972, only about 33 percent of those polled occupied position *1*.

Some believe that an important part of women's rights is the right to purchase abortions without government interference. Chapter 3 relates this issue directly to the problems of externalities and ideology. Any movement toward someone's most-preferred position creates a public good, while any movement away from that position creates a public bad. Figure 5.20 shows the 1978 preference distribution on the abortion issue. The distribution is bimodal but not symmetric; a majority prefers a less-than-complete repeal of

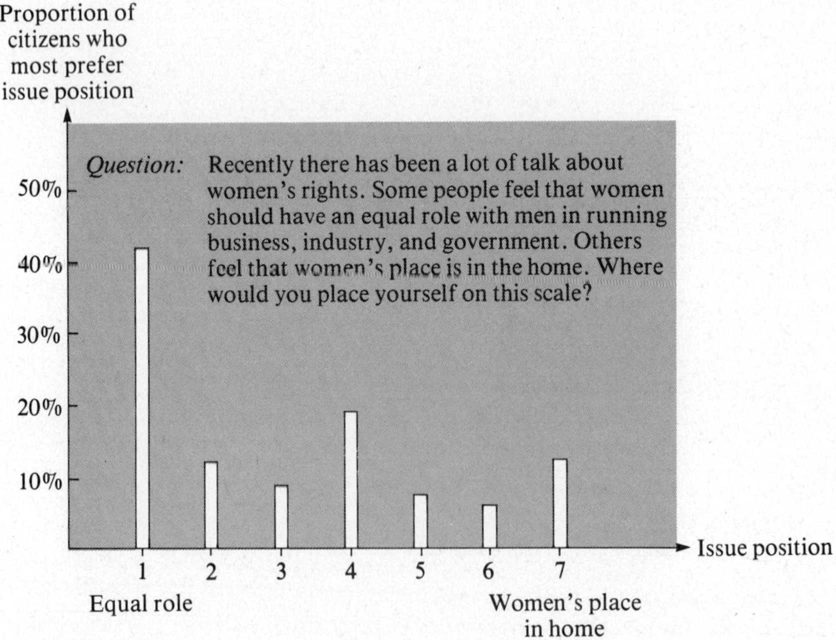

Figure 5.19 Equality for women, 1978 preference distribution.

Source: Data are from a Center for Political Studies 1978 Election Study and are made available by the Inter-University Consortium for Political Research.

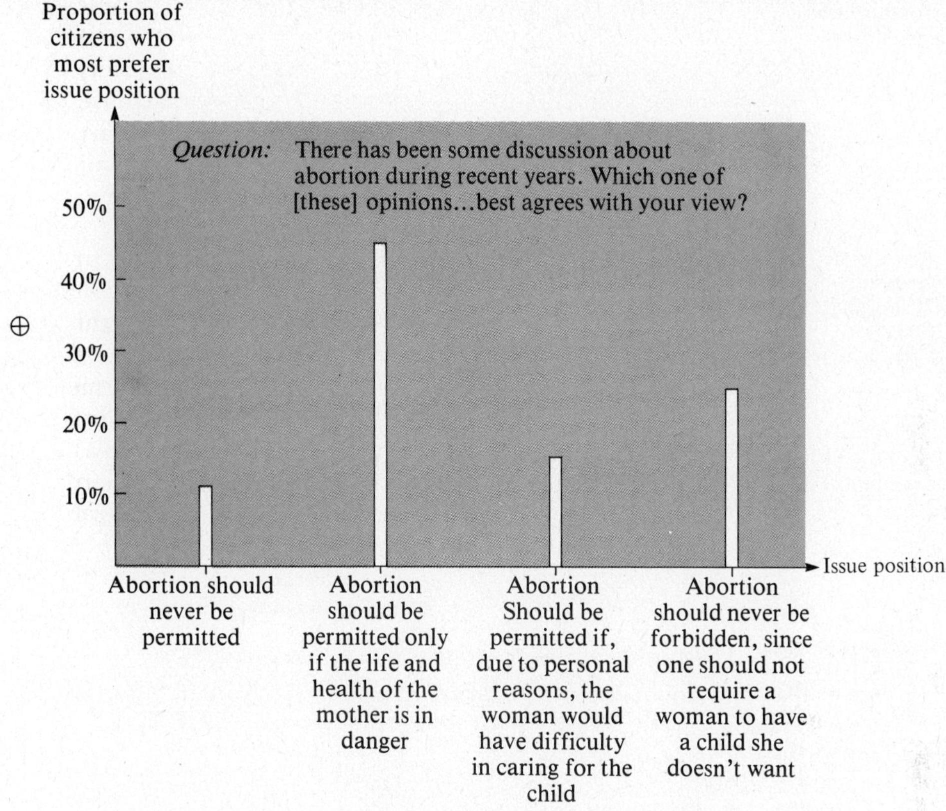

Figure 5.20 When abortions should be allowed, 1978 preference distribution.

Source: Data are from a Center for Political Studies 1978 Election Study and are made available by the Inter-University Consortium for Political Research.

anti-abortion laws. Thus, there is likely to be continued resistance to the 1973 Supreme Court opinions striking down these laws.[19]

Marijuana. On the question of legalizing marijuana use, as Figure 5.21 illustrates, in 1976 a surprising number (38.6 percent) of citizens preferred harsher penalties as opposed to legalization. However, in 1972 a larger percentage, about 55 percent of those answering this question, fell at position 7. Hence, while a majority of adult Americans seem to agree on controlling the personal habits of others, opinions on this subject are rapidly changing.

---

[19] *Roe v. Wade,* 35 L.Ed. 2d 147 (1973), and *Doe v. Bolton,* 35 L.Ed. 2d 201 (1973).

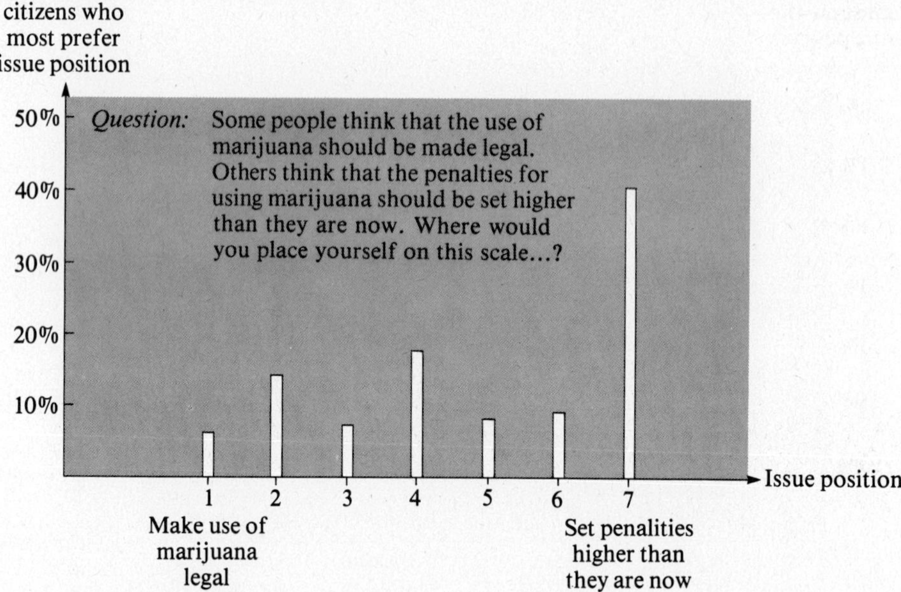

Figure 5.21 Legalize marijuana, 1976 preference distribution.

Source: Data are from a Center for Political Studies 1976 Election Study and are made available by the Inter-University Consortium for Political Research.

Busing. On the issue of busing, there is more approval for one position than exists for any other issue. Figure 5.22 shows that in 1976, 68.9 percent of those taking a position opposed busing and favored keeping children in neighborhood schools. Here, as with the abortion issue, one can expect continuing resistance to Supreme Court decisions that oppose majority sentiment.[20] Interestingly enough, the question on busing measures opinion on an instrumental issue. As the Harris poll cited earlier in this chapter suggests, there remains substantial agreement in favor of equality for blacks (89 percent), school desegregation (73 percent), and an end to prejudice (95 percent).[21] These are primary issues; specific disagreement usually occurs on the instrumental issues of implementing various antidiscriminatory policies.[22]

---

[20] But see *Milliken v. Bradley* 418 U.S. 717 (1974).

[21] Harris, "The Harris Survey," p. 2c.

[22] A substantial argument remains that busing achieves temporary integration at the cost of violence, segregated cities, and a decline in the quality of education and the degree of long-run integration. Hence, the instrumentality of busing to achieve the primary goals of integration, racial equality, and racial amicability is in doubt. Others might argue that busing is worth the cost, as the Constitution requires integration. There is no simple and universally correct answer to the school integration problem, as

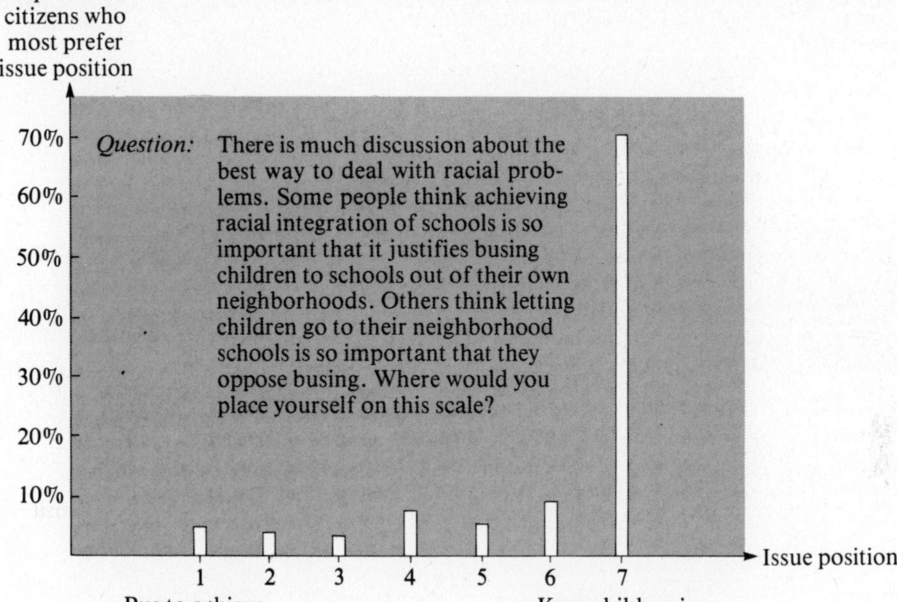
Proportion of citizens who most prefer issue position
70%
60%
50%
40%
30%
20%
10%
Question: There is much discussion about the best way to deal with racial problems. Some people think achieving racial integration of schools is so important that it justifies busing children to schools out of their own neighborhoods. Others think letting children go to their neighborhood schools is so important that they oppose busing. Where would you place yourself on this scale?
Issue position
1
2
3
4
5
6
7
Bus to achieve integration
Keep children in neighborhood schools

Figure 5.22 Busing to achieve racial integration, 1976 preference distribution.

Source: Data are from a Center for Political Studies 1976 Election Study and are made available by the Inter-University Consortium for Political Research.

National health insurance. Figure 5.23 shows the 1978 preference distribution on the issue of whether a national health insurance program should be collectively provided or not. There are more people at position *1* than at position *7*, and the distribution would be bimodal were it not for some fence-sitters at position *4*.

Liberal-conservative scale. Some observers believe that people respond intuitively to a liberal-conservative dimension that summarizes positions on all other issues. For example, support of busing, women's rights, legalization of marijuana and abortions, and national health insurance are all liberal positions while their opposites are all conservative positions. Figure 5.24 shows the 1978 distribution on this scale. It is plainly unimodal but not quite symmetric, as slightly more people place themselves on the conservative side than on the

---

all solutions, including the solution to maintain the status quo, are costly. For a fuller—and different—interpretation of polling data about racial equality, one that points out the instrumental versus primary issues involved, see Mary R. Jackman, "General and Applied Tolerance: Does Education Increase Commitment to Racial Integration?" *American Journal of Political Science,* 32 (May 1978), pp. 302–324.

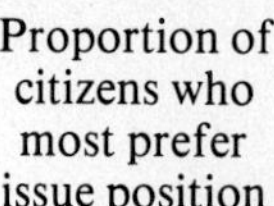

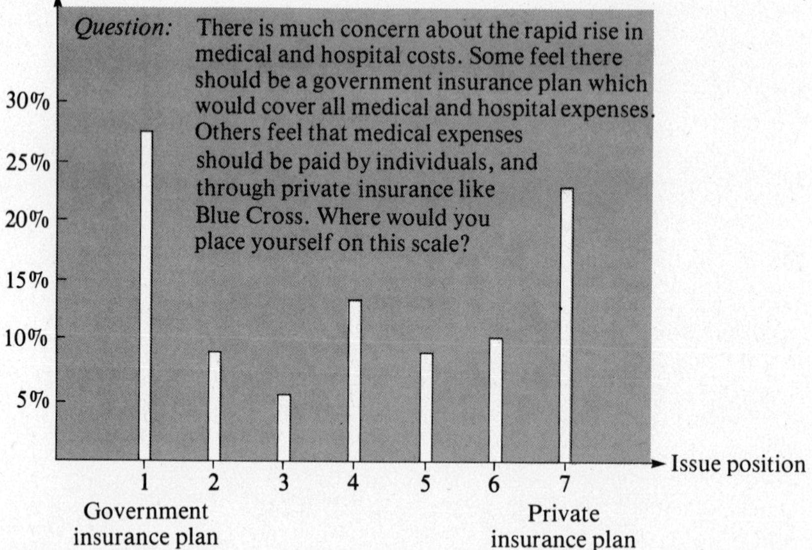

Figure 5.23 National health insurance, 1978 preference distribution.

Source: Data are from a Center for Political Studies 1978 Election Study and are made available by the Inter-University Consortium for Political Research.

liberal side. Such scales should be interpreted with extreme caution, for most people are not purely conservative or liberal. For example, Libertarians would probably approve of legalizing marijuana and abortions but oppose busing and national health insurance. Hence, widespread consistency among issues on the basis of a liberal-conservative scale may be difficult to find.

VOTING AND ABSTAINING

The preceding discussion explains the citizen's first decision—to prefer one candidate rather than another. Citizens act as if they have a utility difference between two candidates: a Republican, r, and a Democrat, d. For example, if a citizen prefers the Democrat to the Republican, then his utility difference, B, is $B = U_d - U_r$. The citizen's own issue preferences and his evaluations of the candidates' issue positions and characteristics form the bases for these utilities.

Now the citizen's second decision—to vote for the candidate he prefers

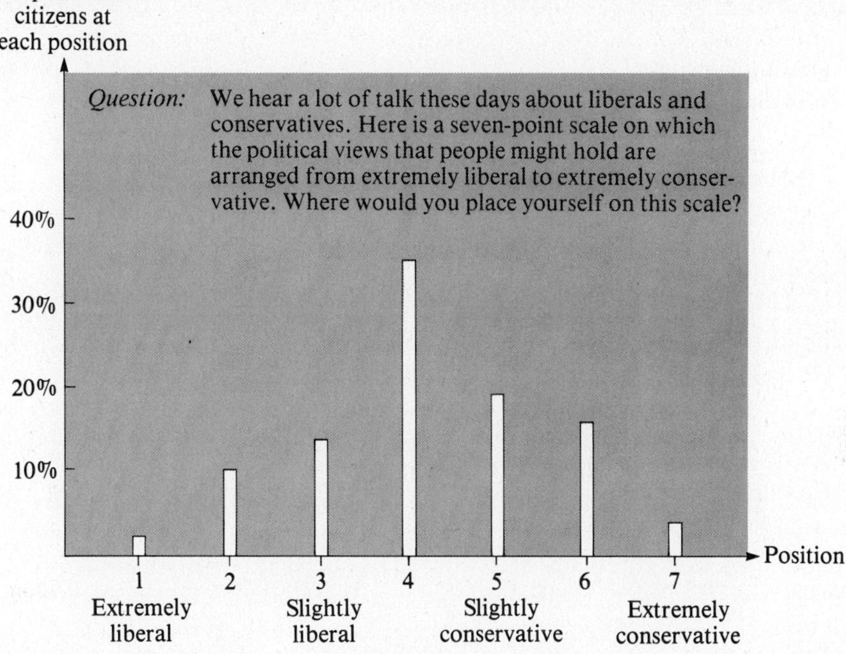

Figure 5.24 Liberal–conservative scale, 1978 distribution.

Source: Data are from a Center for Political Studies 1978 Election Study and are made available by the Inter-University Consortium for Political Research.

or to abstain—becomes important.[23] This decision is simplest to view as one occurring under conditions of risk.[24] Therefore, to explain and predict citizens' decisions, we must know their alternatives, outcomes, utilities for out-

---

[23] Most of the initial work on voting and abstaining, apart from arguments about that work, appears in three places: William H. Riker and Peter C. Ordeshook, "A Theory of the Calculus of Voting," *American Political Science Review,* 62 (March 1968), pp. 25–42; Richard D. McKelvey and Peter C. Ordeshook, "A General Theory of the Calculus of Voting," in J. F. Herndon, ed., *Mathematical Applications in Political Science, VI* (Charlottesville: University of Virginia Press, 1972), pp. 32–78; and Peter H. Aranson, "A Theory of the Calculus of Voting for Alternative, Three-Contestant Election Systems," unpublished Ph.D. dissertation, the University of Rochester, Rochester, New York, 1972. Here, the discussion relies heavily on these essays.

[24] An alternative view is that voting is a process of decision making under conditions of uncertainty. For a well-reasoned exposition of this view and its consequences, see John A. Ferejohn and Morris P. Fiorina, "The Paradox of Not Voting: A Decision Theoretic Analysis," *American Political Science Review,* 68 (June 1974), pp. 525–536.

comes, and subjectively estimated probabilities. In most American elections, citizens have a set of three alternatives to choose from: to vote for the Democratic candidate, to vote for the Republican candidate, or to abstain. The problem is to explain and predict which alternative they will choose.

Private Consequences of Voting

Voting and abstaining have both private and collective consequences.[25] A major difference between private-choice procedures (such as markets without externalities) and collective-choice procedures (such as elections) centers on the difference between private and public consequences of actions. When people in Portland, Maine, buy bread, they have no explicit desire for someone in Portland, Oregon, to buy the same kind of bread. Their actions and intentions are private because they do not affect others, nor are they intended to. By contrast, if people in Portland, Maine, vote for the Republican presidential nominee, then they intend someone in Portland, Oregon, to have that nominee as president. Voting is collective—it has both private and collective consequences, and voters intend the collective consequences, the outcomes, to be collective. However, there are purely **private consequences of voting.**

The private cost of voting. For example, one outcome of voting is its private cost, which depends on the citizen's circumstances. It takes time to get to the polls, to wait in line to vote, and to return home or to work. This time is costly because a voter loses the opportunity to use it for other purposes. Transportation to the polls and baby-sitters are also costly. The citizen has a utility for the costs of the resources he uses in voting, which are denoted here by the letter C. This consequence of (the collective act of) voting is private because it is unrelated to the actual election outcome of who wins or loses and because each citizen's private cost is not borne by someone else.

The private benefit of voting. Many voters do not believe that their vote affects an election's collective outcome. Indeed, it has been remarked that the probability of a person's vote changing the winner of an election is lower than the probability of his being killed in an automobile accident on the way to the polls.[26] Considering the very real cost of voting, C, why do people vote? For many, the answer lies in the private benefits of voting such as "The satisfaction from compliance with the ethic of voting . . . from affirming allegiance to the political system . . . from affirming a partisan preference . . . the satisfaction of deciding, going to the polls, etc. . . . [and] of affirming one's efficacy in the

---

[25] The terms "private and collective consequences of voting" are borrowed from William H. Riker and Peter C. Ordeshook, *An Introduction to Positive Political Theory* (Englewood Cliffs, N. J.: Prentice-Hall, 1973), pp. 58–62.

[26] This theme is explored in Gordon Tullock, *Toward a Mathematics of Politics* (Ann Arbor: University of Michigan Press, 1967), p. 109, *passim*.

political system. . . ."[27] These benefits are private consequences of voting because, like the cost of voting, they do not depend directly on the election outcome. People can gain intrinsic utility from voting, independent of who wins the election. The letter D denotes these benefits.

Collective Consequences of Voting

The citizen's expected utility from voting is the sum of his expected utility from the collective consequences of voting and from the private consequences of voting. Let R equal this sum. The expected utilities from the private consequences of voting are C and D. Therefore, R = *expected utility from collective consequences of voting* $+ D - C$. If R is greater than zero, the citizen votes; otherwise the citizen abstains—or flips a coin to decide what to do, if R equals zero.

The **collective consequences of voting** refer to the effects you expect your vote to have on the election outcome. Therefore, the expected utility you receive as a collective consequence of voting depends on how many citizens you believe will vote for each candidate. As in Chapter 4, let V_d and V_r represent each candidate's vote. Suppose that for you, U_d is greater than U_r. The number of votes each candidate receives if you abstain is actually the state of nature you face in this risky-choice decision problem. If you abstain, there are five possible configurations of votes, or states of nature, which Table 5.7 summarizes with their corresponding outcomes and utilities.

If S_1, S_2, or S_5 prevails, your vote would have no collective consequence. You cannot affect who wins or create a favorable tie. In these cases, you would vote only if D exceeds C. However, if S_3 prevails—$V_d = V_r$—your vote changes a tie into the election of your favored candidate, the Democrat. Your utility for a tie is the same as an equiprobable lottery for U_d and U_r, which turns out to be $(U_d + U_r)/2$. So if a tie prevails before you vote, then by voting, your

Table 5.7 Voting Problem: States of Nature, Outcomes, and Utilities

State of Nature (Votes)	Outcomes	Utilities
S_1, V_d exceeds $V_r + 1$	Democrat wins	U_d
S_2, V_d equals $V_r + 1$	Democrat wins	U_d
S_3, V_d equals V_r	tie	$\frac{U_d + U_r}{2}$
S_4, V_d equals $V_r - 1$	Republican wins	U_r
S_5, V_d less than $V_r - 1$	Republican wins	U_r

[27] Riker and Ordeshook, "A Theory of the Calculus of Voting," p. 28.

utility goes from $(U_d + U_r)/2$ to U_d. The difference between these two utilities is

$$U_d - \frac{U_d + U_r}{2} = \frac{U_d - U_r}{2}.$$

Let P be the probability that S_3 actually prevails. Your expected utility from voting, given this state of nature, then becomes $P(U_d - U_r)/2$.

If S_4 prevails—$V_d = V_r - 1$—your vote changes a Republican victory into a tie. That is, your utility goes from U_r to $(U_d + U_r)/2$. The difference between these two utilities is

$$\frac{U_d + U_r}{2} - U_r = \frac{U_d - U_r}{2}.$$

Let Q be the probability that S_4 actually prevails. Your expected utility from voting, given this state of nature, then becomes $Q(U_d - U_r)/2$.

Since your vote for the Democrat would have a collective consequence only if S_3 or S_4 prevails, the sum of your expected utilities from voting under these states of nature is the relevant expected collective consequence of voting. This sum of expected utilities can be rearranged as follows:

$$\frac{P(U_d - U_r)}{2} + \frac{Q(U_d - U_r)}{2} = (P + Q)\frac{(U_d - U_r)}{2}.$$

Notice that P is the probability that the election is a tie if you abstain, and Q is the probability that the election is a tie if you vote for the Democrat. In large electorates, these two numbers are approximately equal, so P can be substituted for Q in the previous expression. Thus, $P + Q$ becomes $P + P$, or simply $2P$. The 2 cancels out the 2 under $(U_d - U_r)$, and the entire expression for your expected utility from the collective consequences of voting becomes $P(U_d - U_r)$. That is, your expected utility from the collective consequences of your vote is your *subjective estimate* of the probability of a tie times your utility difference between the election of the Democrat and of the Republican. However, recall that $(U_d - U_r)$ equals B. Hence, the expected utility you attach to the collective consequence of your vote simply becomes PB.

The Calculus of Voting

We now have a full expression for a **calculus of voting.** A citizen's expected utility from voting, R, is R = *the expected utility from collective consequences of voting plus the expected utility from private consequences of voting.* But the expected utility from the collective consequences is PB, and the expected utility from the private consequences is $D - C$. Hence, R becomes $R = PB + D - C$.

A hypothetical case. It is useful to work through some explanations based on a hypothetical example. Suppose that it is 1972 and in the presidential election campaign, a citizen prefers Senator McGovern to President Nixon. Right after the nominating conventions, this preference is quite strong. Let P_0 be the citizen's estimate of the initial probability that the election would be a tie, $U_0(M)$ the citizen's initial utility for a McGovern victory, $U_0(N)$ the citizen's initial utility for a Nixon victory, and C_0 and D_0 the citizen's initial private costs and benefits of voting. The interpreted voting calculus for this citizen thus becomes $R_0 = P_0[U_0(M) - U_0(N)] + D_0 - C_0$.

Suppose R_0 is greater than zero: the citizen expects to vote for McGovern. However, during the campaign the psychiatric record of Senator Eagleton, McGovern's running mate, is revealed, and the citizen is not sure that Eagleton should be "one heartbeat away" from the presidency. The citizen also grows less and less sure of McGovern's thoroughness and judgment. Consequently, $U_0(M)$ diminishes to a new utility, $U_1(M)$, which remains greater than $U_0(N)$. But the new difference between the two, $B = U_1(M) - U_0(N)$, is not as great as it once was. Hence, R_0 diminishes to a new value, R_1, such that $R_1 = P_0[U_1(M) - U_0(N)] + D_0 - C_0$.

What are we to make of this reduction from R_0 to R_1? Probably, the citizen is less likely to vote. Thus, for those citizens who continue to prefer McGovern to Nixon, the probability that they will actually vote for McGovern declines, while the probability that they will abstain increases. Of course, the news about Eagleton is expected to have the opposite effect on voting turnout among those citizens who prefer Nixon.

As the campaign continues, the citizen finds that more and more people are becoming increasingly disenchanted with McGovern. Although the citizen still prefers McGovern to Nixon, Nixon's lead in the polls grows. Accordingly, the chance that a vote may affect the election outcome—the probability of a tie—grows ever smaller, and P_0 diminishes to a new value, P_1. The citizen's entire calculus becomes $R_2 = P_1[U_1(M) - U_0(N)] + D_0 - C_0$. R_2 is smaller than R_1, and the likelihood that the citizen will vote continues to decline. The likelihood that a citizen who prefers Nixon will vote also diminishes with a decline in P.

Later in the campaign, the citizen learns about the break-in at the Democratic National Committee Headquarters in the Watergate complex. This incident adversely affects his assessment of Nixon, and therefore $U_0(N)$ diminishes to $U_1(N)$. The citizen's new expected utility from voting, R_3, becomes $R_3 = P_1[U_1(M) - U_1(N)] + D_0 - C_0$. This decline in the citizen's utility for a Nixon victory increases the value of B. R_3 is greater than R_2, and the citizen is now more likely to vote. The effect of revelations about Watergate on those who prefer Nixon is difficult to predict without more information.

On the morning of the election, the citizen's car won't start. The cost of a taxicab ride to the polls increases from the cost of voting C_0 to C_1, and the citizen decides to abstain. But his children remind him that it is a duty to vote, which increases his utility for the private consequences of voting from D_0 to

D_1. Though he refuses to go to the polls on his own, some Democratic party volunteers come by and drive the recalcitrant citizen there, and Senator McGovern receives another vote.

Testing the calculus of voting. This interpreted case of the calculus of voting shows the operation of these four general explanations and predictions:

If ceteris paribus	*then the likelihood that the citizen votes*
the P term increases (decreases),	increases (decreases);
the B term increases (decreases),	increases (decreases);
the D term increases (decreases),	increases (decreases);
the C term increases (decreases),	decreases (increases).

A partial test of these hypotheses has been conducted, based on Center for Political Studies data for the 1952, 1956, and 1960 presidential elections.[28] In the surveys for those years, people indicated whether they thought the election would be "close" or "not close." Their answers give an estimate of P: "close" means a relatively high value of P, while "not close" means a relatively low value of P. People also indicated whether or not they "cared" about the election. "Caring" means a relatively high value of B, while "not caring" means a relatively low value of B. Responses to several other questions formed a "sense of civic duty" scale, which placed D into one of three categories: high D, medium D, and low D.

Table 5.8 shows the results of the test. To see how to read the table, notice that the upper left-hand cell records the percentage of persons who believed the 1952 election to be close (high P), who cared about the election outcome (high B), and who had a high sense of civic duty (high D). Of these people, 89 percent reported that they voted. Contrast this turnout with the turnout among citizens in the lower right-hand corner of the second row (1952 election, low P, low B, and low D), of whom 50 percent reported that they voted. The voting and abstaining reported in Table 5.8 provides reasonably satisfactory evidence in support of hypotheses drawn from the calculus of voting.

Off-year voting turnout. The differential turnout rate in congressional and presidential elections provides another example of rational choice in voting. Figure 5.25 shows the turnout rate for congressional and presidential elections from 1930 to 1976. The percentages are estimates of the proportion of the voting-age population that voted. Voting turnout in congressional

[28] Riker and Ordeshook, "A Theory of the Calculus of Voting," p. 34–39.

Table 5.8 Test of the Calculus of Voting

		High *D*		Medium *D*		Low *D*	
		B		*B*		*B*	
1952		high	low	high	low	high	low
P	high	89%	84%	84%	67%	57%	46%
	low	86	78	77	65	61	50
1956							
P	high	89	81	80	65	57	40
	low	81	77	74	73	52	26
1960							
P	high	94	83	90	82	74	46
	low	90	67	79	75	73	42

Source: William H. Riker and Peter C. Ordeshook, "A Theory of the Calculus of Voting," *American Political Science Review,* 62 (March 1968), p. 38.

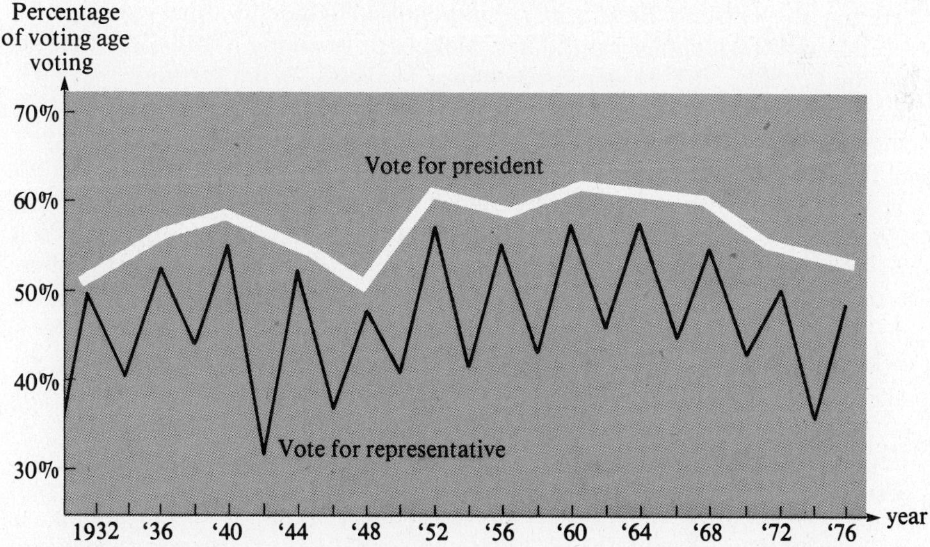

Figure 5.25 Percentage of estimated voting-age population casting ballots in congressional and presidential elections, 1930–1976.

Source: U.S. Bureau of the Census, Statistical Abstract of the United States: 1978, 99th ed. (Washington, D.C.: Government Printing Office, 1978), p. 520.

elections always trails turnout in presidential elections, and congressional election turnout rises in presidential election years and falls in off years.

Let R_1 and R_2 be the citizen's expected utility from voting for a congressional and a presidential candidate, respectively. Congressional elections do not get the attention that presidential elections do. Citizens have less information about the nominees' positions and likelihood of winning. Hence, if P_1 and B_1 are the respective P and B terms for congressional elections, while P_2 and B_2 are for presidential elections, then B_1 is probably less than B_2, while (because of a lack of information) P_1 is probably less than P_2. Accordingly, for congressional elections alone, $R_1 = P_1B_1 + D - C$ is probably less than $R_2 = P_2B_2 + D - C$.

Citizens get the same private benefits and costs from voting in presidential elections as from voting in congressional elections, so if citizens decide to vote for a presidential candidate, their congressional vote is costless. For years of presidential elections, $R_1 + R_2 = P_1B_1 + P_2B_2 + D - C$. $R_1 + R_2$ is larger than R_1, which explains the pattern found in Figure 5.25.

Voting in three-candidate elections. The calculus of voting in three-candidate elections is more difficult to derive than that for two-candidate contests, and therefore we do not formally develop it here.[29] The C and D terms remain unchanged. However, the sets of outcomes and states of nature are expanded to include the possibility that a vote will make or break ties between the citizen's first- and second-choice, first- and third-choice, and second- and third-choice candidates. Making or breaking a three-way tie also may be possible. As Chapter 2 suggests, a pivotal question for voters in such elections emerges if their first choice is unlikely to win, while the race is much closer between their second and third choices. A vote for a particular voter's first choice may be thrown away, allowing his third choice to defeat his second choice. Table 5.9 shows how such considerations can affect voting decisions. This table generates predictions about who a citizen might vote for based on a "feeling thermometer" used in surveys by the Center for Political Studies. Respondents were asked to translate their feelings toward various candidates into a warm-cold "thermometer" score from zero to one hundred degrees, with fifty degrees as the neutral point. The actual degrees reported may be taken as a surrogate for utility. The first set of entries in Table 5.9 shows that voting predictions based on thermometer scores work well in the 1972 presidential election, between Senator McGovern and President Nixon. The few persons who did not vote as predicted might have either answered incorrectly or felt "cold" toward a candidate but nevertheless thought he might make a better president than his opponent.

The second set of entries in Table 5.9 shows that in one instance the thermometer score worked less well than it did for the 1972 election. That

[29] For a study of the three-candidate calculus of voting, see Aranson, "A Theory of the Calculus of Voting for Alternative, Three-Contestant Election Systems," and McKelvey and Ordeshook, "A General Theory of the Calculus of Voting."

Table 5.9 Thermometer Vote Predictions and Actual Votes, 1968 and 1972 Presidential Elections

Thermometer Predicted Preference For	1972: *Actual Vote Cast For*				
	Nixon	McGovern			(N)
Nixon	97.4%	2.6		(100%)	(945)
McGovern	2.9	97.1			(448)
Tie	37.8	62.2			(98)

Thermometer Predicted Preference For	1968: *Actual Vote Cast For*				
	Humphrey	Nixon	Wallace		(N)
Humphrey	96.7%	2.2	1.1	(100%)	(272)
Nixon	1.9	96.0	2.2		(322)
Wallace	1.3	13.9	84.8		(79)
H-N tie	52.9	45.1	2.0		(51)
W-H tie	100.0	0.0	0.0		(3)
N-W tie	0.0	50.0	50.0		(8)
H-N-W tie	57.1	42.9	0.0		(7)

Source: John Aldrich, "Voting in Two U.S. Presidential Elections: An Analysis Based on the Spatial Model of Electoral Competition," unpublished Ph.D. dissertation, University of Rochester, Rochester, New York, 1975, p. 37.

instance concerns the 1968 presidential candidacy of former Alabama Governor George C. Wallace. He had almost no chance of winning the election, and nearly 14 percent of those who preferred him to Nixon and former Vice-President Hubert H. Humphrey transferred their votes to Nixon, the second choice of all but two of them. This kind of voting must be considered rational. But those who continued to vote for Wallace also acted rationally, for they might have believed that Wallace had a chance to throw the election into the House of Representatives or that a vote denied to the other two candidates had public policy implications for future elections.

These general decision patterns carry forward to the three-candidate presidential election of 1980. As we noted in Chapter 2, many citizens preferred independent candidate John Anderson to the Democratic party candidate Jimmy Carter, and preferred Carter to the Republican party candidate Ronald Reagan. Indeed, most polls showed Anderson as the first-place choice of a much larger percentage of voters than the seven percent he collected on election day. Jimmy Carter obviously reflected on these decision patterns, for in the final days of the campaign, he and his associates dwelt on the issues of nuclear non-proliferation, energy, and the Equal Rights Amendment. They repeatedly stressed that a vote for Anderson would be a vote for Reagan, because it would split the number of votes on the liberal side of the political spectrum. Of course, Anderson responded that "a vote for Anderson is a vote for Anderson," insisted that he was no "spoiler," and stated emphatically that a loss for Jimmy Carter would be Jimmy Carter's fault.

George Wallace's third-party candidacy in 1968 probably did not affect the election outcome, and John Anderson's independent candidacy in 1980 certainly did not affect it. However, in both elections, the potential for a change in outcome caused by the presence of third-party candidates was evident. We report these examples here to illustrate the nature of the calculus of voting in three-candidate elections. The calculated vote for a second choice in the two cases examined, as well as in others, has served to draw votes away from independent or minor party candidates, thus further diminishing their electoral performance beyond the normal two-party tendencies of single-member district system elections.

Voting, Abstaining, and Public Policy

The calculus of voting lets us link up the citizen's fundamental participatory decisions with the public policies that candidates advocate. For purposes of discussion, suppose that throughout an election campaign, a citizen's estimates of P, D, and C remain constant, and all variations that occur in R do so because of variations in B. Now, consider again Figure 5.8, which shows a factory worker's utility curve over various levels of government spending as a percentage of GNP. The worker's most-preferred position is at 45, and she believes the Democratic candidate to be at 40 and the Republican at 30 (d and r respectively denote these two issue positions). Figure 5.8 shows the worker's utility for each candidate's position, U_d and U_r. To be clearer, B is now written as $B = U_d(40) - U_r(30)$.

Abstention from indifference. Suppose that with d at 40 and r at 30 the worker votes. If the Republican moves r to 40, then B becomes $B = U_d(40) - U_r(40) = 0$. That is, the convergence of the two candidates to the same issue position reduces the value of B to zero for the worker. If government spending is the *only* issue that matters to the worker, then her vote has no collective (public policy) consequences whatever. And, if D is less than C, then she abstains. This kind of abstention is called **abstention from indifference.**

Abstention from indifference also can occur even if the worker sees a great difference between the candidates' issue positions. For instance, suppose r remains at 30 and d moves to 60. Clearly, $B = U_d(60) - U_r(30) = 0$. The worker is halfway between the two candidates' positions and receives an equal utility from both positions. Or the worker might believe that both candidates are right at her bliss point—for example, both d and r lie at 45. Again, B is zero. Obviously, then, *indifference* does not mean that citizens care little about the issues or about the election. It simply means that if citizens abstain, it is because they perceive insufficient *utility* differences (B) between the candidates' positions. Among other reasons, that is why people who see the candidates as Tweedledum and Tweedledee often do not vote.

Abstention from alienation. Abstention from indifference derives directly out of the B term of the calculus of voting. However, a second influence on voting and abstaining, called **abstention from alienation,** has also been observed.[30] This form of abstention takes place if the citizen's preferred candidate is not close enough to his own position. We do not know why abstention from alienation occurs. One possible explanation is that an election or series of elections in which the citizen's preferred candidate is less than satisfactory tends to erode the citizen's "sense of civic duty," as measured by D.[31] Hence, there may be an apparent interaction between D and the utility citizens receive over time from their preferred candidate.

The aggregate effects of public policy positions on abstention. This analysis of voting and abstention becomes central in Chapter 7's discussion of candidate strategies. To understand why candidates propose the public policies they do, we must know the aggregate effects their policy proposals have on abstention. Accordingly, consider Figure 5.26a, which places two candidates at d and r about the median of a symmetric, unimodal preference distribution. If indifference induces abstention, then the horizontal line—percentage voting—represents the voting turnout rate among citizens at various points along the issue dimension. Citizens to the left of d and to the right of r on average have an equal chance of voting, because they see the same difference in the candidates' positions. Citizens between d and r are less likely to vote, however. A citizen at exactly the median position gets no utility differential—B equals zero. Therefore the turnout rate is lowest at that point and increases to either side of it.

Figure 5.26b moves the candidates' positions closer together, thus reducing the average voting turnout rate for citizens to the left of d and to the right of r as a result of the decline in B. People at the median continue to vote as before. In Figure 5.26c, the candidates are converged at the median. All citizens find B equal to zero; hence, the average voting turnout rate is constant and uniformly low.

Now consider Figure 5.27a, corresponding to Figure 5.26a, except that here alienation induces abstention. As citizens' positions become more distant from their preferred candidate's position, they grow less likely to vote, regardless of where their less-preferred candidate is located. This effect is carried through in a parallel manner in Figures 5.27b and 5.27c as it was in Figures 5.26b and 5.26c.

[30] See V. O. Key, Jr., *Public Opinion and American Democracy* (New York: Knopf, 1963), pp. 231, *passim.*

[31] Peter C. Ordeshook, "Theory of the Electoral Process," unpublished Ph.D dissertation, the University of Rochester, Rochester, New York; 1969, p. 126–128.

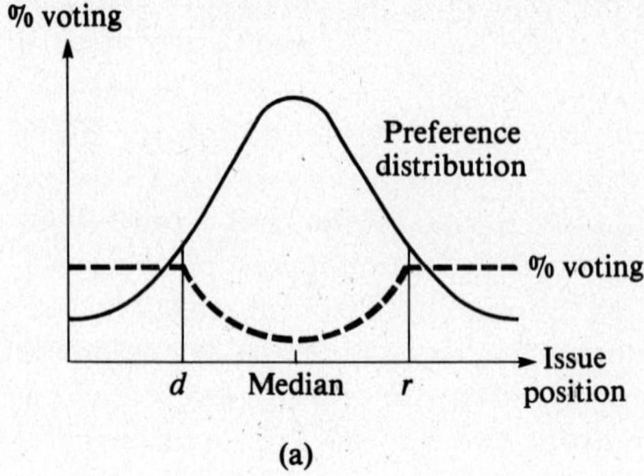

(a)

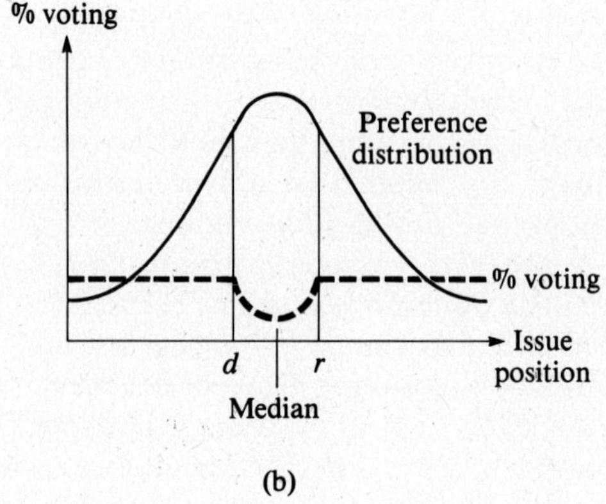

(b)

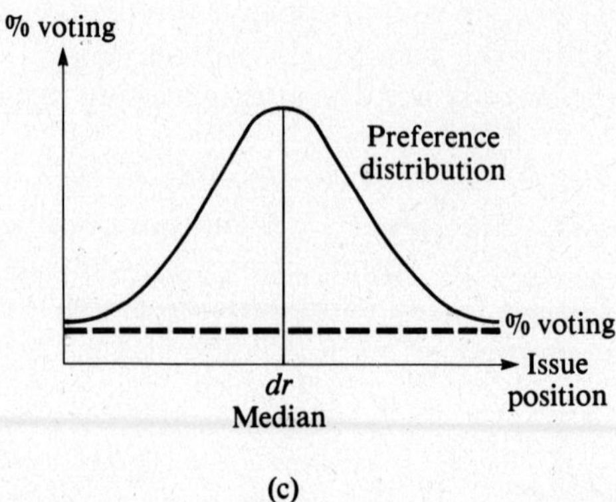

(c)

Figure 5.26 Aggregate effect of candidates' issue positions on abstention: abstention from indifference.

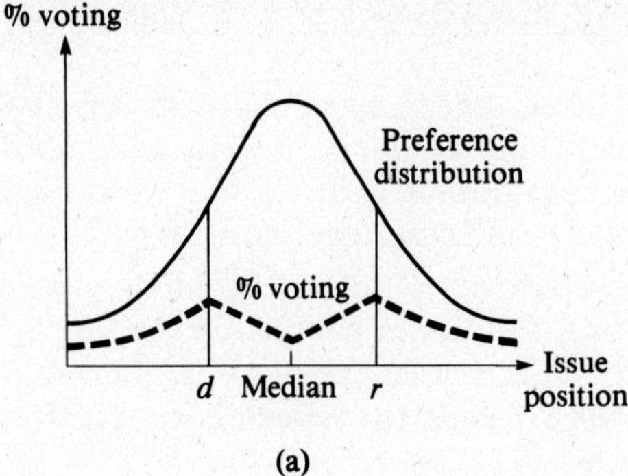

(a)

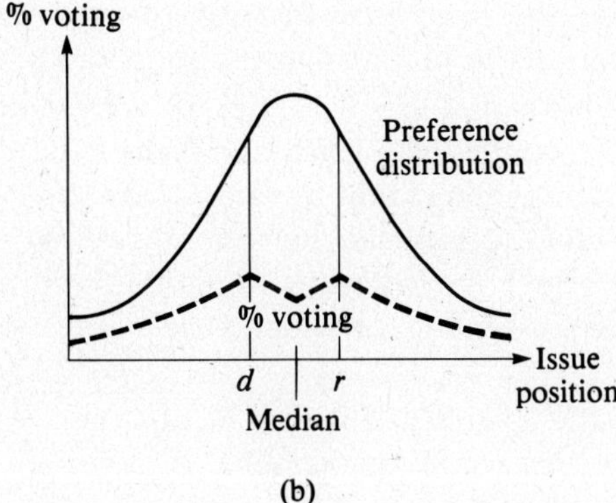

(b)

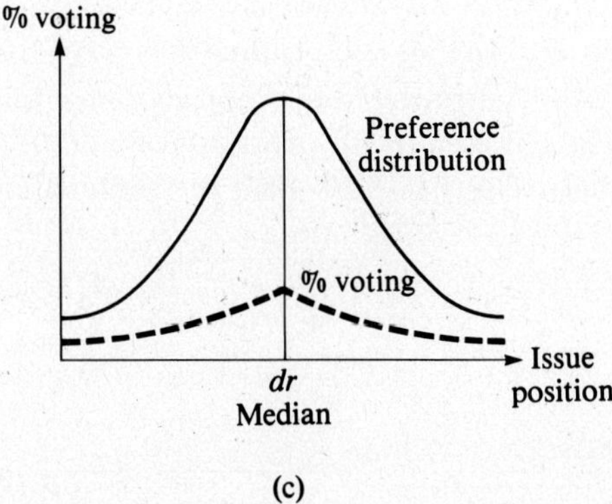

(c)

Figure 5.27 Aggregate effects of candidates' issue positions on abstention: abstention from alienation.

QUESTIONS FOR DISCUSSION AND REVIEW

1. Is rational choice theory, as revealed in this chapter's study of the voting decision, equivalent or not equivalent to a deterministic theory of voting? In what instances do the two views explain and predict the same and different voting decisions? Why?
2. How is retrospective voting in the public sector like using brand names to buy products in the private sector? Are there important differences? What public policy consequences might be expected because of the similarities between retrospective voting and brand-name buying?
3. What costs would be imposed by a law requiring everyone to vote? Would these costs fall more heavily on some than on others? Who? What public policy consequences might follow from such a law? Are there comparable laws requiring the production or consumption of various goods and services in the private sector? Do such laws make any real difference in private consumption and production decisions?
4. The use of information surrogates in voting decisions sometimes implies that group leaders learn about the candidates' positions and then tell group members how to vote. Could such a process be abused by group leaders to mislead their members? Would this practice be correctable? How? Are interests of leaders and members in recommending and endorsing candidates always compatible? Why? Why not?
5. How would the calculus of voting be changed if our elections were not conducted by secret ballot? What differences in voting or public policy might emerge? Why?
6. The League of Women Voters and local newspapers often conduct campaigns to get people to vote. What terms in the calculus of voting do such campaigns affect? How? Do these campaigns have public policy consequences or otherwise affect election outcomes? Do you believe those supporting such campaigns have these effects in mind?
7. In the past, the right to vote in American elections was given only to those who passed wealth or property ownership tests or who were white and male. Do you think such restrictions had any public policy consequences? Why? Why not?

NEW CONCEPTS AND TERMS

abstention from alienation
abstention from indifference
bimodal preference distribution
bliss point

calculus of voting
classificatory group
collective consequences of voting
determinism
instrumental issue
issue
issue salience
mean
median
mode
preference distribution
primary group
primary issue
private consequences of voting
retrospective voting
secondary group
symmetric preference distribution
unimodal preference distribution

6

Activists and Political Organizations

Activists are those participants in politics who do "more" than simply vote but "less" than run for public office. Some examples of what they do include: talking to other people and writing letters to newspapers about candidates, elections, and public policy; wearing campaign buttons and placing bumper stickers with political subjects on their cars; contributing labor or money to election campaigns and attending campaign meetings; working as paid employees of election candidates or interest groups; endorsing candidates and attending nominating conventions or caucuses; bugging the opponents' offices, participating in demonstrations or riots, and assassinating candidates or public officials. Activists also try to affect legislative, executive, judicial, and bureaucratic decision making, matters discussed in later chapters. However, the preceding list is unmanageably large, and therefore this chapter is limited principally to a consideration of activists' election decisions.

Chapter 5 shows how citizens act in **simple elections,** those in which the candidates' main resources are the public policy positions they take on each issue. However, when activists participate in elections, they inject resources other than policy positions into the campaign. The inclusion of activists' decisions and resources turns a contest into a **complex election.**

What do activists accomplish? A brief example gives one partial answer to this question. Figure 6.1a shows a simple, one-issue election between a Democrat at d and a Republican at r. The candidates' positions are fixed equidistant from the median of a symmetric, unimodal preference distribution. By stereotype, the Democrat is to the left of the median while the

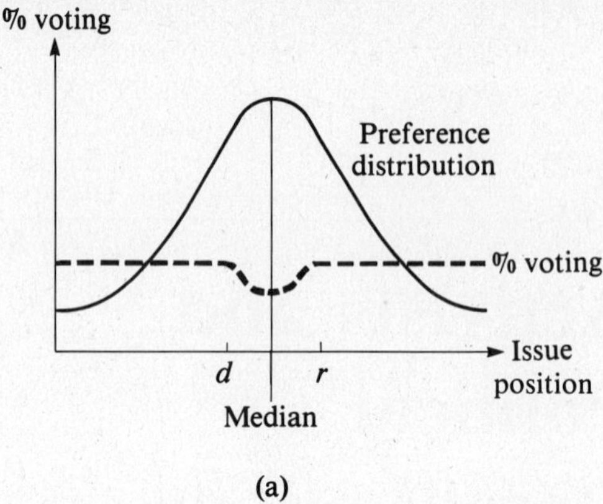

(a)

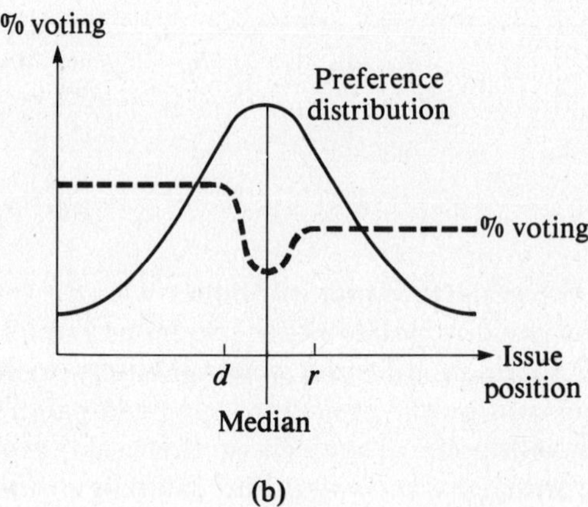

(b)

Figure 6.1 (a) Simple election (no activists). (b) Complex election (Democratic activists).

Republican is to the right. Everyone to the left of the median prefers the Democrat, and everyone to the right prefers the Republican. Most citizens to the left of the median are also Democrats, and most to the right, Republicans. Indifference, a low value of B, causes some abstention. About as many citizens vote for the Democrat as for the Republican, and the election is a tie.

Figure 6.1b shows a complex election with activists who happen to be Democrats but without Republican activists. On election day, the activists drive registered Democrats to the polls, which reduces the cost of voting, C, for many of those whom the activists expect to prefer the Democratic candidate. Naturally, some Democrats who are driven to the polls prefer the Republican candidate, which creates a small increase in the Republican's vote. But the positive effect on turnout is greater for the Democratic candidate than for the Republican. Hence, the Democrat wins the election, even though as many citizens actually prefer the Republican as prefer the Democrat.

This example shows only one collective consequence of activist electoral participation. In this case, we expect public policy to fall to the left of the median voter's preference instead of being a lottery of policies to the left and the right. Obviously, there may be other collective consequences as well as private ones. For instance, the participation of Democratic activists might lead to a Republican victory if they demand that their candidate move too far to the left in exchange for their support, because at some point along the issue dimension, as *d* moves leftward, the increase in turnout—as a consequence of Democratic activist participation—among citizens preferring *d* to *r* will fail to offset the declining number of citizens who actually prefer *d* to *r*. Alternatively, suppose activists demand from the Democrat either illegal payments or favoritism in the awarding of government contracts if he should win the election. At some point, unfavorable public reaction or prosecution for graft and corruption might erode the Democrat's electability.[1]

INDIVIDUAL CHOICE AND GROUP ACTION

The central fact of activist political participation is that it occurs within the structure of groups, organizations. Some of these groups, such as political parties, are put together explicitly for fielding candidates and winning elections. Others, such as interest groups (sometimes called pressure groups), field no candidates but exist to advance the welfare of their members through political action. Still others, such as corporations and labor unions, have ordinary private-sector activities but sometimes delve into politics in the interest of shareholders or members. Activist political participation outside of organizations appears to be of sporadic and unpredictable importance. In sum, to study activist decision making requires an understanding of group action in politics. Explaining how and why organizations such as interest groups and political parties form in the first place, however, poses something of a puzzle.

---

[1] This example does not put activist participation in the best light. Probably Republican activists would be present in the next election; if so, and if they matched Democratic activists' strategies, then public policy emerging from the election would be the same whether or not activists participated. The activists in such a situation would actually be playing a prisoners' dilemma game. If they "solved" it, they would agree not to participate. Of course, voting turnout would be increased by activist participation, and perhaps that is for the good. However, such participation fails to educate voters about the issues, clarify the issues, or change public policy. The limited impact of activists in this example grows out of the particular assumptions we have made about the election.

Group Theory

Political science is heir to an old and popular intellectual tradition about the origin, importance, and structure of human groups in general and of political groups in particular. The pervasiveness, longevity, and legitimacy of this tradition remained unchallenged until 1965, when its relevance was first seriously questioned. Embedded as **group theory** is in political analysis, a description of that theory and the central challenge to it is important for understanding activists and their organizations.

Federalist Paper No. 10. An early and notable discussion of the importance of groups in American politics was provided by James Madison. Writing in *Federalist Paper No. 10,* Madison described a faction in unapproving terms as "a number of citizens, whether amounting to a majority or a minority of the whole, who are united and actuated by some common impulse of passion or of interest, adverse to the rights of other citizens, or to the permanent and aggregate interests of the community."[2] Madison contributed to the *Federalist Papers* to convince the members of various state constitutional conventions to ratify the Constitution: "Among the numerous advantages promised by a well constructed Union," he believed, "none deserves to be more accurately developed than its tendency to break and control the violence of faction." In describing this alleged virtue of the proposed Constitution, Madison set the groundwork for an elaborate theory of political groups.

Madison first observed that human nature leads to differences of opinion and of action: "As long as the reason of man continues fallible, and he is at liberty to exercise it, different opinions will be formed. As long as the connection subsists between his reason and his self-love, his opinions and his passions will have a reciprocal influence on each other; and the former will be objects to which the latter will attach themselves." Madison then identified the origins of these "different opinions" as "the diversity in the faculties of men, from which the rights of property originate." He believed that different talents and assets produce a difference in the ability to acquire property and that differences of property ownership create differences of opinions about the laws of property and its distribution, although other factors also stimulate differences of opinions and therefore factions.

> Different opinions concerning religion. . . , government, and many other points. . . ; an attachment to different leaders, ambitiously contending for pre-eminence and power; or to persons of other descriptions, whose fortunes have been interesting to the human passions, have . . . divided mankind into parties, inflamed them with mutual animosity, and rendered them much more disposed to vex and oppress each other, than

---

[2] This and all subsequent quotations of Madison's *Federalist Paper No. 10* are from Paul L. Ford, ed., *The Federalist* (New York: Holt, 1898), pp. 54–63.

> cooperate for their common good. So strong is this propensity of mankind, to fall into mutual animosities, that where no substantial occasion presents itself, the most frivolous and fanciful distinctions have been sufficient to kindle their unfriendly passions, and excite their most violent conflicts.

Still, differences in economic interests, such as differences in property and wealth, remained for Madison the most frequent causes of differences of opinion, and thus of factions:

> The most common and durable source of factions has been the various and unequal distribution of property. Those who hold, and those who are without property, have ever formed distinct interests in society. Those who are creditors, and those who are debtors, fall under a like discrimination. A landed interest, a manufacturing interest, a mercantile interest, with many lesser interests, grow up of necessity in civilized nations, and divide them into different classes, actuated by different sentiments and views.

Madison concluded that "the latent causes of faction are thus sown in the nature of man; and we see them everywhere brought into different degrees of activity, according to the different circumstances of civil society." Factions are more likely to occur in free nations than in dictatorships because "liberty is to faction what air is to fire, an aliment without which it instantly expires."

Contemporary group theory. Because public policies affect people differently, animosities will arise in public debates about which public and private goods the public sector should or should not provide. But how do political groups arise out of these animosities? Contemporary group theorists take membership in groups as a given of human nature. Like Aristotle, who believed that "man is by nature a political animal," they claim that "man is a social animal."[3] However, contemporary group theorists view interest groups more favorably than did Madison, and their definition of "interest group" does not include the ethical condemnation explicit in Madison's definition of faction. As one major group theorist puts it, "interest group refers to any group that, on the basis of one or more shared attitudes, makes certain claims upon other groups in society for the establishment, maintenance, or enhancement of forms of behavior that are implied by the shared attitudes."[4]

Group theorists believe that groups form spontaneously in response to mutually perceived threats or opportunities. As a hypothetical example, consider the set of male residents of the United States between the ages of eighteen and twenty-six who are without mental or physical maladies. Al-

[3] David B. Truman, *The Governmental Process: Political Interests and Public Opinion* (New York: Knopf, 1951), p. 14.

[4] Truman, *The Governmental Process,* p. 33.

though these men have nothing in common except some superficial characteristics, they are the members of a "potential" interest group. Imagine what might happen if the president and a majority of the members of Congress took steps to reinstate the military draft beyond the present system of registration. Some of these men might organize into an actual interest group to oppose the draft, especially during an unpopular war. That is, a shared potential attitude or interest, when triggered by an external event, turns a potential interest group into an actual one.

The power elite. The group theory of politics underlies several competing theories about American politics and government, all of which center about the basic question of which group rules the nation. For instance, those who accept the **power-elite theory** believe there is a "power elite in America . . . composed of men whose positions enable them to transcend the ordinary environments of ordinary men and women: they are in positions to make decisions having major consequences." These men "command . . . the major hierarchies and organizations of modern society. . . rule the big corporations . . . run the machinery of state and claim its prerogatives. . . direct the military establishment. . . [and] occupy the strategic command posts of the social structure in which are now centered the effective means of the power and the wealth and the celebrity which they enjoy."[5] The power-elite theory rests squarely on the intellectual foundations of group theory. Its major premise holds that a group of people whose shared interests weld them into a cohesive body runs the nation. At times, this view is equivalent to a charge of conspiracy. More commonly, the shared interests motivate open and legal political action rather than conspiracy.[6]

The Marxists. The **Marxist theory** of politics is not far from the power-elite view. One major difference between the two is that believers in the power-elite theory might conclude that such an elite is desirable, or that moral judgments about it are inappropriate. By contrast, Marxists lace their discussions with moral fervor. Their theory holds that some groups are good and others evil, and that political and economic history records the clash of competing groups. For Marxists, these groups are economic classes whose actual identity depends upon the state of economic development. According to traditional Marxist doctrine, the United States today might be entering an age of warfare between the workers—the proletariat—and the owners of industry—the capitalists. Each class receives motivation from "its" economic interest and property ownership. Thus, the Marxist view bears some resemblance to Madison's.

---

[5] C. Wright Mills, *The Power Elite* (New York: Oxford University Press, 1951), p. 4.

[6] A modified view holds that those with great wealth can afford to pay for political expertise and lobbying, leaving those who cannot buy such skills at a political disadvantage. See E. E. Schattschneider, *Politics, Pressures and the Tariff: A Study of Free*

The pluralists. Pluralists believe that power-elite and Marxist views oversimplify reality. **Pluralist theory** argues that a unitary class interest simply does not exist and that there is no single ruling elite. But many "spheres of influence" do exist. For example, in a local community an economic sphere of influence, a political sphere, and a sphere of public education may coexist. Not everyone has an equal share of political resources to affect decisions made in each sphere, but "inequalities" of influence between groups are "non-cumulative" because the influence or resources that one group uses to control one sphere do not help its leaders to control another sphere. For instance, those with substantial influence over mass transit decisions have little or no influence over public education. Accordingly, pluralists describe American politics as the politics of "dispersed," rather than cumulative, inequalities.[7] Many pluralists view group political action as desirable, for the potential influence each group exercises in the political process is believed to benefit its members. More important, the mechanism of group action is thought to be responsible for the collective allocation of benefits to the previously disadvantaged.

Group Action and Collective Goods

Interest-group formation as a collective good. The mechanism implicit in all of these variants of group theory is the same: given a threat or opportunity, a shared interest automatically leads to formation of a group. The group then influences the political process. The validity of this mechanism seems obvious and logical. However, this mechanism has been demonstrated to be neither valid, nor obvious, nor logical.[8] For, a contribution by one person to support group formation and maintenance to further a common attitude or interest is identical to a private action to supply a collective (with respect to the group's members) good. Individual action to further common, group interests thus

---

Private Enterprise in Pressure Politics, as Shown in the 1929–1930 Revision of the Tariff (Hamden, Conn.: Archon, 1963), and Schattschneider, *The Semisovereign People* (New York: Holt, Rinehart, and Winston, 1960). This view is incorrect because people will pursue the expected benefits of lobbying and electoral activities as long as they exceed the expected costs of those activities. Finding opportunities for political "investments" is the function of the political entrepreneur, whose actions and decisions are discussed later in this chapter. Payment for political action among even those of little wealth can often come out of the expected proceeds, or returns, from such activities. Hence, wealth itself does not convey a substantial political advantage, nor poverty a real disadvantage. In recent years the effective political mobilization of the poor, such as welfare recipients, offers an example of the absence of poverty's alleged political disadvantages.

[7] Robert A. Dahl, *Who Governs? Democracy and Power in an American City* (New Haven, Conn.: Yale University Press, 1961), p. 85.

[8] The following discussion relies on the work of Mancur Olson, Jr., *The Logic of Collective Action: Public Goods and the Theory of Groups*, rev. ed. (New York: Schocken, 1971).

shares all of the problems of private action to supply collective goods. Therefore, group theories of politics seem fundamentally at odds with rational human choice, because (as Chapter 3 observes) the private supply of collective goods hardly appears to be automatic.

To understand the equivalence of the group formation and maintenance problem on the one hand and the collective goods problems on the other, consider the hypothetical example of some citizens in a community of one million persons who want to fluoridate their water supply. Fluoridation would reduce dental-care costs by $100 for each resident each year, so the aggregated savings would be $100 million per year. For an average family—father, mother, and three children—the savings would be $500 per year. The citizens call on the water commissioners, who mumble something about planning, budgets, introducing foreign substances into pure water, and constitutional rights: their answer is *no*.

At this point, the citizens try a referendum vote directing the commissioners to fluoridate. To get the referendum on the next ballot requires a petition signed by 10 percent of the number of votes cast in the last election—say 35,000 signatures. Then, the referendum needs a majority to pass. An effort of this magnitude requires organization, time, and money. How much? Certainly far more than fluoridation is worth to an individual citizen. Acting alone, a citizen might collect 35,000 signatures in a year, but he or she would have to abandon all other work and leisure in pursuit of the family's $500 annual benefit. This would make little sense inasmuch as family members could buy their own liquid or tablet fluoride supplies for far less than $500 per year. Costs for campaigning to pass the referendum if it got on the ballot would only add to the potential burden. Thus, the costs of providing political support for community-wide fluoridation far exceed the benefits for an individual citizen.

The next step is to convince several families to contribute to the political fight. The citizens approach their neighbors and say, "We need to get a few thousand people together to pass this thing. Will you contribute $10 to help us start FIG (*F*luoridation *I*s *G*ood), Inc.?" The neighbors agree that fluoridation is good; they want it. But, like citizens who refuse to install antipollution equipment on their automobiles, as discussed in Chapter 3, the neighbors do not want to spend $10, since they believe that everyone else will do so and that no one will miss their small contributions. Their families will get the benefits of fluoridation for nothing. So the neighbors mutter something about not wanting to get involved in politics, and FIG founders.

Now, let us dissect this example. Suppose a poll shows that 300,000 persons, each expecting a $100-per-year benefit, favor the fluoridation referendum. Ignoring the rather minor cost of actually fluoridating the water, this means that the value—not utility—to this group is $30 million per year. The cost of organizing FIG and of getting the referendum passed is perhaps $1 million. Hence, the net positive benefit to this group of would-be supporters is $29 million. However, any individual citizen who bore the full cost of FIG would pay $1 million but receive $100 in the form of lower dental bills, for a net loss of $999,900. Clearly, if all 300,000 FIG supporters would pay only $3.33 each, then FIG, and therefore community-wide fluoridation, would become a reality. Each person's net benefit from such cooperative action would be $96.67 per year. But each citizen reasons that his or her contribution represents only one three-hundred-thousandth part of the total FIG cost. Why pay?

In sum, giving political support to fluoridation is a classic case of a collective good that displays a positive externality for those who want it. (The problem of forming an organization to oppose community-wide fluoridation for those who oppose it, for whom it is a public bad, parallels the problem of supporters.) Therefore, the formation of and contribution to an organization whose members prefer community-wide fluoridation is equivalent to supplying a collective good—the increased probability that community-wide fluoridation will be adopted. As Chapter 3 demonstrates and as we have just seen again, the major problem of supplying such goods is that private-choice mechanisms sometimes fail to provide them, or fail to provide enough of them. (Later in this chapter we shall see that the same problem afflicts public-choice mechanisms.) Hence, the formation of a political interest group is not automatic, no matter what its members' shared interests might be.

Private goods and group formation to supply collective goods. The paradoxical character of this insight is that people fail to contribute to the formation and maintenance of political organizations precisely because their interests and attitudes are commonly shared. A mutual preference, a shared interest, by itself indicates the possibility of a jointly supplied and consumed—collective—good. Fluoridated water—or the increased probability of its collective supply resulting from FIG's activities—could not reasonably be denied to someone who failed to support FIG, just as national defense could not be denied to draft dodgers or tax evaders.

How, then, do groups form? The answer lies partly in Chapter 3's observation that people sometimes supply public goods for private reasons. This answer provides an important clue about political organizations. They are unlikely to form unless they provide some private, divisible benefits as well as collective benefits to their members and supporters. One example is the health and life insurance policies that unions offer their members; others include social gatherings and various contrivances to promote a personal but divisible warmth toward the group. Appointments to leadership positions within an organization, which are valued for their prestige, also represent private benefits flowing from organizational support—for instance, the pronounced incidence of wealthy persons as officers and trustees of voluntary charitable organizations hardly seems accidental. Sometimes the private benefits are negative, disincentives for those who do not contribute to the organization. Examples include social ostracism or the threat of violence against free riders or "scabs," which sometimes accompanies the organization of unions.

People ordinarily contribute large amounts of money to political organizations, such as political parties or candidates' campaign committees, to further their own private goals. Contributions take the form of money and endorsements and often are the result of explicit bargains. The private benefits that contributors expect include private, divisible goods that derive from general public policy decisions. For example, the amount of government spending on highways is much like a public good, but the divisible goods associated with such programs include the allocation of road construction contracts and routings advantageous to different landowners. In other cases, the divisible goods that contributors—activists—receive include federal judgeships and ambassadorial appointments.

Another set of private goods associated with supporting political organizations involves private benefits of a psychological nature. Moral fervor often requires satisfaction in practice. This fervor shows itself in the allegiance that charismatic leaders can often exact from their followers. Ralph Nader's success might be partially attributed to this allegiance. Altruistic actions or actions that involve a sense of moral obligation fulfilled provide another source of private psychological benefits. For example, in 1968 many college students delayed their education to campaign for the presidential nomination of Senator Eugene McCarthy. The costs of this private provision of a collective (for McCarthy supporters) good were great, while the probability of success appeared to be nil. Private psychological benefits—the psychological satisfaction of fighting the perceived immoralities of the Vietnam War and Lyndon Johnson's presidency—probably accounted for much of this phenomenon and provided the private benefits in question.

Group formation and maintenance. In spite of the preceding observations, interest-group formation and maintenance remain a paradox, because if interest groups had to rely solely on internally generated private benefits, esprit de corps, and moral fervor, then few organizations would form, and those that did would be short-lived.[9] There are limited numbers of leadership positions in any group, and proliferating them to reward participation cheapens the currency. Private benefits such as insurance policies can also be sold at a lower price by firms that need not pay the added costs of promoting the public policy in question.[10] Esprit de corps, too, wanes in even the most closely knit group, and moral fervor rises and falls as quickly as issues change. Even intractable anger is difficult to maintain eternally. Moreover, those groups whose existence depends upon moral outrage or purpose "are

---

[9] This argument is forcefully stated in Robert H. Salisbury, "An Exchange Theory of Interest Groups," *Midwest Journal of Political Science,* 13 (February 1969), pp. 1–32.

[10] George J. Stigler, "Free Riders and Collective Action: An Appendix to Theories of Economic Regulation," *Bell Journal of Economics and Management Science,* 5 (Autumn 1974), p. 360.

especially vulnerable to slight changes in circumstances, including many over which the group has no control. For example, America First and the Committee to Defend America by Aiding the Allies were wiped out organizationally by Pearl Harbor."[11] Vietnam Veterans Against the War, like many other such groups, died of its own success. What, then, explains the formation and maintenance of interest groups?

Some groups are already organized and maintained for reasons other than politics before they enter the political process. For example, corporations are put together to increase the wealth of their owners, the shareholders. Before going into politics, corporate officers need only calculate whether political action might be legal and profitable; therefore, corporate officers do not experience the free-rider problems of interest-group organization and maintenance. All benefits they might receive are fully internal or sufficiently internal to the firm, not external to other firms. By contrast, trade or industrial associations made up of several corporations do experience free-rider problems of organizing for political action. However, such associations are often supported almost entirely by the largest firm in the industry, whose managers find it individually rational to maintain an association even though all other firms enjoy a free ride.

Other groups are not already organized and maintained before they enter the political process. These groups must partially rely on internally generated private benefits to sustain members' contributions. However, beyond these private benefits, groups often are supported by the very government whose policies their members seek to influence. Both the grange movement and the Farm Bureau Federation received government support; labor unions often rely on the force of law to compel union membership; professional organizations of doctors (in the past) and lawyers (currently) require membership for licensure; and the two major political parties are protected against third-party challenges by laws that make it difficult to get on the ballot or to get government-supplied campaign funds. Recently, many public interest groups have received government contracts and have secured government subsidies for participating in the rule-making proceedings of various federal regulatory agencies. Indeed, a general policy concerning such subsidies is under active consideration in the Congress.

Finally, in terms of the group-theory definition of "interest group" we offered earlier, federal departments, bureaus, and agencies, as Chapter 11 notes, are themselves merely special kinds of interest groups. Bureau heads lobby the members of Congress on behalf of their clients as well as bureau employees, although the members of Congress regularly appropriate funds to maintain bureau operations. Thus, the Social Security Administration and the Department of Agriculture are as much interest groups as are the American Association of Retired Persons and the National Farmers Union.[12] Of course,

---

[11] Salisbury, "An Exchange Theory of Interest Groups," p. 19.

[12] Peter Woll, *American Bureaucracy,* 2nd ed. (New York: Norton, 1977), p. 31.

government bureaus exist before they undertake political action, but they also rely for their survival on government action.

The political entrepreneur. Plainly, the relationship between interest groups and government seems complex. Interest-group leaders and members demand and sometimes receive preferred public policies from those who govern. Many of these public policies benefit only their groups' members, and sometimes those policies help to keep their organizations going. The flow of benefits in the opposite direction largely consists of monetary and nonmonetary electoral support to incumbent and would-be officeholders, although sometimes benefits from interest groups take the form of covert illegal cash payments.

The person on the other end of this exchange of votes, payments, endorsements, labor, and public policy is the **political entrepreneur.**[13] As Chapter 9 notes, the political entrepreneur at the national level is most often an elected official, such as a member of the House or Senate, although frequently cabinet secretaries, presidents and their assistants, party functionaries, and sometimes even interest-group leaders themselves forge the bargains between group members and those in government.

Political entrepreneurs, and especially those who survive as entrepreneurs, must act efficiently in developing public policies that enable groups to form and to continue in existence. After all, political entrepreneurs operate in an extremely competitive environment in which challengers enjoy regular opportunities in elections to seize their jobs. *Ceteris paribus,* the entrepreneur who can create the best exchange with an interest group enjoys a distinct electoral advantage. But political entrepreneurs' resources are limited, and they cannot satisfy the demands of each member of every political group. Their decisions about which groups to support and which to ignore thus affect not only the character of the interest groups and political entrepreneurs that do survive, but also the nature of public policies formed in the process of exchange.

Political competition and scarcity, as well as the pursuit of their own self-interest, lead political entrepreneurs to follow very general patterns of action concerning the organizations they benefit and help to sustain.[14] First,

---

[13] See Norman Frohlich, Joe A. Oppenheimer, and Oren R. Young, *Political Leadership and Collective Goods* (Princeton, N.J.: Princeton University Press, 1971); Salisbury, "An Exchange Theory of Interest Groups"; and Richard E. Wagner, "Pressure Groups and Political Entrepreneurs: A Review Article," *Papers on Non-Market Decision Making,* 1 (1969), pp. 151–170.

[14] Peter H. Aranson and Peter C. Ordeshook, "A Prolegomenon to a Theory of the Failure of Representative Democracy," in Richard D. Auster and Barbara Sears, eds., *American Re-evolution: Papers and Proceedings* (Tucson: University of Arizona Department of Economics, 1977), pp. 23–46, and Aranson and Ordeshook, "The Political Bases of Public Sector Growth in a Representative Democracy," paper prepared for delivery at the annual convention of the American Political Science Association, Washington, D.C., September 1978.

interest-group leaders' relative abilities to deliver votes and other forms of payment remain the central consideration. Groups that lack voting strength or the internal discipline to mobilize electoral support find small sympathy when bargaining with political entrepreneurs. By contrast, larger groups, or those with competent organizational capabilities, do better than groups without these attributes.[15] For instance, as a result of its better organization and vote mobilization, the National Rifle Association consistently defeats various and diffuse citizens' groups in political battles over gun control.

The superior ability of organizations to produce votes and other forms of political support explains why the central fact of activist political participation is that it occurs within the structure of groups. Consider the extreme case of two sets of one thousand citizens, the first of which is organized and the second of which is not. Understandably, a political entrepreneur will greatly prefer bargaining with the first set, rather than with the second. With the first set only one transaction, or bargain, is required; with the second, 1,000. With the first set, the fact of organization usually indicates the presence of a means to monitor members' compliance with the terms of any agreement made. With the second set, such a mechanism seems entirely absent. With the first set, some efficient, focused procedure for ongoing communications is available. With the second, communications remain unfocused and not fully productive. Though interest-group leaders can exact greater benefits from political entrepreneurs as a consequence of these advantages, the benefits of organization are mutual. Naturally, some groups are better organized than others, and these will be able to extract the greatest benefits from entrepreneurs.

The second consideration concerning entrepreneurs' decisions about which benefits to allocate to which interest groups focuses on free riders. As Chapter 9 observes at much greater length, the benefits flowing to a group's members should be divisible, private, in the sense that members of some other group will not receive benefits as a result of the original transaction. Were this not so, the entrepreneur could not withhold benefits from groups that did not satisfy their end of the bargain. Put differently, political entrepreneurs prefer operating with private benefits (divisible among groups) to operating with collective ones. For example, an interest group whose members demand a 10 percent general increase in total defense spending will not do as well politically as an interest group of retired military personnel who demand a 25 percent increase in their pensions—a divisible benefit. (Notice that a 10 percent increase in total defense spending might follow anyway as a result of the expanded pension benefits.)

The political entrepreneur's third consideration is that groups must benefit enough from his activities to pay for his work. Sometimes, as in the case of compulsory labor union membership, political entrepreneurs can legislate to aid group formation and maintenance and then collect votes,

---

[15] George J. Stigler, "The Theory of Economic Regulation," *Bell Journal of Economics and Management Science,* 2 (Spring 1971), pp. 3–21.

endorsements, and other payments, which would have been impossible if the group had not formed and survived. The importance of a group's ability to pay political entrepreneurs should not be doubted. Group strength (for example, membership) rises and falls with the members' abilities to purchase the services of political entrepreneurs. Those services can also aid group strength. But many organizations find their memberships and political strength rising and falling as a result of changes in such external influences as the business cycle, which affect their ability to pay the entrepreneur.[16]

Interest-Group Public Policy Demands[17]

Demands for public and private goods. As just noted, political entrepreneurs prefer to make bargains about public policies whose benefits are divisible, because indivisible benefits go even to those groups whose members fail to support the entrepreneurs. Of course, if we view different groups as individual actors, then divisible and indivisible benefits respectively become indistinguishable from private and public goods whose costs are both collective.[18]

Offered the choice of politically pursuing a collectively produced private good or a public good, which will interest-group leaders select? Not surprisingly, in most instances they, like political entrepreneurs, will choose to deal in public policies that create private, divisible benefits for them and their members. This preference rests on the same decision structure that leads those who share a common goal or attitude not to contribute to the creation and maintenance of an organization. More generally, this preference rests on the same decision structure that leads people not to contribute to the supply of a public good.

A simple game illustrates the nature of the interest-group leader's decision problem. Arbitrarily, suppose two organized groups, *1* and *2*, make up an electorate. Each group's political resources can be used to pursue at most one public policy, which will be enacted—collectively supplied—if the group's leaders pursue it. Each group's leaders must choose to ask political entrepre-

---

[16] Salisbury, "An Exchange Theory of Interest Groups," p. 8.

[17] This section relies heavily on Aranson and Ordeshook, "A Prolegomenon to a Theory of the Failure of Representative Democracy," and Aranson and Ordeshook, "The Political Bases of Public Sector Growth in a Representative Democracy."

[18] The collective goods problem appears at several levels and therefore may seem confusing. Chapter 3 cites the public goods problem as a general explanation for the use of public choice. In the FIG case, this chapter points out that achievement of a goal shared by all members of a *particular* group is a collective good with respect to each member of that group. Allocating private goods selectively to individual group members might be one way of overcoming the attendant free-rider problem. In the present discussion, a public good goes to the members of all groups, while a private good goes only to all the members of a single group. Essentially, this last context treats groups as individual human beings, but not objectionably so.

neurs either for a policy that produces a public (indivisible) good for their members *and* the members of the other group, or for a policy that produces a private (divisible) good for their members only. Finally, suppose that the monetary costs, C, and benefits, B, of each program are the same.

Table 6.1 shows the resulting two-person game. Notice that if each group seeks its own private good $\{a_2, b_2\}$, each receives a benefit of B. But suppose that the members of each group pay equal tax shares for the cost of each program. For instance, all taxpayers support private benefits such as federal subsidies to ship manufacturers, even though most of the benefits are private. Since two such programs are enacted in this example—one for each group—each group's cost (tax share) for each program becomes $C/2$, for a total cost of C. Hence, each group's payoff from $\{a_2, b_2\}$ is $B - C$.

However, suppose each group seeks the public policy that creates a public good $\{a_1, b_1\}$. Because a *public* good is created, each group receives a benefit of B from this decision, and the cost of producing the program, as before, is divided equally between the two groups, becoming $C/2$. Hence, each group's payoff from $\{a_1, b_1\}$ is $B - C/2$.

Finally, suppose the leaders of group *1* pursue the private-good program while those of group *2* pursue the public-good program. That is, $\{a_2, b_1\}$ is chosen. Group *1* will now receive B from its private-good program and B from the public-good program group *2* pursues, for total benefits of $2B$. Group *1* will also pay its equal share for the two programs, for a total cost of $C/2 + C/2 = C$. Hence, its total payoff from $\{a_2, b_1\}$ is $2B - C$. But notice that group *2*'s members only get B from the public-good program their leaders pursue, although they must pay for their share of supplying that program as well as their share of supplying group *1*'s private-good program. Group *2*'s payoff from $\{a_2, b_1\}$ thus becomes $B - C$. Of course, the payoffs are reversed for $\{a_1, b_2\}$.

If group *2*'s leaders choose b_2, then group *1*'s leaders are indifferent as between a_1 and a_2. However, if group *2*'s leaders choose b_1, then group *1*'s leaders will choose a_2 if $2B - C$ exceeds $B - C/2$. This occurs if B exceeds $C/2$. Put differently, group *1*'s leaders will choose to pursue the collective supply of their group's private-goods program if the benefit associated with that program exceeds their tax share ($C/2$) to pay for it. If B is less than $C/2$, then they will not choose a_2. However, notice that a_1, pursuing the public-goods legislation, would not then be profitable, for with B less than $C/2$, $B - C/2$ would

Table 6.1 Policy Game Between Interest Groups

	Group 2's Strategies	
Group 1's Strategies	b_1, seek public good	b_2, seek private good
a_1, seek public good	$B - C/2, B - C/2$	$B - C, 2B - C$
a_2, seek private good	$2B - C, B - C$	$B - C, B - C$

become negative, and therefore all political activity would be counterproductive.

The game described in Table 6.1 is a slightly modified form of a prisoners' dilemma, and the paradox of the dilemma remains unchanged.[19] The two groups arrive at $\{a_2, b_2\}$ for individual payoffs of $B - C$, even though with $\{a_1, b_1\}$ each would receive $B - C/2$, a greater payoff. As has been noted earlier and will be discussed again in Chapter 9, political entrepreneurs have little incentive to enforce an $\{a_1, b_1\}$ play of the game, for they can exact small payment from legislating programs that produce purely public goods.

This game has been extended to situations containing many interest groups, in which communications among groups as well as coalitions are possible, and in which members of different groups can oppose each others' demands for the collective supply of private goods.[20] With only minor variations, the prisoners' dilemma remains intact. In sum, interest-group leaders and members enter the political process in search of private goods. The members of one group do not ordinarily oppose the collective provision of another group's program unless it is granted principally at their expense. To give such opposition would be equivalent to supplying a public good—the tax share all other groups would not have to pay for the defeated program—to the members of all other groups. The major restraint on any one group's demands seems to be that its members' tax share to pay for its program not exceed the benefit its members receive from the program.

Interest groups and collective action. The implications of this discussion seem troubling.[21] Chapter 3 reviews various reasons for preferring the outcomes of public-choice mechanisms over those of private choice. One reason stands out: the inability of private decision procedures to produce the correct level of public goods, such as national defense, clean air, and police protection. By contrast, the analysis of political interest-group decision making offered here shows that group leaders will seldom pursue politically exactly those public policies that would create public goods. Instead, they pursue public policies that would create private goods for themselves and their members. The demands placed on elected officials, then, bear little or no relation to the theoretical reasons most often given for collective action. Indeed, the more successful interest-group leaders become in communicating

---

[19] The modification arises because group *1*'s payoff from $\{a_1, b_2\}$ and group *2*'s from $\{a_2, b_1\}$ are the same for each as from $\{a_2, b_2\}$. However, for groups *1* and *2* respectively, a comparison of $\{a_2, b_1\}$ and $\{a_1, b_2\}$ with $\{a_1, b_1\}$ remains as in the original prisoners' dilemma. The play of the game is unaffected by this modification.

[20] Aranson and Ordeshook, "A Prolegomenon to a Theory of the Failure of Representative Democracy."

[21] Some of these implications are intuitively but brilliantly revealed in Theodore S. Lowi, *The End of Liberalism: The Second Republic of the United States,* 2nd ed. (New York: Norton, 1979).

with their members, the more extensively such tendencies as those identified here carry over into the electoral process generally.

Elected officials do understand and probably act on diffuse demands to produce public goods. Such issues as the strategic arms balance with the Soviet Union, the inflation rate, and the spread of crime occasion the standard campaign rhetoric, but promises of new army bases and airplane contracts, subsidies for pensioners living on fixed incomes, and grants for experimental nighttime lighting of business districts form the real substance of campaigns. Officeholders often supply public goods apparently largely because constitutional form (limits on what elected officials can do) and propagandistic purposes require them to do so.

The optimality of public policies that are approved in response to such demands for private goods seems to be random. Of course, optimality is difficult to judge, because everyone must pay taxes to support the program that only the members of a particular group enjoy. Nevertheless, suppose that B and C represent dollar amounts, that an electorate is made up of n groups of equal size, and that everyone pays equal taxes. That is, the membership of a particular group pays C/n in taxes to support its own collectively supplied program or that of any other group. The only constant limitation on the political demands of interest-group leaders is that B must exceed C/n. For example, assume that a national electorate has 100 million taxpayers, each of whom belongs to one and only one of 1000 groups of 100,000 persons each. A particular interest-group's leaders might successfully demand a program whose total benefits to group members was little more than 1/1000 of its cost.

In a large electorate, a particular group's leaders can demand much of the political entrepreneurs because the costs (taxes) of satisfying such demands are spread out over the entire population. In the instance of 1000 groups in an electorate of 100 million, a particular group's leaders can demand a program costing $200 million, for which the average taxpayer covers only $2. The benefit to a member of the group must equal only $2.01, or $201,000 for the entire group. Thus, a cost of $2 levied on each of 100 million taxpayers is imposed to produce a benefit worth $2.01 to each of 100,000 group members.

This arrangement is not Pareto preferred, because each group member could receive a check for $2.02 at a cost of $202,000 spread across the taxpaying population. Each taxpayer would then pay two-tenths of a cent in the form of a simple wealth transfer to support this new program. Plainly, benefited group members and taxpayers would both be better off. The reason that Pareto preferred arrangements are not more common follows from the nature of entrepreneurial and group-member preferences for bargaining in private goods rather than public ones. Simple cash wealth transfers are difficult to restrict to a single group. Beneficial laws, regulations, and subsidies-in-kind such as food stamps or monies earmarked for particular kinds of expenditures such as medical expenses or home insulation are not so difficult to make divisible and excludable.

The example of 1000 groups interprets interest-group demands in the worst possible light. Perhaps B exceeds not only C/n but also C itself. However, notice that if B does exceed C, group leaders might be sensible to purchase the benefits of the program in the private sector, especially if the group's budget is limited and group members want programs for which B is less than C. For example, suppose a group's leaders can use their *political* resources in pursuit of a program for which B exceeds C, or one for which B is less than C, but not both. Although we must seriously qualify predictions about such choices, there is some reason to conclude that the group's leaders will pursue the inefficient program, which all taxpayers must help to supply, since they can buy the efficient program privately.

In sum, we find that interest-group leaders demand the collective supply of benefits that are not merely private but also not Pareto preferred. If elected officeholders constantly acceded to such demands, the growth of government described in Chapter 1 would be at least partially explained. Of course, we must examine the decisions of election candidates, officeholders, and bureaucrats before we can fully verify such an explanation for government growth. We would also have to account for the failure of government to spend 100 percent of GNP.

A TYPOLOGY OF ACTIVISTS

Studying the interplay of activists' goals and the pursuit of collective and private goods helps us to understand activist decision making. However, activists in the United States are relatively fewer in number than are voters, as Table 6.2 shows. Extensive involvement in politics beyond voting is not usual, and therefore information about it is more difficult to collect. Rather than examine each and every form of activist electoral participation, we can more usefully construct a typology of activists: a set of different categories into which they can be placed, which seems to make sense in terms of differences in their decisions and actions.

Private and Collective Goods

The first distinction is between activists whose major goals of political participation are the securing of private goods and those whose major goals are the securing of collective goods. A few examples illustrate the difference between these two forms of activists' goals.

Private goods as activist goals. Political appointments are highly divisible benefits. For example, lawyers wishing to become federal judges must acknowledge that the president appoints them and that he usually chooses his appointees from among party supporters. Therefore, would-be federal

Table 6.2 Forms of Political Participation, 1972

Voted	72.8%
Talked to people "to show them why they should vote for one of the parties or candidates"	31.6%
Wore a campaign button or put a bumper sticker on car	14.0%
Gave money to a political party	10.4%
Went to political meetings, rallies, dinners	8.9%
Worked for party or candidate	5.0%

Source: Data are from a Center for Political Studies 1972 Election Study and are made available by the Inter-University Consortium for Political Research.

judges often enter party politics as contributing activists.[22] They will probably join and work for the party whose candidates hold positions they perceive to be closer to their own public policy preferences, although sometimes they will work instead for the party most likely to prevail in presidential elections over the years. Federal judgeships are distinctly divisible, private goods with very real collective consequences. This form of political exchange, work for appointment, is called **patronage.**

Government contracts are also divisible goods. For instance, a construction-firm executive who is in pursuit of government contracts on bridge-building projects might find out that the members of the county board of supervisors make all decisions about who gets the contracts. The executive then contributes large sums of money to the candidates who are apparently most likely to win the supervisors election. Contributions to both candidates in a particular race are not uncommon in the absence of laws requiring the disclosure of contributions.[23] The executive expects a private good, the contract, in return. This form of exchange—money for contracts—is called **graft** provided it is illegal.

Finally, more general laws convey private benefits to the members of particular groups while damaging the interests of others. For example, perhaps a labor leader in a southern state must decide about endorsing one of two equally strong potential Democratic nominees for the governor's office. He offers to endorse the candidate who promises to campaign for the repeal

[22] Harold W. Chase, *Federal Judges: The Appointing Process* (Minneapolis: University of Minnesota Press, 1972). Senators in the president's party conduct initial screenings, and (as Chapters 9 and 12 note) the Senate Judiciary Committee and then the entire Senate must approve the nominations. Recent attempts to make judicial appointments less partisan do not seem very successful.

[23] Peter H. Aranson and Melvin J. Hinich, "Some Aspects of the Political Economy of Election Campaign Contribution Laws," *Public Choice*, 34 (1979), pp. 435–461.

of the state's right-to-work law. The president of the state's association of manufacturers, which opposes repeal, faces the same decision problem from the opposite view.

The goods that activists in these examples pursue are private because they are divisible. One and only one person can receive a particular judgeship or contract. The repeal of a right-to-work law is a private good for union members compared with the rest of the population. Of course, these private goods have their collective aspects. Taxpayers must pay for and drive over the construction executive's bridges. Citizens must live with a particular judge on the bench. Industrialists and, arguably, consumers and those opposed to compulsory union membership must abide with the bargain struck between union leaders and potential governors. Everyone must also accept a possible change in the outcome of an election as an indirect but collective consequence of the incentives for contributions that these private goods create.

Public goods as activist goals. Activists often profess a desire to achieve goals—to enact public policies—that produce public goods. Such matters first induced many of them to become activists. The key differences between enacting private and collective goods as activist goals are divisibility and intent, though sometimes these differences seem hard to detect. For instance, an older person might become an activist to support a candidate who promises higher Social Security payments. Considering the present structure of Social Security, this increase in payments represents an indivisible public good, because nearly everyone either pays Social Security taxes or receives payments from the system. Of course, higher Social Security payments do represent a private benefit for the activist.

The pure pursuit of public goods is extremely rare and is usually connected to emotional issues that seldom persist. Such issues infrequently enjoy widespread support on either side. For example, a few stalwarts continue to press for prohibiting the manufacture and sale of alcoholic beverages. The abortion issue is similar, although both those who oppose and those who support the legality of abortions have maintained their numbers and their fervor for some years.

Most activists at one time or another pursue the collective supply of both private and public goods. But, the more public-goods-oriented activists' goals become, the less likely are they to be responsive to organizational discipline. Divisible benefits, which can be withheld from them, lose meaning. However, activists driven by the pursuit of public goods are also less likely to find real political success. This generalization holds true precisely because collective goods are indivisible: benefits from them accrue even to mavericks who ignore party or interest-group discipline. Yet the cost of such independence often is overall organizational and political failure. Therefore, political organizations specializing in the collective production of private goods are likely to be more successful than those specializing in the collective production of public goods.

Amateurs and Professionals

An **amateur activist** is one whose regular source of income is not politics, while a **professional activist**'s regular source of income *is* politics. These definitions differ somewhat from traditional ones, but various definitions are not contradictory. Most commonly, people use the terms *amateur* and *professional* to emphasize that the professional is in politics largely for "intrinsic rewards" that he or she might find in other lines of work.[24] For a professional, a position in the party or sustaining the organization or winning elections comes before principles. Candidates chosen by professionals are likely to be electable rather than losers who take principled but unpopular issue positions. Understanding the requirements of organization, professionals will bargain in the currency of private goods, "private advantage, sectional loyalties, and ethnic and nationality claims."[25] Issues themselves, especially those that engage highly conflicting positions on public-goods legislation, "will be avoided except in the most general terms or if the party is confident that a majority supports its position."[26] The party will change positions on issues if electoral success requires it.

A description of amateur politicians would emphasize the difference in political action between the pursuit of public and of private goods. Amateurs prefer candidates and campaigns of "commitment," those attached to "some set of principles or goals."[27] They would avoid private goods as political goals, for a "politics of principle would necessarily attach little value to—and indeed would criticize—appeals to private, group, or sectional interest. . . , which for the professional are the motive force of politics, [but for] the amateur [are] irrelevant, irrational, or immoral."[28]

Professionals thus operate with private goods, although they are likely to use any collective goods (general public policy proposals) necessary to win elections. But they want to win elections to maintain their positions and their salaries. By contrast, amateurs operate with collective goods and find the use of private benefits distasteful and perhaps even unprincipled and unethical. They want to win elections not for political position, but to promote their preferences concerning the creation of public goods. Any distinction between professional and amateur activists must place position and salary (as compared to the lack of them) as more highly valued goals of the professional activist. A concern for winning elections, for extrinsic benefits, and for party

---

[24] James Q. Wilson, *The Amateur Democrat: Club Politics in Three Cities* (Chicago: University of Chicago Press, 1966), p. 17. This discussion of the difference between amateurs and professionals relies heavily on Wilson's work.

[25] Wilson, *The Amateur Democrat,* p. 17.

[26] Wilson, *The Amateur Democrat,* p. 17.

[27] Wilson, *The Amateur Democrat,* p. 18.

[28] Wilson, *The Amateur Democrat,* p. 18.

discipline occurs precisely because the professional's bread and butter depend on these things. Amateurs can always return to private life, sometimes at little personal cost. Usually, their political action is only temporary, so they can afford to be more "honest" about political principles.

Political Parties and Interest Groups

The third distinction is between activists who work for political parties and those who work for interest groups. A **political party** is an organization whose members actually nominate candidates for elective offices, whereas an **interest group** is an organization whose members seek private and collective benefits from the electoral and governmental processes—by helping to elect a "friendly" candidate or by lobbying, for example—but who do not directly offer candidates for nomination and election. Activists sometimes move between parties and interest groups and very often occupy positions in each kind of organization, but the stated intentions of each organization's members concerning the fielding of candidates usually differ.

ACTIVIST PREFERENCES, STRATEGIES, AND DECISIONS

The preceding discussion generates a typology of activists along three dimensions: party and interest group activists, amateurs and professionals, and those who seek private goods or collective goods in the public sector. These dimensions generate eight kinds of activists: 1. party professionals in pursuit of private or, 2. collective goods; 3. party amateurs in pursuit of private or, 4. collective goods; 5. interest-group professionals in pursuit of private or, 6. collective goods; and, 7. interest group amateurs in pursuit of private or, 8. collective goods. Activists who fall in different categories should exhibit different preferences and make different decisions, which in turn should affect the conduct and outcomes of elections and public policy decisions.

Here we examine the nature of decision making by activists in different categories. First we consider party activists according to whether they face decisions in primary or general elections. Then we examine the decisions of interest-group activists, particularly decisions about contributing money to campaigns, according to their visibility.

Party Activists in Primary Elections

Party professionals. Because politics represents a regular source of income to professional activists, they try to achieve those outcomes that make their positions secure and add to their value. As we have noted, party professionals may prefer particular public policies, but they use political activity to generate private goods. The heads of the Democratic and Republican National Committees are party professionals, as are the big-city bosses, such as Atlanta's Mayor Maynard Jackson, the late Mayor Richard J. Daley of Chicago, and Mayor Kevin White of Boston.

The party professionals' principal goals are to win presidential, gubernatorial, and mayoral elections and to have their party's candidates win a sufficient number of legislative offices to gain control of the legislature. Winning candidates—those who become officeholders—control usable resources, such as appointments, government contracts, and the passage of divisible public policies. Thus, in primary elections and in other nomination contests, party professionals will ordinarily support those candidates who seem most able to win their general elections.

However, on many issues the distribution of preferences among activists and citizen identifiers in both major parties is quite broad. Each party has its center and right and left wings. If party professionals successfully support nomination candidate A at one issue position over candidate B at a different position, then A might lose the general election support of B's backers. But if party professionals back B, who loses the nomination, then they might lose their jobs, if A retaliates. Their decision problem may become even more difficult if several candidates vie for several nominations.

Party professionals are reluctant to lose control of nomination procedures, and they give up control only if trying to maintain it might threaten their jobs. Many threats come from party amateurs, who wish to change nomination procedures to favor their candidates. However, as Chapter 7 reveals and as Chapter 4 has already suggested, this conflict has an unusual implication. Most people view a tightly controlled nomination process as less "democratic" than a loosely controlled one. However, the party professional's purpose in controlling nominations is not just to preserve a job but also to nominate winning candidates. By definition, a winning candidate in a general election receives more votes than his opponent. But an election victory at least partially reflects popular—democratic—approval, so the professional party activist's control of nominations may be important to democratic assent because the general election candidates he chooses please more voters than would be the case if amateurs controlled the nomination process.

Party amateurs. The preferences of amateurs and of the general electorate may fortuitously coincide, although candidates nominated by party amateurs seem less likely to be acceptable to the general electorate than those nominated by party professionals. The amateur activist's livelihood does not directly depend on electoral success, and consequently he tends to satisfy his own public policy preferences, not those of the general electorate. This is especially true if the amateur's primary interests are in collective goods. But if activists are also concerned with the private consequences of nominations, they may be more likely to nominate a candidate with a better chance of winning the general election. The lawyer who seeks appointment to the bench or the contractor who wants to build a road may enter party politics to fulfill such desires, and supporting a loser for nomination can defeat such purposes. Of course, whether we should view such people as amateurs or professionals is problematical.

Because most party amateurs seem to be concerned with the collective consequences of the nomination, they may be more willing than professionals to support losers over winners. For example, amateur activists might prefer strict environmental protection legislation and nominate an agreeable candidate. Even if this ideologically satisfying candidate loses the general election, amateur activists at least enjoy the symbolic satisfaction of calling everyone's attention to the issue—of raising consciousness. That their candidate lost probably indicates to them that a winning nominee would not have advanced their cause anyway.

Voting in primaries. As Chapter 4 notes, primary elections are gaining ever wider use in the United States to choose each party's general election candidates at the state and local level as well as delegates to the national presidential nominating conventions. Because many voters participate in primaries, they are much like general elections. Thus, the citizen's voting decision process, as Chapter 5 explains it, helps to describe voting in primaries, although primary voting differs somewhat from voting in general elections. Compared to general elections, primaries often have more than two candidates in each race. The change in many primaries to proportional representation in selecting presidential nomination convention delegates partially explains this phenomenon. In its analysis of PR and SMD election systems, Chapter 4 points out why this is so.

The n-candidate calculus of voting in primaries is more complex than the two-candidate representation described in Chapter 5. However, one pattern seems to emerge: in deciding for whom and whether to vote, primary voters act as if they calculate utilities and *two* sets of probabilities. The first set concerns each nomination candidate's electability in the primary election or subsequent convention; primary voters should try not to throw their votes away on sure nomination losers. The second set of probabilities concerns each nomination candidate's potential electability in the general election, if he wins the nomination.

The more concerned activists become about party victory, the more likely they are to vote for a potential general-election winner rather than an ideologically pleasing candidate (if a conflict between ideology and electability emerges). Professional party activists probably rest most of their primary voting decisions on general-election electability, while amateurs rest theirs on ideological acceptability. Again, the amateurs' decision criteria partially depend on whether private or collective goods and consequences motivate their actions. However, we should expect ideological voting in most primaries because amateurs always greatly outnumber professionals.

Party Activists in General Elections

Party professionals. In general elections, party professionals hold preferences and confront strategic decisions that in many ways are indistinguishable from those of candidates. Chapter 7 describes these preferences and decisions at greater length, especially as they apply to party platforms and public policy. Here, though, we describe organizational aspects of the professional in the party's general-election campaign.

The professional party activist's major goal is electing party candidates. To do so, he must generate electoral resources and disperse them among candidates and activists, hoping that they will win elections and generate additional resources. Two simplified examples show how difficult these tasks might become. First, suppose the professional is in charge of distributing $30,000 in campaign funds among three of the party's candidates, who are running for Senate seats in Utah, Oregon, and Maine. All three states are alike in that $15,000 in advertising adds one more percentage point in the polls. The candidate in Utah has 29 percent of the votes in the polls, the candidate in Oregon has 79 percent, and the one in Maine has 49 percent. The professional ought to ignore the Utah and Oregon races and "buy" a victory in Maine. But the original $30,000 comes from contributors in Utah and Oregon as well as Maine. Ignoring the Utah and Oregon candidates may dry up party funds. Or, these other candidates might begin to raise their own money and spend it on their own campaigns, which leaves the win in Oregon and the loss in Utah unchanged but might also assure defeat in Maine.

Second, suppose the professional is in charge of distributing campaign funds to the party's congressional, senatorial, and presidential candidates. The party's incumbents have solid control of the House and Senate, so the professional decides to distribute all of the money to the presidential campaign, since that is a close race. After all, minimum winning coalitions may be sufficient in the House and Senate, but they will require a two-thirds vote rather than a majority if the president is of the other party. This decision is fine for the party, but *losing* candidates in individual House and Senate races might complain bitterly. Similarly, winning candidates may be so angry that they are less than enthusiastic about their newly elected president.[29]

These two problems are simple compared to some that professionals, and an occasional amateur, must solve. The solutions to those real, terribly complicated problems depend upon one critical assumption: that the party whose activists can resolve them is more likely to win elections than one whose activists cannot. Such a party often is led by a well-disciplined organization of professionals rather than by a loose confederation of amateurs.

---

[29] The clash of goals is discussed in Joseph A. Schlesinger, "The Primary Goals of Political Parties: A Clarification of Positive Theory," *American Political Science Review,* 69 (September 1975), pp. 840–849.

Party amateurs. The party amateur is the bane of the party professional, since their preferences seem likely to differ. The professional works either for the entire party or for a large segment of it, while the amateur works for one or a few candidates or for a desired public policy. The professional's livelihood depends upon party success while the amateur's does not. Often, the professional's major concern is in receiving and disbursing private goods, while the amateur's is in producing public goods. To sum up, professionals must rely on organization, reward, discipline, and efficiency, while amateurs remain less concerned about these matters. Worse yet, professionals must use amateurs' resources to win elections, but amateurs are reasonably independent from professionals.

While the professional operates in an environment of uncertainty (deciding in a gaming context) the amateur operates in an environment of risk, much like a citizen does. Only those few amateurs who contribute sufficient resources to affect a general election campaign (make a material difference in the election outcome) are in a gaming situation. Furthermore, the professional's game is often as much one of bargaining *with* the amateur's candidate as it is a game *against* the opposing candidate. The party professional also must bargain and compete to get private goods to the right people to produce votes and other resources, while the amateur more often engages in decision making under conditions of risk to help an ideologically pleasing candidate win office. In this battle, professionals usually win, for they are willing to do what the ideologically committed amateur often is not: wheel and deal and provide private goods.

Table 6.3 reports some data supporting this view. Polls of New Jersey professionals and New York City amateurs show quite a remarkable difference in the services they perform for their constituents. The professionals typically seek to distribute private, individualized benefits to constituents, while the amateurs show little interest in such activities. These differences permeate the political styles of party professionals and amateurs in the entire electoral process.

Interest-Group Activists in Elections

Real differences between the electoral decisions of party and interest-group activists are often difficult to find. Both prefer a particular candidate, and both seem willing to contribute resources beyond their votes to that candidate's victory. Interest-group members often enter into party organizations and sometimes even control the allocation of party resources.[30] From time to time, interest groups and political parties seem indistinguishable, which reflects the common perception of American political parties as large

---

[30] See, for example, Fay Calkins, *The CIO and the Democratic Party* (Chicago: University of Chicago Press, 1952).

Table 6.3 Differences Between Actions of Amateurs and Professionals

The Service	Percentage of New Jersey Politicians Performing it "often"	Percentage of New York Reform Democrats Performing it "often"
Helping deserving people get public jobs	72	0
Showing people how to get their Social Security benefits, welfare, unemployment compensation, etc.	54	5
Helping citizens who are in difficulty with the law (Do you help them get straightened out?)	62	6

Source: Reprinted from "The Changing Pattern of Urban Party Politics" by Fred I. Greenstein, in volume number 353 of *Annals of the American Academy of Political and Social Science.* The New Jersey statistics are from Richard T. Frost, "Stability and Change in Local Politics," *Public Opinion Quarterly,* 25 (Summer 1961), pp. 231–232. The New York statistics are from Vernon M. Goetcheus, "The Village Independent Democrats: A Study in the Politics of the New Reformers," unpublished senior distinction thesis, Honors College, Wesleyan University, 1963, pp. 64–66.

coalitions of formal and informal interest groups.[31] Yet party activists must maintain political organizations to field election candidates. The robustness of these organizations is not quite as important to interest-group activists, for they can go shopping from party to party to find candidates who will support a particular public policy position.

The bad reputation of interest groups. As we fully acknowledged earlier in this chapter, entrepreneurs forge public policies that create private, divisible benefits for interest-group members, and in exchange, interest-group leaders promise organizational support for the entrepreneurs' election campaigns as well as other, sometimes illegal, payments. Not surprisingly, interest group activities are often frowned upon. Interest group participation in election campaigns is often regarded as inappropriate, at best, and more often as dishonest and unethical.

The form of support activists give candidates can vary greatly. Newspaper editors, interest-group leaders, and community notables not usually

[31] This view is advanced in Samuel J. Eldersveld, *Political Parties: A Behavioral Analysis* (Chicago: Rand McNally, 1964), and in V. O. Key, Jr., *Politics, Parties, & Pressure Groups,* 5th ed. (New York: Crowell, 1964).

associated with politics might issue public endorsements. Support to one candidate can even take the form of an expected endorsement withheld from another. Contributions of labor and expertise are especially important when they come from those groups without substantial financial resources. Campaign workers can do everything from stuffing envelopes and distributing literature to engaging in sophisticated strategic planning. Again, the withholding of an expected contribution of labor can be as important as a positive contribution of labor. The most interesting and controversial form of campaign contribution is money, and we devote the rest of this section to it, while understanding that nonmonetary contributions share many characteristics of monetary ones.

Financial contributions provoke the most serious attacks and the most concerted efforts at control, even though it is seldom clear either what money does buy or what it should buy in an election campaign. Recent compilations of campaign contribution data by Common Cause, the citizen interest group, indicate a statistical relationship between interest-group campaign donations and voting in committees of the House of Representatives.[32] For example, in the election year of 1976, maritime union political committees donated some $102,763 to members of the House Merchant Marine and Fisheries Committee. In the following year, committee members voted favorably for a bill that would require at least 9.5 percent of the oil imported to the United States to be carried in American ships. The twenty-four committee members who voted in favor of the bill each received average contributions of $3428 from maritime union political committees. The five representatives voting against the bill each received average contributions of $200 (three received nothing).

Patterns of contributions followed by votes such as these occur regularly, and Common Cause has documented several similar instances. For example, voting on the Carter administration's 1978 hospital cost containment bill was correlated with the presence and amount of contributions to House members from the American Medical Association. An amendment to that bill that would let hospitals pass through to patients additional expenses created by increases in labor costs, was more heavily supported by those receiving labor union contributions than by those not receiving such contributions. Campaign contributions by milk producers are alleged to have sustained federal milk price support systems, which add substantially to the price consumers pay for dairy products.

What campaign contributions mean. Whether of money or of other goods and services, campaign contributions can carry three different but not always mutually exclusive interpretations. The first interpretation might be called the civics-book view, which holds that contributions to election campaigns resemble contributions to charitable organizations. Contributors give money in support of a public policy goal already shared by a particular candidate,

---

[32] Common Cause, *How Money Talks in Congress* (Washington, D.C., 1978; xerox).

HOW MONEY TALKS IN CONGRESS

A Common Cause Study of the Impact of Money on Congressional Decision-Making

October 1978

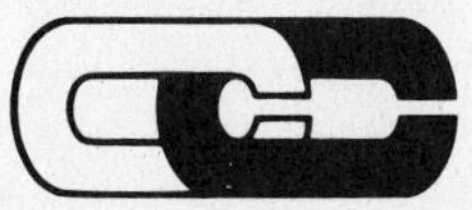

Common Cause

Recent campaign contribution disclosure laws have made it possible for organizations such as Common Cause to publish studies reporting a clear association between interest group contributions to members of Congress and subsequent votes favorable to those groups by the legislators who got the money.

and they expect nothing in return but the enhanced probability that the goal will be achieved. Such contributions require no communications or bargaining between donor and recipient. In political applications of this view, contributors donate to the campaign of their preferred candidate or party with no thought that the recipient will change his public policy positions as a result. If the candidate or party wins, perhaps because of the contribution, then the donor expects nothing in return save what the candidate or party would have done if elected in the absence of the contribution. In the examples of the maritime unions, the AFL-CIO, the American Medical Association, and the milk producers, the civics-book interpretation would hold that contributions by these groups merely reflect the preferences of donors who have no expectations of altered decisions on the part of the legislators.

The civics-book view probably accurately describes contribution decisions by givers of small amounts of money and labor. Candidates could not possibly negotiate separately with hundreds of thousands of contributors, each of whom offered less than, say, $100. But contributors of substantially higher levels of funds probably do not fit well within the civics-book view. More often, a large contribution results from explicit bargaining in which the contribution represents a payoff to the candidate for specific public policy concessions or for access to the officeholder. This second view of campaign contributions, the view of political money as "bribery," is most forcefully argued by those who wish to reform the electoral process, either through stricter contribution limits and disclosure-of-contribution requirements or through public financing of all campaigns.

The metaphor of bribery may seem overly simplistic. Some would argue that the real market for contributions is one of "extortion" by those who hold a monopoly on the use of coercion—the officeholders. For example, in 1974 the late Nelson A. Rockefeller offered a glimpse at the possible extortionate nature of campaign contributions. Testifying before both House and Senate committees on his nomination to the vice-presidency, Rockefeller responded to several questions about his own and his family's campaign giving. He suggested that his family welcomed the new campaign contributions legislation passed in 1974 because it limited the amount of money any one person could give.[33] In earlier years, family members had contributed to several campaigns.

Why should the Rockefellers welcome this legislation? Surely any family members who did not wish to do so could refrain from contributing—or could they? Apparently some Rockefellers, as well as many other wealthy people, view campaign donations as "protection money" or "insurance," a response to political extortion. After all, Rockefeller business interests are

---

[33] United States House of Representatives, Committee on the Judiciary, "Nomination of Nelson A. Rockefeller to be Vice-President of the United States," *Hearings,* 93rd Cong., 2nd Sess., 1974, p. 115; United States Senate, Committee on Rules and Administration, "Nomination of Nelson A. Rockefeller of New York to be Vice-President of the United States," *Hearings,* 93rd Cong., 2nd Sess., 1974, pp. 617–618.

widespread. David Rockefeller is "chairman of the board of directors of the Chase Manhattan Bank; member of the board of directors of the B. F. Goodridge Company, of the Rockefeller Brothers, Inc., and of the Equitable Life Insurance Society; a trustee of the Rockefeller Institute for Medical Research, of the Council on Foreign Relations, of the Museum of Modern Art, of Rockefeller Center, and on the Board of Overseers of Harvard College." James Stillman Rockefeller is "chairman and director of First National City Bank of New York; member of the board of directors of the International Banking Corporation, of the National City Foundation, of the First New York Corporation, of the First National City Trust Company, of the Mercantile Bank of Canada, of the National City Realty Corporation, of Kimberly Clark Corporation, of the Northern Pacific Railway Company, of the National Cash Register Company, of Pan American World Air Lines, and of Monsanto Company."[34]

Financial holdings of other family members are almost as extensive, and few substantial government actions could occur that would not affect Rockefeller family interests in some manner. The Rockefellers know this, and so do House and Senate candidates in search of campaign contributions. Did Rockefeller family contributions to political campaigns represent a principled action of concerned citizens, as in the civics-book view? Did they represent the *quid pro quo* of political "bribery?" Or, were at least some of the contributions responses to a perceived form of political "extortion" by those who staff the tollgates of modern political society, the members of the legislature? Nelson A. Rockefeller's happy acceptance of the legislated limits on contributions indicates that at least some of the monies that family members donated represented a form of "insurance."

Other examples of this third interpretation of campaign contributions are not uncommon. One observer wrote of Illinois legislators that "a few . . . go so far as to introduce some bills that are deliberately designed to shake down groups which oppose them and which pay to have them withdrawn. These bills are called 'fetchers,' and once their sponsors develop a lucrative field, they guard it jealously."[35] The New York *Times* characterized the payments made by an engineer to former Vice-President Spiro T. Agnew, when he was governor of Maryland, as follows:

> These payments . . . reflected . . . [the engineer's] understanding, based upon experience, of the system in which a firm such as his had to participate . . . to insure its survival and growth in Maryland. . . . [T]he selection of engineers for state roads contracts has rested exclusively in the discre-

---

[34] Thomas R. Dye and L. Harmon Zeigler, *The Irony of Democracy: An Uncommon Introduction to American Politics* (Belmont, Calif.: Duxbury, 1971), pp. 103–104.

[35] Paul Simon, "The Illinois Legislature: A Study in Corruption," *Harpers Magazine* (September 1964), pp. 74–75, as quoted in William J. Keefe and Morris S. Ogul, *The American Legislative Process: Congress and the States,* 3rd ed. (Englewood Cliffs, N. J.: Prentice-Hall, 1973), p. 11.

> tion of public officials—in Maryland, the Governor and the members of the State Roads Commission. They have had virtually absolute control. There are many engineering companies which seek contracts, but price competition was not allowed under the ethical standards of this profession until October 1971. Therefore, engineers are very vulnerable to pressure from public officials for both legal and illegal payments.[36]

This third interpretation of contributions, which emphasizes the aim of giving as an attempt to satisfy "extortionist" demands or to buy "insurance" against untoward legislative decisions, goes beyond mere campaign contributions into the area of personal aggrandizement for purposes other than financing a political campaign. However, the structure of the shakedown problem remains similar to that of legal payments for campaign contributions, except that the contributor and recipient must calculate the probability of exposure and prosecution.

Terms such as *bribery* and *extortion* carry no implications for the public policies eventually enacted as a result of campaign contributions. Suppose that everyone could agree that a particular law is better than others. Legislators might have to be "bribed" to pass such a law. Alternatively, those whom such a law would adversely affect might be targets of extortionist threats by those legislators who will pass it unless they are paid off. Thus, these heavily laden terms refer only to the relationship between contributor and candidate and not to specific public policy effects or even to moral judgments.

Congressional action to control political money. Several methods are available to regulate campaign contributions. First, contributions might be completely uncontrolled and unregulated, so that what passes between contributors and candidates would be a private matter entirely of their own concern. Any disclosure or limitations that occur would be at the candidate's discretion. Conceivably, under such a system some candidates would voluntarily limit the size, or possibly the source, of campaign contributions they accept, and they would make all campaign financial records public. Limited voluntary actions of this sort were not unprecedented before recent legislative enactments, and some candidates in earlier elections voluntarily publicized their personal financial records as well.

A second possibility for regulation would place a limit on the amount of money any person or organization can contribute to a particular campaign or to all campaigns in a given election year. A third variation would require the public disclosure of the names of campaign givers and the size of their contributions to each candidate. Such a regulation might incorporate a threshold amount below which contributors' names or the amounts they contribute would not be publicized. The enforcement problem of such an

[36] The New York *Times,* October 11, 1973, p. 37, as quoted in William P. Welch, "The Economics of Campaign Funds," *Public Choice,* 20 (Winter 1974), p. 85.

arrangement is that a contributor of $10,000 under a $1000 limit could give $1000 each to nine friends, who would then contribute that amount to the target candidate. Successful prosecution against such an arrangement has occurred, though detection remains extremely difficult. A fourth regulatory possibility would simply limit the amount of spending for a given campaign. This attempt to control expenditures instead of the source of revenues is quite difficult, because inflation and variations of competitiveness among campaigns make it somewhat unrealistic to set any particular limitation.

Finally, the British system of publicly financing all national campaigns might be adopted. Public financing (which is discussed at greater length in Chapter 13) seems attractive because it avoids more overt problems of "buying" and "selling" elections. However, it would probably shift the flow of political money into even less acceptable channels, such as direct bribes and extortion. Also, the formation of new political parties represents a serious problem for public funding. Ideally, everyone who wishes to appear on the ballot would get access to public funding, but the availability of funds would almost certainly create an incentive to form new parties, often merely for nuisance value. On the other hand, the establishment of any size threshold that a party must meet to qualify for access to public campaign funds would pose a serious political problem inasmuch as present legislators, who are major-party incumbents, would set the threshold. Their interest would be to set the threshold as high as possible to eliminate minor-party competition.

Various combinations of these regulatory alternatives have been enacted in recent years. State law, which varies widely, governs political money in elections for state offices, and much of that law tries to outlaw overtly fraudulent practices. Registration and reporting requirements are common, as are limitations on giving and spending. Federal legislation passed in 1971 and 1974 has made substantial changes in campaign finance practices. The Federal Election Campaign Act of 1971 imposed contribution limitations on both individual donors and groups: neither could contribute more than $1000 to any particular candidate for federal elective office, while a political committee was limited to contributions of $5000. Total annual contributions to all campaigns by individual donors or groups could not exceed $25,000, and a person could not spend more than $1000 independently on a campaign for the election or defeat of a clearly identified candidate for federal office. Congressional candidates were limited by the 1971 act to spending no more than ten cents per voting-age person in their constituency. The 1971 act also required reports by candidates of anyone contributing more than $10 each year to their campaigns and the availability for public inspection of the names of those contributing more than $100 each year.

In 1971 the members of Congress also enacted various tax subsidies to encourage small contributions to candidates and to provide for public financing of presidential campaigns. In particular, taxpayers are allowed to take a small tax credit (up to $12.50 for those filing separate returns and $25 for those filing joint returns) or a tax deduction (a maximum of $50 for those filing separately and $100 for those filing jointly). Partial public funding of presidential campaigns is provided by the use of a checkoff on income tax returns whereby each taxpayer can allocate $1 ($2 for joint returns) to a special fund, with no additional tax liability. Legislation passed in 1974 creates a full-scale mechanism for the public financing of presidential nominating and general-election campaigns, to be overseen by the Federal Election Commission. The 1974 legislation increased limits on spending for congressional elections, but also placed limits on spending by presidential candidates.

Much of this legislation was challenged in the Supreme Court case of *Buckley v. Valeo,* decided in 1976.[37] The justices held that the legislative imposition of ceilings on political contributions did not violate the First Amendment guarantee of free speech and association, nor did it discriminate against challengers and third-party candidates. However, the justices did find limitations on independent political expenditures—those not formally connected with a particular candidate—to be unconstitutional, because they restricted the right of free expression under the First Amendment. Similarly, the justices held that limitations on the amount of his own money someone could spend on his own campaign were unconstitutional under the First Amendment, but that the reporting and disclosure provisions were not unconstitutional. The Court also upheld the provision for public financing of presidential nominating conventions and primary election campaigns. Public financing of presidential election campaigns also received the Court's approval, but the justices took issue with the manner of appointing the members of the Federal Election Commission.

Debate over public policy concerning political money continues unabated. Recent attempts to extend public financing to House and Senate campaigns have failed to gain the necessary support. Yet, the trend of campaign financing in the United States is toward ever more inclusive public financing, with the associated outlawing or limitation of private contributions.

Contribution decision making: small contributors. A more formal discussion of campaign contributions helps improve our understanding of activist decision making and the political money problem. The first activist to be considered is the contributor or potential contributor of small amounts of money or labor. Defining what *small* means is difficult. One possibility is that the contribution cannot materially affect the election outcome. By this standard, most contributions would be small. Another possibility is that small contributions are those that candidates fail to notice or acknowledge by some specific action or payment. Small contributors would be those that most closely accord with the civics-book view of campaign giving, would most likely be amateurs, and would probably be contributing in support of public- rather than private-goods legislation.

The analysis of voting in Chapter 5 offers a close approximation of the

[37] 46 L.Ed. 2d 659 (1976).

small giver's calculus of contributions. Recall that the calculus of voting deduced that $R = PB + D - C$. R is the expected utility from voting for the preferred candidate, and B represents the utility difference that the citizen experiences between the candidates. These two terms would remain unchanged in a calculus of contributions, except that R would become $R(x)$—read "R is a function of x"—which would be the expected utility from contributing \$$x$ or other valued goods or services to a candidate's campaign. P would become $P(x)$ to represent the increase in the probability of making or breaking a tie in favor of the preferred candidate as the result of contributing \$$x$. The C term would now be replaced by $C(x)$ to state the utility loss from not having the money to spend for other purposes. Similarly, D would become $D(x)$ to show how the intrinsic utility of contributing based on philosophical, psychological, or other values would increase with a contribution of \$$x$. The entire calculus of contributions thus becomes $R(x) = P(x)B + D(x) - C(x)$.

The present tax credit for contributions changes $C(x)$ to $C(x - \$25)$. For larger contributions taken as a tax deduction rather than as a credit, $C(x)$ is reduced fractionally up to \$100, the fraction depending upon the citizen's marginal tax bracket. In either case, such tax loopholes encourage contributions.

Another variation concerns $D(x)$. The calculus of voting includes D to represent the sense of civic duty fulfilled. Few people would argue that a campaign contribution is morally obligatory. Thus, $D(x)$ seems more likely to measure party loyalty or the intrinsic attractiveness of supporting charismatic or ideologically distinguishable candidates. For example, in the presidential campaigns of 1968 and 1972 respectively, Governor George C. Wallace and Senator George S. McGovern captured record contributions from small givers.

Contribution decision making: large contributors.[38] The contributor of large sums probably expects either to gain public policy concessions from the candidate or to avoid the punishment that might accompany an unfavorable public policy. Large contributors thus conform either to the "bribery" or "extortion" view of campaign giving. We shall assume initially that such contributors are unconcerned about party identification or ideology.

Now, suppose that the law does not limit contributions or require public disclosures of contributions, and that a contributor gives x_r and x_d dollars respectively to the Republican and Democratic candidates in a particular race. Let $U(x_r)$ and $U(x_d)$ be the contributor's utility from giving x_r and x_d. Both $U(x_r)$ and $U(x_d)$ incorporate the utility lost from giving the money, so a $C(x)$ term is unnecessary. For instance, $U(x_r)$ increases, reaches a maximum, and then declines, as in Figure 6.2 (which we discuss momentarily). Beyond the maximum point of $U(x_r)$, an additional dollar spent on contributions produces

[38] This section relies heavily on Aranson and Hinich, "Some Aspects of the Political Economy of Election Campaign Contribution Laws."

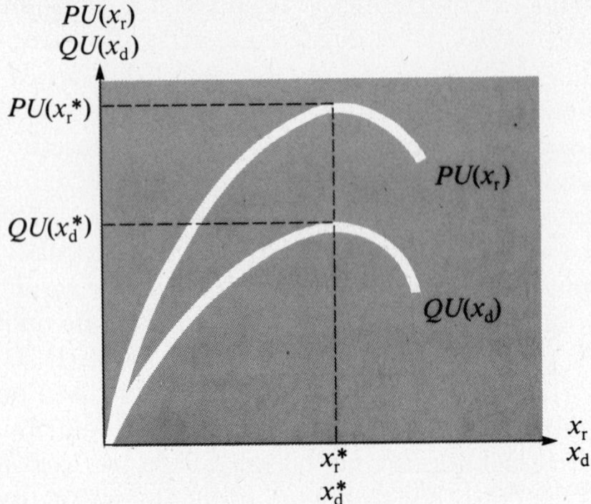

Figure 6.2 Payoffs to a large contributor.

Source: Peter H. Aranson and Melvin J. Hinich, "Some Aspects of the Political Economy of Election Campaign Contribution Laws," *Public Choice,* 34 (1979), p. 442.

less utility than some alternative use of that dollar. Before the maximum point, an additional dollar spent elsewhere creates less utility than a dollar spent on campaign contributions.

Let P and Q be the respective probabilities that the Republican and the Democrat win. Of course, $P + Q = 1$. The contributor supposes that P and Q remain unaffected by x_r and x_d. The D term is absent because the large contributor is interested only in completely private, "non-civic" payments. The contributor's total expected payoff, $R(x_r, x_d)$, now becomes, $R(x_r, x_d) = PU(x_r) + QU(x_d)$.

$U(x_r)$ and $U(x_d)$ are identical because the contributor is uninterested in party identification. Figure 6.2 shows $PU(x_r)$ and $QU(x_d)$. These curves, with the first higher than the second, incorporate the assumption that the contributor believes that the Republican is more likely to win; that is, P is greater than Q. However, because $U(x_r)$ and $U(x_d)$ are the same, the contributor gives an equal amount to each candidate's campaign and donates up to the point where expected utility is maximized on each curve: $x_r^* = x_d^*$. Hence, a contribution system lacking disclosure or limitations on giving yields no advantage to those candidates expected to win.

To show the effects of a limitation, consider Figure 6.3, which depicts the expected *marginal* (added) utilities based on the curves in Figure 6.2. Marginal utility is the added utility the contributor receives from giving one more dollar. For example, if the contributor has given nothing to either candidate and is limited to giving only one dollar, then he would give this dollar to the Republican because the added utility from such a contribution

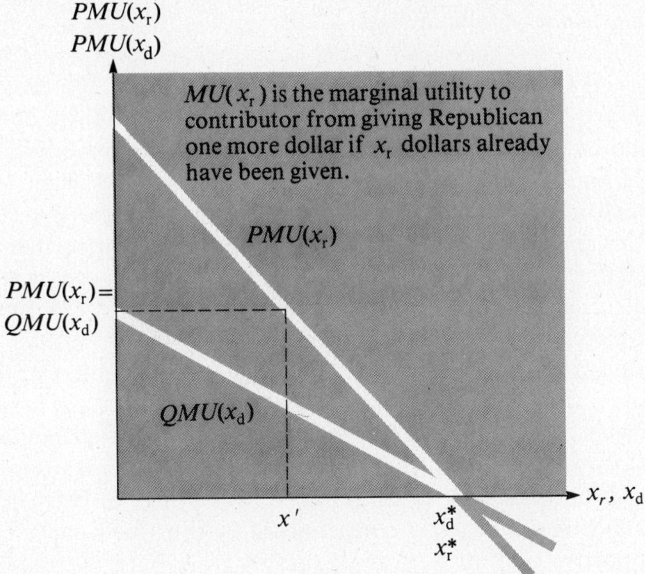

Figure 6.3 Expected marginal payoffs to a large contributor.

Source: Peter H. Aranson and Melvin J. Hinich, "Some Aspects of the Political Economy of Election Campaign Contribution Laws," *Public Choice,* 34 (1979), p. 443.

exceeds the amount gained from giving the dollar to the Democrat. If the contribution were limited by law to x' dollars, it would all go to the Republican. After the limit of x' is exceeded, the contributor would give money to each candidate until x_r^* and x_d^* are reached. Since $x_r^* = x_d^*$, each candidate would then receive the same amount, as Figure 6.2 illustrates.

In most American elections, the incumbent candidate holds a distinct advantage over the challenger, which is reflected by differences in contributors' estimates of P and Q. Therefore, legal contribution limitations of the sort expressed here as x' often lead campaign givers to contribute their entire political budgets to incumbents. That is why the recent campaign contribution laws have been called "acts for the relief of incumbents."

Now, suppose it becomes unlikely that a contributor will give to both candidates in a particular race, because of traditional party loyalties or objections of group members (in the case of a group leader). The advantages that limitations give to incumbents do not change materially. Contributors give first to the incumbent candidates, who are most likely to be reelected, until they reach their legal contributions limit—and contributors to the other party's candidates do the same. Again, challengers suffer a disadvantage because contributors believe that they are less likely to win.

Conclusive evidence about contribution decisions is difficult to find, because disclosure requirements are a recent phenomenon and these requirements, along with limits on giving, change the calculus of contributions in predictable ways. Nevertheless, Table 6.4 provides some evidence in support of the preceding view of large contributors. Political action committees (PACs), which are voluntary campaign contribution groups attached to various organizations, have become an increasingly popular method of giving since the 1974 legislation limiting individual contributions. Table 6.4 shows the traditional affinities of labor unions and corporations for the Democratic and Republican parties respectively. More important, notice that in 1977–1978, 57 percent of PAC money ($20 million) went to incumbents, 22 percent ($7.7 million) to challengers, and about the same amount ($7.4 million) to candidates in elections without incumbents.

Developing a calculus of contributions in the presence of disclosure becomes more complicated, since expected payoffs from a particular candidate can vary with contribution levels to the opponent. Nevertheless, in many instances disclosure appears to increase the incumbent's advantage further. Third-party challengers are even more disadvantaged, because if *either* major-party candidate wins, the contributors to the third-party challenger may be in jeopardy.

THE IRON LAW OF OLIGARCHY

Chapter 4 introduces some nomination rules of American political parties and raises the possibility that "democratic" or "open" parties might enjoy

Table 6.4 1977–78 Political Action Committee Contributions to Federal Candidates (in millions of dollars)

	Total Contri-butions	*Party Affiliation**		*Candidate Status**		
		Dems.	**Reps.**	**Incum-bent**	**Chal-lenger**	**Open**
Trade, membership, health	$11.5	$5.0	$ 6.5	$ 6.7	$2.3	$2.5
Labor	10.3	9.7	0.6	6.1	2.2	2.0
Corporations	9.8	3.6	6.1	5.8	2.0	2.0
Non-connected organizations	2.5	0.7	1.9	0.7	1.1	0.7
Cooperatives	0.9	0.6	0.2	0.6	0.1	0.2
Corporations without stock	0.1	0.1	0.0	0.1	0.0	0.0
Total	$35.1	$19.7	$15.3	$20.0	$7.7	$7.4

Source: Federal Election Commission, as reported in *Congressional Quarterly Weekly Report,* 37 (June 2, 1979), p. 1044.

* Figures within the party-affiliation and candidate-status columns do not always equal the total contributions figure because of rounding.

less electoral success than more nearly "dictatorial" or "closed" parties. This chapter provides a somewhat more comprehensive view of political organizations, including parties, and now we can explain this phenomenon more completely. A venerable observation in political science is that no matter how democratic their avowed purpose, *successful* political organizations must become tightly controlled, dictatorially directed oligarchies. This **iron law of oligarchy,** which was first propounded to explain the failure of European mass parties, such as labor and socialist parties, to run their internal affairs democratically even though their purpose was avowedly the spread of democracy, also describes American political parties.[39] Generally, a candidate whose party is weakly organized has little chance of defeating an opponent from a well-organized party, for poorly organized and disciplined interest groups and parties find comparatively little success in the political process.

The public-goods interpretation of political organizations partially explains this phenomenon. Although American political parties are far less tightly controlled than European ones, nevertheless as local organizations they are reasonably centralized and bureaucratic (with the exception of occasional intraparty political fratricide). The reason for this centralized, nondemocratic control is that parties and other political organizations exist in a competitive environment. The opposition party's members are almost always willing to take over control of any elected office. Therefore, *ceteris paribus,* an efficient political organization—one that can best allocate private rewards and resources—must succeed over an inefficient one.

One aspect of efficiency mentioned earlier concerns the use of campaign funds in different congressional or senatorial elections. For instance, a party slate will include candidates for all elective offices: president, senators, congressional representatives, governor, state representatives and senators, county commissioners, city councilors, mayors, and so forth. Some of these candidates might be nearly certain of victory, while others might be nearly certain of defeat. Still other candidates might come from constituencies where the election outcome is a toss-up. The efficient use of party or interest-group resources in a competitive environment implies that only token allocations go to sure winners or losers and heavy allocations go to toss-up candidates.

The actual allocation to marginal contests depends on the relative utility to party leaders of winning the corresponding offices. Furthermore, efficiency implies a careful allocation of *different* resources in any given election contest. However, it is often difficult, and sometimes impossible, to get party activists as well as interest-group leaders and members to go along with these allocations. Candidates (even those of the same party) differ in the public policy positions they advocate, in personal characteristics, and in the loyalty of the activists they command. Left to their own devices, activists seldom expend their own resources efficiently from the "party point of view." At least up to the point of legislative control and allowing for the importance of contests,

[39] Roberto Michels, *Political Parties,* translated by Eden and Cedar Paul (New York: Free Press, 1958).

party leaders want to maximize the expected number of offices they win; by contrast, activists often want a candidate to whom they are personally attached to win.

We can restate this entire problem in the language of public and private goods. Suppose an activist has worked out an agreement to contribute to congressional candidate Smith's campaign committee in return for some private benefit—perhaps merely psychological satisfaction. Smith is guaranteed a victory, while Jones, another congressional candidate, is in an extremely tight race. Further, suppose Jones would represent the party's controlling vote in the Congress. Smith and all other party members would be much better off in the majority than in the minority, so contributions to Jones are equivalent to contributions to the supply of a public good with respect to *all* party members. The party leader's problem is to get the contributor to forgo private agreements with Smith and channel resources to Jones.

Manifestly, a party whose leaders exercise the tightest control of resource use is going to be successful, while a more nearly "open" or "democratic" party is bound to fail. However, tight control means control and the efficient distribution of *private,* divisible benefits—the private goods that figure into the bargains among party and interest-group leaders and political entrepreneurs. To distribute private goods efficiently to those who earn them, party and interest-group leaders must successfully monitor what activists do and how much they contribute to the organization's resources. A well-disciplined, closely monitored party or interest group has an obvious advantage. Commands and expectations are clear, and leaders can monitor the degree and direction of effort more easily than in a loose organizational structure. Well-disciplined parties and interest groups sometimes are not advantageous, especially if creative leadership and innovation are of value, but for winning elections and extracting benefits from the political process, these organizational structures remain superior.

QUESTIONS FOR DISCUSSION AND REVIEW

1. Suppose the game in Table 6.1 is modified so that each group can lobby for a separate *public*-goods program; if each group does so, two such programs will be produced collectively, yielding each group a benefit of $2B$. Will the resulting game be played differently or have different public policy consequences?
2. Most third-party movements in the United States have failed to elect candidates or to survive, but they have occasionally succeeded in getting their public policy proposals adopted. These parties usually are single-issue organizations that take a strong position on the production (suppression) of a particular public good (bad). The Prohi-

bitionist party and the Right to Life party are good examples. Using the view of political organizations developed in this chapter, why do you think third parties succeed in their public policy goals but fail politically? How would you organize a politically successful third party?

3. How could political organizations be given incentives to pursue the public supply of public rather than private goods? Are constitutional provisions helpful in this regard? Which ones? What other such constitutional provisions might be adopted?
4. What would be the costs and benefits of government financing of all election campaigns? Of repealing all laws regulating campaign contributions and expenditures? Can the perfect campaign finance system be devised? By what criteria should we judge it?
5. Compare and contrast the organization of a firm in the marketplace and of a political group in elections. What are the major similarities and differences in the problems the "managers" of each must solve? Who "owns" a political group? Do problems of ownership account for any of the differences between private- and public-sector groups? Do private-sector firms do better in politics than other groups? What reasoning explains your answer?
6. Are elected officeholders members of an interest group? What evidence supports your answer? What are the public policy consequences of your answer?
7. Imagine an election system in which members of the House and Senate represented and were explicitly nominated by interest groups rather than districts and states. How would public policy in this system resemble or differ from public policy under the present system?

NEW CONCEPTS AND TERMS

activist
amateur activist
complex election
graft
group theory
interest group
iron law of oligarchy
Marxist theory
patronage
pluralist theory
political entrepreneur
political party
power-elite theory
professional activist
simple election

7

Candidates, Strategies, and Public Choice

Chapters 4, 5, and 6 depict elections as complex combinations of rules, citizens whose preferences and decisions combine in a variety of ways, and activists whose electoral demands, organizations, and resources can assume many forms. In this complicated environment, candidates compete for public office by clearly or ambiguously advocating public policies and by stressing their personal qualities and qualifications. Of course, the extent to which candidates come to resemble the officeholders they once promised to be remains for later chapters to explore.

A PRELIMINARY EXAMPLE

To analyze candidates' strategic decision making and its effects on election outcomes and public choice, we begin with a simplified hypothetical example. Suppose a Democrat and a Republican compete in a simple election, one without activists. The election has only one issue, government spending as a percentage of GNP, and the candidates' positions are d and r respectively. All citizens vote, and each votes for the candidate whose position is closest to his or her own. The distribution of citizens' preferences is symmetric and unimodal, and the candidate with most votes wins the election. Each candidate's goal is to win; we shall assume that each candidate gets a utility of $+1$ from winning, 0 from a tie, and -1 from losing.

Figure 7.1 illustrates this election. Suppose each candidate is thinking

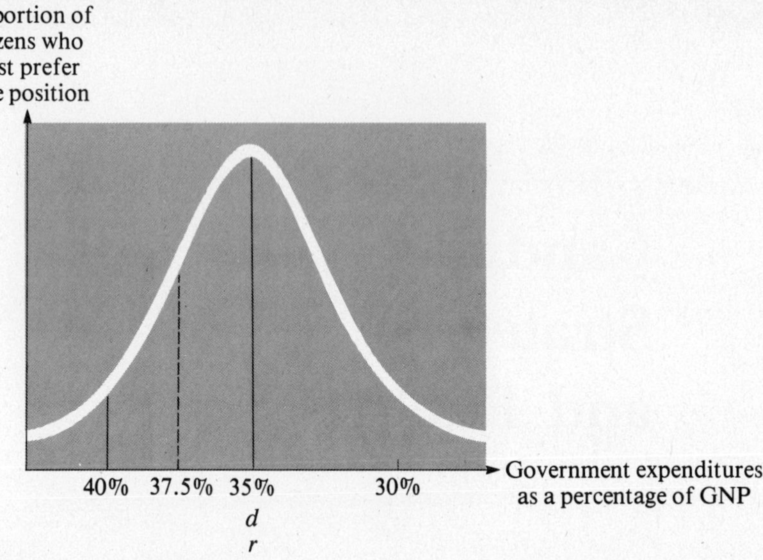

Figure 7.1 Hypothetical election with symmetric unimodal preference distribution and no abstentions.

about advocating one of three issue positions: government spending at 30, 35, or 40 percent of GNP. The median voter's preference is placed at 35 percent. Now, consider the election from the Democratic candidate's point of view.

First, looking at Figure 7.1, suppose the Republican advocates government spending at 40 percent. If the Democrat also advocates 40 percent, then every voter is indifferent between *d* and *r,* the expected outcome of the election is a tie, and each candidate receives a utility of zero. However, if the Democrat advocates 35 percent with *r* at 40, then every voter who prefers spending levels higher than halfway between 35 and 40—that is, higher than 37.5—is closer to *r,* and all other citizens are closer to *d.* But one-half of the citizens prefer positions less than 35, so the additional votes of those who prefer positions between 35 and 37.5 give the Democrat more than one-half of the votes, and he wins. Finally, if the Democrat advocates 30 percent with *r* at 40, then every voter who prefers spending levels higher than halfway between 30 and 40—that is, higher than 35—is closer to *r,* and all other citizens are closer to *d*. In this instance, one-half of the citizens prefers each candidate, and the election is a tie. The election outcomes and candidates' utilities with *r* at 40, and *d* at 40, 35, and 30 are summarized in the first part of Table 7.1. *Second,* suppose the Republican advocates 35 rather than 40 percent. Going through the previous exercise to account for this change in *r* generates the entries in the middle part of Table 7.1. *Finally,* moving *r* to 30 generates the entries in the bottom part of the table.

Table 7.2 gathers together all of these possible combinations of issue position strategies and shows the candidates' payoffs. The election is obviously

Table 7.1 Outcome and Utility Possibilities for Simple Election

r at 40%, *d* at

	40%	35%	30%
Election Outcome	**Tie**	**Democrat Wins**	**Tie**
Democrat's Utility	0	+1	0
Republican's Utility	0	−1	0

r at 35%, *d* at

	40%	35%	30%
Election Outcome	**Republican Wins**	**Tie**	**Republican Wins**
Democrat's Utility	−1	0	−1
Republican's Utility	+1	0	+1

r at 30%, *d* at

	40%	35%	30%
Election Outcome	**Tie**	**Democrat Wins**	**Tie**
Democrat's Utility	0	+1	0
Republican's Utility	0	−1	0

Table 7.2 Simple Election Game

		Republican's Strategies 40%	35%	30%
Democrat's Strategies	40%	0, 0	−1, +1	0, 0
	35%	+1, −1	0, 0	+1, −1
	30%	0, 0	−1, +1	0, 0

a two-person zero-sum game because the candidates' utilities sum to zero for each strategy pair chosen.[1] Several deductions flow from this discovery. First, the candidates choose public policy positions under conditions of uncertainty. Second, the candidates' issue positions become strategies in the game-theoretic sense. Here we call these **issue position strategies,** or simply issue strategies. Third, since the game is zero-sum, its solution finds the candidates adopting minimax strategies: they maximize their security levels.

[1] One might argue that the game is zero-sum only because we have assigned the candidates utilities of +1, 0, and −1 for winning, tying, and losing respectively. Actually, this assignment of utilities is only a convenience. Another utility structure that gives candidates utilities in proportion to their pluralities produces the same

To solve this election game, we must compute each candidate's security level for each strategy. The Democrat's security level from advocating 40 percent is -1, because he loses and receives a utility of -1 if the Republican advocates 35. Similarly, the Democrat's security level from advocating 35 is zero, which occurs with r at 35. Finally, the Democrat's security level from advocating 30 is -1, which again occurs with r at 35. Thus, the Democrat's maximum security level falls at 35. The Republican's maximum security level also falls at 35. Hence, the solution to the game is the strategy pair $\{d = 35, r = 35\}$. That is, the candidates adopt minimax strategies by converging to the median citizen's preference.

The median citizen's preference also represents a unique equilibrium strategy pair. For example, if the Republican adopts the security-level-maximizing strategy of 35, then the Democrat must do the same, and vice versa. Put differently, if the Republican adopts his best strategy, then the Democrat has no incentive to use a strategy other than his best. If both candidates are at their respective best strategies, then neither has an incentive to change. While this example appears to rest on very restrictive assumptions, we may begin to understand why candidates sometimes tend to appear identical in the policies they advocate. Moreover, since most of these assumptions are about citizens and *their* decisions, it would be unkind to blame only the candidates for their convergence on the issues.

CANDIDATE STRATEGIES

The preceding example allows candidates to use only issue positions as strategies, but campaign or election strategies can be anything a candidate might vary to achieve (or help to achieve) an election goal, including issue strategies, attribute strategies, allocation strategies, and coalition strategies.[2]

Issue Strategies

Issue position strategies. Issue strategies concern public policy alternatives about which candidates can advocate the adoption of a particular posi-

---

result. Recall from Chapter 4 that a candidate's plurality is his vote minus his opponent's vote. For instance, if Pl_d is the Democrat's plurality, then $Pl_d = V_d - V_r$. Of course, $Pl_r = V_r - V_d$, and $Pl_d + Pl_r = 0$ for any pair of policies. Therefore, the election is also a zero-sum game if we use pluralities to represent the candidates' payoffs. Table 7.1 merely sets the utility for a plurality that is greater than zero equal to $+1$, for a plurality equal to zero at 0, and for a plurality less than zero equal to -1.

[2] Peter H. Aranson, Melvin J. Hinich, and Peter C. Ordeshook, "Campaign Strategies for Alternative Election Systems: Candidate Objectives as an Intervening Variable," in Hayward R. Alker, Jr., Karl W. Deutsch, and Antoine H. Stoetzel, eds., *Mathematical Approaches to Politics* (New York: Elsevier, 1973), pp. 193–229; and Aranson, Hinich, and Ordeshook, "Election Goals and Strategies: Equivalent and Nonequivalent Candidate Objectives," *American Political Science Review,* 68 (March 1974), pp. 135–152.

tion. The previous example restricts candidates to one simple issue position strategy. In campaigns with several issues, the candidate's issue strategy problem becomes one of finding positions on each issue that help to achieve election goals. However, as members of the electorate grow more sophisticated about public policy, they learn that issues are related. For example, people have come to understand that inflation, unemployment, government spending, and interest rates are intertwined problems—that a policy toward one affects the others. Hence, candidates today often must go beyond thinking about issues one at a time and must approach public policy comprehensively.

Issue salience strategies. In campaigns with more than one issue, candidates must also decide how much time and emphasis to give to each. That is, they must develop **issue salience strategies.** Candidates sometimes enjoy an advantage on some issues that they lack on others. For instance, part of American political lore in this century holds that Democrats start wars while Republicans start recessions. Although the logic of this maxim seems doubtful, nevertheless some voters believe it. As a result, Republican candidates might emphasize foreign policy and ignore domestic issues, while Democratic candidates might do the opposite. Candidates usually try to increase the citizens' salience for the issues on which they believe they have an advantage. For example, during the 1976 Republican Presidential Nominating Convention most speakers, including President Ford, stressed the Democrats' role in the Vietnam War while emphasizing that no American troops were at war at the time of the convention. In the aftermath of Watergate, the Democrats countered by emphasizing "morality in government." Speakers at the 1980 Republican National convention stressed the problems of inflation and unemployment, while criticizing the Carter administration for the perceived weakening of the American position abroad.

Candidates' attempts to vary issue salience are ordinarily strategies that depend heavily on retrospective voting, which Chapter 5 describes. Candidates usually stress certain issues rather than others when a historical record or an economic or international condition breeds either great satisfaction or discontent. For instance, in 1980 President Jimmy Carter's campaigners lauded the Camp David Accords and the peace treaty between Israel and Egypt, while former Governor Ronald Reagan continually harped on the high rate of inflation and the failures he perceived in American foreign and military policy.

Citizens also differ on which issues are important to them. For instance, presidential candidates who talk to Iowa farmers about urban problems or to stockbrokers about medical care for the aged are wasting time and probably alienating voters. Least successful of all are those candidates who take unfavorable positions on high-salience issues before interested groups of people. Senator Barry M. Goldwater's 1964 proposals to modify the Social Security system, which he made before audiences of retired residents in Florida, and

Senator George S. McGovern's 1972 economic proposals on income redistribution and changes in the tax treatment of capital gains, which he detailed to audiences of stockbrokers on Wall Street, are two cases in point.

Chapter 5 describes how changes in issue salience affect citizens' voting decisions. As issue salience increases, a citizen's utility curve grows steeper, increasing $B = U_d - U_r$ (or $U_r - U_d$, if U_r is greater than U_d). As B increases, R increases in turn, and the citizen is more likely to vote. Candidates thus receive a disproportionate advantage in turnout among supporters from a carefully targeted increase in salience. Candidates can allocate their resources to reflect a salience pattern that already exists among the electorate by concentrating their campaign time on higher-salience issues that favor them and ignoring those that favor their opponents. Or, candidates can try to increase citizens' salience for issues on which they enjoy a natural or pre-existing advantage.

Issue ambiguity strategies. Candidates can also advocate public policies with varying degrees of certitude. There are at least four reasons that they might use **issue ambiguity strategies.** First, early in their campaigns, they might not know what policies citizens prefer. For instance, in the hypothetical election we discussed previously, early and incomplete polling mistakenly might tell a candidate that the median preference is 38 rather than 35 percent. If the candidate adopts this issue strategy, his opponent might advocate 35 and win by a small margin. The desire for accurate information about citizens' preferences and the difficulty in getting it—perhaps because even citizens have not made up their minds—are reasons that candidates are sometimes ambiguous early in their campaigns.

Second, most candidates, and especially those running for the presidency, must win nomination before entering general elections. In seeking nomination, a candidate must not forget to provide for "the maintenance of coalitions inclusive enough to contend for the presidency." Hence, "platforms must conform with that necessity," and "there is no simpler way . . . to destroy an electoral coalition than for its majority to insist on precise, forthright, and advanced policy positions unacceptable to other elements of the coalition."[3] Therefore, candidates may remain ambiguous simply to maintain party support. For example, a Democratic candidate's coalition typically includes heavy concentrations of activists and citizens from labor unions, from the black population, and from those concerned about the natural environment. These people often hold conflicting goals and preferences; for instance, unionized workers in heavy industry are understandably suspicious of strict environmental regulations that might shut down their factories and leave them without work. A Republican candidate's coalition also includes people with conflicting goals and preferences. Republican activists and voters typically come from the skilled trades, from clerks and merchant groups, from professions such as law and medicine, and from industry. Conflicts among

[3] V. O. Key, Jr., *Politics, Parties, & Pressure Groups,* 5th ed., rev. (New York: Crowell, 1964), p. 421.

these groups are a commonplace, and early, forthright campaign statements can mean early political demise.

Third, recall from Chapter 2 that some zero-sum games have no pure strategy equilibria and that the players must adopt mixed strategies. One example, shown in Table 2.8, reveals that if one player adopts a pure strategy, then his opponent can always win. But election candidates cannot play mixed strategies in the game-theoretic sense. To use such strategies, each would have to use a randomizing device such as a spinner or die, and they would simultaneously announce the pure strategies that the randomizing devices selected. This is an impracticable procedure. Elections in which it was used would become waiting games, because the candidates would put off announcing strategies until their opponents did so. The alternative to mixed strategies is a strategy of ambiguity, which is investigated more carefully later in this chapter.[4]

A fourth and related problem, which is also examined more carefully later in this chapter, concerns the presence of **intense minorities** in opposition to or support of a particular issue position. The members of certain secondary or classificatory groups may vote against a candidate who opposes them on such an issue position no matter how well that candidate does for them on all other issues. Intense minorities can also implicitly form coalitions to topple a candidate even though a majority on each issue prefers that candidate. Depending on the structure of preferences, those running for office try to avoid these problems either by being as ambiguous as possible on all such issues or by taking the minorities' positions.

Attribute Strategies

Chapter 5 interprets a candidate's personal attributes as campaign issues and perhaps even as questions of public policy. However, these issues differ fundamentally from what people usually consider to be issues and questions of public policy because, unlike other public policy positions, candidates cannot readily vary their personal attributes. These attributes include sex, physical appearance, race, ethnic and national origin, religion, age, geographical origin, military record, past employment and education, health, marital status, affectional preferences, and party identification. Senator William Proxmire's (D-Wisconsin) hair transplant and Senator Henry Jackson's (D-Washington) facial plastic surgery attest that candidates try to make limited changes in

---

[4] An excellent analysis of this problem is provided by Kenneth A. Shepsle, "The Strategy of Ambiguity: Uncertainty and Electoral Competition," *American Political Science Review,* 66 (June 1972), pp. 555–568. See also Shepsle, "Parties, Voters, and the Risk Environment: A Mathematical Treatment of Electoral Competition Under Uncertainty," in Richard G. Niemi and Herbert F. Weisberg, eds., *Probability Models of Collective Decision Making* (Columbus, Ohio: Merrill, 1972), pp. 273–297; Benjamin I. Page, "The Theory of Political Ambiguity," *American Political Science Review,* 70 (September 1976), pp. 742–752; and Richard D. McKelvey, "Ambiguity in Spatial Models of Policy Formation," *Public Choice,* 35 (1980), pp. 385–402.

personal attributes. Indeed, even a virile Texan such as Lyndon Johnson dyed his hair. Washington hairdressers, wig fitters, and plastic surgeons probably enjoy a strong demand for their services, especially around election time.

The real and significant variations of personal **attribute strategies** involve the salience of the attributes. For example, during the 1960 presidential campaign, Senator John F. Kennedy's researchers reported to him that he had lost about as many votes as he was going to lose because of his religion, but that his Catholicism had not generated very much support among Catholic citizens. Therefore, Kennedy decided to increase the salience of this issue among Catholics, because such a strategy could do no further damage among non-Catholic voters. One tactic he used as part of this attribute strategy was a forceful address to the Greater Houston Ministerial Association on September 12, 1960. Kennedy publicly expressed his anger at the very idea of the religious issue. "This is the kind of America I believe in—and this is the kind of America I fought for in the South Pacific and the kind my brother died for in Europe. No one suggested then that we might have a divided loyalty, that we did not believe in liberty or that we belonged to a disloyal group that threatened the freedoms for which our forefathers died." Kennedy went on to personalize the matter for all Catholic citizens. "[I]f this election is decided on the basis that 40 million Americans lost their chance of being President on the day they were baptized," he said, "then it is the whole nation that will be the loser in the eyes of Catholics and non-Catholics around the world, in the eyes of history, and in the eyes of our own people."[5] By thus identifying the religious attack on his candidacy as an attack on *all* Catholic citizens, Kennedy increased the salience of the religion issue among Catholic voters. Increased salience led to increased turnout among Kennedy's Catholic supporters, and some scholars believe that this strategy won the election for him.

Candidates stress their ethnic, religious, or racial backgrounds if this strategy yields a net plurality advantage—votes gained minus votes lost. Otherwise, they try to ignore the matter. However, a complementary strategy is available to a candidate whose opponent's background is a political liability. Such a candidate can begin each speech by saying, "First, this is going to be a clean campaign. Appeals to racial or religious bigotry are no part of a decent electoral process. Just because my opponent is a ______ is no reason that he should not be elected. I will have no part of intolerance." This candidate, while devious, enjoys the best of both worlds, and there is little or nothing an opponent can do about it. Citizens who share the opponent's attribute are usually only mildly offended, while all other citizens are constantly reminded

---

[5] As quoted in Theodore H. White, *The Making of the President 1960* (New York: Cardinal Edition Pocket Books, 1961), pp. 470–471. For a discussion of the religion issue in the 1960 presidential election, see Chapter 5. See also Ithiel de Sola Pool, Robert P. Abelson, and Samuel Popkin, *Candidates, Issues, and Strategies: A Computer Simulation of the 1960 and 1964 Presidential Elections,* rev. ed. (Cambridge, Mass.: M.I.T. Press, 1965), p. 68, *passim,* and Philip E. Converse, "Religion and Politics: The 1960 Election," in Angus Campbell, Philip E. Converse, Warren E. Miller, and Donald E. Stokes, eds., *Elections and the Political Order* (New York: Wiley, 1966), pp. 96–124.

about it. Sometimes such reminders are even more indirect. For example, early in the 1980 Democratic presidential nomination campaign, President Jimmy Carter stressed that he was not one to panic in a crisis. The indirect reference to the experience at Chappaquidick of his nomination opponent, Senator Edward M. Kennedy, was all too apparent.

Party identification, which is central to retrospective voting, is much like other personal attributes, such as race, religion, and ethnic background. While candidates seldom change their party identification, they do manipulate their campaigns according to whether or not their party identification is the same as that of a majority of citizens in their constituency. For instance, a Democratic candidate in a heavily Democratic district might put up campaign signs that look like the upper one in Figure 7.2, while the same candidate in a heavily Republican district might use signs like the lower one. A candidate who can identify one area of his district as heavily Democratic and another as heavily Republican might actually use two different signs.

Allocation Strategies

Candidates use resources such as money, time, and paid volunteer labor, which they must decide how to allocate most efficiently and within a specified budget. **Allocation strategies** concern decisions such as how much time to spend campaigning in various areas of a constituency, what part of limited funds to use for billboards, bumper stickers, and radio and television adver-

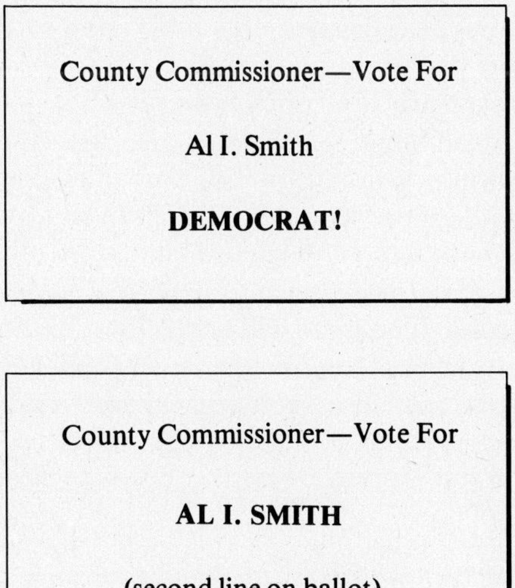

County Commissioner—Vote For

Al I. Smith

DEMOCRAT!

County Commissioner—Vote For

AL I. SMITH

(second line on ballot)

Figure 7.2 Democrat's campaign sign in Democratic and Republican districts.

tisements, and at what point in the campaign and at what rate to spend these resources.

Some allocation strategy problems have intuitive solutions. For example, as a general rule presidential candidates should spend little time campaigning in states they are certain to win or lose; rather, they should concentrate their campaigning in toss-up states. Following this rule, Jimmy Carter campaigned little or not at all in most western states during the 1980 presidential campaign, while Ronald Reagan spent few hours in Georgia. But, allocation strategies can become far more complex than this rule suggests. For instance, much of the debate about the effects of the electoral college asks whether or not its rules of representation induce presidential candidates to allocate more resources to campaigning in some states than in others. Presumably, more extensive campaigning leads to a relatively greater number of campaign promises and therefore to favorable public policy obligations to those states. Existing research about the electoral college seems ambiguous, although informed speculation holds that larger states, such as California, New York, Illinois, Ohio, and Pennsylvania, are favored over smaller ones if the closeness of the vote in each state is taken into account.[6]

Allocation strategies now figure importantly in presidential primary elections and caucuses. Each nomination candidate is faced with a series of individual state contests over a four-month period, and each must decide which contests to enter, which to avoid, and what level of resources to commit to each. "Momentum" waxes and wanes in importance as the candidates play out a set of dynamic games over a long period of time. Political scientists are only now beginning to understand the nomination decision-making problems that are common to most candidates.[7] Each decision is an allocation strategy problem in which the preferences of citizens in each contest help to form some of the states of nature the candidates face.

The decisions of all other candidates also affect the states of nature. Campaigning in multiple primaries—or, for that matter, in presidential elections—is like a game called "Colonel Blotto." In this game, "Blotto has four units of armed forces with which to oppose an enemy of three units. Between the opposing forces is a mountain with four passes; in each pass is a fort. War is declared in the evening. The issue will be decided in the morning. Decisions are based on who outnumbers the other at each pass. One point is scored for each fort taken, and one point for each unit taken."[8] Plainly, the forts are like

---

[6] Steven J. Brams and Morton D. Davis, "The 3/2's Rule in Presidential Campaigning," *American Political Science Review,* 68 (March 1974), pp. 113–134; Claude S. Colantoni, Terrence J. Levesque, and Peter C. Ordeshook, "Campaign Resource Allocations Under the Electoral College," *American Political Science Review,* 69 (March 1975), pp. 141–154; see also the "Comment" and "Rejoinder" in *American Political Science Review,* 69 (March 1975), pp. 155–161.

[7] John Aldrich, *Before the Convention: Strategies and Choices in Presidential Nominating Conventions* (Chicago: University of Chicago Press, 1980).

[8] John McDonald and John W. Tukey, "Colonel Blotto: A Problem of Military Strategy," *Fortune* (June 1949), p. 102, reprinted in Martin Shubik, ed., *Game Theory and Related Approaches to Social Behavior* (New York: Wiley, 1964), pp. 226–229.

state primaries or caucuses, and the units are like the campaign resources of each candidate. The major difference between Blotto and the primary election problem is the timing aspect, but the zero-sum nature of both games assures us of a solution to the allocation strategy problem, although it might be in mixed strategy form.

Coalition Strategies

Candidates must decide which persons or organizations of persons to include in their electoral coalitions. As Chapter 6 points out, this **coalition strategy** consideration can be especially important for decisions about activist organizations. For example, a candidate might receive the endorsement and support of black organization leaders only to lose the support of trade unionists who fear busing. Or, a candidate might receive the support of an importers' lobby only to lose the endorsements of those industrial leaders who prefer tariff protection. Public goods are indivisible, and this aspect of public policy lies at the root of most coalition strategy problems, because often the members of one group cannot be satisfied except at the expense of another group. Also, the presence of certain groups in a candidate's electoral coalition might signal real policy intentions no matter how ambiguous the candidate's actual pronouncements might be. Electoral coalitions made up of amateur activists can be especially troublesome, for such activists can also be uncompromising in their demands on the candidate.

CANDIDATE GOALS

The simple election described at the beginning of this chapter restricted candidates to issue position strategies. However, as the preceding discussion shows, other and more complex strategic possibilities abound. This chapter pays most attention to issue position strategies because they form the basis of public policy decisions for both citizens and candidates, but we should not overlook the importance of other strategies.

Our initial example also restricted candidates to a simplified form of security-level maximization (of plurality) even though the goals candidates hold in elections are many and varied. Candidates may pursue what they regard as political power, they may wish to enact what they believe to be good public policy, or they may enjoy the exhilaration of public exposure. Some—though surely not many—might even enjoy the exotic foods they consume along the campaign trail. Candidates who are asked why they are running usually utter platitudes about duty to country and the importance of meeting new challenges, but we cannot construct a theory of candidate decision making that depends on idiosyncratic goals such as these. Nor need we try to do so. The question is not "What are the candidate's goals in life?" The question is "What are the candidate's goals in the election campaign?" Put differently, the question is "By what criteria, or to accomplish which outcomes or objectives, will a candidate choose campaign strategies?"

Stated in these terms, the problem of reducing many personal goals to a few campaign goals becomes easier to resolve. Consider again the election described in Figure 7.1, and suppose the Democrat believes that good public policy requires government expenditures at 40 percent of GNP. The Republican can beat him at 35, so even if the Democrat "believes in" 40, his only recourse against the plurality equilibrium strategy is to lie in the campaign, advocate 35 percent, and seek higher expenditures once in office. (Reelection might then be difficult.) Manifestly, the enactment of good public policy as the candidate sees it first depends on being elected.

An equilibrium strategy's importance can be formulated as a general principle. As just noted, the strategy of 35 percent in the earlier election maximizes the candidates' security levels in plurality, represents an equilibrium strategy in plurality, is a solution to the two-person (candidate) zero-sum game (election), and does as well or better than any other strategy each candidate might choose, no matter what strategy his opponent adopts. A general principle of two-candidate, single-member district elections follows directly from the minimax theorem of two-person zero-sum games: *In simple two-candidate, single-member-district elections, a party's candidates for a particular office in the long run adopt pure plurality equilibrium strategies if these strategies exist.*

Ideological variations. As examples in Chapters 1 through 3 suggest, the existence of pure strategy electoral equilibria cannot be guaranteed. Two-person game theory shows that mixed strategies are often the appropriate solutions to zero-sum games. Furthermore, the intransitivities associated with Arrow's paradox—cyclical majorities—create a closely related phenomenon. Indeed, election games in the presence of intransitivities require that candidates not adopt pure strategies, because such games *are* zero-sum games without pure strategy equilibria. Later, this chapter investigates at greater length the problems candidates face on those frequent occasions when pure strategy equilibria do not exist. However, when such strategies do exist, then the general principle just stated, which we shall call the **plurality equilibrium principle,** is quite robust. Indeed, short-run variations from it by particular parties and candidates show just how robust it is.

Consider a series of five presidential elections, and suppose Figure 7.1 depicts the underlying preference distribution. In the first election, the two candidates converge to the plurality equilibrium strategy, 35 percent. As chance would have it, the Democrat wins by a few votes, which deprives the Republicans of patronage appointments. The utility a person receives from being a Republican party member declines, and several party activists, including professionals and contributors of money, leave the party for private employment.

Since the value of Republican party membership has fallen, the party's right-wing members seem almost unopposed when they fill the resulting vacuum and take over the next Republican National Convention. They nominate a candidate who adopts a platform of 30 percent to run in the second election. Their defeat is resounding compared to the party's earlier defeat by a few votes. Meanwhile, because of this Republican ideological variation, the Democrats have put together an overweighted winning electoral coalition, which begins to fall apart.

The Republican party moderates realize that the voters have repudiated Republican appeals for lower levels of government spending and that the Democrats' coalition is in disarray. The moderates take over the next Republican National Convention and nominate a candidate at 35 percent, the plurality equilibrium strategy. The Democrats try to pull themselves together and also nominate a candidate at 35, but their electoral coalition cannot achieve victory. Even though the vote is close, the Republicans win the third election.

In the fourth election, the Democrats, now deprived of patronage, have fallen apart for the same reasons that the Republicans fell apart after the first election. The left-wing members of the party take over the Democratic National Convention and nominate a candidate at 40 percent. The Republican incumbent wins renomination, advocates 35, and wins the fourth election by a landslide, just as the Democrat had done in the second election.

In the fifth election, the Republicans have an overweighted coalition in disarray while the Democratic moderates have taken their party back from the left wing. The Republican candidate stays at 35, but the Democrats have converged to 35 and win the election by a small margin. Table 7.3 summarizes this sequence of elections.

One familiar with American presidential politics might recognize this sequence as a highly simplified and stylized version of the presidential elections of 1960, 1964, 1968, 1972, and 1976. Table 7.4 shows the corresponding data for these elections. We must regard the hypothetical sequence of elections as highly simplified and stylized for several reasons.

First, unlike the hypothetical sequence, in the real sequence there is more than one issue and issues change from election to election. In 1964, Barry Goldwater's conservative domestic economic policies and widely perceived international belligerence occupied most of the campaign. Retrospective voting on the Vietnam War strongly affected the outcome of the 1968 election. In 1972, George McGovern's liberal domestic economic policies and widely

Table 7.3 Hypothetical Sequence of Presidential Elections

Election	Democrat's Strategy	Republican's Strategy	Winning Strategy	Election Outcome
1	35%	35%	35%	small Democratic victory
2	35%	30%	35%	landslide Democratic victory
3	35%	35%	35%	small Republican victory
4	40%	35%	35%	landslide Republican victory
5	35%	35%	35%	small Democratic victory

Table 7.4 Actual Sequence of Presidential Elections

Election	Democratic Candidate	Republican Candidate	Winner	Winner's Two-Party Vote Proportion
1960	John F. Kennedy	Richard M. Nixon	*d*	50.01%
1964	Lyndon B. Johnson	Barry M. Goldwater	*d*	61.34%
1968	Hubert H. Humphrey	Richard M. Nixon	*r*	50.41%
1972	George S. McGovern	Richard M. Nixon	*r*	61.79%
1976	Jimmy Carter	Gerald R. Ford	*d*	51.06%

perceived international isolationism contributed to his defeat. Certainly, in 1976 the Watergate affair and Gerald Ford's pardon of Richard Nixon were on voters' minds when they elected Jimmy Carter. However, the departures from the political center (median voter) by Goldwater and McGovern in 1964 and 1972 respectively correspond to the departures in elections 2 and 4 of the hypothetical sequence and for much the same reasons as are given in the discussion of that sequence. So, too, does the return of the parties to the political center in the following elections correspond to the hypothetical sequence.

Second, in the hypothetical sequence issue salience remains unchanged (there is only one issue). *Third,* citizens' preferences are also assumed to remain constant. *Fourth,* real candidates do not necessarily converge to the same strategy when they reach equilibrium. These conditions do not hold true of the real election sequence. Inflation and unemployment appear and reappear as issues, with no consistent pattern over the period examined. There is a marked change in citizen preferences on the Vietnam War issue from 1968 to 1972. The salience of the civil rights issue also falls sharply from the 1960s to the 1970s. Finally, no one could argue that Kennedy and Nixon had converged in 1960, nor Nixon and Humphrey in 1968.

Nowhere is the shift of issue preferences and saliences more apparent than in the 1980 presidential election. If we project the sequence begun with the five elections in Table 7.3 and assume that they correspond to the five real elections in Table 7.4, then Jimmy Carter should have defeated Ronald Reagan in 1980, perhaps by as much as a 3-to-2 vote. Instead, Reagan won 55 percent of the two-party popular vote and 91 percent of the electoral vote. Furthermore, the Republicans gained control of the Senate for the first time since 1952.

The Reagan victory shows that the hypothetical sequence does not portray a cyclical phenomenon, for by 1960 through 1976 standards Reagan's 1980 positions were analogous to Goldwater's and Jimmy Carter's to Johnson's in 1964. Yet Reagan won a landslide victory. What accounts for this reversal of the expected pattern? Scholars now differ over the answer to this question. Some see it as a dislike for Carter and an unshakeable belief in his incompetence. Others hold that Carter lost because of last-minute opinion shifts caused by his handling of the Iranian seizure of American hostages and by double-digit inflation. Still others argue that Reagan took positions that many voters believe in on issues such as abortion and busing, which other presidential candidates had played down. Finally, some commentators advance the view that citizens' preferences had shifted to the positions Reagan had taken for many years. To these explanations we might add that there might not have been a pure strategy equilibrium in the 1980 presidential election. The election outcome thus might have resulted from complex strategic interactions and, quite frankly, from the luck of the draw.

It will be some time (if ever) before we fully understand the 1980 election. The elections of 1982 and 1984 will certainly help to put it in perspective. We describe the hypothetical election sequence and link it to a series of real elections merely to show that if a pure strategy equilibrium exists, then it strongly affects all parties and candidates, including those who temporarily ignore it.[9] Of course, in real elections a pure strategy equilibrium may not exist or it may be a moving target that candidates can only track imperfectly.

In this hypothetical sequence of five elections, even though each party departs once from the plurality equilibrium strategy (the Republicans in election 2 and the Democrats in election 4), that issue strategy still wins. Hence, *both* candidates need not be at the "correct" strategy for it to be the public policy advocated in the election, but the structure of the election game provides a powerful incentive over time for candidates to advocate that position, and in our hypothetical sequence both parties eventually return to it.

Information variations. The preceding discussion includes some heroic assumptions about candidates' information. Do candidates actually know what the underlying preference distribution looks like? Can they estimate the effects their strategies have on abstention? How do candidates' strategies affect their opponents' strategies and fortunes? The answers to these and similar questions involve highly complex matters of polling and decision theory. Moreover, if they are made public, polls themselves might affect abstention and hence election outcomes.[10]

---

[9] Most political scientists would regard this accounting for the 1960–1976 presidential election outcomes as somewhat fanciful and surely oversimplified. After all, there is a clear explanation in each election for what happened. While I share some of this disbelief, nevertheless I am struck by the virtue of this simple explanation and the emerging pattern.

[10] The evidence about the effect of polls on subsequent voting is mixed. For a theoretical discussion, see Herbert A. Simon, *Models of Man* (New York: Wiley, 1957), chapter 5. An empirical study of a related problem is developed by Kurt Lang and Gladys Engel Lang, *Voting and Nonvoting: Implications of Broadcasting Returns Before Polls Are Closed* (Waltham, Mass.: Blaisdell, 1968). Articles in *Public Opinion Quarterly,* 17 (Spring 1973), discuss the effects of polling generally; these include Morris Janowitz,

Even without information about matters such as preference distributions and opponents' reactions, though, candidates might still obey the plurality equilibrium principle. For example, suppose that in the election described in Figure 7.1 neither candidate knows what the actual preference distribution looks like. Either by guessing or by substituting their own preferences for those of the electorate, the Democrat and Republican advocate 40 and 37 percent respectively, and the Republican wins. In a second election, the Democrat converges to the Republican's position at 37, and the election is an expected tie. But suppose the Democrat wins by a few votes. In a third election, the Republican is now in a quandary. Advocating 37 produces a small loss, and when the Democrat advocates more than 37, the Republican wins. So in this election, the Republican will probably advocate a small shift to the right, say to 36, and will win. If preference distributions remain unchanged from election to election, the long-run reiteration of this process moves the candidates closer and closer to the median preference. Therefore, even without information about the preference distribution, candidates have a way of eventually coming close to obeying the plurality equilibrium principle.

Several factors can interfere with this process, however, even though it seems robust. The equilibrium strategy might change, perhaps because the underlying preference distribution changes. But such a change would merely call forth new entrepreneurial skills on the part of the candidates, moving their actual strategies toward new theoretical equilibria as the result of rivalrous political activity.

Candidates' information actually seems better than we might think. Primary elections convey substantial information: the frequency of these elections in 1976 provided both President Gerald R. Ford and Governor Jimmy Carter with a great amount of information. The extended number of primaries in 1980 gave Carter and Governor Ronald Reagan even more state-by-state information about voters' preferences. Although that information contained the bias of party voting, each general-election candidate could learn much about voter preferences from how his opponents fared in each primary. Conventions also sometimes distill political wisdom about reality. Hence, candidates themselves need not always move along the issue space to find plurality equilibrium strategies for those strategies to hold good in the general election. Party delegates to a convention might be able to shift their loyalties to a more nearly viable general-election candidate (although this is not possible for those delegates whose votes are committed on the first ballot).

"Political Polling," pp. 1–2; Louis Harris, "Polls and Politics in the United States," pp. 3–8; Mark Abrams, "Public Opinion Polls and Political Parties," pp. 9–18; and Martin Meadows, "Public Opinion Polls and the 1961 Philippine Election," pp. 19–27. Polls would affect the P term in the calculus of voting and the $P(x)$ term in the calculus of contributions. Polls' results are sometimes reported for various groups in the electorate. If group members use this knowledge (about how others like themselves react to the candidates) as an information surrogate, then polls can also affect the B term. Whether different groups of voters are systematically affected remains unknown.

Polls, too, can be extremely useful, provided they are carefully executed and cautiously interpreted.

Evidence about candidates' issue strategies. Frankly, the evidence concerning how candidates respond to the election game they confront is quite sparse. As we point out in the next section, American elections are extremely complex, inviting candidates to be ambiguous about their issue positions, to take different positions on the same issue before different audiences, and to take no position at all on the "hard" issues. Nevertheless, some evidence about candidates' responsiveness to citizens' preferences is available.

One study used existing polling data to divide the population into quartiles on several issues.[11] Each quartile contains 25 percent of those stating a preference on the relevant issue. The study carefully located candidates' positions (strategies) on the issues by analyzing their statements. Then, it asked whether candidates adopted positions falling close to the median, which was assumed to fall somewhere in the two middle quartiles (50 percent of those citizens stating a preference). Table 7.5 shows the results for the 1968 presidential election. Clearly, Richard M. Nixon did better at finding the median—the hypothesized plurality equilibrium strategy—than did Hubert H. Humphrey, which might partially explain Nixon's electoral success.

A division of the electorate into quartiles was not possible on certain issues because appropriate polling data were unavailable. Nevertheless, in several cases it was possible to identify the *plurality* preference—the issue position that had more support than any other—on various issues. Table 7.6 reports how often various candidates advocated the plurality opinion. The Nixon and Humphrey percentages are about as expected, as is the report of Senator Goldwater's poor matching with plurality preferences. Somewhat surprising is Senator McGovern's relatively better performance in early 1972. However, the study points out that McGovern went against plurality prefer-

Table 7.5 Closeness of Presidential Candidates' Issue Positions to the Median of Public Opinion, 1968

	Nixon		Humphrey	
Candidate's Stand		(*N*)		(*N*)
In the second or third quartile	90%	(19)	65%	(15)
In the first or fourth quartile	10%	(2)	35%	(8)

Source: Reprinted from *Choices and Echoes in Presidential Elections: Rational Man and Electoral Democracy* by Benjamin I. Page, by permission of the University of Chicago Press. From table 2, p. 39.

[11] Benjamin I. Page, *Choices and Echoes in Presidential Elections: Rational Man and Electoral Democracy* (Chicago: University of Chicago Press, 1978).

Table 7.6 Agreement of Candidates' Positions with Plurality Preferences of the Public

	Nixon (1968)	(N)	Humphrey (1968)	(N)	McGovern (early 1972)	(N)	Goldwater (early 1964)	(N)
In agreement with plurality opinion	79%	(65)	69%	(59)	70%	(14)	32%	(9)
Opposed to plurality opinion	21%	(17)	31%	(26)	30%	(6)	68%	(19)

Source: Reprinted from *Choices and Echoes in Presidential Elections: Rational man and Electoral Democracy* by Benjamin I. Page, by permission of the University of Chicago Press. From tables 3, 4, and 5, pp. 40, 54, and 55.

ences on several highly salient issues by advocating reduced penalties for marijuana possession, amnesty for draft evaders, and busing to achieve school integration; he also proposed a guaranteed income plan and increased taxes for wealthier Americans.[12] When we weight issues for salience, McGovern's poor showing in the general election becomes more understandable.

Parties, elections, and firms. Citizens' preferences and majority rule combine to reward with victory candidates who advocate plurality equilibrium strategy positions and to punish with defeat those who do not. Even variations in candidates' ideologies and information cannot long suppress these fundamental electoral forces. A striking parallel exists between how competitive forces affect parties in elections and how they affect firms in the marketplace. A decline in a firm's profitability provides an incentive for corporate takeovers and mergers. The decline may result from the firm's management not attending to innovations, changes in consumer preferences, or poor management practices. The takeover or merger by people who believe they can run the firm more profitably is an extremely important mechanism in economic life.[13] As is evident in our example of the series of five elections, a similar takeover mechanism is also central to the movement of parties toward public policy issue strategies that can win elections.

A parallel between economics and politics also exists for the information problem. Firms in the marketplace operate in an environment of uncertainty. Their managers plan for future plants and products in great ignorance of future technological developments and innovations, the availability of supplies, and changes in consumer tastes. How such managers should go about maximizing profits in the face of this uncertainty seems theoretically

---

[12] Page, *Choices and Echoes in Presidential Elections,* p. 55.

[13] Henry G. Manne, "Some Theoretical Aspects of Share Voting," *Columbia Law Review,* 64 (December 1964), pp. 1426–1445, and Manne, "Mergers and the Market for Corporate Control," *Journal of Political Economy,* 73 (April 1965), pp. 110–120.

impossible to calculate, but capital and profits flow to those firms that take the correct actions, even if by accident. Managers probably do not try to maximize profits absolutely, but they do try to maximize profit relative to other firms, even though they suffer under uncertainty about future conditions. The result is the survival and flourishing of firms whose actions are more nearly "correct," and the destruction or decline or takeover by more efficient managers of firms whose actions are less so. Firms thus appear to be maximizing profit even if their managers are only guessing at random or by copying the strategies of their most successful competitors.[14] Similarly, candidates respond to uncertainty about citizens' preferences by judging the relative performance of different strategies based on their own experiences and those of others.

PLURALITY EQUILIBRIA AND THE PUBLIC INTEREST

The election described in Figure 7.1 relies on strong assumptions to guarantee not only that the election has a pure strategy equilibrium pair, but also that the candidates converge to the same equilibrium strategy. When one or more of these assumptions is not satisfied, convergence may not occur, and pure strategy equilibria may not exist. However, elections without pure strategy equilibria are just as (or perhaps more) interesting and important as those with pure strategy equilibria, for an evaluation of democratic institutions.

The paradox of voting. Chapters 1 and 2 describe games and elections without pure strategy equilibria, and Chapter 3 analyzes this phenomenon in greater detail.[15] These discussions show first that no group decision mechanism can simultaneously satisfy five very reasonable conditions while generating a connected and transitive public choice (Arrow's impossibility theorem). Second, in the example in Chapter 3 of an election on the Vietnam War issue, a cyclical majority prevails. That example shows that if citizens' utility curves, or preferences, over an issue dimension do not satisfy certain conditions of "reasonableness," no pure strategy equilibrium may exist. Therefore, candidates who publicly state clear, forthright policies on such issues before their opponents commit themselves are bound to lose. There is no pure winning or tying strategy for the plurality election game; any strategy can be defeated by some other strategy. Third, the candidates' only recourse in such elections is to be as ambiguous as possible about their issue positions.

---

[14] Armen A. Alchian, "Uncertainty, Evolution, and Economic Theory," *Journal of Political Economy,* 58 (June 1950), pp. 211–221.

[15] See particularly Chapter 1, Table 1.2; Chapter 2, Tables 2.3 and 2.4 for elections; Table 2.8 for a discussion of two-person zero-sum games without pure strategy equilibria; and the end of Chapter 3, following the subheading "The paradox of voting," for a discussion of Arrow's paradox.

Mechanics of the paradox. The election in Figure 7.1 has a pure strategy equilibrium with both candidates converged to the median. Here, we identify some conditions that might destroy the existence of such pure strategy equilibria. However, first we consider an election with a pure strategy equilibrium to which candidates might converge, which differs from the election in Figure 7.1. In particular, look again in Chapter 5 at Figure 5.6, which depicts the utility curves of three citizens on the issue of government spending as a percentage of GNP. Suppose these three citizens are the entire electorate in a particular election and that each votes. The reasoning applied to the election depicted in Figure 7.1 will also show that position *Y*, the baker's bliss point, is the pure strategy equilibrium to which candidates in a two-candidate plurality-rule election will converge. The proof consists merely in showing that a strategy at 35 percent defeats one to the left or right of it by a vote of two to one, and of course it ties itself. In sum, *Y* is the minimax strategy for each candidate.

The elections in Figures 5.6 and 7.1 are identical except that the number of citizens in the first is countably finite while the number in the second is uncountably infinite. But suppose the three citizens in the first election were asked to vote in an election in which the issue was United States policy in the Vietnam War. We might define the three hypothetical positions as in Chapter 3, in the discussion of private and collective choice as paradox generators: *X* becomes escalation of the war, the hawk position; *Y* becomes the status quo, or LBJ position; and *Z* becomes de-escalation, the dove position. Say the factory worker is a classic hawk, preferring *X* to *Y* and *Y* to *Z*. Her utility curve is shown in Figure 7.3 as the solid line sloping downward from left to right. We have normalized her utility so that U_x equals 1.0, U_y equals 0.5, and U_z equals 0.0. Of course, the linear nature of this curve and the particular assignment of utilities are entirely artificial.

The baker is an LBJ supporter who prefers the status quo, *Y*, to the dove position, *Z*, and the dove position to the hawk position, *X*. His utility curve is shown in Figure 7.3 as a dashed line. Again, the curve is linear for convenience, and for the baker U_y equals 1.0, U_z equals 0.5, and U_x equals 0.0. Finally, the pensioner most prefers *Z*, de-escalation of the war, to *X*, an escalation, but least prefers *Y*, the status quo. His pithy remark concerning the war is, "Fish or cut bait." Figure 7.3 shows his utility curve as a line made by a series of long and short dashes. Again, we have normalized utility so that for him, U_z equals 1.0, U_x equals 0.5, and U_y equals 0.0.

The earlier general discussion and the analysis of this particular preference ordering on the Vietnam War policy in Chapter 3 have already shown that no pure strategy equilibrium exists. A candidate at *X* defeats one at *Y* by a vote of two to one. Similarly, *Y* defeats *Z* and *Z* defeats *X*. A cyclical majority occurs, and no strategy defeats or ties all other strategies.

Why? How does this election differ from the ones described in Figures 5.6 and 7.1? The answer is that citizens voting in those elections had utility curves with at most one peak (single-peaked utility curves are explicitly drawn

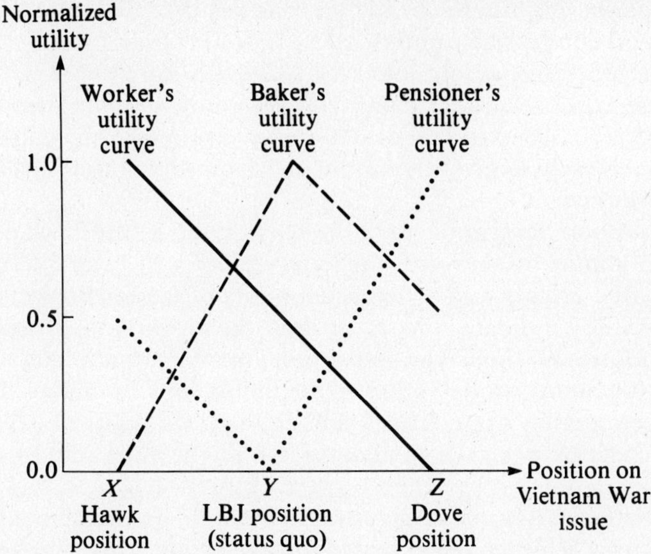

Figure 7.3 Three utility curves on Vietnam War issue aggregated to form a cyclical majority.

in Figure 5.6 and implicitly assumed in the election based on Figure 7.1). However, in Figure 7.3, the pensioner's utility curve has two peaks, one at *Z* and the other at *X*. Even if we relabeled the figure by switching the positions of *X* and *Y*, or *Y* and *Z*, or *X* and *Z*, one of the citizens would turn out to have a double-peaked utility curve. If citizens' utility curves cannot be arranged along the issue dimension so that they all become single-peaked, the absence of a pure strategy equilibrium remains a distinct possibility.[16]

The paradox of voting and the strategy of ambiguity. Game theory proves that all two-person zero-sum games of the sort described in this book have equilibrium pairs, even if they are mixed strategy equilibria—and two-candidate plurality-rule elections are zero-sum games. But candidates cannot realistically adopt mixed strategies in a campaign, for they cannot simultaneously use spinners and announce the pure strategies the spinners select. Each candidate would delay his announcement. In place of mixed strategies, when pure strategy equilibria are absent, candidates tend either to present citizens with what amount to lotteries over possible issue positions, or to avoid talking about issues altogether.

The election based on the Vietnam War issue and represented by Figure 7.3 can be used to demonstrate the logic of the strategy of ambiguity. Suppose

[16] Duncan Black, *The Theory of Committees and Elections* (Cambridge: Cambridge University Press, 1958).

that by avoiding the issue or by giving conflicting signals, one of the candidates offers an equiprobable lottery called L_1, over positions X, Y, and Z. Each voter's expected utility in the lottery, EU, equals $\frac{1}{3}U_x + \frac{1}{3}U_y + \frac{1}{3}U_z$. For example, the factory worker's expected utility for the lottery would become $EU = (1.0)/3 + (0.5)/3 + (0.0)/3$, or 0.5. It is also simple to show that the baker and pensioner each receive a utility of 0.5 from this lottery over the three possible positions.

Now, suppose one candidate proposes position X, the hawk policy, while the other candidate offers voters the lottery L_1 over X, Y, and Z. The worker has a utility of 1.0 for X and an expected utility of 0.5 for the lottery. Hence, she votes for the candidate at X rather than the one adopting the strategy of ambiguity. However, the baker gets a utility of 0.0 from X but an expected utility of 0.5 from L_1, so he votes for the ambiguous candidate. Finally, the pensioner gets a utility of 0.5 from X and an expected utility of 0.5 from L_1, so he is indifferent between the candidates. He might flip a coin to decide how to vote.

In sum, the strategy of ambiguity that a candidate carries out by offering voters a lottery achieves an expected tie—one vote for, one against, one randomly chosen—against the unambiguous advocacy of X. We can show by the same reasoning that the lottery also ties Y and Z. But in the election game based on pure strategies, no single strategy can beat or tie all other pure strategies. The equiprobable lottery, a particular strategy of ambiguity, does tie all three pure strategies, however.

But this is not the end of the story, for the problem of incoherence in public choice goes much deeper than we might have supposed. In particular, let us define three other lotteries: $L_2 = 0.8X, 0.0Y, 0.2Z$; $L_3 = 0.2X, 0.8Y, 0.0Z$; and $L_4 = 0.2X, 0.0Y, 0.8Z$. Table 7.7 shows the worker, baker, and pensioner's expected utility for each of these lotteries as well as for L_1, based on their utilities in Figure 7.3.

Notice that by a vote of two to one in every case: L_2 defeats L_3; L_3 defeats L_1; L_1 defeats L_4; and L_4 defeats L_2. That is, there is a cycle among the lotteries over the pure strategy alternatives. (Indeed, X now defeats L_3, Y defeats L_4, and Z defeats both L_2 and L_4.) This result is fully general.[17] If there is an underlying cycle among the pure strategy alternatives, then there will be no single mixed strategy—lottery—that defeats all other lotteries. The incoherence in elections is therefore extremely profound. Candidates fail to guarantee themselves a victory or a tie even with ambiguous stands on the issues. Indeed, they are led by the logic of this incoherence to say nothing about public policy issues. Instead, they kiss babies, salute the flag, eat various ethnic dishes, and carry on about their opponents' inadequacies.

Several examples of the strategy of ambiguity have occurred in real elections. Nicholas Biddle, President William Henry Harrison's campaign

---

[17] Peter C. Fishburn, *The Theory of Social Choice* (Princeton, N.J.: Princeton University Press, 1973), pp. 251, *passim.* See also Richard D. McKelvey and Jeff Richelson, "Cycles of Risk," *Public Choice,* 18 (Summer 1974), pp. 41–66.

Table 7.7 Expected Utilities of Worker, Baker, and Pensioner for Four Hypothetical Election Lotteries

	Lottery 1, L_1 (⅓X, ⅓Y, ⅓Z)	**Lottery 2, L_2 (0.8X, 0.0Y, 0.2Z,)**	**Lottery 3, L_3 (0.2X, 0.8Y, 0.0Z)**	**Lottery 4, L_4 (0.2X, 0.0Y, 0.8Z)**
Worker	0.5	0.8	0.6	0.2
Baker	0.5	0.1	0.8	0.4
Pensioner	0.5	0.6	0.1	0.9

manager, offered this advice about Harrison's campaign: "Let him say not one single word about his principles, or his creed—let him say nothing—promise nothing. Let no Committee, no convention—no town meeting ever extract from him a single word about what he thinks now, or what he will do hereafter. Let the use of pen and ink be wholly forbidden as if he were a mad poet in Bedlam."[18] Similarly, this anecdote has been provided about the 1920 Harding presidential campaign: "From his deathbed, Boise Penrose, the Pennsylvania machine politician advised: 'Keep Warren at home. Don't let him make speeches. If he goes out on a tour somebody's sure to ask him questions, and Warren's just the sort of damned fool that will try to answer them.' "[19] And, "More recently, presidential candidates have followed Biddle's seemingly ageless advice with ambiguous pronouncements on the salient political issues of the time. In the 1968 presidential campaign, both Nixon's 'I have a [secret] plan' [to end the Vietnam War] statements . . . and Humphrey's 'law and order with justice' slogan . . . suggest that the equivocal pronouncement . . . is a common and recurring theme in American electoral politics."[20]

Jimmy Carter's 1976 campaign for the Democratic presidential nomination illustrates the most masterful use of the strategy of ambiguity in recent political history. The Carter campaign's major pamphlet, *Jimmy Carter: Why This Democrat Should Be Our Next President,* shows the strategy in action. The pamphlet lists nine issue areas as "your problems," including the economy, energy, welfare, environment, agriculture, crime, taxes, health care, and defense.

On the economy, the pamphlet notes that "Jobs for Americans who want to work must be our number one national priority. We will never have a balanced budget, an end to the inflationary spiral, or adequate services for our people as long as we have 8.5 or 9 million people unemployed." Notice all of

[18] Shepsle, "The Strategy of Ambiguity," p. 555, quoting Nicholas Biddle, *Correspondence,* edited by R. C. McGrane (Boston: Houghton Mifflin, 1919), p. 256.

[19] Shepsle, "The Strategy of Ambiguity," p. 555, quoting William E. Leuchtenberg, *The Perils of Prosperity, 1914–1932* (Chicago: University of Chicago Press, 1958), p. 88.

[20] Shepsle, "The Strategy of Ambiguity," p. 555.

JIMMY CARTER IS CONCERNED ABOUT YOUR PROBLEMS.

Economy. "Jobs for Americans who want to work must be our number one national priority. We will never have a balanced budget, an end to the inflationary spiral, or adequate services for our people as long as we have 8.5 or 9 million people unemployed."

Energy. "The mishandling of the energy problem is a primary cause of the current economic crisis. We are the only civilized nation on earth without a national energy policy. This negligence is a crime against the American people."

Welfare. "Our welfare system is an insult to those who pay the bill and those who honestly need help. 2,000,000 employees desperately try to administer over 100 federal programs to about 12,000,000 recipients. Some combined welfare payments exceed the income of the average working family, while other needy families are unable to obtain a bare subsistence. We have heard promises of welfare reform too long. It's time to act."

Environment. "We cannot compromise the commitment of our federal government to play a significant role in the preservation of natural areas and resources."

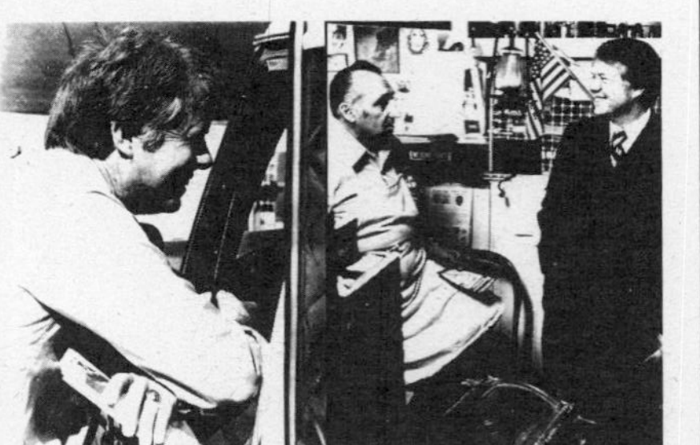

Agriculture. "The United States of America is the greatest agricultural producer in the world. Yet, we now find ourselves in the ridiculous position of seeing the family farmer going broke trying to produce food and fiber the consumer cannot afford to buy."

Crime. "Our best defense against skyrocketing crime is a criminal justice system that can deliver swift, certain, fair and firm justice. The present system has shown itself incapable of doing any of these things."

Taxes. "Our tax system is a disgrace. The average family earning $10,000 or less pays a larger portion of its income in taxes than a family with an annual income of $1,000,000 or more. We need a fair tax system NOW!"

Health Care. "The quality of health care in this nation depends largely on economic status. It is often unavailable or costs too much. We need a national health care system, including national health insurance, that is efficient, workable and fair. We must emphasize preventative medicine, better delivery of services and cost control."

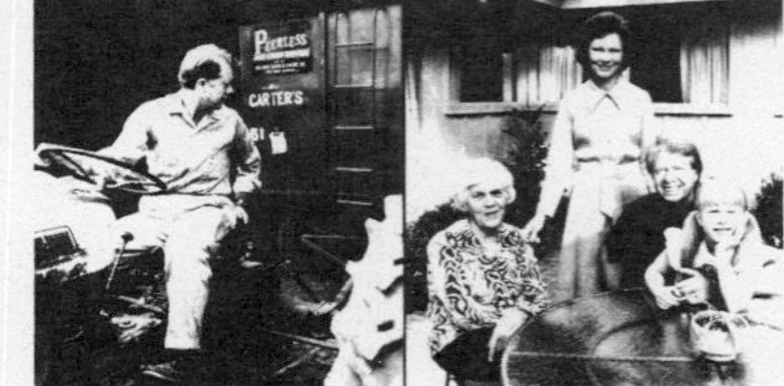

Defense. "Waste and inefficiency are both costly to taxpayers and a danger to our own national existence. Strict management and budgetary control over the Pentagon should reduce the ratio of officers to men and of support forces to combat troops. I see no reason why the Chief of Naval Operations needs more Navy captains on his staff than we have serving on ships!"

This page reproduced from Jimmy Carter's 1976 campaign pamphlet, *Jimmy Carter: Why This Democrat Should be Our Next President,* illustrates the strategy of ambiguity in action. The pamphlet mentions nine salient issues and remains ambiguous on each one.

the things that Carter regarded as bad: an unbalanced budget, an inflationary spiral, inadequate services, 8.5 or 9 million people unemployed. A disdain for these perceived evils in no way distinguished Governor Carter's positions on economic issues from those of any other candidates. What were Carter's positions? "Jobs for Americans who want to work must be our number one national priority." How might this priority be met? Carter the candidate remained ambiguous and merely stated his likes or dislikes, not what he intended to do about them. That is, he implicitly invited citizens to ignore the future and place the full weight of their decisions on retrospective voting.

On energy the pamphlet notes, "The mishandling of the energy problem is a primary cause of the current economic crisis. We are the only civilized nation on earth without a national energy policy. This negligence is a crime against the American people." However, Carter was the only candidate in the presidential race who failed to reveal his energy policy. He thus played on popular dissatisfactions with President Ford while remaining ambiguous about his own proposals.

The strategy of ambiguity is far more difficult for incumbents than for challengers to carry off successfully. Incumbents' positions are often a matter of record, but without such a record challengers can remain ambiguous. For example, Carter also issued conflicting messages to the electorate in the 1976 presidential election. He vacillated on the abortion issue, depending upon his audience. And, he carefully cultivated an alliance with the family of slain civil rights leader Martin Luther King, Jr., at the same time that he voiced his compassion for those who wished to preserve the "ethnic purity" (a euphemism for "segregated") of their neighborhoods. As the incumbent, President Ford could only emphasize Carter's ambiguity to counter this strategy. This defensive tactic failed.

In his 1980 reelection bid, Carter continued to use the strategy of ambiguity concerning his own future plans as president. However, most of his time campaigning was spent criticizing Ronald Reagan and trying to create the impression that Reagan's real issue positions were both unambiguous and undesirable. This tactic eventually backfired, because it led many voters to believe that the president was "mean."

Equilibria in multiple-issue elections. Perhaps cyclical majorities only happen when it is impossible to arrange citizens' utility curves on an issue dimension so that they are all single-peaked. Since single-peakedness might occur more often than not, perhaps we need not worry about this hypothetical problem or about the strategy of ambiguity. Pure strategy equilibria may be likely to exist in most elections, and the candidates can be expected to adopt them. In this view, elections are good procedures for aggregating citizens' preferences, and candidates' public policy positions reflect those preferences accurately.

But these claims do not hold true. First, cyclical majorities can occur with alarming frequency. Second, even with single-peaked utility curves, a pure strategy equilibrium may not exist, turning elections into random generators of public policy. To understand this possibility, consider Figure 5.7, which shows the baker's total utility over the issues of government spending as a percentage of GNP and national defense spending as a percentage of government spending. For convenience, let us call these issues X and Y, respectively. On both issues taken singly, the baker's utility curve is single-peaked, and on both issues taken together, the curve—now an upside-down bowl—remains single-peaked. Labeling the baker's preferences with the letter *a*, his most-preferred position on X becomes X_a, or 35, and his most-preferred position on Y becomes Y_a, or 40.

Figure 7.4 shows what we would see if we "looked down" on the baker's utility curve. The single point at *a* is the baker's most-preferred position on the two issues taken together. The concentric circles around *a* are called **indifference contours.** The baker receives the same utility from any two points on a particular circle, so he is indifferent as among all public policy combinations on the same circle. Finally, the larger the radius of the circle, the less utility the baker receives, which means he prefers a public policy closer to *a* to one that is further away.

Figure 7.5 shows a similar configuration for the baker, whom we shall now refer to simply as *a*, and for two other citizens, *b* and *c*. Arbitrarily, let X_b equal 75 percent, Y_b equal 20 percent, X_c equal 55 percent, and Y_c equal 75 percent. Suppose these three citizens are the entire electorate, and each votes for the candidate whose public policy proposal (issue strategy) is closest to his own bliss point. That is, each votes for the candidate whose issue strategy is on the higher indifference contour (the one with the smaller radius). Figure 7.5 illustrates portions of the indifference contours, which are projections of total utility curves, of these three citizens on the two issues in the election. Each citizen has a single-peaked utility curve.

What pure strategy equilibrium should candidates adopt? One likely answer is the center of the triangle whose vertices are the citizens' bliss points—*a, b,* and *c*. This center is marked by *r*. However, consider another point, say *s*, which bisects the shortest side of the triangle. With respect to citizen *a*, *r* falls on an indifference contour with a larger radius than the one *s* falls on. Hence, *a* prefers *s* to *r*, and *a* will vote for *s* over *r*. Similarly, with respect to *c*, *r* also falls on an indifference contour with a larger radius than the one *s* falls on. So, *c* also prefers *s* to *r*. While *b* prefers *r* to *s*, *s* defeats *r* by a vote of two to one. Now consider point *t*, which lies outside the triangle. Obviously, both *a* and *b* prefer *t* to *s*, so *t* defeats *s* by a vote of two to one. But notice that both *b* and *c* prefer *r* to *t*. Hence a cycle exists: *s* defeats *r*; *r* defeats *t*; and *t* defeats *s*. No pure strategy equilibrium appears to exist.

The proof that no pure strategy equilibrium exists for this election is reserved for advanced texts, although the proposition now seems obvious.[21]

[21] The technical background for the preceding example and a proof of the proposition is in Charles R. Plott, "A Notion of Equilibrium and Its Possibility Under Majority Rule," *American Economic Review,* 57 (September 1967), pp. 787–806.

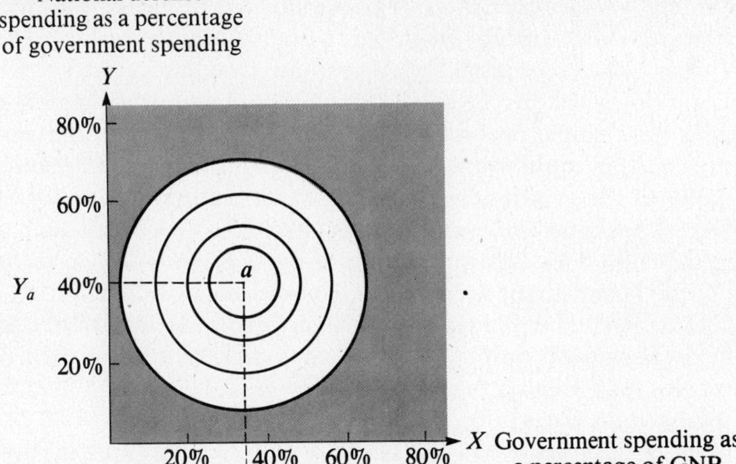

Figure 7.4 Projection of baker's total utility curve on two issues.

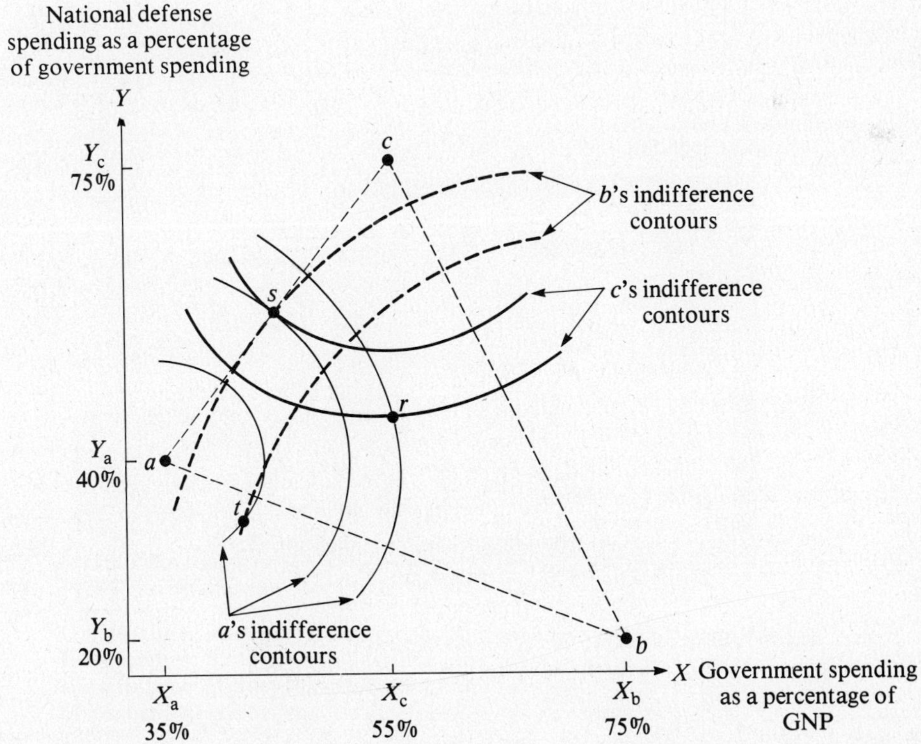

Figure 7.5 Hypothetical three-voter, two-issue election.

We can search in vain for a pure strategy equilibrium; it simply does not exist. The election outcome appears random. If one candidate is the first to announce a clear policy proposal, his opponent can always find a winning strategy. Candidates will thus be driven to adopt ambiguous strategies. Yet, all three citizens have single-peaked utility curves. What explains *this* result?

A pure strategy equilibrium fails to emerge in this election because there exists no point in the two-dimensional issue space around which the citizens' most-preferred positions are symmetrically arrayed. Notice that such a pure strategy equilibrium does exist on either of the two issues voted on separately. It falls at X_c for government spending as a percentage of GNP and at Y_a for national defense spending as a percentage of government spending. But these equilibria exist because X_c and Y_a represent median positions for their respective issues. No such median exists when the issues are combined in one election, unless votes are symmetrically distributed about some such position. For example, if *a*, *b*, and *c* were points on a straight line in this two-dimensional space, then the middle point would be the pure strategy equilibrium for two-candidate plurality-rule elections. Simply for illustration, Figure 7.6 depicts a five-voter election in which citizen *c*'s most-preferred position is the pure strategy equilibrium. Notice that citizens *a* and *e* are symmetrically located around *c*'s position, as are *b* and *d*.

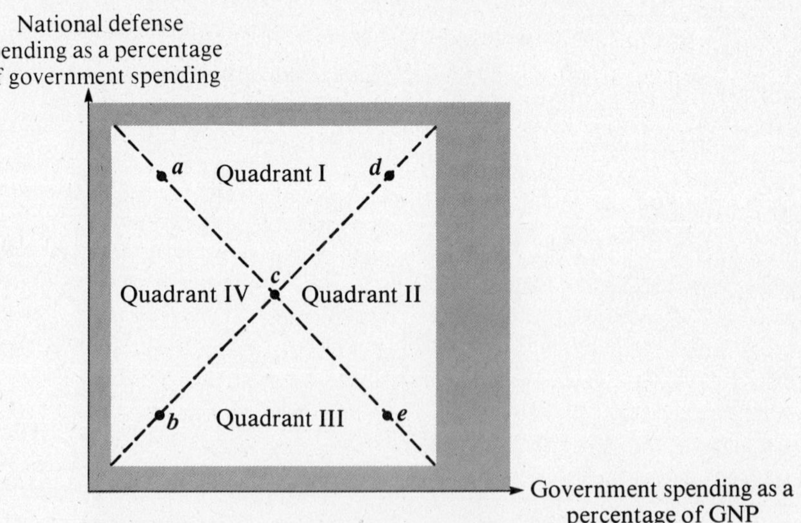

Voters *b*, *c*, and *e* vote for motion *c* against any motion in quadrant I.
Voters *a*, *b*, and *c* vote for motion *c* against any motion in quadrant II.
Voters *a*, *c*, and *d* vote for motion *c* against any motion in quadrant III.
Voters *c*, *d*, and *e* vote for motion *c* against any motion in quadrant IV.

Figure 7.6 Hypothetical five-voter, two-issue election with pure strategy equilibrium at *c*.

Intense minorities. Electoral instability (not to mention a severe philosophical problem) also arises in elections in the presence of minority groups whose members hold intense preferences about particular issues.[22] For our purposes in this discussion, a minority or minority group is merely a set of people numbering less than a majority whose members share the same preference about a particular issue or issue position. Calling the group members' preference about the issue "intense" implies no interpersonal comparison of utilities but means only that a candidate who satisfies the members' preference on the issue will defeat one who does not, no matter what positions the candidates take on all other issues. For example, the Democratic candidate might advocate national health insurance, wage and price controls, higher taxes for the wealthy, and a national handgun confiscation law, while the Republican takes opposing positions on all of these issues. A voter with an intense preference against the handgun act might agree with the Democrat on the three other issue positions, but because he holds his preference about the handgun issue intensely, he will vote for the Republican.

If a majority holds an intense preference, then no special philosophical problems arise for believers in representative democracy, provided the majority gets its way. Of course, cyclical majority problems might intervene, but these we have encountered before. However, if minorities hold intense preferences, then two problems immediately arise and a third problem soon emerges from them.

First, suppose there are two groups in the electorate whose members hold diametrically opposed but intense preferences on a particular issue. The abortion issue is again a good example. Members of right-to-life groups or of organizations such as Moral Majority would oppose any move to liberalize abortion policies, while members of women's rights groups such as the National Organization for Women would prefer the opposite policy. If these preferences are intensely held, a candidate who takes a clear and forthright stand on either side of this issue will lose the opposing group's support; its members will vote for his opponent, even if the opponent does not commit himself. The use of a strategy of ambiguity in this kind of situation is not at all surprising.

Second, even with strong preferences on only one side of an issue, an implicit or explicit coalition of minorities with intensely held preferences is possible and quite troublesome. This coalition can be the result of a consciously employed strategy by candidates of a party not in office. To illustrate the nature of this coalition strategy, let us suppose that an electorate is divided

---

[22] Anthony Downs, *An Economic Theory of Democracy* (New York: Harper and Row, 1957), pp. 55–60. See also David H. Koehler, "Vote Trading and the Voting Paradox: A Proof of Logical Equivalence," *American Political Science Review,* 69 (September 1975), pp. 954–962; and Joe A. Oppenheimer, "Relating Coalitions of Minorities to the Voters' Paradox or Putting the Fly in the Democratic Pie," paper prepared for delivery at the annual meeting of the Southwest Political Science Association, San Antonio, Texas, March 30-April 1, 1972. Some theoretical evidence supports the notion that cyclical majorities and coalitions of minorities are related phenomena.

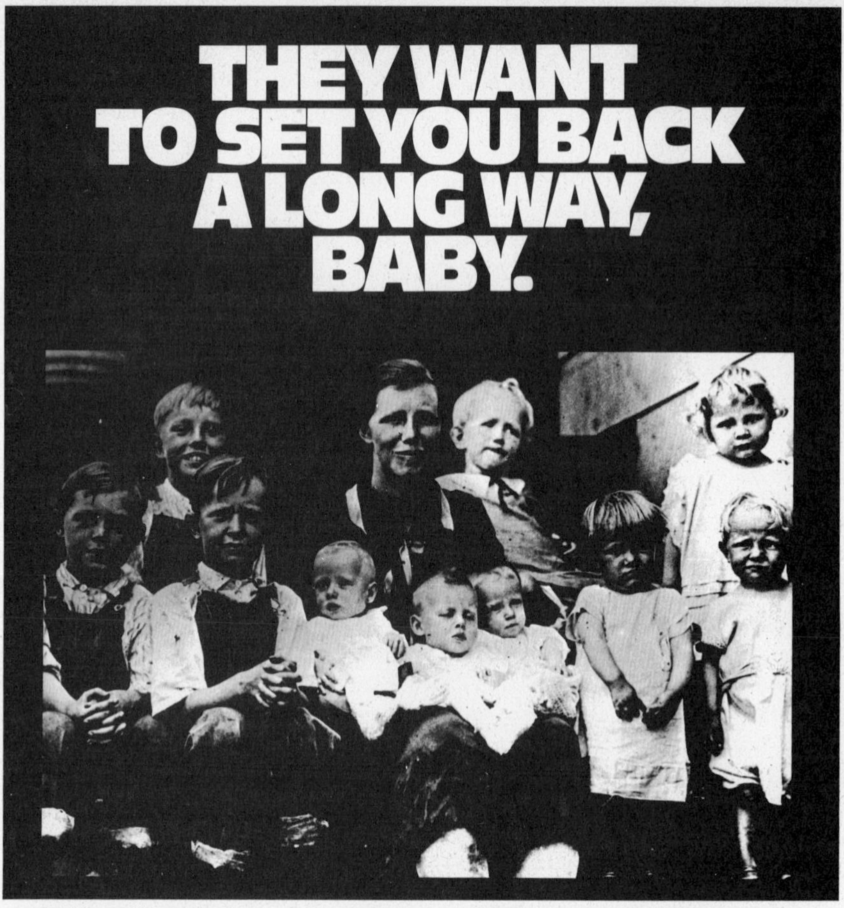

THEY WANT
TO SET YOU BACK
A LONG WAY,
BABY.

The "right-to-life" movement wants to deprive you of your freedom of choice. By imposing its beliefs on everyone.

On your friends.

On your children.

On you.

Some of your most important rights are being challenged:

The right to have any number of children you want. When you want them. Or to have none at all.

The right to use contraceptives.

The right to an abortion even when it's essential to your health.

The right to terminate a pregnancy even if it resulted from rape.

Don't stand by silently and let outrage become law. Fight back.

Take pen in hand and fill out the Planned Parenthood coupon. Give generously of your time and money.

Your most important possession is being threatened: your freedom.

JOIN PLANNED PARENTHOOD

Planned Parenthood of New York City, Inc
380 Second Avenue, New York, NY 10010 (212) 777-2002

☐ I want to help. Keep me informed. Add me to your mailing list.
☐ Send me the voting records of my legislators.
☐ I want to make a tax-deductible contribution. Here is my check in the amount of $________

NAME ________

ADDRESS ________

This advertisement has been paid for with private contributions.

A copy of our annual report can be obtained from us or from the New York State Board of Social Welfare, Office Tower, Empire State Plaza, Albany, NY 12223

THE TIME HAS COME AGAIN WHEN AMERICANS MUST FIGHT FOR THEIR FREEDOM.

These two documents illustrate the uncompromising language used by those who hold intense preferences concerning abortion. The advertisement on the left, taken out by Planned Parenthood of New York City, Inc., attacks the position of organizations such as the National Committee of the Movement to Restore Decency, whose statement concerning abortion is reproduced on the right.

Reprinted by permission of Planned Parenthood of New York City, Inc.
Photo courtesy of The Bettman Archive, Inc.

National Committee Of
The Movement To Restore Decency

★★★★★★★★★★☆☆☆☆☆☆☆☆☆☆

MOTOREDE ☆ 4 Hill Road ☆ Belmont, Massachusetts 02178 ☆ Telephone (617) 489-0600

A Statement Concerning Abortion

The most fundamental of man's God-given rights is the right to life itself. The Movement To Restore Decency wishes to speak for this right on behalf of that significant portion of the human race that cannot speak for themselves – those who are not yet born.

MOTOREDE believes that abortion is murder. When, therefore, we note the cries for relaxation of laws prohibiting abortion, liberalized attitude toward abortion, or abortion on demand, we read instead, relaxation of laws prohibiting *murder,* liberalized attitude toward *murder,* or *murder* on demand.

We believe that any people who will permit their leaders to legalize and legitimatize mass abortion will be unable to restrain those same leaders from further deciding who shall live and who shall not. In just a few years, the trickle of abortion "reform" has become a flood of wholesale murder (the extermination of the unborn), now including the support of the highest levels of the Nixon Administration. We note with horror and apprehension a new trickle of "reform" which will result in the killing of the old and the sterilization of the prolific.

Confusion can well be introduced into this issue by raising the one case in one hundred thousand where a choice might have to be made between the life of a mother and her unborn child. While this extreme situation may be food for discussion in a study of ethics, it has little place in the face of an increasing acceptance of what clearly amounts to a widespread assault on life. The monstrous fact is that thousands of unborn infants are being murdered every week.

Unfortunately, this current assault on life is not an isolated turning away from morality, but is instead one more step in a downward plunge toward barbarism. To discuss the prevalence of drug abuse, sexual promiscuity, rampant crime, *etc.* is to belabor the obvious.

The abortionists, however, do not have to have their way, and this nation does not have to sink to additional depths of depravity. If decency is to be restored, and with it the morals, manners, customs, values, and traditions which have always characterized our nation, we must begin the restoration by realizing that our contemporary degeneration is not entirely the effect of normal causes. Our situation is deliberately being promoted by powerful and sinister human forces for their own evil purposes.

Those forces who propose to destroy traditional morality were alluded to in a short admonition many years ago. It was William Penn who said: "You will either be ruled by God or by a tyrant." We expand on his wise counsel to conclude that those who would legalize murder, or who have already done so, are either unwittingly inviting tyranny, or are themselves the tyrants.

Additional copies of this flyer are available at 25 copies for one dollar from MOTOREDE, 4 Hill Road, Belmont, Massachusetts 02178

equally into three groups of citizens, A, B, and C, and that three proposed changes of law make up the issues in the election campaign: legalizing abortions, confiscating handguns, and decriminalizing the use of marijuana. Table 7.8 summarizes the preferences of each group's members on these three issues.

Suppose a candidate adopts the minority position on each issue, even though a majority of two to one exists in support of all three changes. If each group is an intense minority, that candidate will defeat an opponent who espouses all three majority positions. For each member of A, the utility received from a candidate who opposes legalizing abortions but who also opposes handgun confiscation and marijuana decriminalization is greater than the utility from a candidate who is *for* all three proposals. For each member of B, the utility for the same candidate is also greater than the utility from a candidate who is for all three proposals. The members of A and B will support the candidate who opposes all three proposals, and they will make up a winning coalition of minorities. The members of group C will also join in, for they too hold intense preferences. All three proposals will be defeated in any case, even though a majority of citizens supports each one. If the intense minority on all issues is always constituted of the members of the *same* group, then a coalition of minorities will not win, because the majority defeats the minority. But if there is some separateness of groups on these issues, and if the members of a majority of groups have a greater salience for a particular issue than for all other issues combined, then the coalition of minorities strategy works.

The third problem, a philosophical one, is now apparent. In the first instance of two groups, the presence of citizens with opposing but intensely held preferences led candidates to mask their true issue positions—a most unexpected result. In this second case of three groups, the majority is defeated on all issues. Should it be? That depends on whether one believes that majorities should always prevail or that more or less indifferent majorities should stand aside for intense minorities. Of course, to take a position on that issue would require interpersonal comparisons of utilities.

Electoral equilibria, intense minorities, and the public interest. Chapter 3 used the Arrow problem to question seriously the concept of the public interest. Here, the same problem applies to pure strategy electoral equilibria: such equilibria are sometimes impossible to find—they do not exist. Perhaps electoral equilibria would be located and maintained more easily if we abandoned our narrow insistence on the goal of plurality maximization. Perhaps candidates really wish to advocate what they believe to be the "public interest" as revealed by the "democratic process," which identifies the "collective wisdom" of the electorate. Candidates with such a belief in the electoral process would hold that a public policy achieving the approval of the majority of the electorate is the public policy that wins elections and is identical to the public interest.

Table 7.8 Coalition of Minorities Election Strategy

	Issue		
	Legalization of Abortion Law	**Handgun Confiscation Law**	**Decriminalization of Marijuana Use Law**
Group A	Anti	Pro	Pro
Group B	Pro	Anti	Pro
Group C	Pro	Pro	Anti

If a pure strategy equilibrium exists, these candidates have no problem. But if it does not, then they cannot possibly know what the public interest is. What can we tell them? "The public interest is a lottery over several policies"; or, "The citizens prefer a gamble to a certainty"; or, "The public interest is what the last candidate to announce his platform says it is"—or even, "The public interest is the aggregated preferences of a coalition of minorities." Surely none of these ideas is satisfactory, but as Chapter 3 argues, neither is the concept of the public interest itself. A belief in elections is certainly misplaced if it grows out of the notion that these collective-choice procedures render something that does not exist. Candidates and public policies chosen by elections thus might not acquire any special properties by virtue of their having been voted on. Therefore, a reliance on elections rather than on another choice mechanism to make decisions must rest on a belief other than that voting identifies the public interest. Often, such a belief has less to do with the outcomes of elections than with the use of a democratic procedure itself, in which all citizens are "consulted."

THE SPATIAL THEORY OF SIMPLE ELECTIONS

The conditions under which pure strategy electoral equilibria do exist now seem more important, and equally important are the conditions under which such equilibria do not exist. Since 1958, a theory of the electoral process has been developing using the concept of issue spaces, or issue dimensions.[23] Called **spatial theory,** it seeks to understand the electoral process by identifying conditions under which pure strategy equilibria exist and fail to exist as well as by finding the locations of such equilibrium strategies as do exist.

A Spatial Typology of Elections

Chapter 5 describes several different characteristics of citizens in elections. These characteristics provide the basis for a typology on which a spatial

[23] Downs, *An Economic Theory of Democracy,* is the seminal work.

theory of simple elections has been constructed. The first characteristic identifies one of four possibilities regarding abstention in a particular election: (1) there are no abstentions—all citizens vote; (2) there are some abstentions caused by indifference; (3) there are some abstentions caused by alienation; and (4) there are some abstentions caused by indifference or by alienation or by both. The second characteristic describes the distribution of citizens' bliss points, which can take two interesting forms in a theoretical election: either preference distributions are symmetric and unimodal (*a*), or they are symmetric and bimodal (*b*).

The third characteristic isolates the candidates' goals. Most work in spatial theory assumes that candidates follow the plurality equilibrium principle; that is, they adopt plurality equilibrium, security-level-maximizing strategies. But other goals are possible and often can be shown to be equivalent to the goal of maximizing plurality.[24] However, for simple (no activist) two-candidate, single-member-district elections, the goal of moving to a strategy that maximizes the candidate's security level in plurality ordinarily seems reasonable. Put simply, spatial theory usually assumes that elections are two-person zero-sum games, since the plurality of both candidates sums to zero for any pair of strategies they might adopt. If we assume plurality maximization, this typology generates eight possibilities: 1*a,* 2*a,* 3*a,* 4*a,* 1*b,* 2*b,* 3*b,* and 4*b*. Table 7.9 summarizes the results of spatial theory in locating the policies candidates advocate for each of these eight possible combinations of conditions.

Some Interesting Findings

Table 7.9 shows the median citizen's bliss point to be the plurality equilibrium strategy in many cases.[25] However, some of the findings listed in this table intuitively appear to be nonobvious, or are of special interest in and of themselves. Because these findings are unusual and because they reveal much about the logic of elections, some are examined here.

Case 1*b*, no abstentions and symmetric, bimodal preference distribution. Figure 7.1 illustrates case 1*a*, an election with no abstentions and a symmetric,

---

[24] See Aranson, Hinich, and Ordeshook, "Election Goals and Strategies," and Joseph A. Schlesinger, "The Primary Goals of Political Parties: A Clarification of Positive Theory," *American Political Science Review,* 69 (September 1975), pp. 840–849.

[25] Recent developments in spatial theory show that even in cases for which we cannot identify an equilibrium strategy, such a strategy nevertheless exists in the neighborhood of the median voter's bliss point. See Richard D. McKelvey and Peter C. Ordeshook, "Symmetric Spatial Games Without Majority Rule Equilibria," *American Political Science Review,* 70 (December 1976), pp. 1172–1184. But the robustness of the median voter strategy is seriously questioned in Melvin J. Hinich, "Equilibrium in Spatial Voting: The Median Voter Result Is an Artifact," *Journal of Economic Theory,* 16 (December 1977), pp. 208–217.

Table 7.9 Candidates' Plurality Equilibrium Strategies for Simple Elections

	a—Symmetric Unimodal Distribution	*b*—Symmetric Bimodal Distribution
1. No Abstention	median	median
2. Abstention from Indifference	median	median*
3. Abstention from Alienation	median	no general solution
4. Abstention from Indifference and Alienation	median	median or no general solution*

* Solution depends on the shape of citizen's utility functions.

unimodal preference distribution. The median voter's position, 35 percent, is the plurality equilibrium strategy, the public policy both candidates will advocate. Case 1*b* is interesting because it is not as obvious which strategy candidates will adopt. Figure 7.7 depicts such an election and indicates seven representative strategies, six of which are placed in pairs symmetrically about the seventh, the median voter's position (35). It was once intuitively believed that this preference configuration would lead candidates to diverge, with one positioned at each mode: the Republican might go to 25 while the Democrat went to 45. It seemed reasonable to speculate that the bimodal quality of the distribution would induce candidates to draw apart so that they might better represent what appear to be two distinct bodies of opinion within the electorate.

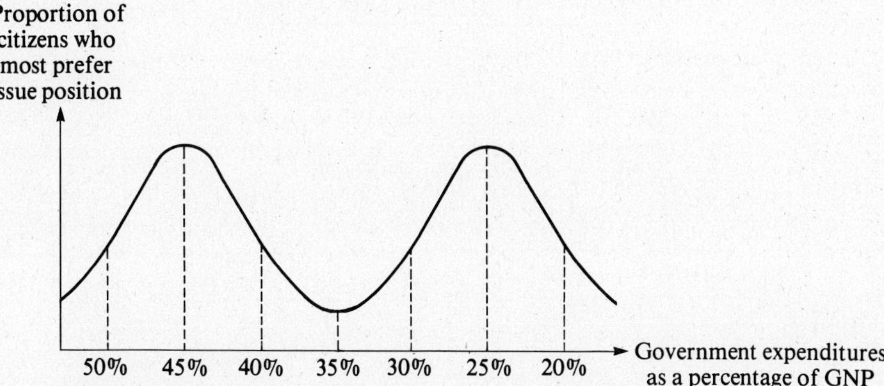

Figure 7.7 Hypothetical election: symmetric, bimodal preference distribution, no abstention.

Table 7.10 Utilities for Candidates in Simple Election: Symmetric, Bimodal Preference Distribution, No Abstention

		The Republican's Strategy							
		50%	45%	40%	35%	30%	25%	20%	*Republican's Security Level*
The Democrat's Strategy	50%	0, 0	−1, +1	−1, +1	−1, +1	−1, +1	−1, +1	0, 0	[−1]
	45%	+1, −1	0, 0	−1, +1	−1, +1	−1, +1	0, 0	+1, −1	[−1]
	40%	+1, −1	+1, −1	0, 0	−1, +1	0, 0	+1, −1	+1, −1	[−1]
	35%	+1, −1	+1, −1	+1, −1	0, 0	+1, −1	+1, −1	+1, −1	[0]
	30%	+1, −1	+1, −1	0, 0	−1, +1	0, 0	+1, −1	+1, −1	[−1]
	25%	+1, −1	0, 0	−1, +1	−1, +1	−1, +1	0, 0	+1, −1	[−1]
	20%	0, 0	−1, +1	−1, +1	−1, +1	−1, +1	−1, +1	0, 0	[−1]
Democrat's Security Level		[−1]	[−1]	[−1]	[0]	[−1]	[−1]	[−1]	

However, using the same assumptions to analyze this election as those used to analyze the one that Figure 7.1 illustrates, we find that the candidates' plurality equilibrium strategy is again at the median voter's bliss point, 35. Table 7.10 reports the payoffs for each candidate in a manner analogous to those listed in Table 7.2. Advocating 35 maximizes each candidate's security level, so that which seemed intuitively obvious is false. Even with bimodal preference distributions, candidates converge to the median citizen's bliss point if everyone votes. This finding strongly implies that the cause (or lack) of abstentions affects the location of electoral equilibria.

Case 2a, abstention from indifference with symmetric, unimodal preference distribution. With case 2*a*, abstention enters the analysis. Suppose the preference distribution is symmetric and unimodal, and indifference is the source of abstentions. In other words, some citizens have *B* terms that are not great enough for them to vote.

Figure 7.8a shows two candidates, a Republican at *r* and a Democrat at *d*, converged in an election with a symmetric, unimodal preference distribution. Notice the horizontal line, which is the turnout function. If it were higher (or lower), more (or fewer) people would be voting. In Figure 7.8a, for each citizen $B = U_r - U_d = 0$. The only question for a particular citizen is whether *D* exceeds *C*, in which case he or she votes instead of abstaining. The expected outcome of this election is a tie.

Now suppose the Democrat decides to move to the left, to advocate 40. The Republican remains at the median, 35. Figure 7.8b shows the resulting configuration. Notice that for citizens halfway between *d* and *r*—those at 37.5—*B* continues to be zero, and the turnout function does not change. However, for all other citizens *B* increases.

Several things happen. First, because of the increase in *B*, the Democrat gets more votes at 40 than at 35. Yet, as the Democrat moves to the left while the Republican's strategy remains at 35, the Republican picks up votes at a faster rate than the Democrat. Clearly, 35 is not a vote-maximizing strategy for the Democrat, as he can get more votes elsewhere. However, 35 is an equilibrium strategy in plurality. This is an important distinction. These candidates do not maximize votes if they want to win! They maximize their respective security levels in plurality. Although they gain additional votes, candidates who leave the median lose the election, for an opponent who *remains* at the median gains even more voter support.

The significance of this result goes beyond the simple finding that the median in case 2*a* is the minimax strategy. The issue in question, government spending as a percentage of GNP, represents a collective good, which can be at only one level at a particular time. People must accept that level of spending whether they prefer it or not. However, suppose the issue space measured some aspect of a private good, such as automobile horsepower. Two automobile producers, each of whom could make only one kind of car, would not act in the same way as two candidates advocating the level of a collective good,

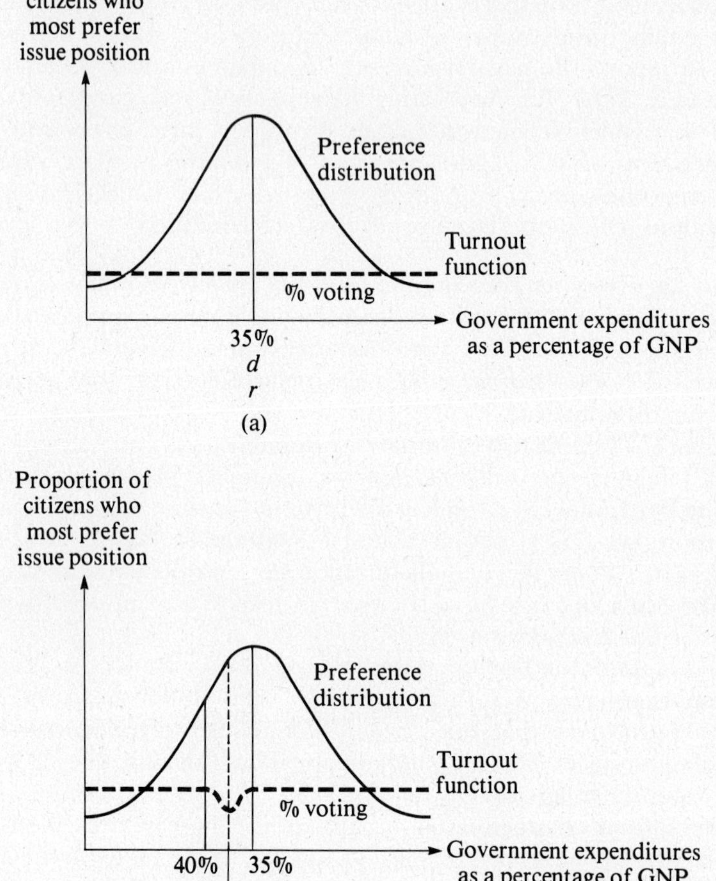

Figure 7.8 Hypothetical election: symmetric, unimodal preference distribution, abstention from indifference.

simply because the success of private producers is less dependent upon their competitors' sales.

Given the underlying assumptions of case 2*a*, private producers would try to maximize profit, which is much like trying to maximize votes. Therefore, two producers would probably diverge from the median. Perhaps one would go to 37.5 and the other to 32.5 (the actual positions depend upon automobile prices, the shape of the preference distribution, and the propensity to consume). But if an election were to choose only one of them, then they would converge. Thus, the different rules under which markets and elections operate lead producers and candidates to adopt different strategies. Different private entrepreneurs will create products with different attributes. Political entrepreneurs—candidates—when dealing in *public* goods will converge to offer to produce identical public policies.

Case 2*a* provides one other insight into the electoral process. Many Americans regard voting as a civic duty. However, the nature of two-candidate elections makes it unlikely that turnout will be as great as possible. To see why this is so, consider Figures 7.8a and 7.8b again. In Figure 7.8a, the candidates are apart on the issue, but the presence of abstention caused by indifference drives them together to the median citizen's bliss point. However, convergence minimizes turnout because B goes to zero. Hence, the same forces that create convergence also create the conditions of low voter turnout.

Convergence and the doctrine of responsible parties. Since before the turn of the century, political scientists and journalists have been concerned with the **doctrine of responsible party government.**[26] This doctrine addresses two separate though related concerns. First, it argues that political parties and their candidates should offer citizens clear and distinct policy positions in elections. Second, they should also hold themselves accountable to carry out their promises if they win public office. Woodrow Wilson spoke to this second point when he criticized the lack of party discipline in the offices of government: "Provided with parties in abundance, and entertained with many nice professions of political principle, we lack party responsibility. American parties are seldom called to account for any breach of their engagements, how solemnly soever those engagements may have been entered into. . . . 'Platforms' are built only for conventions to sit on, and fall into decay as of course when conventions adjourn. Such parties as we have, parties with worn-out principles and without definite policies, are unmitigated nuisances."[27]

Our concern with the doctrine of responsible party government lies more with the failure of parties and candidates to offer distinct programs in elections than with their failure to carry out nonexistent policies once they are in office. Wilson also pointed out this failure: "I, for my part, when I vote at a critical election, should like to be able to vote for a definite line of policy with regard to the great questions of the day—not for platforms, which Heaven knows, mean little enough—but for *men* known and tried in public service; with records open to be scrutinized with reference to these very matters; and

[26] A thorough treatment of the history of this doctrine is in Austin Ranney, *The Doctrine of Responsible Party Government* (Urbana: University of Illinois Press, 1962). The discussion here relies on Peter C. Ordeshook, "Extensions to a Model of the Electoral Process and Implications for the Theory of Responsible Parties," *Midwest Journal of Political Science,* 14 (February 1970), pp. 43–70.

[27] Woodrow Wilson, "Committee or Cabinet Government?" in *The Public Papers of Woodrow Wilson: College and State,* edited by R. S. Baker and W. E. Dodd (New York: Harper and Brothers, 1925), vol. I, p. 109, as quoted in Ranney, *The Doctrine of Responsible Party Government,* p. 33.

pledged to do this or that particular thing, to take definite course of action. As it is, I vote for nobody I can depend upon to do anything—no, not if I were to vote for myself."[28]

Three explanations for this long-documented lack of clear, unambiguous party positions immediately come to mind. First, underlying citizen preferences might aggregate into an intransitive ordering, making a lottery or even complete silence more profitable than a clear pronouncement for an individual candidate. Second, activist and citizen preferences might seem dissimilar, leading candidates to remain ambiguous lest they offend someone important to their chances of electoral victory. Finally, the very real possibility of a coalition of minorities might lead candidates to soft-pedal their stands on certain issues if particular groups in the electorate are unalterably opposed to those stands.

The doctrine of responsible party government goes beyond the problem of ambiguity, however, and attacks parties for convergence itself, whether they converge clearly or not. Spatial election theory offers some clarification of this part of the doctrine. Table 7.9 shows that in many cases, candidates who try to be responsible in the sense of being distinct are likely to be defeated. This problem stems from the nature of citizens' demands for public policy, and in these demands lies a paradox. Suppose indifference causes abstentions: candidates do not offer those citizens who abstain sufficiently distinct issue positions. Yet the very presence of abstention from indifference leads candidates to converge to identical public policy positions.

On the other hand, suppose abstention is caused by alienation, and the preference distribution is bimodal. Candidates will diverge—adopt distinct platforms—if citizens have a high sense of citizen duty, *D*, which is quickly eroded by their preferred candidate moving away from them. "Thus an alert electorate whose response to unsatisfactory candidates is to abstain, which, in the classical theory, responsible parties are supposed to create, is itself a precondition of responsible parties."[29] However, the paradox deepens if we interpret abstention from alienation differently. Citizens who abstain because their preferred candidate "is just not good enough" certainly fail to conform to contemporary notions of responsibility, especially if voting symbolizes responsible citizenship. Therefore, it is the presence in an electorate of "irresponsible" citizens that leads candidates to be "responsible"—to diverge. By contrast, "responsible" citizens (those who always vote) virtually guarantee the existence of "irresponsible" candidates (those who always converge).

---

[28] Woodrow Wilson, "Leaderless Government," an address before the Virginia Bar Association, August 4, 1897, in Baker and Dodd, *The Public Papers of Woodrow Wilson: College and State,* p. 355, as quoted in Ranney, *The Doctrine of Responsible Party Government,* p. 33.

[29] William H. Riker and Peter C. Ordeshook, *An Introduction to Positive Political Theory* (Englewood Cliffs, N. J.: Prentice-Hall, 1973), p. 360.

COMPLEX ELECTIONS

Complex elections include activists as well as citizens.[30] The spatial theory developed in the last section helps us to find out how activists affect candidates' strategies. To simplify matters, we shall assume that activists must only decide which candidate to nominate for the general election and not how much to contribute to that candidate. The candidate's problem is to find a strategy that works best against both general election and nomination opponents. Figure 7.9 illustrates the problem. The general electorate, with a preference distribution shown as symmetric and unimodal with a median at *g*, decides the general election. By convention, the median of the Democratic activists' preference distribution is to the left of *g*, while the Republicans' is to the right.

This preference configuration is not uncommon. For example, consider Figure 5.23 in Chapter 5, which shows the 1978 preference distribution on the national health insurance issue for the entire electorate. While this distribution is roughly bimodal, unlike the general electorate's preference dis-

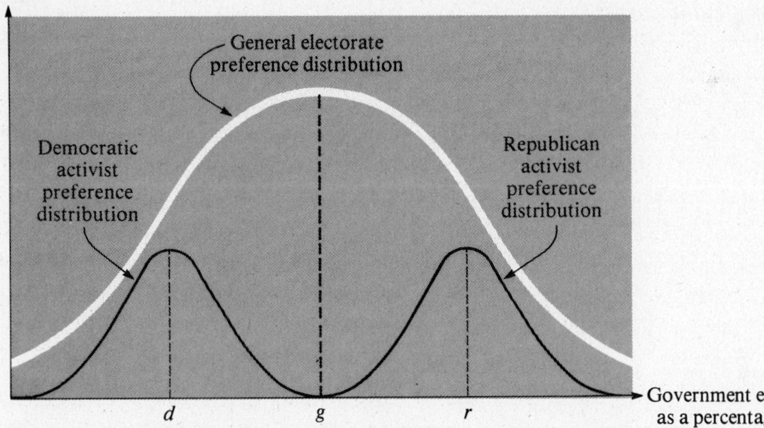

Figure 7.9 Hypothetical complex election with activists as nominators.
Source: Adapted from Peter H. Aranson and Peter C. Ordeshook, "Spatial Strategies for Sequential Elections." in Richard A. Niemi and Herbert F. Weisberg, eds., *Probability Models of Collective Decision Making* (Columbus, Ohio: Merrill, 1972), p. 307.

---

[30] The following discussion relies on Aranson and Ordeshook, "Spatial Strategies for Sequential Elections," in Richard G. Niemi and Herbert F. Weisberg, eds., *Probability Models of Collective Decision Making* (Columbus, Ohio: Merrill, 1972), pp. 298–331.

tribution in Figure 7.9, it will serve our purposes. Figures 7.10a and 7.10b show the same distribution of preferences on the same issue, only now the polling sample is restricted to strong Democrats (Figure 7.10a) and strong Republicans (Figure 7.10b). While not all strong party identifiers are activists, surely most activists are strong party identifiers. Hence, these distributions may be taken as typical of those found among activists. More to the point, notice that the median preference among strong Democrats is at *2* and among strong Republicans at *6*, but the median preference among the entire electorate, *g*, is at *4*. The candidate's decision will now depend on the activists' decision rule as well as on how citizens make their choices.

Professional activists. Recall from Chapter 6 that professional activists use public policy proposals principally to win elections. To win the general election in Figure 7.9, the party's candidate must be at *g*, the median citizen's preference, so the professional activists of each party will seek to nominate whichever primary or caucus candidate is closest to *g*. Professional activists in charge of nominations thereby reinforce the importance of the median general-electorate preference. Nomination candidates in these circumstances should converge to the median.

Amateur activists. By contrast, amateur activists in primaries and conventions will ordinarily vote to nominate candidates who seem closest to their own bliss points. Consider the problem from the Democratic candidate's viewpoint. The winning nomination strategy is at *d*, but the winning general-election strategy is at *g*. The candidate's problem is severe if he cannot lie, if people hold him to earlier policy pronouncements. Otherwise, he could seek nomination at *d* and election at *g*. But, his probable strategy remains ambiguity. He will try to offer both the citizens and the activists a lottery over strategies between *g* and *d*. The expected value of this lottery might be $(g + d)/2$, although its actual location depends on what he expects his nomination and general-election opponents to do.

Activists with mixed motives. Some activists might be part professional and part amateur in that they are concerned about both public policy and winning elections. Or, a party's nominators might have both professional and amateur activists among their numbers. In either case, candidates will continue to offer activists and citizens a lottery, but its expected location moves closer to *g* as the ratio of amateurs to professionals declines.

Activists' decisions and party democracy. The problem of "democratic" versus closed nomination procedures finds yet another interpretation in the preceding discussion. Chapters 4 and 6 point out that as methods for nominating candidates, primary elections appear to be more "democratic" than conventions, and conventions more "democratic" than old-style cau-

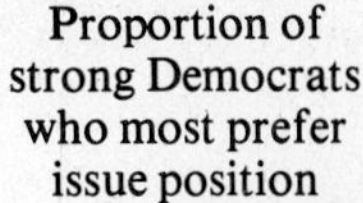

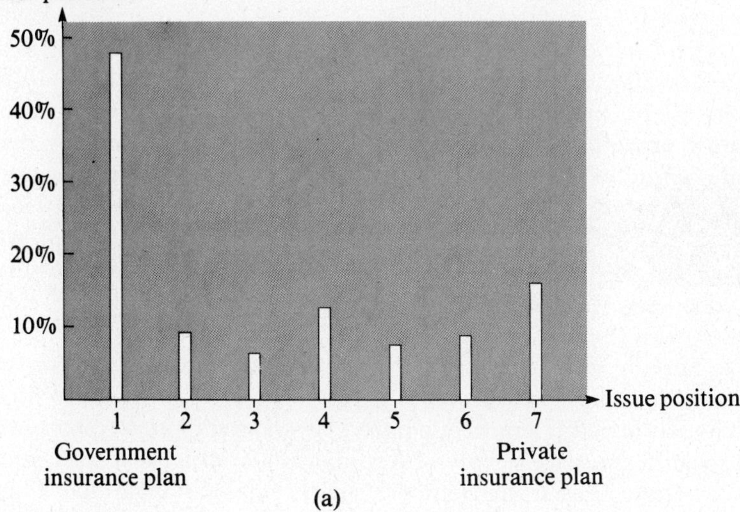

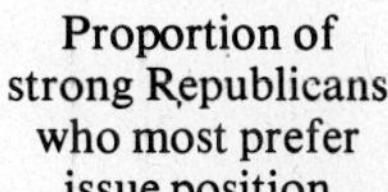

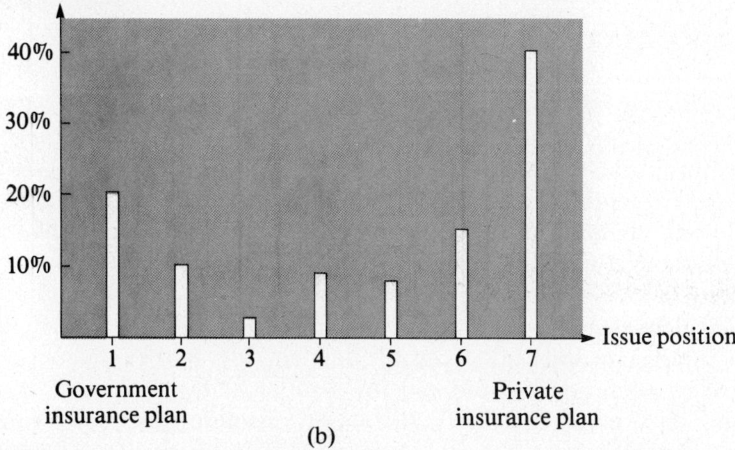

Figure 7.10 (a) National health insurance, 1978 preference distribution among strong Democrats. (b) National health insurance, 1978 preference distribution among strong Republicans.

Source: Data are from a Center for Political Studies 1978 Election Study and are made available by the Inter-University Consortium for Political Research.

cuses. But as nominating procedures enlarge to include greater numbers of people, they are more likely to include a relatively larger proportion of amateurs.

Suppose both parties begin with old-style caucus nominations to select candidates for various races. Caucus members are likely to be professionals. Both Democrats and Republicans will nominate candidates at *g*, and the elections will be ties. If one party, say the Democrats, "democratizes" its nomination procedure by going to a primary or convention system, then it will nominate candidates whose expected strategies are at some distance to the left of *g*. These more "democratically" nominated opponents in turn will be defeated in general elections.

Here lies a fundamental problem with nomination processes. *Ceteris paribus,* the more "democratic" they become, the less likely the candidates nominated with them are to win. Again, TANSTAAFL! There is yet another reason to find an *iron law of oligarchy* observed in the conduct of party affairs. As Chapter 4 argues, this problem represents a great difficulty for the recently "democratized" Democratic party. "Democracy" in nominations probably will mean a greater number of Republicans in office—at least, more than there would have been if the Democrats had remained oligarchic. This generalization holds true especially in presidential contests, because the Democrats' proportional representation primaries make it far simpler for amateurs to get to the national convention, particularly in those years when the incumbent in the White House is a Republican.

PRIVATE GOODS AS ELECTION ISSUES

A common assumption of spatial election theory is that citizens and candidates perceive the same set of issue dimensions, which are often taken to measure proposals about the level at which a particular public good will be produced. For example, one dimension might gauge national defense spending; another might measure the general tax level; a third might index the extent of air and water pollution remaining after the imposition of various antipollution laws. Yet these dimensions could also measure the level of particular private goods that candidates promise to deliver to the members of distinct interest groups but that will be paid for at collective expense. Of course, each such good would call for a separate dimension.

Chapter 6 points out that political entrepreneurs (especially candidates) would rather do their campaign bargaining with interest-group leaders in the currency of private goods than with individual, unconnected citizens in the currency of public goods. Interest groups provide readily available channels for communicating political information, including voting recommendations, to their members. The organization and leadership of these groups can also help to monitor the contributions individual members make toward the election of favorite candidates and can then reward or punish them individually for their actions or inactions. Divisible, private benefits do not flow to members of groups that provide little backing to candidates. Therefore, candidates are more likely to satisfy the demands of organized interest-group members for private goods than those of diffuse unorganized citizens for public goods.

The popular view of elections. For most American citizens, two forces combine to divert attention from the private-goods aspects of elections and to focus it on larger issues concerning the production and consumption of public goods. The first force is that citizens generally devote more attention to national elections than to state-wide ones, and more to state-wide elections than to local ones. Hence, the average citizen is likely to be better informed about a presidential than a senatorial or gubernatorial race, and better informed about senatorial or gubernatorial races than about congressional or mayoral ones. By this view, citizens will pay closer attention to the personalities and issue positions of national than of state and local candidates. Various reports have documented that most people know who the president is, while large numbers of people are unaware of their senators' or representatives' names. Figure 5.25 in Chapter 5 illustrates the corresponding turnout differences between presidential and congressional elections.

The second force leading citizens to pay more attention to the public-goods aspects of elections than to their private-goods components derives from the logic of campaigning. Candidates ordinarily will try to use their campaign resources, and in particular their campaign funds, in the most cost-effective manner; that is, they try to allocate their resources to maximize their return in plurality for each dollar they spend. Now, consider the resource allocation of a major presidential candidate. He will use some of his resources for national advertising, most prominently on network television. The rest of his funds will finance travel and local appearances before the largest possible audiences. Because of these campaign allocation decisions, most citizens will have an opportunity to see the candidate in their own community at most once or twice during the campaign, but their exposure to him through television will be far more frequent.

However, messages to the entire electorate cannot possibly enumerate all of the private benefits the candidate promises to allocate to the members of clearly identifiable interest groups within the population. Such messages would take too long and would probably be highly counterproductive, because most voters would be appalled by their crassness. By contrast, the national message will concentrate almost completely on great national issues such as the rates of unemployment and inflation, the problems of energy and the environment, and military preparedness. National candidates thus will fashion their television appeals in the broadest possible terms, with small regard for individual groups in the population. Candidates' most common messages to citizens will be about public goods.

Nevertheless, when national candidates travel to local communities, their attention to larger national issues often seems almost perfunctory. These candidates, who on national television speak in terms of general, public goods, in Portland, Maine, promise cheap electric power from a new tidal power system, in Philadelphia, pledge that the shipyard will receive an important government contract, in Des Moines, promise to maintain a high level of agricultural price supports and to export more grain to the Soviet Union, and in Miami Beach, guarantee that Social Security payments will more than keep pace with inflation. At the local level, the individual constituencies thus become transformed into interest groups, and along the campaign trail and in visiting each constituency the national candidate promises to deliver private, divisible benefits on a district-by-district basis. Understandably, campaign promises to particular interest groups are made in even smaller and more intimate forums.

Local candidates and individual congressional candidates (compared to presidential candidates, say) would receive little attention for their pronouncements on large public issues such as national defense or inflation. Not only do they receive less attention generally, but also (as Chapters 8 and 9 suggest) their promises to do something about these larger issues simply are not credible. Hence, the campaigns of state-wide or district-wide candidates are almost entirely involved with promises about locally beneficial programs that create private goods at collective costs.

Theories of elections with private goods. This general discussion of public and private goods as campaign issues rests on theoretical findings concerning the voter's level of political information.[31] In a world of perfect information, voters would know precisely what to expect from the candidates they help to elect. They would know what each candidate has promised to every single person or group in the electorate, the kinds of benefits and costs that might occur as a result of those promises, the direct costs of the promises to the voter as a taxpayer, and the likelihood that the candidate would do what he promised if elected. In such a world, we might expect candidates to promise private benefits to a little more than one-half of the electorate at the expense of the less than one-half that remains. Or, possibly, all government programs that passed would be Pareto preferred, unlike the hypothetical case concerning interest-group demands, discussed in Chapter 6.

However, this assumption about perfect information is violated in at least two ways. First, candidates face real incentives to create **fiscal illusions,** which are designed to make voters underestimate program costs and overes-

---

[31] Peter H. Aranson and Peter C. Ordeshook, "Incrementalism, The Fiscal Illusion, and the Growth of Government in Representative Democracies," in William Meckling, ed.. *The Growth of Government* (Hingham, Mass.: Martinus Nijhoff, forthcoming).

[32] Charles J. Goetz, "Fiscal Illusion in State-Local Finance," in Thomas E. Borcherding, ed., *Budgets and Bureaucrats: The Sources of Government Growth* (Durham, N. C.: Duke University Press, 1977), pp. 176–187, and Richard E. Wagner, "Revenue Structure, Fiscal Illusion, and Budgetary Choice," *Public Choice,* 25 (Spring 1976), pp. 45–61.

timate their benefits.[32] This practice is common enough; we seldom hear candidates emphasizing the costs of the programs they propose or underestimating their benefits. Taxing and spending usually are divided in legislative decision making, and politicians constantly search for new ways in which to tax citizens with as little political damage as possible. For example, periodic income-tax withholding spreads out tax payments over an entire year, so that citizens are not required to accumulate the sum involved and pay it all at one time. Small sales taxes on individual purchases are another method of inducing fiscal illusions. The division of taxes among various sources, such as those on sales, property, income, and inheritance, also spreads out the citizen's total tax burden, so that each payment is less noticeable than a single tax (even one paid monthly) would be. Candidates who can generate such illusions about taxes and also about program benefits usually defeat those who cannot.

We have already encountered the second reason why perfect information eludes the voter. As Chapter 5 points out, information itself is costly to obtain. It simply does not pay for the ordinary voter to calculate how much a new tariff on imported shoes might cost next year in higher prices for shoes. However, because of interest-group organization and the concentrated nature of private benefits, it certainly does pay for shoe producers and leaders of shoemakers unions to find out which candidates will support the tariff and which will oppose it. Any public policy that creates a private good generates both benefits and costs. Unless those benefits or costs exceed some threshold, which rises or falls with the cost of accumulating political information, the public policy in question is unlikely to enter into the citizen's decisions. To extend the previous example, we find that most citizens will not usually vote on the basis of the $2 or $3 added annual cost resulting from the imported-shoe tariff. By contrast, shoemakers—who stand to gain or lose thousands of dollars from this public policy—are most likely to vote on this issue and this issue alone. They will make up an intense minority. And, many, perhaps most, other voters are like shoemakers in some respect.

Elections, private goods, and the growth of government. When citizens enjoy less-than-perfect information about the programs that candidates propose, then candidates in politically competitive environments will search out new opportunities to find interest groups who will then benefit from new programs. These programs create more and more private goods, each at collective cost. The aggregate result of this tendency is an increase in the size of the public sector relative to that of the private sector. Sometimes these programs will take the form of direct money subsidies; at other times they will appear as regulations favorable to members of the benefited group.

The predicted sequence of candidates' proposing one private-goods program after another rests on an incremental electoral process. Candidates are presented with or discover the actual or potential demands of one group after another. At some point, when the size of the public sector and the tax burden that supports it become noticeably larger, citizens will demand an abandonment of *legislative* (not electoral) incremental decision making. People will begin to insist on considering federal expenditures all at once, and perhaps even on limiting them.

A slowdown in public-sector growth might result. However, the impetus to grant private-goods legislation will probably soon reassert itself. Candidates who espouse "economy in government" will really be proposing a public good, while their opponents who propose private-goods legislation will really be following a politically advantageous and superior strategy. Campaign rhetoric at the national level will continue to emphasize the desirability of reducing the size of government, while campaign reality at the local level will continue to appeal to private, divisible interests. Hence, one finds little possibility in the electoral process of reducing the drive for an expanding public sector and a proliferation of private-goods legislation, which derives from interest-group demands. Tax limitation legislation resembling California's Proposition 13 will succeed on few occasions, and its results will be eroded during the intervening years.

QUESTIONS FOR DISCUSSION AND REVIEW

1. If a strategy of ambiguity wins elections, is it what voters really want? Is it Pareto preferred to pure strategies? Why? Why not?
2. Should coalitions of minorities prevail over those who are less intense? Why? Why not? Does this question make sense without interpersonal comparisons of utilities?
3. Do public opinion polls affect candidates' strategies? How? Would election outcomes and public policy be different without polls? How? Can polls distort a "majority sentiment?" Can they be used to do so intentionally? What, if anything, should be done about it?
4. Are election candidates who take any position on important public issues just to get elected morally inferior to private-sector producers who continuously adjust the goods and services they sell in response to changing consumer tastes merely to maximize profits? Why? Why not? Who is more to be feared, a candidate who changes his positions to get elected, or one who does not?
5. How do direct and indirect elections respond to problems raised by coalitions of minorities? Lack of pure strategy equilibria? Strategies of ambiguity? How would a referendum election handle problems raised by demands for private goods to be collectively supplied?
6. Suppose a three-candidate election occurred with the preference distribution in Figure 7.1. Would this contest have an equilibrium? Where? How would the public policy emerging from such an election differ from the policy emerging from a two-candidate election?

7. Can candidates change preference distributions on issues? If so, how would the results reported in this chapter be changed? Are such changes likely to occur? Why? Why not?

NEW CONCEPTS AND TERMS

allocation strategy
attribute strategy
coalition strategy
doctrine of responsible party government
fiscal illusion
indifference contours
intense minority
issue ambiguity strategy
issue position strategy
issue salience strategy
plurality equilibrium principle
spatial theory

8

Government: Between Elections and Public Policy

Chapters 4 through 7 describe election politics in the United States. When a biennial American election ends, 435 people sit in the House, 100 in the Senate, one in the White House, and another in the Vice-President's Mansion, not to mention their counterparts in state, county, and local governments and members of the judiciary and bureaucracy. What happens? What should happen? Which public policies are or should be adopted? Answers to these questions strongly depend on the rules and structures of the institutions of government. They depend, too, on the goals, strategies, and choices of those elected and appointed to populate those institutions: the members of Congress, the president and vice-president, the bureaucrats, and the judges.

THEORETICAL DIMENSIONS OF REPRESENTATION

The connection between officeholders and members of the electorate should not be ignored. Presumably, the electoral process in the United States makes a difference for collective action because it affects the public policies eventually adopted by those elected to serve. Here, the theoretical nature of the connections between officeholders and members of the electorate are examined. The possible effects of different aggregation rules are explored. And, reasons for changing franchise requirements are explained.

Simple Spatial Representations

Suppose an election occurs in a congressional district of five citizens, whose bliss points are distributed as in Figure 7.6 and all of whom vote. A candidate for this district's seat wins election or ties by advocating *c*. *Ceteris paribus,* representation in its simplest form means that the new member enters Congress with a single intention: to get at least one-half of the other 434 representatives and other members of the national government to enact a public policy as close to *c* as possible. Given the opportunity to vote in Congress, the new member will consistently vote for policies closer to *c* rather than for ones further away.

Why should the representative try to enact such a public policy? One possible answer is that he personally believes that *c* is a good public policy. After all, *c* is the constituents' median preference. Representatives often share their constituents' preferences, especially if they also share common backgrounds, interests, and attitudes. Thus, while the winning candidate prefers *c*, perhaps this preference is an incidental by-product, an artifact of the electoral process. Alternatively, the winner's preferences may have nothing whatever to do with his social background. A representative may prefer *c* for purely philosophical reasons.

A representative might also try to enact public policies close to *c* because his constituents "prefer" *c*. As Chapter 7 points out, some believe that constituents' preferences are revealed in the electoral process. Members of Congress might believe that this process creates a reasonable approximation of constituents' interests, and might conceive the job of a representative to be that of enacting constituents' "preferred" public policies. Such representatives see themselves as delegates, who should inject as many of their constituents' preferences as possible into the lawmaking process. Elections alone give such representatives their public policy instructions.

A representative might also believe that these same five voters, or others like them, will be casting ballots in the next election, and that their preferences are not likely to change very much. As a consequence, his chances of reelection depend not only on advocating *c* in the next campaign, but also on advancing *c* as a desirable public policy in the Congress. Such a judgment engages not merely the representative's sincerity and honesty, but also his legislative effectiveness.

Lawmaking Problems If Officeholders Maximize Plurality

There are serious objections and counter examples to each of these explanations for the legislative attractiveness of *c*. Here, though, we begin with the working assumption that representatives, senators, and presidents advocate and try to enact public policies as close as possible to their constituents' electoral equilibria (if such exist), because this lawmaking strategy maximizes plurality in the next election. This assumption need not always imply that legislators' personal beliefs or ethical attachments to some public policy other than a hypothetical median voter's preferences must be ignored. Nevertheless, the assumption of plurality maximization does follow from the electoral equilibrium principle: In simple two-candidate, single-member district elections, a party's candidates for a particular office in the long run adopt pure plurality equilibrium strategies if these strategies exist. The parallel strategies in the lawmaking process consist of finding ways to advocate and enact public policies closest to electoral equilibria. Our working assumption thus provides the most direct link imaginable between the electoral process and the lawmaking process. However, it soon becomes clear that even this simple link can create incredibly complex possibilities.

Legislative districting effects: The House of Representatives. Consider Figure 8.1a, which spatially represents an election much like the ones in Figures 7.5 and 7.6.[1] Here, nine voters make up the entire American electorate. Suppose these voters elect the president by majority vote and without an electoral college. A two-candidate election with this preference distribution has a plurality equilibrium at E_P, citizen *5*'s bliss point. Given the previous assumption about the president's motivation, he advocates the passage of a public policy at or near *5* (50%, 50%).

Figure 8.1b shows the same nine voters divided into three states: Maine, Illinois, and California. The lines are meant not to represent a geographical map but merely to identify those citizens who live in the same state. Suppose these are the only three states in the Union and that each has only one congressional district. The Maine district electorate, made up of voters *1, 2,* and *3*—all of whom prefer to allocate 80 percent of government spending to national defense—elects a representative at citizen *2*'s bliss point, E_M; Illinois, made up of voters *4, 5,* and *6,* elects a representative at citizen *5*'s bliss point, E_I; and California, made up of voters *7, 8,* and *9,* elects a representative at citizen *8*'s bliss point, E_C. The Congress now has three members who respectively advocate E_M, E_I, and E_C as national public policy. If each representative seeks to maximize plurality in the next election, then together as legislators they become like a committee of three voters, with bliss points at E_M, E_I, and E_C respectively. The congressional equilibrium is at E_I, which is identical to E_P in Figure 8.1a. That is, the president and the members of the House propose the enactment of identical laws.

However, suppose congressional districts are bounded as in Figure 8.1c. The Maine district electorate is now made up of voters *1, 2,* and *4*; Illinois of voters *3, 5,* and *6*; and California remains as in Figure 8.1b, made up of voters

[1] This section, beginning with Figure 8.1a, uses a technique for mapping voters' preferences into legislative preferences developed in Melvin J. Hinich and Peter C. Ordeshook, "The Electoral College: A Spatial Analysis," *Political Methodology* (Summer 1974), pp. 1–29.

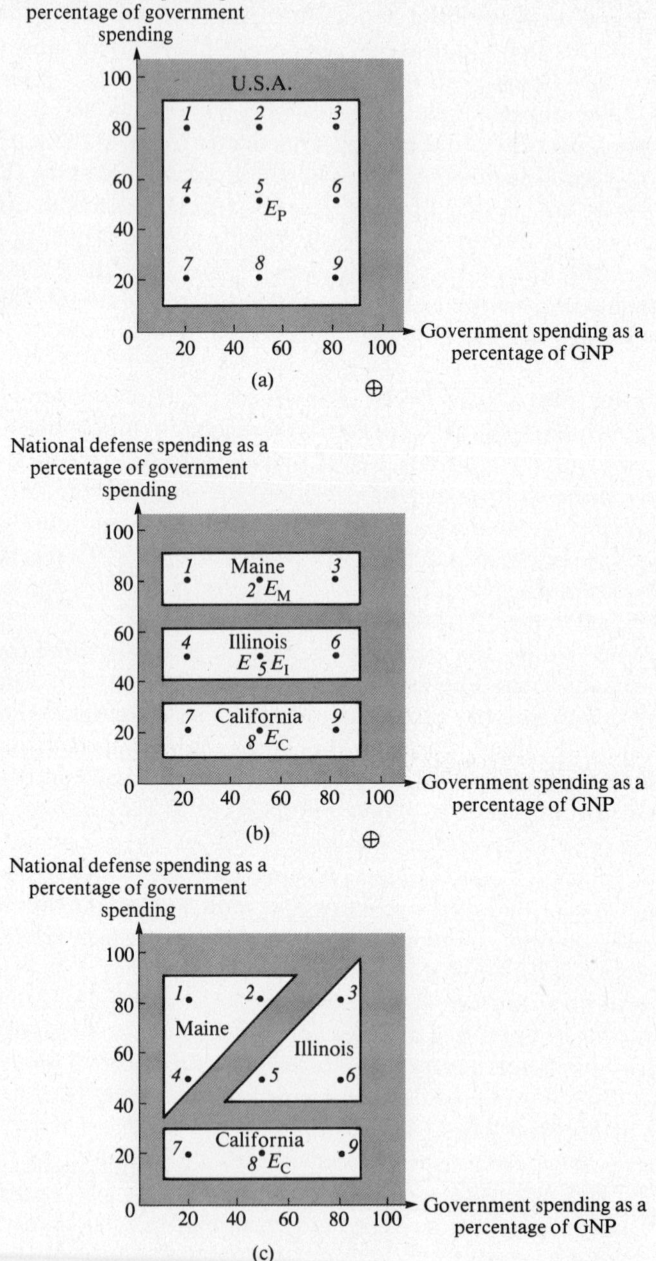

Figure 8.1 (a) Direct presidential election, nine voters, two issues, and equilibrium at E_P. (b) Three congressional elections, nine voters, two issues, and House equilibrium at E. (c) Three congressional elections, nine voters, two issues, and no House equilibrium.

7, 8, and *9*. Of course, the California equilibrium remains at E_C, but in Maine and in Illinois there are no pure strategy electoral equilibria. Elections in these two states are identical to the one in Figure 7.5. If congressional candidates in Maine or in Illinois advocate any pure (unique) public policy, their respective opponents can find some other policy to defeat them. This does not mean that voters in these states elect no members to the House; it simply means that no pure strategy guaranteeing victory or a tie exists. Any strategy might win, but winning candidates will wait for their opponents to announce first and then will choose a strategy to defeat them—or, complete ambiguity might prevail.

The implications of this hypothetical example are telling. Suppose the election winners in Maine and Illinois are respectively at the bliss points of voters *2* and *5*. Nothing guarantees that the Maine and Illinois representatives will advocate and support these positions in the House. There is nothing special about the policies, in an electoral sense. More important, if the two representatives earn reputations for supporting these positions in the Congress, their opponents surely will find strategies to defeat them in the next election; as a consequence of retrospective voting, the incumbents' lawmaking activities are like campaign announcements, and in these states whichever candidate announces first (in this case, the incumbent) loses. Therefore, the representatives from Maine and Illinois will try to hide their lawmaking activities, and policies *2* and *5* thus become unlikely pure lawmaking strategies. Of course, all other pure strategies suffer from a similar defect.

While we cannot say which policies these representatives will support, we can reasonably eliminate the exact bliss points of voters *2* and *5*. These are but single points, and each triangle, or state, holds an uncountable infinity of such points. The California representative's public policy preference is at E_C, voter *8*'s bliss point. But if the Maine and Illinois representatives choose to advocate policies that do not fall on a line connecting the bliss points of voters *2, 5,* and *8*, then there is no lawmaking equilibrium in the House of Representatives! No law, no public policy, no set of collective goods exists that can command a majority of the votes in the House over all others. Hence, the president's position, E_P, is the only one that remains stable. However, notice that if the president is elected by an electoral college in which each state has one vote (as in the hypothetical House) and is bounded as in Figure 8.1c, then presidential candidates face the same problem of finding a pure strategy equilibrium as do representatives in Congress.

The "small" matter of drawing the boundaries of states or congressional districts and the differences in equilibria or lack of equilibria in various districts thus can wield an enormous effect on public policy and lawmaking. Different boundaries might create pure congressional lawmaking equilibria and electoral equilibria as well as destroy an underlying electoral equilibrium, such as voter *5*'s bliss point. Even if representatives try to "represent" their districts, what this would mean in terms of links with their constituencies, public policy, and lawmaking remains unclear and may vary under different districting arrangements.

Legislative districting effects: The Senate and the electoral college. The preceding discussion gives each state three citizens, incorporating the constraint that congressional districts must contain approximately equal numbers of citizens. But in Senate and presidential elections, the boundaries for districting are the states themselves, rather than geographically bounded equal fractions of the population. Hence, in these elections, more widely varying preference structures are possible than was true of House elections.

Suppose each state elects one senator and has one electoral vote: population does not matter. (This is a realistic view of the Senate, but not of the electoral college.) Now consider Figure 8.2a, which spatially illustrates a fifteen-voter, two-issue Senate election or presidential election with an electoral college. An underlying electoral equilibrium—if the nation were considered as one state—exists at voter *8*'s bliss point. The Maine electorate has seven voters (*1, 2, 3, 4, 5, 6, 7*) and an electoral equilibrium, E_M, at citizen *4*'s bliss point; Illinois has one voter, *8,* and an equilibrium, E_I, at that citizen's bliss point; and California has seven voters (*9, 10, 11, 12, 13, 14, 15*) and an equilibrium, E_C, at citizen *12*'s bliss point. Senators win elections at E_M, E_I, and E_C respectively; the lawmaking equilibrium *in* the Senate is at E_I, which is also the underlying electoral equilibrium.

Suppose that in the presidential election, candidates cannot adopt different strategies, one for each state, and notice that a presidential candidate at E_I wins the electoral vote from Illinois (assuming his opponent is not at E_I). If the other candidate advocates a position "above" E_I, then the Illinois winner also wins the California electoral vote and then the presidency by an electoral college vote of two to one; if the other candidate advocates a position "below" E_I, then the Illinois winner also wins the Maine electoral vote and again wins the presidency by an electoral college vote of two to one. Thus, E_I is the equilibrium not only *in* the Senate but also in the presidential election with an electoral college.

However, consider the election in Figure 8.2b, which incorporates the same underlying preference structure as the election in Figure 8.2a. Voter *8*'s bliss point remains the underlying electoral equilibrium, but state boundaries are different. The resulting new equilibria in the Senate elections are at citizen *2*'s bliss point for Maine, *4*'s for Illinois, and *10*'s for California. The new Senate lawmaking equilibrium remains at the Illinois senator's equilibrium strategy, but it has shifted upward from (50%, 50%) in Figure 8.2a to (50%, 70%) in Figure 8.2b. Similarly, the equilibrium strategy for the presidential election with the electoral college now also falls at (50%, 70%).

But consider Figures 8.3a and 8.3b, which depict two presidential or Senate elections, each with eleven voters but with different preference structures.[2] In Figure 8.3a, an underlying pure strategy electoral equilibrium exists at voter *6*'s bliss point. Yet, if we disaggregate this electorate into

---

[2] Figure 8.3a is a modification and Figure 8.3b a replication of the configuration in Hinich and Ordeshook, "The Electoral College: A Spatial Analysis," p. 20.

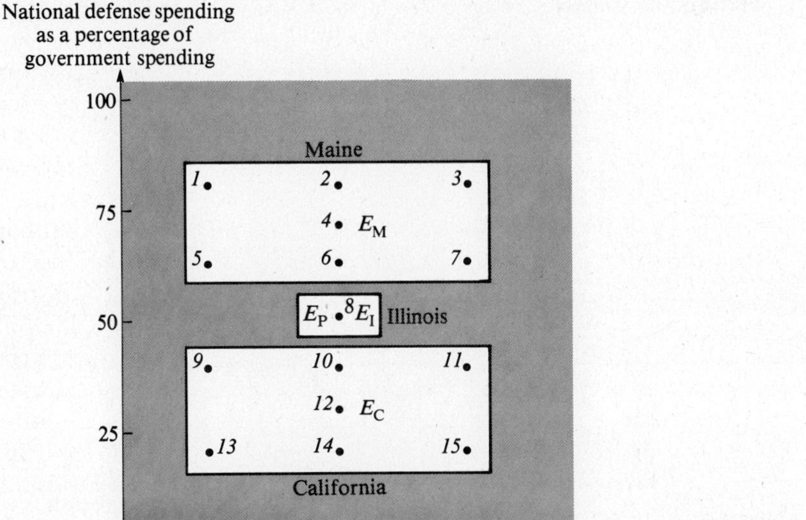

(a)

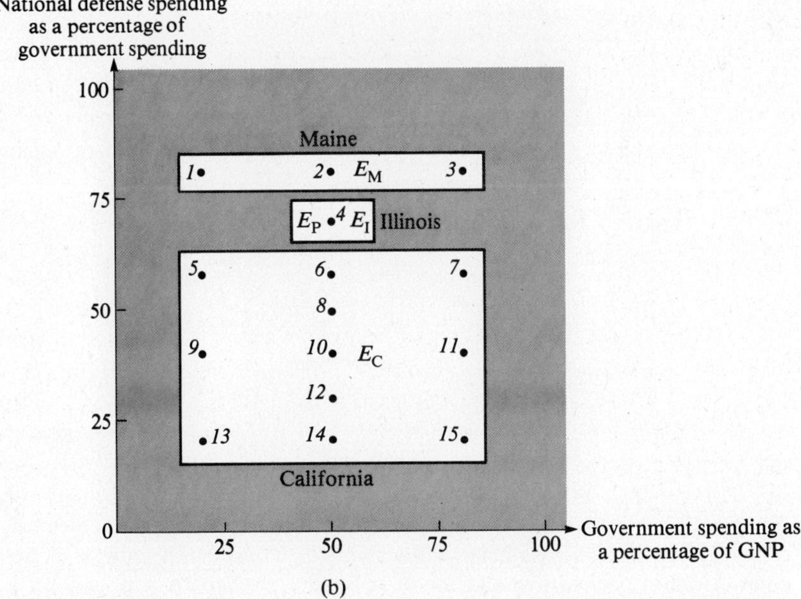

(b)

Figure 8.2 (a) Senate or presidential election with equal-vote electoral college; fifteen voters, two issues; presidential election and Senate equilibrium at E_P (8). (b) Senate or presidential election with equal-vote electoral college; fifteen voters, two issues; presidential and Senate equilibrium at E_P (4).

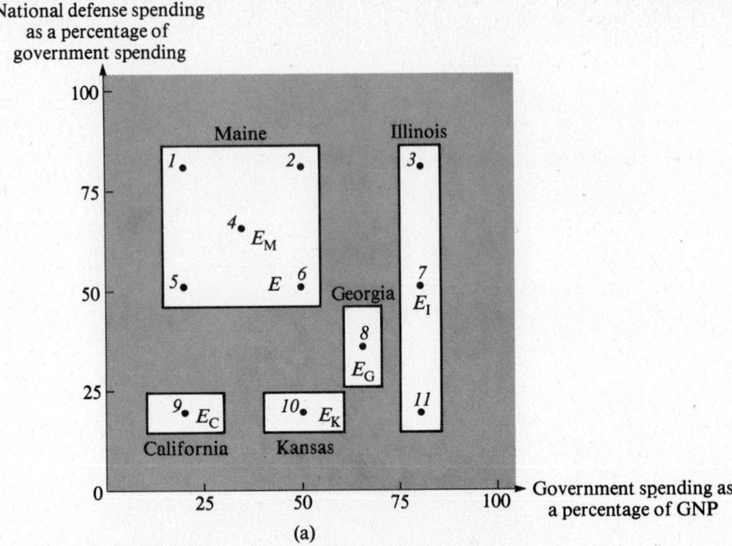

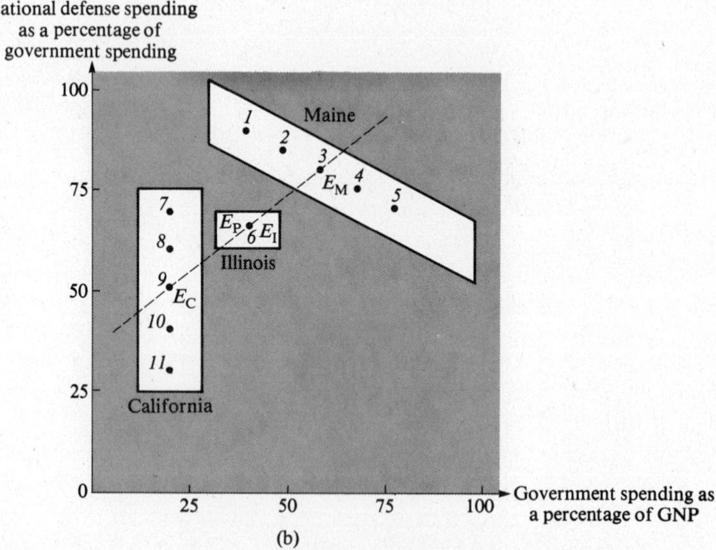

Figure 8.3 (a) Senate or presidential elections with equal-vote electoral college; eleven voters, two issues; underlying electoral equilibrium at E; no equilibrium in presidential election or in Senate. (b) Senate or presidential elections with equal-vote electoral college; eleven voters, two issues; no underlying electoral equilibrium; presidential election and Senate equilibrium at E_P.

Source: Adapted from Melvin J. Hinich and Peter C. Ordeshook, "The Electoral College: A Spatial Analysis," *Political Methodology* (Summer 1974), p. 20.

five states and locate the states' equilibria at E_M, E_I, E_C, E_K, and E_G, respectively, it becomes apparent that a pure strategy equilibrium exists neither in the Senate nor in the presidential election with an electoral college. Thus, forming a particular pattern of states as election units (here, each with its own equilibrium) destroys the underlying pure strategy electoral equilibrium.

Figure 8.3b illustrates a different configuration of citizen preferences for which no underlying pure strategy equilibrium exists. But disaggregating this electorate into three states and locating their equilibria at E_M, E_I, and E_C respectively, turns E_I into a lawmaking equilibrium in the Senate and in the presidential election with an electoral college. Thus, forming a particular pattern of states as election units now creates an electoral college and Senate pure strategy lawmaking equilibrium where none existed in the underlying electorate preference structure.

Creating institutional conflicts. Even if the same citizens vote in presidential and congressional elections, it is most likely that the resulting lawmaking equilibria in the House and Senate and at the president's position will be different. This is because the same voters casting ballots in different contests will create two lawmaking bodies and a chief executive, all with different "views" (equilibria) on public policy. Of course, this expectation assumes that in-district and in-chamber pure strategy equilibria do exist, even though the discussion in Chapter 7 indicates that they may not. Furthermore, if pure strategy equilibria fail to exist, public policies advocated in each institution will probably vary considerably.

Such differences in equilibria will provide incentives for the members of one institution, say the House, to propose collective actions that differ substantially from those advocated by the members of another, say the Senate. Here, then, is one reason that presidents, senators, and representatives so often clash on public policy, even though their constituents are largely the same people. Different ways of aggregating citizens—drawing boundaries and defining constituencies—become crucially important, since they can lead to variations in public policy equilibria between different institutions.

Controlling the Franchise

The preceding discussion of how constituency boundaries or preference differences eventually might affect the public policies that legislators adopt takes those boundaries as "givens." Yet, Chapter 4 describes the central importance of election rules and districting arrangements—rules for drawing district boundaries—for determining who wins and loses elections. Gerrymanders created by members of the majority party give them very real electoral advantages over the other party. Legislative malapportionment before *Baker v. Carr* usually weighted state representative assemblies disproportionately in favor of rural interests. Chapter 4 concludes that districting practices are not merely givens of the political process; they are rationally manipulated by legislators and others to maximize legislative strength. Even legal battles for representational equality are aimed at improving legislative strength.

The mechanics of franchise extension. Here, we have pursued, in a very preliminary way, the theoretical connection between constituents' preferences and legislative action. But legislators do more than define the boundaries of their districts; they also can set the rules governing who has the right to vote or who might be encouraged or discouraged from voting. Changes in franchise requirements nicely illustrate the rational manipulation of election rules and the subsequent effects—or the absence of such effects—on public policy. Historically, legislators and courts have almost exclusively been the ones empowered to extend the franchise to new classes of people, or to contract it. Strangely, members of the present electorate seem to be the only ones who have no direct say in fixing the qualifications of future voters.

As Chapter 4 notes, the Constitution grants to state governments control over most elections. However, the constitutional amendment process, the courts, and the members of Congress can preempt decisions taken at the state level. The Fifteenth Amendment (ratified in 1870) gave blacks the right to vote by forbidding the denial of franchise "on account of race, color, or previous condition of servitude." The Seventeenth Amendment (ratified in 1913) gave citizens the right to elect their senators directly. The Nineteenth Amendment (ratified in 1920) gave women the right to vote, although most states had already done so.[3] The Twenty-third Amendment (ratified in 1961) gave residents of the District of Columbia the right to choose electoral college members, which meant they could vote for the first time in presidential elections. The Twenty-fourth Amendment (ratified in 1964) eliminated the payment of poll taxes as a qualification to vote in federal elections; poll taxes increased the *C* term in the calculus of voting. Finally, the Twenty-sixth Amendment (ratified in 1971) extended voting rights to eighteen-year-olds.

Subsequent court decisions and congressional actions have extensively embroidered upon these amendments. For example, in 1965 the members of Congress passed a comprehensive voting rights act to fulfill the terms of the Fifteenth Amendment, and in 1966 the Supreme Court extended the Twenty-fourth Amendment to declare poll taxes unconstitutional in *all* elections.[4] Sometimes the actions of those sitting in different institutions have addressed the same question. For example, the congressionally approved Voting Rights Act of 1970 gave eighteen-year-olds the right to vote in all elections, but the Supreme Court then ruled that the Act could only apply to voting in federal elections.[5] The Twenty-sixth Amendment subsequently

---

[3] Kirk Porter, *History of Suffrage in the United States,* (Westport, Conn.: Greenwood, 1979).

[4] *Harper v. Virginia Board of Elections,* 383 U.S. 603 (1966).

[5] *Oregon v. Mitchell,* 400 U.S. 112 (1970).

eliminated the confused ballot procedures that might have occurred in future elections because of the possibility of different age qualifications in different races.

Franchise extension as a prisoners' dilemma. Decisions to grant voting rights to a new class of people represent something of a paradox. For example, suppose that left-handed people cannot vote. Except for preferences about the placement of watch stems and the construction of scissors, golf clubs, and baseball gloves, few systematic preference differences between left- and right-handed people come to mind. Politically, left-handed people are as likely to be Democrats (or Republicans) as are right-handed people. Their preferences concerning issues such as government spending, national defense, government regulation of the economy, or even prohibitions on marijuana use, handgun ownership, or abortions should not differ systematically from those of right-handed people. Therefore, as far as public policy matters are concerned, left-handed people should not really care very much whether they have the right to vote or not. This is because right-handed people seem likely to produce the same public policies with left-handed people voting as without.

But two other concerns might lead left-handed people to prefer having the right to vote. First, if R in their voting calculus would be positive for some elections, then for them voting would be a preferred activity to its alternatives. Indeed, R might represent one measure of utility lost from disenfranchisement. Second, legislators might withhold ombudsman services (described in Chapters 9 and 11) from those who cannot vote. These services can be important, especially in a highly bureaucratized economy. Beside these factors, "only" a psychological sense of deprivation would lead left-handed people to petition for the vote. However, their interests would probably be so diffuse as to make political organization to achieve their common goal most unlikely.

Right-handed citizens and legislators would have reasons for denying the vote to left-handed people. Enfranchising left-handed people would increase the size of the electorate by, say, 15 percent. This expansion would dilute the probability (P from the calculus of voting) that each right-handed voter might be pivotal (or cast the deciding vote) in any given election. Hence, *ceteris paribus,* the expected utility (R) of each right-handed voter would decline if left-handed people could vote. Legislative ombudsman services for right-handed people would also decline, and legislators would not necessarily wish to work harder to keep an expanded constituency happy. "Only" a philosophical or psychological intolerance of discriminatory rules would lead right-handed voters or legislators to petition for a left-handed franchise.

This fanciful example in some respects approximates decisions about extending the franchise to eighteen-year-olds. Apart from issues such as conscription, the drinking age, and the legal age of majority, few systematic political or public policy differences separate late adolescents from their elders. Time itself spans the much overrated "generation gap." Differences about the responsiveness of elected representatives in their ombudsman capacities disappear entirely, for adolescents soon will be voters and their parents usually share their children's concerns in dealings with federal bureaus. Therefore, House and Senate members would probably service disenfranchised eighteen-, nineteen-, and twenty-year-olds as fully as they attend to those who have reached twenty-one.

Legislators would also be indifferent about the matter as far as public policy is concerned. The campaign promises they make and the laws they pass seem unlikely to change much after eighteen-year-olds begin to vote. Of course, legislators would have to pay slightly more to poll a slightly larger number of constituents to get accurate information about preference distributions. They would also have to spend their time going through the legislative or constitutional amendment process. And, they would gain the enmity of those diehards opposed to the franchise extension who prefer neither their own voting strength to be diluted nor their constitutional traditions disturbed. For all of these reasons, legislators would tend privately to oppose franchise extension. But, if the eighteen-year-old franchise issue actually comes to a vote in the legislature, perhaps as the first stage in the constitutional amendment process, the strategic situation legislators face changes radically as public attention comes to bear.

Suppose the members of each party must publicly vote for or against the voting-rights motion. Table 8.1 represents this decision problem as a two-person game. The entries in the table rest on two assumptions. First, if one party votes for the motion and it passes, while the other party votes against it, then the supporting party gains +10 while the opposing party loses −10. Second, the added cost of representing the new voters is taken to be −1. If both parties vote against the motion, it fails and nothing happens (0, 0). If both vote for it, the motion carries and a cost of −1 is imposed on each party to reflect the added costs of representation. Suppose one party votes for the motion and the other against it. We shall assume that it passes, either because the pro-extension party is in the majority or because some anti-extension party members understand the game in the table, fear retribution, and defect to the pro-extension side. The supporters gain +10 because adolescent voters reward them for granting the right to vote; but they also pay a cost of −1 in added representational effort, and perhaps in diehard enmity. The net payoff is +9. Opponents pay the same added cost in representational effort, −1, but are punished by the new voters. Their net payoff thus becomes −11.

Table 8.1 illustrates a prisoners' dilemma game. It may appear surprising that legislators do not respond to such games by instantaneously giving the vote to anyone who asks for it. Usually, though, legislators protect themselves against such prisoners' dilemma situations as these by bottling up the associated proposals in committees, where they die for lack of attention. However, once these proposals reach the floor of the House or Senate, they gain nearly unanimous approval, which is what we might predict from the

Table 8.1 Two-Party, Eighteen-Year-Old Voting-Rights Game in the Legislature

	Republicans' Strategies	
Democrats' Strategies	vote against	vote for
vote against	0, 0	−11, +9
vote for	+9, −11	−1, −1

structure of the game. For example, House members approved the Twenty-sixth Amendment by a vote of 401 to 19, and Senators by a vote of 94 to 0.

***Franchise extension as* force majeure.** In the preceding example, granting voting rights to eighteen-year-olds has only minor public policy consequences. However, the process of franchise extension seems quite different from this simple prisoners' dilemma if real public policy conflicts are engaged. For, when legislators extend the franchise with public policy at issue, this action affects not only their own reelection campaigns but also the existence and location of electoral and lawmaking equilibria. A very different analysis must explain franchise extensions under these conditions.

The struggle for black voting rights in the United States provides the best example of franchise extension associated with real public policy consequences. While the history of this struggle is long and complicated, some of its legislative, judicial, and constitutional highlights deserve mention.[6] Following Reconstruction, the Fifteenth Amendment did little to ensure black voting rights. Physical coercion against blacks, along with state control of election procedures, kept most blacks disenfranchised in southern states. For example, literacy tests prevented many blacks from registering to vote, but whites whose fathers or grandfathers voted before 1866 were exempted from taking the tests, even though many of these whites were themselves illiterate. In 1915 the Supreme Court found the "grandfather clause" in violation of the Fifteenth Amendment.[7]

In spite of this decision, control of Democratic primary elections continued to be particularly effective for disenfranchising blacks in the one-party, Democratic, Solid South. Blacks were excluded from voting in Democratic primaries, and this practice was defended on the theory that political parties are private organizations, beyond the reach of federal law. Through a series of cases, the white primary was eventually overturned completely in 1944.[8]

---

[6] This narrative closely follows Lucius J. Barker and Twiley W. Barker, Jr., *Civil Liberties and the Constitution: Cases and Commentaries,* 2nd ed. (Englewood Cliffs, N.J.: Prentice-Hall, 1975), p. 372, *passim.* A discussion of legislative reapportionment and gerrymandering are omitted, as these subjects are considered at length in Chapter 4.

[7] *Guinn v. U.S.,* 238 U.S. 347 (1915).

[8] *Smith v. Allwright,* 321 U.S. 649 (1944).

During the 1950s and 1960s, congressional action dominated attempts to fulfill the promise of the Fifteenth Amendment. Civil rights acts were passed in 1957, 1960, 1964, and 1965. The 1965 legislation, called the Voting Rights Act of 1965, allowed for federal registration of voters and the elimination of literacy tests in districts with low voter registration levels. The Act eliminated poll taxes if their use was found to be discriminatory and provided for criminal penalties against those who might threaten or harm people seeking to register or vote. The Supreme Court quickly affirmed the Act's constitutionality.[9]

The Voting Rights Act of 1965 fulfilled the purpose of the Fifteenth Amendment. (Several important court cases and some additional legislation remained to be completed, but these were in the nature of mopping-up operations.) However, passage of the Voting Rights Act, like the approval of voting by eighteen-year-olds, represented something of a paradox, for real public policy consequences were sure to follow from granting black citizens the right to vote. As Chapter 5 observes, black voters tend to support Democrats relatively more than do whites. Public opinion polls consistently show that blacks, compared to whites, prefer higher levels of government spending, especially for redistributive public policies said to aid the poor. For example, a poll taken in early 1979 asked a national sample of respondents: "If the federal budget were to be balanced it would be necessary to reduce spending. For which of these programs do you think a cut in spending should be made in order to balance the budget?"[10] Of black ("nonwhite") respondents, 35 percent mentioned defense, and 27 percent, welfare. Comparable figures for white respondents were 29 percent in favor of defense spending cuts and 59 percent in favor of welfare spending cuts. This question and the responses to it indicate a fundamental difference over the perceived desirability of present spending levels for various government programs.

The paradox involved with passage of the 1965 Voting Rights Act concerns this difference. Suppose the median voter's bliss point is the pure strategy equilibrium in a national election. Plainly, the median bliss point among potential black voters is quite a bit different from the (white) median voter's bliss point. Adding blacks to the electorate by enfranchising them would move the median bliss point away from the present median voter's most-preferred issue position. Why, then, would the median voter support black voting rights?[11] *Ceteris paribus,* the median voter would probably do no such thing. But extension of the franchise is a direct result of legislation and judicial action, not of popular voting. The Voting Rights Act of 1965 resulted

---

[9] *South Carolina v. Katzenbach,* 383 U.S. 301 (1966).

[10] *The Gallup Opinion Index,* 164 (March 1979), p. 25.

[11] The question was suggested to me by Dr. Thomas G. Moore of the Hoover Institution for the Study of War, Revolution, and Peace.

from a decisive shift in the Congress in the wake of the 1964 presidential election, in which Lyndon Johnson won a landslide victory over Barry Goldwater. Straight ticket voting changed the political nature of the Congress. Northern (non-southern) Democrats, who made up 37.5 percent of the House in 1964, made up 47.3 percent of that body in 1965. Northern Republicans fell from 38.6 percent to 29.1 percent after the 1964 congressional election. In the Senate, the number of northern Democrats went from 47 to 50, and the number of northern Republicans fell from 31 to 29.

With one exception, congressional voting on the 1965 Voting Rights Act was as expected. The Act passed in the House by a vote of 333 to 85. Republicans supported it 112 to 24, northern Democrats 188 to 1, and southern Democrats 33 to 60. Senators passed the bill by a vote of 77 to 19. Republican senators voted for it 30 to 2, northern Democrats 42 to 0, and southern Democrats 5 to 17. This Republican voting is something of a surprise until it is recalled that Republicans knew the bill would pass anyway. This knowledge put them in a position similar to that of the parties depicted in Table 8.1. Southern Democrats largely opposed the measure, but it was passed over their objections by simple, straightforward *force majeure.*

Implementation of the act effectively shifted the location of the median voter's bliss point in *southern* elections in general, and those filling House and Senate seats in particular. Black voters in the South were probably closer in public policy preferences to those preferences found in northern Democratic districts than to those found in southern districts. Thus, newly elected members from the South would have legislative preferences closer to those of northern Democrats than was true before the 1965 Voting Rights Act was passed. Legislative success could then be won more easily by northern Democrats, whose certainty of reelection and seniority in Congress would grow as a consequence.

Politics, principles, and voting rights. This discussion of franchise extension shows in two particular ways how legislators are affected by their constituencies and in turn can remake and redefine their constituencies as well as the constituencies of other legislators. Rules matter, and thus are subject to self-interested manipulation. Surely, though, principles also matter, especially when symbolic issues such as the right to vote are involved. Certainly Republicans and northern Democrats might have voted for the 1965 Act from considerations of principle. Just as certainly, the Twenty-sixth Amendment reflected an emotion-laden congressional response to the political activism of the young in the wake of the Vietnam War. How can these actions be interpreted as self-serving? That they turned out to be self-serving cannot be doubted. Whether they were intended to be so or not, no one knows for sure. Nevertheless, the logic of each situation suggests that conscious self-interested decision making would have produced the same legislative results in the absence of principle.

THE PREFERENCES OF ELECTED OFFICIALS

The preferences of challengers and incumbents sometimes extend beyond a desire for election or reelection, although for reasons enumerated in Chapter 7, these electoral preferences must remain central in the long run. The importance of electoral considerations reflects the political vulnerability of those who ignore them. However, a desire to run in future elections (beyond the present contest) for the same or a different office, as well as policy preferences and institutional ambitions, can also affect an officeholder's decisions.

Preferences about Future Elections

Elected officials might contemplate one of three future actions: not to run again for public office, to run for the same office they now occupy, or to run for some other office. Career plans can make these actions complex. For example, a representative might consciously plan to remain in the Congress for two more terms, return home to run for governor, then run for the Senate, and after a term or two run for the presidency.

The problems of incumbents who want to run again for the same office go beyond identifying the electoral equilibria in their districts and advocating the corresponding public policies. Pure strategy equilibria may not exist, and even if they do, there is no guarantee that they will continue to exist or remain unchanged over the next two years (for a representative), or four years (for a president), or six years (for a senator). Therefore, today's public policy equilibrium might create tomorrow's electoral disaster. Furthermore, sophisticated constituents might believe that an officeholder who represents their preferences is useless if he cannot put together a legislative coalition to enact those preferences. What is worse, new issues may emerge about which an officeholder cannot judge the location of electoral equilibria. Those constituents who write letters to their representative may be an unrepresentative sample of all or even most citizens.

Sometimes, especially because of retrospective voting, officeholders have little or no control over events; no matter what they do, they lose plurality. Adverse economic conditions or setbacks in foreign policy are obvious examples. Generalized attitudes about all politicians, or about those in one of the parties, can produce large turnovers in office, as with the 1974 Republican losses in the House and Senate following the Watergate hearings and President Nixon's resignation.

Officeholders who seek election to higher office exhibit a **progressive ambition:** a representative might run for a governorship or the Senate, a senator might run for the presidency, or a vice-president might run for the presidency.[12] Of our recent presidents, Reagan and Carter were governors;

---

[12] The term *progressive ambition* is from Joseph A. Schlesinger, *Ambition and*

Ford was a congressman and an appointed vice-president; Nixon was a vice-president, senator, and congressman; Johnson was a vice-president, senator, and congressman; Kennedy was a senator and congressman; Truman was a vice-president and senator; and Roosevelt was a governor. Eisenhower alone of the last eight presidents held no prior elective office.

Lawmakers with progressive ambition have all of the problems of incumbents in addition to the obvious problems of changing constituencies. For instance, House members who seek election to the Senate might encounter severe problems if the public policy equilibria in their districts differ substantially from a state-wide equilibrium. The misfortune of former Senator Charles Goodell in the 1970 election is a case in point. Goodell was an upstate New York Republican House member until Governor (later Vice-President) Nelson A. Rockefeller appointed him to fill the unexpired term of the assassinated Senator Robert F. Kennedy. Goodell's House constituents were conservative compared to the state-wide New York constituency. Goodell quickly shifted "to the left" to improve his chances of winning the election; for instance, he opposed President Nixon's Vietnam policies, which led Vice-President Spiro T. Agnew to say, "If you look at the statements Mr. Goodell made during his time in the House and compare them with some of the statements I have been referring to, you will find he is truly the Christine Jorgenson of the Republican party."[13] Goodell's move to the left seemed futile, for he came in a poor third, losing to James Buckley, the Conservative party candidate.[14]

I spoke with Goodell during the campaign and asked him about his new positions. He remarked that as a representative from Jamestown, New York,

---

Politics: Political Careers in the United States (Chicago: Rand McNally, 1966). This work is the first in an important body of research, which indicates that politicians act rationally in deciding whether or not to run for office, and for which office to run. Those who seek the same office have **static ambition.** See also Gordon S. Black, "A Theory of Professionalization in Politics," *American Political Science Review,* 64 (September 1970), pp. 865–878; Black, "A Theory of Political Ambition: Career Choices and the Role of Structural Incentives," *American Political Science Review,* 66 (March 1972), pp. 144–159; and David W. Rohde, "Risk Bearing and Progressive Ambition: The Case of the United States House of Representatives," *American Journal of Political Science,* 23 (February 1979), pp. 1–26.

[13] Jorgenson, a transsexual, responded in a telegram to Agnew, "The blatant use of my name in connection with your feud with Senator Goodell is not only unfair, but totally unjustified. . . . I request that some effort be made to correct the erroneous impression that has been given such wide publicity." New York *Times,* October 9, 1970, col. 1, p. 49.

[14] Richard Ottinger, a Democrat, was the third candidate. Actually, the leftward movement of Goodell's pronouncements might have been more nearly appropriate for a two-candidate race. Such a strategy worked well in election after election for another New York Republican Senator, Jacob Javits, until he was defeated by a conservative Republican in the 1980 primary election. However, what occurred spatially in the 1970 election was that Goodell and Ottinger divided the votes to the left of the median, while Buckley stood alone and won the votes to the right of the median.

he had an obligation to represent the people of Jamestown, while as a senator from New York, he had an obligation to represent all of the people of New York. He seemed sincere, but he acted *as if* he sought to maximize his reelection plurality.

The problems of election to a new office are great even if the constituency remains unchanged. A senator who wants to be a governor, a governor who wants to be senator, or a representative from a state with only one representative who wants to be governor or senator, all have problems if their constituents view these offices differently. People might expect one set of policies from a state's governor and a different set from its representative or senator. Activists especially may express more interest in one officeholder's activities than they do in another's; for example, members of an anti-war group might be more concerned about a senator's position on defense spending than about the positions of a governor from the same state. Even when candidates seek election in an enlarged constituency, the old constituency may look with disfavor on their ambitions. For example, Senator George S. McGovern did not carry his home state of South Dakota in the 1972 presidential elections. South Dakotans, it seems, approve of McGovern as a senator but not as a president. (However, they changed their minds and voted him out of the Senate in 1980.)

Those seeking to represent an expanded constituency, particularly senators who become presidential contenders, face serious problems. Should they support legislation corresponding to a state-wide or a national electoral equilibrium? If they lose the presidential nomination, they may have difficulties in their next Senate reelection bid—or they may satisfy their state constituents, thus effectively excluding themselves from the presidency. Incumbent vice-presidents who want to be president have the worst of all possible worlds. Their principal claim to the nomination is their support of the president. Yet, they operate with the full liabilities of the current administration. A case in point is then Vice-President Hubert H. Humphrey's unsuccessful attempt as a presidential candidate in 1968 to forge a Vietnam policy that differed from President Johnson's.

The political nature of progressive ambition has been calculated for members of the House of Representatives.[15] First, House members are more likely to run for Senate seats than for four-year governorships, and they are more likely to run for four-year governorships than for two-year governorships. This ordering reflects the value of the offices pursued as well as the positive value officeholders place on infrequent elections. Second, the fewer congressional districts there are in a state, the more likely are House members to run for state-wide office. This finding reflects the problem of differences in equilibria between present constituencies and future ones; in a state with only one congressional district, electoral equilibria are presumably the same for House, Senate, and gubernatorial elections. This finding also reflects the

---

[15] This discussion about the progressive ambition of House members is from Rohde, "Risk Bearing and Progressive Ambition."

difference in campaign costs between large and small states. Depending on competition, a congressional candidate in a state with only one congressional district must campaign before as large a constituency as a senate candidate does. Why not run for the Senate, then? Third, risk-takers seem more likely to exhibit progressive ambition than will others. (Risk-takers are identified as those who ran against an incumbent or a candidate of the dominant party in their first election to the House.) Finally, House members are more likely to run for higher office if their probability of winning appears high. In sum, a rational choice calculus of progressive ambition appears to explain decisions to seek or not to seek higher office.

The public policy consequences of progressive ambition are not entirely clear. However, House or Senate members with an eye to higher office probably bring broader considerations to bear on public policy questions than do those with a narrower, district- or state-wide focus. But this tendency must be tempered by the incentives for officeholders with progressive electoral ambitions to remain ambiguous about their positions on certain public policy issues. Concerning issues on which their positions are advantageous in elections, politicians with progressive ambition can be expected to use their legislative bodies as forums for publicity rather than as deliberative assemblies.

Preferences about Public Policy

Senators, representatives, and presidents do hold personal preferences about good public policy, and they occasionally try to educate citizens to accept these preferences. Elected officeholders have been known to vote their consciences on some matters, even if doing so means the loss of office. Senators, representatives, and an occasional president have acted according to their own policy preferences in spite of adverse public reaction. For example, Lyndon Johnson once said wryly, "I think [my grandchildren] will be proud of two things. What I did for the Negro and seeing it through in Vietnam for all of Asia. The Negro cost me 15 points in the polls and Vietnam cost me 20."[16] One observer describes another case:

> In 1970 the "liberal" abortion bill passed by the New York Senate lay dead in the House apparently, 74-74 (a majority of the full membership of the House—76—is required to pass legislation). But before the Chair could announce the defeat of the bill, Representative George Michaels, a Democrat from a heavily Catholic district . . . changed his vote from "nay" to "aye." Speaker Perry Duryea then cast the 76th and winning vote. Michaels . . . [said] his vote switch was political suicide. . . . [He] was correct. Michaels was denied the nomination of the local party, defeated in the primary, and

---

[16] As quoted in John E. Mueller, "Presidential Popularity from Truman to Johnson," *American Political Science Review,* 64 (March 1970), p. 18.

> trounced in a three-way election. . . . Michaels, a Jew, reported acting as he did from family pressures (one son called him a "political whore").[17]

Like Michaels, many officeholders hold some core of policy preferences that they are unwilling to violate even at the cost of electoral defeat. Realistically, it is difficult to know when an official is acting from conscience and when from electoral or other motives. With some politicians, we cannot discern personal values and preferences. With others, conflicts between the dictates of conscience and those of reelection strategy or of some other preference, such as those growing out of party loyalty, almost never emerge. Hence, political observers cannot often clearly identify a politician's struggle with conscience.

The link between an officeholder's personal policy beliefs and legislative actions remains as ambiguous as the link between constituency preferences and legislative actions. Policy and reelection questions seldom become either-or situations. Most officeholders prefer reelection, and most prefer their versions of good public policy to be enacted. However, when officeholders confront choices, those choices usually are between a little more or a little less likelihood of reelection, or a policy a little closer or a little further away from an ideal.

Imagine a situation in which two representatives want government spending as a percentage of GNP to be as high as possible. But, their districts are conservative about government spending, and the electoral equilibrium is near zero on this issue. As the representatives support more and more government spending, their probability of reelection declines.[18] Figure 8.4 depicts indifferent curves for two such representatives, A and B. Both prefer to advocate and enact higher rather than lower levels of government spending, and both prefer higher to lower probabilities of reelection. However, their constituents' preferences are such that reelection probabilities are inversely related to an advocacy of increased government spending.

Notice that A is indifferent as between an 80 percent chance of reelection while advocating a 22 percent level of government spending, on the one hand, and a 60 percent chance of reelection while advocating a 32 percent level of spending on the other. Stated differently, if his probability of winning is at 80 percent, A is willing to forgo a 20 percent increment in chance of reelection in exchange for being able to advocate a public spending increment of 10 percent. By contrast, B is willing to forgo the same absolute increment in

---

[17] Morris P. Fiorina, *Representatives, Roll Calls, and Constituencies* (Lexington, Mass.: Heath, 1974), p. 45.

[18] Earlier references to candidate goals are to maximizing plurality. Here we have chosen maximizing the probability of reelection. These two goals may lead candidates (in this case, incumbents) to adopt identical strategies under a wide variety of conditions. Moreover, maximizing reelection probability is an appropriate goal in this discussion. See Peter H. Aranson, Melvin J. Hinich, and Peter C. Ordeshook, "Election Goals and Strategies: Equivalent and Nonequivalent Candidate Objectives," *American Political Science Review,* 68 (March 1974), pp. 135–152.

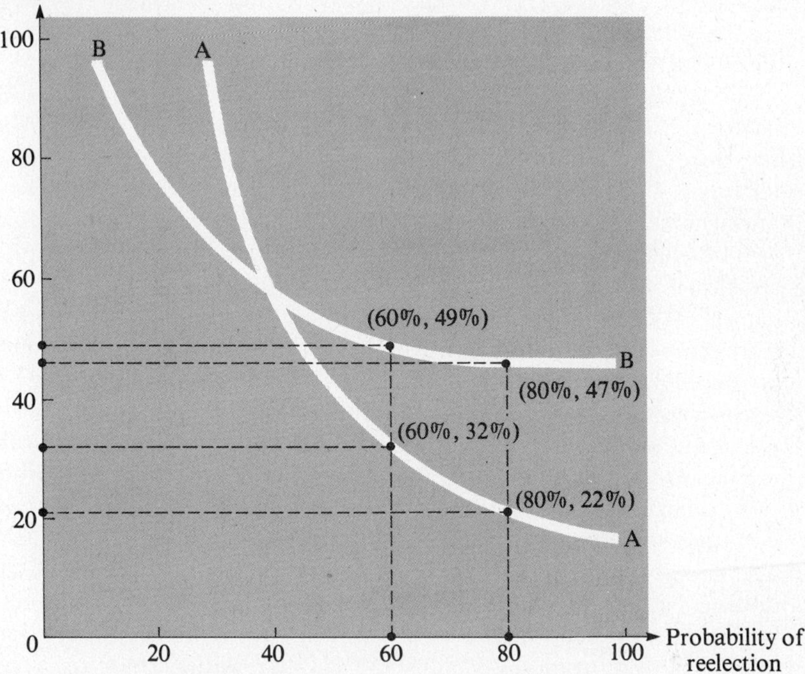

Figure 8.4 Policy position and reelection probability trade-offs for two representatives, *A* and *B*.

reelection chances in exchange for being able to advocate a public spending increment of only 2 percent.

Is B more principled than A? After all, B would be willing to give up 20 percentage points of reelection probability in return for only a small change in advocacy. By comparison, A would demand a far larger change in advocacy for the same decline in reelection probability. However, comparisons among legislators concerning how principled they are seem inappropriate for several reasons.

First, this is only one issue. On another issue—say, how strictly secret government wiretaps are controlled by the courts—A might be willing to forgo reelection entirely for a small increase in control, while B might remain unconvinced that the issue is important. A willingness to stand on principle can thus vary from issue to issue. Therefore, judgments about which legislator is more principled would reflect the observer's own weightings of the (moral) importance of different issues.

Second, there is no mention of how effective A and B's respective advocacies actually might be. While B might seem willing to trade more reelection probability than A relative to a change in issue position, this greater willingness might have nothing whatever to do with principle. Perhaps B can get a real policy change through Congress, while A has no effect on congressional decisions whatever. Why, then, should A throw away reelection probability while not affecting public policy?

Third, B might be independently wealthy, while A is barely able to make ends meet. Without comparing utilities, one should find it obvious that A will think more carefully before throwing away a congressional career. On the other hand, B can afford to be less careful about reelection chances. If their financial positions were reversed, A might then become as principled as B.

The matter of principle among lawmakers thus is far from settled, especially if "principle" refers to advocating and supporting one's own preferences. Most officeholders enjoy some leeway. Political issues change quickly; some rapidly lose importance while others gain prominence. Not many people remember their senator's position on the beef shortage of 1972; perhaps a greater number have some idea where their senator stood on a more recent shortage. Furthermore, the lengths of their terms of office may influence how much leeway officeholders enjoy. Senators at the beginning of a six-year term can probably afford to be more principled than can those at the end of one. Senators can also probably afford to be more principled than can House members, who only serve two-year terms. Perhaps this is why the Founding Fathers arranged House and Senate terms—and the methods of election—as they did. Senators are supposed to be more contemplative and further removed from the vagaries of public opinion than are representatives.[19] Supreme Court justices, allegedly the most principled of all officeholders, serve for life "during good Behaviour."

Preferences about Institutions

Political commentators sometimes distinguish between an office and its current occupant. For instance, a particular president is not "the Presidency," a particular representative is not "the House of Representatives," and a particular senator is not "the Senate." Such distinctions are common. For example, during the Watergate affair, television viewers had to ponder such questions as "Did the president do irreparable damage to the presidency?" and "Is the president a blight on the presidency?" Since Watergate, several revelations about House and Senate members who acted improperly lead one to ask about the effects these revelations have on "congressional prestige." Elected officials act on these organicist judgments about their institutions as well as on their preferences concerning their positions in those institutions.

---

[19] See Alexander Hamilton, *Federalist Paper No. 62,* and James Madison, *Federalist Paper No. 63,* for discussions of the Senate's six-year term. These men valued permanence as a foundation for stability.

Legislators' positions in the institution. Most organizations contain both formal and informal hierarchies, chains of command and deference, and sometimes hierarchies exist within hierarchies. How people achieve certain positions in a hierarchy is important. Most elected officials, especially those in lawmaking bodies, prefer positions at a higher level in both formal and informal hierarchies because those who occupy such positions enjoy what amounts to a property right to control public policy, which then aids them in seeking reelection. However, some actions that improve reelection chances or help a legislator to enact a desired public policy can diminish the likelihood that he will gain a higher position in the institution. Young representatives and senators who upstage their elders may find themselves with the worst positions—for example, committee assignments—and least commodious offices in their respective lawmaking bodies. Clamorous advocacy may be an effective short-run election strategy with dire long-run institutional consequences. Those who cannot or will not bargain or compromise within a legislature have nothing to offer their fellow lawmakers in exchange for election to positions of institutional leadership.

The institution's position in the government. The members of different institutions sometimes disagree about institutional rights, limitations, and jurisdictions. For instance, there is constant disagreement about what presidents should or should not do and about what the members of Congress should or should not do. Does the president have an *executive privilege* that allows him to keep information from representatives and senators? Can members of congressional committees subpoena the president? Who should initiate what legislation? Can the president legally impound funds that members of Congress have appropriated? To whom—if anyone—are federal bureaucrats responsible? Should one house of the Congress have a veto over a federal bureau's decisions?

These questions emerge as a natural outgrowth of conflicting preferences among elected officials. Some of these conflicts derive from differences in their election rules of aggregation, in constituency preferences, and in personal public policy preferences. Most officeholders—especially those who belong to legislative majorities—probably would prefer their particular institution to hold a superior position when it comes to matters of jurisdiction over lawmaking, for the utility that representatives derive from their tenure in office is related directly to the position of their institution in the government. (Constant conflicts among members of different branches of government often take the form of arguments over legality. For instance, if a House or Senate member disapproves of something the president does, one line of attack is to claim that he has no legal authority to do it.)

Institutional position in lawmaking derives from many sources, not the least of which is the personal reputation of the institution's members. Hence, if the members of a lawmaking body can maintain discipline among themselves, then they might improve their position in the lawmaking process relative to the members of other, sometimes competing institutions. Ultimately, the voter is the judge of that position. For example, a senator who offends public decency creates a public bad for all other senators, by affecting not only the capabilities of the Senate in lawmaking, but also every other senator's reelection chances.

Party preferences. House and Senate members organize much of their business along party lines. Party leaders and organizations in the Congress assign members to legislative committees and influence the appointment of committee chairmen. Hence, elected officials are bound to hold some preferences related to party success. Such preferences are a problem especially for presidents, as the success of their legislative programs partially depends on the relative party balance in the Congress. Similarly, representatives of a particular party share in the reputations and notorieties of their colleagues.

Personal Preferences and Motives

Personal motives—a desire for fame and glory, public adulation, and the undefinable (and therefore not analytically useful) quality of political power—inform the actions of most elected officeholders. A desire for wealth in particular can sometimes influence a lawmaker's actions, with graft or corruption as the result. An occasional representative is for sale, though for obvious reasons the extent of the market or the price charged is unknown.[20]

RULES AND PROCEDURES

We have learned that an understanding of election outcomes requires a knowledge of the rules under which elections occur. This observation also holds true for procedural rules in the institutions of government. For example, Figure 8.5a illustrates the preferences of a three-member Senate on the issues of government spending as a percentage of GNP and defense spending as a percentage of government spending. Senator A prefers levels of 35 percent government spending and 50 percent defense spending, B prefers 20 and 35, and C prefers 50 and 20. This preference configuration resembles the election in Figure 7.5, and as in that election, here no pure strategy lawmaking equilibrium exists in the Senate: no public policy motion concerning these two issues exists that can defeat all other motions. Thus, it is impossible to say what public policy will be produced by Senate voting on this pair of issues.

---

[20] See Susan Rose-Ackerman, *Corruption: A Study in Political Economy* (New York: Academic Press, 1978). The Abscam affair seems to have established the price many congressmen will accept to do small legislative favors as $50,000.

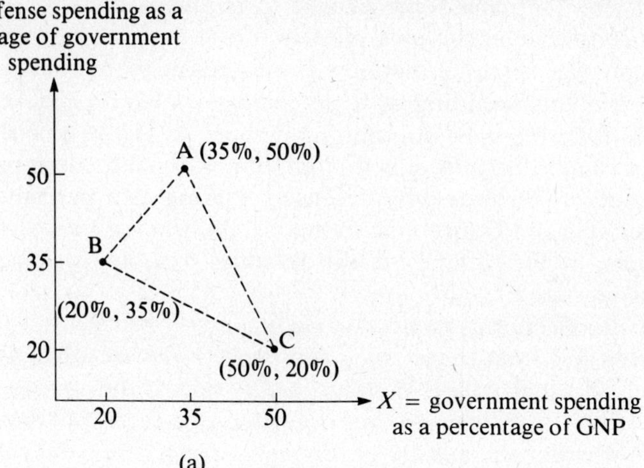

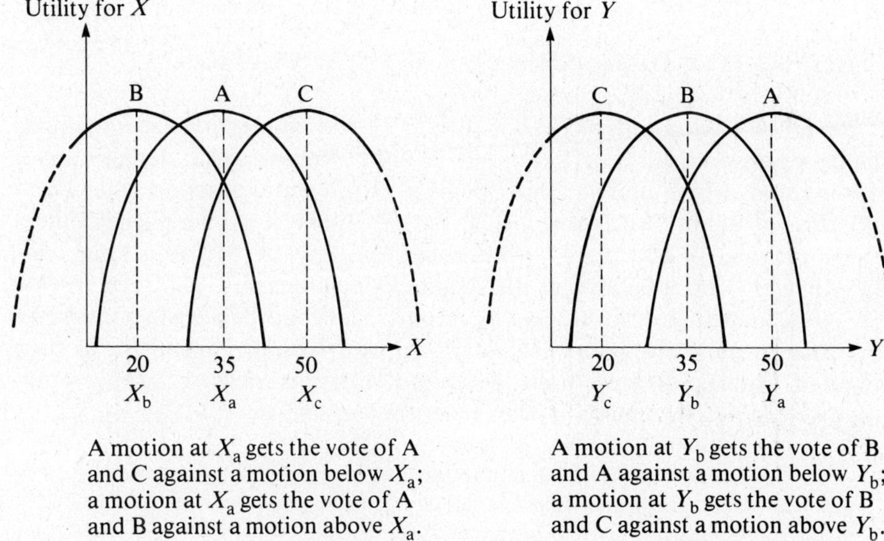

Figure 8.5 (a) Preferences on two issues in a three-member Senate; no Senate equilibrium. (b) Question divided in three-member Senate; equilibrium at X_a = 35 percent for government spending issue. (c) Question divided in three-member Senate; equilibrium at Y_b = 35 percent for defense spending issue.

However, suppose senators vote to require a **division of the question,** which means that a complex motion must first be broken down to the simplest possible separate motions. In this instance, the first motion concerns only government spending as a percentage of GNP. The Senate vote that follows finds X_a, 35, to be the winning motion. As Figure 8.5b shows, it defeats any other motion because it is the one-dimensional median preference. The second motion concerns only defense spending as a percentage of government spending. As Figure 8.5c shows, Y_b, 35, wins this vote. (For all of these possibilities, in Figures 8.5a-c, the senators' reasons for these preferences need not be stated.)

As with elections so with lawmaking: who controls the rules and voting procedures and what those rules and procedures are strongly influence the final form of public policy. Without the division of the question, public policy outcomes cannot otherwise be predicted. A clever parliamentarian can influence whether the question is divided or not. As Chapter 9 shows, he can also control the agenda and thus the order in which motions are considered, so that the last motion considered wins. Plainly, what happens to constituency preferences in the legislature depends on the rules and procedures used in the legislature.

NORMATIVE DIMENSIONS OF REPRESENTATION

Burke on representation. What should be the connection between constituents' preferences and officeholders' actions? Philosophical debates about representation, while ancient, must begin with Edmund Burke's "Speech to the Electors of Bristol," of November 3, 1774.[21] Burke, a British parliamentarian and political philosopher, represented the city of Bristol, along with Henry Cruger, who was born in the American colonies and who, like Burke, was a Whig. In a speech to the voters, Cruger said that their wishes would be his, no matter what the issue. He would act and vote in Parliament as they demanded. Burke fundamentally disagreed with this view of a representative's obligations. His speech is worth quoting at length.

> He [Cruger] tells you, that "the topic of instructions has occasioned much altercation and uneasiness in this city;" and he expressed himself . . . in favour of the coercive authority of such instructions.
>
> Certainly . . . it ought to be the happiness and glory of a representative, to live in the strictest union, the closest correspondence, and the most unreserved communication with his constituents. Their wishes ought to have great weight with him; their opinion high respect; their business unremitted attention. It is his duty to sacrifice his repose, his pleasures, his satisfactions, to theirs; and, above all, ever, and in all cases, to prefer their

---

[21] *The Works of Edmund Burke, with a Memoir* (New York: Harper and Brothers, 1860). The subsequent quotation is from volume 1 of this work, p. 219, *passim.*

> interest to his own. But, his unbiased opinion, his mature judgment, his enlightened conscience, he ought not to sacrifice to you; to any man, or to any set of men living. These he does not derive from your pleasure; no, nor from the law and the constitution. They are a trust from Providence, for the abuse of which he is deeply answerable. Your representative owes you, not his industry only, but his judgment; and he betrays, instead of serving you, if he sacrifices it to your opinion.
>
> My worthy colleague says, his will ought to be subservient to yours. If that be all, the thing is innocent. If government were a matter of will upon any side, yours, without question, ought to be superior. But government and legislation are matters of reason and judgment, and not of inclination; and, what sort of reason is that, in which the determination precedes the discussion; in which one set of men deliberate, and another decide; and where those who form the conclusion are perhaps three hundred miles distant from those who hear the arguments?
>
> To deliver an opinion, is the right of all men; that of constituents is a weighty and respectable opinion, which a representative ought always most seriously to consider. But *authoritative* instructions; *mandates* issued, which the member is bound blindly and implicitly to obey, to vote and to argue for, though contrary to the clearest conviction of his judgment and conscience; these are things utterly unknown to the laws of this land, and which arise from a fundamental mistake of the whole order and tenour of our constitution.
>
> Parliament is not a *congress* of ambassadors from different and hostile interests; which interests each must maintain, as an agent and advocate, against other agents and advocates; but parliament is a *deliberative* assembly of *one* nation, with *one* interest, that of the whole; where not local purposes, not local prejudices ought to guide, but the general good, resulting from the general reason of the whole. You chuse a member indeed; but when you have chosen him, he is not a member of Bristol, but he is a member of *parliament.* If the local constituent should have an interest, or should form an hasty opinion, evidently opposite to the real good of the rest of the community, the member for that place ought to be as far, as any other, from any endeavour to give it effect. . . .
>
> To be a good member of parliament, is . . . no easy task; especially at this time, when there is so strong a disposition to run into the perilous extremes of servile compliance or wild popularity. To unite circumspection with vigour, is absolutely necessary; but it is extremely difficult. We are now members for a rich commercial *city;* this city, however, is but part of a rich commercial *nation,* the interests of which are various, multiform, and intricate. We are members for that great nation, which, however, is itself part of a great *empire.* . . . All these wide-spread interests must be considered; must be compared; must be reconciled if possible.

Burke's view of proper representation is far more complex than this quotation may seem at first, yet his words contain references to most arguments about how representatives ought to act. Burke holds that representatives ought to be fiduciaries, acting as trustees for the entire nation, rather than self-seekers, acting as instructed delegates for a particular constituency.

Fiduciaries and self-seekers. Burke believes that a representative should "above all, ever, and in all cases . . . prefer [his constituents'] interest to his own." This is a **fiduciary** relationship. It means that representatives must always act in the interest of their constituents. They must not advocate and support public policies that benefit themselves while harming their constituents.

Some conflict-of-interest cases violate the fiduciary relationship. For example, a senator who owns a domestic oil field and votes for duties on imported oil, thus improving his profits and raising the cost of petroleum to his constituents, is in violation of the fiduciary relationship. The creation of blind trusts or the divestiture of financial interests before taking office are (imperfect) ways of maintaining the fiduciary relationship as a desirable standard for public officials' actions.

The focus of representation.[22] While ignoring problems such as cyclical majorities, we still have questions as to how one can best benefit a constituent and whose judgment a representative should follow in deciding what is best for the constituent, the constituent's judgment or his own? In response, Burke's view of good representation really concerns two separate matters. The first is that of **representational focus;** the second, of **representational style.** Focus refers to the people whom a public official seeks to represent. Burke sees the problem as one of representing the nation rather than the district. For example, Detroit representatives might believe that a higher tariff on imported automobiles would aid their constituents, though it might create an economic setback for everyone else. If the focus of Detroit representatives' lawmaking activities is Detroit, they will support higher duties; however, if their focus is the entire population, they will oppose them.

Representational focus has several important characteristics. First, the ability to have a wider rather than a narrower focus is partly a function of district electoral characteristics. If districts are competitive and elections are close, then representatives must attend to the narrow focus of constituents' preferences. Otherwise, representatives might enjoy a wider focus. Indeed, one study finds that in three separate states—California, New Jersey, and Ohio—the more competitive state legislative districts are, the more likely are legislators to have a narrow focus. As Table 8.2 indicates, in competitive districts the plurality equilibrium principle probably adversely affects lawmakers' abilities to consider more than narrow district interests.

The second characteristic of representational focus—one subject to some dispute for reasons discussed momentarily—rests on constituency size. It seems less costly for a president than for a senator to have a wide focus, and simpler for a senator than for a representative (unless the representative's

---

[22] This discussion relies on Heinz Eulau, John C. Wahlke, William Buchanan, and Leroy C. Ferguson, "The Role of the Representative: Some Empirical Observations on the Theory of Edmund Burke," *American Political Science Review,* 53 (September 1959), pp. 741–756.

Table 8.2 Relationship Between District Electoral Competitiveness and Legislator's Focus in Three States

	District Electoral Competitiveness		
Legislator's Focus	**Competitive**	**Semi-Competitive**	**One-Party**
District	53%	48%	33%
District and State	28	34	33
State	19	18	34

Source: Heinz Eulau, et al., "The Role of the Representative: Some Empirical Observations on the Theory of Edmund Burke," *American Political Science Review,* 53 (September 1959), p. 753.

state has only one House seat or exactly replicates in miniature the state-wide electorate). This generalization is a natural implication of how constituents derive their interest. Some districts are urban and others rural; some have poor citizens and others wealthy ones; districts also differ as to racial, occupational, and religious composition. Thus, *ceteris paribus,* the larger the population of a constituency, the wider the lawmaker's focus would seem to be.

As we noted in our discussion of progressive ambition, the third characteristic of representational focus is that officeholders who seek election to a higher office are more likely to have a wider focus than those who seek reelection to the same office. This characteristic derives from the previously mentioned relationship between district size and focus, and from the observation that higher offices usually have larger constituencies.

The fourth characteristic of representational focus concerns the relationship between the public goods problem and the lawmaker's focus. Consider again the focus of Detroit representatives on the automobile tariff issue. If all representatives have a strictly narrow focus, then the House of Representatives or the Senate at best might become the arena for an *n*-person zero-sum game, in which coalitions of representatives form to pass laws favoring their districts at the expense of others. Indeed, many argue that Congress is just that. But representatives with a national focus by their actions help to supply public goods for all other representatives and their constituents. However, people usually do not supply these goods except for private reasons. Thus, the fundamental lawmaking problem of enlarging a representative's focus is really the problem of producing public goods.

When constituencies (districts) become interest groups or seem closely identified with interest groups, demands from members of those groups will be for granting them private goods at collective expense: a dam here, a post office there, a new protective tariff, or an enlarged subsidy. Therefore, the representational focus problem is really the same as the problem of the public-sector supply of private benefits, which we have confronted since Chapter 3. In sum, legislators with a narrow focus see their jobs as producing private, divisible goods, whose production bears no apparent relationship to the reasons usually advanced for collective action. The reason why the second characteristic of representational focus is subject to some dispute now becomes clear. We have not yet proved that representatives of larger constituencies, such as presidents, can be more successfully isolated from narrow demands for private benefits than can representatives of smaller constituencies, such as House members.

The style of representation. Burke's speech also contains a prescription about representational style. Representatives can be **delegates,** who seek to enact their constituents' wishes directly into law, or they can be **trustees,** who reflect on the matter and try to serve their constituents' best interests as they, and not their constituents, see those interests. A simple example clarifies the difference between delegates and trustees. Many young children, and not a few adults, abhor medical injections. Parents who act as delegates—who act according to the child's wishes of the moment—tell the doctor, "Our child does not want the shot, so forget it." But parents who act as trustees—who act according to *their* judgment of their child's best interest—tell the doctor, "Get it over with." If children had the knowledge, wisdom, and judgment of their parents, trustees believe, they too would accept injections.

Delegate-trustee distinctions may seem too crude, for surely some public officials act both as delegates and as trustees, depending on the issue and on what their constituents will accept. These people are called **politicos.**[23] Representational style can also interact with representational focus, so lawmakers can be trustees or delegates for their districts, for their states, for their regions, for the nation, or even for the world.

The trustee style seems inherently paternalistic, or perhaps maternalistic. Nevertheless, the—perhaps justified—presumptuousness of trustees compared to delegates still leaves trustees with ambiguous decision rules. Should trustees, based on their superior wisdom, take their constituents' preferences into consideration and enact laws that maximize constituents' utilities? Or, should trustees actually substitute their own preferences for those of their constituents? Trustees who accept constituents' preferences say, "We know what you want; now, leave it to our judgment to find the best way of getting it for you." Trustees who rely on their own preferences say, "We know what you should want if you were as wise as are we." Put differently, trustees must decide whether the aims of legislation should be their own or those of their constituents.

The ever-present problem of defining constituency interests and preferences remains. Burke and those who study him often ignore the problems of defining and locating electoral equilibria. However, even if equilibria do exist, they cannot cover the bliss points of all constituents. Therefore, any change in public policy must hurt someone. Hence, representatives might not know who to represent.

---

[23] Eulau, et al., "The Role of the Representative."

QUESTIONS FOR DISCUSSION AND REVIEW

1. If no pure strategy equilibrium exists in a legislator's district, would he be most likely to act as a trustee, delegate, or politico? Why? If the legislator's district contains several intense minorities, would he be most likely to act as a trustee, delegate, or politico? Why?
2. Did New York State Representative George Michaels act as a trustee, delegate, or politico? Was his representational focus district-wide or state-wide? How should he have acted? Why?
3. Which representational style and focus would you prefer your senators and congressman to take? Why?
4. Would a candidate with progressive ambition prefer to run in a district with or without a pure strategy equilibrium? Why? With or without intense minorities? Why?
5. Would the right to vote ever be expanded if the decision were entirely and exclusively left up to those presently allowed to vote? If so, how?
6. Suppose one legislator accepts a monetary bribe to change his vote in Congress, while another accepts an endorsement carrying with it a substantial number of votes. Is one morally inferior to the other? Why?
7. Would the presence of nation-wide interest groups, compared with district-wide groups, appreciably change the connection between legislators and constituents, or change representational focus or style? How?

NEW CONCEPTS AND TERMS

delegate
division of the question
fiduciary
politico
progressive ambition
representational focus
representational style
static ambition
trustee

Part III

Institutions

We now consider the institutions of American national government. The Constitution first provides for a Congress, and our initial concern in Chapter 9 is with the Constitution's requirements for congressional legislative procedures and its enumeration of the rights that representatives and senators enjoy to make laws. (Later, Chapter 9 examines congressional activities in approving presidential appointments, ratifying treaties, overseeing the national government, carrying on investigations, and impeaching and convicting federal officeholders.) As we describe each congressional right of action derived from the Constitution, we try to link that right to the reasons for collective action that Chapter 3 describes. Next, we reexamine the connections between voters and officeholders, paying special attention to how members of Congress respond to reelection problems. Chapter 9 then explains the formal lawmaking process in the House and Senate and analyzes the consequences of various congressional rules and procedures for legislative decision making and public policy. We pay special attention to logrolling and legislative coalition building. Next, we discuss the organization of Congress and explain the committee system as a rational response to the preferences, goals, and strategic environments of House and Senate members. Chapter 9 then turns to voting in the Congress and shows how the public policy preferences revealed in roll call votes reflect each member's political preferences as those preferences correlate with each member's region and party identification. We then consider the changing ideological makeup of the Congress and conclude with a discussion of other congressional activities.

Chapter 10 examines the American presidency. We begin the discussion of presidential decision making as we began the discussion of Congress, by considering the president's constitutionally granted rights. Then, we enumerate the extra-constitutional rights that presidents have acquired over the years and consider presidential leadership within the framework of collective choice and collective action. Presidents sometimes act as "elected dictators," and we explain why. Chapter 10 next considers presidential decision making. We first describe the criteria under which presidents make decisions and characterize presidential decision making according to the uncertainty that prevails in the president's political and governmental environment. We also examine problems of information and conflict, which exist in most decisions presidents must make. We then turn to the ambiguous problem of presidential personality and its effect on presidential decision making. The chapter concludes with a discussion of the executive branch of government.

Chapter 11 examines the federal bureaucracy, which has developed outside formal constitutional provisions (although the Constitution certainly contemplates the existence of a bureaucracy). We first consider the theoretical functions of bureaus in terms of the reasons for collective action that Chapter 3 describes. Next, we investigate problems of bureaucratic action, and especially problems of measuring a bureau's output both in terms of actual output of goods and services and in terms of assessing the value or importance of that output. We then examine decision making in bureaus. Our descriptions of congressional and presidential decision making could assume that elected officials "merely" try to maximize their chances of reelection. The bureaucrat's objective is much more complicated. Here, therefore, we construct an "operational code" for bureaucrats, which is a set of rules that captures many of the incentives they face. Chapter 11 then examines bureaucrats' actions in the political process, and the strategies and choices bureaucrats adopt in working with the members of Congress, the president, and the federal judiciary. Finally, Chapter 11 dicusses the divergence between the theory of bureaucracy and the actual practice of bureaucratic decision making.

Chapter 12 examines the judicial branch of government, the courts. When we discussed the Congress in Chapter 9 and the presidency in Chapter 10, we had the benefit of the discussion in Part II, which analyzed the electoral environment of presidents and House and Senate members. When we discussed bureaucratic decision making in Chapter 12, we enjoyed the advantage of understanding the preferences and decisions of presidents and House and Senate members, which strongly affect the strategies and choices of bureaucrats. But we consider judicial decision making without first having carefully investigated the external environment in which judges operate. Nor have we considered decision making by litigants (plaintiffs, prosecutors, and defendants). Litigants stand in their relation to judges and juries much as citizens, voters, and interest group members stand in their relation to candidates and elected officeholders. Because we must sketch out a theory of litigants' decision making, our examination of the judiciary must be longer and more involved than our analysis of the Congress, the presidency, and the bureaucracy.

Chapter 12 first discusses the common law. This is "judge-made" law, which developed in Great Britain and in certain other former British colonies, such as the United States. The common law is a body of rules concerning rights, obligations, and liabilities, which form a body of precedents that has evolved over the centuries. Litigants' decisions (to sue, go to trial, or settle out of court) in particular classes of cases affect the kind of common-law rules that emerge from the judicial process. And, the nature of these decisions is believed to lead to the adoption of common-law rules (precedents) that are themselves economically efficient. Indeed, the common law has been used in the past to control many activities that are now controlled by bureaucratic decision making. Accordingly, we must contemplate private action controlled by the judicial process as an explicit alternative when we consider preferences among various forms of private and collective choice.

Chapter 12 then describes criminal law and interprets crimes as public bads. We discuss procedures in criminal cases, emphasizing decisions concerning conviction or acquittal, sentencing, parole, and probation. We also describe constitutional protections in criminal cases. Next, we consider the federal judiciary: the Supreme Court, the circuit courts of appeal, and the federal district courts. We enumerate constitutional provisions concerning the structure and jurisdictions of federal courts and then analyze the important and central problem of Supreme Court decision making. Chapter 12 concludes by reflecting on judicial activism and judicial restraint.

9

The Congress

This chapter describes the Congress and congressional activities. It asks what members of Congress actually do and what they should do if they hold certain preferences. It explores the effects that different congressional rules and procedures have on the shape of public policy, and it draws upon our understanding of the nature of collective action to explain congressional choice as public choice.

CONGRESS, THE CONSTITUTION, AND COLLECTIVE ACTION

The Constitution of the United States begins with a Preamble, after which these words appear: "All legislative Powers hererein granted shall be vested in a Congress of the United States, which shall consist of a Senate and House of Representatives" (Article 1, Section 1). This provision means that no members of the national government save House and Senate members may 'pass a law." Of course, for the last century the members of Congress have empowered various government agencies and bureaus to make laws in the form of "rules." And, Supreme Court decisions and presidential agreements with foreign rulers are also "the law of the land." But the Constitution nevertheless recognizes the preeminence of Congress in lawmaking.

The Constitution (in Article 1, Section 8) also enumerates the rights enjoyed by the members of Congress to pass laws in certain areas of human action. Most of these areas concern some aspect of producing public goods or suppressing public bads. Hence, the delegates to the Constitutional Convention seem to have had in mind the theoretical reasons for collective action described in Chapter 3.

National defense. Much of Section 8 is concerned with producing national defense, which is the clearest known example of a public good. The members of Congress can "define and punish Piracies and Felonies committed on the high Seas and Offenses against the Law of Nations." They can also "declare War, grant Letters of Marque and Reprisal, and make Rules concerning Captures on Land and Water."

The president is commander-in-chief of the armed forces, but House and Senate members have a considerable involvement in their upkeep and governance. The members of Congress can "raise and support Armies . . . ; provide and maintain a Navy . . . ; make Rules for the Government and Regulation of the land and naval Forces . . . ; provide for calling forth the Militia to execute the Laws of the Union, suppress Insurrections, and repel Invasions . . . ; [and] provide for organizing, arming, and disciplining the Militia, and for governing such Part of them as may be employed in the Service of the United States."

State governments control "the Appointment of the Officers" and have "the Authority of training the Militia," but these activities shall be done "according to the discipline prescribed by Congress." Moreover, Congress can "exercise . . . authority over all Places purchased by Consent of the Legislature of the State in which the Same shall be, for the Erection of Forts, Magazines, Arsenals, dock-Yards, and other needful buildings."

The encouragement of commerce. The members of Congress can also "establish . . . uniform laws on the subject of Bankruptcies throughout the United States . . . ; coin Money, regulate the Value thereof, and of foreign Coin . . . , fix the Standards of Weights and Measures . . . ; [and] provide for the Punishment of counterfeiting the Securities and current Coin of the United States."

A common, stable currency benefits anyone directly or indirectly involved in any kind of economic transaction. Since money changes hands in most exchanges, agreement on its value diminishes the costs of bargaining and satisfying the terms of contracts. Standardized weights and measures accomplish a similar purpose. Money also can easily be stored and saved or moved at will. With stable and reliable money and weights and measures, the costs of making economic exchanges decline, which means that people will make such transactions more often, thereby increasing everyone's utility. Bankruptcy is the end result of certain patterns of exchanges, and the congressional right to make uniform bankruptcy laws, when exercised, can stabilize the expectations of both creditors and debtors. Since uniform currencies, weights and measures, and bankruptcy laws affect nearly everyone by reducing risk and the costs of transactions, they are themselves public goods.

The members of Congress also hold the right "To regulate commerce with foreign Nations, and among the several States, and with the Indian Tribes." These rights, especially the right to regulate interstate commerce, have been broadly defined to allow the members of Congress to regulate nearly anything they choose. But the original intent of this clause, and one that partially survives to this day, was to prevent the states from embarking upon economic warfare with each other. For example, Table 4.5 in Chapter 4 shows the deleterious effects that interstate tariff warfare has on commerce generally. The Founding Fathers intended congressional regulation of foreign and interstate commerce to suppress the public bad of state-by-state tariff barriers, which, if permitted to continue, would impose an economic loss on the entire population.

The Constitution (in Article 1, Section 9) also specifically enjoins the members of Congress from themselves becoming parties to possible interstate conflicts.[1] Congress could not tax citizens in one state at a different rate from those in another. "No Capitation, or other direct Tax shall be laid, unless in Proportion to the Census. . . ." (This provision, but not its intent, was overturned by the Sixteenth Amendment.) Nor do the members of Congress have the right to become belligerents in a tariff war among the states: "No Tax or Duty shall be laid on Articles exported from any State." And, "No Preference shall be given by any Regulation of Commerce or Revenue to the Ports of one State over those of another; nor shall Vessels bound to, or from, one State be obliged to enter, clear, or pay Duties in another."

Other congressional rights concerning commerce enumerated in Section 8 include the right to guarantee property rights for authors and developers of innovations. New knowledge often shares certain characteristics of public goods because once someone produces it, it is sometimes available to everyone at little or no cost. To nurture the production of new knowledge, the members of Congress have the right "To promote the Progress of Science and Useful Arts by securing for limited Times to Authors and Inventors the exclusive Right to their respective Writings and Discoveries." The patent and copyright laws follow from these congressional prerogatives.

Support of collective action. To insure the supply of public goods, potential free riders must be compelled to share the cost. Accordingly, Article 1, Section 8 grants the members of Congress the very general right to tax, borrow, and spend: "The Congress shall have Power to Lay and Collect

[1] The possibility that an agent of government would join a coalition with one citizen to exploit another is discussed in Peter H. Aranson, "Public Goods, Prisoners' Dilemmas, and the Theory of the State," paper prepared for delivery at the annual meeting of the American Political Science Association, Chicago, Illinois, September 1974.

Taxes, Duties, Imposts and Excises, to pay the Debts and provide for the common Defense and general Welfare of the United States. . . ." Of course, the right to tax overcomes the free-rider problem. Furthermore, Congress can "borrow Money on the credit of the United States."

At the end of Section 8, the Constitution also gives the members of Congress legislative authority to ensure that all of their rights to act can find expression in law. House and Senate members can "make all Laws which shall be necessary and proper for carrying into Execution the foregoing Powers, and all other Powers vested by this Constitution in the Government of the United States, or in any Department or Office thereof."

Relations with other branches of government. The Constitution gives Senate members the formal right to advise and consent in several presidential nominations and decisions, including Supreme Court appointments and the approval of treaties. House and Senate members respectively control the impeachment and conviction of all federal officers except for members of the House and Senate, who are answerable only to their peers in their own house of the Congress. Other constitutionally delegated House and Senate rights include selecting the president and vice-president if there is no electoral college majority, confirming an appointed vice-president, judging the president's ability to "discharge the powers and duties of his office" if it should come into question, regulating most elections, determining the line of presidential succession, regulating their own business, and passing on and proposing constitutional amendments.

THE ELECTORAL CONNECTION AND LEGISLATIVE ACTIVITY

Those legislative rights of House and Senate members that are derived from the Constitution in many instances parallel the reasons for collective action described in Chapter 3. Therefore, in an idealized model of lawmaking that reflects constitutional mandates, senators and representatives would be instructed by the electoral process as to what level of which public goods (or bads) constituents wanted produced (or suppressed). They would then enter the Congress, thrash out the details, and hand over appropriately fashioned bills to the president to be considered, signed, and faithfully executed.

However, the analysis of interest-group decision making in Chapter 6 alerts us to a different possibility. Demands from the electorate might be for the enactment of sometimes Pareto-inferior programs that create private benefits at collective cost. An apparently unrestrained public-sector growth is sometimes said to result. Chapter 7 points out that aggregated demands from the electorate might seem ambiguous, leading to endless preference cycles, or might reflect the preferences of intense minorities. A strategy of ambiguity on the candidate/legislator's part is induced as a consequence. Chapter 8 also

Form **1040** Department of the Treasury—Internal Revenue Service
U.S. Individual Income Tax Return **1980**

For Privacy Act Notice, see Instructions | For the year January 1–December 31, 1980, or other tax year beginning , 1980, ending , 19

Use IRS label. Otherwise, please print or type.
Your first name and initial (if joint return, also give spouse's name and initial) | Last name | Your social security number
Present home address (Number and street, including apartment number, or rural route) | Spouse's social security no.
City, town or post office, State and ZIP code | Your occupation ▶ | Spouse's occupation ▶

Presidential Election Campaign Fund ▶ Do you want $1 to go to this fund? . . . Yes / No
If joint return, does your spouse want $1 to go to this fund? . . . Yes / No
Note: *Checking "Yes" will not increase your tax or reduce your refund.*

Requested by Census Bureau for Revenue Sharing ▶
A Where do you live (actual location of residence)? (See page 2 of Instructions.) State | City, village, borough, etc.
B Do you live within the legal limits of a city, village, etc.? ☐ Yes ☐ No
C In what county do you live?
D In what township do you live?

Filing Status
Check only one box.
For IRS use only
1 ☐ Single
2 ☐ Married filing joint return (even if only one had income)
3 ☐ Married filing separate return. Enter spouse's social security no. above and full name here ▶
4 ☐ Head of household. (See page 6 of Instructions.) If qualifying person is your unmarried child, enter child's name ▶
5 ☐ Qualifying widow(er) with dependent child (Year spouse died ▶ 19). (See page 6 of Instructions.)

Exemptions
Always check the box labeled Yourself. Check other boxes if they apply.
6a ☐ Yourself ☐ 65 or over ☐ Blind
b ☐ Spouse ☐ 65 or over ☐ Blind
Enter number of boxes checked on 6a and b ▶
c First names of your dependent children who lived with you ▶
Enter number of children listed on 6c ▶

d Other dependents: (1) Name	(2) Relationship	(3) Number of months lived in your home	(4) Did dependent have income of $1,000 or more?	(5) Did you provide more than one-half of dependent's support?

Enter number of other dependents ▶
7 Total number of exemptions claimed . . . Add numbers entered in boxes above ▶

Income
Please attach Copy B of your Forms W-2 here.
If you do not have a W-2, see page 5 of Instructions.
Please attach check or money order here.

8	Wages, salaries, tips, etc.	8
9	Interest income *(attach Schedule B if over $400)*	9
10a	Dividends *(attach Schedule B if over $400)* , **10b** Exclusion	
c	Subtract line 10b from line 10a	10c
11	Refunds of State and local income taxes *(do not enter an amount unless you deducted those taxes in an earlier year—see page 9 of Instructions)*	11
12	Alimony received	12
13	Business income or (loss) *(attach Schedule C)*	13
14	Capital gain or (loss) *(attach Schedule D)*	14
15	40% of capital gain distributions not reported on line 14 (See page 9 of Instructions)	15
16	Supplemental gains or (losses) *(attach Form 4797)*	16
17	Fully taxable pensions and annuities not reported on line 18	17
18	Pensions, annuities, rents, royalties, partnerships, etc. *(attach Schedule E)*	18
19	Farm income or (loss) *(attach Schedule F)*	19
20a	Unemployment compensation (insurance). Total received	
b	Taxable amount, if any, from worksheet on page 10 of Instructions	20b
21	Other income (state nature and source—see page 10 of Instructions) ▶	21
22	**Total income.** Add amounts in column for lines 8 through 21 ▶	22

Adjustments to Income
(See Instructions on page 10)

23	Moving expense *(attach Form 3903 or 3903F)*	23
24	Employee business expenses *(attach Form 2106)*	24
25	Payments to an IRA (enter code from page 10 ....)	25
26	Payments to a Keogh *(H.R. 10)* retirement plan	26
27	Interest penalty on early withdrawal of savings	27
28	Alimony paid	28
29	Disability income exclusion *(attach Form 2440)*	29
30	**Total adjustments.** Add lines 23 through 29 ▶	30

Adjusted Gross Income
31 **Adjusted gross income.** Subtract line 30 from line 22. *If this line is less than $10,000, see "Earned Income Credit" (line 57) on pages 13 and 14 of Instructions. If you want IRS to figure your tax, see page 3 of Instructions* ▶ 31

☆ U.S. GOVERNMENT PRINTING OFFICE: 1980—313-252 EI 52-0237640
Form **1040** (1980)

The "Power to lay and collect Taxes," which the Constitution gives to the members of Congress, stands behind the entire tax system. Most Americans are made aware of this power, whose exercise supports nearly all collective actions, when they file their income tax returns on April 15.

points out that even if pure strategy electoral equilibria exist in particular congressional districts, no pure lawmaking equilibrium may prevail in the House and Senate. Therefore, the public policy outcomes of congressional deliberations might be subject to parliamentary manipulation and agenda control.

The kinds of public policies that actually emerge from Congress depend on the aggregated individual decisions of individual House and Senate members. Here, the connections between lawmakers and their constituents are considered.[2] After the effects of those connections on lawmakers' strategies and choices are identified, later sections analyze the effects of internal institutional arrangements in the House and Senate on public policy.

Attention to their districts. The most immediate effect of the electoral connection is the close attention House and Senate members pay to their respective districts and states. In 1973, not an election year, House members took an average of thirty-five trips home to their districts; the actual numbers ranged from a low of four to a high of 365 for those living in nearby Maryland, Virginia, and Pennsylvania districts.[3] Congressional staffs have been growing over the years, and the percentage of staff members working in congressional district offices rather than in Washington, D. C., has also increased. In 1960, 14 percent of House members' staffs were assigned to their district offices; this fraction grew to 26 percent in 1967, 34 percent in 1974, and 36 percent in 1977.[4] In 1978, senators allocated an astonishing 45 percent of their staffs to district (state) offices.[5]

Electoral activities and lawmaking. House and Senate members constantly engage in three sorts of activities in pursuit of reelection: advertising, credit claiming, and position taking.[6] **Advertising** is purely an attempt to "package" senators and representatives and give them public recognition. The importance of name recognition, which is analogous to brand-name recognition, is not lost on most legislators, and they seldom refuse an opportunity to place their names and their persons before the electorate.

---

[2] Much of this section is informed by the highly original and extremely useful work of David R. Mayhew, *Congress: The Electoral Connection* (New Haven, Conn.: Yale University Press, 1974).

[3] Richard F. Fenno, Jr., "U.S. House Members and their Constituencies: An Exploration," *American Political Science Review,* 71 (September 1977), p. 891.

[4] Reported in Samuel C. Patterson, "The Semi-Sovereign Congress," in Anthony King, ed., *The New American Political System* (Washington, D.C.: American Enterprise Institute, 1978), p. 149. Data are from Morris P. Fiorina, *Congress: Keystone of the Washington Establishment* (New Haven, Conn.: Yale University Press, 1977), p. 58, and from calculations based on information reported in the 1977 *Congressional Staff Directory.*

[5] From calculations based on information reported in the 1978 *Congressional Staff Directory.*

[6] These activities are identified and discussed in Mayhew, *Congress: The Electoral Connection,* p. 49, *passim.*

Credit claiming is more complex than advertising. It concerns the nature of the legislation that House and Senate members succeed in passing. Writings about legislation refer variously to distributive benefits, particularized benefits, and the pork barrel. These benefits of legislation are often similar to, and more often identical to, private, divisible goods. Literature about the Congress identifies their opposites as programmatic activities and universalistic benefits, which more closely resemble public goods.[7]

Individual senators and representatives usually find that claiming credit for the passage of universalistic or programmatic laws—public goods—is not credible.[8] Constituents simply will not believe that a particular legislator single-handedly pushed a new voting rights act or general income-tax cut through the legislative labyrinth. Similarly, voters today ordinarily will not seriously entertain the notion that some individual House or Senate member did or could diminish the rates of inflation and unemployment.

Legislators must thus claim credit for the passage of specific private-goods legislation, particularized benefits, which must flow principally to distinguishable constituents, a group of constituents, or the entire constituency to the exclusion of all or most other constituencies. It follows that House and Senate members try to claim credit for nearly every benefit that flows from the federal government to their respective districts and states. But to do so, they must have something to claim. Hence, the electoral connection leads legislators to bend their efforts and allocate their legislative resources to supplying constituents with private, divisible benefits rather than public, indivisible ones.

The legislative process reflects attempts to claim credit for delivering private benefits in yet another way. Increases in the size of congressional staffs in general and of district staffs in particular grow out of an expansion of legislators' ombudsman activities. The increasing size and complexity of the federal bureaucracy at once make constituents more dependent on it, more subject to its random (and not so random) arbitrariness and capriciousness, and less able to understand how to pursue their rights when faced with administrative denial. Senators and representatives now hire *caseworkers* who specialize in helping constituents press their claims on federal bureaus. Each constituent satisfied receives the most divisible sort of private good from such activities. And, the political profit House and Senate members receive in return when they claim credit for personal services has created curious and surprising relationships between legislators and bureaucrats (which Chapter 11 explores at some length).[9]

---

[7] See Theodore J. Lowi, "American Business, Public Policy, Case-Studies and Political Theory," *World Politics,* 16 (1960), pp. 541–563; Mayhew, *Congress: The Electoral Connection,* p. 53, *passim*; and Fiorina, *Congress: Keystone of the Washington Establishment,* pp. 45–46. See also V. O. Key, Jr., *Politics, Parties & Pressure Groups,* 5th ed. (New York: Crowell, 1964), pp. 149–150.

[8] Mayhew, *Congress: The Electoral Connection,* p. 53, *passim.*

[9] These relationships are described in Fiorina, *Congress: Keystone of the Washington Establishment.*

Position taking, like credit claiming, reflects other problems we have encountered before. Position-taking activities range from making speeches on issues to voting on motions under House and Senate consideration. As far as reelection chances are concerned, position taking is nearly always analytically equivalent to choosing an election strategy, as described in Chapter 7. Hence, senators and representatives, *first,* can take the same positions as the electoral equilibria in their districts. When these do not exist or cannot be identified, legislators, *second,* become ambiguous. If intense minorities might form coalitions against officeholders because of their advocacy of an opposing view, *third,* ambiguity again comes to the rescue. The first and third of these cases, and possibly even the second, find reflection in this discussion:

> A solid consensus in the constituency calls for ringing declarations; for years the late Senator James K. Vardaman (D., Miss.) campaigned on a proposal to repeal the Fifteenth Amendment. Division or uncertainty in the constituency call for waffling; in the late 1960s a congressman had to be a poor politician indeed not to be able to come up with an inoffensive statement on Vietnam ("We must have peace with honor at the earliest possible moment consistent with the national interest"). On a controversial issue a Capitol Hill office normally prepares two form letters to send out to constituent letter writers—one for the pros and one (not directly contradictory) for the antis.[10]

THE FORMAL LAWMAKING PROCESS

The legislative preferences of senators and representatives, not to mention presidents and others, are aggregated in the lawmaking process, out of which comes some form of public policy. The connection between legislators' preferences and the resulting public policy is not direct and unambiguous. (Again, we have encountered this problem before.) A set of rules governing legislative procedures in both the House and Senate intervenes. The nature of those rules and procedures affects the character of public policies that eventually emerge—or fail to emerge—from the Congress.

Outline of the Lawmaking Process

An overview. All laws begin as bills, and bills become laws through several possible routes. However, most bills go through a similar process, some parts of which derive from constitutional provisions, and others from formal and informal House and Senate rules. Before we consider the lawmaking process in each chamber, it is helpful to get an overview of this process, which Figure 9.1 provides.

Article 1, Section 7 of the Constitution specifies that "all bills raising

[10] Mayhew, *Congress: The Electoral Connection,* p. 64.

He Thinks! Fascell has helped create practical, intelligent solutions to solve the local and national problems facing our people and government. He leads with his heart. And his mind.

He Fights! His Legislative Leadership has helped achieve many of the important goals of the nation and much more for the people of Dade and Monroe Counties, whom he serves.

You Win! With Fascell, we know we have a strong, clear voice in Congress!

Democrat. 15th Congressional District.

Refugees . . . a national responsibility

From the first day of the present refugee influx, Fascell has strongly and repeatedly urged the Administration to recognize the problem and take steps to relieve the impact on South Florida. Fascell . . .

○ demands that the federal government assume the full responsibility for all costs, present and future, to remove the financial burden from Dade County Citizens; Fascell authored, and successfully passed legislation that reimburses cities, counties, states and voluntary agencies for incurred and future costs (Fascell-Stone Amendment).

○ calls for stronger and increased efforts to put an end to illegal immigration as well as strict enforcement of immigration laws.

○ insists that any permanent refugee center be located outside South Florida; and that every effort be made to relocate refugees without families in South Florida to other states.

Fighting Inflation

Fascell has voted to reduce federal spending; Fascell continues to vote in Congress to reduce government spending. In the years 1975 through 1980, he voted to cut federal spending by 95 billion dollars.

The Cost of Energy

Fascell voted for major initiatives to move the nation toward energy independence and eliminate America's heavy dependence on foreign oil. The cost of foreign oil is a major cause of inflation. His votes include measures for:

○ development and use of all forms of synthetic fuel and gasohol production.

○ accelerated development of solar energy technology.

○ industrial, commercial and residential energy conservation.

○ mandated higher gas mileage for American cars.

National Defense

Fascell has voted for increased defense spending in order to maintain a strong national defense. He has also supported measures to assure a high quality of protection, an effective nuclear defense capability and improved intelligence capability.

Senior Citizens

Fascell consistently votes for needed increases in Social Security benefits and other programs designed to assist the elderly. He fights for legislation to guarantee that the future of the Social Security Trust Fund remains financially sound.

Fighting Crime

Fascell is fighting for a massive and comprehensive federal effort to assist local law enforcement agencies in their struggle against drug traffic and the high rate of crime.

Health Care

Fascell and his family know what it's like to bear the burden of costly medical bills. He supports quality and affordable national health care.

Strengthening Our Economy

Fascell supports a strong, healthy economy, with growth for both individuals and businesses by:

○ increasing productivity and full employment.

○ providing inducements for greater savings and investments.

○ reducing government regulations and red tape.

Lower Taxes

Fascell votes to cut federal taxes for individuals, businesses, middle-income taxpayers, homeowners, and small businesses. And to provide incentives for capital investment to create more jobs. Fascell supports further tax cuts as soon as we can responsibly afford them.

He supports the elimination of tax discrimination against working married couples.

Fascell is fighting against the proposed 15% withholding tax on stock dividends and interest on savings accounts.

More Jobs

Fascell votes for programs to put people to work, especially youth employment and training programs, in order to help reduce our welfare burden.

Honesty in Government

Fascell knows that full confidence in government can only be achieved when people know what our government is doing and how our public officials are serving the public interest. To achieve these goals, Fascell:

○ sponsored and won enactment of the Fascell-Chiles Government in the Sunshine Act, which opened Executive Branch meetings to the public.

○ successfully sponsored rules changes which opened votes and meetings of Congressional Committees to the public.

Agriculture

Fascell has strongly supported South Dade tomato growers' efforts to fight unfair competitive measures from Mexico. He has also fought proposals which would have threatened our mango and avocado industries.

He Fights for Dade and Monroe Counties. Here Are a Few of the Significant Programs He Helped Obtain in the Past Few Years:

○ $118 million to replace and repair bridges on the Homestead-Key West Overseas Highway.

○ $63.2 million loan to help improve Monroe County's water system and to replace the water pipeline with a new and larger pipe support system.

○ Funds to restore the beaches of Miami Beach.

○ The establishment and expansion of Biscayne National Park.

○ The retention and full operation of Key West Naval Air Station.

Authorized and paid for by Fascell Campaign Committee, George Korge, Treasurer. A copy of our report is filed with and available for purchase from the Federal Elections Commission, Washington, D.C.

pd. for by Fascell Campaign Fund. George Korge, Treas.

This campaign pamphlet issued by the Fascell Campaign Committee during the 1980 congressional elections shows the skillful mixture of advertising, credit claiming, and position taking that has made Dante Fascell (D-Fl.) one of the most senior members of the House of Representatives.

95TH CONGRESS
2D SESSION

H. R. 11280

IN THE HOUSE OF REPRESENTATIVES

MARCH 3, 1978

Mr. NIX (for himself and Mr. DERWINSKI) (by request) introduced the following bill; which was referred to the Committee on Post Office and Civil Service

A BILL

To reform the civil service laws.

Be it enacted by the Senate and House of Representatives of the United States of America in Congress assembled,

SHORT TITLE

SECTION 1. This Act may be cited as the "Civil Service Reform Act of 1978".

SEC. 2. The table of contents is as follows:

TABLE OF CONTENTS

I—O

J. 29-001—B4——1

Bills submitted in the House and Senate appear in the form of those whose front pages are reproduced here.

95TH CONGRESS
1ST SESSION

S. 270

IN THE SENATE OF THE UNITED STATES

JANUARY 14, 1977

Mr. KENNEDY (for himself, Mr. ABOUREZK, Mr. BAYH, Mr. BROOKE, Mr. CHURCH, Mr. DURKIN, Mr. FORD, Mr. HUMPHREY, Mr. JAVITS, Mr. MAGNUSON, Mr. MATHIAS, Mr. METCALF, Mr. PELL, Mr. RIBICOFF, and Mr. WILLIAMS) introduced the following bill; which was read twice and referred to the Committees on Government Operations and the Judiciary jointly by unanimous consent and second committee has thirty days after first report

---

A BILL

To amend chapter 5 of title 5, United States Code (commonly known as the Administrative Procedure Act), to permit awards of reasonable attorneys' fees and other expenses for public participation in Federal agency proceedings, and for other purposes.

Be it enacted by the Senate and House of Representatives of the United States of America in Congress assembled, That this Act shall be cited as the "Public Participation in Federal Agency Proceedings Act of 1977".

SEC. 2. (a) Subchapter II of chapter 5 of title 5, United States Code (relating to administrative procedure), is

VII—O

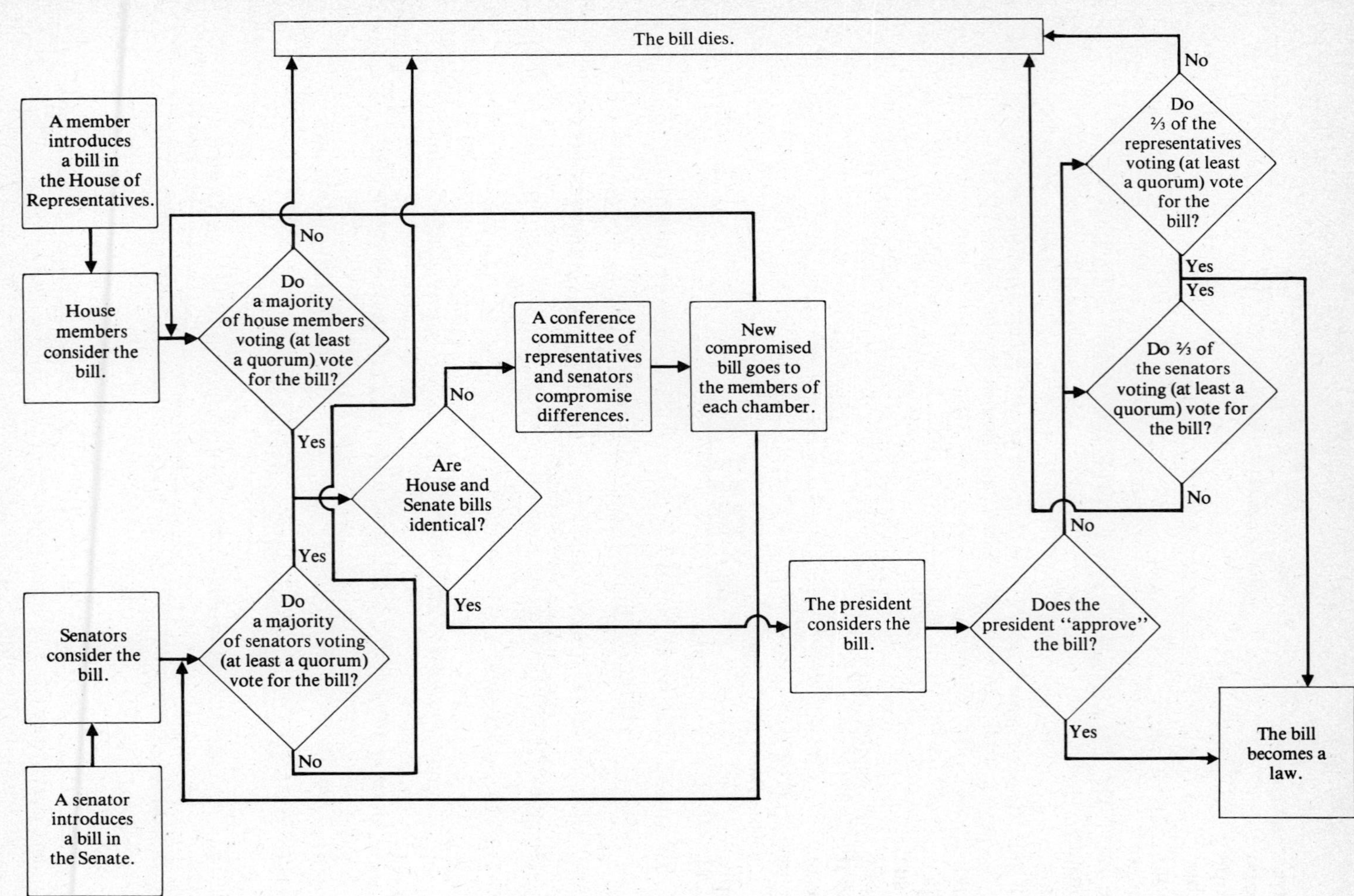

Figure 9.1 How a bill becomes a law: A general view.

Revenue shall originate in the House of Representatives; but the Senate may propose or concur with Amendments as on other Bills." Traditionally, appropriations bills also originate in the House; all other bills may originate in either the House or the Senate. Representatives and senators introduce bills in their respective chambers. A bill goes through a process of consideration, sometimes never reaching a vote. Those bills that do come to a vote require the assent of a majority of at least a quorum of each chamber's members. The Constitution sets a quorum at a minimum of one-half of the members for each chamber. If a bill fails to reach the voting stage in either chamber, it dies; and, if it fails to get enough votes in either house, it dies.

Suppose a bill passes in both chambers. If the House and Senate versions of the bill are not identical, the members of a conference committee, made up of legislators from each chamber, must negotiate to make them so. If bargaining is successful, the new, compromised bill goes back to each chamber for another vote. If the revised bill receives the necessary votes in both the House and the Senate, it goes to the president. If the House and Senate versions of the bill are identical (before a conference committee)—an infrequent event for important bills—the original bill goes directly to the president.

The president considers the bill and must decide whether or not to approve it. He can indicate approval in one of two ways: first, he can sign the bill, in which case it becomes a law; second, he can fail to sign it, but if the Congress has not yet adjourned ten days after the president receives the bill for consideration, then again it becomes a law. The president can also withhold approval in two ways. First, he can **veto** the bill, sending it back to the chamber in which it originated and stating his reasons for disapproval; second, he can fail to sign it, and if the Congress has adjourned within ten days of his receiving it for consideration, it does not become a law. This method of withholding presidential approval is known as a **pocket veto.**

If the president vetoes the bill, the members of Congress can make it law anyway. The bill returns to the chamber in which it originated, and if two-thirds of a quorum of that chamber votes to pass it, then the bill goes to the other chamber, in which a similar process occurs. If two-thirds of a quorum of the second chamber passes the bill, then the House and Senate are said to have overridden the president's veto and the bill becomes a law. Otherwise, it dies. The Constitution prescribes this entire process in Article 1, Section 7.

Lawmaking in the House of Representatives. This overview considerably simplifies the lawmaking process as it occurs in each chamber, reducing it to *introduction, consideration,* and *voting.* Figure 9.2 more fully describes procedures used in the House of Representatives, although even this figure is a simplification. The lawmaking process in the House begins when a member introduces a bill. The speaker of the House, who is elected by members of the majority party to be the House's presiding officer, assigns the bill to a committee, whose members consider it. The committee members can report the bill to the House, or they can "bury" it by failing to report it.

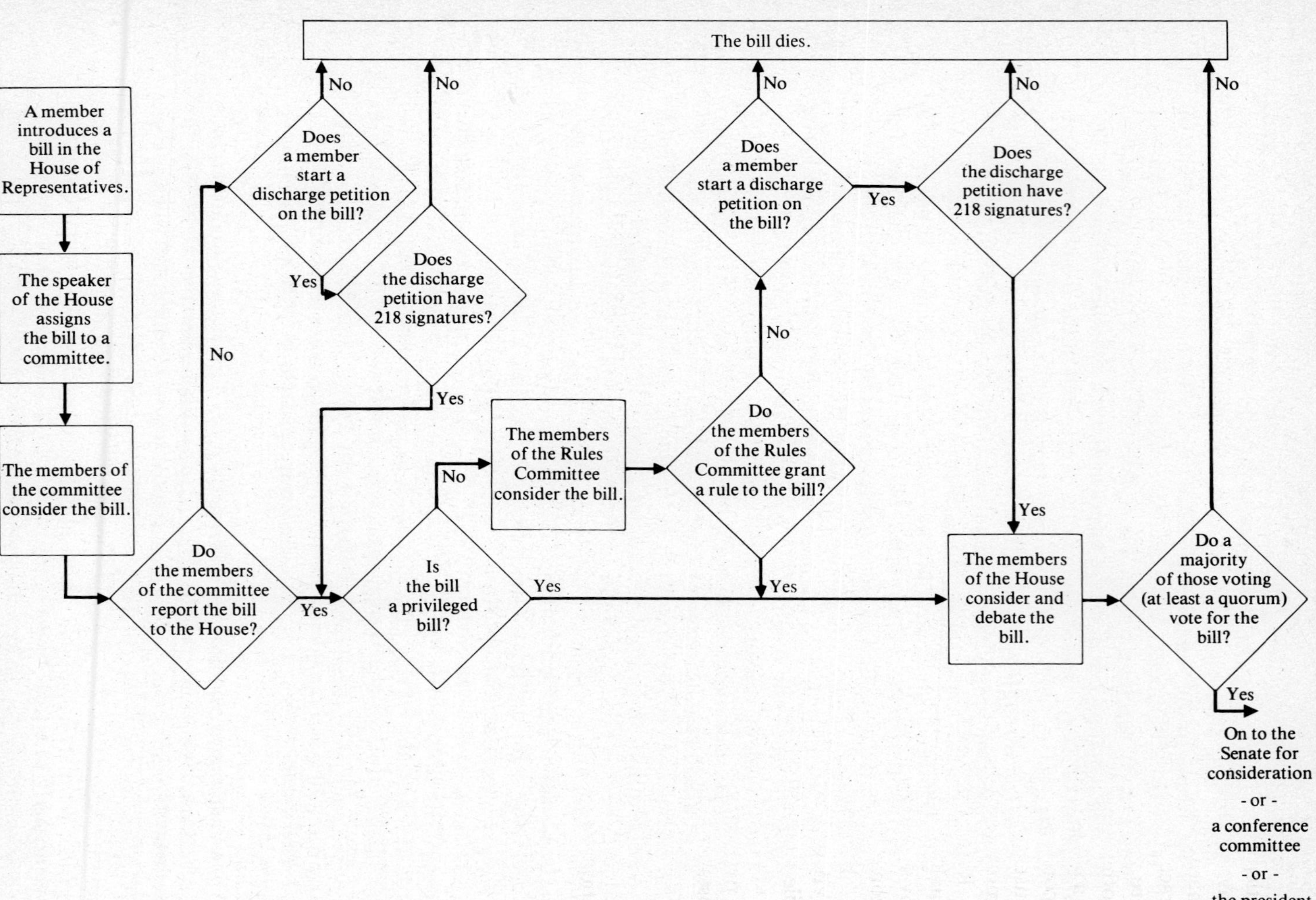

Figure 9.2 How a bill becomes a law: The House of Representatives.

The bill's supporters have several strategies for removing it from a particular committee's jurisdiction if that committee's members try to kill or delay it. One strategy is to use a **discharge petition,** which requires the signatures of more than one-half of the members of the House. If the petition attracts enough signatures, the bill goes on a **discharge calendar** and remains there for at least seven days, after which House members may consider it. Another strategy for getting a bill out of committee is to ask House members for a **suspension of the rules,** which allows representatives to bypass any rules or committees if at least two-thirds of a quorum agrees. The speaker of the House controls this procedure, since he must recognize a member who wishes to move for a suspension of the rules. A third strategy is for the members of the Rules Committee to report the bill directly to the floor. These three strategies are seldom tried and less often successful. Thus, committee approval usually remains necessary, though not sufficient, for most bills to become laws.

Bills that come out of committee may be privileged or not privileged. **Privileged bills** go directly to the members of the House for consideration, while bills without privilege must go through the Rules Committee. Privileged bills fall into several classes. **Private bills,** which are submitted to aid particular persons, go on a **private calendar.**[11] Limited bills without controversial substance might go on the **consent calendar.** Bills from the Appropriations Committee (concerning raising federal revenues), the Public Works and Transportation Committee, and the Veterans Affairs Committee (for certain bills), and from the Rules Committee itself (for resolutions on how the consideration of a bill will be conducted), are similarly all privileged.

Bills without privilege must go to the Rules Committee. The members of this committee, once called the "traffic cop of the House," decide whether to report each bill they consider to the House.[12] If Rules Committee members so decide, a bill can die in their committee, unless a discharge petition on the bill's behalf gets enough signatures, or unless a motion to suspend the rules succeeds on the floor of the House. Rules Committee members also set the

---

[11] Unlike private-sector corporations, the federal government enjoys sovereign immunity protecting it against lawsuits for damages caused by the negligence of its agents and employees. Legislators might submit private bills to compensate persons who have been injured on government property (for example, someone who slips and falls on a wet floor in the Capitol). They might also submit such bills to propose variances for persons seeking to bypass a government regulation (for example, would-be immigrants who fail to meet immigration requirements).

[12] The Rules Committee has undergone substantial political changes in recent years because of attempts to limit its control. In early 1975, the speaker (when a Democrat) was given the formal right to appoint Democratic Rules Committee members. He may remove them at the beginning of each new Congress. However, the Rules Committee continues to act both as "traffic cop" and as some observers have recently suggested, as the Democratic leadership's legislative "field commander." See Bruce I. Oppenheimer, "The Rules Committee: New Arm of Leadership in a Decentralized House," in Lawrence C. Dodd and Bruce I. Oppenheimer, eds., *Congress Reconsidered* (New York: Praeger, 1977), chapter 5.

terms of full House consideration for bills they do send to the floor: such bills are accompanied by one rule that specifies the time allowed for debate and another stating whether the bill can be amended on the floor of the House or not. Bills with an **open rule** can be amended; bills with a **closed rule** cannot. Finally, if a bill gets to the House floor through one of these many routes, it minimally requires a vote of over one-half of a quorum—at least 110 of at least 218 representatives—to pass.

Process in the Senate. The Senate's lawmaking process resembles that of the House, but with important differences. First, while a presiding officer in the Senate refers bills to committees, as in the House, bills can also come to the floor of the Senate for consideration through other means. Senators may vote to suspend the rules, but they can also offer **rider amendments** to bills already under consideration by the full Senate. Unlike requirements in the House, Senate rider amendments need not be germane to the original bill. A rider amendment to a bill already under consideration can put an entirely new bill before the Senate for debate, thus entirely avoiding the committee process. Senators may directly consider any bill that the House has passed, and, as in the House, they can use discharge petitions to dislodge bills from Senate committee consideration.

While the Senate has no Rules Committee, its majority and minority party leaders act as one by scheduling debate. Senate committees are somewhat less important in lawmaking than are House committees, but they are more important in other matters, such as conducting hearings on presidential appointments and on treaties—in both instances, the first step for the Senate to advise and consent to presidential decisions.

The **filibuster** is a Senate device that can stall legislation quite as effectively as can the members of a House committee. Senate floor debate is almost unlimited. Hence, senators literally can continue to talk about a bill—or about anything else that comes to mind—until the desire to get on with other business leads the bill's supporters or Senate leadership to drop its consideration. A vote of **cloture** to end a filibuster requires an affirmative vote from 60 percent of all senators. (Before 1975, cloture required a vote of two-thirds of the senators present and voting.) A successful cloture vote is difficult to achieve.

Congressional Rules and Public Policy

Information costs and procedural efficiency. Standardized rules and procedures such as those just described reduce the costs of information and decision making. In the absence of detailed procedural rules, House and Senate members would have to adopt new rules for each bill they considered. Because rules can affect outcomes, a repetitive consideration of new rules for each bill would be a time-consuming business in which those who favored a bill would vote for rules favorable to its passage and those who opposed it would vote for unfavorable ones. Legislators would also have to adopt more general rules to choose procedural rules for considering each specific bill.

Members of Congress can suspend their own rules or create new ones. However, these actions usually require more than a majority vote. For example, a suspension of the rules requires two-thirds of a quorum. The explanation for this requirement probably lies with considerations about decision rules, as described at the beginning of Chapter 4. Suspension of the rules sometimes carries with it the possibility that larger-than-normal external costs will be imposed on individual House and Senate members. By contrast, a regularized process reduces decision costs. The related costs associated with gaining information about the legislative process also decline. By using a clear set of rules, representatives and senators usually can easily find out what becomes of the bills they introduce in their respective chambers. They can also follow the process more closely and know how to affect it. Much of this process depends on learning, but learning would become impossible without a regularized set of procedures to learn about.

Rules, procedures, and redistribution. Despite the advantages for lawmakers of regularized rules and procedures, these rules and procedures are not neutral. Which rules and procedures are chosen affects the kinds of public policies that emerge from the Congress and gives different advantages to different lawmakers and groups of lawmakers. For instance, from 1948 to 1963, the filibuster in the Senate and the committee structure in the House gave southern legislators an advantage beyond their numbers. They used this advantage to maintain the status quo in several public policy areas, such as school integration. However, in recent years northern liberal Democrats have used both of these provisions to some advantage. Thus, at a particular time in history the rules seem not to be neutral. Of course, over many years one group of lawmakers can also lose rule-related advantages to some other group.

The central property of congressional rules and procedures is their bias toward protecting the statutory status quo. Legislating change seems most difficult. True, economic and social conditions change while the laws remain unaltered. But, altering public policy to prevent such external changes from occurring is also difficult. To pass, bills usually require more than simple majorities, because unconvinced lawmakers can use any number of lethal and dilatory strategies for defeating, or delaying, or substantially modifying them. There are many ways to kill a bill, and lawmakers opposed to a bill need not be in a majority to defeat it. From introduction to enactment, a bill travels a perilous route. The speaker of the House can send it to a hostile committee. The members of a House or Senate committee can fail to report it. The House Rules Committee also can fail to report it, or can report it with an unfavorable rule. Opposed senators can filibuster the bill to death or lose it in the labyrinth of Senate procedures. The president can also veto it.

Possibly the speaker, an exact majority of the appropriate House and

Senate committees, an exact majority of House and Senate members, and the president will all simultaneously favor the bill. This is so unlikely that coalitions larger than bare majorities are almost always required to pass important measures. A filibuster supported by forty-one senators can stop the entire process, though if they come from the smallest states, these forty-one senators may represent less than 10 percent of the population. The president alone can override the desires of up to two-thirds of the members of the Congress. In sum, the chances of aligning a bare majority coalition to pass any important bill are small indeed.

If this were not the case, one might expect minimum winning coalitions of poor states and districts to withdraw resources from rich ones, because less wealthy states and districts have less to tax away than rich ones. But as Chapter 2 indicates, such redistributions seldom happen, and sometimes the poor are taxed more heavily than middle-income citizens.[13] Nor do energy-poor states succeed in legislatively extracting fuel from those with abundant supplies. In sum, the logic of congressional rules and procedures prevents coalitions of less wealthy or fuel-poor states from forming and winning simply because coalitions larger than bare majorities remain necessary to pass most important legislation.

The tendency of congressional rules and procedures to preserve the statutory status quo protects against the legislation of wholesale redistributions. Each year, House and Senate members pass bills that extract wealth from the electorate and give it back again. As Chapter 1 observes, the amount of wealth extracted, either directly through taxes or indirectly through regulation, represents a growing fraction of GNP. However, total economic resources, both public and private, remain more or less constant in any given year, which makes legislative coalition formation an n-person constant-sum game. As Chapter 2 suggests, the size principle should operate in such situations. That is, 51 senators and 218 representatives should secure benefits for their respective states and districts at the expense of the other 49 senators' and 217 representatives' respective states and districts.

The probability of being in a legislative minimum winning coalition is about one-half, as is the probability of falling among the losers. Hence, in an aggregate sense this variety of legislative redistribution merely accomplishes an increase of risk, since the expected value of such redistributive games is zero. Only a legislative gamble would determine whether the House or Senate member is in the winning or losing coalition. If legislators or their constituents have diminishing marginal utility curves, a dollar added in the process would represent less utility gained than a dollar subtracted would take away. As a consequence, public choice—the legislative gamble—would seem inferior to leaving the resources in the private sector. Congressional rules and procedures partially avoid the hazards of such gambles by making sure that winning

[13] See Chapter 2, footnote 8, and its associated discussion of resource redistributions in the publicly supported higher-education system.

coalitions are very large. Everyone gets some benefit. But as we shall now see, and as Chapter 6 has already pointed out, that too is a problem.

Rules, procedures, and private benefits: logrolling. If lawmaking procedures in the Congress limit the most obvious forms of redistributive legislation, they seem irresistibly to encourage laws that spread private benefits at collective cost all over the political landscape. Such laws do redistribute, but less obviously so, and that is the problem. This represents something of a paradox, because legislators should be able to perceive program costs even when the programs themselves, not to mention their costs, remain unknown to the constituents who pay for them. Put differently, House and Senate members should have far more public policy information than do voters. Even if the legislator's electoral imperative is to create particularized benefits—**pork-barrel legislation**—nevertheless one might expect practices that discipline the associated urges to develop in the House and Senate. The paradox represented by the lack of such discipline is partially explained by studying the fascinating process variously called **logrolling,** vote trading, and back-scratching.

The successful enactment of much complex legislation results from logrolling. This practice requires the consideration of at least two separate motions, though a single bill incorporating at least two motions can satisfy this requirement. To see how logrolling might work, consider two separate, unrelated motions and a Congress of three representatives, A, B, and C. The first motion is called *X*. If two out of three members vote for *X*, it passes and becomes public policy. Otherwise, it fails. The second motion is called *Y*. Again, if two out of three members vote for *Y*, it passes. Otherwise, it does not. Table 9.1 summarizes the members' preferences and utilities for these two motions.

Table 9.1 Preferences and Utilities for a Simple Logroll

		Motion X	
	Member prefers *X* to:	**Member's utility if *X* passes**	**Member's utility if *X* fails**
Member A	pass	2	0
Member B	fail	−1	0
Member C	fail	−1	0
		Motion Y	
	Member prefers *Y* to:	**Member's utility if *Y* passes**	**Member's utility if *Y* fails**
Member A	fail	−1	0
Member B	pass	2	0
Member C	fail	−1	0

Member A wants X to pass, while B and C do not. Member B wants Y to pass, while A and C do not. If all three members vote their preferences on both motions, X and Y fail, and all three members receive a utility of zero. However, suppose that A approaches B and offers to vote for Y if B will vote for X. The message A gives to B goes something like this: "We each receive zero utiles from voting against each other's motion. If we both vote for X, I receive two utiles and you lose one; if we both vote for Y, I lose one utile and you receive two. But if we both vote for X and Y, we each receive a net of one utile, which is better than nothing. Come now, let us reason together." Of course, C loses two utiles if the trade occurs.

This coalition of two members on two issues differs from the simple redistributive coalitions discussed previously. Here, one representative tries to win a program, say a public works project, for his district, while the program's cost is divided among all districts, *including* his own. The utilities in Table 9.1 derive from such simple but highly realistic assumptions as (for instance) that a program in one district, say motion X for member A, is worth three dollars (utiles), the cost being divided equally among the constituents of all three districts. The situation in Table 9.1 is a three-person zero-sum cooperative game.

As early as 1885, Woodrow Wilson wrote of this practice:

> It is principally in connection with appropriations that what has come to be known in our political slang as "log-rolling" takes place. Of course, the chief scene of this sport is the private room of the Committee on Rivers and Harbors, and the season of its highest excitement, the hours spent in the passage of the River and Harbor Bill. "Log-rolling" is an exchange of favors. Representative A. is very anxious to secure a grant for the clearing of a small watercourse in his district, and representative B. is equally solicitous about his plans for bringing money into the hands of the contractors of his own constituency, whilst representative C. comes from a seaport town whose modest harbor is neglected because of the treacherous bar across its mouth, and representative D. has been blamed for not bestirring himself more in the interest of schemes of improvement afoot amongst the enterprising citizens of his native place; so it is perfectly feasible for these gentlemen to put their heads together and confirm a mutual understanding that each will vote in Committee of the Whole for the grants desired by the others, in consideration of the promise that they will cry "aye" when his item comes on to be considered.[14]

Plainly, logrolling is designed to create private benefits at collective cost, but scholars disagree on its merits. Some argue that it produces a more nearly market-like and therefore a more efficient resource allocation.[15] Others say it

---

[14] Woodrow Wilson, *Congressional Government,* with an Introduction by Walter Lippmann, 15th ed. (New York: Meridian Books, 1956), p. 121.

[15] James M. Buchanan and Gordon Tullock, *The Calculus of Consent: Logical Foundations of Constitutional Democracy* (Ann Arbor: University of Michigan Press, 1962), chapters 11 and 12.

Table 9.2 Utilities of Representatives for Outcomes of Voting

	Motion X			*Motion Y*		
	Member prefers *X* to:	**Utility if motion: fails**	**passes**	**Member prefers *Y* to:**	**Utility if motion: fails**	**passes**
Member A*	fail	1	−2	fail	1	−2
Member B	fail	1	−1	pass	−2	2
Member C	pass	−2	2	fail	1	−1
	Motion W			*Motion Z*		
	Member prefers *W* to:	**Utility if motion: fails**	**passes**	**Member prefers *Z* to:**	**Utility if motion: fails**	**passes**
Member A	fail	1	−1	pass	−2	2
Member B	pass	−2	2	fail	1	−1
Member C*	fail	1	−2	fail	1	−2
	Motion T			*Motion V*		
	Member prefers *T* to:	**Utility if motion: fails**	**passes**	**Member prefers *V* to:**	**Utility if motion: fails**	**passes**
Member A	pass	−2	2	fail	1	−1
Member B*	fail	1	−2	fail	1	−2
Member C	fail	1	−1	pass	−2	2

Source: Adapted from William H. Riker and Steven J. Brams, "The Paradox of Vote Trading," *American Political Science Review*, 67 (December 1973), p. 1241.

* Not trading

does not. For instance, one logrolling example has been developed that is both bizzare and paradoxical.[16] Table 9.2 shows three legislators trading on six motions. By voting their true preferences without logrolling, members A and B vote against *X* and *V*; A and C against *Y* and *W*; and B and C against *Z* and *T*. All six motions—programs—are defeated, and the sum of each representative's utility from voting his true preference is zero. Now consider motions *X* and *Y*. Members B and C might combine to pass them, in which case each receives one utile while A receives minus four utiles. If A and B make a similar trade to pass *W* and *Z*, while A and C pass *T* and *V*, then all programs pass and the sum of each representative's utility from all of these logrolls becomes minus two.[17]

---

[16] William H. Riker and Steven J. Brams, "The Paradox of Vote Trading," *American Political Science Review*, 67 (December 1973), pp. 1235–1247.

[17] This analysis can be criticized because other trades are possible. For example, in considering *X* and *Y*, A receives minus four utiles from a trade between B and C. Hence, A might approach C and offer to vote for *X* if C will vote against *Y*. From this

This result is disturbing because the structure of representatives' preferences may lead them to do exactly the wrong thing. The situation appears worse if legislators use logrolling to win congressional support of programs for their districts that cost more than they are worth. This is the case in Table 9.2 if money is substituted for utility. For example, the trade by B and C on *X* and *Y* would produce one dollar for each of them but cost four dollars for A. Nationally, such logrolls will lead to Pareto-inferior results. The purposes of logrolling as suggested by this example thus bear little relationship to those given for collective action in Chapter 3. Logrolls involve divisible—district-wide—goods. And, the programs enacted as a result of logrolls may be—collectively—more expensive than they are worth. Legislators' incentives to create private goods at collective cost by logrolling also seem fully compatible with those of interest-group members and leaders, described in Chapter 6.

The connection between logrolling and congressional procedures now becomes apparent. As noted earlier, congressional procedures usually require aproval by more than one-half of each house for bills to become laws. The logroll helps to add the requisite number of legislators to the winning coalition. Acts of Congress very often assume the form of omnibus legislation with something for everyone. These acts commonly appear to be the product of implicit logrolls. A subject for legislative attention is announced in the House or Senate, and by the time of final passage nearly everyone has extracted some form of private, divisible benefit from the process. The importance of congressional committees in sustaining this process will be considered momentarily.

Rules, procedures, and parliamentary manipulation. Congressional procedures also enable clever House and Senate members to manipulate for their own advantage the order in which motions are considered. Suppose a motion is made, and then an amendment to the motion is offered. In the House of Representatives, as in many other legislatures following ordinary parliamentary procedure, the amendment must be voted on first. If the amendment carries, then the amended motion is voted on against the status quo.

Now consider a voting cycle in which motion *X* defeats *Y*, *Y* defeats *Z*,

---

exchange, A receives minus one utile (instead of minus four), and C receives three utiles (instead of one). Of course, B receives minus three utiles, which might lead him to offer a vote trade to A. (Which one?) See Gordon Tullock, "Communications," *American Political Science Review,* 68 (December 1974), pp. 1687–1689. The logrolling situation represented in Table 9.2 is highly unstable. First, B trades with C, then A trades with C; then, A trades with B; and then B trades again with C. This leads to the suggestion that the vote-trading paradox in Table 9.2 is logically equivalent to Arrow's voting paradox—the cyclical majority problem. See David H. Koehler, "Vote-Trading and the Voting Paradox: A Proof of Logical Equivalence," *American Political Science Review,* 69 (September 1975), pp. 954–960. The generality of this suggestion is questioned seriously in Peter Bernholz, "Logrolling and the Paradox of Voting: Are They Really Logically Equivalent? A Comment," *American Political Science Review,* 69 (September 1975), pp. 961–962.

and *Z* defeats *X*. And, suppose *X* is the status quo. If *Z* is brought against *X*, *Z* wins and the status quo loses. But if *Z* is first put to a vote against *Y*, an amended version of *Z*, then *Y* defeats *Z*. But, then *X* defeats *Y*, and the status quo is preserved.

A similar situation arose during the 1950s in House of Representatives consideration of a bill granting federal aid for school construction.[18] As before, let *X* represent the status quo, no federal aid. *Z* represents a simple school construction aid bill, and *Y* represents the same aid bill amended to deny funds to states that do not comply with the Supreme Court's 1954 desegregation decision in *Brown v. Board of Education.*[19] Northern Democrats in the Congress preferred *Y* to *Z* to *X*. Southern Democrats wanted federal school construction money but not integration; they preferred *Z* to *X* to *Y*. Republicans were opposed to school aid in any form, but they were willing to vote for the integration amendment, called the Powell Amendment, to scuttle the unamended bill by parliamentary manipulation.

This strategy worked. The original bill, *Z*, was submitted. The Powell Amendment, *Y*, was offered, and Republicans joined with northern Democrats to support *Y* over *Z*. *Y* carried, but in the final vote of *Y* against the status quo, *X*, Republicans joined southern Democrats to defeat *Y*. The result was *X*, no federal aid for school construction, exactly what the Republicans preferred—and against the preference of a congressional majority for a simple, unamended school construction bill, *Z*, over the status quo, *X*.

This agenda manipulation process has been identified as working in congressional voting on the Seventeenth Amendment, on highway appropriations bills, and on federal aid to parochial schools.[20] It seems common enough in actual practice and shows how underlying preference structures can make the manipulation of public policy outcomes a very real possibility. Of course, since the speaker of the House or any other presiding officer recognizes members for the purpose of offering motions and amendments to motions, he can often determine the order of consideration, and consequently the public policy adopted.

THE ORGANIZATION OF CONGRESS

Table 9.3 lists the twenty-two standing committees of the House, the fifteen of the Senate, and the 1979 party division in each committee. The

---

[18] William H. Riker, "Arrow's Theorem and Some Examples of the Paradox of Voting," in John M. Claunch, ed., *Mathematical Applications in Political Science* (Dallas: Arnold Foundation, Southern Methodist University, 1965), pp. 41–60.

[19] 347 U.S. 483 (1954).

[20] See Riker, "Arrow's Theorem and Some Examples of the Paradox of Voting"; Riker, "The Paradox of Voting and Congressional Rules for Voting on Amendments," *American Political Science Review,* 52 (June 1958), pp. 349–366; Kenneth S. Arrow, *Social Choice and Individual Values,* 2nd ed. (New York: Wiley, 1963), p. 3; and Robin Farquharson, *A Theory of Voting* (New Haven, Conn.: Yale University Press, 1969), pp. 52–53.

Congress also has conference committees, joint committees, special committees, and select committees, which usually exist for short periods of time to handle unusual problems, though some are almost permanent. The problems of lawmaking mentioned earlier in this chapter are reflected in committee deliberations. For this and other reasons, the structure and operation of committees influence the public policies that eventually emerge from the Congress.

The preeminence of the committees in the lawmaking process is well documented. Woodrow Wilson wrote:

> In form, the Committees only digest the various matter introduced by individual members, and prepare it, with care, and after thorough investigation, for the final construction and action of the House; but, in reality, they dictate the course to be taken, prescribing the decisions of the House not only, but measuring out, according to their wills, its opportunities for debate and deliberation as well. The House sits, not for serious discussion, but to sanction the conclusions of its Committees as rapidly as possible. It legislates in its committee-rooms; not by the determinations of majorities, but by the resolutions of specially-commissioned minorities; so it is not far from the truth to say that Congress in session is Congress on public exhibition, whilst Congress in its committee-rooms is Congress at work.[21]

Wilson concluded, "We are ruled by . . . 'little legislatures.' "[22]

The Nature of Committees

The hierarchy of committees. Three committees in the House—Appropriations, Ways and Means, and Rules—and two in the Senate—Appropriations and Finance—are preeminent in legislative matters. The members of most of the other committees, most of the time, concern themselves with particular substantive public policy subject matters. In the House, the members of two of the preeminent committees, Appropriations and sometimes Ways and Means, must decide whether to fund the programs the members of substantive committees are successful in passing through the lawmaking process. The members of the Rules Committee usually must decide whether those programs will indeed get through that process in the first place.

This arrangement of committees can dramatically increase the problems of getting public policy through Congress. For example, suppose that a representative wanted to provide national health insurance through the Social Security system. This legislation might take many different routes. For instance, in the first stage, the bill might be submitted in the House. The speaker might assign the bill to the Education and Labor Committee, while a similar

---

[21] Wilson, *Congressional Government,* p. 69.

[22] Wilson, *Congressional Government,* p. 89.

Table 9.3 Standing Committees of the 96th Congress, 1st Session (1979)

House Committees	Senate Committees
Agriculture (D 22; R 15)	Agriculture, Nutrition, and Forestry (D 10; R 8)
Appropriations (D 36; R 18)	Appropriations (D 17; R 11)
Armed Services (D 28; R 15)	Armed Services (D 10; R 7)
Banking, Finance, and Urban Affairs (D 27; R 15)	Banking, Housing, and Urban Affairs (D 9; R 6)
Budget (D 17; R 8)	Budget (D 12; R 8)
District of Columbia (D 9; R 5)	Commerce, Science, and Transportation (D 10; R 7)
Education and Labor (D 23; R 13)	Energy and Natural Resources (D 11; R 7)
Foreign Affairs (D 22; R 12)	Environment and Public Works (D 8; R 6)
Government Operations (D 25; R 14)	Finance (D 12; R 8)
House Administration (D 16; R 9)	Foreign Relations (D 9; R 6)
Interior and Insular Affairs (D 26; R 14)	Governmental Affairs (D 9; R 8)
Interstate and Foreign Commerce (D 27; R 15)	Judiciary (D 10; R 7)
Judiciary (D 20; R 11)	Labor and Human Resources (D 9; R 6)
Merchant Marine and Fisheries (D 25; R 14)	Rules and Administration (D 6; R 4)
Post Office and Civil Service (D 16; R 9)	Veterans' Affairs (D 6; R 4)
Public Works and Transportation (D 31; R 17)	
Rules (D 11; R 5)	
Science and Technology (D 27; R 15)	
Small Business (D 25; R 14)	
Standards of Official Conduct (D 6; R 6)	
Veterans' Affairs (D 21; R 14)	
Ways and Means (D 24; R 12)	

Source: As reported in *Congressional Quarterly Weekly Report,* 37 (April 14, 1979), pp. 295–301.

bill in the Senate would probably go to the Labor and Human Resources Committee. The bills that *might* come out of these committees would be authorization bills. Even if the House bill got through the Rules Committee and the Senate bill through a possible filibuster, and even if both chambers passed the respective bills and the conference committee compromises, and even if the president signed the resulting bill into law or the members voted to override the president's veto, the resulting law would have no effect. There has been no appropriations bill to pay claims against the insurance fund, and there are no tax revenues to supply the fund. An appropriations bill would first have to go to the Appropriations committees of the House and Senate, and the revenue bill would go to the House Ways and Means Committee and to the Senate Finance Committee: the lawmaking process would begin again.

MARTIN LUTHER KING, JR., NATIONAL HOLIDAY, S. 25

JOINT HEARINGS

BEFORE THE

COMMITTEE ON THE JUDICIARY

UNITED STATES SENATE

AND THE

COMMITTEE ON

POST OFFICE AND CIVIL SERVICE

HOUSE OF REPRESENTATIVES

NINETY-SIXTH CONGRESS

FIRST SESSION

ON

S. 25

MARCH 27 AND JUNE 21, 1979

Serial No. 96–14

Printed for the use of the Committee on the Judiciary

CARIBBEAN REFUGEE CRISIS: CUBANS AND HAITIANS

HEARING

BEFORE THE

COMMITTEE ON THE JUDICIARY

UNITED STATES SENATE

NINETY-SIXTH CONGRESS

SECOND SESSION

MAY 12, 1980

Serial No. 96–58

Printed for the use of the Committee on the Judiciary

These four reports illustrate the wide-ranging concerns of a single congressional committee, the Senate Judiciary Committee. Moving clockwise from the upper left, the joint hearings with the House Post Office and Civil Service Committee concerned a Senate bill (S. 25) to make Martin Luther King, Jr.'s birthday a national holiday. The hearings on a balanced budget amendment reflect the committee's control over constitutional matters in general and the amendment process in par-

PROPOSED CONSTITUTIONAL AMENDMENT TO BALANCE THE FEDERAL BUDGET

HEARINGS
BEFORE THE
SUBCOMMITTEE ON THE CONSTITUTION
OF THE
COMMITTEE ON THE JUDICIARY
UNITED STATES SENATE
NINETY-SIXTH CONGRESS
FIRST SESSION
ON
S.J. Res. 2, 4, 5, 6, 7, 9, 10, 11, 13, 16, 18, 36, 38, 45, 46, 56, 76, 79, 86, and 93

MARCH 12, MAY 23, JULY 25, OCTOBER 4, 11, AND NOVEMBER 1, 1979

Serial No. 96–41

Printed for the use of the Committee on the Judiciary

HEALTH CONSEQUENCES OF MARIHUANA USE

HEARINGS
BEFORE THE
SUBCOMMITTEE ON CRIMINAL JUSTICE
OF THE
COMMITTEE ON THE JUDICIARY
UNITED STATES SENATE
NINETY-SIXTH CONGRESS
SECOND SESSION
ON
MARIHUANA USAGE

JANUARY 16 AND 17, 1980

Serial No. 96–54

Printed for use of the Committee on the Judiciary

ticular. The hearings on marijuana use and the refugee crisis are examples of the committee's oversight and investigation activities. The Federal Judiciary Committee also screens nominations for federal judgeships and law-enforcement appointments requiring Senate confirmation.

At the end of the process, most public policies involving money, including a national health insurance bill, must proceed through the money committees, the members of which enjoy "the power of the purse." The Rules Committee members must decide whether to report the authorization bill or not and, if requested, must decide again on the appropriations and revenue bills. Rules Committee members also set the terms for floor debates and the permissibility of floor amendments on any bills they report. While the national health insurance example is hypothetical, it emphasizes the centrality of these three House and two Senate committees.

Committee appointment procedures. House and Senate members' fortunes are closely tied to the committee assignments they receive. Generally, legislators prefer seats on one of the preeminent committees. Secondarily, they may also seek appointments to committees whose substantive concerns are related to their respective constituents' interests. The importance of committee assignments to House and Senate members should not be underestimated. Even those assigned to committees of little substantive connection with their constituents' interests use their positions to advantage. For example, one Brooklyn congressman who was assigned to the Agriculture Subcommittee of the House Appropriations Committee was at first angered by what appeared to be a nonsensical assignment. He eventually exploited this appointment by becoming an expert on Food Stamps and other agriculture-related programs of interest to his district.[23]

Legislators try to extract constituency benefits from their committee assignments. For example, the locations of urban renewal programs were shown to be sensitive to whether a district's representative sits on the House Banking and Currency Committee.[24] Now called the Banking, Finance, and Urban Affairs Committee, its members are responsible for urban renewal programs. While committee members made up 5 percent of House membership during the period studied, their districts received 9 percent of all urban renewal projects and 10 percent of all expenditures for urban renewal. In three other public policy areas—military employment, water and sewer grants, and model cities grants—"Depending on the program, between 10 and 30 percent of [bureaucrats'] allocational decisions may be adjusted in accordance with particular congressmen's preferences."[25] Figures 9.3a and 9.3b show the extensive positive effects that Armed Services Committee membership exerts on military employment in a representative's district.

---

[23] As reported in Richard F. Fenno, Jr., *The Power of the Purse: Appropriations Politics in Congress* (Boston: Little, Brown, 1966), pp. 215–219.

[24] Charles R. Plott, "Influences of Decision Processes on Urban Renewal" (Ph.D. dissertation, University of Virginia, 1966). See also Plott, "Some Organizational Influences on Urban Renewal Decisions," *American Economic Review,* 58 (May 1968), pp. 306–321.

[25] R. Douglas Arnold, *Congress and the Bureaucracy: A Theory of Influence* (New Haven, Conn.: Yale University Press, 1979), p. 214.

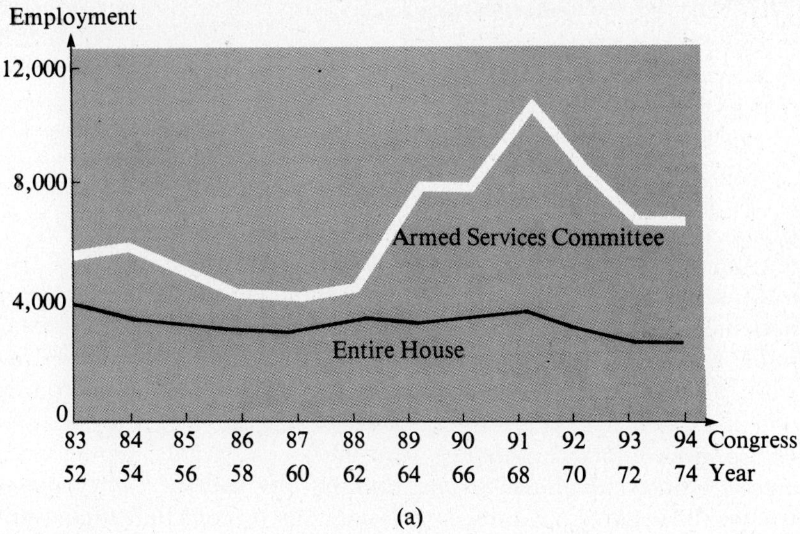

(a)

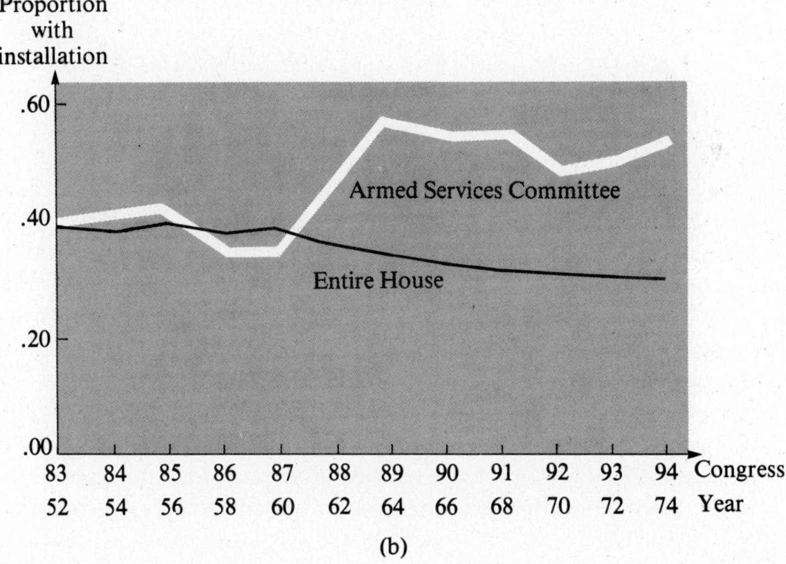

(b)

Figure 9.3 (a) Mean Army and Air Force employment for congressional districts with representative on Armed Services Committee, 1952–1974. (b) Proportion of congressional districts with representative on Armed Services Committee with at least one Army or Air Force installation, 1952–1974.

Source: R. Douglas Arnold, *Congress and the Bureaucracy: A Theory of Influence* (New Haven, Conn.: Yale University Press, 1979), p. 105.

Members request assignments, but because they are competing for the scarce resources that assignments represent, conflicting preferences and demands for committee positions constantly arise. As a result, the members of each party in the Congress have developed elaborate committee assignment procedures to reduce the otherwise inevitable conflict over committee positions. Before 1974, the Democratic members of the House Ways and Means Committee made Democratic committee assignments; since 1974, the members of the Democratic Steering and Policy Committee have assigned members to committees with the approval of the Democratic Caucus. The speaker of the House, if a Democrat, names Democratic members to the House Rules Committee. In the Senate, the Democrat Steering Committee members make committee assignments with the approval of the Senate Democratic Caucus.

House Republicans use a Committee on Committees to make committee assignments. The Republicans in each state delegation appoint one member to their Committee on Committees, who has as many votes as the state has Republican House members. Senate Republicans use the same committee appointment procedure as do Senate Democrats, except that their ratifying body is the Republican Conference rather than the Democratic Caucus. Party leaders in the Senate appoint the members of their respective Steering committees.

Committee appointment characteristics. The actual appointment process is highly complex.[26] The leaders of each party in each chamber agree on the respective party division in each committee. After that, the committee assignments of each party member become a party matter. Certain rules of assignment usually seem to be followed in requesting and granting committee positions, however. First, returning members enjoy an implied property right in their assignments of the previous Congress. They may exercise this right or give it up to request assignments on other committees. Second, an informal seniority rule operates to decide between claimants to the same committee seat. **Seniority** refers to the number of terms a member has been in the office. For instance, a representative with five consecutive terms is senior to one with four. But, seniority ends with a break in service, though a newly elected representative with a previous (nonconsecutive) term is senior to one without prior service. Former holders of other public offices, such as governorships, also receive priority.

---

[26] The standard work on this subject is Nicholas A. Master, "Committee Assignments in the House of Representatives," *American Political Science Review,* 55 (June 1961), pp. 345–357. Some recent works using a rational choice perspective are David W. Rohde and Kenneth A. Shepsle, "Democratic Committee Assignments in the House of Representatives: Strategic Aspects of a Social Choice Process," *American Political Science Review,* 67 (September 1973), pp. 889–905; Shepsle, "Congressional Committee Assignments: An Optimization Model with Institutional Constraints," *Public Choice,* 22 (Summer 1975), pp. 55–78; and Shepsle, *The Giant Jigsaw Puzzle: Democratic Committee Assignments in the Modern House* (Chicago: University of Chicago Press, 1978).

Third, certain *ad hoc* rules affect seat assignments. In the House, the Appropriations, Rules, and Ways and Means committees are **exclusive committees:** with few exceptions, representatives cannot simultaneously be members of one of these committees and sit on another committee as well. Senate Democratic committee assignments follow the (Lyndon) Johnson rule, by which low-seniority senators get to sit on at least one important committee. Certain regions and state delegations also exercise traditional claims to seats on some committees, if only to maintain regional balance or to protect a substantive interest shared by citizens of the state or region.

These assignment rules and procedures lead to an interesting gaming situation for new representatives. If they ask for positions on preeminent committees, they are likely to be refused and to receive somewhat arbitrary assignments to less important committees instead. Thus, they usually ask for appointments to committees of intermediate importance. But, if all lawmakers followed this strategy for requesting committee assignments, it would pay for a few to ask to sit on preeminent committees. If that is true, then all may decide to ask for prestigious assignments. The decision problem then becomes one of conjectural variation, uncertainty.[27] However, one study develops evidence that members approach the problem of requesting assignments as decision making under conditions of risk: they maximize expected utility.[28]

Committees and seniority. Appointment procedures generate a tendency for preeminent committees to include members more senior than do the less important ones. The exact relationship between committee importance and seniority is not precise. Before the Ninety-fourth Congress (1975–1976), a positive relationship between seniority and committee importance seemed fairly obvious. In the Ninety-fourth Congress, because of the large number of newly elected representatives, the relationship became less clear (although it still remained). This murky trend continued in the Ninety-sixth Congress. Taking representatives' seniority rankings (for example, for the Ninety-sixth Congress 1 is most senior and 54 among Democrats and 35 among Republicans is least senior), the average seniority for Democrats is 35.5 and for Republicans, 21.8. Rules Committee Democrats have an average ranking of 34.6, and Republicans 11.6. The rankings for the Ways and Means Committee are 36 and 18.9, but for the Appropriations Committee they are 28.2 and 15.9. Table 9.4 summarizes these data.

The seniority criterion also strongly influences the appointment of committee leaders. In earlier years, the majority-party member with the longest tenure on a committee automatically became chairman, but in their Caucus meeting, Democrats in the Ninety-fourth Congress changed this procedure and ousted three standing committee chairmen. Today, Democratic

---

[27] I am indebted to Matthew Cohen for describing this game to me. See also Rohde and Shepsle, "Democratic Committee Assignments," and Shepsle, *The Giant Jigsaw Puzzle,* which examines this problem in great detail.

[28] Shepsle, *The Giant Jigsaw Puzzle.*

Caucus approval has grown more important for those nominated to become committee chairmen. But, as the data in Table 9.4 show, seniority still provides a presumptive—though not absolute—right to committee leadership.

Committees, Member Goals, and Public Policy

The committee system in both the House and Senate makes sense from the ordinary perspective of a division of labor. It is especially useful in competing with the executive branch, the president, for control over public policy. Members of a single committee who are personally knowledgeable about a particular subject can efficiently direct staff members and collect information. They can also focus public attention on a problem to balance the president's natural publicity advantage. This was surely true of the Senate Foreign Relations Committee's Vietnam War hearings in the late 1960s and of the various Watergate hearings of 1973–1974. Similarly, committee control of legislative proceedings can offset the chief executive's superior unity of purpose.

Committees have also become personally useful to most members. If bills often die in committee, it is because members want it that way. Constituents and interest-group leaders may place unreasonable demands on legislators, who in the face of these demands can maintain their chances of reelection by submitting a bill that goes nowhere except to a committee instead of filing no bill at all. Of course, committee leadership positions also

Table 9.4 Seniority Data for Preeminent House Committees in 96th Congress, 1st Session, 1979

	Democrats			*Republicans*		
	Average Seniority	**Median Seniority**	**Chairman's Seniority**	**Average Seniority**	**Median Seniority**	**Ranking Minority Member's Seniority**
Appropriations Committee	28.2	26	1	15.9	15	3
Rules Committee	34.6	35	9	11.6	4	5
Ways & Means Committee	36.0	43–44	3	18.9	20	8
Committee on Committees*	24.4	29–30	4	18.6	22	1
Entire House	35.5	44	7.6	21.8	22	7

Source: Compiled from data reported in *Congressional Quarterly Weekly Report,* 37 (January 13 and April 14, 1979).

* Democratic Steering and Policy Committee and Republican Committee on Committees.

enhance a particular member's stature and help his reelection chances. And, the more committees and subcommittees there are, the greater the number of available leadership positions.

The committee system has also helped to create and sustain two informal rules of operation in the Congress.[29] The first of these is **universalism,** which requires that each legislative action include benefits for as many members as possible. The second is **reciprocity,** by which each committee or subcommittee decision is supported, or at least not interfered with, by everyone else. These rules actually represent two symmetrical aspects of the same arrangement. Universalism is the granting of benefits by one subgroup, say a subcommittee, to everyone else. Reciprocity is the granting of jurisdiction over a particular subject by everyone else to the subgroup.

Universalism implies that a bill from a particular committee or subcommittee will reflect the interests of everyone imaginable. But there are two ways to accomplish this near-unanimity. The first is to write bills creating public, nondivisible goods; the second is to write bills creating private, divisible benefits. Plainly, any petition from someone outside a particular committee or subcommittee (or from inside, for that matter) will more likely be granted if there is *quid pro quo* than otherwise. But, as noticed earlier in this chapter, producing public-goods legislation creates no claimable benefits for the petitioner-legislator. Hence, successful external (and some internal) congressional demands on the committees will be for legislation that creates private, rather than non-divisible benefits.

Reciprocity makes universalism possible in committee decisions. For if the members of each committee tried to exercise constantly challenged and unsure control over their respective subject matter jurisdictions, they would have nothing to bargain with in exchange for their universalism. Members could go elsewhere to have their individual demands for private-benefits legislation satisfied. No superior advantage—for example, monopoly control over subject matter—would attach to committee membership, so no one would have an incentive to provide the internally efficient forum for public policy bargains that committees now offer.

In this view, the seniority system becomes crucial for maintaining universalism and reciprocity. Reelection pressures on legislators, both individually and in committees, always seem intense. These pressures would ordinarily lead members to place unreasonable demands on committees, to attack the jurisdictional subject matter control of other committees, and to imperialize through their own committees. Placing the most senior members on the most important committees, and in the chairmanships of other committees as well,

---

[29] This discussion is informed by Morris P. Fiorina, "Legislative Facilitation of Government Growth: Universalism and Reciprocity Practices in Majority Rule Institutions," in Peter H. Aranson and Peter C. Ordeshook, eds., *The Causes and Consequences of Public Sector Growth* (forthcoming), and Barry R. Weingast, "A Rational Choice Perspective on Congressional Norms," *American Journal of Political Science,* 23 (May 1979), pp. 245–262.

diminishes this problem. By their seniority alone, these members prove their relative invulnerability to attack, both in the Congress and in the electorate. (Of course, this invulnerability is not guaranteed, as the 1980 congressional elections so abundantly demonstrated.) Senior members also have comparatively small electoral incentives to imperialize, which otherwise would jeopardize universalism and reciprocity.

The committee system, along with seniority and the informal rules of universalism and reciprocity, appears to be more important in the House than in the Senate, because reelection pressures on House members occur at more frequent intervals. The recent decline of seniority's importance in the House has been partially overcome by rules changes that enlarge the independence of subcommittees and subcommittee chairmen.[30]

House and Senate members thus have succeeded in evolving a system of formal and informal rules and practices that solves their *n*-person prisoners' dilemma. Uncontrolled individual demands by legislators scrambling for reelection would lead to the creation of few divisible constituency benefits. Legislators would simply have far too many opportunities to scuttle each other's programs (bills). Universalism and reciprocity, supported by the committee system and seniority, promote the passage of bills to satisfy nearly everyone's reelection concerns. Thus, House and Senate seats grow in value beyond what their worth would be without these rules and practices.

What about constituents? Of course, they receive the programs their senators and representatives secure, and these programs are widespread. For example, public works omnibus bills were found to benefit between 350 and 400 congressional districts.[31] "The recent 'Park barrel' bill was estimated to have a direct effect on more than 260 districts as well as spillovers into other neighboring districts."[32] Other examples come to mind, including multifaceted tariff bills that provide protection against competition from imports for someone in nearly every congressional district.[33] Even recent tax "reform" acts are virtually crenelated with various exemptions and loopholes to benefit this, that, or the other constituent.

However, as Chapter 6 argues, constituents and interest groups themselves are in a prisoners' dilemma situation. They would often be better off without many of these divisible programs, since the costs of these programs

---

[30] The causes and effects of the 1973 "Subcommittee Bill of Rights" are discussed in Norman J. Ornstein, "Causes and Consequences of Congressional Change: Subcommittee Reforms in the House of Representatives, 1970–73," in Ornstein, ed., *Congress in Change: Evolution and Reform* (New York: Praeger, 1975), pp. 88–114.

[31] John A. Ferejohn, *Pork Barrel Politics* (Stanford, Calif.: Stanford University Press, 1974). As cited in Fiorina, "Legislative Facilitation of Government Growth."

[32] Fiorina, "Legislative Facilitation of Government Growth"; *Congressional Record*, June 26, 1978, pp. H6059–H6073.

[33] The best case study is E. E. Schattschneider, *Politics, Pressures and the Tariff: A Study of Free Private Enterprise in Pressure Politics, as Shown in the 1929–1930 Revision of the Tariff* (Hamden, Conn.: Archon Books, 1963).

sometimes exceed the benefits. This means that the members of Congress have solved *their* legislative prisoners' dilemma while perpetuating the associated dilemma among constituents and interest groups. House and Senate members win reelection term after term for service to their individual states and districts, but public dissatisfaction with the Congress generally grows apace. People do not seem to have made the connection, and cannot yet answer one congressional scholar's question: "If, as Ralph Nader says, Congress Is 'The Broken Branch,' How Come We Love Our Congressmen So Much?"[34]

ROLL CALLS, PARTY, AND REGION

Chapter 5, *first,* considers citizens' preferences for public goods of concern to *all* citizens, and Chapter 6, *second,* examines interest groups' demands for private goods. Chapter 7, in its analysis of candidate strategies, reflects that ordering by first considering elections where public goods are issues and then elections in which private goods are issues. Here, the nature of the legislative process in the House and Senate has compelled us to reverse the order. The legislative provision of private goods has been discussed first, and we can now examine some very broad attitudes among lawmakers as revealed by their roll-call votes. These attitudes, as summarized by various ratings of how legislators vote, tend to measure a conservative-liberal dimension much like the one depicted in Figure 5.24 in Chapter 5. Hence, these ratings also reflect legislators' general attitudes toward public goods such as defense spending and law enforcement. These attitudes vary systematically across legislators as a function of their background characteristics.

Party identification and roll-call votes. A pronounced and general consistency appears between legislators' party memberships and their other activities, including roll-call votes on bills. For example, Americans for Democratic Action (ADA), a very liberal organization made up mostly of Democrats, each year checks several recorded roll-call votes and rates House and Senate members according to how they voted. For instance, in 1978 House ADA roll calls included votes on a new consumer protection agency, on a constitutional amendment granting House and Senate representation to Washington, D. C., and on a full employment act. ADA supported all three. In 1978, ADA chose nineteen such Senate and twenty House roll-call votes on which to base its ratings.

Table 9.5 shows the results for all roll calls on all ADA-rated votes. In the House, Democratic legislators are two-and-a-half times more likely to vote for ADA supported—liberal—legislative positions than are their Republican

[34] Richard F. Fenno, Jr., "If, as Ralph Nader Says, Congress Is 'the Broken Branch,' How Come We Love Our Congressmen So Much?" in Ornstein, *Congress in Change,* pp. 277–287.

Table 9.5 Roll-Call Votes in Agreement with ADA Positions, 95th Congress, 2nd Session, 1978

	House	Senate
Northern Democrats	61.5%*	67.6%
Southern Democrats	30.5%	32.2%
All Democrats	52.0%	57.0%
Republicans	20.6%	30.2%
Entire Chamber	41.3%	46.7%

Source: Compiled from data reported in *Congressional Quarterly Weekly Review,* 37 (June 2, 1979).

* Percentages are calculated by summing all Democratic members' votes *for* all ADA positions and dividing by all Democratic members' votes for *and* against ADA positions. Other entries are computed in a similar manner.

counterparts. In the Senate, roll-call votes in support of ADA positions are a little less than two times greater among Democrats than among Republicans.

Region. A second variable that affects roll-call voting is the lawmaker's region. Table 9.5 shows this influence, as well as the effects of party, quite explicitly. While Republicans in each chamber vote more conservatively than Democrats, the degree of voting in support of ADA positions varies markedly. In particular, southern Democrats seem much closer to Republicans than to the rest of their party.

Figures 9.4a–d show Americans for Constitutional Action (ACA) ratings of House members in 1978 (ACA is a conservative counterpart to ADA). Ratings are based on percentage agreement with ACA positions on various roll-call votes, but unlike ADA ratings, ACA ratings do not penalize representatives for abstaining. Interestingly, the House itself is roughly bimodally distributed. However, Republicans and northern Democrats are roughly unimodally distributed toward the ends of the implicit issue dimension, which (as noted earlier) may tap some measure of liberalism-conservatism. As becomes evident in a moment, the relative conservatism of southern legislators has been an important determinant of public policy.

Other factors. The occupational backgrounds of party members also differ, as Table 9.6 reports. Republicans in both houses are slightly more likely than Democrats to be farmers or to have worked in business or banking. Similarly, race and religion correlate with congressional party membership. Jews and Catholics are proportionately more likely to be found among Democratic than among Republican House and Senate members. What influence such factors as occupation and religion have on roll-call voting or on other congressional actions remains unclear. However, the pronounced tendency of lawyers to run for Congress seems apparent.

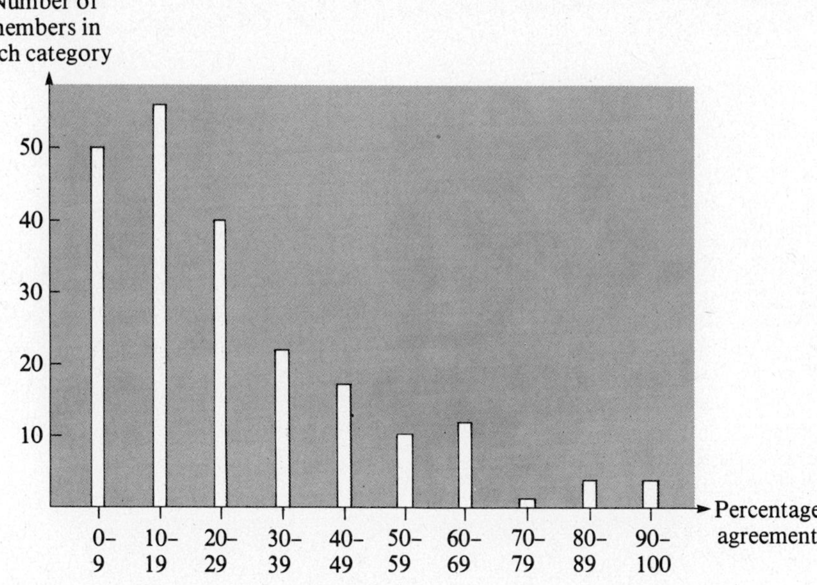

(a)

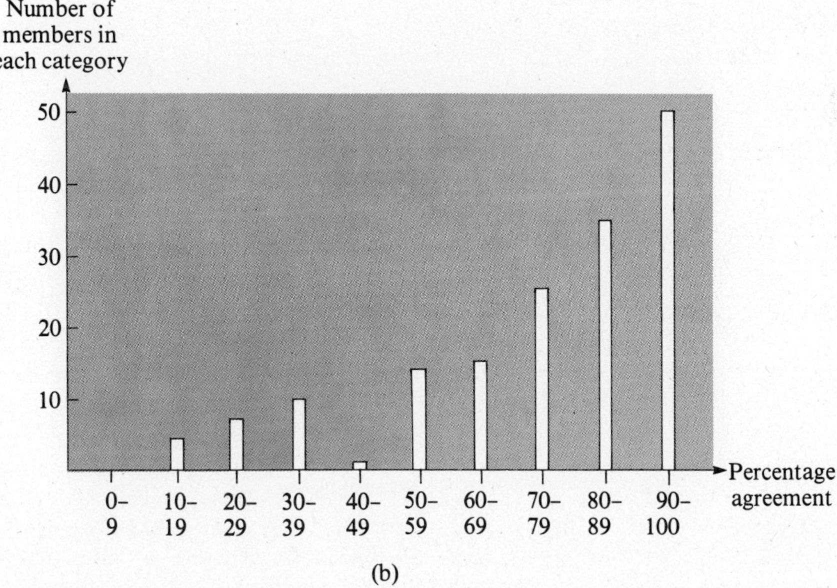

(b)

Figure 9.4 (a) Percentage roll-call vote agreement with ACA positions, House northern Democrats, 95th Congress, 2nd session, 1978. (b) Percentage roll-call vote agreement with ACA positions, House Republicans, 95th Congress, 2nd session, 1978.

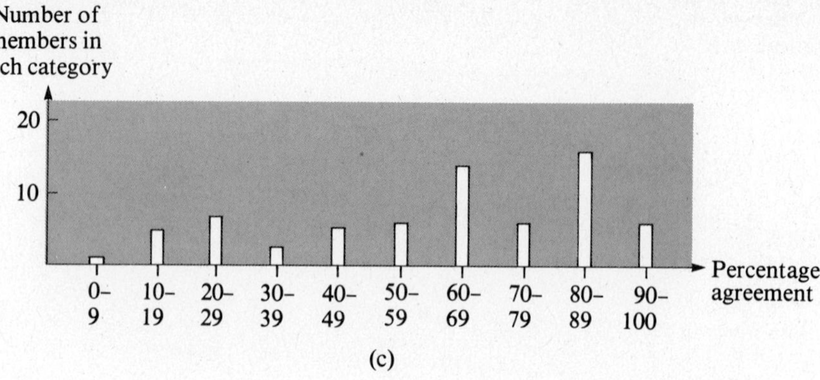

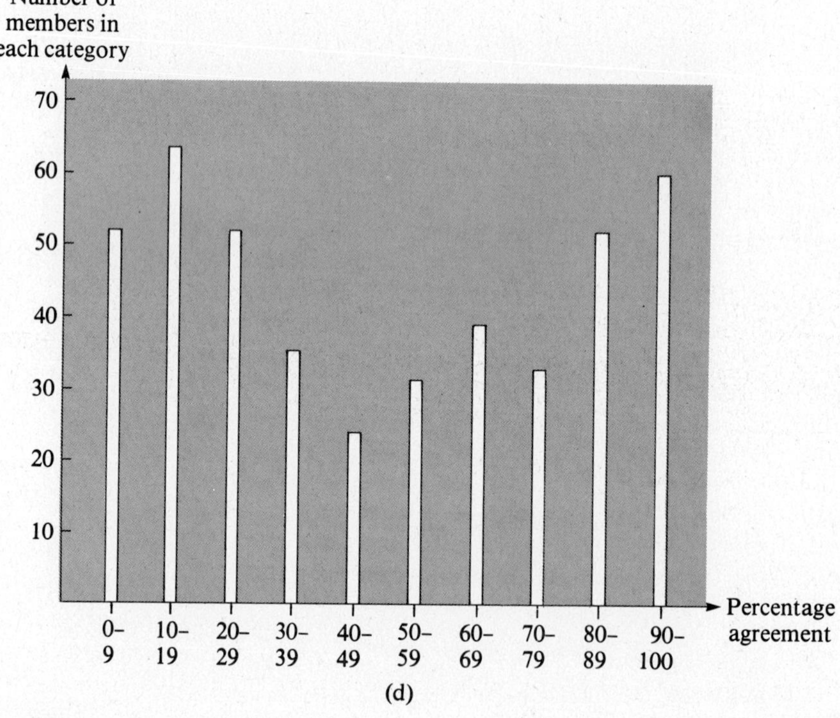

Figure 9.4—*Cont.* (c) Percentage roll-call vote agreement with ACA positions, House southern Democrats, 95th Congress, 2nd session, 1978. (d) Percentage roll-call vote agreement with ACA positions, entire House of Representatives, 95th Congress, 2nd session, 1978.

Source: Computed from data reported in *Congressional Quarterly Weekly Report,* 37 (June 2, 1979).

Table 9.6 Previous Occupations of Members of Congress, 96th Congress, 1st Session, 1979

	House		*Senate*	
	Democrats	**Republicans**	**Democrats**	**Republicans**
Agriculture	3.3	4.9	2.7	8.0
Business or Banking	23.5	30.6	20.0	28.0
Educator	14.6	7.1	5.3	6.0
Engineering	0.0	1.1	0.0	0.0
Journalism	2.0	2.7	2.7	0.0
Labor Leader	1.0	0.5	0.0	0.0
Law	44.7	38.3	57.3	44.0
Law Enforcement	1.3	0.5	0.0	0.0
Medicine	0.3	2.7	1.3	0.0
Public Service/Politics	7.3	10.4	9.3	10.0
Clergyman	1.3	1.1	0.0	2.0
Scientist	0.7	0.0	1.3	2.0

Source: Computed from data reported in *Congressional Quarterly Weekly Report,* 37 (January 20, 1979), p. 81.

The conservative coalition. The configuration of party and region in the Congress has led in past years to the formation of a **conservative coalition** made up of Republicans and southern Democrats, who joined together to prevent the passage of many laws concerning civil rights and government intervention in economic matters. While some bills passed even with conservative-coalition opposition, many of these bills were far less extensive than their supporters had wished, since they had to be watered down to attract the votes of a few conservative-coalition members. The conservative coalition is interesting because it demonstrates the weakness of congressional party (especially Democratic) unity, it shows the importance of seniority, and it reveals some interesting properties of congressional public policy formation. The effectiveness of conservative-coalition members resulted from their voting strength and from the committee and seniority systems.

Southern House and Senate members gained comparatively more seniority than others by enjoying relatively less two-party competition in their states and districts. The result was a presumptive claim on committee leadership positions by southerners, in greater proportion than their numbers would warrant. For example, in 1973 southerners made up 28.6 percent of House Democrats but held 38.5 percent of House committee chairmanships; that same year they made up 25.9 percent of Senate Democrats but held 47.1 percent of Senate committee chairmanships. The committees that conservative-coalition members chaired were also the most important in the Congress. For instance, in 1973–1974, the chairmen of the House Appropriations and Ways and Means committees were both southerners. In the Senate, Appropriations and Finance committee chairmen were also southerners.

Thus, before 1975 southerners enjoyed substantial control over the power of the purse.

Of course, that control has weakened with the loss of the chairmanships of the House Ways and Means Committee and the Senate Appropriations Committee. More generally, as Figure 9.5 shows, the *proportion* of southerners among congressional Democrats has declined markedly in recent years. (Chapter 8 discussed this decline in connection with the Voting Rights Act of 1965.) The results for committee leadership positions are most pronounced. Figure 9.6 illustrates the percentage of times House and Senate committee chairmen voted and are expected to vote in the future with the conservative coalition on roll-call votes. The *projected* decline is substantial, especially among Senate committee chairmen. In sum, conservative-coalition members

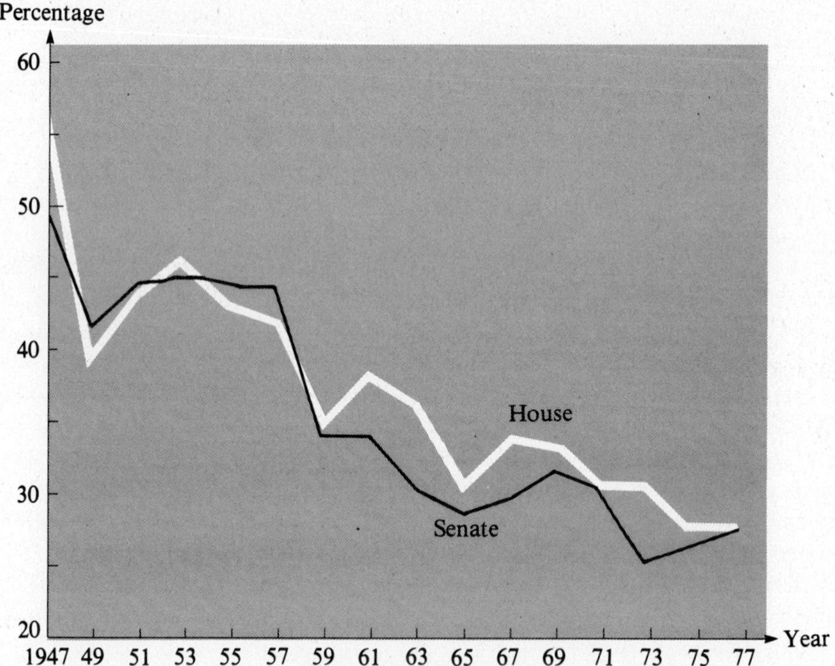

Figure 9.5 Proportion of southerners among congressional Democrats, 1947–1977.

Source: Norman J. Ornstein and David W. Rohde, "Seniority and Future Power in Congress," from *Congress in Change: Evolution and Reform,* edited by Norman J. Ornstein. Copyright © 1975 by Praeger Publishers, Inc. Reprinted by permission of Holt, Rinehart & Winston, p. 74; as updated in Samuel C. Patterson, "The Semi-Sovereign Congress," in Anthony King, ed., *The New American Political System* © 1978 by American Enterprise Institute for Public Policy Research, Washington, D.C., p. 462.

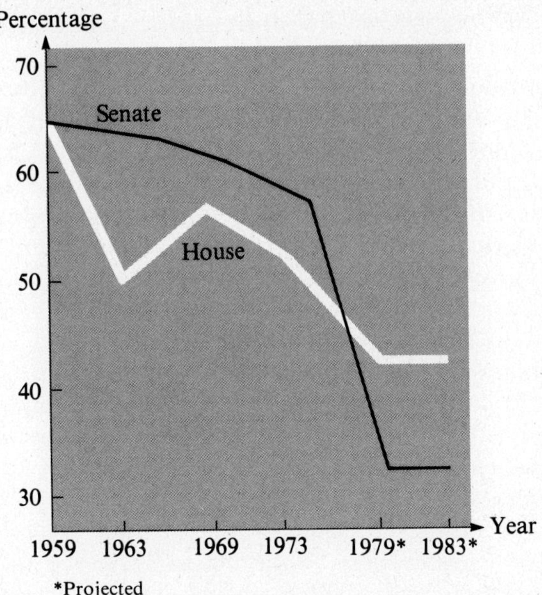

Figure 9.6 Mean (average) conservative coalition roll-call voting support percentages of committee chairman, 1959–1983.

Source: Norman J. Ornstein and David W. Rohde, "Seniority and Future Power in Congress," from *Congress in Change: Evolution and Reform,* edited by Norman J. Ornstein. Copyright © 1975 by Praeger Publishers, Inc. Reprinted by permission of Holt, Rinehart & Winston, p. 80.

have lost ground in their attempts to control public policy emerging from the Congress. If anything, after 1974 congressional control passed to the members of a liberal coalition within the Democratic party. This coalition's major problem was unity among its members. With the Republican presidential and and Senate victories of 1980, however, the conservative coalition will probably grow stronger again, as many southern Democrats try to deal with the Republican leadership.

OTHER CONGRESSIONAL ACTIVITIES

This chapter pays closest attention to congressional rules, procedures, and preferences as they apply to formal lawmaking. However, the members of Congress do many other things besides making laws, and most of these other activities usually have some effect on public policy. These include Senate **advice and consent** on treaties and presidential appointments, congressional **oversight** and **investigation,** and **impeachment.** Congressional ombudsman activities were discussed earlier in this chapter and are referred to again in Chapter 11.

Approval of Presidential Appointments

The Constitution specifies in Article 2, Section 2 that the president "shall nominate, and by and with the Advice and Consent of the Senate, shall appoint Ambassadors, other public Ministers and Consuls, Judges of the Supreme Court, and all other Officers of the United States, whose Appointments are not herein otherwise provided for, and which shall be established by law; but the Congress may by Law vest the Appointment of such inferior Officers, as they may think proper, in the President alone, in the Courts of Law, or in the Heads of Departments."

The importance of appointments. The appointment process bears a crucial relationship to public policy because, as Chapters 11 and 12 reveal, many of the people presidents nominate and senators confirm fill positions that allow them to make or implement public policy. Chapter 11 points out that while the members of the independent regulatory agencies are supposed to implement and execute acts of Congress, these people also make public policy based on their own preferences and intentions. Chapter 12 shows that Supreme Court justices as well as the members of lower courts are themselves often in the business of lawmaking and regulating; they can declare acts of Congress unconstitutional and can prescribe what public policy will be. Judicial activities in civil rights and civil liberties are obvious examples of legislation.

Many presidential appointees hold office through several presidencies. Supreme Court justices and judges of other federal courts "shall hold their Offices during good Behaviour," which usually means that justices serve as long as they desire. Other presidential appointees serve for specified terms. For example, governors of the Federal Reserve Board serve fourteen-year terms, and their influence on public policy is extensive.

Nevertheless, even those appointed only for the tenure of a given president can strongly influence public policy. Former Secretary of State Henry Kissinger is a good example, as is former Secretary of Defense Robert McNamara. Senators understandably do not take their place in the appointment procedure lightly. The importance of these appointments generates considerable political acitivity in the Senate, and opportunities to extract presidential concessions in exchange for approval of a controversial nomination are seldom overlooked.

The politics of appointments. The right to make appointments represents an important resource for most presidents. Appointments allow them to give voice to a particular view of public policy. For example, President Carter in 1977 and again in 1979 appointed monetary conservatives to head the Federal Reserve Board. This strategy helped to strengthen the dollar in international markets. In 1980 he appointed Senator Edmund S. Muskie to fill Secretary of State Cyrus Vance's position, which signaled toughness toward the Soviet Union and shored up the prestige of the Carter cabinet. (Some commentators also believed that Carter appointed Muskie to remove him from contention as a potential opponent in Carter's renomination bid.) Presidents usually appoint or nominate someone who shares their ideologies, but occasionally a nominee's views seem to change upon taking office. Presidents can also use nominations to gain electoral support, even if the nominations fail in the Senate. One example of this strategy is President Nixon's Supreme Court nominations of Clement Haynsworth and Harold Carswell. Both nominations failed in the Senate, but Nixon did not lose, for he had kept his promise to nominate southerners to the Court. The onus of failure fell on liberal Democratic senators. Appointments are also useful in paying off campaign workers and supporters. Patronage appointments remain numerous and important despite civil-service reforms dating from the turn of this century.

Senators consider presidential nominations in much the same way they consider bills. A nomination goes to the most relevant substantive committee. For instance, the nomination of an attorney general or of a Supreme Court justice goes to the Senate Judiciary Committee, while the nomination of a secretary of state goes to the Senate Foreign Relations Committee. First, the committee members conduct hearings, interviewing the nominee and others who have an interest in the matter. Second, they report to the full Senate on the nomination, either favorably or unfavorably. Third, the senators then vote on the nomination.

Senators use several criteria in their confirmation decisions. Many federal government officers serve in a particular state. If the president and one senator of that state are of the same party, the president must clear a nomination with him. This practice, which is all but binding, is known as **senatorial courtesy.** Senators usually try to apply minimum standards of competence, honesty, and impartiality. For example, Lyndon Johnson's nomination of Abe Fortas to be chief justice of the Supreme Court failed because of alleged conflicts of interest. Carswell and Haynsworth were attacked for their "racial insensitivity." More recently, President Carter's nomination of Thomas Bertram Lance to be director of the Office of Management and Budget (OMB) raised concern because of alleged overdrafts, manipulation of loan collateral, and loans in excess of $4 million that Lance's bank made to Carter's business interests. Lance eventually resigned from OMB under pressure, but in a trial that followed he was not convicted of any wrongdoing. Carter's nomination of Griffin W. Bell as attorney general brought forth objections because of his membership in social clubs that excluded blacks and Jews.

Senators apply political and ideological standards in their confirmation decisions. Interest-group leaders often pay close attention to the nominee's record both in and out of government. Senators try to respect the opinions of those leaders in confirmation hearings. Frequently, if the objections to a nomination are over public policy, opposed senators will go even further than usual into the nominee's background in search of other grounds for rejection.

Treaties

Article 2, Section 2 of the Constitution specifies that the president "shall have Power, by and with the Advice and Consent of the Senate, to make Treaties, provided two thirds of the Senators present concur. . . ." Treaties with other nations proceed through the Foreign Relations Committee. They are important not only because they affect international relations but also because they affect domestic matters and are the law of the land.[35] Modern presidents have come to use executive agreements more often than treaties. These are like treaties except that they do not require the advice and consent of the Senate. Often, though, executive agreements receive congressional approval as with other bills and resolutions. But the use of executive agreements is said to diminish congressional control of foreign affairs.

Tensions between presidents and Senate members over foreign policy questions seem commonplace. Chapter 10 explains why presidential autonomy in this area might often be desirable. But senators do have the right to advise and consent, and they cannot be expected to abdicate such a right willingly. Presidents with some sophistication in foreign *and* domestic politics try to bring Foreign Relations Committee senators into the treaty formation process. Otherwise, senators are handed a *fait accompli* to ratify, which is something they strongly resent. Woodrow Wilson failed to get Senate approval for United States membership in the League of Nations because he excluded senators from treaty deliberations. (They might have opposed him anyway.) Jimmy Carter's protracted problems over Senate ratification of the Strategic Arms Limitation Treaty with the Soviet Union, SALT II, might have partially stemmed from the same source. However, his conflict with the Senate over SALT II became moot with the Soviet invasion of Afghanistan.

Oversight and Investigation

Through committee hearings, House and Senate members can examine the workings of the laws and agencies they create. This is the practice of congressional oversight. Similarly, they can study problems before, during, or even after the consideration of bills, which is called congressional investigation. While the Constitution does not expressly authorize these practices, nevertheless they are "inherent powers" because they provide clear and useful resources for lawmaking.

The relationship between oversight and investigation on the one hand,

---

[35] The matter of how to terminate treaties has not been definitively settled. Toward the close of 1978, Senator Barry M. Goldwater (R-Ariz.) joined with other senators to oppose President Carter's unilateral termination of a United States treaty with Taiwan (Republic of China) upon recognition of the Peoples Republic of China. In December of 1979, the Supreme Court said this was a matter to be settled between the president and the Senate, a ruling that went against Goldwater's position. See *Goldwater v. Carter,* 100 S.Ct. 533 (1980).

and lawmaking on the other, seems obvious. Not so obvious is the strategic nature of oversight and investigation hearings for accomplishing other goals. Senate hearings have become extremely useful vehicles for launching presidential and vice-presidential campaigns. They cost the would-be candidate no money, they appear "apolitical," and news reporters give them extensive coverage. For instance, in 1976 several Democratic senators were mentioned as possible presidential nominees: Bayh (Ind.), Muskie (Me.), Kennedy (Mass.), Humphrey and Mondale (Minn.), Bentsen (Tex.), Jackson (Wash.), and Proxmire (Wisc.). Committee oversight and investigation hearings had been politically useful to all of them. The publicity of investigative hearings eventually led Harry S. Truman and Richard M. Nixon to the White House by way of the vice-presidency.

While publicity during hearings is helpful for election and reelection, hearings can also be an effective device for controlling agency staffs and the administration. Investigatory and oversight hearings "educate" and "propagandize," and in so doing they also mobilize public opinion. However, one major problem is the possibility that committee hearings might lead lawmakers, in their search for publicity or "the facts," to violate the civil liberties of witnesses. As Chapter 10 briefly notes, another problem is executive reluctance to reveal what lawmakers want to know.

Impeachment and Conviction

Constitutional provisions. An impeachment is analogous to an indictment. It is a charge against an officeholder for some offense. It is not a conviction on that offense, and it has no legal effect without a conviction. The Constitution states that "The House of Representatives shall chuse their Speaker and other Officers, and shall have the sole Power of Impeachment" (Article 1, Section 2). Furthermore, "The Senate shall have the sole Power to try all Impeachments. When sitting for that Purpose, they shall be on Oath or Affirmation. When the President of the United States is tried, the Chief Justice shall preside: And no Person shall be convicted without the Concurrence of two thirds of the Members present. Judgment in Cases of Impeachment shall not extend further than to removal from Office, and disqualification to hold and enjoy any Office of honor, Trust, or Profit under the United States; but the Party convicted shall, nevertheless, be liable and subject to Indictment, Trial, Judgment, and Punishment, according to law" (Article 1, Section 3). Finally, "The President, Vice President and all civil Officers of the United States, shall be removed from Office on Impeachment for, and Conviction of, Treason, Bribery, or other High Crimes and Misdemeanors" (Article 2, Section 4).

As Chapter 10 recalls, the members of the House have impeached only one President, Andrew Johnson; by a margin of one vote, Senate members refused to convict him. The members of the House Judiciary Committee approved a report issuing articles of impeachment against President Richard

Nixon. Although a nearly unanimous House accepted the report, this did not constitute a vote of impeachment. All told, there have been twelve House votes to impeach and four Senate votes to convict. Federal judges seem to be a favorite target.

Impeachment and the president. Before the Watergate break-in and the subsequent suppression of evidence about it, most people viewed the impeachment of a president as a near impossibility. Had Richard Nixon not resigned, he would probably have been impeached and convicted. Thus, the right to impeach has grown more important than was formerly believed. Perhaps impeachment and conviction will never be carried out against a president; nevertheless, these remain important congressional rights, because a president must calculate that some actions might result in impeachment and conviction. What those actions are only becomes clear when they are contemplated. Of course, the meaning of "Treason, Bribery, or other High Crimes and Misdemeanors" includes many gray areas of law and of constitutional interpretation.

QUESTIONS FOR DISCUSSION AND REVIEW

1. Suppose that the president and vice-president were elected by the Congress—just as the British Parliament chooses the prime minister—rather than by the electorate through the electoral college. How might public policy be affected? Would logrolling, or the formation of coalitions of minorities, or the absence of pure lawmaking equilibria, or even the public pursuit of private benefits be more or less prevalent? Why?
2. How would public policy be changed if the Senate were abolished and all of its tasks given to the House? If the House were abolished and all of its tasks given to the Senate? Does **bicameralism,** a two-house legislature, as compared with **unicameralism,** a single-house legislature, affect public policy? How?
3. Would Congress work more or less effectively if committees sat as "little legislatures" and were able to pass bills without consent of the House or Senate? Why?
4. Why do members of Congress grant each other universalism and reciprocity but do not extend these courtesies to the president?
5. How would public policy and the day-to-day operation of the House and Senate be changed if members were elected in nonpartisan contests? Why? Would these changes be beneficial? Why? Why not?

6. Would the members of Congress be able to pass bills creating public goods or suppressing public bads if these bills did not also have strong private-goods components? Why? Why not? Which component is more important, the private-benefits component or the public-benefits component? Why?
7. Should a president prefer his party to have a small (minimum winning) majority in Congress or greater than a two-thirds majority? Why?

NEW CONCEPTS AND TERMS

advertising
advice and consent
bicameralism
closed rule
cloture
consent calendar
conservative coalition
credit claiming
discharge calendar
discharge petition
exclusive committee
filibuster
impeachment
investigation
logrolling
open rule
oversight
pocket veto
pork-barrel legislation
position taking
private bill
private calendar
privileged bill
reciprocity
rider amendment
senatorial courtesy
seniority
suspension of the rules
unicameralism
universalism
veto

10

The Presidency

This chapter's principal concerns are with presidential decisions and their effects on public policy. However, focusing directly on these concerns becomes difficult when the object of study is the president. More than other officials, the president often brings together in one person all that citizens believe to be good or bad about their lives, their government, and their politics; their attitudes toward him reflect their satisfactions or frustrations. The unstated relationship that citizens experience between themselves and their presidents can become intensely personal. For instance, after the assassination of John F. Kennedy, many psychiatrists reported a surge in the number of patients suffering from symptoms of deep personal grief, depression, and acute anxiety. More recently, the events surrounding Richard M. Nixon's resignation were said to have caused "a national catharsis."

No president has escaped the acerbity of the most intemperate personal attacks.[1] Whether or not these attacks are deserved, their very existence establishes the psychological centrality of presidents. For example, recall that terrible chant during Lyndon B. Johnson's second term: "Hey, hey, LBJ, how many kids did you kill today?" The lines are frightening if deserved, and

[1] "Every President . . . with but one exception, when he has been in office has been denounced as a despot, a tyrant, a dictator, as one who was using the power of the government . . . to achieve his own personal ambitions. The only President who was not so denounced was William Henry Harrison; he lived only one month after he was inaugurated." Louis Brownlow, *The President and the Presidency* (Chicago: Public Service Administration, 1949), pp. 17–18; as quoted in Marcus Cunliffe, *American Presidents and the Presidency,* 2nd ed., rev. (New York: McGraw-Hill, 1976), p. 163.

disgusting if not. At least Johnson was in good company, for over a century earlier the noted jurist Chancellor Kent, corresponding with Mr. Justice Story, wrote somewhat injudiciously, "I look upon [President Andrew] Jackson as a detestable, ignorant, reckless, vain and malignant tyrant. . . . This elective monarchy frightens me."[2] More recently, former Senator James Abourezk (D-S.D.) called President Carter a "liar" for the latter's alleged role in ending Senate debate over a natural-gas deregulation bill. Senator Ted Stevens (R-Alaska) later questioned the president's emotional health following the shake-up of the Carter cabinet during the summer of 1979. On the other hand, one finds a nostalgic yearning for the return of Kennedy's Camelot and a public adoration of such men as Franklin D. Roosevelt and Abraham Lincoln.

THE PRESIDENT, THE CONSTITUTION, AND PUBLIC CHOICE

Public and private reactions to presidents and their leadership only become important for this discussion if they affect presidents' decisions and others' acceptance or rejection of those decisions. Furthermore, an understanding of presidential decision making must go far beyond purely emotional reactions to consider the opportunities, and obligations and boundaries placed on presidents by the Constitution and by custom.

Formal Rights

The Constitution gives the president a centrality and preeminence in public life and public policy that no other officeholder or collection of officeholders can match. He enjoys a right to act in several areas of national life and public policy making. The most enduring description of those areas divides the president's formal, constitutionally derived rights into five categories: **chief of state, chief executive, commander-in-chief, chief diplomat,** and **chief legislator.**[3]

Chief of state. Most governments have major ceremonial figures. Cities have mayors, states have governors, and nations have presidents, monarchs, and dictators. The chief of state need not govern but may instead occupy a wholly ceremonial position. This is true of the Israeli, Italian, and Indian presidents and the monarchs of Britain and of several other European countries. Israel, Italy, and Great Britain also have prime ministers, who, along with their parliaments, cabinets, and bureaucracies, do the real job of govern-

[2] As quoted in Cunliffe, *American Presidents and the Presidency,* p. 154.

[3] Clinton Rossiter, *The American Presidency,* 2nd ed. (New York: Harcourt, Brace and World, 1960). The following discussion relies on Rossiter's work.

ing. But because the United States has no national officer whose principal duties are ceremonial, these tasks fall to the president.

The Constitution's only explicit provision that presidents should fill a ceremonial role appears in Article 2, Section 3: "[H]e shall receive Ambassadors and other Public Ministers." However, logic dictates that the president would have ceremonial duties even without this provision, for he and the vice-president are the only nationally elected officers in the United States. The president's obvious uniqueness cannot escape the notice of those who wish to associate themselves with the person who is to the American people, as President Taft said, "the personal embodiment and representative of their dignity and majesty."[4] Those who actually get to meet the president seem thereby honored.

The president's ceremonial duties often assume an importance beyond pomp. Such was the case when President Gerald Ford extended an elaborate and extensive welcome to Egyptian President Anwar Sadat during his 1975 visit to Washington, D.C. Ford's gracious hospitality signaled a clear shift in American policy toward Middle Eastern nations—a shift that was less supportive of Israeli interests. A different kind of symbolism attached to Ford's refusal that same year to invite to the White House Soviet dissident and expatriate author Aleksandr Solzhenitsyn, who openly criticized the Ford administration's policy of *détente* with the Soviet Union. Neither President Ford nor Secretary of State Henry Kissinger wished to endanger that policy by extending a White House invitation to such an outspoken and notable Russian opponent of Soviet-American *détente* and of the Kremlin leadership. (After leaving office in 1977, Ford said he regretted his decision not to meet with Solzhenitsyn, however.) President Carter showed no such reluctance to meet with Russian dissidents at the White House, and he used his contacts with them to reaffirm his dedication to the human-rights component of his foreign policy.

While ceremonial duties are costly and time-consuming, most presidents would probably be unwilling to give them up because they help presidents to do so many other things better. Well-planned ceremonial occasions enable presidents to signal threatened policy changes without actually executing them, a tactic that is especially important in foreign policy. A president may not wish to break a treaty or cause an international incident or realignment; he may want merely to express his displeasure with a particular foreign leader without explicitly saying so. A meeting with that leader's adversary, either foreign or domestic, along with a full-course banquet, often can convey such displeasure without a break in relations. Hence, ceremonial duties can effectively expand a president's available strategies, especially those required of him as chief diplomat.

If a president is popular in a given congressional district, he can use his popularity to gain its representative's support for his administration's legisla-

[4] As quoted in Rossiter, *The American Presidency,* p. 18.

tive program. He need only appear in the district for highly visible ceremonial occasions during which he praises the representative, who usually takes pains to sit on the same platform. Chief-of-state activities thus are an asset to the president as chief legislator.

A president can also use ceremonial occasions to claim credit for various public policies. If he dedicates a new dam or highway or school building, he simultaneously emphasizes his involvement in supporting the project. Bill-signing ceremonies have little meaning other than to take and distribute credit (as well as pens); the electorate sits as an audience. Thus, the president can use his position as chief of state to remain chief of state.

Chief executive. The president's position as chief executive derives concretely from the Constitution, which grants him a capacity unmatched in any western democracy. Article 2 states that "The executive Power shall be vested in a President of the United States." With "the Advice and Consent of the Senate," the president also appoints "public Ministers and Consuls . . . and all other Officers" not mentioned in the Constitution. The members of Congress "may by Law vest the Appointment of such inferior Officers, as they think proper, in the President alone. . . ." Further, the Constitution grants the president the right "to fill up all Vacancies that may happen during the Recess of the Senate, by granting Commissions which shall expire at the end of their next Session." The president "may require the Opinion, in writing, of the principal Officer in each of the executive Departments, upon any Subject relating to the Duties of their respective Offices. . . ." As a result of these provisions, the president today exercises varying degrees of control over an executive branch of some 2.8 million persons, not including civilian and military defense personnel. (The comparable figures for the legislative and judicial branches of the national government are about 35,000 and 9000, respectively.)

As Chapter 11 points out, the members of Congress cannot possibly legislate American public policy to the last detail. The laws they pass include general directions about goals but seldom specify exactly what is to be done. Therefore, these laws almost always authorize the president to appoint people, who appoint people, who appoint people . . . to execute the laws. Hence, executive-branch personnel must promulgate and enforce rules and regulations in keeping with and in execution of the laws that the members of Congress pass and the president signs. Furthermore, if the provisions of two or more laws conflict or if limited budgets do not permit the complete enforcement of all provisions of all laws, these people must also make judgments as to which law or provision has priority.

Presidential appointees are also a major source of information for the members of Congress in their activities of oversight, investigation, and law-making. Therefore, a chief executive who successfully controls his appointees not only can affect the manner in which the laws are executed, but also can shape the kinds of laws the members of Congress pass. However, as Chapter

presidential documents

Title 3—The President

[3195-01]

Executive Order 12044 **March 23, 1978**

Improving Government Regulations

As President of the United States of America, I direct each Executive Agency to adopt procedures to improve existing and future regulations.

SECTION 1. *Policy.* Regulations shall be as simple and clear as possible. They shall achieve legislative goals effectively and efficiently. They shall not impose unnecessary burdens on the economy, on individuals, on public or private organizations, or on State and local governments.

To achieve these objectives, regulations shall be developed through a process which ensures that:

(a) the need for and purposes of the regulation are clearly established;

(b) heads of agencies and policy officials exercise effective oversight;

(c) opportunity exists for early participation and comment by other Federal agencies, State and local governments, businesses, organizations and individual members of the public;

(d) meaningful alternatives are considered and analyzed before the regulation is issued; and

(e) compliance costs, paperwork and other burdens on the public are minimized.

SEC. 2. *Reform of the Process for Developing Significant Regulations.* Agencies shall review and revise their procedures for developing regulations to be consistent with the policies of this Order and in a manner that minimizes paperwork.

Agencies' procedures should fit their own needs but, at a minimum, these procedures shall include the following:

(a) *Semiannual Agenda of Regulations.* To give the public adequate notice, agencies shall publish at least semiannually an agenda of significant regulations under development or review. On the first Monday in October, each agency shall publish in the FEDERAL REGISTER a schedule showing the times during the coming fiscal year when the agency's semiannual agenda will be published. Supplements to the agenda may be published at other times during the year if necessary, but the semiannual agendas shall be as complete as possible. The head of each agency shall approve the agenda before it is published.

At a minimum, each published agenda shall describe the regulations being considered by the agency, the need for and the legal basis for the action being taken, and the status of regulations previously listed on the agenda.

Each item on the agenda shall also include the name and telephone number of a knowledgeable agency official and, if possible, state

As chief executive, the president may order changes in the procedures of various federal agencies and bureaus. This page from the *Federal Register* records one of President Carter's attempts to affect federal regulatory actions.

11 observes, executive-branch members—including many bureaucrats—sometimes hold preferences that differ from the president's, so the president as chief executive is limited by the independence of his own cabinet members and of other executive branch officials. Various cabinet shuffles, especially in the Nixon and Carter administrations, attest to the problems of cabinet-member loyalty and independence.

The actions of government bureaucrats figure importantly in the lives of most Americans. If presidents can control those actions, they can also benefit those whose lives are touched by the agencies or departments in question. For instance, a president in firm control of the Department of Agriculture usually has only himself or the weather to blame if House and Senate members from farming states are not part of his legislative coalition. Thus, the president's performance as chief executive can affect his success as chief legislator. Similarly, his relations with the State Department, another government bureau, affect how successfully he accomplishes his goals as chief diplomat.

Commander-in-chief. Article 2 says "The President shall be Commander-in-Chief of the Army and Navy of the United States, and of the Militia of the several States when called into the actual Service of the United States. . . ." The Constitution thus grants the president control over all military forces. Over the years this right has grown to the point where the possibility of thermonuclear war has virtually placed the president's finger on the trigger of total annihilation. While the members of Congress must authorize and appropriate funds for all military programs, as well as declare war, until the 1960s they had been satisfied merely to criticize presidential military decisions. Only recently have they lost some of their reluctance to tamper with the president's control of the armed forces and national defense.

As commander-in-chief, the president exercises control over many important subsidiary questions of public policy. The stockpiling and international trading of strategic materials, such as uranium, petroleum, and chromium, come under his control. High-level technological equipment, such as advanced computers, cannot be sold abroad without presidential approval. During World War I, President Wilson even nationalized the railroads. Yet, the justices of the Supreme Court rejected President Truman's contention that "the authority vested . . . by the Constitution and Laws of the United States" allowed him to nationalize the steel industry to avoid the economic and military damage that he argued would come from a strike.[5] Nonetheless, the president appears to be a dictator in matters of national defense, at least in the short run.

While defense spending is not the largest part of the federal budget, it remains substantial. Defense spending in 1979 was estimated at $118 billion. Veterans benefits accounted for another $19 billion, and interest on the national debt, much of which was incurred to pay for national defense,

---

[5] *Youngstown Sheet and Tube Co. v. Sawyer,* 343 U.S. 579 (1952).

represented yet another $49 billion. The president is as much the chief executive of the Department of Defense as of any other federal bureau. Through the secretary of defense, he can select the locations of airbases and shipyards, divisible benefits about which House and Senate members are vitally concerned. He can thus gain congressional support, helping to accomplish his goals as chief legislator by allocating defense dollars to the "right" congressional districts. Of course, his successes and failures as commander-in-chief also affect his relations with leaders of other nations in his activities as chief diplomat.

Chief diplomat. Article 2 gives the president the "Power, by and with the Advice and Consent of the Senate, to make Treaties, provided two-thirds of the Senators present concur. . . ." Similarly, the president "shall nominate, and by and with the Advice and Consent of the Senate, shall appoint Ambassadors. . . ." The president's agents—ambassadors and secretaries of state—negotiate all foreign agreements, fill all diplomatic posts, and are the principal contacts in all matters of foreign relations. Hence, the president stands at the center of this nation's international relations and conducts its foreign policy.

Controlling foreign policy is important both domestically and internationally. Domestically, international agreements are the law of the land. Because these agreements (for example, trade treaties) concern economic arrangements as well as military ones, the president's decisions as chief diplomat can benefit or harm particular sectors of the economy. President Carter's partial boycott in 1980 of export grain sales to the Soviet Union following that nation's invasion of Afghanistan is a case in point. An adverse reaction quickly spread through Farm Belt states, spurred on by the challenges to Carter's renomination of Senator Kennedy and Governor Brown. (Governor Reagan, too, opposed the embargo.) Carter's embargo on Iranian trade following unsuccessful attempts to have the American hostages released is a second example of how foreign-policy decisions affect domestic commerce.

The members of Congress, particularly senators, try to exercise some control of foreign policy by using the Senate's constitutional authority to advise and consent to treaties, by exercising the power of the purse, and by broadly interpreting the need for congressional declarations of war or congressional approval of any military action short of declared war that the president might order. However, sometimes the president can circumvent congressional authority by forging **executive agreements** with the heads of other nations or by promulgating "doctrines," such as the Monroe Doctrine, concerning Latin America; the Truman Doctrine, concerning Greece; the Eisenhower Doctrine, concerning Lebanon; the Nixon Doctrine, concerning Southeast Asia; and the Carter Doctrine, concerning the Persian Gulf.

The kinds of interactions among tasks that occur with the chief-of-state, chief-executive, and commander-in-chief positions apply equally to the president as chief diplomat. For instance, annual assistance to foreign governments is in the neighborhood of $7.7 billion, most of which buys American goods, which are subsequently shipped overseas. The domestic profit from foreign aid and anticipation of this profit can keep in line a congressman whose district has, say, a tractor factory. After all, tractors are useful for farmers in other countries. Import and export policies concerning tariffs, quotas, and trade agreements, which often represent distinctly divisible, private goods for particular congressional districts, may be as effective as military bases and defense contracts for buying legislative support. In sum, the public good of foreign policy carries a distinctly private dimension.

While the most apparent interactions are between the presidential positions of chief of state and chief diplomat, the most important connections are between the positions of chief diplomat and commander-in-chief. The president's success in negotiating with other world leaders influences the kinds of military preparations and actions that national defense requires, and vice versa. These relationships between diplomacy and military planning are complex because they involve many games with many players—nations. International coalitions may change without warning, and little stability may remain in arrangements based on yesterday's agreements.

Chief legislator. The provisions in Article 1 for veto and legislative recommendation provide the machinery for presidential leadership of the Congress. Difference of opinion in the Congress—a natural result of vastly different constituencies—and the fundamental collective inability of 535 self-interested persons to initiate legislation provide the motivation for that leadership. No public policy matters of substance get through the lawmaking process without some consideration of the president's preferences. He is an important, though not always necessary, member of the coalition that forms to pass or defeat each bill. Even bills that a president might veto are likely to reflect his wishes, for a veto raises the requisite vote in each chamber of the Congress from one-half to two-thirds. It may be easier to compromise with the president over the bill's substance than to achieve a two-thirds vote in each house.

The president is the primary initiator of legislation, and he and his agents are also a fundamental source of information for congressmen concerning most important policy proposals. Thus, he can often substantially alter the shape public policy assumes compared to what legislators would do without his direction and without the information he provides. Congressmen are much like patrons in a new restaurant. The chef—the president—sets the menu, and the patrons—the legislators—have only his word on whether the prime ribs are indeed better than the filet mignon. All of the president's other constitutional rights are helpful in accomplishing his goals as chief legislator. Plainly, though, the relationships between Congress and the president remain reciprocal. The president's success with the members of Congress, and especially with senators in matters of appointment and foreign policy, affect his success as chief executive, chief diplomat, and commander-in-chief.

Informal Rights

While the Constitution gives him broad instruments with which to govern, the president has gained substantial extra-constitutional rights from these instruments and from the accretion of nearly two centuries of custom and necessity. These informal rights have also been divided into five categories: **chief of party, voice of the people, protector of the peace, manager of prosperity,** and **world leader.**[6] Although today one or more of these titles might be disputed, nevertheless their vestiges surely remain and can be quickly reinvigorated.

Chief of party. That the president is chief of his political party follows from his constitutional rights. As chief executive he directly or indirectly appoints the members of his cabinet and the occupants of a few thousand other federal positions. He also appoints the chairmen of his party's national organization. The principal recipients of these appointments are usually his party's faithful and especially his own personal loyalists, for they make up the core of his support. The bases of agreement between the president as political entrepreneur and his supporters are readily discernible: The president grants patronage and provides leadership for certain public policy concerns; his followers supply him with legislative and election votes and with other forms of political support. Though useful, complete issue agreement between presidents and their supporters is not always absolutely necessary.

Members of the president's electoral coalition are usually identifiable at his nomination. Commonly, the nomination of a presidential candidate who can win the general election begins with well-bargained agreements among those who speak for major factions of the candidate's party. The substance of those agreements represents a consensus on the candidate's acceptability and seldom leaves potentially serious conflicts unresolved.[7] While overt evidence of such bargains is sometimes lacking, the failure of candidates who do not enjoy full party support seems all too apparent. As Chapter 7 points out, Barry Goldwater, the 1964 Republican presidential nominee, failed to gain the support of liberal and moderate Republicans; similarly, George McGovern, the 1972 Democratic nominee, could not command the support of moderate and conservative (especially southern) Democrats. Both Goldwater and McGovern met resounding defeat in the general election.

The effects of the failure to make prior stable bargains with party leaders over patronage and public policy can be seen in the political fate of vice-presidents who attain the presidency upon a president's death or resigna-

---

[6] Rossiter, *The American Presidency,* pp. 33–40.

[7] It may be misleading to claim that all major conflicts are resolved. It is more likely that leaders of major factions agree not to let any remaining conflicts interfere with the success of their presidential candidate's campaign.

tion. All earlier bargains made with the former president are terminated, and time does not allow the complete consummation of new ones. Thus, Harry Truman, who succeeded Franklin Roosevelt in 1945, could barely win the 1948 election and did not even enter the 1952 contest. Partially as a result of the Goldwater campaign, Lyndon Johnson's electoral fortunes in 1964 were better than Truman's in 1948, but four years later the former Kennedy vice-president, like Truman, threw in the towel without seeking another term. Gerald Ford, just as Truman and Johnson before him, could put together neither his party nor a winning electoral coalition, so the former Nixon vice-president was not even elected to a full term of his own.

The indifferent political success of vice-presidents who succeed to the presidency suggests that the president's position as chief of party conveys neither instant loyalty nor complete support among followers. Political support results from successful bargaining and does not precede it. However, the president is chief of party for much the same reason he is chief of state: no other person can claim such a widespread constituency. Whether this position carries with it real advantages depends on who the chief of party might be and on what kinds of bargains he can strike, and when.

Voice of the people. The term "voice of the people" at once suggests too much and too little. By one view, the president is "the leading formulator and expounder of public opinion in the United States. While he acts as political leader of some, he serves as moral spokesman for all."[8] Woodrow Wilson echoed this view of the president.

> His is the only national voice in affairs. Let him once win the admiration and confidence of the country, and no other single force can withstand him, no combination of forces will easily overpower him. His position takes the imagination of the country. He is the representative of no constituency, but of the whole people. When he speaks in his true character, he speaks for no special interest. If he rightly interprets the national thought and boldly insists upon it, he is irresistible; and the country never feels the zest for acting so much as when its President is of such insight and character.[9]

Seldom in the history of the United States have presidents found that "no . . . single force can withstand" them or that they are "irresistible." But such moments occasionally do occur at times of great national peril. The wartime speeches of President Roosevelt are one example; such a moment also happened in the midst of the Cuban missile crisis (October 22, 1962), and it is revealing to consider President Kennedy's words on that occasion.

> [L]et no one doubt that this is a difficult and dangerous effort on which we have set out. No one can foresee precisely what course it will take or what

[8] Rossiter, *The American Presidency,* p. 32.

[9] As quoted in Rossiter, *The American Presidency,* p. 32.

> costs or casualties will be incurred. Many months of sacrifice and self-discipline lie ahead—months in which both our patience and our will will be tested, months in which many threats and denunciations will keep us aware of our dangers. But the greatest danger of all would be to do nothing.
>
> The path we have chosen for the present is full of hazards, as all paths are; but it is the one most consistent with our character and courage as a nation and our commitments around the world. The cost of freedom is always high—but Americans have always paid it. And one path we shall never choose, and that is the path of surrender or submission.[10]

Kennedy seemed to embody a president speaking as the voice of the people. A nearly complete national consensus emerged that the Soviet missiles would have to be removed from Cuba, whatever the cost. Kennedy's popularity in the polls, which had been declining markedly in the preceding six months, promptly surged to its earlier high levels. However, beginning in 1966, a similar appeal concerning the Vietnam War was difficult for President Johnson to sustain. By 1972, President Nixon was referring to the American disposition of that same conflict as "peace with honor," which by the days of President Ford's administration had become synonymous with an "orderly withdrawal" of American forces. The final withdrawal was less than orderly.

Today, Kennedy's rhetoric might sound alien. It has been many years since American presidents have spoken of "courage," of "commitments around the world," and of "sacrifice and self-discipline." On those few occasions when presidents since Kennedy have tried such appeals, they have met with increasing popular disbelief, if not outright hostility. For example, in his speech to the nation on July 15, 1979, Jimmy Carter tried to rally public support to fight what he regarded as a national "crisis of confidence." Dependence on the Organization of Petroleum Exporting Countries (OPEC) for imported oil was the real subject of his talk, but he tried to rekindle the spirit that was Kennedy's in the fall of 1962. Carter's popularity momentarily stabilized, yet he could not sustain his advantage. However, five months later he fully reflected the widespread quiet anger and determination of the American people in his words and deeds concerning the Iranian seizure of Americans in the Tehran embassy. His popularity soared in the polls, and the incident probably derailed the nomination campaign of his major opponent, Senator Edward M. Kennedy. Perhaps if the Cuban missile crisis occurred today, an American president could not respond as John Kennedy did but would need a quieter approach. Ronald Reagan's presidency promises to test that view. In any case, the president's strength as voice of the people may be limited by time, by place, by presidential personality and reputation, as well as by what people believe before the president tries to voice their beliefs.

We should not overlook the strategic importance of presidents' speaking

---

[10] As quoted in Robert F. Kennedy, *Thirteen Days* (New York: Norton, 1969), p. 139.

as voice of the people, for presidents can sometimes succeed in telling people what they should believe. A president is often the first elected official to learn about new national problems, issues, and crises. Consequently, he holds a temporary monopoly on information, which sometimes allows him to define an issue, his position on it, and the positions of those who might oppose him. This ability to manipulate citizens' perceptions of public policy issues is substantial. On many issues, the president is not only the voice of the people but also their teacher. The first words they hear about a missile crisis or a new Middle East peace proposal often come from the president or his agents. Regarding complex public policy questions, such as gasoline shortages, inflation, or unemployment, people often look to the president to simplify the problem, to give them an understanding of it, and even to tell them what to believe.

The sturdiness of the president's "bully pulpit," as Theodore Roosevelt called it, may be crucial for carrying out most of his other tasks. For example, House and Senate members respond to public opinion, and the president's ability to form that opinion can often be pivotal to the congressional success or failure of his public policy proposals. The strategy of mobilizing public opinion against a stubborn Congress is a standard presidential ploy. The president's ability to speak as the voice of the people thus undergirds his fortunes in other matters, such as legislation.

Protector of the peace. As protector of the peace, the president is called upon to respond to emergencies and disasters. This authority does not derive directly from the Constitution, but its pedigree shows constitutional ancestry. For, over the years the members of Congress have granted to the president the right to take unilateral action in the face of emergencies and disasters. After storms and earthquakes and during strikes, riots, financial crises, or military attacks, the president enjoys the congressionally granted right to act on his own.

The president's reach as protector of the peace often seems innocuous. No one objects when he sends family or cabinet members to inspect disaster areas and then makes the appropriate declarations, activates the necessary personnel (for example, the National Guard), and provides emergency relief supplies and low-interest government loans for rebuilding damaged homes and businesses. At other times, the president's activities as protector of the peace may be hotly disputed, especially if they invoke presidential prerogatives more closely associated with direct constitutional provisions, such as those of chief executive or commander-in-chief.

For example, the president may act the part of a dedicated statesman by calling labor and management representatives together to settle a violent or economically damaging strike. People might even demand presidential intervention. But if White House negotiations fail, the president probably will receive much of the blame. On the other hand, if the president tries to prod the negotiations along by exerting pressure on one of the bargainers, he

EMBARGOED FOR RELEASE
UNTIL THE PRESIDENT'S SPEECH

MARCH 2, 1978

Office of the White House Press Secretary

THE WHITE HOUSE
FACT SHEET

The President announced today a comprehensive program to reorganize the Federal Civil Service system. The program is designed to improve government performance by establishing (1) genuine merit incentives for federal employees, (2) more legitimate management flexibility in federal personnel matters, and (3) greater protections against political abuse of the civil service.

The reform program includes legislation sent to the Congress today and a reorganization plan to be submitted later this month. The reorganization plan is authorized by legislation enacted in April 1977, and will go into effect unless either House votes to disapprove it within 60 legislative days.

The legislation provides:

1. Measures to increase employee incentives:

   —creation of a new merit-based Senior Executive Service for top government managers;

   —authorization of a merit pay system for about 72,000 managers and supervisors below the Senior Executive Service level;

   —establishment of a fairer, speedier appeals system.

2. Measures to ensure greater management flexibility:

   —modifications in veterans preference provisions;

   —decentralization of personnel management decision-making;

   —expansion of the manager's range of choice in hiring employees;

   —consolidation of the regulations affecting the hiring of state and local employees under grant programs.

This press release put out by the White House Press Secretary on March 2, 1978, illustrates the president's ability to manipulate the presentation of newsworthy information while acting as "voice of the people." Notice the caption at the head of the fact sheet: "EMBARGOED FOR RELEASE UNTIL THE PRESIDENT'S SPEECH." The subject of the fact sheet is federal civil service reform, a matter falling under the president's constitutionally derived authority as chief executive.

might lose that bargainer as a future political ally. Sometimes presidents are forced into these situations, and whether they succeed or fail, the popular expectation that they should be protectors of the peace can be as costly for them to fulfill as not.

Manager of prosperity. The members of Congress have given the president broad controls over American economic life. The president, with the advice and consent of the Senate, appoints the members of the principal economic regulatory commissions and boards; he affects the economic activity of the nation in countless ways; he can even close the banks during financial emergencies. The president and his agents, most notably the secretary of the treasury, negotiate currency exchange arrangements and foreign trade agreements with the leaders of other nations. Through the secretary of commerce, the direction of the Department of Commerce is in the president's hands, and his annual budget message to the Congress sets the agenda for all subsequent economic discussions and debates.

The president's management of the economy is often a no-win situation. During times of economic expansion, there is political credit enough to go around. However, during periods of economic reversals each politician tries to place the blame on everyone else. For example, if inflation becomes severe, the president's congressional opponents might try to give him the right to impose wage and price controls. If he fails to impose these controls, he loses support for failing to act, but if he imposes them, he loses support for being an "economic dictator." Such was the course of events in 1971, when President Nixon imposed wage, price, and rent controls and AFL-CIO president George Meany blasted him for limiting economic freedom. President Ford understandably asked Congress not to give him the right to control wages and prices during his administration. President Carter's "voluntary wage and price guidelines" were also attacked by the AFL-CIO, this time in court. The suit challenged the president's right to deny government contracts to those who did not follow the guidelines. A court of appeals ruling found against the AFL-CIO, and the Supreme Court refused to review the ruling.[11]

That people hold presidents responsible for the state of the economy through retrospective voting is evident in the results of public opinion polls and elections, as Jimmy Carter found out to his dismay in the 1980 presidential election. "Outcomes of national elections, taken as a whole, are partially the product of pre-election changes of ordinary magnitude in national economic conditions, taken as a whole. Short-run changes in real disposable income per capita have had a strong effect on the fortunes of the presidential party in mid-term congressional elections, on-year congressional elections, and presidential elections since 1948. The effect is a strong and persistent one, statistically secure and politically significant."[12] Moreover, "A decline of

---

[11] *AFL-CIO v. Kahn,* 99 S.Ct. 3107 (1979), *cert. denied.*

[12] Edward R. Tufte, *Political Control of the Economy* (Princeton, N. J.: Princeton University Press, 1978), p. 136.

[presidential] popularity of about 3 percentage points is suggested for every percentage point in the unemployment rate over the level holding when the president began his present term."[13] But presidents are not entirely helpless, even in the face of events they cannot completely control. As noted later in this chapter, presidents can and do manipulate economic policy in ways calculated to ensure reelection, if not long-term economic health.

World leader. Plainly, "The President has a much larger constituency than the American electorate: his words and deeds in behalf of our own survival as a free nation have a direct bearing upon the freedom and stability of at least several score other countries."[14] But, while presidents are world leaders, one president may not interpret the mandate of this leadership as does another, and observers of presidents may also differ over what world leadership entails and what it ought to entail.

The line of presidents from Truman to Johnson took world leadership to mean "containing" communism by nuclear armament, "brinkmanship," armed confrontation, and sometimes by limited war. The presidencies of Nixon and Ford stressed negotiation and *détente* more than confrontation. The Carter administration initially viewed the Soviet Union's foreign-policy strategies as less of a threat to American security, but that view changed markedly after the Soviet invasion of Afghanistan. President Carter otherwise formed his world leadership into a concern for how nations treat their citizens. He also used American influence and his personal intervention to try to settle the long-term conflict between Israel and Egypt.

While presidents differ over how to be world leaders, so too do their critics. People disapprove of presidential leadership they believe to be in the wrong direction. For example, the picture of the United States and of its president that emerged from the Korean War was that of the "world's policeman." While the legal characterization of the Korean War as a "police action" probably contributed to this view, nevertheless it seemed accurate. However, by the end of the Vietnam War many Americans had come to reject explicitly this world-leader-as-police-chief mandate of the presidency.

Notwithstanding continuing disagreements over how and whether presidents should be world leaders or not, the debate seems beside the point. Even if presidents were to avoid all possible foreign-policy initiatives, they would find themselves pivotal members of several international coalitions. Some of these are formal, as with the "alphabet" treaty organizations: NATO, SEATO, ANZUS, CENTO, OAS, and OACS. Other alliances are completely informal and may last only briefly, as when the United States and the Soviet Union opposed the invasion of Egyptian territory by Israel, Great Britain, and France during the Suez crisis of 1956.

---

[13] John E. Mueller, *War, Presidents, and Public Opinion* (New York: Wiley, 1973), p. 240.

[14] Rossiter, *The American Presidency,* p. 39.

American presidents must be world leaders whether or not they approve of an aggressive foreign policy. Heads of other nations will demand that presidents honor prior agreements in each new crisis. When presidents choose to take sides, they once again become world leaders. Their position is inescapable, and most presidents welcome it to the exclusion of all other activities. For example, one firsthand observer noted of President Carter, "As he grew more deeply involved in his international human rights campaign, the Panama Canal negotiations, the delicacy of *détente* with the Russians, and, especially, his quest for peace in the Middle East, his efforts on the domestic front suffered from his inattention. Returning from a triumphant journey to Nigeria or Germany, his eyes would noticeably glaze as he forced himself to discuss such a matter as reorganization of the Commerce Department."[15]

Presidential Leadership and Public Choice

American presidents exercise a greater control over American political and governmental processes and over the shape of public policy than does any other person or collection of persons. The scope of presidential decision making from time to time may expand or contract, and the members of Congress and the Supreme Court now and then may constrain a president's programs or thwart the achievement of his goals. However, in the long run, presidential influence on the political process and public policy remains superior.

Limitations on the presidency. Before analyzing the reasons for a president's influence and centrality, it is well for us to pause briefly to list the restrictions on presidential action. For, while presidential "rights" seem comprehensive, nevertheless an account of limitations on the presidency is equally so.[16] These limitations include the Twenty-second Amendment, which allows a president only two four-year terms (provided the voters believe he has earned the second). The independent status of the Congress, the Supreme Court, and several regulatory agencies and commissions provides others with the ability to make decisions beyond the president's control and against his wishes. The members of the Congress can override the president's veto; the members of the Supreme Court can judge his actions unconstitutional or otherwise contrary to law; and, the members of independent commissions and boards can impose policies in direct opposition to his preferences.

The members of Congress enjoy specific rights that limit presidential discretion. As noted earlier, senators in particular must advise and consent to major presidential appointments and to treaties. The enumeration of congressional rights in Section 8 of Article 1, especially the power of the

---

[15] James Fallows, "The Passionless Presidency: The Trouble with Jimmy Carter's Administration," *The Atlantic Monthly* (May 1979), p. 40.

[16] Rossiter, *The American Presidency,* chapter 2.

purse, makes the members of Congress coequal with the president in many policy areas. The threat of impeachment is always present, although as Chapter 9 points out it has only twice been a serious possibility. Finally, the president is limited by the concrete constitutional and common-law rights of other people and by the existence of the federal system. The structure of federalism reserves to state and local governments a degree of self-rule that the president can overturn only with great difficulty, and the body of law protecting private property helps draw a line across which presidents can tread only lightly, if at all.

The general problem of presidential rights. In spite of these limitations, the president's tools of governance and action are as great as can be found in the West. However, disagreement emerges over whether or not presidents should be more or less limited in the scope of their rights. This disagreement is very old, beginning with debates about the "divine right" of kings and finding voice in newly independent America during the Constitutional Convention. According to James Madison's *Journal,* Roger Sherman of Connecticut "said he considered the executive magistracy as nothing more than an institution for carrying the will of the Legislature into effect; that the person or persons ought to be appointed by and accountable to the Legislature only, which was the depository of the supreme will of society. As they were the best judges of the business which ought to be done by the executive department, and consequently of the number necessary from time to time for doing it, he wished the number might not be fixed, but that the Legislature should be at liberty to appoint one or more as experience might dictate."[17] This proposal to have the officer who today is called "the president" appointed from time to time by the Congress, in varying numbers, hardly seemed outlandish in Sherman's day. Some delegates to the Convention feared to make one person the chief executive officer of the government; for example, Edmund Randolph of Virginia viewed a presidency by one person "as the foetus of monarchy."[18]

Alexander Hamilton, on the other hand, had little patience with those who thought "a vigorous executive is inconsistent with the genius of republican government."[19] Hamilton believed that "Energy in the executive is a leading character in the definition of good government," and he advocated not only an energetic executive, but also ample constitutional provisions to exercise that energy.[20] Though they disagreed about the scope of presidential authority, Sherman, Randolph, Hamilton, and others were vitally interested

---

[17] James Madison, *Journal of the Federal Convention,* edited by E. H. Scott (Chicago: Albert, Scott, 1893), p. 85.

[18] Madison, *Journal of the Federal Convention,* p. 86.

[19] Paul L. Ford, ed., *The Federalist* (New York: Henry Holt, 1898), p. 466; hereinafter cited as *Federalist Paper No. 70.*

[20] *Federalist Paper No. 70,* p. 466. See also *Federalist Papers Nos. 67–77.*

in defining the rights and obligations of an office whose occupants they would sometimes want to be effective and strong, and always they would mistrust.

Presidents have also debated the same problem. Theodore Roosevelt and William Howard Taft did much to set the agenda of this debate. Roosevelt's view was that the president could do anything not expressly prohibited by constitutional or statute law. His *Autobiography* argues this position while reflecting on his own presidency:

> I declined to adopt the view that what was imperatively necessary for the Nation could not be done by the President unless he could find some specific authorization to do it. My belief was that it was not only his right but his duty to do anything that the needs of the Nation demanded unless such action was forbidden by the Constitution or by the laws. Under this interpretation of executive power I did and caused to be done many things not previously done by the President and heads of the departments. I did not usurp power, but I did greatly broaden the use of executive power. In other words, I acted for the public welfare, I acted for the common well-being of all our people, whenever and in whatever manner was necessary, unless prevented by direct constitutional or legislative prohibition. I did not care a rap for the mere form and show of power; I cared immensely for the use that could be made of the substance. . . .[21]

William Howard Taft, on the other hand, believed that the president could only take those actions for which the Constitution or an act of Congress gave him a direct right. "[T]he President can exercise no power which cannot be fairly and reasonably traced to some specific grant of power or justly implied and included within such express grant as proper and necessary to its exercise. Such specific grant must be either in the Federal Constitution or in an act of Congress passed in pursuance thereof. There is no undefined residuum of power which he can exercise because it seems to him to be in the public interest."[22]

The two philosophies of the presidency expressed by Roosevelt and Taft have come down to the present day with only modest changes to adjust them to modern circumstances. In the 1950s and 1960s, many academic writers became upset with formal, constitutional limitations on the presidency. They preferred a "strong" president, comporting with Roosevelt's view, to a "weak" one, which Taft's restricted comprehension of the chief executive implied. For, as some believed, "The great Presidents were also strong Presidents, magnifying the executive branch at the expense of other branches of the government. . . . From Washington's time onward, each conceived of the

---

[21] Theodore Roosevelt, *An Autobiography* (New York: Charles Scribner's Sons, 1924), p. 357; as quoted in Sidney Warren, ed., *The American President* (Englewood Cliffs, N. J.: Prentice-Hall, 1967), p. 25.

[22] William Howard Taft, *Our Chief Magistrate and His Powers* (New York: Columbia University Press, 1925), pp. 138–140; as quoted in Warren, *The American President*, p. 26.

office in heroic proportions, and each left it more powerful and influential than he found it."[23]

One perennial student of the American presidency has looked to the office of the presidency itself and bemoaned the president's constitutionally created inability to overcome congressional opposition to his programs. "When the realities of presidential power are examined more closely, they reveal an office far less strong than those who attack it would lead us to suppose."[24] In this view, the American president often cannot command House and Senate members' support of his programs. "The President has no dependable way, as the British Prime Minister does, to command the legislature's support. . . . The likelihood is that a President who seeks important—and therefore controversial—social and economic legislation will face a hard wall of opposition from legislative leaders of his own party. . . . Checks and balances and the President's legislative and party weaknesses affect his other functions. . . . Even where his authority is presumably great, in foreign affairs and as Commander in Chief, the President depends on congressional support."[25]

One cure proposed for this alleged weakness is the simultaneous election of House and Senate members and the president every four years. This change is expected to "produce a President and two houses of Congress in better harmony on party and policy outlook than the present fragmented elections permit."[26] The president would also receive an "item veto," so that he could selectively approve or disapprove of expenditures in any omnibus appropriations bill. Congressional committee chairmen would be chosen by secret ballot, thus further reducing the ability of senior House and Senate members to use their positions to oppose the chief executive's wishes. (This proposal has already been adopted among congressional Democrats.) Also, the Twenty-second Amendment, which now limits the president to two terms, would be repealed.

Students of the presidency are not all of one mind in favoring a stronger president and in endorsing proposals such as these. Some firmly believe that "[t]he chief constitutional value which overextension of presidential power threatens is . . . the concept of a 'government of laws and not of men'—the 'rule of law' principle."[27] In a similar vein, the events following the Watergate

---

[23] Arthur M. Schlesinger, *Paths to the Present* (New York: MacMillan, 1949), p. 105; as quoted in William H. Riker, *Democracy in the United States,* 2nd ed. (New York: Macmillan, 1965), p. 188.

[24] Louis W. Koenig, "More Power to the President (Not Less)," *The New York Times Magazine,* January 3, 1965, p. 7.

[25] Koenig, "More Power to the President (Not Less)," p. 7.

[26] Koenig, "More Power to the President (Not Less)," p. 7.

[27] Edward S. Corwin, "The Steel Seizure Case: A Judicial Brick Without Straw," *Columbia Law Review,* 53 (June 1953), pp. 53–66; as quoted in Richard Loss, ed., *Presidential Power and the Constitution: Essays by Edward S. Corwin* (Ithaca, N. Y.: Cornell University Press, 1976), p. 126.

break-in and the resignation of President Nixon triggered a widespread reconsideration of the desirability of a strong presidency. Earlier disagreements over Lyndon Johnson's handling of the Vietnam War helped to enhance the belief that more restrictions on presidential action might be appropriate. Some scholars now see in these examples a clear signal that strong presidencies easily get out of control. Constitutional law experts have also attacked the notion that presidents and their aides have an "executive privilege" to refuse to cooperate with congressional investigations.[28] Others have drawn back from their earlier adulation of strong presidents such as Andrew Jackson and Franklin D. Roosevelt; they now write of the "imperial presidency" and of the "runaway presidency."[29]

Preferences for presidential action. Rational choice theory can explain differences of opinion over just how strong presidents should be. The source of the preference for a strong or weak president can best be illustrated by working through the most brutal problem imaginable: nuclear warfare. Consider a hypothetical example in which the House and Senate are combined into a one-hundred-member unicameral legislature. Suppose the president and all one-hundred legislators hold identical public policy preferences, that there is no risk or uncertainty involved—their information is perfect—and that each would react as any other to a given situation.

Now, how many of these people should be required to decide whether or not to "pull" the nuclear trigger in response to a Soviet nuclear first strike? Should the president call the members of Congress together to vote by majority rule "to declare War," as the Constitution requires? Nonsense. Very likely none of the lawmakers would survive the first strike. There would be no vote, and therefore our adherence to constitutional strictures requiring a congressional declaration of war would itself greatly reduce any deterrent effects our nuclear arsenal might now have on Soviet military decision makers. Indeed, if the intentions of the Soviet military leadership were actually aggressive, then Soviet knowledge that the legislators must vote to launch a nuclear counterstrike could only serve to encourage a Soviet nuclear first strike. As one summary has it, "[W]ar comes in many shapes and a variety of ways. The Marquis of Queensbury rules do not apply. We have learned that we can be attacked without warning, and [also] that we can slowly move one small step after another into a genuine shooting war before we fully realize what has happened. It is not always possible for a prudent President to wait for a Congressional declaration before he acts."[30]

---

[28] Raoul Berger, *Executive Privilege: A Constitutional Myth* (New York: Bantam, 1975).

[29] Arthur M. Schlesinger, Jr., "The Runaway Presidency," *The Atlantic Monthly* (November 1973), pp. 43–45; see also Schlesinger, *The Imperial Presidency* (Boston: Atlantic Monthly Press, 1974).

[30] Harold W. Chase and Craig R. Ducat, eds., *Edward S. Corwin's The Constitution and What it Means Today* (Princeton, N. J.: Princeton University Press, 1973), p. 83.

The chief consideration in nuclear response is the time it takes to decide to launch a counterattack. Presumably, the more people who are required to vote on this decision, the longer it will take to order the counterstrike. The length of time involved is a measure of cost, and this cost is a decision cost in precisely the way such costs are defined in Chapter 4. *Ceteris paribus,* if one person alone makes the decision to launch a counterattack, the decision costs are minimized.

But, suppose uncertainty enters this scenario, because what appears to be a Soviet attack might possibly be so, or, it might be an attack launched from some other nation, a meteor shower, the individual action of an American or Soviet field commander gone beserk, or a malfunction in monitoring equipment. The uncertainty now introduced greatly complicates the decision problem formerly entrusted to the president alone. Table 10.1 illustrates the president's altered decision problem.

Assume that the president and legislators agree that a counterattack following a Soviet attack and no counterattack in any other situation represent "correct" decisions. An error occurs, first, if the president falsely believes that the Soviets have not attacked and launches no counterattack. An error occurs, second, if he falsely believes that there is a Soviet attack and launches a counterattack against the USSR. Statisticians and decision theorists refer to these errors as type-I and type-II errors respectively. Here, they are referred to simply as Error I and Error II.

Once certainty is removed from the president's decision problem, the legislators' *evaluations* of the president's decision problem will change. A difference of opinion can then emerge that was not present before. Some lawmakers—call them *hawks*—might be somewhat more willing than other lawmakers for the president to commit Error II rather than Error I. Hawks would require the president to have less evidence confirming a Soviet attack before he launched a counterattack. Other lawmakers—call them *doves*—might be somewhat more willing, compared to hawks, for the president to commit Error I rather than Error II. Doves want the president to refrain from launching a counterattack unless he can confidently reject the idea that the Soviets have *not* launched a first strike.

It is in the nature of such decisions that a president can reduce the likelihood of committing Error I only by increasing the likelihood of commit-

Table 10.1 Nuclear Attack Decision Problem

	States of Nature	
President's Strategies	Soviet attack	not Soviet attack
launch counterattack	Correct decision	Error II
do not launch counterattack	Error I	Correct decision

ting Error II, and vice versa. Thus, a new issue dimension emerges along which legislators might array themselves. At one end of this dimension sit extreme hawks, who would pull the nuclear trigger at the first sign of a Soviet attack. At the other end sit extreme doves, who would restrain the president's hand until all possibilities except a Soviet attack have been rejected. Between these two extremes, legislators would position themselves according to the risk they would be willing to accept of making one error rather than the other.

Now, recall that the legislators are unanimous and agree with the president in the case without uncertainty. Here, uncertainty creates a difference of opinion, which injects a new possibility—the likelihood that the president is going to do something the legislator does not want him to do—into each legislator's evaluation of the president's decision problem. Moreover, the trade-off between the probabilities of committing the two kinds of errors might have become an issue in congressional elections. A congressional policy equilibrium might exist on this issue, but given what we know about such equilibria from Chapter 8, it seems highly unlikely that the president's most-preferred position on this issue would coincide with the congressional equilibrium. Thus, the president and the members of Congress would probably be at odds with one another over choosing the "correct" public policy, or trade-off of errors, for deciding to order nuclear retaliation.

To say that a president and a legislator differ over a decision to launch a counterstrike means that the president imposes a cost on the legislator beyond the cost the legislator would impose on himself if the counterstrike decision were his alone to make. This cost is an external cost in precisely the way such costs are defined in Chapter 4. If unanimous consent of the legislature is required to make such decisions, this external cost will be minimized. Under a rule of unanimity, any legislator would have to be compensated for the external cost imposed on him, or else he would not consent to the policy question at hand—in this case, a particular trade-off between the likelihood of committing the two kinds of errors.

When the president faced no uncertainty and when each legislator agreed completely with whatever he chose to do, the only concern was the decision cost. This cost increased as the number of people who must be consulted grew. Decision cost, measured in response time, was minimized by leaving the choice to attack or not entirely in the president's hands. However, the presence of uncertainty appears to tap a previously-undetected source of disagreement. If the president continues to decide alone, an external cost is imposed on anyone who does not exactly agree with him—on anyone who prefers a different combination of probabilities of committing Error I and Error II.

As with most external costs, the level any given legislator can expect is inversely related to the number of legislators the president must consult before he decides to return fire or stand down. This inverse relationship holds because the greater the number of legislators who must give their consent, the greater the likelihood that any given legislator, or another legislator with like preferences, will be among those consulted. And, those whose consultation and consent is required are more likely to be compensated or to experience less external cost from the president's decision.

Estimates about how great the external cost can become relative to the decision cost for any given legislator seem purely speculative. The consensus in the United States today appears to be that as long as there *is* a nuclear trigger, the president's finger and the president's finger alone ought to be on it. Thus, we can reasonably infer that the decision cost and external cost curves look like the ones in Figure 10.1. External cost declines as the number of people who must agree increases, but the corresponding increase in decision cost is great enough to swamp the external cost variations. The curve depicting the summed costs shows that they are minimized if the president alone decides.

While most legislators prefer presidential nuclear autonomy, the introduction of uncertainty, and thus external costs, can lead to perfectly under-

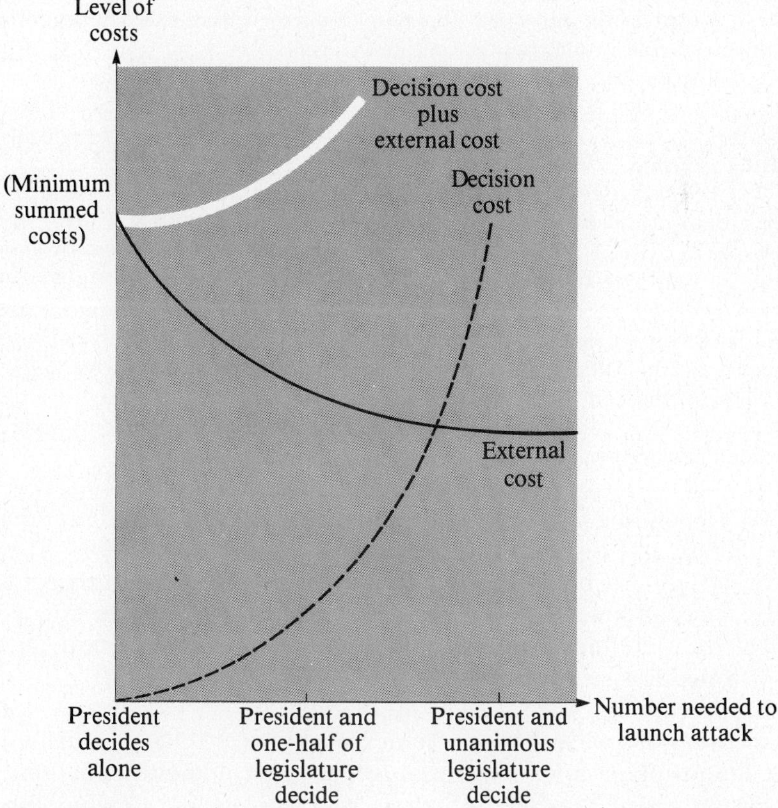

Figure 10.1 Decision cost and external cost for nuclear attack decision problem.

standable legislative actions. The Armed Services committees of the House and Senate will meet in secret sessions to learn how accurate our DEW-Line detection systems really are.[31] Congressional investigators will probe witnesses from the Department of Defense and the White House to find out how the president would, or should, react to this, that, or the other contingency. Whether or not NATO field commanders have the authority to launch a nuclear strike may become a presidential election campaign issue, as it did in the 1964 contest between Barry Goldwater and Lyndon Johnson. House and Senate members may even try to legislate contingency plans for the president to follow in the event of nuclear attack. However, after all is said and done, the president remains the sole decision maker, and only those who oppose a nuclear arsenal in principle would wish to deprive him of this nuclear dictatorship.

In his last State of the Union message (January 12, 1977), Gerald Ford summarized the case for presidential supremacy in military and foreign affairs:

> I express the hope that this new Congress will re-examine its constitutional role in international affairs.
>
> The exclusive right to declare war, the duty to advise and consent on the part of the Senate, and the power of the purse on the part of the House, are ample authority for the legislative branch and should be jealously guarded.
>
> But because we may have been too careless of these powers in the past does not justify congressional intrusion into, or obstruction of, the proper exercise of Presidential responsibilities now or in the future. There can be only one Commander-in-Chief. In these times crises cannot be managed and wars cannot be waged by committee. Nor can peace be pursued by parliamentary debate. To the ears of the world, the President speaks for the Nation. While he is, of course, ultimately accountable to the Congress, the courts and the people, he and his emissaries must not be handicapped in advance in their relations with foreign governments as has sometimes happened in the past.

Ford was responding to limits the members of Congress placed on the president's military and diplomatic discretion during the early 1970s. These included the Case Act of 1972, which requires the president to report to the Congress any agreements he makes with other nations, and the War Powers Act of 1973, which limits presidential authority to commit troops in battle short of a declaration of war.[32]

One recurring fear is that presidential military and international preeminence will spill over into domestic politics. While presidents could muster little support for a dictatorial role in most domestic situations, they have a wide range of discretion short of complete dictatorship. Because

[31] DEW stands for "distant early warning."

[32] These are PL 92–403 and PL 93–148 respectively.

decision costs seem very much smaller in domestic public policy choices than in military and foreign affairs, people disagree as to how extensive presidential control of domestic policy ought to become. Generally, those whose preferences completely coincide with the president's domestic programs are satisfied to grant him a greater control over domestic public policy choices, simply to minimize decision costs, or to block contradictory congressional preferences. But those who oppose most of the president's domestic programs would prefer to shift control to the members of Congress, provided their views are more congenial—would impose a lower external cost—than the president's. The president would then become a congressional errand boy, executing the laws as written.

The interaction of public policy agreement and disagreement, presidential and congressional demands for public policy control, and partisan interests have led to curious but understandable reversals of publicly stated opinions, sometimes bordering on hypocrisy. Both political parties make such reversals. In the 1960s, Republican members of the House and Senate viewed John Kennedy's and Lyndon Johnson's domestic actions as an assault on the Constitution, on the "separation of powers," and on the delicate "checks and balances" among the three branches of the federal government. They insisted on returning public policy control to the Congress. A decade later, many of these same legislators supported Richard Nixon's impoundment of congressionally-appropriated funds and the secret war he ordered waged in Cambodia. Many Democrats who in the early 1960s had celebrated the expansionist presidencies of Kennedy and Johnson and scoffed at Republican cries of alarm now spoke of Nixon's impoundment of funds—something first done by President Thomas Jefferson—as the usurpations of a tyrant.

Clearly, the Vietnam War was a watershed in the scholarly reappraisal of strong presidencies. "It . . . forced scholars to face a disturbing question: Had they promoted the cult of the strong Presidency simply because, up to 1965, strong Presidents had mostly been doing things which historians and political scientists had mostly wanted done? The spectacle of a strong President doing things they mostly did not want done suddenly stimulated many of us to take a fresh look at the old problem of presidential power."[33] Not surprisingly, views on presidential rights are very much affected by expectations about presidential policies.

PRESIDENTIAL DECISION MAKING

Whatever decisions presidents are called upon to make, they are among the most difficult imaginable. With each public policy decision, the president must begin anew to decide how to decide—which decision criteria to choose. He must depend on information that might be biased, inaccurate, incomplete,

[33] Arthur M. Schlesinger, Jr., "The Limits and Excesses of Presidential Power," *Saturday Review* (May 3, 1969), p. 17, *passim.*

or irrelevant. He must make endless trade-offs, and he must understand that any significant decisions he makes in one area can affect all other areas and can even close off other alternatives in future decisions.

Criteria for Presidential Decision Making

Presidents can have a terribly difficult time selecting decision criteria—deciding how to decide. For example, in a particular case should a president maximize expected utility, or expected value, or his security level? The answer to this question might appear uncomplicated, but the president's advisers may differ on decision criteria, especially if one recommendation is from a diplomat and another from a soldier. An essay from the early 1960s, while arguing against certain applications of military decision criteria, helps to describe the president's problem when advisors disagree over criteria.

> The military are always disposed to make their estimates in terms of theoretical military capacity. If Guatemala is under a hostile regime . . . , they may express alarm . . . that the oil fields of Texas are within bombing range of it, even though there is no possibility that Guatemala will bomb Texas. In 1950 they were alarmed because, by sending our occupation forces out of Japan into Korea, we were leaving the way open for China to invade and conquer Japan. In practical terms this was nonsense, since it was not realistically conceivable that, under the circumstances of the day, China would actually undertake the reduction of Japan and the military pacification of the Japanese people. It was, however, in response to the insistence of the military, based on this fantastic fear, that we were moved to intervene in the Chinese Civil War, sending our fleet into the Formosa Channel to create a diversionary threat to the Chinese flank. Our present entrapment on Formosa and the Chinese offshore island is the direct consequence of a move that had no other purpose than that of preventing an invasion of Japan which was quite out of the question. . . .
>
> It is simply not true that the military know best when it comes to matters which can be denominated military-strategic. The vision to which they are trained is too narrow, too technical, too crude. The fact that they are human, moreover, repeatedly makes it proper to discount their recommendations in terms of a political bias that may be unconscious. . . . [T]he President and his civilian advisers, including the Secretary of State, may *agree* with the judgments of the men in uniform, but should never feel themselves obliged to accept them.[34]

Accordingly, suppose the president asks the Joint Chiefs of Staff whether he ought to pursue a particular treaty. Having been schooled in

---

[34] Louis J. Halle, "Lessons of the Cuban Blunders," *The New Republic,* 144 (June 5, 1961), pp. 13–17; as quoted in James N. Murray, Jr., "Military Policy," in Jack W. Peltason and James M. Burns, eds., *Functions and Policies of American Government,* 2nd ed. (Englewood Cliffs, N. J.: Prentice-Hall, 1962), pp. 111–112. Reprinted by permission of *The New Republic,* © 1961, The New Republic, Inc.

military strategy, the Joint Chiefs will treat the question as one of decision making under conditions of uncertainty. After all, potential signatories to the treaty are intelligent participants, as are potential adversaries whose actions the treaty would guard against. Therefore, the Joint Chiefs recommend to the president a strategy associated with minimax—best of the worst—thinking. Should the president follow the advice of his military staff? That depends on how he views the problem, what his concept of national defense entails, and whether he believes the Joint Chiefs have come to the correct decision or not (even conceding that their decision criterion is appropriate). Perhaps "the vision to which they are trained is too narrow, too technical, too crude." A better response may lie with diplomats, who calculate probabilities and maximize expected utility instead of identifying the minimax strategy. Perhaps not.

One can only speculate that the president is as sensible about choosing decision criteria as anyone else. That is, he should know in advance that military advisers will recommend strategies selected by minimax criteria, and he should ask for their opinions with that in mind. When he wants recommendations based on other criteria, he might ask people whose background or training is different. In the life-and-death matters of military policy and national defense, presidents probably apply minimax criteria. In other cases, they probably implicitly choose criteria to fit the decision contexts they face at the moment. However, the problem of choosing a decision criterion will always be with a president, because, as one observer remarked, "Every decision a President makes involves uncertainty. Every decision involves risk."[35]

Information and Presidential Decision Making

Presidents often must anticipate entire sequences of decisions, especially in international conflicts. They must predict what actions both friends and adversaries might take over several moves. Presidents can even try to structure the conflict present in a particular game, as when John Kennedy left room for Soviet Premier Nikita Khrushchev to maneuver during the Cuban missile crisis. Kennedy's care in structuring the conflict prevented it from turning into a game of "chicken" between the United States and the Soviet Union in which neither player could turn back from nuclear confrontation.

Incomplete or inaccurate information. The choice of a decision criterion becomes more difficult if the quality of a president's information leaves him casting about simply for a definition and delimiting of his problem. Incomplete information may lie at the heart of a president's difficulties either because he is unaware of the preexisting facts or because he cannot predict the future with a comfortable degree of confidence. Information about any

[35] Theodore C. Sorensen, *Decision-Making in the White House* (New York: Columbia University Press, 1964), p. 11.

decision-making component might be incomplete or inaccurate. The president may seem unaware of a superior strategy's existence; he may fail to anticipate an outcome; he can wildly misguess probabilities or misspecify states of nature; and he might draw the connection between strategies and outcomes incorrectly. Of course, these information failures do not make it impossible to predict a president's decisions, provided that the state of his information, inaccuracies and all, is known.

Examples abound of adverse consequences resulting from presidential decisions made with incorrect or incomplete information. President Herbert Hoover's failure to increase the supply of money, which brought on the full force of economic depression, was an error created by a lack of understanding of macroeconomic policy. Hoover misspecified the connection between strategy (tight money) and outcome (deflation). Some believe that John Kennedy's misreading of both Cuban public opinion and the strength of anti-Castro forces allowed the Bay of Pigs disaster to occur.[36] Many said that Lyndon Johnson failed to gauge accurately the tenacity of the North Vietnamese and the Viet Cong just as surely as he overestimated the willingness of American citizens to support a sustained, limited war. Richard Nixon's errors in deciding what to do about the Watergate break-in and the White House tapes are now well known, if poorly understood.

Bad judgments based on incomplete or inaccurate information are not confined to contemporary presidents. In historical perspective, Thomas Jefferson's decision to embargo trade with Europe because of British and French interference with American trade and shipping was an astonishing mistake. In 1807 Jefferson proposed to the members of Congress that American ships remain in port. They consented to this proposal and in December of that year passed the Embargo Act, which was an immediate failure. It "not only failed to force Britain and France to respect American rights on the high seas, but also brought economic paralysis to the trading cities of the Northeast and the farms and plantations of the West and South."[37]

Judged by Jefferson's preferences regarding the social and economic structure of the nation, the Embargo Act was also a long-run failure, for Jefferson preferred an agrarian society of "yeoman farmers" to one of industrial workers. Jefferson believed that "Those who labor in the earth are the chosen people of God, if ever He had a chosen people . . ." and "Corruption of morals in the mass of cultivators is a phenomenon of which no age or nation has furnished an example." Jefferson concluded, "I think our governments will remain virtuous for many centuries; as long as they remain agricultural; and this will be as long as there shall be vacant lands in any part of America. When they get piled upon one another in large cities, as in Europe, they will

---

[36] Arthur M. Schlesinger, Jr., *A Thousand Days: John F. Kennedy in the White House* (Boston: Houghton Mifflin, 1965).

[37] Richard Hofstadter, *The American Political Tradition* (New York: Alfred A. Knopf, 1949), p. 39. Copyright 1948 by Alfred A. Knopf, Inc.

become corrupt as in Europe."[38] More to the point, "the proportion which the aggregate of the other classes of citizens bears in any State to that of its husbandmen, is the proportion of its unsound to its healthy parts, and is a good enough barometer whereby to measure its degree of corruption. While we have lands to labor then, let us never wish to see our citizens occupied at a work bench or twirling a distaff. . . . Let our workshops remain in Europe."[39]

Jefferson's agrarian preferences could be fulfilled only if Europe provided the manufactured goods that an agricultural economy required. The Embargo closed off the United States from its supply of such goods, creating a demand for the development of domestic manufacturing. The Embargo thus encouraged what amounted to an industrial revolution in the United States. "The period of the Embargo and the War of 1812 proved to be the seedtime of American industrialism; Henry Adams remarked on the ironic fact that 'American manufacturers owe more to Jefferson than to Northern statesmen who merely encouraged them after they were established.' "[40]

Information overload. Presidents have ample opportunities to use incorrect and incomplete information, often resulting in serious mistakes. But some mistakes occur not because of a lack of information but because of an **information overload.** The president's centrality in public policy decision making virtually guarantees that thousands will try to tell him "their side of the story." Anyone who enjoys a monopoly in supplying information to the president about some issue can usually control the outcome of the president's decisions on that issue, an advantage that is limited only by the president's own good sense and prior knowledge.

Real and persistent information monopolies seldom last. More often, the nearly universal imperative to inform the president creates "inexorable tides of official memoranda, reports, cables, intelligence briefings, and other government documents, and the occupant of the White House becomes subject to drowning in paper. All presidents, at least in modern times, have complained about their reading pile, and few have been able to cope with it."[41]

Information overload is something presidents must live with. "To make informed decisions, the President must be at home with a staggering range of information—about history, economics, politics and personalities in fifty states and now in a hundred or more countries. He must know all about the ratio of cotton acreage to prices, of inventory accumulations to employment, of corporate investment to earnings, of selected steel prices to the economy, and of the biological effects of fall-out to the effects of natural radiation."[42]

---

[38] As quoted in Hofstadter, *The American Political Tradition,* p. 27.

[39] As quoted in Hofstadter, *The American Political Tradition,* p. 27.

[40] Hofstadter, *The American Political Tradition,* p. 40.

[41] Sorensen, *Decision-Making in the White House,* p. 37.

[42] Sorensen, *Decision-Making in the White House,* p. 39.

Nor can the president ignore much of the information that comes his way, for "only if he immerses himself in the problems will a President know what questions he must ask if he is to find the answers he must give."[43]

Information closure. The information avalanche presidents encounter creates another problem, that of **information closure.** The president's time is a scarce commodity, and the cost of reading one report can often be measured as the opportunity forgone to read another. Hence, before making a decision, the president must decide what information to assimilate. He needs a system to filter out irrelevant or less important information and to call his attention only to the most important. Yet, "There is a temptation . . . to cut out all that is unpleasant. . . . [and] to require more screening of information, with only the more salient facts filtering through on one-page memoranda."[44] However, presidents must resist these temptations, because a lack of information can lead to serious mistakes.

A lack of information may be neutral, random, and unbiased in a public policy sense. More often, opinions and data supporting positions contrary to the president's or to the preferences of those who control what the president sees, will be concealed. "For there will always be subordinates who are willing to tell a President only what they want him to hear, or, what is even worse, only what they think he wants to hear."[45] Like most of us, presidents can only assimilate so much criticism before they protest in the strongest possible terms. Criticism seems endless, and aides must know how to "tell it like it is" without alienating their boss. This quality is all too rare among presidential advisers and less common still among those who remain so.

Conflicts in Presidential Decision Making

Whatever the decision criteria presidents decide to use and no matter how accurate their information, every presidential decision represents serious conflicts: "conflict[s] between departments, between the views of various advisors, between the administration and Congress, between The United States and another nation, or between groups within the country: labor versus management, or race versus race, or state versus nation."[46] Everywhere he turns, the president finds conflict. "The claims of domestic and foreign policy sooner or later collide. Congressional checks and balances are written into law. Public and political needs will often be incompatible. Competing policies or interest groups are sometimes equally deserving."[47] Nor can presidents avoid

---

[43] Sorensen, *Decision-Making in the White House,* p. 38.

[44] Sorensen, *Decision-Making in the White House,* pp. 37–38.

[45] Sorensen, *Decision-Making in the White House,* pp. 36–37.

[46] Sorensen, *Decision-Making in the White House,* pp. 14–15.

[47] Sorensen, *Decision-Making in the White House,* p. 15.

conflict, because "the heat that is generated by all of this friction will naturally rise to the top—to the presidential office."[48]

Private goods and public bads. Chapters 6 through 9 describe in detail the problem of political entrepreneurs who, at collective cost, create private, divisible goods for distinct groups in the electorate. For these entrepreneurs, public policy becomes a way to create private goods and public bads. Chapter 9 particularly singles out the members of Congress as being responsible for enacting and sustaining such policies, which often turn out to be Pareto-inferior. Therefore, one conflict in presidential decision making would arise between presidents who wish to stem legislation favorable to "special interests" and House and Senate members who want present trends to continue.

Some scholars believe presidents to be well suited to accomplishing this task, especially if they are able to stop federal bureaucrats from acting as agents of House and Senate members in distributing private benefits.[49] However, there is no theoretical reason that presidents would either try or succeed. First, problems of information overload lead them to consider public policy demands incrementally, one at a time. Grand schemes for government reorganization or for righting all of the wrongs of the tax code simultaneously, pass by the board quickly. The president learns that advancing such schemes against congressional wishes can be extremely costly and time-consuming. Presidents talk about a wholesale "reordering of national priorities," but few do anything about it. Fewer yet succeed.

As Chapter 7 pointed out, incremental decision making is one of the two conditions underlying the electoral and legislative tendencies to create private benefits at collective cost. The other condition is a perceptual threshold below which a large number of citizens do not notice the costs of supporting the new public programs of particular groups. This condition seems to apply as much to public policies developed by presidents as to those advanced by other political entrepreneurs. In sum, on theoretical grounds presidents would probably resolve conflicts between demands for private benefits on the one hand, and an unrepresented interest in minimizing collective costs on the other, in favor of supplying the private benefits.

While evidence concerning this prediction seems mixed, the fact of continued public production of private benefits strongly suggests presidential acquiescence in the enabling legislation. Indeed, most presidents have overtly constructed electoral and legislative coalitions out of various interest groups. The Carter administration at first seemed less prone to this tendency than others, but that is probably because early in his presidency, Jimmy Carter paid very little attention to domestic politics. The members of Congress

---

[48] Sorensen, *Decision-Making in the White House,* p. 15.

[49] Morris P. Fiorina, "Control of the Bureaucracy: A Mismatch of Incentives and Capabilities," paper prepared for a conference on "Congress and the Presidency: A Shifting Balance of Power?" Lyndon B. Johnson School of Public Affairs, Austin, Texas, November 1977.

proceeded in his absence to continue legislating private, divisible benefits. However, even Carter eventually used programs that were particularized to distinct constituencies to help win renomination and to try to win reelection. In 1979 he channeled federal funds into programs in central Florida just before a nonbinding Democratic preference straw vote there, and Neil Goldschmidt, his secretary of transportation, threatened a cutoff of aid to Chicago because Mayor Jane M. Byrne defected to the Kennedy camp. Carter also targeted new government loans to farming states just before the 1980 Democratic National Convention and with great fanfare released a large number of federal grants shortly before the general election. Thus, presidents either partake in the process of private-benefits production or ignore it. The process continues in either case, and government growth therefore seems less constrained by a regard for the costs and benefits imposed on the undifferentiated electorate.

Present payoffs and future costs. Presidents must also make decisions whose resulting costs and benefits are spread out over a long period of time, perhaps even beyond the next election. For example, they can often manipulate national economic policy to produce short-term reductions in unemployment. However, it is argued that in the long run this strategy creates greater inflationary pressures and eventually even more unemployment. Presidents who strongly prefer an immediate economic boom, perhaps because an election is close at hand, will be greatly tempted to forgo long-run economic stability in exchange for short-run economic stimulation.

While evidence concerning the political use of economic stimuli is mixed as to its political effects, little doubt remains that most presidents view the short-run economic stimulation strategy as effective. Monetary policy, affecting the availability of money in the economy, seems to be manipulated to create economic expansion in election years; increases in Social Security payments and veterans' benefits usually come just before elections, and tax increases to pay for them come afterward.[50] Presidents apparently have few incentives to plan beyond the next election, so in conflicts between present political goals and future economic stability, their decisions often reflect a "live today" attitude. Table 10.2 shows the hypothesized expected effects in terms of economic conditions in the United States in election years as compared with other years. The evidence about the results of manipulation seems fairly convincing.

Coalitions of minorities. Conflicts requiring presidential decisions can be structured by the president's political opponents. Presidents are targets for the opposition party's members, who can often manipulate to his political disadvantage the kinds of issues he must confront. Sometimes as a result of this strategic manipulation and sometimes for other reasons, presidents have

[50] Tufte, *Political Control of the Economy.*

Table 10.2 Inflation, Unemployment, and Presidential Elections, 1946–1976

Yearly Change in Unemployment Rate and Inflation (Real GNP Deflator)	Presidential Election Years (8)	All Other Years (23)
less unemployment and less inflation	50%	9%
less unemployment but more inflation	13	30
less inflation but more unemployment	38	43
more inflation and more unemployment	0	17

Source: *Political Control of the Economy* by Edward R. Tufte (© 1978 by Princeton University Press): Table 1–2, p. 22. Reprinted by permission of Princeton University Press.

to face a succession of no-win decisions. Each decision alienates the members of some identifiable group, or "minority," who happen to hold intense preferences.

As mentioned earlier, presidents ordinarily can and do grant private benefits to various interest groups. However, as Chapter 7 points out, sometimes two such groups face off in political battle. Examples include such intractable conflicts as those concerning abortion and busing. One group wins only if the other loses. Presidents try to avoid these situations by using a strategy of ambiguity, but they do not succeed if their *political* opponents have any say in the matter. Opponents continually raise divisive issues to the level of presidential decision making, and eventually the members of one group after another become disappointed with the president and go into permanent opposition. The result is a coalition of minorities, and as a consequence of its formation, the president finds political support increasingly more difficult to generate. As the discussion of coalitions of minorities in Chapter 7 suggests, this is exactly what the president's political opponents had in mind.

The effects of a coalition of minorities on presidential popularity are apparent both in recent public opinion survey data and in voting in the Congress. As Figure 10.2 shows, during their administrations Presidents Truman, Kennedy, Johnson, Nixon, Ford, and Carter experienced progressive declines in the percentage of persons approving of how they did their job.[51] Only President Eisenhower seemed to have escaped this phenomenon. This erosion of popular support provides evidence that disaffection with a president's decisions grows over time. Figure 10.3 illustrates that the coalition of minorities problem is also reflected in voting on bills by House and Senate

---

[51] A good discussion of this polling data is in Mueller, *War, Presidents and Public Opinion,* chapter 9.

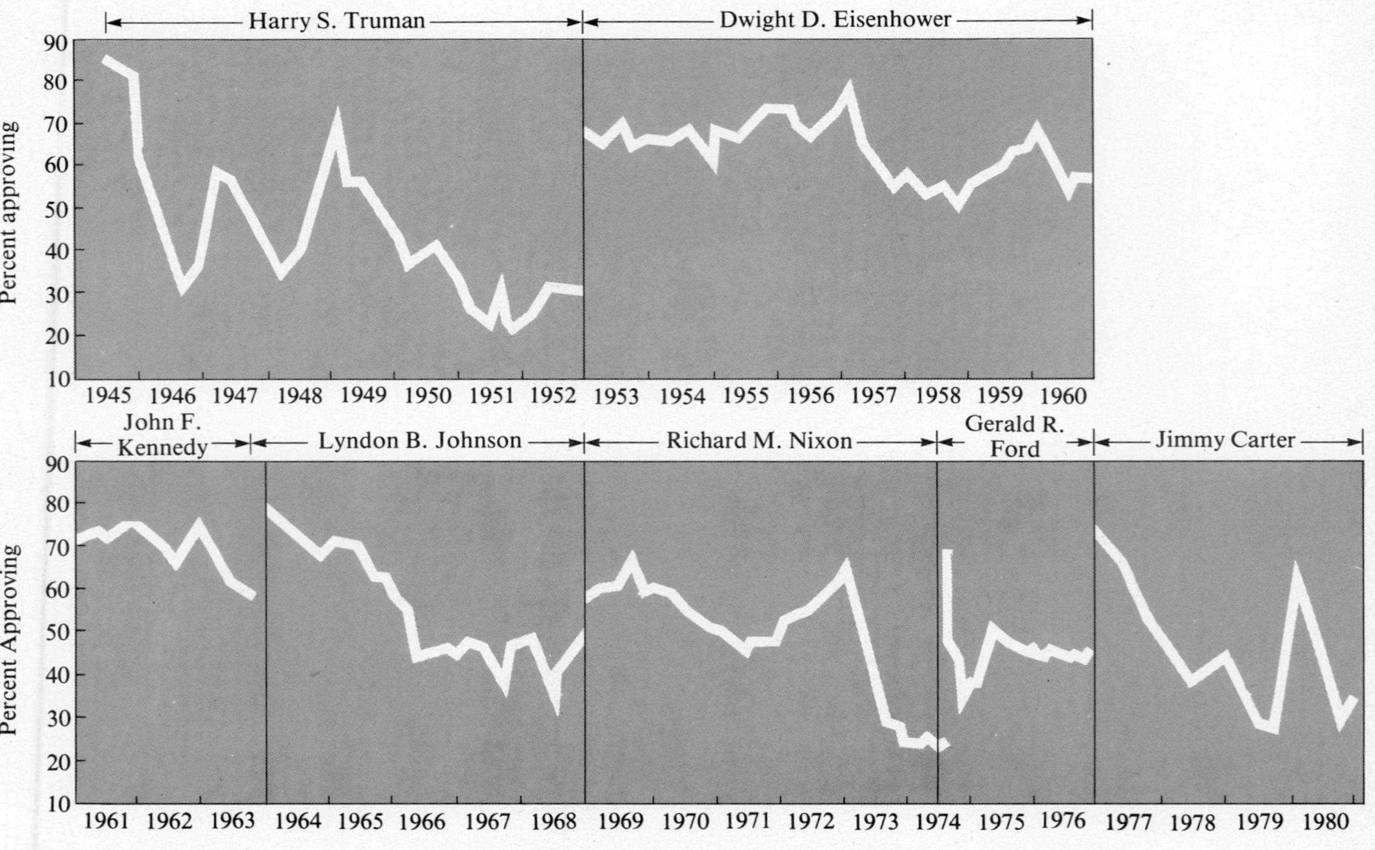

Figure 10.2 Public approval of how presidents do their jobs, June 1945–September 1980.

Source: Adapted from Thomas E. Cronin, *The State of the Presidency,* 2nd ed. (Boston: Little, Brown, 1980), pp. 328–329. Data are from George Gallup, Gallup Poll Index, 1935–1971 (New York: Random House, 1972), and the Gallup Opinion Index, monthly reports.

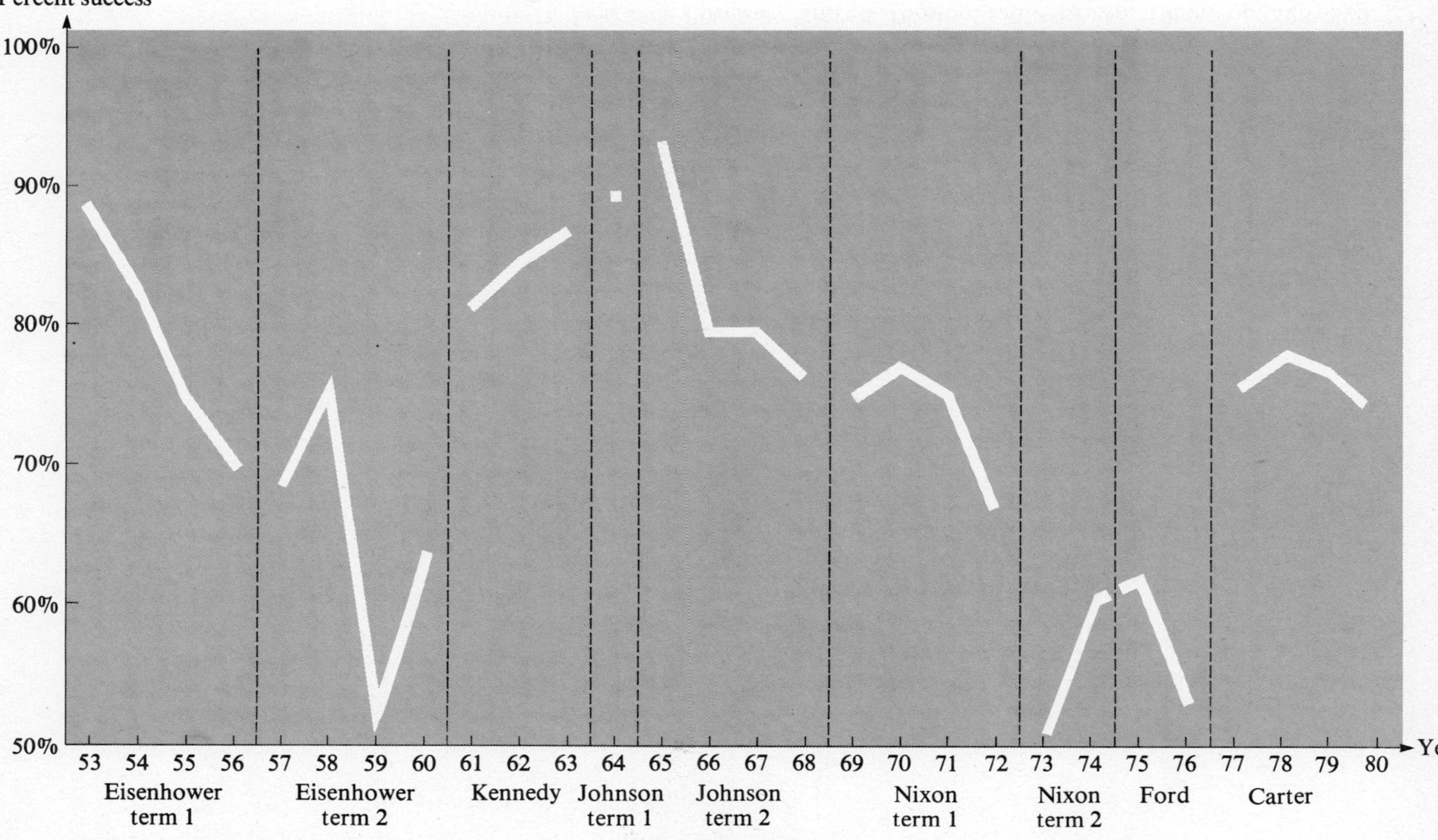

Figure 10.3 Presidential success on votes in Congress, 1953–1979.

Source: Data are from *Congressional Quarterly Weekly Report,* 38 (January 12, 1979), p. 91. Similar figures appear in Randall B. Ripley, *Congress: Process and Policy,* 2nd ed. (New York: Norton, forthcoming), and Samuel C. Patterson, "The Semi-Sovereign Congress," in Anthony King, ed., *The New American Political System,* © 1978 by American Enterprise Institute for Public Policy Research, Washington, D.C., p. 173.

members. The percentage of congressional votes in favor of the president's position on various issues declines as his term wears on. Thus, presidents must come to expect that their present decisions will erode the support they require for future ones.

PRESIDENTIAL PERSONALITY AND PRESIDENTIAL DECISION MAKING

In this book, preferences have been taken as "given," and the analysis of the origin of preferences, itself an important subject, has been declared a subject of concern to psychologists. Ordinarily, deep-seated psychological aspects of personality are not a concern in the study of voters, activists, or even members of Congress. It is not farfetched to assume that too many voters and legislators are sane and stable for insanity or instability to prevail. By contrast, presidents remain singular and central in national decision making. Their personalities and psychological traits thus have become a matter of some concern and increasing scrutiny.

Personality traits by themselves may be unimportant for explaining and predicting presidents' decisions. It may be irrelevant whether presidents are happy or sad, well-adjusted, neurotic, or unadjusted, paranoid, or manic-depressive. The president's personality itself matters much less than how and whether his personality affects his decisions. At one extreme, mental illness may distort the president's view of reality, rendering him suicidal or otherwise incapable of correctly identifying the probabilistic links between alternatives and outcomes. However, most presidents are neither insane nor suicidal. Some may exhibit more paranoid tendencies than others, and the actions of some may give evidence of troublesome insecurities. But personality descriptions themselves do not provide the tools to connect presidential personality with presidential decision making.

Presidential character. One recent attempt to provide that connection categorizes presidents along two dimensions.[52] The first is activity-passivity. "How much energy does the man invest in his Presidency? Lyndon Johnson went at his day like a human cyclone, coming to rest long after the sun went down. Calvin Coolidge often slept eleven hours a night and still needed a nap in the middle of the day."[53] The second dimension is a positive-negative one, which taps a president's attitude toward life in general and toward what he is doing in particular. The positive personality enjoys his work and sees in it a

---

[52] James David Barber, *The Presidential Character: Predicting Performance in the White House,* 2nd ed. (Englewood Cliffs, N. J.: Prentice-Hall, 1977). This section relies on Barber's work.

[53] From the book *The Presidential Character,* 2nd ed. by James David Barber. © 1977 by James David Barber. Published by Prentice-Hall, Inc., Englewood Cliffs, NJ 07632.

purpose of improvement, while a negative personality interprets his travail as an inescapable burden. He carries this burden to ward off and even throw back the evils that everywhere beset him and his people.

The combination of these two dimensions yields four presidential types: active-positive, active-negative, passive-positive, and passive-negative. Each type is said to react predictably to presidential decision problems. For an **active-positive president,**

> There is a congruence, a consistency, between much activity and the enjoyment of it, indicating relatively high self-esteem and relative success in relating to the environment. The man shows an orientation toward productiveness as a value and an ability to use his styles flexibly, adaptively, suiting the dance to the music. He sees himself as developing over time toward relatively well-defined personal goals—growing toward his image of himself as he might yet be. There is an emphasis on rational mastery, on using the brain to move the feet.[54]

These presidents "are more open to evidence because they have less need to deny and distort their perceptions for protective purposes."[55] They are flexible and willing to experiment. But this kind of president also can experience great difficulty because "he may fail to take account of the irrational in politics. Not everyone he deals with sees things his way and he may find it hard to understand why."[56] Thomas Jefferson, Franklin Roosevelt, Harry Truman, John Kennedy, and (perhaps mistakenly) Jimmy Carter are classified by this categorization as active-positive presidents.[57]

John Adams, Woodrow Wilson, Herbert Hoover, Lyndon Johnson, and Richard Nixon are believed to have been **active-negative presidents.** They worked very hard at their jobs but received little satisfaction. Furthermore,

> The activity has a compulsive quality, as if the man were trying to make up for something or to escape from anxiety into hard work. He seems ambitious, striving upward, power-seeking. His stance toward the environment is aggressive and he has a persistent problem in managing his aggressive feelings. His self-image is vague and discontinuous. Life is a hard struggle to achieve and hold power, hampered by the condemnations of a perfectionist conscience. Active-negative types pour energy into the political system, but it is an energy distorted from within.[58]

---

[54] Barber, *The Presidential Character,* p. 12.

[55] Barber, *The Presidential Character,* p. 454.

[56] Barber, *The Presidential Character,* p. 12.

[57] James David Barber, "An Active-Positive Character," *Time* (January 3, 1977), p. 17.

[58] Barber, *The Presidential Character,* pp. 12–13.

Active-negative presidents confront us with "the risk of disaster."[59] Public policy may have to change quickly in a world of sometimes unpredictable events and rapidly eroding loyalties. But the active-negative president cannot easily remove himself from a course of action to which he is committed. Withal "there is the perseveration in a policy despite strong evidence that it is proving counter-productive." And, "there is the fact of the President's strong emotional investment in the failing policy."[60]

By contrast, a **passive-positive president** is a "receptive, compliant, other-directed character whose life is a search for affection as a reward for being agreeable and cooperative rather than personally assertive."[61] James Madison, William Howard Taft, and Warren G. Harding are classified as passive-positives. These presidents expose us to the danger of "a President-people romance that diverts popular attention from the hard realities of politics and twists the President's own thinking from his larger purposes to his dear friends."[62]

Finally, the **passive-negative presidents**—people such as George Washington, Calvin Coolidge, and possibly even Dwight Eisenhower—are the most difficult to understand. Each "does little in politics and enjoys it less."[63] What explains the passive-negative's participation in politics?

> The answer lies in the passive-negative's character-rooted orientation toward doing dutiful service; this compensates for low self-esteem based on a sense of uselessness. Passive-negative types are in politics because they think they ought to be. They may be well adapted to certain nonpolitical roles, but they lack the experience and flexibility to perform effectively as political leaders. Their tendency is to withdraw, to escape from the conflict and uncertainty of politics by emphasizing vague principles (especially prohibitions) and procedural arrangements. They become guardians of the right and proper way, above the sordid politicking of lesser men.[64]

The passive president may satisfy the desire for "breathing spells, times of recovery in our frantic political life." In the larger picture, however, they create a "danger of drift," for unfortunately "the price of relaxation may be too high." It seems all too clear that "social problems do not disappear because a President neglects them. . . . What passive Presidents ignore active Presidents inherit."[65]

---

[59] Barber, *The Presidential Character,* p. 140.

[60] Barber, *The Presidential Character,* p. 141.

[61] Barber, *The Presidential Character,* p. 13.

[62] Barber, *The Presidential Character,* p. 206.

[63] Barber, *The Presidential Character,* p. 13.

[64] Barber, *The Presidential Character,* p. 13.

[65] Barber, *The Presidential Character,* p. 145.

Predicting decisions from character. This analysis of presidential character links personality with the *general* nature of presidential action and choice. It shows that the emotional framework affecting how presidents might react to the issues they confront—or even create themselves—can be predicted by examining their life histories to find out, among other things, if they are active or passive, positive or negative. But problems remain even with this careful attempt to get at the personality roots of presidential decision making. The personality "types" are loaded with emotional connotations: "active" and "positive" are portrayed as good traits, while "passive" and "negative" are not. Not a little ideology enters the analysis, for "active" becomes synonymous with "activist." This typing of presidents would clearly embrace Theodore Roosevelt's view of the Presidency rather than Taft's. In a like manner, the liberal activist presidents of the twentieth century—Roosevelt, Truman, and Kennedy—would be praised, while others—Hoover and Nixon, not to mention Woodrow Wilson (for the rigidity of his foreign policy in general) and Lyndon Johnson (for the rigidity of his Vietnam policy in particular)—would be denigrated.

Moreover, even a close study of presidents' lives can leave scholars with the problem of assigning presidents to categories. In this analysis, Jefferson is assigned an active-positive label, though others might find him more appropriately called an active-negative. Lincoln is a clear active-negative, but Lyndon Johnson seemed every bit an active-positive before the enlargement of American participation in Vietnam. The difference between positive and negative presidents, which lies at the heart of this analysis, thus becomes a matter of some confusion. The positive president sees a political environment to be manipulated and enjoyed. The negative president interprets the environment, including his own personality, as hostile, to be controlled or at least held off. But who can say which of these attitudes toward the environment is incorrect? What would active-positives such as Franklin D. Roosevelt, Harry Truman, or John Kennedy have done with the kind of intractability and political opposition that surrounded the Vietnam War era? Might not Lyndon Johnson have been another Franklin D. Roosevelt, without Vietnam? Some political environments are beyond manipulation. Such is the case when opponents become many and implacable and political survival grows doubtful.

In spite of these problems, this categorization produced impressively accurate predictions about the Nixon presidency. Less impressive are its briefer predictions for Carter. While Carter was first judged to be an active-positive, he might equally be placed somewhere between active and passive, and more nearly negative than positive. For example, in the face of charges of banking management improprieties, Carter persisted in the futile cause of supporting Bert Lance, his Office of Management and Budget director. He did so far longer than Nixon supported his personal aides, H. R. Haldeman and John Ehrlichman, who also left the White House under a cloud of suspicion. Neither Nixon nor Carter could easily change course. Carter showed the same tendency as did Nixon and Johnson to "tough it out," but he had neither Nixon's nor Johnson's energy. That his presidency has been described as "passionless" also attests to his passive character.[66] His emphasis on reduced expectations and his negative campaign against Ronald Reagan similarly gave evidence of a man at war with his environment.

Psychological studies of presidential personality make more sense of how presidents' personalities affect their attitudes—friendships, likes, and dislikes—than of how their personalities affect their decisions. But personality is, and shall remain, a worrisome issue in presidential decision making. Because of the Darwinian political and social processes that select them, we believe presidents to be extraordinary people under extraordinary pressure with great capacities for doing both good and evil. Thus, we worry about their emotional stability.

THE EXECUTIVE BRANCH

The president's immediate staff began with a few aides in George Washington's day and now numbers over 3000 persons. The members of various executive departments, such as Treasury, State, and Defense, exclusive of soldiers and postal workers, number over 700,000. Total civilian employment in the Department of Defense is about one million persons. Nearly 3.8 million civilians now work for the federal government, and most of these are responsible to the president in some way or another. Chapter 11 considers the problem of the federal bureaucracy in its entirety, but those offices, councils, and departments closest to the president are discussed here.

The president's cabinet. The Constitution contemplated the existence of **executive departments,** whose heads must respond to a president's demand for "opinions" and who are chosen by the president with the advice and consent of the Senate. However, the Constitution did not anticipate a president's **cabinet.** This organization is made up of the president and vice-president, the heads of departments, and such other persons as the president might choose. The 1980 Carter cabinet and the Reagan cabinet-designate are listed in Table 10.3 (It is customary to name the department secretaries and their departments in the order in which they were established.

The cabinet grew out of George Washington's failure to get the members of the Senate and the Supreme Court to participate in executive-branch activities. Since its earliest development, presidents have used their cabinets for every imaginable purpose. Some, such as Dwight Eisenhower, employed the cabinet as a formal advisory and decision-making body. More recent presidents, such as Kennedy and Johnson, believed that cabinet meetings were a waste of time and acted accordingly.

The makeup of the cabinet has become symbolic of the president's larger

---

[66] Fallows, "The Passionless President."

Table 10.3 The Cabinet, 1980

	Carter Cabinet	Reagan Cabinet Designate
President	Jimmy Carter	Ronald Reagan
Vice-President	Walter F. Mondale	George Bush
Secretary of State	Edmund S. Muskie	Alexander Haig
Secretary of the Treasury	G. William Miller	Donald T. Regan
Secretary of Defense	Harold Brown	Caspar W. Weinberger
Secretary of the Army	Clifford L. Alexander, Jr.	John O. Marsh
Secretary of the Navy	Edward Hidalgo	John Lehman
Secretary of the Air Force	Hans Mark	Vern Orr
Attorney General (Justice Department)	Benjamin Civiletti	William F. Smith
Secretary of the Interior	Cecil D. Andrus	James Watt
Secretary of Agriculture	Bob S. Bergland	John R. Block
Secretary of Commerce	Philip M. Klutznick	Malcolm Baldridge
Secretary of Labor	F. Ray Marshall	Raymond J. Donovan
Secretary of Health and Human Services	Patricia Harris	Richard S. Schweiker
Secretary of Housing and Urban Development	Moon Landrieu	Samuel R. Pierce, Jr.
Secretary of Transportation	Neil E. Goldschmidt	Andrew Lewis, Jr.
Secretary of Energy	Charles W. Duncan, Jr.	James B. Edwards
Secretary of Education	Shirley M. Hufstedler	Terrel Bell

purposes. Today, many citizens have come to expect that their economic, ethnic, or geographic group will be represented in the cabinet. Women and blacks are more often appointed to cabinet posts now than in the past. The backgrounds and other characteristics of those who become secretaries of the departments of the Treasury, the Interior, Agriculture, Labor, and Health and Human Services provide signals about administration intentions to the members of relevant interest groups in the electorate.

The loyalty that cabinet secretaries give to presidents varies from case to case. Richard Nixon had problems with some cabinet members early in his first term; Jimmy Carter cleaned house during the summer of 1979. Loyalty was at issue in both instances. Whether or not presidents rely heavily on their cabinets, the secretaries remain important. Together, these people exercise eventual control over nearly 90 percent of the federal budget, although this percentage includes some funds beyond immediate control. Their rule-making and regulatory purview is exceedingly broad, and they are the central executive agents of the federal government.

The Executive Office of the President. Begun in 1939, the Executive Office of the President includes the president's immediate aides and assistants as well as leaders of several councils and public policy groups. By convention, the Central Intelligence Agency is also included. The most recent listing of the Executive Office includes the following principal offices, organizations, councils, and groups: The president and White House Office; The Executive Residence; Office of Management and Budget; Council of Economic Advisers; Council on Environmental Quality; Council on Wage and Price Stability; Domestic Policy Staff; Economic Policy Group; National Security Council (including the Central Intelligence Agency); Office of Science and Technology Policy; Office of the U.S. Trade Representative; and Office of the Vice-President. The White House Office includes those most closely attached to the president: his immediate assistants, legal counsels, national security adviser, press secretary, and congressional liaison assistants. It also includes several special assistants to handle issues that seem to cross departmental lines—for example, problems of aging, health, and consumer affairs. With few exceptions, those who serve in the Executive Office of the President do so entirely at his pleasure. They are not usually subject to Senate confirmation. Unlike the cabinet, whose members often represent special interests, the members of the Executive Office are entirely the president's servants and are expected to have interests and incentives paralleling his own.

How the Executive Office of the President arches over all other departments and agencies is best understood by considering its Office of Management and Budget (OMB). All budgetary requests from all federal agencies and departments must clear OMB. Its personnel must see to it that each request is in line with the president's goals and objectives. OMB also exercises an implicit oversight of all federal agencies and departments. In a very real sense, OMB is the president's form of the power of the purse as well as his accountant.

What OMB is to the budgetary process, the National Security Council (NSC) is to military and geopolitical problems. The NSC is made up of the president, vice-president, secretary of state, secretary of defense, and assistant to the president for national security affairs; the director of the Central Intelligence Agency and the chairman of the Joint Chiefs of Staff serve as advisers to the Council. In military and other international crises, the NSC is the president's most immediate advisory and decision-making body.

The executive branch and presidential decision making. The make-up of the executive branch represents the accumulation of two centuries of growth and custom, some of it purposive and much of it idiosyncratic. The theory behind the executive branch, and especially behind the Executive Office of the President, is that a large number of people can operate as the president's eyes, ears, and hands, screening information and problems, separating that which is significant from that which is not. The ultimate goal of this process is for the president to be able to accomplish all that statute law, the Constitution, and the members of the electorate require, even though this task would be impossible for him to perform alone.

Such a view of a rationally constructed executive branch shares all of the weaknesses of any simplistic view of most complex organizations. Supposedly, each person in the executive branch will act exactly as the president would want if that person knew what the president knew, and vice versa. But, presidents cannot be cloned. Their preferences cannot be transferred unaltered to their assistants. Even if it were possible to make such a transference, an overly active zeal for achieving goals such as reelection or the enactment of a particular policy could result in another scandal such as Watergate.

Sometimes a president's own preferences might seem contradictory. He wants aides and assistants to give him all of the news and their most accurate assessment of it, and he seeks the best possible policy recommendations. Information closure is a very real problem if his aides are weak-willed, but aides who would be able to avoid closure are also likely to have strong personalities. Their independent judgments will signal the presence of independently-formed preferences, which might clash with the president's preference for loyalty. Thus the conflict: loyal aides are seldom independent, and independent aides may be less loyal.

Aides and department heads must often speak for the president. The result can be a confusion about what the president wants, since each aide might offer a slightly different interpretation of the president's position. In domestic policy, the ambiguity generated can hamper the success of the president's legislative program. On the other hand, as Chapter 7 points out, ambiguity is often an appropriate election strategy. But in foreign and military policy, ambiguity generated by the contradictory statements of different presidential aides can lead to dangerous confrontations. For example, if administration personnel *seem* to be saying that the United States "might" not be willing to go to war over Berlin, then those who say so invite the opportunity to find out if that is true. During the first three years of the Carter administration, a similar problem arose because Secretary of State Cyrus Vance took a "soft line" toward the Soviet Union, while National Security Adviser Zbigniew Brzezinski took a "hard line." Each expressed his own view, and it remained unclear where President Carter stood. Even when Vance finally resigned in protest over the ill-fated Iranian rescue mission, speculation continued about whether Brzezinski or Vance's successor, Edmund S. Muskie, would speak for the president.

Ambiguity on an international scale can thoroughly defeat a president's purpose. For instance, recall the discussion in Chapter 2 about the game of chicken. In its cooperative form, chicken strongly resembles several international confrontations, such as the Cuban missile crisis, the Berlin blockade, and the hostage crisis in Iran. If the president wants to "win" such a confrontation, it is absolutely imperative for him to communicate his commitment to a "no-swerve" strategy—his determination not to back down—to his adversary, in the strongest possible and most convincing manner. Those who speak for the president cannot give the slightest impression that he might back down—"swerve." On the other hand, these devilishly sensitive situations might be approached by a mutual agreement for each party to "swerve"—back down—thereby saving face and not giving the lasting impression of weakness—an impression that might prove catastrophic for managing future conflicts successfully. The president thus must not merely coordinate the actions of his aides; he must also see to it that they speak with one voice—his own.

As this discussion indicates, the executive branch is a complex organization of complex persons holding diverse preferences and with all of the problems associated with any such organization. It will seldom work with one will in the service of the president, although his is the paradoxical job of managing and directing the members of an organization who must both propose and execute the laws. As Chapter 11 makes clear, the problems with such a group are immense.

QUESTIONS FOR DISCUSSION AND REVIEW

1. Can a president ever make a foreign-policy or military decision without domestic consequences? Why? If not, are presidential decisions about foreign policy and military matters less than perfect? Would it be possible to have two presidents, one who conducted foreign policy and the other, domestic policy?
2. Can you imagine arguments for or against a "strong" presidency that are not related to the public policies such presidents would pursue? What are they?
3. The present debate about strong presidents is cast in terms of the relative strength of Congress versus the president. Using the discus-

sion of collective action in Chapter 3, could you describe a second debate, cast in terms of the relative strength of private choice versus public choice? How would the positions advocated in this second debate affect or constrain positions taken in the first debate?

4. This chapter describes the problems of presidents whose advisers state different and opposing views on foreign-policy matters. Would this practice ever be advantageous in foreign policy? In domestic policy? In what circumstances?
5. Are the president and his advisers more or less susceptible to problems of cyclical majorities and coalitions of intense minorities? Why?
6. What would be the public policy effects of restricting the president to a single six-year term? Why?
7. Can you explain the Watergate scandal in terms of the discussion in this chapter? Do so.

NEW CONCEPTS AND TERMS

active-negative president
active-positive president
cabinet
chief diplomat
chief executive
chief legislator
chief of party
chief of state
commander-in-chief
executive agreement
executive department
information closure
information overload
manager of prosperity
passive-negative president
passive-positive president
protector of the peace
voice of the people
world leader

11

The Federal Bureaucracy

When elected officials legislate new public policies, they often state their goals explicitly in the laws and resolutions they enact. For example, the members of Congress and the president may respectively pass and sign bills calling for a cut in the unemployment rate to 4 percent, for a lowering of the inflation rate to zero, for a 90 percent reduction in air pollution, for a 20 percent increase in the nuclear missile arsenal, and for sending troops to some foreign land to protect American interests. But seldom does enacting such goals into law make them come true, for laws usually transfer goal achievement to new or existing government organizations. Sometimes the laws say precisely how the personnel of such organizations must do their jobs. More commonly such personnel enjoy some discretion, because limitations on information, expertise, and time seriously curtail just how specific elected officials might become in the laws they write. Therefore, elected representatives delegate the achievement of legislated goals to unelected personnel for the same reasons that they grant those personnel discretion about means (instrumental goals) and sometimes about ends (prime goals).

Elected officials set goals and establish, fund, and try to oversee the organizations created to achieve them. But they cannot easily administer aptitude tests to job-training applicants, they do not send field personnel out to monitor pollution sources, they never hire steam fitters and welders to build battleships, and they seldom deploy troops in battle. Instead, elected officials delegate these tasks to organizations called **bureaus.** A group of such organizations is called a **bureaucracy,** a term that merely denotes the unelected, nonjudicial organizations within a government.[1] While the bureaucrats—the directors and employees of such organizations—involve themselves more fully with the implementation of public policy than do elected officials, nevertheless bureaucrats themselves also "enact" public policy, and they frequently adjudicate disputes arising from their activities and from the laws and regulations they enforce.

The Constitution places the selection and control of "public ministers" with the members of Congress and with the president but says little else about them. As Chapter 10 points out, not even the president's cabinet, which is made up of the secretaries of the principal bureaucracies (departments) within the executive branch, finds mention in the Constitution. Yet, the citizen's most frequent and significant contact with government at all levels remains with bureaucrats. They collect and process tax returns, they write all government checks and provide for benefits in kind (such as food stamps), and as Chapter 1 observes, they regulate ever-expanding areas of human action. Today, nearly one member of the work force in five is employed by some level of government in the United States.[2] As noted later in this chapter, this fact alone carries great political and public policy significance.

THE THEORETICAL FUNCTIONS OF FEDERAL BUREAUS

The reasons for public choice listed in Chapter 3 provide a framework for describing and evaluating the functions of federal bureaus. These reasons include supplying public goods, suppressing public bads, redistributing resources, controlling monopolies, and establishing property rights. Of course, program costs and benefits are appropriate considerations in carrying out these functions. By this view, an ideal, or perfect bureaucrat in a perfect

---

[1] Some bureaus, especially regulatory commissions, have developed internal judicial systems and employ administrative law judges. The armed forces conduct their own court-martial procedures, and in recent years individual federal judges have acted as bureaucrats by taking over partial administrative control of entire school districts to enforce desegregation edicts. On the other hand, some bureaucrats in state and local governments, such as public service commissioners, insurance commissioners, and dogcatchers, are popularly elected.

[2] This figure includes military personnel on active duty. In round numbers, there are 2.8 million federal employees in nondefense activities, 1 million civilian defense employees, and 2.1 million soldiers on active duty, for a total of 5.9 million federal employees. Additionally, there are 3.3 million state government workers and 8.8 million local government workers, some of whom are paid by the federal government. The grand total is 18 million people. Moreover, several federal bureaus have evaded legislated ceilings on the size of their work forces by farming out various jobs to private firms specializing in government contracts. One estimate, which includes state and local officials paid with federal funds, puts the number of such persons at 3 to 4 million. See Donald Lambro, "In and Out at HEW: Doing Well by Doing Good Through Consulting," *Policy Review,* 7 (Winter 1979), p. 109.

bureau, responding to a legislative directive to supply a public good, would produce it at the optimum level and to the extent possible would use cost-minimizing methods of production. The same bureaucrat, charged with suppressing a public bad, would use the most cost-effective method of suppression. Asked to enforce antitrust laws and given the choice of pursuing two equally expensive lawsuits, a perfect bureaucrat would choose the one that represented the greater economic gain to consumers of the allegedly monopolizing firm's product. And, given the job of redistributing resources to the poor, the same bureaucrat would see to it that people spend as little time on welfare as possible, because lifting people above the poverty level and off the welfare rolls seems a reasonable measure of success.

In sum, ideal bureaucrats in ideal bureaus proceed efficiently to fulfill one or more of the purposes for preferring public choice over private action identified in Chapter 3, and not to fulfill other, conflicting purposes. Therefore, a useful starting point in studying American bureaucracy is to describe the theoretical goals of some major federal bureaus and bureaucrats in ideal, abstract terms, according to the goals of collective action described in Chapter 3.

Producing public goods. The free-rider problem, which often plagues the production of public goods, sometimes leads those goods not to be supplied or to be supplied inadequately. National defense provides a classic example of a jointly supplied and consumed public good, and Americans supply themselves with national defense by using public-choice procedures in general and bureaucratic methods in particular. The Internal Revenue Service (IRS), a division of the Department of the Treasury, is charged with collecting taxes to pay for national defense and other federal expenditures. However, the bureau overseeing the actual production of national defense is the Department of Defense (DOD). DOD expenditures in 1979 were estimated at $118 billion, which represented nearly 24 percent of the federal government's budget and about 6 percent of GNP. The DOD employs about one million civilians and two million people in uniform, for a total of slightly more than 3 percent of the work force. During times of war, these numbers have increased dramatically. For example, in 1944 defense-related expenditures reached nearly 89 percent of federal expenditures and 42 percent of GNP. In that year of World War II, more than 17 percent of the work force was in uniform.

The "simple" management of this large, complex, and expensive organization goes far beyond the direct capacity of the members of Congress or of the president's staff, and delegation of decision making becomes imperative. But how an abstract, ideal DOD would operate remains a mystery. What mix of weapons systems to buy, how to target intercontinental ballistic missiles, and what level of conventional military readiness to achieve are interrelated analytical decision problems whose simultaneous solution often defies human imagination. The successes and failures of the State Department only serve to make definitive solutions to DOD problems more difficult to identify. Thus, ideal, Pareto-preferred DOD actions may not even be possible to define, especially since the good called "national defense" remains collective and is extremely difficult to measure.

Sometimes the rationale for collective action may seem evident, but it is not easy to identify in terms of the categories listed in Chapter 3. For example, the Food and Drug Administration (FDA) was established by the Agricultural Appropriation Act of 1941. It was originally in the Department of Agriculture but was moved to the Department of Health, Education, and Welfare (HEW), the predecessor to the Department of Health and Human Services (HHS), when HEW was formed in 1953. The FDA's original purpose was to keep adulterated food and medicines from consumers, but its functions have expanded over the years. The FDA is now responsible for carrying out the original act of 1931 as well as the Food and Drug Act of 1906; the Food, Drug, and Cosmetic Act of 1938, which was enlarged by the Food Additives Amendments of 1958 (the Delaney Amendment), the Color Additives Amendments of 1960, the Drug Amendments of 1962, and the Medical Devices Amendments of 1976; the Fair Packaging and Labeling Act of 1966; and the Radiation Control for Health and Safety Act of 1968. Additionally, the FDA enforces portions of the Tea Importation Act of 1897, the Filled Milk Act of 1923, the Public Health Services Act of 1944, and the Federal Hazardous Substances Act of 1966.[3] In sum, the FDA now regulates many aspects of the development, use, and marketing of foods, drugs, and medical equipment and appliances.

In terms of categories listed in Chapter 3, among other things the FDA is in the business of providing information, which can be a public good. Alongside the primary market for a particular good or service there exists the possibility of a second, parallel market. Information about the good or service traded in the primary market would be bought and sold in this secondary market. Such information would concern prices, quantities, locations where the good or service is available, quality, usefulness, durability, and safety.

For many goods and services, the secondary market for information fails to form because consumers themselves are expert, because costs of search and error are low, and because competitive market forces minimize prices by driving out inefficient, high-cost, or low-quality producers. For instance, consumers ordinarily do not buy independently generated information about markets in pencils, paper clips, bubble gum, clothes, and books and magazines (although book reviews appearing in periodicals are popular).

For other kinds of goods and services, the secondary information market forms explicitly. For example, people buy and sell houses through real-estate brokers, who are actually providing a market for information. Consumer-oriented magazines evaluate goods for the home and everyday living; auto-

---

[3] The enumeration of FDA statutory authority is from Ronald J. Penoyer, *Directory of Federal Regulatory Agencies,* 2nd ed. (St. Louis: Washington University Center for the Study of American Business, 1980), p. 59.

mobile magazines publish articles rating the latest sedans; trade and hobby journals offer detailed accounts of how effectively specialized equipment operates. And, producers' own brand-name reputations and advertising remain the most extensive information sources about various products.

However, information is sometimes a public good. One person's use of it need not affect another's ability to use the same information, and once it is produced (discovered) it may become available to everyone.[4] Whether people produce and disseminate information in optimal quantities or not thus depends on the existence of a patent or copyright system, or some other property-rights arrangement to ensure payment for production and dissemination. Sometimes the creation of such a system appears difficult or impossible, and some would argue that an effective, orderly market for information about the efficacy and safety of drugs similarly will not appear spontaneously. The cost of generating such information exceeds any one consumer's budget, while the total benefits all consumers would receive from its availability exceed the cost of generating it. Nor could such information easily be withheld from those who failed to pay their share for its production. Therefore, FDA action to create such information might be expected to improve citizens' welfare generally. Since most people are actual or potential users of pharmaceutical products, FDA regulations requiring drug companies to generate test data about their products are equivalent to creating the public good of product information.

This rationale puts FDA activities in the best possible light, for privately created information about drugs has always been plentiful, and physicians are legally responsible for the correct use of pharmaceuticals. Moreover, as this chapter points out later, FDA regulations are the subject of extremely sharp debate because they go far beyond the generation of information. The FDA

---

[4] Sometimes it is profitable to be the first to get certain kinds of information. As Chapter 9 points out, patent and copyright laws are intended to protect those who first make commercially useful discoveries or write original works. It is profitable to be the first to discover a gold or oil deposit, or to learn about changes in a particular firm's earnings. By various rulings of the Securities and Exchange Commission (SEC), exploiting "insider" information about publicly traded firms is illegal, although laws against it seem largely unenforceable. See Henry G. Manne, *Insider Trading and the Stock Market* (New York: Free Press, 1966). The decision-theoretic analysis of markets for information is extremely complex. See Jack Hirshleifer, "The Private and Social Value of Information and the Reward to Inventive Activity," *American Economic Review,* 61 (September 1971), pp. 561–574, and George J. Stigler, "The Economics of Information," *Journal of Political Economy,* 69 (June 1961), pp. 213–225. One should also notice that some consumers seek out information about prices and products. Their actions lead producers to reduce prices and to offer goods of optimal—not necessarily perfect—quality. But this consumer information-seeking activity benefits other consumers, who accept market prices and product quality as they are. Hence, consumers who conduct price and quality searches create a public good for those consumers who do not. Economists refer to such public goods as "pecuniary externalities." Their presence usually makes *perfect* information about products unnecessary for market exchange to work efficiently.

now licenses some drugs and prohibits the sale of others for which licenses have not been approved. Many believe the costs that such regulations impose on consumers and on the drug industry may be substantial.

Other federal bureaus, and especially the **independent regulatory commissions,** enforce laws and promulgate rules and regulations that make certain information more readily available to citizens. (Independent regulatory commissions are created by acts of Congress and are directed by commissioners appointed by the president, with the advice and consent of the Senate, to legislatively determined, staggered terms. They are supposedly independent of presidential, congressional, or political influence and control.)

One agency compelling the publication of information is the Federal Trade Commission (FTC). Established by the Federal Trade Commission Act of 1914, the FTC enforces several laws that require products to be labeled according to their contents, including the Wool Products Labeling Act of 1940, the Fur Products Labeling Act of 1951, the Textile Fiber Products Identification Act of 1958, and the Fair Packaging and Labeling Act of 1966. The FTC also enforces the Truth-in-Lending Act of 1969, the Fair Credit Reporting Act of 1970, the Fair Credit Billing Act of 1974, and the Debt Collection Act of 1977, which variously require a standardized notification of interest rates and other loan costs to borrowers, impose safeguards on the use of credit reporting agencies, and regulate the "aggressiveness" with which debts may be collected. The FTC also operates under the Magnuson-Moss Warranty-Federal Trade Commission Improvement Act of 1975, which seeks to clarify warranty language, and the Hart-Scott-Rodino Antitrust Improvement Act of 1976.[5] Among its other tasks, the FTC monitors the "truthfulness" of private-sector advertising and packaging. For example, a toy sold in an oversized box might elicit FTC disapproval because such packaging is alleged to mislead buyers about the toy's size. The FTC is also responsible for requiring cigarette manufacturers to print health warning labels on cigarette packs.

Several other agencies share in compelling the publication of information. The Consumer Product Safety Commission (CPSC) regulates labeling, and the Federal Deposit Insurance Corporation (FDIC) regulates compliance with truth-in-lending rules, as does the Federal Reserve Board (FRB). Similarly, the SEC requires those who sell stocks to disclose information periodically about their firms. The Office of Consumer Affairs and Regulatory Functions of the Department of Housing and Urban Development (HUD) requires the publication of similar information about interstate land sales and also enforces the Real Estate Settlement Procedures Act of 1974, which requires that buyers be informed of all closing costs before a real-estate transaction is completed.

Like national defense and certain forms of information production, governmental establishment of a legal system of property rights is also a

---

[5] Penoyer, *Directory of Federal Regulatory Agencies,* p. 37.

public good. Chapter 3 points out that more people build or buy homes and businesses if their rights to them are secure.[6] Productivity, investment, and employment greatly expand with an optimal property-rights system, compared with a regime in which rights are absent or poorly or inefficiently specified. The explicit allocation of such rights often falls under the jurisdiction of particular federal agencies. The Constitution grants the Congress "the Power . . . to promote the Progress of Science and useful Arts, by securing for limited Times to Authors and Inventors the exclusive Right to their respective Writings and Discoveries. . . ." Pursuant to this grant of legislative authority, the Copyright Office of the Library of Congress gives property rights to authors and publishers, while the Patent and Trademark Office of the Department of Commerce administers various patent and trademark laws.[7] To the extent that the policies of these bureaus act to increase inventions, publications, and productivity generally, the associated property rights they establish create public goods.

Of course, the collective creation of a property right need not be desirable or correctly done. For example, a municipal parking bureau might allocate the right to set up tollgates on every road leading into or out of a city. The toll collector could keep the tolls, and would be granted this right for five-year periods. Such a right would inefficiently reduce traffic flows and the number of parking spaces demanded. On balance, it would create public bads—the toll and delays—and a pointless resource redistribution to the toll collector. The correct pricing of parking spaces themselves would represent a superior system for reducing the number of parking spaces demanded.

The external effects of bureau activities can become ambiguous, especially if the creation of property rights is involved. For example, the Federal Communications Commission (FCC) regulates the conditions under which various persons, corporations, and government units have the right to use certain portions of the radio frequency spectrum. There is only so much "room" in radio frequencies, and two radio or television stations cannot occupy the same channel unless they are geographically separated. But, whoever receives the property right to a particular frequency for, say, television or AM or FM radio broadcasts enjoys a limited monopoly. Plainly, the collective frequency-allocation system is a public good. In its absence, the chaos resulting from radio frequency interference might reduce the aggregate value of the spectrum as a productive resource. But, the monopoly power that the present system creates is a public bad, which the members of Congress and the FCC have not yet seen fit to avoid by changing that system.[8]

This kind of ambiguity concerning the extent and location of relative benefits and costs pervades the activities of several other regulatory agencies.

---

[6] Gordon Tullock, *Private Wants, Public Means: An Economic Analysis of the Desirable Scope of Government* (New York: Basic Books, 1970), chapter 2.

[7] See footnote 4.

[8] One regulatory alternative that has been suggested is to auction off channels to the highest bidder. The money received would go to the public treasury and in an

The Civil Aeronautics Board (CAB), established in 1938, for many years granted routes and set fares for all domestic commercial airlines. The granting of a route to an airline is equivalent to the vesting of a property right. The justifications given for this activity were, first, that without a guaranteed number of passengers, a national air transportation system could not develop in an orderly, predictable, and dependable manner, since investment would be too risky and not sufficiently profitable. Second, it was argued that the absence of regulation would leave small communities without air transportation, since airlines no longer would be required to service (principally small) unprofitable routes. Thus, the regulatory apparatus not only established property rights in routes supposedly to produce the associated public good of reliable air transportation, but also compelled a resource redistribution from riders on heavily traveled routes who paid higher fares to subsidize riders on unprofitable routes.[9]

Deregulation and the eventual dismemberment of the CAB began in 1978. However, other agencies regulate other areas of commerce as the CAB once did in aviation and as the FCC now does in communications and broadcasting. The FDIC, the Federal Home Loan Bank Board (FHLBB), and several state agencies regulate entry into the banking business and limit the number of banks and the degree of intra- and interstate competition in banking. The Federal Energy Regulatory Commission (FERC) regulates natural-gas pipelines and licenses private hydroelectric facilities. The Federal Maritime Commission licenses common carriers on the high seas. The Federal Reserve Board regulates interest rates. The International Trade Commission creates a property right for domestic manufacturers in domestic markets by acting against "dumping," a practice said to result from foreign manufacturers selling goods in the United States below their cost of production to ruin American businesses. And, activities equivalent to CAB regulatory practices are the major grist of the Interstate Commerce Commission (ICC). Established in 1887, the ICC is the oldest of the independent regulatory commissions. It regulates routes and rates of all interstate railroad and truck transportation, as well as inland waterways and coastal shipping. Following the

---

active auction market would represent nearly all of the monopoly rate of return the owner could secure. The owner could then sell the station if he chose to do so. Other suggestions include the more active encouragement of cable television and radio. See these essays in the *Journal of Law and Economics:* Ronald H. Coase, "The Federal Communications Commission," 2 (October 1959), pp. 1–40, and "The Interdepartment Radio Advisory Committee," 5 (October 1962), pp. 17–47; Harvey J. Levin, "Federal Control of Entry in the Broadcast Industry," 5 (October 1962), pp. 49–67, and "The Radio Spectrum Resource," 11 (October 1968), pp. 433–501; Jora R. Minasian, "Television Pricing and the Theory of Public Goods," 7 (October 1964), pp. 71–80, and "Property Rights in Radiation: An Alternative Approach to Radio Frequency Allocation," 18 (April 1975), pp. 221–272; Paul A. Samuelson, "Public Goods and Subscription TV: Correction of the Record," 7 (October 1964), pp. 81–83.

[9] Richard A. Posner, "Taxation by Regulation," *Bell Journal of Economics and Management Science,* 5 (Spring 1971), pp. 22–50.

CAB, the ICC appears to be the next target for dismemberment, and trucking and railroads the associated targets for deregulation. Indeed, some deregulation of trucking and railroads is already underway.

Public goods arise from information, patents, copyrights, and the creation of other forms of property rights. Education is also said to carry public-goods aspects, because it is believed by some to create a stable democracy, which they view as a public good whose production justifies its subsidy, if not its outright supply.[10] Hence, certain education-related activities of the Department of Education fall under the category of supplying public goods. Others argue that government sponsorship of research follows the same line of reasoning that explains FDA information-creating activities. Thus, National Science Foundation and National Institutes of Health grants are said to stimulate higher levels of discovery and research—products of information-generating activities. Finally, the provision of a stable currency—the job of the Department of the Treasury and the FRB—greatly reduces commercial transactions costs and therefore produces the public good of increased levels of commerce.[11]

The suppression of public bads. As Chapter 3 notes, creating public goods and suppressing public bads are mirror images of each other. Not surprisingly, therefore, the justifications offered for CAB, ICC, and banking regulations rest on the notion that entry into various markets must be limited. For otherwise, competitors would rush in, profits would disappear, and services would be provided either sporadically or not at all. Entry, route, and rate regulations are said to avoid prisoners' dilemma situations among producers that would show up as external diseconomies—public bads—for consumers in the form of inadequate service. However, such justifications find little support among economists, who point to any number of stable, competitive markets without such regulations.[12]

A clearer example of a public bad whose suppression has become the task of collective action is environmental pollution. The Environmental Pro-

[10] Milton Friedman, *Capitalism and Freedom* (Chicago: University of Chicago Press, 1962), pp. 85–107.

[11] The taste of double-digit inflation in recent years shows what happens when currencies are destabilized. Everyone finds it most difficult to contract for the future delivery of goods and services because producers cannot correctly judge how much the money they are paid will be worth. For a discussion of currency stability as a public goods and constitutional problem, see the analysis of constitutional bargains in Chapter 4 and the review of the constitutionally granted authority of Congress to control the currency in Chapter 9.

[12] Some economists approve of programs to limit output in agriculture and to regulate food prices, because market supply cannot respond rapidly to instantaneous changes in demand. Crops planted and cattle bred today are harvested and butchered some time from now. Other economists argue that an unregulated commodity futures market would do better at regulating long-run supply than the Department of Agriculture, which now controls farm production.

tection Agency (EPA), established in 1970, is responsible for enforcing the Clean Air Amendments of 1970 and 1977; the Federal Water Pollution Control Act of 1972; the Noise Control Act of 1972; the Federal Insecticide, Fungicide, and Rodenticide Act of 1972; the Toxic Substances Control Act of 1976; the Marine Protection, Research, and Sanctuaries Act, 1972; the Safe Drinking Water Act of 1974; the Water Quality Improvement Act of 1970; the Clean Water Act of 1977; and the Resource Conservation and Recovery Act of 1976; the EPA also shares responsibility for enforcing provisions of the Energy Supply and Environmental Coordination Act.[13] In sum, the EPA is responsible for the abatement of air, water, and noise pollution as well as the containment of radioactivity and solid waste. The EPA also regulates the use of pesticides and other toxic substances. Its principal activities are rule making, monitoring compliance with rules, and enforcement.

Several other agencies also administer various safety regulations. For example, the CPSC enforces (among others) the Flammable Fabrics Act of 1954, the Refrigerator Safety Act of 1956, the Hazardous Substances Act of 1960 as amended, and the Poison Prevention Packaging Act of 1970.[14] The Refrigerator Safety Act plainly suppresses a public bad, for it reduces the danger of suffocation for all children and thereby eliminates the negative externality associated with the production, use, and eventual discarding of refrigerators. However, it is difficult to place many of these other acts of Congress under the general rubric of suppressing the production of public bads. Buyers bear most of the costs and benefits of making products safer. Therefore, laws such as the Flammable Fabrics Act essentially require some consumers to purchase more "insurance" against burns, a private good, by purchasing safer products than they would in an unregulated marketplace. Since wealthier people generally prefer to buy more insurance than do poorer ones, the enforcement of such acts creates a resource redistribution of a private good from less wealthy consumers to those with higher incomes. Similar descriptions of agency activities concerning redistribution and the production of private goods characterize the Occupational Safety and Health Administration (OSHA) and the National Highway Traffic Safety Administration.

Various federal law enforcement agencies, such as the Federal Bureau of Investigation and the Drug Enforcement Administration in the Department of Justice, as well as the Treasury Department's Secret Service and Bureau of Alcohol, Tobacco, and Firearms, are charged with suppressing the public bad of certain criminal activities. However, by and large, enforcement of criminal law is the task of state, county, and local bureaus: police forces.

Resource redistribution. Resource redistribution is a major task of federal bureaus and bureaucrats. Transfer payments to individual citizens, in-

---

[13] Penoyer, *Directory of Federal Regulatory Agencies,* p. 27.

[14] Penoyer, *Directory of Federal Regulatory Agencies,* p. 23.

cluding income security (principally Social Security payments and public assistance), veterans benefits, and subsidies for education and training programs, now make up about 41 percent of the federal budget.[15] Huge bureaus such as HEW, which in 1979 (its last year before a separate Education Department was formed) had a proposed budget of $181 billion, and the Veterans Administration (VA), with a proposed 1979 budget of $19 billion, administer the related programs.

Hundreds of other federal agencies also daily allocate millions of dollars in the form of direct and indirect subsidies to various persons. These subsidies represent resource redistributions from the general, nondescript taxpayer to the definable persons or groups of persons receiving them. A tariff on imported shoes is a resource redistribution from consumers and foreign shoemakers and workers to domestic shoe manufacturers and their employees. A new post office in Tempe, Arizona, is a resource redistribution from taxpayers everywhere to the construction industry in Tempe, Arizona. The deepening of a harbor to receive pleasure boats is a resource redistribution from all taxpayers to those who own homes, businesses, and yachts in the harbor town. And, as mentioned earlier, a regulation forcing airlines to offer excessive services on sparsely traveled routes is a resource redistribution from all passengers to users of the unprofitable services.[16]

A government redistribution completely untouched by a bureau is unthinkable. Even simple changes in the tax code require IRS rule making, monitoring, and enforcement. Indeed, the entire tax system itself contains large numbers of implicit and often intentional redistributions. As becomes apparent later in this chapter, the effect bureaucrats have on redistributive decision making processes is substantial and not neutral.

Control of monopoly. Theoretically, monopolistic firms produce too little and charge too much. Several other practices, such as price fixing among firms as well as predatory pricing by a large firm trying to undercut the prices of a smaller one, also are taken as reasons for government action. There are two principal collective-choice approaches to monopoly. The first is to accept the monopoly, even outlaw potential competition, and then create a bureau to regulate the monopoly's prices and pricing structure. As Chapter 3 points out, this mode of regulation is thought to be suitable for controlling natural monopolies, such as electric power companies, natural-gas pipelines, and telephone companies. The very size of these monopolies creates a reduced cost of producing each unit of the associated goods and services. That is why such monopolies can destroy smaller competitors: they can afford to sell at a lower price per unit since their average production costs are lower. State agencies

[15] Social Security payments are transfers because those who are working now carry nearly the full cost for payments to those who are retired and drawing Social Security benefits. The system is almost completely subsidized by present payers. It is not a self-supporting pension fund.

[16] Posner, "Taxation by Regulation."

regulate most electric power companies and most intrastate telephone rates. Federal bureaus, such as the FCC, regulate interstate telephone service. The FERC regulates the interstate grid of natural-gas pipelines. The theoretical intent of such regulatory processes is to realize the low-cost benefits of size while shifting such benefits to consumers.

The second approach to monopolies is invoked when they are thought to result from anticompetitive practices, or when firms, monopolistic or otherwise, are alleged to engage in such practices. This second approach is embedded in antitrust laws such as the Sherman Act of 1890 and the Clayton Act of 1914. The FTC Bureau of Competition and the Antitrust Division of the Department of Justice hold responsibility for detecting and litigating various antitrust violations. They usually sue to break up the accused firm or to fine it (triple damages) for its alleged violation of the law. However, private antitrust suits alleging price fixing or predatory practices by one firm against another represent a widespread form of private regulation and have themselves been cited as having severe anticompetitive effects.[17]

PROBLEMS OF BUREAUCRATIC CONTROL

Federal bureaus, like private-sector firms, have structures, exist in a competitive environment, and produce various goods and services. However, bureaus confront decision-making problems unlike those faced by firms in the private sector.

Ambiguity about products. First, and perhaps most important, the owners of a private-sector firm usually agree on what their product is and why they produce and sell it. For example, Du Pont develops, manufactures, and sells chemicals, explosives, dyestuffs, fabrics, and paints. The goal of these activities is profit maximization.[18] Now, consider the DOD. What does it produce and sell? Some would answer "deterrence of foreign aggression." Others would say "the potential to thwart foreign aggression." Still others would regard the DOD's product as "the potential to wage aggressive, offensive war." But the DOD also provides training and social mobility to disadvantaged

[17] Robert Bork, *The Antitrust Paradox* (New York: Basic Books, 1978).

[18] Owners of publicly traded corporations do not necessarily agree on a simple measure of profit. Businesses differ according to the amount of risk and return they offer their owners. Stockholders may prefer different tradeoffs between risk and return on investments. They might also differ on whether they want the firm to pay out all earnings immediately in the form of dividends, or whether they wish the firm to reinvest profits, a strategy that can be reflected in higher future earnings and thus higher share prices as well as lower immediate personal income taxes. However, the voluntary nature of share ownership largely diminishes the importance of these preference differences. As we shall note momentarily, people can select the form of private-sector investment that suits them best. However, "investment" in (payment of taxes to support) a public-goods-producing bureaucracy is ordinarily compulsory.

citizens, an economic stimulus to particular communities and private firms, and several inventions of use in the private sector. This list hardly seems exhaustive.

Moreover, the DOD produces and sells a vague, undefinable, unmeasurable, and perhaps psychological good called national defense. The physical implements that create this undefinable good are things such as tanks, bombers, fighter planes, troop carriers, submarines, aircraft carriers, battleships, mine sweepers, a bevy of missile systems, infantry battalions, army bases, and an officer corps led by a joint chiefs of staff. How does each entity and its deployment contribute to this elusive entity called national defense? Would one more nuclear aircraft carrier add more or less to national defense than, say, 1500 more tanks would add? Would the cost of a new manned bomber system be worth more than the national defense forgone from not building such a system? Does an all-volunteer army produce more or less national defense than a partially conscripted army? Would additional expenditures on a new missile system not be cost-effective if relations with the Soviet Union improved? While similar questions might be difficult to answer for a large, multidivision, private-sector firm in search of profit, they could prove impossible to answer for a gigantic public-sector bureaucracy in search of national defense or, for that matter, in search of health, or education, or welfare.

Goal and strategy differences. To complicate matters further, the "owners" of the DOD, in this case the citizens of the United States, who are also "consumers" of the DOD's products, do not speak with one voice on the DOD's goal or goals, or on the strategies or product lines that might best achieve those goals. Some citizens would most prefer a greater emphasis on offensive weapons than on defensive ones; others would prefer the opposite. Some would prefer a greater reliance on diplomacy than on deterrent capability; others would most prefer to rely on naked military threat. Similarly, some would prefer the DOD to grow larger, while still others would prefer it to retrench.

Such goal and strategy differences are mirrored in the workings of most government agencies, and to a large extent the same differences pervade private-sector activity. For example, automobile buyers hold vastly different preferences among automotive styles, body types, colors, and engineering designs, and investors disagree over a firm's managerial strategies for maximizing profit. Yet, the dynamics that determine the structures and actions of private-sector firms do not determine those of public-sector bureaus. As a consequence, goal and preference differences resolved in one way by firms in a voluntary marketplace are resolved in quite another way by nonvoluntary public-sector bureaus, as agencies of the citizenry. Nor does the resolution of conflicting preferences by bureaus necessarily lead to Pareto-preferred results sanctioned by the theoretical justifications for public choice described in Chapter 3 and earlier in this chapter.

Political goals and bureau actions. In the first place, bureau structure and action are bounded and often defined by presidential and congressional decisions. As this chapter argues later and as Chapters 9 and 10 point out, presidents and representatives structure bureaus and bureau actions to maximize their chances of reelection as well as to improve their positions in the national government. Bureau output is at least two steps removed from citizen preferences: elections and the legislative process intervene. Bureau decision making itself, as described later in this chapter, adds yet a third step.

The connection between political and governmental processes and bureau decisions means that each problem associated with political and governmental processes affects what bureaucrats do. Citizens' preferences and legislative action get caught up in cyclical majorities, strategic ambiguities, coalitions of minorities, and a variety of sometimes perverse logrolls and prisoners' dilemmas. Bureaucrats cannot make any more sense out of incoherent *aggregated* preferences than can we, and their actions well might reflect that incoherence. Hence, citizens' *individual* preferences for bureau action sometimes become distorted beyond recognition; that bureaucrats themselves vote only exacerbates these problems.

Moreover, as we have noted before, citizens often seek the collective supply of distinctly private goods through political action. Bureau decisions frequently reflect attempts to satisfy the associated political demands. In sum, the political process, with all of its indeterminacies, is firmly interposed between citizen preferences and bureau performance. Thus, messages from the electorate have small chance of arriving undistorted and affecting bureau structure and performance in a stable, predictable manner.

Bureaus as monopolies. Federal bureaus also tend to be monopolies, with all potential competitors being outlawed. As Chapter 3 notes and as was just pointed out again, monopolies sometimes arise in the private sector because of the nature of production costs. The most efficient (least-cost) producer would be so large that only one firm could survive to manufacture a particular product. However, there is no theoretical reason that some government agencies that are now monopolies should continue to be so. The Post Office's delivery of first-class mail could be carried on by several competing private firms. There might be forty competing private- or public-sector veterans administrations and fifty bureaus of prisons. Or, VA and prison functions could even be contracted out to private-sector firms. The concept of competing bureaus has obvious limitations, but its strangeness merely reflects how seldom it becomes a reality and not a theoretical impossibility.

That some bureaus are monopolies, then, stems not from a natural response to market forces and production costs. They are so because the president and members of Congress want it that way.[19] However, the

---

[19] Indeed, the Supreme Court, using impeccable constitutional authority (Article 6, Section 2), grants monopoly *jurisdiction* to the federal government whenever its laws, regulations, and administrative actions conflict with the wishes of individual state

monopolistic organization of the bureaucratic "industry" sometimes bears no apparent relationship to citizens' preferences. Monopoly-bureaus also face little or no competition, so they have a reduced incentive to seek out and adopt more efficient structures, procedures, and allocations. As noted earlier in this chapter, bureau goals remain ambiguous, so efficiency may go undefined. Monopoly-bureaus, then, can accept inefficient structures, procedures, and allocations, and even if their directors wished to act as competitors, they might not know how to do so.[20] The cumulative impact of these forces is a perpetuation of present organizational modes and actions.

The monopoly problem is compounded in bureaus because shareholders of a private-sector firm, whether that firm is a monopoly or not, can sell their shares (stock) and spend the proceeds of the sale or invest the money in another firm. Firms that persist in doing business badly will experience falling share prices relative to the share prices of other, more efficiently organized firms, as more and more disenchanted stockholders sell out. As Chapter 7 points out in developing a parallel between private-sector corporations and political parties, failing firms become targets for takeover by those who believe they can manage them better. If consumers of a firm's product become dissatisfied, they can seek out a higher-quality or lower-price product. Even if the firm is a monopoly, consumers can try to find substitute products; at the very least, consumers can reduce their purchases of a private monopoly's product in response to higher prices.

By contrast, federal bureaus do not leave much room for shareholders and consumers to respond as they would in the private sector. For, at least some of the things that bureaus do create public goods that must be consumed, such as national defense. Other agencies dispense private, divisible goods but the provision of these goods must be supported out of taxes, which are public bads. Furthermore, tax law enforcement leaves no way for citizen-owner-consumers to divest themselves of "shares" in federal bureaus without either leaving the country or going through a complex, uncertain political process to seek changes in bureau action. Because both moving and politics are expensive and unlikely to succeed—most countries to which one might

---

authorities. See *McCulloch v. Maryland,* 4 Wheat. 316 (1819), and *Gibbons v. Ogden,* 9 Wheat. 1 (1824). Of course, the challenged federal action itself cannot be constitutionally impermissible.

[20] Recall from Chapter 3 that one facet of monopolistic inefficiency partially derives from the guarantee of relatively larger profits. Monopolies or regulated industries (which are often monopolies) were said to engage in discriminatory hiring because there was no way for a manager to convert a worker's lower salary into profits. See Harold Demsetz, "Minorities in the Market Place," *North Carolina Law Review,* 43 (February 1965), pp. 271–297. Federal bureaus share these problems despite many legislative and presidential attempts to overcome them by regulating bureau hiring and promotion procedures. Even HEW (now HSS), which shares with other agencies substantial responsibility for eliminating discriminatory hiring practices, found its own hiring to be discriminatory in result, if not by intent.

move will have similar bureaus—few citizens adopt either alternative. Therefore, federal bureaus, unlike private-sector firms, sometimes remain relatively immune to citizen-owner-consumer preferences. Too, citizens have relatively less opportunity to adjust their actions in response to bureau actions than in response to private-sector monopolies. Individual citizens "buy" defense and the tax code whether they want them or not.

DECISION MAKING IN BUREAUS: AN OPERATIONAL CODE

The common view of bureaucrats is that they merely transmit the wishes of the courts, the Congress, the president, and their bureau superiors. For example, an IRS bureaucrat who checks the accuracy of all additions and subtractions on a personal income tax return enjoys little discretion. An FTC clerk who compiles the bylaws of each county medical society in the United States may have latitude only about the final mode of presentation. And, the VA director, blessed by the Congress with funds to build a new hospital in Louisiana, cannot decide to build it instead in Kentucky. Certainly, bureaus can cause delays and fail to notice or correct serious cost overruns. Bureaus might even be riddled with corruption, as was alleged in 1978 about the federal government's major housekeeping and purchasing bureau, the General Services Administration (GSA). But the common view remains that bureaus are merely imperfect extensions of legislative and presidential preferences. Indeed, some argue that bureaucrats follow orders all too well.

Facts quickly overtake this view of bureaucracy. For example, one IRS bureaucrat also decided that some private schools were really operated to help parents avoid public-school desegregation; it was therefore proposed that any private schools that failed to meet minimum quotas on racial composition of their student bodies, as set by the IRS, would lose their tax-exempt status. One FTC bureaucrat used information compiled by the Commission to sue a county medical society for restraint of trade—an antitrust violation—because the society's bylaws prohibited its members from advertising. And, as this chapter notes later, VA bureaucrats keep patients in VA hospitals anywhere from two to three times longer than they would stay in private hospitals for the same procedures.[21] None of these activities has a specific legislative mandate, though each may have a general mandate. These examples simply provide evidence about the enormous discretion bureaucrats enjoy.

But what goals do bureaucrats pursue? What decisions do they make? First, we know that carrying out "the goals of the Congress" or of the president would be difficult because these are seldom clearly defined. Even if they were, bureaucrats usually must exercise too much discretion for congressional or presidential intent to provide more than general boundaries on the public

---

[21] Cotton M. Lindsay, "A Theory of Government Enterprise," *Journal of Political Economy*, 84 (October 1976), p. 1073.

policies that are eventually adopted. Second, we know that carrying out "the public interest" would be difficult because that interest is seldom revealed by the electoral process. Bureaucrats who seek "the public interest" would probably substitute their own judgments of what such an interest requires, which almost always is to say that bureaucrats would choose the public policy they prefer. Third, even if "the will of the Congress" and of the president and "the public interest" were plainly identifiable and coincided, and even if bureaucrats sought policies consistent with these concepts, bureaucrats still enjoy so much discretion that their decisions often could not be accurately predicted merely by reference to the wishes of other people.

To explain and predict bureaucrats' decisions, it proves useful to assume that bureaucrats themselves act *as if* they are rational decision makers: they choose alternatives to maximize expected utility or security levels, depending on the decision context. By this view, bureaucrats have consistent preference orderings, prefer more of positively valued outcomes and less of negatively valued ones, and prefer less risk to more risk.[22] But assuming that bureaucrats are rational decision makers means we believe "that bureaucrats are people who are, at least, not entirely motivated by the general welfare or the interests of the state."[23] Put differently: "It is not from the benevolence of the bureaucrat that we expect our research grant or our welfare check, but out of his regard to his own, not the public interest."[24]

---

[22] People often speak of a "bureaucratic" personality type, as if something sets government employees apart from others. In ordinary conversation, to call someone a bureaucrat is to insult that person. Writers occasionally note certain "dysfunctional" ways of thinking that sometimes characterize bureaucrats' decisions. See particularly Robert K. Merton, *Social Theory and Social Structure* (New York: Free Press, 1949), pp. 151–160. My own view is that there is no single bureaucratic personality type but that certain character traits are found more often among bureaucrats than among the general population. One such trait is an enhanced degree of risk aversion, which becomes manifest in several ways. First, bureaucratic positions have more job security than do most positions in the private sector. (Of course, private-sector positions are riskier but potentially more rewarding financially.) Thus, a self-selection process staffs government agencies with those less inclined to accept risk. Second, bureaucrats appear more likely to follow rules than to depart from established procedures, even when following those rules leads to entirely nonsensical results. Obsessive concern for details, as a corollary, is part of the bureaucrat's risk-avoiding ritual. However, compulsive rule following would probably characterize any organization whose product is ambiguous and not clearly measurable. Third, bureaucrats, by their rulings on such matters as safety regulations, demonstrate an aversion to risk far in excess of the population's preferences, as revealed by actual consumption decisions made in the marketplace.

[23] William A. Niskanen, Jr., *Bureaucracy and Representative Government* (New York: Aldine Atherton, 1971), p. 36.

[24] James M. Buchanan, in "Foreword" to Gordon Tullock, *The Politics of Bureaucracy* (Washington, D. C.: Public Affairs Press, 1965), p. 2. The quotation is adapted from Adam Smith's pivotal observation about the marketplace in *The Wealth of Nations*: "It is not from the benevolence of the butcher, the brewer, or the baker, that we expect our dinner, but from their regard to their own interest."

Even so, interpreting bureaucratic decision making as rational choice is difficult because bureaucrats must pursue many different goals just to pursue their self-interest. To understand how these goals affect bureaucratic action, it is helpful to construct an **operational code of the bureaucrat.**[25] Such a code is a set of decision rules that an outside observer believes people under study act as if they use when they are choosing to develop and implement various public policies. It is not possible to construct an operational code that can explain and predict all bureaucratic action. However, five rules of such a code seem evident, substantially researched, and descriptive of how bureaucrats make decisions.

Maximize the bureau's budget. An important analysis of bureaucrats' decision making has been developed assuming that bureaucrats seek to maximize their bureaus' budgets.[26] This assumption follows from the observation that increases in certain measures create increases in a bureaucrat's utility. These measures include the bureaucrat's "salary, perquisites of office, public reputation, power, patronage, [and] output of the bureau. . . ."[27] In turn, each of these measures usually increases with an increase in an agency's budget.

We do not know whether larger budgets actually cause outcomes such as greater public reputation or power, or whether causality runs *from* reputation or power *to* budget increases. However, the conjecture about the positive relationship between each of these measures and budget size seems reasonable. For example, the budgets of HEW and DOD were expected to be about $185 billion and $128 billion respectively for fiscal year 1979. The less prestigious Departments of Agriculture and Commerce had projected budgets of $20 billion and $2.7 billion respectively. The Department of Energy budget was at $2.5 billion. Even though the more prestigious State Department had a projected budget of only $1.5 billion, nevertheless a tenfold increase of the State Department's budget to $15 billion, while holding all other departments' budgets constant, would certainly indicate an enhancement of reputation and patronage for the secretary of state.

Budget maximization is positively related to the bureaucrat's probability of success and survival. For instance, bureau employees hold well-established expectations about a bureau director's actions, and those expectations are substantially connected to the director's pursuit of ever larger budgets. A bureau director's dependence on employees for survival is probably far more pronounced in the public sector than among private-sector firms. Members of Congress can exploit disagreements within a bureau, while shareholders of a private-sector firm ordinarily have no such incentive. For example, a deputy assistant secretary of state may become incensed over the

[25] The notion of an operational code is developed in Nathan Leites, *The Operational Code of the Politburo* (New York: McGraw-Hill, 1951).

[26] Niskanen, *Bureaucracy and Representative Government.*

[27] Niskanen, *Bureaucracy and Representative Government.* p. 38.

secretary of state's position on South Korean domestic politics and give information embarrassing to the secretary to minority-party members of the Senate. Dissatisfied generals and admirals can "plant" questions adverse to the secretary of defense, who then will confront them for the first time at a Senate Foreign Relations Committee hearing on approving a strategic arms limitation treaty with the Soviet Union. Bureaucrats' employees can make life miserable and, in extreme cases, drive their bosses from office. "They can be cooperative, responsive, and efficient, or they can deny information to the bureaucrat, undermine his directives, and embarrass him before the constituency and officers of the [Congress]. . . ."[28]

Larger budgets allow bureaucrats to hire subordinates with greater skills and enhanced loyalties. Subordinates' performances depend "on their perceived rewards of employment in the bureau. The employees' interests in larger budgets are obvious and similar to those of the bureaucrat: greater opportunities for promotion, more job security, etc., and more profits to the contract suppliers of factors" (for example, steel manufacturers who supply steel plates for DOD-contracted battleships).[29] Hence, "A bureaucrat's life is not a happy one (tra la) unless he can provide increasing budgets for his subordinate bureaucrats."[30]

Members of Congress, acting as the agents of various groups, *ceteris paribus* also prefer increasing bureau budgets to stable or declining ones. The members of most groups in the electorate presently receiving benefits from a bureau, and therefore their legislator-agents, want the bureau to sponsor ever more and larger programs. Bureaucrats who fail to comply with such preferences can expect severe attack from congressional critics. For example, if the secretary of defense suddenly decided to advocate the abandonment of manned aircraft as part of the nation's strategic arsenal, his severest critics would be senators and representatives whose states and districts have aircraft plants and air bases. Even the secretary's failure to push for a *larger* Air Force would provoke sharp questioning on Capitol Hill. The same relationship holds true for districts with shipyards and Army bases. The secretary of defense is thus under constant pressure to seek larger and larger DOD budgets, and the members of Congress can reward or punish a secretary who complies with or ignores this pressure.[31]

---

[28] Niskanen, *Bureaucracy and Representative Government,* p. 40. This strategy occurs in the private sector, but it is less effective. A corporate director's superiors and customers enjoy fairly clear performance measures, such as price and profit. The absence of these measures in the public sector has been discussed earlier in this chapter. But additional information offered by subordinate "tattletales" in the private sector is unlikely to have real value unless it suggests ways for increasing profit.

[29] Niskanen, *Bureaucracy and Representative Government,* p. 40.

[30] Niskanen, *Bureaucracy and Representative Government,* p. 40.

[31] While legislators approve of bureaucrats who push for enlargement of a favored program's budget, they also prefer bureaucrats who argue forcefully for an overall enlargement of the agency's *total* budget. Legislators see their job as one of deciding among competing claims for limited resources. They exercise monopoly

Budget maximizing also results from the nature of bureaucrats' incentives and rewards. The "not-for-profit" environment in which bureaucrats produce public goods requires them to pursue a goal other than profits. For the reasons already suggested, maximizing budget size is an appropriate goal. A corollary of budget maximizing is that bureaucrats should act to maintain their agencies' budgets against attack, which means that they may even sometimes have to accept smaller budget cuts from angry legislators to avoid larger ones.

The descriptive validity of this first rule of the bureaucrat's operational code distinguishes sharply between older, traditional views of bureaucratic action, which perceive bureaus as mere conduits for legislative commands, and more recent views, which see bureaucratic action as a source of utility for bureaucrats. Under the older view, heads of bureaus should not much care (within limits) if their budgets are cut, as long as that is what legislators prefer. Under more recent views, budget cuts would call forth some form of counterattack.

For example, California's tax-cutting Proposition 13, which was followed by threatened and occasionally successful parallel actions in other states, meant that some bureau budgets would be cut. Bureaucratic attacks on Proposition 13 were fierce and predictable. Before the vote, school superintendents issued preliminary layoff notices to thousands of teachers and cancelled summer school programs. They predicted double sessions, larger classes, elimination of bands, orchestras, and sports programs, and a general decline in the quality and quantity of public education in California. Police commissioners spoke menacingly of 30 to 40 percent reductions in the number of officers on the beat. Librarians predicted three-day weeks and widespread branch closings. Welfare-agency directors publicly acknowledged the likelihood of large cuts in benefits to welfare recipients. Sanitation-department directors voiced fears that garbage pickups at private residences would end. The message from most bureaucrats was the same: "Cut our budget and expect the immediate loss of the most highly valued services we supply."

Notice that *before* the passage of Proposition 13, school superintendents did not promise to try to maintain educational levels by running schools more efficiently or by paring the size of the superintendents' staffs or the number of vice-principals. Nor did police commissioners pledge more efficient opera-

---

control over the resulting allocations and often collect benefits—for example, campaign contributions—for "choosing wisely." Representatives seem not especially interested in having bureaucrats make these allocation decisions for them by providing honest, and possibly humble, assessments of the value of the existing and proposed government programs they oversee. Legislators' preferences for forceful advocacy by bureau directors follow in part from the view of legislators as agents for their constituents. But this preference is obviously more complicated than that, and it reflects a complex pattern of relationships that is not well understood. However, my guess is that legislators prefer budget-maximizing bureaucrats principally because of their treatment of the constituents' pet projects. See Niskanen, *Bureaucracy and Representative Government,* p. 40.

tions and fewer assistant chiefs. Librarians failed to acknowledge the possibility of less expensive operations; sanitation-department heads did not admit that private-sector entrepreneurs could collect garbage for a lower price. Of course, welfare-agency directors did not publicly discuss the possibility of maintaining payments to recipients by laying off administrators and caseworkers. The California bureaucrats responded as bureaucrats almost always respond to impending budget cuts: they threatened to eliminate their most highly valued services rather than improve efficiency or fire administrators. Their use of this strategy is a direct consequence of seeking larger budgets or of trying to maintain present budget levels.[32] The California experience notwithstanding, this strategy seldom fails. Indeed, it succeeded in the 1980 effort to defeat California's Proposition 9, a referendum to cut state income taxes.

Expand the bureau's jurisdiction. Sometimes budgets grow larger because bureau jurisdictions expand, and sometimes jurisdictions expand because budgets grow larger. This second rule of the bureaucrat's operational code may seem indistinguishable from the first rule, but it may also fail to operate as often. Bureaucrats might be invited into new areas but draw back from entering them because their controversial nature would threaten the bureau's overall budget. And, sometimes bureaucrats believe that new activities would simply be too costly in terms of other bureau goals.

Nevertheless, the drive for new activities and expanded jurisdictions remains a constant characteristic of bureaucratic action. Old tasks are completed or regularized, and uninterrupted employment itself requires that new tasks be found. Members of Congress exert continual pressure on behalf of their constituents, and the satisfaction of congressional demands must often come from the expansion of some bureau's jurisdiction. As a corollary, bureau jurisdiction must be maintained against encroachments and threats of cutbacks. This corollary gains importance in an environment of several bureaus, all of whose directors are pursuing expanded jurisdictions. Conflicts may be unavoidable, and agency heads often must formulate explicit agreements among themselves about which agency is responsible for which problems.

For example, the Department of Justice and the FTC have developed

---

[32] Later, this chapter describes the close correspondence between bureau and legislative decision making. Here, though, it is interesting to note that certain members of the House and Senate responded like bureaucrats to a threatened national Proposition 13. The Constitution provides in Article 5 that on petition of the legislatures of two-thirds of the states, Congress must "call a convention for proposing amendments . . . ." By early 1979, thirty state legislatures had petitioned Congress to propose and consider various forms of taxing and spending limitation amendments to the federal Constitution. Former Senator Edmund S. Muskie (D-Maine) threatened that following the adoption of such an amendment, the first program to be cut would be federal Revenue Sharing with state governments. Another proposed constitutional amendment that would limit federal spending has been introduced in the Congress and is reproduced here in Appendix B.

understandings to separate their overlapping jurisdictions in antitrust cases. Such agreements are not difficult to maintain when federal revenues and agency budgets are increasing. However, if revenues decline relative to bureau expenditures, then bureaucratic "cartels" quickly dissolve in the scramble for funds. For instance, the Departments of the Army, Navy, and Air Force entered into the Key West Agreement in 1947 to reduce competition among them for funds and program authorizations, but a subsequent cutback in defense revenues proved too much for this armed forces "cartel," which then quickly dissolved.[33]

In and of itself, expanding an agency's jurisdiction is not difficult and often can be accomplished through rule-making procedures. The IRS decision referred to earlier, to monitor private schools' racial compositions and to grant or deny tax exemptions based on its findings, provides an example of a bureau's (eventually unsuccessful) search for an expanded jurisdiction. The ICC's decision to deregulate interstate trucking partially—before the members of Congress or the president acted more harshly—provides an example of a bureau trying to protect its jurisdiction by retrenching.

An extreme example of expanding jurisdictions is that of the Equal Employment Opportunity Commission (EEOC), a regulatory commission established by Title VII of the Civil Rights Act of 1964. The EEOC is responsible for enforcing the 1964 Act and the Equal Employment Opportunity Act of 1972, which amended the 1964 Act. The EEOC is a good example of an "imperializing bureaucracy." Estimates show its staff growing from 1970 to 1981 by nearly 400 percent, from 780 to 3891.[34] This is a larger staff than the ICC, the oldest of the independent regulatory commissions, employs. EEOC budget outlays rose from $12 million in 1970 to an estimated $135 million in 1979, an increase of over 1000 percent.[35]

The EEOC is responsible for seeing to it that private-sector as well as state and local employers carry out the legal requirement of "equal pay for equal work." Doing this job means that the EEOC must learn about various forms of job and pay discrimination as between races, sexes, and age groups. Then, the Commission must take legal actions to enforce nondiscriminatory practices. The basic fodder of EEOC cases involves situations in which the average female clerk-typist II in a firm—and sometimes in a public-sector bureau—receives a significantly lower rate of pay than the average male clerk-typist II in that firm, without any nonprejudicial explanation for the difference.

Recently, EEOC bureaucrats have become interested in a new area of alleged discrimination. As an example of this new area, they have observed that the plumbers a large corporation employs are mostly men, while the clerk-typists are mostly women. Furthermore, plumbers earn a higher rate of

---

[33] Niskanen, *Bureaucracy and Representative Government,* p. 195, *passim.*

[34] Penoyer, *Directory of Federal Regulatory Agencies,* p. 28.

[35] Penoyer, *Directory of Federal Regulatory Agencies,* p. 28.

pay than do clerk-typists. Such systematic wage-rate differentials could be discriminatory, depending upon the "true" relative values to the firm of plumbers' and clerk-typists' labor. Corporate executives might even be using job classifications to mask discriminatory wage rates. Accordingly, the EEOC has under active consideration a policy of requiring "equal pay for comparable work," or for work of "comparable value."[36]

EEOC employees would have to evaluate and continually monitor the economic nature—supply, demand, wage rate, job amenities, and required training costs—of every job classification of every firm in the United States simply to establish that this newly discovered form of alleged discrimination actually exists in a particular firm. Ensuring nondiscrimination among different job classifications thus would require a huge growth of the bureau. Expanding jurisdiction into this new area is precisely the kind of action expected of a bureau complying with the second rule of the operational code. Notice that its budget would also have to grow enormously to monitor private-sector wage patterns. For an imperializing bureaucracy such as the EEOC, the discovery of this form of alleged discrimination is heaven-sent.

The drive to expand an agency's jurisdiction partially explains why so many bureaus exercise monopoly control over the goods and services they produce. Sometimes jurisdictions collide, and either the legislature, or the president, or a court of law must decide which agency will prevail. As suggested earlier, on other occasions the agencies themselves divide the territory. Whatever the resolution of jurisdictional disputes might be, bureaus seem to expand in the direction of least resistance until monopoly control or near-monopoly control results.

Maximize the bureau's output. *Ceteris paribus,* bureaus with growing budgets and expanding jurisdictions will have increasing outputs. Budget increases and jurisdictional imperialism may themselves require that bureau heads try to maximize output. The postmaster general goes to Congress with tales of handling an ever-increasing volume of mail. Welfare agencies proudly count clients served. Public schools—especially universities—compute credit hours taught. And, United States attorneys report on the number of cases successfully prosecuted or plea bargained. Bureau output indicates to the members of Congress how extensive and important bureau activities have become to their constituents. Expansions of output often go hand-in-hand with increases in constituents' reliance on and support for a bureau's activities.

As noted earlier, though, bureau output may be difficult to define or measure. For example, an antipoverty agency has many different ways of measuring its output. One measure might report the amount of money or the value of the benefits in kind the agency distributes to indigents. Another might count the number of poor people receiving benefits in a given year. A

---

[36] For an analysis of this policy, see Cotton Mather Lindsay, *Equal Pay for Comparable Work: An Economic Analysis of a New Antidiscrimination Doctrine* (Coral Gables, Fla.: University of Miami Law and Economics Center, 1980).

third might count the agency's present caseload. A fourth, suggested earlier in this chapter, might gauge the number or percentage of the agency's welfare recipients lifted permanently above the poverty level in a given year.

One could go on indefinitely listing various measures of the agency's output. Such measures usually tap different and often conflicting aspects of agency output. For instance, suppose the poverty agency's employees try successfully to maximize the fourth measure, the number or percentage of welfare recipients lifted permanently above the poverty level in a given year. If they are successful, then the agency's caseload will probably be reduced below what it would have been using some other measure, since some of its clients no longer will ask, or qualify, for its services. By contrast, one perverse way in which the agency can maximize output measured as a caseload is to fail systematically to make permanent improvements in its clients' economic independence. Its caseload will then simply continue to expand.

Another problem with the code's third rule is the inherent unmeasurability of some public goods. This problem has already been discussed with reference to national defense. The DOD often responds to this problem by counting its output in terms of the number of people in uniform, the number of tanks in Europe, the number of missile-firing submarines at sea, and the throw weight of its ICBMs. Then, comparisons are drawn between United States forces and Soviet forces or between NATO forces and Warsaw Pact forces. National defense itself never seems to be directly measured or estimated, except in relative terms: "We are stronger than they are."

Maximize output that can be monitored. Some bureau outputs are monitorable and measurable, while others are not.[37] Hence, the DOD output-measuring strategy makes sense. Bureaucrats will usually produce a larger output of easily monitored product attributes than of not-so-easily monitored ones. They will also usually produce attributes of output that seem to have a greater connection to the bureau's legislated "mission" than attributes of output for which the connection is less clear. This often means that those who monitor bureau performance, the members of the relevant congressional committees overseeing the bureau, will monitor bureau *activity* rather than bureau *output.* Activity measurements represent a substitute for more difficult indices of real output. For example, legislators will count the number of people living in HUD-financed dwellings rather than assess HUD's profitability or even the net improvement in living standards created by HUD programs. Legislators will also ascertain the number of patient-days spent in VA hospitals rather than seek some yardstick of net health improvements from VA programs, and, they will carefully measure the number of arrests for dealing in illegal drugs rather than try to assess the impact of those arrests and other Drug Enforcement Administration activities on quality of life, on life expectancy among adolescents, or even on the street price of heroin.

[37] This section restates the argument in Lindsay, "A Theory of Government Enterprise."

This kind of direct monitoring of bureau activity rather than of bureau output itself leads bureaucrats to produce outcomes that differ systematically from those produced by comparable private-sector firms. In particular, bureaus will ordinarily produce a higher level of output at a lower level of quality than their private-sector counterparts. The reason for this difference is that the members of Congress find it far more difficult to monitor output quality than output quantity. Output is often free to users of bureau services, and therefore they respond slowly to a deterioration in its quality. By contrast, private-sector consumers quickly take their business elsewhere, so that quality deterioration rapidly affects the profits of private-sector firms. However, unhappy users of services provided in the public sector, and especially services monopolized by bureaus, can only write to their congressman and hope for the best.[38]

These propositions about bureaus have been tested by studying hospital care, an area in which private- and public-sector institutions offer comparable services. Government VA hospitals coexist with private-sector voluntary (nonprofit) and proprietary (for profit) hospitals. One consequence of differential private- and public-sector monitoring is that to maximize patient-days, VA hospitals should try to keep their beds filled with patients, and one way to do this is to keep patients in the hospital for relatively longer periods. On the other hand, voluntary hospitals should keep patients in the hospital only for as long as good care and patients' preferences dictate. Table 11.1 reports exactly the difference expected.

It would be exceedingly difficult for members of Congress (and also researchers) to monitor variations in the quality of care. Nevertheless, VA hospital administrators can be expected to spend their budgets on increasing patient-days, a variable that House and Senate members can monitor, rather than on quality of care, which legislators cannot directly monitor. The production of a lower quality of goods and services in the public sector than in the private sector is also expected, because dissatisfied private-sector consumers can take their business elsewhere, while public-sector consumers may find a similar exercise of consumer choice more difficult. They may be using the agency's output because it seems costless to them or because it is a public good, which they must consume. Of course, the very inability to find direct measures of quality suggests that this proposition about comparative public- and private-sector quality can only be tested indirectly.

Some of the evidence is impressionistic. Plainly, "The title 'bureaucrat' . . . has developed pejorative overtones. . . . The typical customer of a government bureau expects inconvenience and delay in receipt of service. He is not surprised when the service is unavailable when demanded or defective when delivered, or when it is administered by personnel who are rude and indiffer-

[38] There is a strong argument, discussed later in this chapter, that members of Congress have real incentives to keep the quality of public-sector services at a low level. One reason for this perverse incentive is vote production stemming from performing ombudsman activities on behalf of aggrieved constituents.

Table 11.1 Average Lengths of Stay (reported in days) in VA and Voluntary Hospitals Controlling for Illness or Surgical Procedure for Patients 50–64 Years Old (except where noted)

Procedure	VA	Voluntary
Pilonidal cyst (35–49)	15.7	5.8
Diabetes mellitus	19.0	9.0
Acute coronary occlusion	31.5	21.7
Hemorrhoidectomy	15.3	7.1
Tonsils and adenoids (35–49)	6.4	2.4
Duodenum ulcer	15.2	6.7
Appendicitis	12.1	6.9
Inguinal hernia	17.1	7.2
Gastroenteritis and colitis	11.1	7.7
Gallstones	26.5	11.9
Pyelitis, cystitis, nephritis	11.6	6.0
Kidney stones	18.6	8.2
Prostate	22.1	9.7

Source: Interagency length-of-stay study group (unpublished); reprinted from Cotton M. Lindsay, "A Theory of Government Enterprise," *Journal of Political Economy,* 84 (October 1976), p. 1073, by permission of The University of Chicago Press, © 1976 by The University of Chicago.

ent."[39] Other evidence, though indirect, is less impressionistic. The net cost per patient day in a VA hospital (1973) is $49.09, while the comparable cost for a proprietary hospital is $82.87.[40] As Table 11.2 shows, staff-to-patient ratios in VA hospitals are lower than in proprietary hospitals. These figures imply a lower quality of care for VA hospital patients.

This incentive to maximize monitorable aspects of output while ignoring or trading off unmonitorable ones—compared to private sector incentives—becomes especially acute if the connection between agency output and agency mission remains ambiguous. For example, it is not at all evident exactly what relationship holds between traffic-law enforcement by police and the death rate from automobile accidents. However, when death rates climb, police often respond to gubernatorial prodding by setting up speed traps and quickly increasing the number of speeding citations they issue. They seldom patrol the most dangerous intersections; instead, they set up their surveillance in areas where their presence can go undetected.[41] This strategy maximizes

[39] Lindsay, "A Theory of Government Enterprise," p. 1061.

[40] Lindsay, "A Theory of Government Enterprise," p. 1070, quoting Committee on Veterans Affairs, U.S. House of Representatives, *Hospitals: Guide Issues, 1967–1973,* and *Operations of Veterans Administration Hospitals and Medical Program,* various years, and Lindsay's computations.

[41] Lindsay, "A Theory of Government Enterprise," p. 1067.

Table 11.2 Staff-to-Patient Ratios for VA and Proprietary Hospitals: Various Years

Year	VA General Hospitals	Proprietary Short-Term General Hospitals
1969	1.42	2.44
1970	1.46	2.56
1971	N/A	2.62
1972	N/A	2.67
1973	1.59	2.72

Source: Committee on Veterans Affairs, U.S. House of Representatives, *Operations of Veterans Administration Hospitals and Medical Program,* various years, and *Hospitals: Guide Issues, 1969–1973;* reprinted from Cotton M. Lindsay, "A Theory of Government Enterprise," *Journal of Political Economy,* 84 (October 1976), p. 1072, by permission of the University of Chicago Press, © 1976 by The University of Chicago.

the number of traffic citations issued, but no one knows what it does to accident death rates, compared to some other surveillance strategy.

The problem of monitoring persists even when one bureaucrat (instead of an elected official) monitors another. Junior bureaucrats will use most of their energies to maximize the output of product attributes that their superiors can monitor and allocate few resources, if any, to other attributes. For example, some believe that an extensive firsthand knowledge of the culture, politics, and language of a foreign country seems of little use for an ambitious State Department junior embassy staff member. "The important social contacts for the American diplomat who wishes to rise in the hierarchy are those with other Americans, both important American visitors and members of the American missions. Too much association with natives is likely to involve some slighting of this relationship to other Americans, and is, consequently, likely to retard promotion."[42]

Senior State Department officials cannot easily monitor the staff member's output that most would regard as central to the department's supposed mission. "Influencing foreigners is . . . one object of the American foreign service, but there is no simple way of determining how successful any particular individual has been in this task. As a result, the Department of State tends to overlook this factor in deciding on promotions. The ambitious diplomat will, if he is wise, confine himself to influencing Americans. His reports should be based on an analysis of the Department of State, not upon the country he is ostensibly reporting. Quite naturally, as a polished diplomat, he will not admit all this, probably not even to himself."[43]

Nor does the CIA escape this problem. Both CIA and State Department operatives probably "scored points" with their superiors by cultivating the

[42] Tullock, *The Politics of Bureaucracy,* p. 42.

[43] Tullock, *The Politics of Bureaucracy,* p. 42.

Shah of Iran's staff and SAVAK, the Iranian secret police. Such contacts with Iranian officialdom were extremely important to Americans doing business in Iran, and therefore they were also important to American public servants—CIA and State Department personnel—acting as intermediaries. These operatives were constantly reassured by their Iranian contacts that a successful revolt was impossible. Little credit could be gained *before* the Iranian revolution by State Department or CIA officials from becoming intimately familiar with the aides of the Ayatollah Khomeini. This problem of inappropriate incentives is widespread, and it may help to explain some of the failures of American intelligence operations, including those in Iran.

Minimize the probability of making detectable errors. The code's fifth rule rests on the idea that some errors are easier to detect than are others. The members of Congress monitor bureau output and bureau mistakes—errors—but only where those errors are detectable. Therefore, bureaucrats use resources to minimize the chances of making detectable errors and tend to disregard undetectable ones. Indeed, they may be unaware of certain errors they make simply because those errors *are* undetectable. This fifth rule parallels the fourth, and both rules might be reduced to saying: Do best what customers and superiors can judge you on.

Following the fifth rule can create regulatory imbalances that impose severe costs on the population. The most extensively documented case of such an imbalance concerns the FDA's regulation of new drugs.[44] The theoretical benefits of FDA information-creating activities are noted earlier in this chapter. The licensing and regulatory questions constantly before the FDA are: How extensive must tests of new pharmaceutical preparations be? and How high should efficacy and safety standards be set? Testing and efficacy and safety standards set levels of effectiveness and safety that drugs under required tests must meet. For example, a drug that dissolves dangerous blood clots in fifteen percent of the cases for which it is administered would be judged unacceptable if, say, it induced internal bleeding and killed 20 percent of those who received it.

The FDA's imposition of more extensive testing rules and higher levels of efficacy and safety standards certainly should reduce the probability of error. In this case, an error would mean licensing for use an ineffective or dangerous drug. Sometimes errors appear unavoidable. For example, chloramphenicol, a strong antibacterial drug, can be toxic to bone marrow. But in not more than one in 20,000 cases of use has it been known to cause blood dyscrasias, which sometimes can prove fatal.[45] Still, it is simply not practical to test chloramphenicol on the number of people necessary to uncover this side effect. FDA error therefore seems unavoidable in approving

---

[44] See William M. Wardell and Louis Lasagna, *Regulation and Drug Development* (Washington, D. C.: American Enterprise Institute, 1975).

[45] Wardell and Lasagna, *Regulation and Drug Development,* p. 139.

such drugs, although a practical number of clinical tests may be possible for other drugs with more frequently occurring side effects.

When FDA functionaries set a particular number of clinical trials for the human testing of any drug, they simultaneously accept some probability of making an error by approving an ineffective or unsafe preparation. How large that probability of error might be is inversely proportional to the stringency and thoroughness of the testing requirements and approval standards as well as the number of persons on whom the drug is tried. Each and every previously unexpected side effect from the use of an FDA-approved drug, though, represents an FDA error. Many such errors eventually become detectable through extensive drug use in the population (as was true of chloramphenicol). FDA officials are vitally interested in minimizing the probability that such errors occur. But, as in most other areas of regulation, severe trade-offs are involved with FDA drug-approval procedures. Each time the FDA stiffens testing requirements and standards to reduce its chances of approving an ineffective or dangerous drug, it simultaneously increases the likelihood of preventing the development and use of a safe and effective one. FDA regulations thus are costly, but such costs are well concealed. In short, TANSTAAFL.

The hidden costs of FDA activities are manifested in four ways. First, by increasing the required thoroughness for animal and human testing, the FDA delays the time it takes to get pharmaceutical preparations out of the laboratory and into drugstores, hospitals, and doctors' offices. Delays can be costly. For example, suppose some disease afflicts 100,000 people each year and kills 50,000 of them, even with the use of presently available medication. A pharmaceutical company might develop a drug that reduces deaths from this disease from 50,000 to 40,000 annually. Suppose this drug eventually will prove to have no serious side effects in human beings. Finally, assume that no better therapy is available. If the normal course of testing such a drug requires one year and if the FDA increases its standards so that testing requires two years, then the FDA action has killed 10,000 people. How many people might be saved because unknown side effects were avoided by the year's delay for additional testing remains a purely speculative question. However, the error of incorrectly delaying the approval of a safer and more effective drug remains far less detectable than does the error of approving a drug whose use results, say, in children being born without limbs.

The second cost associated with the error of incorrectly requiring too high a level of testing and efficacy and safety standards is a higher cost for drugs.[46] The order of magnitude is estimated to be between 5 and 10 percent.[47] The third cost occurs because pharmaceutical companies fail to seek

[46] "Too high" levels result from the FDA's failure to calculate *all* of the costs associated with the imposition of its rules, including the costs of relatively undetectable errors. The results are Pareto-inferior.

[47] Sam Peltzman, "An Evaluation of Consumer Protection Legislation: The 1962 Drug Amendments," *Journal of Political Economy,* 81 (September-October 1973), p.

approval for medicines they have developed simply because of a diminished probability of approval and the now substantial cost of applying for approval.

The fourth cost, another manifestation of the increased probability of FDA error, seems almost completely undetectable. The development of pharmaceutical preparations, from research through marketing, represents an investment decision. The most speculative aspects of this decision concern the level of resources a pharmaceutical corporation should allocate to research. Because research expenditure decisions are quite risky, a dollar spent on research must eventually result in more than a dollar added to the firm's revenue. Otherwise, the firm will do no research. However, increased testing standards add to the cost of marketing a drug and delay the time when the firm can realize a cash flow from its research and development investment. Increased efficacy and safety standards reduce the probability that a particular drug will be licensed. The combined effects of FDA activities, then, reduce the investment attractiveness of new-drug development. Pharmaceutical corporations will thus develop fewer new drugs, and some of those that are not developed would probably have been safer and more effective than those now available. Every undiscovered drug that FDA regulations prevent from becoming a reality represents an FDA error. However, this kind of error seems virtually undetectable by those who monitor FDA activities as well as by FDA decision makers themselves. Hence, FDA functionaries are not terribly concerned about the adverse effects their regulations have on drug development. This lack of concern persists even though FDA activities might harm or kill more people than they serve.

Data and analysis reinforce the view that FDA activities take their toll on pharmaceutical research and development. A statistical model published in 1973 very accurately predicted the number of new chemical entities that American pharmaceutical manufacturers had developed annually before 1962.[48] Figure 11.1 shows the model's results. Until 1962, when stiff regulatory amendments to the Food, Drug, and Cosmetic Act of 1938 were passed, the model's predictions very closely tracked the actual number of new chemical entities developed each year. After 1962, the number of new chemical entities produced fell off drastically from what the model would have otherwise predicted. Additional research shows comparable differences between United States and European pharmaceutical manufacturers.[49] European nations have not instituted testing procedures and efficacy and safety standards as strict as the FDA requires.

Another example of the same phenomenon of reducing the probability of making detectable errors while ignoring undetectable ones shows up in

---

1090. Peltzman calculates a *net* loss based, among other things, on savings from not buying ineffective drugs, losses from lack of price competition among drug firms, and losses from forgone innovations that result in new and improved drugs.

[48] Peltzman, "An Evaluation of Consumer Protection Legislation: The 1962 Drug Amendments," pp. 1049–1091.

[49] Wardell and Lasagna, *Regulation and Drug Development.*

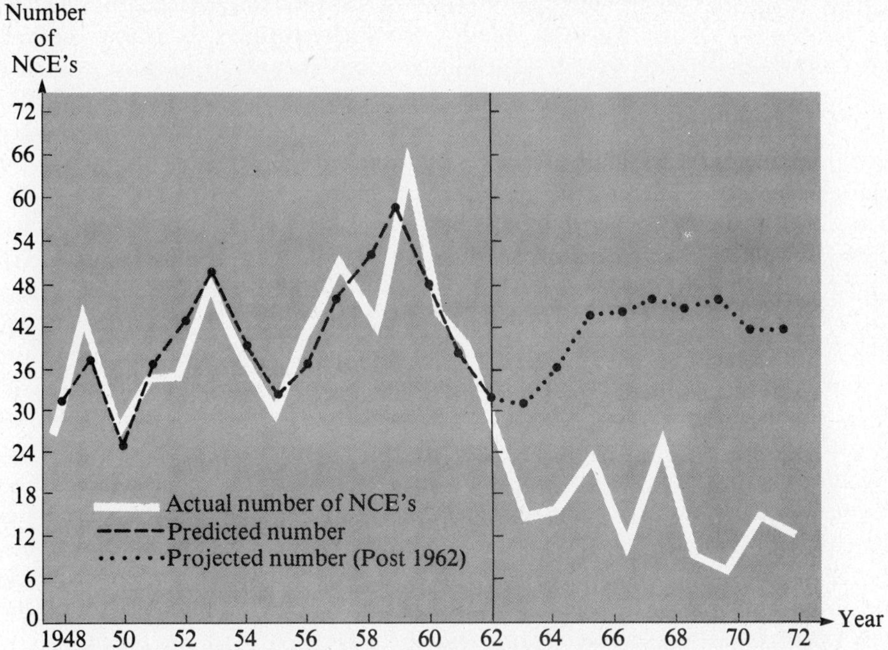

Figure 11.1 Number of new chemical entities produced in the United States, 1948–1972; actual number and predicted number from statistical model.

Source: Reprinted from Sam Peltzman, "An Evaluation of Consumer Protection Legislation: The 1962 Drug Amendments," *Journal of Political Economy,* 81 (September–October 1973), p. 1056, by permission of The University of Chicago Press. © 1973 by the University of Chicago.

OSHA's activities. Following passage of the Occupational Safety and Health Act of 1970, OSHA had very little time in which to issue its regulations. Rather than risk the chance of being blamed for leaving some workplace unsafe, OSHA functionaries combed the rule books of various public and private organizations involved in setting safety standards. They adopted entire series of rules for workplace safety, though without critical review. They disregarded the sensibleness of the regulations they adopted or the costs they might impose on employers, employees, consumers, and stockholders. Many of the regulations OSHA originally adopted are now part of American folklore; for instance, one archaic rule forbids placing ice in workers' drinking water because it might be cut from polluted ponds.[50]

---

[50] Richard Zeckhauser and Albert Nichols, "The Occupational Safety and Health Administration: An Overview Prepared for the Senate Committee on Government Operations" (Cambridge, Mass.: John F. Kennedy School of Government, Harvard University, 1977), p. 50; as cited in Commission on Law and the Economy, *Federal Regulation: Roads to Reform,* exposure draft (Washington, D. C.: American Bar Association, 1978), p. 50.

After severe public ridicule and court battles over whether OSHA inspectors must secure warrants before gaining entrance to plants, OSHA officials finally decided to cull their new regulations and drop those offering little but harassment.[51] OSHA's retrenchment does not mean that the regulations it continues to enforce impose no unknown cost. The effects of making workplaces even marginally safer often can be reflected in lower worker salaries and fringe benefits and higher unemployment levels and consumer prices. Smaller firms using labor-intensive production methods will also face the added risk of failure. But the errors associated with overly harsh safety regulations remain far less detectable than those associated with leaving a workplace unsafe.[52]

The underlying problem involved in the code's fifth rule is that attempts to reduce the probability of error in one direction often increase the probability of error in another. Sensible theoretical solutions to these sorts of problems may exist. For example, in the case of drug regulation, there is some point at which one small increase in the rigor of testing will begin to kill more people than it saves. In the case of occupational safety and health regulations, there is some point at which the added costs of business failures, unemployment, and higher prices begin to exceed the added costs of injury. Comparable problems and solutions occur with regard to activities of the CPSC, the National Highway Traffic Safety Administration, and the EPA. Unfortunately, errors seldom are symmetrical in the ease with which they are detected. Hence, regulators face an inherent incentive to adopt and enforce public policies that represent less-than-optimal trade-offs between varieties of errors and the costs of those errors.

BUREAUS IN POLITICS AND GOVERNMENT

Federal bureaus operate within the structure of national politics and government. The preceding sections of this chapter assume for convenience that members of Congress and chief executives merely make demands on bureaucrats without entering into complicated interactions with them. But the relationships between bureaucrats and others in and out of government are dynamic and complex, and these relationships must be examined more closely.

---

[51] *Marshall v. Barlow,* 430 U.S. 964 (1978).

[52] Much safety regulation encounters a serious additional problem. When people learn that their workplaces or automobiles are safer as the result of regulation, they tend to work or drive less safely. The result is that there are no net gains in accident prevention but the cost of complying with the safety regulations remains. See John Mendeloff, *Regulating Safety: An Economic and Political Analysis of Occupational Safety and Health Policy* (Cambridge, Mass.: MIT Press, 1979); Sam Peltzman, "The Effects of Automobile Safety Regulation," *Journal of Political Economy,* 4 (August 1975), pp. 667–725; and Henry G. Manne and Roger LeRoy Miller, eds., *Auto Safety Regulation: The Cure or the Problem* (Glen Ridge, N.J.: Thomas Horton and Daughters, 1976).

Bureaus in the Political Process

Conventional wisdom holds that bureaus are, or at least should be, wholly apolitical institutions. However, it is obvious to anyone who has worked within a bureau that, in the absence of meaningful, objective productivity measurements for judging the value of each person's work, the *internal* workings of bureaus become almost entirely political.[53] Despite occasional attempts to ensure procedural fairness in bureau promotions by using such means as competitive examinations and merit selection, bureaus remain political, nonmarket institutions in their internal distributions of resources. *Externally,* federal employees are prohibited by law (the Hatch Acts of 1939 and 1940) from participating actively and publicly in election campaigns. In fact, bureau leaders and employees probably represent the most politicized group of citizens in the electorate. Bureaucrats' political actions thus hold the potential for working a profound influence on public policy.

Bureaus as interest groups. Federal bureaus differ little from interest groups in their approach to politics and government. Just as with interest groups, bureau leaders and members participate in the electoral process to elect candidates favorable to their organizations and their members. Just as with interest groups, bureau staffs regularly lobby members of the House and Senate and try to have an impact on presidential and judicial decisions. "It should be realized that there are both governmental and private interest groups, and that any discussion of the problems of reconciling political interest groups must deal, for example, as much with the Department of Defense (or its sub-divisions) as with General Dynamics Corporation; as much with the Department of Agriculture and its sub-divisions as with the Farm Bureau Federation; as much with the Federal Communications Commission as with the American Telephone and Telegraph Company, the National Broadcasting Company, and the numerous other private groups within the jurisdiction of the FCC."[54]

Chapter 6 notes this equivalence of bureaus and interest groups but observes that interest-group leaders face a major difficulty in forming and maintaining their organizations. The free-rider problem associated with the supply of a collective good—usually some aspect of the organization's output—makes group formation problematic. However, the president and members of Congress have already used government revenues to pay for a bureau's establishment and operation, so elected officeholders (and, indirectly, taxpayers) "solve" the free-rider problem for these public-sector interest groups.

One practical consequence of this difference between nongovernmental

---

[53] A strong statement of this view appears in Tullock, *The Politics of Bureaucracy.* The theme is first developed in Ludwig von Mises, *Bureaucracy* (New Haven: Yale University Press, 1944).

[54] Peter Woll, *American Bureaucracy,* 2nd ed. (New York: Norton, 1977), p. 31.

interest groups and bureaus may be to reverse the normal pattern of responsiveness. As Chapters 6 and 9 suggest, members of Congress and other political entrepreneurs ordinarily respond more or less freely to interest-group demands. Bureau personnel, as members of an interest group, press their share of demands on legislators. But members of Congress probably can demand and get more from the Department of Labor than they can demand and receive from the AFL-CIO, because they are paying the department's bills on a year-by-year basis.

The identification of bureaus as interest groups also gains importance when the nature of interest-group demands is compared with bureau goals. Recall from Chapter 6 that interest-group members tend to demand the collective supply of private rather than public goods. Larger budgets and expanding jurisdictions are the private benefits bureaus pursue, and individual bureau leaders can be expected to lobby legislators for them. The theoretical reasons for bureau activity cited at the beginning of this chapter thus might fade into obscurity. However, bureau activity can generate very real collective consequences, as our discussions of VA hospitals and FDA drug-licensing practices indicate.

Bureaus in the electoral process. Our discussion of bureau budget maximization describes how bureaucrats participate in one form of the electoral process, popular referenda to limit taxes or government spending. Bureaucratic participation is also found in other kinds of direct elections, such as those state and local referenda deciding about school budgets and bonded indebtedness. Unions of government employees now figure importantly in federal, state, and local elections to choose officeholders.

Bureaucrats sometimes dictate the wording, or motion, that appears on referendum or budget-setting ballots. One way in which they can enlarge their budgets is to present citizens with the following choice: voters can approve a budget larger than they ordinarily might wish, or they can close down or severely curtail the service provided. This process has been studied in local school-budget-setting elections in Oregon.[55] Figure 11.2 depicts the logic of this budget-setting strategy. The figure shows the median voter's utility curve, assuming that a median exists and represents the pure strategy equilibrium in the budget-setting election. The voter most prefers a budget of $3 million but clearly will vote for one of, say, almost $6 million over no budget at all.[56] Bureaucrats, who control the terms of the election's motion, can there-

---

[55] The theoretical decision problem is worked out in Richard Romer and Howard Rosenthal, "Political Resource Allocation, Controlled Agendas, and the Status Quo," *Public Choice,* 33 (Winter 1978), pp. 27–43. See also Romer and Rosenthal, "Bureaucrats versus Voters: On the Political Economy of Resource Allocation by Direct Democracy," *Quarterly Journal of Economics,* 93 (November 1979), pp. 563–587.

[56] In the Oregon elections, if voters turn down the higher budget proposed by the bureaucrats, school expenditures revert to their 1916 levels adjusted by a 6 percent annual inflator.

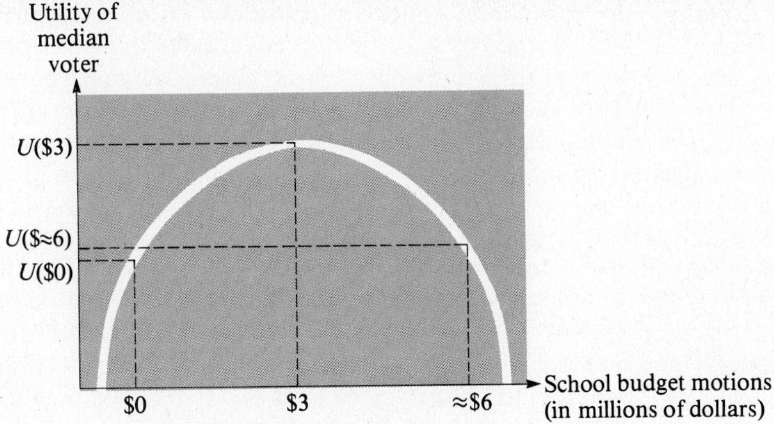

Figure 11.2 Median voter's utility for various school budget levels. *Source:* Adapted from Richard Romer and Howard Rosenthal, "Bureaucrats versus Voters: On the Political Economy of Resource Allocation by Direct Democracy," *Quarterly Journal of Economics,* 93 (November 1979), p. 568.

fore write a motion for nearly $6 million and extract almost $3 million more than a two-candidate election would approve. Bureaucrats can also advantageously control and manipulate agendas, in the same manner that legislators do, if individual citizens' preferences do not combine to form a transitive ordering—if cyclical majorities occur. And, they can "bundle" various provisions offered to voters to maximize bureau advantage.[57]

Bureaucrats' electoral participation goes beyond direct elections. The secretaries of the major departments of the federal government, who make up the president's cabinet, are politically selected officials. Political selection also reaches below cabinet level to the naming of under secretaries, assistant secretaries, deputy assistant secretaries, and bureau chiefs. All of these people serve at the will of the president, and most hold their jobs because of presidential appointment. An overriding consideration for these people is to maximize the chances of the president's reelection or (perhaps less important) the election of their party's presidential candidate if the incumbent does not or cannot seek reelection.

Conflicts occasionally emerge over bureaucrats' carrying out of the department's mandate while simultaneously protecting the president's political viability. For example, HEW Secretary Joseph Califano, Jr.'s attack on cigarette smoking was not well received by North Carolina's voters. President Carter made a special trip to North Carolina in 1978 to promise tobacco

[57] Robert J. Mackay and Carolyn L. Weaver, "Monopoly Bureaus and Fiscal Outcomes: Deductive Models and Implications for Reform," in Gordon Tullock and Richard E. Wagner, eds., *Policy Analysis and Deductive Reasoning* (Lexington, Mass.: Heath, 1978), pp. 141–165.

growers that they were not under attack and that the efforts of the federal government would be devoted to making cigarettes "safer than they already are." From time to time, these conflicts grow severe. Former governors George Romney and Walter Hickel left the Nixon cabinet because of policy differences. Presidential assistant Margaret Costanza gave up her position in the Carter Administration because of such differences. And, President Carter cleaned out a large part of his cabinet in the summer of 1979, an event that was at least partially triggered by questions of loyalty. Defections and changeovers seem inevitable in any "multiproduct" government. The important lesson is that those who remain with an administration are tied to its political, electoral success.

Federal bureaucrats have important strategies for affecting election outcomes. Chapter 9 describes the centrality of pork-barrel legislation and other forms of constituency benefits in helping officeholders to get reelected. Bureaucrats make extremely important allocational decisions about where the money for pork-barrel projects and other government programs should be spent. For example, the secretary of defense exercises a wide discretion about the placement and continued operation of various military bases. He can reward legislators friendly to the DOD and punish its adversaries and detractors. Other federal departments and agencies share similar strategic advantages.

Bureaucrats also affect elections merely by voting. Government workers usually know more about candidates' public policy positions than do other voters. Because they work in government, bureaucrats enjoy an enhanced knowledge of and understanding about political issues. Many agencies have employee organizations that regularly publish newsletters setting forth various candidates' positions on issues affecting them. These newsletters sometimes pretend to be purely informational. But a front-page report that one candidate favors a 10 percent cutback in an agency's budget, while his opponent supports a 15 percent increase, will affect employees' voting decisions in obvious ways.

Since all levels of government combined employ nearly one member of the workforce in five, the direct impact of public employees on the electoral process is now substantial. In state and local politics, groups such as teachers' and police unions participate as both interest groups and bureaus in legislative and election politics. Where government workers are heavily concentrated, such as in large cities, public-sector employees often become pivotal in elections. Many argue that municipal employee voting strength in cities such as New York has forced elected officials to capitulate to demands for extensive wage and pension increases. As a consequence, some larger cities, and New York City in particular, seem near or beyond bankruptcy.

How extensively bureaucrats should participate in politics remains a problem for democratic theorists. Recent years have seen serious attempts to abolish the Hatch Acts. Some believe that the fact of government employment should not prohibit citizens from full participation in the political process.

Bureaucrats as voters are said to bring highly informed opinions into politics. Others argue that allowing government workers to vote and campaign for those who set their salaries creates a conflict of interest. Bureaucrats trying to comply with the first three rules of their operational code find the use of the political process highly attractive. But bureaucrats' political activities, opponents of extensive public employee participation suggest, expand the bureaucracy. As bureaus expand, more and more people become bureaucrats and bureau voting strength increases apace. The spiraling dynamic inherent in this process, some believe, leads to a growing, self-aggrandizing public sector.[58] Indeed, the proposal has even been made that government employees should not be allowed to vote.[59]

Bureaus and the Congress

Bureaucrats' political activities carry over directly into the legislature. Agency heads are lobbyists in the full meaning of the term, and most federal agencies devote some of their personnel to a more or less routinized process of maintaining communications with the members of Congress. For example, the Department of Agriculture has an Office of Congressional and Public Affairs. The Army, Air Force, and Navy Offices of Legislative Liaison maintain quarters on Capitol Hill. The DOD has an assistant secretary and a deputy assistant secretary for legislative affairs. The Department of Commerce employs an assistant secretary for congressional affairs. The Department of Energy has a director for its Office of Congressional Affairs, and the FERC employs a congressional liaison. HHS has an assistant secretary for legislation, and several HHS subdivisions have created their own mechanisms for congressional liaison.

Bureaus and congressional information. Federal bureau directors have at least three formal opportunities to express their views to the members of Congress. The first occurs before substantive committees during hearings to write authorizing legislation. The second occurs at the appropriations stage before subcommittees of the House and Senate Appropriations Committees. The third, though one that bureau chiefs do not often welcome, occurs at the behest of committees exercising congressional oversight of bureau activities.

Compared to other interest groups, bureaus are at an advantage in their relations with House and Senate members. Bureaus represent a major source

---

[58] Winston C. Bush and Arthur T. Denzau, "The Voting Behavior of Bureaucrats and Public Sector Growth," in Thomas E. Borcherding, ed., *Budgets and Bureaucrats: The Sources of Government Growth* (Durham, N. C.: Duke University Press, 1977), pp. 90–99. For a skeptical view of the importance of bureaucrats' political strength, see Paul N. Courant, Edward M. Gramlich, and Daniel L. Rubinfeld, "Public Employee Market Power and the Level of Government Spending," *American Economic Review*, 69 (December 1979), pp. 806–817.

[59] The proposal is attributed to public-choice scholar Gordon Tullock.

of legislators' information. Bureau personnel make and execute public policy; they systematically collect information about the effects of their activities; and they also estimate the effects of their failure to act in particular areas because they lack funds or congressional authorization. The collection, interpretation, and presentation of information are not neutral activities. Clever advocates of particular positions can often make data prove nearly anything they wish. Bureau chiefs, who prefer larger bureaus, larger bureau budgets, and expanding jurisdictions, will present to the members of Congress information consistent with satisfying those preferences.

The collection, interpretation, and presentation of information can also be terribly expensive. Because of their national scope, federal bureaus are better able to carry out these activities than are other interest groups. Furthermore, congressional appropriations to bureaus usually include funds for information gathering. The members of Congress thus provide the resources with which a bureau can give them back information reflecting favorably on the bureau. By contrast, other interest groups face constant free-rider problems in establishing and maintaining the degree of organization necessary to provide legislators with similar comprehensive information. Therefore, if bureau and private interest-group positions collide, the bureau enjoys this information advantage. *Ceteris paribus,* even in the absence of conflict bureaus can be expected to "do better" with legislators than do other groups.

Bureaus and other interest groups. House and Senate constituencies usually contain well-organized pressure groups whose members are vitally interested in what bureaus do. For example, members of the American Association of Retired Persons are quite concerned about Social Security Administration activities. AFL-CIO leaders pay close attention to decisions of the Department of Labor, the National Labor Relations Board (NLRB), and OSHA. Airline and trucking trade organizations and firms closely follow the activities of the CAB and the ICC, respectively. Members of the New York and American Stock Exchanges are vitally interested in the latest SEC directives. Banking organizations often require daily contact with the FHLBB, the FDIC, and the FRB. Members of the American Farm Bureau Federation, the National Farmer's Union, the National Grange, the National Council of Farmer Cooperatives, and the National Milk Producers Federation all pay close attention to what happens inside the Department of Agriculture. Members of the American Legion and the Veterans of Foreign Wars often work hand in hand with VA personnel. Thousands of other interest groups closely track the activities of particular federal agencies.

Earlier scholarship about federal bureaus, and especially about regulatory commissions, suggested that industries and their associated interest groups often "take over," or "capture," the bureaus that were supposed to regulate them. Regulatory agencies were believed to have a **life cycle,** beginning with gestation, going through youth and maturity, and ending up in old

United States
Environmental Protection
Agency

Washington, D.C. 20460

EPA-600/9-79-036
July 1980

Office of Research and Development

ACID RAIN

Many federal agencies exercise dominant control over information of concern to them. In this report on the *acid rain* problem, the Environmental Protection Agency's Office of Research and Development fully explores the cost of acid rain and offers the opinion that "without a firm commitment both to developing improved pollution control methods and to applying those methods rigorously, the problems of the past could be a prelude to an acid rain future." The report fails to mention the effects that EPA regulations requiring "tall stacks" and catalytic converters have had on worsening the acid rain problem. The contents of this publication are fully consistent with all of the rules of the operational code of the bureaucrat.

age.[60] A different variety of activities was said to characterize each stage of the life cycle as a result of the combined decisions of bureaucrats, members of Congress, and interest-group leaders and members.

First, by the time an agency is born in the Congress, public concern over the regulatory problem it is supposed to address has faded. Therefore, the agency's legislatively determined mandate yields principally to the demands of those to be regulated and not to any definable interest of the electorate at large. Regulatory commissions were thus born with weak mandates, bowing to demands for regulations that would create not public but private, divisible goods, such as protection against competition. The regulatory commissions thus seemed compromised in their gestations.

Second, in their youths agencies might have appeared to be actively seeking to control those whom they were supposed to regulate. But as public attention to each bureau's theoretical reason for being subsided, bureau commissioners who acted as adversaries of the regulated industry came under increasing industry attack. A pattern of recruiting commissioners and agency heads from among the regulated began to emerge, and soon a **revolving door** in and out of government to and from the regulated firms developed.[61] The members of Congress often tended to take the side of the industry against the bureau, for they preferred to dispense private goods to the industry than supposed benefits to the electorate at large.

Third, in maturity, commissioners became representatives of industry interests; and finally, in old age, they grew positively protective of those whom they were to have regulated. They lost all creative force. In sum; "these agencies have, for years, been disproving the basic assumptions which led to their creation. Set up to regulate in the public interest, they have more and more tended to equate that concept with the private interests of those being regulated. Designed to remove regulation from politics, they have failed to resist pressures from the political branches. Conceived of as quasi-judicial tribunals, they have acted in a manner grossly contrary to the canons of judicial ethics. Intended to promote competition, they have fostered monopoly."[62]

Many federal bureaus other than regulatory commissions have become sponsors and protectors of those whom their mandates require they regulated. But who has "captured" whom? Firms in most regulated industries will undoubtedly try to influence regulatory commission decisions. Similarly, leaders of the American Association of Retired Persons will try to affect Social

---

[60] This discussion of agency life cycle closely follows Marver H. Bernstein, *Regulating Business by Independent Commission* (© 1955 by Princeton University Press).

[61] Legislation passed in 1978 (P.L. 95–512) sought to limit the revolving-door syndrome by placing restrictions on the rights of former agency personnel to represent private clients in dealings before the agency. A threatened exodus of high-level bureaucrats led Congress one year later to pass a bill (S.869) weakening the law.

[62] Bernard Schwartz, "Crisis in the Commissions," *The Progressive,* 23 (August 1959), p. 13.

Security Administration decisions, and leaders of various farm groups will try to bend Department of Agriculture decisions to their advantage. However, the takeover or **capture hypothesis** may be far too strong. Most bureaus have some latitude in deciding exactly who it is that is going to take them over, and some bureaus and regulatory agencies exhibit a remarkable degree of independence even after old age has set in. For example, the FTC is today very much an imperializing bureaucracy. It has shaken off its once cozy relationship with business, and (much to the displeasure of many members of Congress) it is attacking private firms on many fronts. If anyone has captured the FTC, it is the Nader organizations. The CAB proceeded with deregulation in spite of widespread industry opposition. The SEC, an older agency, constantly tries to impose new and burdensome obligations on corporate boards of directors. The relevant interest group for the SEC may be securities lawyers, whose caseloads derive directly from SEC rulings, rather than buyers of stocks and bonds or the corporations themselves.

The metaphor of capture is further complicated by the multiple interests that focus on agency activities. For example, residents of small communities often used the CAB's control over airline routes to guarantee themselves excessive, economically wasteful levels of service. State power commissioners redistribute resources by adopting "lifeline" rate structures said to benefit the poor and the elderly. These requirements on regulated firms have been characterized as "taxation by regulation."[63]

So the relationship between bureaus and interest groups is more complex than the capture hypothesis would indicate. Bureaus really assume partial control of firms in particular industries and of other private-sector participants. From that point on, the bureaucrats' goals are to maintain and expand their jurisdictions. They protect against competition those firms they are supposed to control to assure that indeed there will *be* firms to control, as well as to keep political entrepreneurs in Congress happy. Bureaus whose regulatory decisions create private-sector monopolies or cartels at public expense give legislators an additional source of support—monopoly or cartel profits—to collect either legally, in pursuit of reelection, or illegally, as Chapter 6 observes, in direct payoffs. Private goods—monopoly or cartel profits and payments to politicians—are thus created, but again, at collective cost.

For example, the Department of Agriculture develops elaborate subsidies for farmers and imposes extensive marketing agreements, which establish cartels among growers of various produce lines, at the expense of consumers, who must pay higher prices for food. Earlier CAB and ICC activities prevented potential competitors from servicing various airline and truck routes already serviced by another company or companies. The FCC for many years limited competition for television and FM stations by inhibiting the use of new technologies, and does so today by making it difficult for new firms to enter into competition against existing broadcasting outlets.

The exchange between interest groups and bureaus is reciprocal, how-

[63] Posner, "Taxation by Regulation."

ever. Interest-group leaders seeking federal subsidies for their members fully understand that their fortunes are tied closely to bureau budgets. Farm subsidies come from the Department of Agriculture, and therefore an increase in the department's budget will often be reflected in larger subsidies for farmers. Veterans' benefits come from the VA, and therefore an increase in the VA's budget will often be reflected in larger benefits for veterans. Similarly, health care administrators and welfare workers and recipients have a vital interest in the size of HHS's budget. Aerospace workers and members of the armed forces closely follow congressional budget debates concerning the DOD. Bureaus protect their "clients," but not surprisingly, the relationship is reciprocal. Bureaus depend mightily upon the lobbying support of those whom they are to control.

Indeed, bureaus go beyond "capturing" constituent groups: they often try to create and sustain their own parallel interest groups. The Grange was founded by federal employees, and the Department of Commerce was midwife to the Chamber of Commerce. Federal bureaus have made direct grants to private organizations. More recently, the EPA, the FTC, the Department of Agriculture, and the Department of Energy, to name but a few, have begun to pay various interest groups to testify in bureau proceedings and to prepare studies for bureau consideration. These subsidies help interest groups to survive. In sum, the bureaus try to guarantee themselves a constituency in their interactions with the members of Congress.

Bureaus and "the Washington Establishment." The capacity of federal bureaucrats to shape public policy may seem extraordinary.[64] Like many other people, bureaucrats pursue their self-interest through politics. However, federal bureaucrats need not face the costs of initiating and maintaining their own interest groups. They enjoy regularized channels of access to the members of Congress. And, sometimes they can independently generate and support their own constituency groups. The members of Congress seem agreeable to present arrangements. Despite occasional reshuffling and reform legislation, bureaus appear to be the way a majority of House and Senate members want them. Those interest groups that have become the camp followers of various bureaus also remain constituents of members of Congress. Bureau activities represent a continuing source of benefits for the members of such groups. Therefore, bureau activities represent a continuing source of electoral benefits for the members of Congress, who vote their budgets and oversee their activities. Representatives and senators also use the agencies as dumping grounds for highly emotional issues. For example, because intense minorities have formed about matters such as abortion and busing, legislators can only lose votes by taking positions on those issues. But by relegating decisions about such issues to bureaus while enacting only very

[64] The title of this section and the basic argument are from Morris P. Fiorina, *Congress: Keystone of the Washington Establishment* (New Haven, Conn.: Yale University Press, 1977).

general guidelines, congressmen can avoid an erosion of electoral support. Of course, such issues do occasionally make it to the floor of the House or Senate.

Bureaucratic and congressional interests usually coincide in support of various interest-group demands. They also coincide on certain aspects of the bureaucrat's operational code. For example, House and Senate members, like FDA personnel, do not wish to appear responsible for the birth of limbless children. Hence, the laws they write tend to minimize the probability of making detectable errors while ignoring undetectable ones.

The relationship between bureaus and the members of Congress has grown far more complex than one might imagine. Fewer and fewer members of Congress are elected from marginal districts, those in which the vote is close. In recent years, incumbents have seemed to enjoy an enhanced ability to get reelected. The growing electoral strength of incumbents at least partially results from the expansion of bureaucratic production of goods and services and the growing pervasiveness of bureaucratic regulation both of the private sector and of the public sector at the state and local levels. The connection between the trends of increasing bureaucratic control and a growing incumbency advantage is fascinating to describe. Centralized bureaucratic production of goods and services as well as regulatory agency attempts to control both the private sector and the public sector at the local level often produce serious hardships, errors, and misallocations of resources. Both those who favor an expansion of bureaucracy and those who favor its contraction recognize the problems of centralized bureaucracy. However, these problems appear to have few satisfactory solutions, and those who wish to use federal bureaus to carry out public policies must include such errors, misallocations, and hardships as costs of bureaucracy.

These errors, misallocations, and hardships provide most of the examples of *Catch-22*-like horror stories about the bureaucracy. For example, a Georgia chemical manufacturer, whose small plant employed only a few people, was required by OSHA to install safety equipment at a cost that would close down the business. Bureaucratic regulations to reduce atmospheric emissions of particulate matter ignore sulfur emissions, which the particulate matter formerly helped to neutralize; the result is "acid rain," a condition worse than that which prevailed before regulation. Federal attempts to protect endangered species at one extreme temporarily led to a halt in production of a hydroelectric dam because of the presence of a small breed of fish, the snail darter. At the other extreme, compliance with federal registration and reporting requirements for zoos owning endangered species has become so expensive that the zoos have stopped breeding those species; every new pregnancy and birth requires paperwork whose cost far exceeds the value of the animal to the zoo. Hence, these species rapidly approach extinction.

Reports of more common problems derived from centralized bureaucratic controls and procedures seldom appear in print. These include lost Social Security payments, arbitrarily deleted medical benefits, lost passport applications that ruin planned honeymoons abroad, failure of the Army to teach photography (as promised) to soldiers, who only learn how to stand guard duty and scrub latrines in Greenland, and an overly strict interpretation of immigration laws, which prevents foreign relatives from entering the United States.

The growth of the congressional incumbency advantage partially reflects the increase in centralized bureaucratic control, which in turn gives the members of Congress ever more opportunities to intervene on behalf of their constituents. As Chapter 9 observes, such legislative activities are almost entirely noncontroversial, they can believably be credited to a particular House or Senate member, and they are by definition unavailable to would-be challengers. Longer tenure in office improves the incumbent's advantage, for *"Experience in Washington and congressional seniority count when dealing with the bureaucracy.* [T]he incumbent . . . is naturally preferred over a newcomer. *This incumbency effect is not only understandable; it is rational.* And it would grow over time as increasing numbers of citizens come to regard their congressman as a troubleshooter in the Washington bureaucracies."[65]

The three-way relationships among members of Congress, bureaucrats, and constituents (whether or not aggregated into organized interest groups) lie at the heart of congressional action concerning the bureaucracy. As special pleader to the bureaucracy for the constituent, the representative or senator is at the hub of the system, and the benefits for congressional incumbents are so great that the bureaus—whose actions sustain the market for congressional entrepreneurial services—ordinarily remain immune from *successful* attack. Indeed, members of Congress in search of further support do what they can to expand this system.

> [B]y working to establish various federal programs (or in some cases fighting their establishment) congressmen earn electoral credit from concerned elements of their districts. Some federal agency then takes Congress' vague policy mandate and makes the detailed decisions necessary to translate the legislation into operating programs. The implementation and operation of the programs by the agencies irritate some constituents and suggest opportunities for profit to others. These aggrieved and/or hopeful constituents then appeal to their congressmen to intervene in their behalf with the bureaucratic powers that be. The system is connected when congressmen decry bureaucratic excesses and red tape while riding a grateful electorate to ever more impressive electoral showings.[66]

Despite furious congressional condemnation of specific bureau actions, a successful attack is seldom mounted on a bureau's jurisdiction. More often, new problems call for new bureaus, and new bureaus call for more intervention by individual congressmen. Election margins widen as House and Senate

---

[65] Fiorina, *Congress: Keystone of the Washington Establishment,* p. 51.

[66] Fiorina, *Congress: Keystone of the Washington Establishment,* p. 71.

seats become the seemingly indisputable personal property of their incumbents.

Bureaus and the Presidency

As Chapter 10 notes, the president's formal authority with regard to the bureaucracy appears to be substantial. As chief executive he can appoint, with the advice and consent of the Senate, a large number of its most important policy makers. His authority to dismiss is inherent in his power to appoint.[67] He seems less an ombudsman for his constituents than are House members. Thus, he also seems more nearly immune from the forces just described. The president can also use the Office of Management and Budget to exercise some control over federal bureaus, and he enjoys a limited statutory authority to reorganize parts of the executive branch, provided that the members of Congress do not explicitly object.

To some extent, presidents can and do affect bureau decisions. However, the changes they can make in bureau policies and activities are limited both as to the number of agencies affected and as to the degree of control exercised over any particular agency. For instance, many programs that come to the president's attention are already mandated by acts of Congress. Scholars differ over how much of federal government activity is premandated, but something on the order of two-thirds of the federal budget falls into expenditure classes over which the president has little or no immediate control. Many regulatory programs seem equally isolated from presidential influence.

The president is also an elected official, and public opinion affects him directly through reelection and indirectly through the Congress. While the president may not pay attention to missing Social Security checks, he does heed the admonitions of congressmen whose districts might lose defense contracts or installations. He is very much tuned in to the demands of the leaders of large interest groups, even if he is not able to satisfy them. Responding to his constituents almost invariably requires that the president interact with the bureaucracy. Hence, he shares with particular bureaus a relationship not unlike the relationship that members of Congress enjoy.

But as chief executive the president simply cannot monitor the actions of a bureaucracy as extensive as the national administration has become. It is useful to think of monitoring in several discrete steps. First, the president can monitor what particular bureaus are presently doing. Second, he can issue orders to change present bureau actions. Third, he might monitor bureaus both to see that his orders are complied with and that they have the desired effect. Fourth, he can continue to monitor to search for further changes in bureau actions that might be desirable.

---

[67] *Myers v. U.S.*, 272 U.S. 52 (1926). For limitations on the president's removal power, see *Humphrey's Executor v. U.S.*, 295 U.S. 602 (1935), and *Wiener v. U.S.*, 357 U.S. 349 (1958).

If a president did nothing else but monitor the activities of the approximately 2200 federal agencies, he could devote no more than one-sixth of a day to each agency each year, which would be equivalent to throwing away the entire year. Hence, the president concentrates on only a few agencies at a time and proceeds incrementally to make decisions about them. He is likely to choose agencies to scrutinize in accordance with crisis management criteria or because agency activities impinge upon significant campaign promises or other electorally or politically sensitive issues. For example, allegations of communist infiltration focused attention on the State Department during the Truman administration. When inflation or unemployment seems out of control, the FRB receives attention. The Kennedy administration concentrated on changing DOD decision-making procedures. The DOE was the object of close scrutiny during the 1979 oil crisis, and in that year the Nuclear Regulatory Commission also came under official investigation by a presidential commission because of the Three Mile Island nuclear reactor accident. NASA attracted congressional attention when it was feared that Skylab might fall from orbit and land in a heavily populated area, and House members quickly focused on the FAA after the tragic 1979 DC-10 crash in Chicago. But these are all crisis-related examples.

Long-term, calculated presidential—or even congressional—control of the bureaucracy is more difficult. President Harry S Truman noted of President-elect Dwight D. Eisenhower, "He'll sit here, and he'll say, 'Do this! Do that!' *And nothing will happen.* Poor Ike—it won't be a bit like the army. He'll find it very frustrating." While Truman in his own presidency plainly overestimated the willingness of Army bureaucrats to do what they are told (*vide* General MacArthur), he properly characterized not merely the Eisenhower presidency but also all presidencies before and after Eisenhower's, including his own. The capacity of presidents to monitor and command quickly reaches physical limitations. Even if bureau leaders tried to find out what it is the president wants done and then bent every effort to do it, their giving up of their own personal interest would not make much difference. The president simply does not have time to make informed judgments about most issues before most federal bureaus. Hence, bureaucrats are usually left on their own, provided they do not draw too much attention.

The president, too, shares with the members of Congress a commonality of interest concerning the activities of federal bureaus. He wants to maximize bureau output that can be measured while not spending money on unmeasurable output. He prefers to minimize the probability that bureau chiefs will make detectable errors, while he seems not particularly concerned with errors that perhaps even he cannot detect. Presidents will use bureaus to reinforce their influence over the course of legislation: they can bring recalcitrant House members into line by the promise of new air bases; they can make senators toe the mark by threatening to take planned major hydroelectric power projects away from their states. Cooperative committee leaders might receive presidential backing for new Department of Labor office buildings in their districts. This kind of control over the members of Congress requires a similar control over bureau personnel, part of which comes to the president through his cabinet officers. For example, as Chapter 10 pointed out, in November of 1979 Secretary of Transportation Neil Goldschmidt said that if possible, he would deny federal funds to Chicago because Mayor Jane Byrne had switched political allegiance away from President Carter to the camp of presidential candidate Senator Kennedy.[68] However, by and large control derives from a real give-and-take between the president and the members of the bureaucracy. It seldom results from presidential actions that bureaucrats perceive as frankly antagonistic.

Can presidents really change the bureaucracy? That depends on their own individual political strengths. First, real changes in bureaucratic structure and action that presidents might wish to impose require that the members of Congress and of the federal judiciary acquiesce in their wishes and that bureaucrats do the same. Second, any opposition to presidential preferences must appear futile to the objects of change. Third, presidents must be willing to forgo popularity to work their will. The simultaneous satisfaction of these three conditions rarely occurs, although the opposite sometimes prevails. For example, President Nixon promised to reform the bureaucracy. But early in his second term, when electoral considerations were not relevant and he might have succeeded, the growing Watergate scandal soon undermined any support he might have had for changes in bureaucratic structure and performance. Indeed, as his second term wore on, his administration began to acquiesce in one bureau's demands after another, simply to try to preserve whatever shreds of popular support remained. President Carter enjoyed some limited success at piecemeal reorganization, but no one is yet sure if it has made a difference for bureau action.

Many commentators have written about the **iron triangles** of Washington, D. C. At one vertex of each triangle stands a particular interest group, such as a firm, labor union, or actual political organization. The second vertex is the bureau that dispenses benefits to the interest group's leaders and members. The third vertex is the congressional committee or subcommittee whose members oversee the bureau and have the interest-group members as part of their constituency and electoral coalition. The incentives of those at each vertex seem almost entirely compatible, and no president to date has gained unambiguous and widespread success in breaking these triangles.

Bureaus and the Judicial Process

Most federal bureaus regularly sue and are sued.[69] Agencies are often defendants to lawsuits that claim they have exceeded their legal authority or

---

[68] New York *Times,* November 21, 1979, p. A1.

[69] This discussion of bureaus and the judicial process must anticipate much of the discussion in Chapter 12. Rereading this section after completing Chapter 12 might be helpful for a richer understanding of bureaucrats' strategic use of litigation.

have failed to follow rule-making procedures required by the Administrative Procedures Act. They also might become plaintiffs in lawsuits, as, for example, when the Antitrust Division of the Department of Justice sues to break up IBM or ITT, which it deems to be monopolies. Many litigation decisions of bureaucrats can be understood by applying the rules of their operational code.

The decision to litigate. Most federal agencies have constant opportunities to be parties to lawsuits. An agency becomes a plaintiff simply by filing a complaint in an appropriate court of law—sometimes its own administrative law court. An agency becomes a defendant simply by failing to settle someone else's complaint against it out of court or by failing to acquiesce immediately in the terms of the complaint. Some bureaus employ their own lawyers to represent them in court while others use the Department of Justice as their law firm. If a bureau litigates for itself, its directors must decide how to allocate their own limited legal resources among alternative litigation opportunities. If the bureau uses the Department of Justice as its law firm, then its director must convince Department of Justice functionaries that the litigation is meritorious.

How should bureaucrats decide to litigate? To answer this question, suppose the FTC has completed work on two antitrust cases. Its own administrative law judge has ordered two separate and unrelated trade associations, say a county medical society and a city's real-estate association, to stop trying to control the prices their respective members charge. Both associations appeal the FTC's decisions in federal court. Faced with limited resources, perhaps the FTC can defend only one of these suits. Which one? If FTC functionaries decide correctly from the consumers' point of view, *ceteris paribus* they will choose to defend the suit representing the larger economic benefit (if any) to consumers. For example, if one trade association has been successful in controlling its members' prices and maintaining those prices above competitive levels, while the other association has not, then the first suit should be defended and the second passed by. A similar reasoning applies to most litigating activities of most agencies.

However, bureau personnel usually decide to sue or defend a suit to satisfy some rule of their operational code. For example, bureaus often undertake activities or issue rulings that seem only remotely connected with their legislative mandates. Those mandates can be very general, and therefore the agencies enjoy a wide latitude in interpreting what they can and cannot do. Federal judges often will agree to adjudicate the issue of whether an agency has exceeded its mandate or not. In deciding such cases, federal judges of necessity must themselves state what they believe an agency's jurisdiction to be. Hence, federal judges are very much in the business of setting boundaries on agency jurisdictions, and in some instances they widen or contract those boundaries.

Federal bureaucrats, especially those who survive as federal bureaucrats, become fairly adept at predicting when they will win and when they will lose in suits concerning their jurisdictions. If they expect to lose a suit, they acquiesce before it comes to trial so that the plaintiffs go their own way, satisfied, while no binding judicial decision concerning the larger jurisdictional question in the specific dispute has been entered. If the bureaucrats expect to win a suit, then they will welcome it because they expect the judicial decision to define new territories into which their bureau might expand. Sometimes, though, the decision may declare an expansion they have already undertaken to be legal. In either case, the bureaucrats' litigation decisions are very much conditioned by the second rule of their operational code: expand the bureau's jurisdiction.

Much of the work of the Antitrust Division of the Department of Justice and the Bureau of Competition of the FTC is expected to concentrate on litigating antitrust matters. Economists have developed the notion of **welfare loss** to measure the cost that monopolistic practices are said to impose on consumers. Welfare losses are extremely difficult to measure, and therefore it is not surprising that the Antitrust Division appears to pay little attention to them in deciding when to sue to break up alleged monopolies. Instead, the evidence suggests that the Antitrust Division uses such measures as sales and profits, neither of which bears any demonstrable relationship either to monopoly practices or to welfare loss.[70] Naturally, sales and profits of various firms are measurable. Furthermore, in abiding by the third rule of the bureaucrat's operational code—maximize the bureau's output—Department of Justice officials are usually reluctant to get involved in a few long and costly suits when they could be litigating hundreds of smaller ones. The result is that Antitrust Division attorneys prefer to pick off weak defendants, non-monopolies, which impose small welfare losses on consumers, rather than to go after larger firms, which have the wealth to fight back. Of course, there are exceptions, such as the Justice Department's lengthy suit against IBM. But even this suit was probably motivated by the political importunings of congressmen who had smaller computer firms in their districts. Hence, the department's budget, controlled by the Congress, was also probably protected by the suit against IBM.

Benefit-cost analysis undertaken by FTC personnel themselves indicates that FTC litigation success in certain instances would raise prices for particular products by 580 percent.[71] The FTC has received severe criticism from the American Bar Association, whose study commission could not make sense out of FTC practices, including litigation decisions. "Over the past 50 years, a

[70] William Long, Richard Schramm, and Robert Tollison, "The Economic Determinants of Antitrust Activity," *Journal of Law and Economics,* 16 (October 1973), pp. 351–364.

[71] Federal Trade Commission, *Fiscal 1975 Mid-Year Budget Review,* as cited in Wesley J. Liebeler, "Should the Federal Trade Commission's Activity be Strengthened and Enlarged?" in M. Bruce Johnson, ed., *The Attack on Corporate America: The Corporate Issues Sourcebook* (New York: McGraw-Hill, 1978), p. 292.

succession of independent scholars and other analysts have consistently found the FTC wanting in the performance of its duties by reason of inadequate planning, failure to establish priorities, excessive preoccupation with trivial matters, undue delay and unnecessary secrecy."[72] Nor can firms decide how to conduct business in response to FTC antitrust policies and threats to sue. One former FTC commissioner noted, "What a young [antitrust] law student needs most after a diploma and a shingle and a client is a good pair of eyebrows and broad shoulders. Then when his client asks him how to stay out of trouble with the government, he can raise the first and shrug the second. . . ."[73]

In sum, government agencies such as the Justice Department and the FTC maximize their output of litigation, as measured in numbers of cases, and use economically meaningless but readily measurable indices such as sales and profits to justify their activities. Agencies often pursue litigation that expands their jurisdictions and settle out of court litigation that could reduce their jurisdictions.

Bureau litigation strategies. As noted earlier of jurisdictional questions, bureau leaders pursue litigation strategies that are understandably designed to maximize their probability of winning. Consider two extreme examples of litigation involving a bureau and a private firm. First, suppose that a monopolist, a power company, is disputing the ruling of a bureau, the state power commission. Presumably, the power company's shareholders, management, and employees would bear the full cost (or benefit) of an adverse (or favorable) court decision.[74] Hence, the firm's officials can rationally decide for themselves how much of their resources, if any, to allocate for prosecuting the suit. Similarly, the power commissioners, as the elected or appointed agents for electric power consumers, can decide how much those consumers would benefit if the agency wins its point in court. From this knowledge, the commissioners can then decide how much of their resources, if any, to allocate for defending the suit. Whatever level of resources each party allocates to litigation, any judicial precedents set by virtue of the suit affect no one besides the power company, its shareholders, management, and employees on the one

[72] As cited in Edward F. Cox, Robert C. Fellmeth, and John E. Schulz, *The Nader Report on the Federal Trade Commission* (New York: Baron, 1969), p. 59.

[73] Lowell B. Mason, speech at Marquette University, April 11, 1950; as quoted in Harold Fleming, *Ten Thousand Commandments: A Story of the Antitrust Laws* (Englewood Cliffs, N.J.: Prentice-Hall, 1951), p. 20.

[74] Short-run costs of state power commission actions leading to lower company revenues will probably be borne by shareholders to the benefit of consumers. But a decline in profitability as a result of such actions will eventually make it more difficult for the company to raise capital for expansion. Therefore, in the long run, consumers might end up paying for the cut in rates in the form of higher capital costs, which must be reflected in the rate structure or in the form of unavailability of service—TANSTAAFL. Naturally, the correctness of these predictions depends upon industry cost and revenue characteristics.

hand and the power commission and the consumers it is said to represent on the other. Stated differently, everyone's interests are fully represented in the lawsuit, and we shall assume that any precedents set affect no one else.[75]

Now, consider as a second extreme example a small firm in a highly competitive product market of several thousand such firms, a used car dealer. The FTC might issue a ruling covering the activities of a particular dealer. The dealer might then decide to sue the FTC on the ground that it does not have jurisdiction to regulate the activities of merchants who sell used products as well as on other (perhaps more pertinent) jurisdictional grounds. The FTC enjoys its full legal capacity to devote to this particular case. On the other hand, the small used car dealer, being a participant in a competitive marketplace, has virtually no resources to devote to the suit. But, all similarly situated dealers, who are *not* parties to this litigation, nevertheless will experience the full effects of any precedents on jurisdictional questions that result. Hence, to the extent that the used car dealer who *is* party to the litigation fights the FTC, he provides a public good that displays a positive externality for all other used car dealers. They, in turn, are free riders on his efforts. Therefore, a less-than-optimal amount of resources will probably be devoted to litigation on the dealers' behalf. Their actions are completely uncoordinated, whereas the actions of the FTC are completely coordinated. Furthermore, the FTC has no free-rider problem, though such a problem fully characterizes the dealers' situation.

Bureaus will thus enjoy far greater judicial success in litigation involving the most competitive and least coordinated areas of the private sector. Any precedent-setting litigation that a smaller, more competitive economic agent enters into will probably be inadequate compared to the stakes at risk for the agent's entire industry. By contrast, commissions are likely to steer clear of larger firms with some degree of monopoly control. As a result, federal bureaus will end up regulating most heavily those parts of the private sector that are relatively more competitive than would otherwise be the case.[76]

Those bureaus that seek to regulate across product lines within the private sector enjoy the additional advantage of developing long-range litigation strategies. These include the FTC, EPA, CPSC, and OSHA. Their decision makers have literally thousands of cases developing before them in diverse industries. They can pick and choose among these cases to pursue sequentially a set of legal precedents so that objections to their activities fall, one after the other. The private litigant has a far more limited set of oppor-

---

[75] Of course, these assumptions are fictitious. State power commissions, as political agencies, share all of the problems of legislatures and other bureaus, including cyclical majorities, intense minorities, and the pursuit of private benefits, collectively supplied.

[76] Many heavily regulated industries are also less competitive. Railroads and interstate trucking are examples. But this observation has less to do with present litigation strategies of agencies and more to do with the reduction in competitiveness that usually follows regulation.

tunities to sue and be sued. Thus, a coordinated long-range litigation strategy eludes firms in the private sector as well as local governments under federal control.

In the areas of civil rights and civil liberties, many organizations have arisen to mitigate the free-rider problem and to counter the ability of government agents to generate long-run litigation strategies. An organization such as the National Association for the Advancement of Colored People (NAACP) for many years whittled away at government-imposed public-school discrimination at the state and local level until in 1954 it succeeded in having the Supreme Court declare all forms of public-school racial segregation unconstitutional.[77] The American Civil Liberties Union (ACLU) has worked on behalf of defendants as well as plaintiffs to expand their "personal jurisdictions" in the area of civil liberties against police bureaus and government prosecutors.

The precedents reached in NAACP and ACLU cases affect everyone. Similar groups concerned with economic regulation are now emerging in the private sector, and several independent legal foundations, such as the Pacific Legal Foundation, the National Legal Center for the Public Interest, the Southeastern Legal Foundation, and the Mid-Atlantic Legal Foundation, now represent many litigants—private firms and state and local governments—in matters of economic regulation. They may come to be as important in tempering economic regulation by bureaus as organizations such as the NAACP and ACLU have been in matters of racial equality before the law, criminal justice, and government regulation of private personal action.

BUREAUS IN THEORY AND PRACTICE

The reasons for collective action cited in Chapter 3 are interpreted at the outset of this chapter as theoretical tasks of various federal bureaus. For example, the DOD and FDA are viewed as producers of public goods, the EPA and CPSC as suppressors of public bads, HHS as an agency involved in resource redistribution, the Department of Justice and the FTC as counterforces to private monopoly, and the FCC, ICC, and CAB as definers of property rights.

Federal bureaus face substantial difficulties in carrying out these theoretical tasks, however. The mandates agencies receive from Congress may be tainted with requirements to produce private goods at collective expense. Nevertheless, because of the environment of public goods and externalities in which agencies operate, their goals may be strongly disputed and ambiguous. There also appear to be no clear motives inducing bureaus to make their constituent parts operate more efficiently. And, those who would—impossibly—monitor and control bureau actions seldom can define even what aspects of output to measure.

---

[77] *Brown v. Board of Education,* 347 U.S. 483 (1954).

Without other direction, bureaucrats seem implicitly to obey an operational code that bears small resemblance to the theoretical purposes for which their respective bureaus were established. Bureaucrats maximize their agencies' budgets and outputs and expand their agencies' jurisdictions. They use agency resources to maximize monitorable output rather than output that is not readily monitorable and to minimize the probability of making detectable rather than undetectable errors. Adhering to this code also leads bureaucrats, just like other interest-group leaders, to use the political and governmental processes to fulfill the goals that the code contemplates. Consequently, bureaus are believed to extract an excessive amount of resources from the private sector and local governments and to impose regulatory costs that often exceed the benefits associated with their activities. The members of Congress extract benefits from the current operation of bureaus and therefore ordinarily try to sustain the present characteristics of bureaus. Even when they are willing, presidents seem unable to change matters much. Bureau leaders also find strategic advantages in judicial proceedings. In sum, the theoretical reasons for bureau action often are lost in the processes of government and politics.

QUESTIONS FOR DISCUSSION AND REVIEW

1. Do bureaucrats control the Congress, or do House and Senate members control the bureaucracy? Neither? Both? What would be the public policy consequences if each hypothesis were true?
2. Are bureaucrats "bad" people? Or, are the problems of bureaucracy the inevitable consequences of producing public goods and suppressing public bads? Could the severity of these problems be reduced by establishing many competing bureaus or by decentralizing bureaus by placing them under state and local governments? Or, perhaps merely by diminishing our reliance on bureaus?
3. Would public policy change if the chief bureaucrats—for example, cabinet secretaries—were themselves elected directly rather than nominated by the president and confirmed by the Senate? How would it change?
4. Compare the members of the "iron triangles" with intense minorities. Do the problems raised by each differ in any respect? What is the connection between intense minorities and those who pursue private goods in the public sector?
5. How are the incentives and environments of bureaucrats like or unlike the incentives and environments of managers of private-sector firms? What public policy consequences follow from these similarities and differences?

6. Should bureaucrats be allowed to vote? Why? Why not?
7. Can the problems of bureaucracy be solved by better management techniques, such as the adoption of improved accounting methods and the use of advanced data processing systems? Why? Why not?

NEW CONCEPTS AND TERMS

bureau
bureaucracy
capture hypothesis
independent regulatory commission
iron triangle
life cycle
operational code of the bureaucrat
revolving door
welfare loss

12

Law and the Judiciary

We now turn to the law, the courts, and their place in making collective choices—public policy—in the United States. In earlier chapters, we have often encountered Supreme Court decisions and we have noted their importance. For example, Chapter 4 describes the significant line of Supreme Court cases, beginning with *Baker v. Carr,* which created a revolution in the apportionment of state legislatures and congressional seats.[1] Chapter 8 points out the central position of the Supreme Court, as well as the members of Congress, in eliminating racial restrictions on the franchise. Other chapters identify cases in which a decision of the Court has affected the relationships among various branches of government and between the agents of government and the citizens.[2]

When referring to these Supreme Court decisions, earlier chapters took them as *given,* without considering the important processes that helped to

---

[1] 369 U.S. 186 (1962).

[2] Discussions about courts and judges commonly refer to "the court," thereby committing an apparent organic fallacy. However, this usage carries a specific meaning. In the first place, a court presided over by a single judge may be referred to as a court. For example, in sentencing a person just convicted of a crime, the judge might declare, "This court sentences you to a term of five years in the state penitentiary." As we will note later, the same language is also used to refer to a written opinion in a Supreme Court case that a majority of the justices voting agreed to. The opinion then becomes the opinion of the Court, and is called by that name. Here, for convenience, we maintain this usage, though we must remain mindful that such an *opinion* results from individual decisions.

create them. However, judges and others associated with the judiciary—litigants and lawyers—use fairly well-defined rules of procedure in arriving at their decisions, and those procedures and decisions, like others considered in this book, can be analyzed using the theory of rational choice. Furthermore, we shall find that the scope and importance of judicial activities go far beyond merely deciding cases and controversies between two litigants making opposing claims. For, in deciding such cases, judges sometimes also establish rules that affect future human decisions and actions in both the private and public sectors. Because such a large part of public choice outside of the judiciary also consists of rule making, judicial proceedings could conceivably be substituted for most activities now carried on in the other institutions of government. Indeed, at one time courts of law were the principal institutions involved in matters that are now largely the province of regulatory commissions.[3] For this reason, it will become evident that people either use or could use the legal process to address many of the problems cited in Chapter 3 as goals for adopting collective choice.

THE COMMON LAW

In our discussion of the Congress and the presidency, we began by considering the formal authority vested in these institutions, as defined and limited by the Constitution. We shall do so here later for the federal courts, but we must begin this analysis by describing and explaining various aspects of law and the judiciary. For in the first place, most people are less familiar with legal decision making than they are with Congress and the presidency. In the second place, the roots of our legal practices pre-date the Constitution by at least six centuries, if not longer.

Varieties of Law

Law in the United States may usefully be divided into three large categories: constitutional law, statutory law, and common law, sometimes called case law or judge-made law. These three categories are neither exhaustive of the varieties of law in existence (for example, the Vatican is governed under ecclesiastical law) nor mutually exclusive (for example, some statutory laws are legislatively enacted codifications of preexisting common law).[4] However, the distinctions among these three categories are important for the decisions of judges and litigants and therefore for public policy.

[3] This is especially true of those regulatory agencies such as the EPA, OSHA, and the FTC, which regulate across industry lines. It is less true of agencies such as the ICC and the CAB, which regulate particular industries.

[4] These categories also fail to include international law, which governs the relationships among nations. Some argue that such a body of law exists only in name and then only concerning matters not affecting the sovereignty of any nation.

Constitutional law. **Constitutional law** is the body of law that includes the dictates of the Constitution itself and all subsequent court opinions that interpret the Constitution or refer to it for authority in finding another law or action constitutional or unconstitutional. Hence, much of constitutional law *is* case law. But it is also statutory law, for the members of Congress sometimes enact statutes to fulfill specific, constitutionally prescribed purposes.

Court opinions that interpret the Constitution must be regarded as continuing precedents for later cases or else they are of no effect. For example, in the case of *Plessy v. Ferguson,* decided in 1896, Plessy asked the Supreme Court to declare that a Louisiana statute requiring black and white passengers to ride in "separate but equal" railroad cars was unconstitutional because it violated, among other things, the Fourteenth Amendment's requirement that states not "deny any person . . . the equal protection of the laws."[5] Plessy, a black man, had been convicted under that Louisiana statute, for riding in a "whites only" coach. Mr. Justice Brown, writing for the Court, said, "The object of the amendment was undoubtedly to enforce the absolute equality of the two races before the law, but . . . it could not be intended to abolish distinctions based on color, or to enforce social, as distinguished from political, equality, or a commingling of the two races upon terms unsatisfactory to either." A majority of the justices thus held that a state law requiring "separate but equal" facilities did not violate the Fourteenth Amendment's requirement of "equal protection of the laws." This interpretation of the Constitution no longer stands as a precedent in constitutional law. In 1954, Chief Justice Warren, citing a number of psychological and sociological studies, delivered the unanimous opinion of the Court that "segregation of children in public schools solely on the basis of race, even though the physical facilities and other 'tangible' factors may be equal, deprive[s] the children of the minority of equal educational opportunities."[6]

Constitutional law provides the rules for setting up the major institutions of government. It also defines the relationships among and obligations, rights, and responsibilities of the citizens and those who occupy various institutions set up under the Constitution. In a profound but nonmystical sense, constitutional law is **organic law,** for it states the fundamental rules by which government is established and under which its agents operate.

Statutory law. Laws created by members of a legislature—for example, laws enacted by the members of Congress—fall in the category of **statutory law.** Such laws are ordinarily called statutes. But statutory law also includes treaties and executive agreements. Scholars usually distinguish statutory law from **administrative law,** which is the body of law controlling the procedures

---

[5] 163 U.S. 537 (1896).

[6] 347 U.S. 483. Warren also said, "Whatever may have been the extent of psychological knowledge at the time of *Plessy,* this finding is amply supported by modern authority."

of various government bureaus, agencies, commissions, and administrations. Part of administrative law is statutory law, in particular the laws passed by the members of Congress controlling the jurisdictions and procedures of federal bureaus. Part of administrative law is issued by the bureaus themselves in establishing their procedures and in doing their jobs. Finally, some administrative law grows out of case law, in particular judicial decisions concerning suits brought by and against the bureaus. Like statutory law, all administrative law must meet standards of constitutionality.

A large part of **criminal law** derived from the common law of England. However, today most criminal law is included as part of statutory law. An exception is the act of treason, which is made a crime by Article 3, Section 3 of the Constitution: "Treason against the United States shall consist only in levying War against them, or in adhering to their Enemies, giving them Aid and Comfort."[7] Furthermore, all federal criminal law is statutory law (there is no federal criminal common law), and by modern constitutional standards most criminal law today must be written, statutory law.

As a general rule, contemporary criminal law is distinguished by three properties. First, it is defined by statutory law. Second, the government (federal or state) is usually named as the plaintiff (prosecution). Third, upon conviction of a crime, defendants may ordinarily receive penalties that are intended to deprive them of more utility than they gained by committing the crime in the first place. That is, the penalty is set high not to compensate the plaintiff or the victim, for they are not compensated in any meaningful sense, but to deter the defendant and others from similar acts in the future.[8]

A crime may be classified as a **felony** or a **misdemeanor.** Felonies are serious crimes. Federal law and the criminal law in most states categorize as felonies those crimes for which a convict may be executed or sentenced to prison for more than one year (hence the frequently imposed sentence of "a year and a day").[9] Misdemeanors are less serious crimes for which judges may impose short prison terms or monetary fines.

The common law. Most **civil law** (as distinct from criminal law) in the United States is case law, judge-made law, usually referred to as **common law.**[10] The common law first developed in England following the Norman

[7] Notice the wording here: "the act of treason . . . is made a crime by Article 3 . . . ." In Western legal systems, legal practice holds to the principle of *nullum crimem sine lege,* "there is no crime without law." By contrast, the Soviet criminal code does not accept "this 'bourgeois' principle," but instead provides "that an act not made punishable by a specific article of the code may, if it is deemed socially dangerous, be punishable under articles relating to analogous acts." See Harold J. Berman, "Legal Systems: Socialist Legal Systems—Soviet Law," in David L. Sills, ed., *International Encyclopedia of the Social Sciences* (New York: Macmillan, 1972), vol. 9, p. 218.

[8] Of course, the maximum possible penalty may not be carried out. Judges give many first-time offenders suspended sentences and a period of parole.

[9] *United States Code Annotated,* § 1.

[10] The term "civil law" has another meaning, which may cause some confusion. Many European nations do not let judges "make" law but instead confine them to

Conquest of 1066.[11] The kings of England in this period sent judges out into the countryside to hear cases in the courts of various towns. While these judges tried to apply local custom to the cases they heard, certain customs made better sense than others. The judges eventually adopted these customs as uniform principles, or rules, for deciding cases. Of course, they also applied some rules of their own. The development of central royal courts at Westminster encouraged this uniformity, because these courts used the rules that the traveling judges had previously adopted. These rules were entirely judge-made or judge-discovered (though today many have been codified by statutes), but they soon became common to the entire kingdom. Hence, the term "common law."

Varieties of Common Law

Common law and equity. Legal experts usually distinguish between common law and **equity.** In a suit at common law, a plaintiff might claim that the defendant's actions have damaged him in some respect. The plaintiff therefore asks the court to force the defendant to pay him compensation for the damages suffered. However, to have standing to sue at common law, a plaintiff usually must be able to show that he has actually been injured.[12] But suppose the plaintiff has not yet been injured, though he is about to be injured as the result of the defendant's actions. For instance, the plaintiff might have contracted to buy the defendant's home, and the contract called for the seller (defendant) to take all necessary legal steps to give the buyer clear title to the property. The buyer discovers before the closing (the actual sale) that the property has a cloud on the title, which the seller has no intention of removing.[13] The buyer can wait until the seller fails to perform under the terms of the contract and then sue for **damages,** or he can decide not to wait but to sue immediately *in equity* to get the seller to clear the title (this is called a suit for **specific performance**). Notice that a suit at common law asks for damages, while a suit in equity calls for performance of a contract or other obligation. The court demands performance by issuing an **injunction** ordering the defendant to comply with the terms of the contract, in which case

---

applying to specific cases complicated statutes covering every imaginable contingency. The body of such statutes is also called the civil law. Civil law in this sense of the term is of Roman origin, as compared to common law, which is of Anglo-Saxon origin.

[11] An excellent brief summary of British legal practices is provided in Gwendolen M. Carter and John H. Herz, *Major Foreign Powers,* 5th ed. (New York: Harcourt, Brace, and World, 1967), pp. 172–187.

[12] *Damage* and *injury* refer to financial injury or injury to reputation as well as to physical injury.

[13] A cloud on a title is an imperfection (perhaps created during a previous sale) that puts the present legal status of ownership in doubt. For example, the IRS may have improperly seized the property from a previous owner to settle a tax payment claim. If so, the former owner may sue (successfully) at some time in the future to have his property restored.

the plaintiff has received **injunctive relief.** (Divorce cases were originally brought in equity.)

A plaintiff may have already been injured but nevertheless decide to sue in equity, not at common law. For example, A may contract to have B store her furniture. If B refuses to return A's furniture as agreed, A can sue B for damages. However, the court will determine damages in this case by ascertaining the value of comparable used furniture. The damages the court will require B to pay A will thus be inadequate if the stored furniture has sentimental value because it has been in A's family for generations.[14] Therefore, A may decide to sue B for specific performance (return of the furniture) rather than for damages.

Plaintiffs sue in equity rather than at common law either because relief at common law is not available or not yet available or because they expect the damages awarded to them at common law to be worth less, say, than specific performance. (However, under traditional common-law rules, one cannot sue in equity if there is an adequate remedy at common law.) Equity emerged as a body of law in England for the express purpose of overcoming the perceived limits of the common law in cases such as those just mentioned. Claims for "equitable relief" were made to the lord chancellor, who for that reason was called "keeper of the King's conscience." Litigants brought cases in equity to the chancery courts. But the case-law development of rules of equity paralleled the development of the common law, and in England chancery courts and common-law courts were combined in the 1870s. Today, both in England and in the United States, equity and the common law are viewed as a single body of judge-made law.

Torts. A **tort** is "A private or civil wrong or injury, other than a breach of contract, for which the court will provide a remedy in the form of an action for damages."[15] Tort law is a major area of the common law. All tort actions must have three elements: "Existence of legal duty from defendant to plaintiff, breach of duty, and damage as a proximate result."[16] In common-law tort cases, where statutory law is silent, the legal duty from defendant to plaintiff either will be defined by the court or will have been defined by the ruling of that court or another court in an earlier case.

Torts may be divided into three categories: intentional torts, torts caused by negligence, and torts arising out of damage where fault is not an issue (where a doctrine of strict liability is imposed). **Intentional torts** include defamation (slander if spoken, libel if written), trespass, conversion (theft), assault, battery, and fraud, all of which have parallels in the criminal law.

---

[14] This case is suggested by *Downing v. Williams,* 191 So. 221 (Ala. 1934). I am indebted to Professor Timothy Muris for bringing it to my attention.

[15] *Black's Law Dictionary,* 5th ed. (St. Paul: West, 1979), p. 1335.

[16] *Black's Law Dictionary,* p. 1335.

Wrongful interference with contractual relations and unfair competition are also intentional torts, though in these matters statutory and administrative law have altered common-law rules. Applying the definition of a tort, we find that all of these intentional torts are examples of acts one person has a duty not to do to another.

A tort arising because of **negligence** occurs as the result of an "omission to do something which a reasonable man, guided by those ordinary considerations which ordinarily regulate human affairs, would do, or the doing of something which a reasonable and prudent man would not do."[17] As with other torts, to prove a tort arising because of negligence there must be a legal duty, the breach of that duty, and damage as a proximate result.

A tort arising under **strict liability,** or liability without fault, holds a person liable for injury caused to others even though the defendant acted as a "reasonable man" would act. Judges usually impose strict liability when the activity causing the injury is inherently and "abnormally" dangerous. For example, the owners of a dynamite-manufacturing firm would be held liable for the damage caused to others if their plant exploded. Their liability would remain even though they had taken every precaution to avoid explosions.

Contracts. The subject of contracts is the second major body of common law. A **contract** is "An agreement between two or more persons which creates an obligation to do or not to do a particular thing. Its essentials are competent parties, subject matter, a legal consideration, mutuality of agreement, and mutuality of obligation."[18] Contract law differs from tort law in that the obligations the parties owe each other under a contract are agreed to by them and those obligations are not binding on others. Obligations incurred in tort law are owed by all persons to each other, even though there has been no contract.

Contract law concerns judgments about such matters as: What is adequate consideration? What is satisfactory performance? Under what conditions may a contracting party be discharged from performance under the contract? and, When is a person legally competent to be a party to a contract? A large number of contract cases involve breach of contract and the appropriate damages to be paid for the breach.[19]

An example of alleged breach of contract illustrates some of the con-

---

[17] *Black's Law Dictionary,* p. 930.

[18] *Black's Law Dictionary,* pp. 291–292. "Consideration" is the "motive" or "inducement to a contract" (p. 277). "Mutuality of obligation" means that *both* parties must be bound by the contract (p. 920).

[19] Lawsuits arising from failure to perform under the terms of a contract may be brought as intentional torts. For example, to satisfy the terms of a contract, a buyer may knowingly issue a worthless check, which violates both the common law of torts and statute law. The overlapping nature of the law thus leads to the saying that "the law is a seamless webb."

cerns of contract law. The case of *Hadley v. Baxendale* was argued and decided in Gloucester, England, in 1854.[20] The Hadleys, owners of a flour mill, contracted with Pickford and Co. to deliver their broken engine shaft to W. Joyce and Co., which would use the broken shaft as a form to make a new shaft. Delivery of the broken shaft took an alleged five days longer than necessary—and longer than promised—because Pickford and Co. used canal transportation rather than rail service for part of the journey. Since the mill was out of commission for an additional five days because canal transport was used, the Hadleys sued Baxendale, managing director of Pickford, for damages.

On appeal of an award of £50 to the Hadleys, the court held: "Where two parties have made a contract which one of them has broken, the damages which the other party ought to receive in respect of such breach of contract should be such as may fairly and reasonably be considered either arising naturally, i.e., according to the usual course of things, from such breach of contract itself, or such as may reasonably be supposed to have been in contemplation of both parties, at the time they made the contract, as the probable result of the breach of it."[21] The court found that Pickford and Co. had not been told of any "special circumstances," such as that the Hadleys were out of operation and losing £60 per day. Hence, Pickford and Co. had no obligation under the contract either to hasten delivery or (after the alleged breach) to pay damages to the Hadleys. For reasons we examine later, the ruling in *Hadley v. Baxendale* is still "good law," an accepted rule for judging such disputes, both in England and the United States.

Property. The third extensive area of the common law is the law of property. We have already encountered cases involving **property law.** This chapter reports a theoretical case concerning an imperfection in a title to real estate—a very important form of property. Chapter 3 analyzed the problem of incompatible uses of land (a plot of ground cannot simultaneously sustain wandering cattle and flourishing gardens).[22] Property law addresses an entire range of problems concerning more or less incompatible uses of land and other resources. For example, trespass and nuisance law can help to resolve problems of public bads, while eminent domain—because it allows bureaucrats to assemble large packages of land for public projects without being stopped by "hold-out" property owners—serves as a tool for reducing the cost of certain projects said to be public goods.

---

[20] 9 Ex. 341, 156 Eng. Rep. 145 (1854). An excellent discussion of this case is provided by Richard Danzig, "Hadley v. Baxendale: A Study in the Industrialization of Law," *Journal of Legal Studies,* 4 (June 1975), pp. 249–284.

[21] 9 Ex. 341, 354, 156 Eng. Rep. 145, 151 (1854). As quoted in Danzig, "Hadley v. Baxendale."

[22] See the text associated with Chapter 3, footnote 23.

The Efficiency of the Common Law

Efficiency and legal rules. Within the last few years, our understanding of legal rules and processes has grown considerably because of the application of decision theory and economic analysis to studying them.[23] A central finding of this application is that in deciding cases at common law, judges tend over time to adopt, sustain, and apply rules that are economically efficient.[24] **Efficiency** in the sense used by economists means that a firm, a government, a person, or a process (for example, the legal system) either maximizes output for a fixed level of input or minimizes input (cost) for a fixed level of output.[25] For example, a company that manufactures fifty bicycles with ten hours of labor and two hundred pounds of steel is more efficient than a company that manufactures the same number of bicycles with eleven hours of labor and three hundred pounds of steel.

We can apply the same reasoning to common-law rules. For example, consider a negligence (tort) action brought about when A was struck on the head by a tree limb that B had just sawed off a tree under which A was walking. B is liable for damages if a judge holds that he must compensate A. A is said to be liable if he must pay for his own damages. To simplify matters, suppose the judge must find only one of them liable—there is no contributory negligence. Was B negligent? The judge can apply the "prudent man" rule to answer this question, but what would a prudent man do to protect passers-by from falling limbs? Here the judge must find a rule of liability in past cases or make one up to apply to this case. If the judge applies an economically efficient rule, and if all other judges adopt it in future cases, then it will minimize the cost of accident avoidance for a given number of accidents. That is, the judge will make the least-cost-accident-avoider—person who can avoid accidents at least cost—liable.[26] In this case, a tree surgeon could bear the cost of accident avoidance more cheaply by placing warning signs around the tree than could pedestrians, who would probably have to inspect every tree under

---

[23] This section, and especially the mathematical discussion, depends for much of its analysis on Paul Rubin, "Why is the Common Law Efficient?" *Journal of Legal Studies,* 6 (January 1977), pp. 51–63. See generally Richard A. Posner, *Economic Analysis of Law,* 2nd ed. (Boston: Little, Brown, 1977).

[24] Rubin, "Why is the Common Law Efficient?"; George L. Priest, "The Common Law Process and the Selection of Efficient Rules," *Journal of Legal Studies,* 6 (January 1977), pp. 65–82; and John C. Goodman, "An Economic Theory of the Evolution of the Common Law," *Journal of Legal Studies,* 7 (June 1978), pp. 393–406. See also the symposium volumes "Private Alternatives to the Judicial Process," *Journal of Legal Studies,* 7 (March 1979), pp. 231–417, and "Change in the Common Law: Legal and Economic Perspectives," *Journal of Legal Studies,* 9 (March 1980), pp. 189–429.

[25] For technical reasons, the two tasks of maximization and minimization cannot ordinarily be performed simultaneously.

[26] Guido Calabressi, *The Costs of Accidents: Legal and Economic Analysis* (New Haven, Conn.: Yale University Press, 1970).

which they walked to avoid the same number of accidents as the signs would eliminate.[27] Hence, if the common law is efficient, the judge will order B to pay damages to A.

Efficiency and Pareto optimality. Why should we be interested in efficiency? After all, in the preceding case the judge must decide whether to award A compensation for his injuries. A will receive what B loses, the game is zero sum, and therefore all outcomes are Pareto optimal.[28] Therefore, we cannot say that one outcome is better than another, for efficiency and Pareto optimality appear to be unrelated concepts—and so they are, within the narrow view of efficiency just proposed. But suppose A and B are trying to fashion a legal procedure for a society in which their specific occupations are unknown to them. Certainly, they would wish to establish a procedure that would develop liability rules to minimize the cost of accident avoidance. Such a procedure—and then such rules—would make both A and B prospectively better off. Therefore, these liability rules would be Pareto optimal and they would also be efficient. (We would similarly call efficient the procedure that produced those rules.) Everyone has an interest in efficient rules and the procedures that discover them; the money or other resources saved (to avoid the same number of accidents) will be used to produce other valued goods, thus increasing the national product.

Common-law dynamic efficiency. How do common-law procedures lead to the adoption of efficient rules? To answer this question, recall that in the absence of statutory law affecting the matter, the judge in the personal injury trial between A and B will probably apply a rule from the decisions of judges in previous cases. That is, he will apply a **precedent:** "An adjudged case or decision of a court, considered as furnishing an example or authority for an identical or similar case afterwards arising or a similar question of law."[29] In deciding to apply precedent, the judge abides by the judicial practice of ***stare decisis,*** the "policy of courts to stand by precedent and not to disturb settled point."[30]

To understand the importance of precedent, we must see how it operates. The tree surgeon's case provides a good example. If a precedent makes the tree surgeon, B, liable, then in all future cases arising from similar accidents, he will face a summed total cost of T_B. This cost is made up of S_B,

[27] Assigning liability to B will probably also reduce the number of accidents. Here, though, we have artificially kept the number of accidents constant by assumption.

[28] Here, we ignore attorney's fees. We also make all subsequent calculations in expected value rather than expected utility. The reason for doing so is *lack* of sufficient reason. We know utility increases with value, but we cannot compare utility. Nor can judges do so. Hence, they are usually interested solely in value.

[29] *Black's Law Dictionary,* p. 1059.

[30] *Black's Law Dictionary,* p. 1261.

the amount B will spend for accident avoidance if he is liable for damages, and $N_B X$, such that N_B is the number of accidents that will occur in the future if B spends S_B on accident prevention, and X is the amount of damages B must pay to each future A in any subsequent accident. In sum,

$$T_B = S_B + N_B X.$$

Similarly, if precedent makes the pedestrian, A, liable (in the sense that he alone must bear the cost the accident imposes on him), then in all future cases in which he is struck by a falling limb, he will face a total cost of T_A, made up of S_A, the amount he will spend (in added caution while walking) to avoid such accidents, and $N_A X$, the number of accidents occurring if he spends S_A, times the cost of each accident.

If T_B is less than T_A, which we here assume to be true, then the judge will find for A and make B and all others like B liable in future cases. With T_B less than T_A,

$$S_B + N_B X < S_A + N_A X.$$

But suppose S_A and S_B produce the same "output" in accidents prevented, so that N_A equals N_B. If so, the previous inequality reduces to $S_B < S_A$, which means that B is the least-cost (more efficient) accident avoider. Of course, N_A and N_B may not be equal, in which case the judge may act *as if* he calculates the full expression in finding a rule.

When an accident occurs, both A and B must decide whether to proceed with a suit or to settle out of court. Suppose that the rule the courts have imposed is *inefficient* because it assigns liability to A, not to B. Let P_A be the probability that precedent will be overturned and accordingly that A will win the suit against B. P_B is the probability that *stare decisis* will prevail, that the precedent will be sustained in favor of B. Of course, $P_B = 1 - P_A$. Each party faces court (litigation) costs of C.

If B wins, A will have to bear the cost of *this* accident by himself. That is, he will receive an amount equal to $-X$. But if A wins, he will no longer face a future total cost of T_A. Therefore, EV_A, A's expected value of going to trial, becomes

$$EV_A = P_B(-X) + P_A T_A - C.$$

By a similar logic, if precedent is not overturned, B will not have to pay damages of X in this case. But if A wins, B expects to pay T_B in all future cases. B's expected value of going to trial, EV_B, therefore becomes

$$EV_B = P_B(X) + P_A(-T_B) - C.$$

The tendency for the common law to adopt efficient liability rules depends crucially on the decisions of the litigants to settle out of court or to go to trial. A will be willing to settle for an amount greater than EV_A, and B, for an amount greater than EV_B. For example, suppose A believes EV_A to be \$1000 and B believes EV_B to be −\$1500. B can offer to settle A's claim for any amount less than \$1500 (greater than −\$1500) and be better off than he would be going to court. Similarly, A should accept an offer from B of more than \$1000. But if A believes EV_A to be \$1500.01 or more, then no settlement is possible.

The general condition for settlement out of court is that $-EV_A$ is greater than EV_B (or that EV_A is less than $-EV_B$). Spelling out the full expressions for EV_A and EV_B, this settlement condition means that

$$-[P_B(-X) + P_A T_A - C] > P_B(X) + P_A(-T_B) - C.$$

Rearranging terms, this expression for *settlement* becomes

$$P_A(T_B - T_A) > -2C,$$

or, *litigation* occurs if

$$P_A(T_A - T_B) > 2C.$$

This last expression is the key to the efficiency of common-law rules. By assumption, precedent is inefficient and favors B. This means that P_A, the probability that A will win in court, is less than 50 percent. However, the amount $(T_A - T_B)$ shows just how much more it costs A than it costs B to be held liable under the rule in future cases. "$T_A - T_B$ is the cost of the inefficient legal rule."[31] As T_A and T_B diverge, reflecting an even greater inefficiency, $(T_A - T_B)$ grows larger, making an out-of-court settlement less and less likely and litigation more and more likely.

Precedent cannot be changed by out-of-court settlements. Therefore, if $(T_A - T_B)$ were negative, reflecting an efficient rule, *ceteris paribus* there would be no litigation of disputes arising over accidents of the sort in question. Precedent would remain unchallenged. But if $(T_A - T_B)$ were positive and growing larger, litigation would surely follow, thus challenging precedent in case after case. Even if judges used spinners or other randomizing devices to decide cases and choose rules (which would be reflected in the value of P_A), eventually the inefficient liability rules set by precedent would be overturned, and the more inefficient those rules were, the faster and more frequently they would be challenged. The resulting new precedent would be efficient and seldom challenged.

Precedents as public goods. This discussion of the efficiency of the common law suggests that it is an extraordinary system for collective decision

[31] Rubin, "Why is the Common Law Efficient?" p. 54.

making. Indeed, it is so, as evidenced by its continuous development in most English-speaking nations since it began in Great Britain over eight centuries ago.[32] However, certain problems do emerge with common-law rules, which we shall consider momentarily. First, though, we must consider the nature of precedents.

It should now be apparent that by their effects on costs and benefits (inputs and outputs), precedents are public goods. For example, liability rules that are adopted today affect the welfare of all potential future accident victims and perpetrators. A precedent based on an efficient rule is a public good that displays a positive externality; one based on an inefficient rule is a public good that displays a negative externality. But the common law proceeds in such a way that efficient rules are likely to remain in force, simply because they are infrequently challenged.

More surprising, the common law gets potential litigants to help create these public goods while pursuing their self-interest. Indeed, this precedent-creating activity occurs with greatest frequency just when it is most beneficial. For instance, when precedent is clearly in B's favor, P_A equals zero. But if there have been no judgments about a particular situation, or if judgments seem contradictory, then P_A may appear to equal approximately 50 percent. At that point, $P_A(T_A - T_B)$ is more likely to exceed $2C$ than when P_A is at or near zero. Therefore, litigants "come out of the woodwork" and push the courts to establish precedent. Trial courts may continue to differ on the best rule. However, as more and more **appellate courts**—those to which litigants appeal for a review of a lower-court ruling—find trial courts fashioning contradictory rules, these higher courts will try to find an efficient rule amid the muddle of conflicting lower-court opinions. Here and there courts may continue to issue aberrant decisions, but in the long run the common law tends toward the adoption of efficient rules.

Asymmetric interests. The example of the tree surgeon and the pedestrian is somewhat contrived, because the tree surgeon will have a substantial ongoing interest in any precedent set in the case; the pedestrian will not. Therefore, T_A is likely to be zero or very, very small compared to T_B. In such situations of asymmetric interests, the decision to go to trial will principally reflect the level of litigation costs and the concerns of the party with the long-term interest.[33] Whether such cases result in efficient rules or not is difficult to say.

Three developments in law help to restore the likelihood that judges will apply efficient rules even if the interests of the parties are asymmetrical,

---

[32] Indeed, judges at common law often cite the opinions of other common-law judges in other nations as authority. Even judges in nations with civil (Roman) law codes have been known to cite decisions of common-law courts. See Roscoe Pound, *The Spirit of the Common Law* (Boston: Marshall Jones, 1921), pp. 3–4.

[33] In cases with asymmetric interests, the parties will proceed to trial if $P_B(T_B) > 2C$. See Rubin, "Why is the Common Law Efficient?" p. 56.

however. First, there may continue to be suits between parties with symmetric interests in the future, and those suits may elicit precedents that control decisions in cases involving litigants with asymmetric interests. For example, consider an action for breach of contract between a bank and an armored truck company that transports money for the bank. A robbery occurs and the bank sues the truck company for its losses. Did failure to deliver the money constitute a breach of contract? Did failure to prevent or deter the robbery constitute negligence? Both the bank and the truck company have a long-run interest in any precedent set in this case. More to the point, such a precedent may control the decision in a future case between a parcel delivery service and a woman who sends her grandchildren gifts using the service and who suffers a loss when a robbery occurs. The grandmother has little or no precedential interest in the bank case, but the delivery service certainly does. Of course, while the grandmother and the bank are in analogous positions, the precedent set in the bank's suit may not be efficient for deciding any action the grandmother brings against the delivery service. However, the precedent set in the bank's suit is more likely to be efficient for deciding the grandmother's suit than not, especially as the two cases grow more alike in detail.

Second, one of the litigants in a suit again may have no particular interest in precedent but only in his or her recovery of damages in the case at hand. However, such a litigant's situation may resemble the situation of thousands or even millions of other future potential litigants, who individually would also have no interest in precedent. This problem could occur in tort or contract cases, or even in property cases if the event initiating the suit is most unlikely to happen to such a litigant more than once in a lifetime. But the present litigants and all such potential litigants may belong to a trade association whose attorneys have an interest in the precedent. Or, the litigants may have insured themselves against the very loss at issue in the trial, in which case the insurance company has an interest in precedent. If either contingency has occurred, then the interests of these potential future litigants may be aggregated, so that the present litigant's legal fees are paid and he or she is represented by the association or insurance company's counsel. In any case, an interest in the precedent the case sets, or breaks, or maintains, might again become symmetric.

Third, the **class action** has been proposed and is sometimes used as a means to establish a symmetry of legal capability, though not explicitly a symmetry of interest in precedent. In many situations, the interests of one potential litigant are not sufficient to go to trial, and without the threat of a suit the other litigant has no incentive to settle. For example, suppose a department store credits a customer's account for returned merchandise but systematically fails to credit the sales tax the customer paid. When challenged about this practice, the store's management claims that the money withheld is an unannounced "service charge," and in any event the store has discontinued this practice for the foreseeable future. The plaintiff learns that this case will cost $25,000 to litigate successfully, but he calculates that in the last year the store has withheld \$50 from him, so he can only ask the court for \$50 in damages. It would obviously be irrational to proceed to trial. However, if 4999 other customers are in the same position, then the total loss to this "class" would be \$250,000, ten times the legal fees. Clearly, bringing the suit against the store would be equivalent to providing a collective good for the members of the class. And, an adequate interest in precedent also might then be created by the class action.

In recent years, the Supreme Court has made it very difficult to bring a class action concerning purely economic matters in federal court.[34] However, class actions are sometimes easier to bring in state courts or in federal courts when constitutionally guaranteed rights are at issue.

Litigants without interest in precedent. When neither party is concerned about precedent, EV_A becomes $-P_BX - C$ and EV_B becomes $P_BX - C$. The parties again settle if $-EV_A$ is greater than EV_B, which occurs if

$$P_BX + C > P_BX - C,$$

which is always true.[35] Of course, this inequality holds no implications for the character of any precedents set in any trial that occurs.

Notice, however, that the parties will settle out of court if they agree on the value of P_B, but they might not settle otherwise. One cause of disagreement about P_B in a particular case is the absence of a clear precedent. But if estimates of P_B vary widely between plaintiffs and defendants for a particular kind of case, because there is no clear precedent, then the number of such cases brought to trial will probably increase. Therefore, a lack of interest in precedent, coupled with the absence of a clear precedent, might actually create the conditions under which a clearer precedent might be judicially formulated. Of course, even though two particular opposing parties have no interest in precedent, as we found with asymmetric interests, the chance remains that other cases may be brought by parties with such an interest. Nevertheless, in cases in which neither party has an interest in precedent, the likelihood that they will go to trial stands posed as a loose cannon, which occasionally might overturn efficient rules as well as inefficient ones.

Judicial Decision Making

Our discussion of common-law efficiency included no mention of judges' incentives or judicial decision making. The analysis merely assumed that the

[34] A review of cases is provided in Arthur R. Miller, "Of Frankenstein Monsters and Shining Knights: Myth, Reality, and the 'Class Action Problem,'" *Harvard Law Review,* 92 (January 1979), pp. 664–694.

[35] Rubin, "Why is the Common Law Efficient?" p. 57.

parties to a conflict, litigants, must rationally decide whether to sue or settle out of court. The analysis then showed that even if judges decide cases randomly but with a bias toward precedent, the common law tends toward the adoption of efficient rules governing the allocation of rights and duties in torts, property, and contract disputes.[36]

This finding grows in importance when we learn that in most cases at common law or in equity, the attorneys argue the claims of their clients, not the future consequences for efficiency of any precedent to be set. The job of the judge or jury is to do justice as between the litigants in the courtroom, not to set a precedent to rule future cases involving similar litigants.[37] For instance, in the hypothetical case of the tree surgeon and the pedestrian, nothing guarantees that a judge trying to rule wisely for these two litigants will establish an efficient rule to control all similar cases in the future. Furthermore, there is no reason to believe that a judge has an incentive to make an efficient ruling. However, our analysis demonstrates that judges will ordinarily not get to hear cases for which efficient rules are already controlling, since litigants tend to settle such cases, not to bring them to trial.

Judges' incentives. In spite of the theory that the decisions of litigants are largely responsible for common-law efficiency, judges are hardly passive participants in judicial processes. They could conceivably create and adhere to an inefficient precedent even in the face of the expanding caseload that it creates. Eventually, potential litigants might get the message that the judges will stand by the inefficient rule no matter what the cost. Nothing except the intervention of the legislature or the judicial selection process itself could possibly prevent such a result if most judges had an incentive to keep the inefficient rule.

An enumeration of judges' incentives shows, however, that they are at least neutral where efficiency is concerned, and probably biased toward it. First, for most judges the effects of an electoral connection are either muted or nonexistent. Federal judges are appointed for life "during good Behaviour." While their salaries and other perquisites of office are set by the ordinary lawmaking process, the Constitution requires that they "receive for their Services, a Compensation, which shall not be diminished during their Continuance in Office" (Article 3, Section 1). Nor do most federal judges intend to seek higher positions in the government. Hence, the electoral connection of progressive ambition affects them less than it affects, say, members of the House of Representatives.

---

[36] All three of these areas of common law, as well as others such as family law, can be analyzed within the same framework we used to study the negligence case between the tree surgeon and pedestrian. See Richard A. Posner, *Economic Analysis of Law,* 1st ed. (Boston: Little, Brown, 1973), chapter 5.

[37] Indeed, a jury trial sets no precedents, except for the judge's procedural rulings. But it might give future litigants estimates of the probability that they would win in a particular kind of case if tried by a jury.

State judges are popularly elected in twenty-five states. They are elected by the legislatures in four states. Thirteen states use the Missouri plan, under which a nonpartisan commission initially nominates judges, who thereafter stand periodically for the approval of the voters in elections without opponents. [The ballot reads, "Shall Judge ______ of the ______ Court be retained in office? Yes ( ) No ( ) (Scratch One)."][38] In four states judges are elected by the legislature, and in seven they are nominated by the governor and confirmed by the state senate. Many states in which judges are popularly elected also allow governors to make permanent appointments to fill vacancies on the bench. Hence, the actual proportion of elected judges is far less than these numbers might otherwise indicate.[39]

Even if judges are elected, in many cases, and especially those at common law or in equity, the conflicts they decide do not raise the kinds of highly publicized issues about which large numbers of citizens will have preferences on which they would vote. Though precedent may be involved, usually only two litigants appear before the court. In such cases, even elected judges need not think about how voters will react to their decisions. Therefore, in cases of this nature, an electoral connection ordinarily does not bias elected judges one way or another.

If the preferences among members of the electorate or the legislature might affect the judge's decision, all is not lost. Previous chapters argue the propensity of legislators, voters, and bureaucrats to support inefficient programs. They may also support inefficient judicial rulings, but not necessarily. More to the point, the appellate process—especially in cases involving constitutional issues that many voters follow closely—can be used to raise a case to the judgment of an appointed court. In sum, where efficiency is concerned, the electoral connection counts for much less in judicial decision making than in legislative decision making.

Second, unlike bureaucrats, judges are probably not extremely interested in the size of their budgets or in the numbers of workers their courts individually employ. Certainly, most judges would prefer to work in commodious and pleasantly decorated surroundings, and most judges would also prefer to have more bailiffs and other court personnel available. However, the appearance of court facilities and the number of personnel bear only a slight relationship to the quality and quantity of a single judge's output. For the judge's capacity to process cases is itself limited. Even justices of the Supreme Court have only two law clerks each. Not surprisingly, therefore, instead of pursuing a course that would maximize output of cases, as would a bureau-

---

[38] Henry J. Abraham, *The Judicial Process: An Introductory Analysis of the Courts of The United States, England, and France,* 3rd ed., rev. (New York: Oxford University Press, 1975), p. 36.

[39] John Paul Ryan, Allan Ashman, Bruce D. Sales, and Sandra Shane-DuBow, *American Trial Judges: Their Work Styles and Performance* (New York: Free Press, 1980), chapter 6.

NONPARTISAN JUDICIAL

JUSTICE OF THE SUPREME COURT

Shall Justice James C. Adkins be retained in office?

YES	134	➡
NO	135	➡

Shall Justice James E. Alderman be retained in office?

YES	138	➡
NO	139	➡

Shall Justice Joseph A. Boyd be retained in office?

YES	142	➡
NO	143	➡

Shall Justice Arthur J. England be retained in office?

YES	146	➡
NO	147	➡

Shall Justice Parker Lee McDonald be retained in office?

YES	150	➡
NO	151	➡

Shall Justice Ben Overton be retained in office?

YES	154	➡
NO	155	➡

6 (11/4/80) TURN TO NEXT PAGE

This is a Missouri plan ballot, used in a 1980 Florida judicial election.

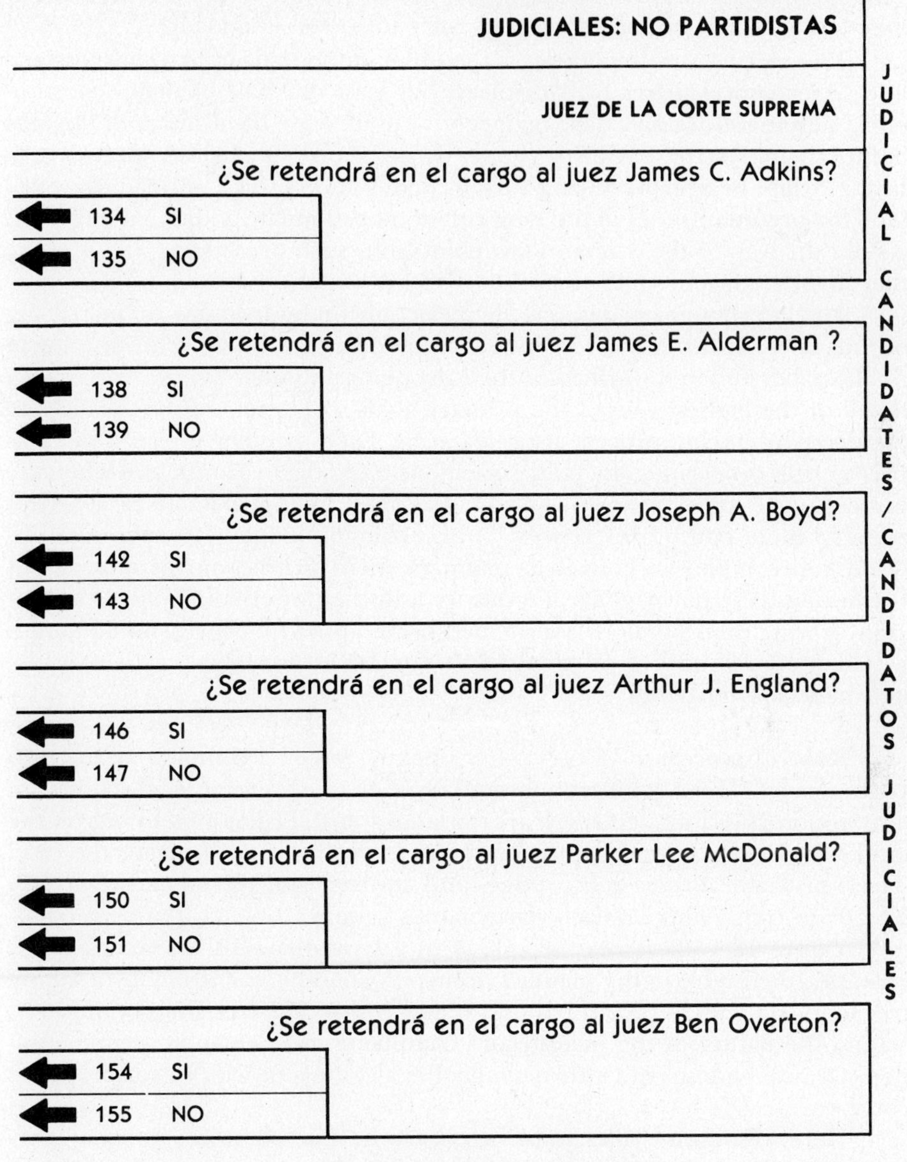

JUDICIALES: NO PARTIDISTAS

JUEZ DE LA CORTE SUPREMA

¿Se retendrá en el cargo al juez James C. Adkins?

134 SI

135 NO

¿Se retendrá en el cargo al juez James E. Alderman ?

138 SI

139 NO

¿Se retendrá en el cargo al juez Joseph A. Boyd?

142 SI

143 NO

¿Se retendrá en el cargo al juez Arthur J. England?

146 SI

147 NO

¿Se retendrá en el cargo al juez Parker Lee McDonald?

150 SI

151 NO

¿Se retendrá en el cargo al juez Ben Overton?

154 SI

155 NO

JUDICIAL CANDIDATES/CANDIDATOS JUDICIALES

SIGA A LA PAGINA SIGUIENTE (11/4/80) 6A

crat, most judges consider their available resources as fixed. As a consequence, they will probably adopt procedural rules to *reduce* case loads.

Reinforcing this hypothesis is the observation that, unlike congressmen and bureaucrats, judges will "displease" at least one-half of their "constituents," and therefore they have no incentive to increase the number of litigants before them. For these reasons, judges do not share bureaucrats' incentives to be inefficient by overproducing various goods and services; instead, they will look for precedents that in the long run do not stimulate additional litigation. As our analysis of the common law points out, such precedents will be those that invoke efficient rules.

Finally, though an interest in reelection or budget size or increasing output does not usually affect judges' decisions, they do have an interest in public policy and in the effects of their decisions on public policy. As has been noted of the highest court, "the primary goals of Supreme Court justices in the decision-making process are *policy goals.* Each member of the Court has preferences concerning the policy questions faced by the Court, and when the justices make decisions they want the outcomes to approximate as nearly as possible these policy preferences."[40] Accordingly, judges will have sophisticated and complex incentives to maintain their jurisdictions as a means of furthering their policy goals. To this we add that lower-court judges do not enjoy having their opinions overturned by an appellate court, and all judges would prefer to have good reputations for fairness, judicial craftsmanship, and judicial scholarship.

Rules of procedure. Most courts operate under a common set of procedural rules. These rules are substantially the same even for legal actions not at common law, although there are variations in the rules depending on the kind of legal action taking place and the particular court hearing the case. These procedural rules guide judges and attorneys for the litigants, but they also place constraints on each participant's actions.

Figure 12.1 illustrates the course of a typical lawsuit. In our previous example, the injury to the plaintiff occurred when he was struck by a falling tree limb. He goes to his attorney, who may contact the tree surgeon directly, stating the nature of the pedestrian's complaint and demanding compensation. Or, the pedestrian's attorney may file a complaint with the appropriate court.

Here, significant rules must be observed. The plaintiff's attorney may have to explain in the **complaint** why his client has standing to sue and why the court in which he is filing the complaint has jurisdiction over the case. For example, a military court cannot hear the case if both litigants are civilians and if the accident occurred on private property, nor can a federal tax court hear the case. The military court lacks ***in personam*** **jurisdiction,** in this instance

[40] David W. Rohde and Harold J. Spaeth, *Supreme Court Decision Making* (San Francisco: W. H. Freeman, 1976) p. 72.

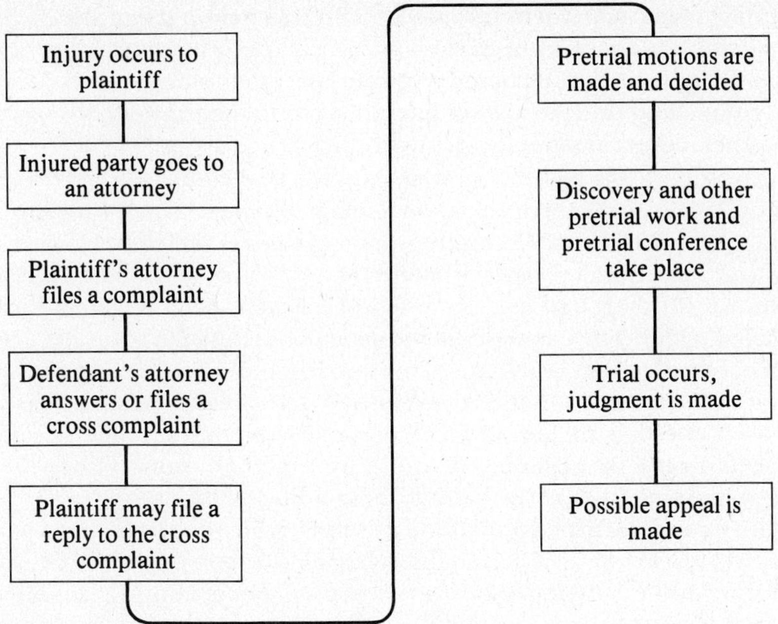

Figure 12.1 Steps in a civil lawsuit.

Source: Reproduced by permission from *West's Business Law: Text and Cases* by Kenneth W. Clarkson, Roger Leroy Miller, and Bonnie Blaire, copyright © 1980, West Publishing Co. All rights reserved.

jurisdiction over civilian litigants; the tax court lacks **subject-matter jurisdiction.**

Standing to sue has several aspects and is often limited by law. It usually means "that a party has sufficient stake in an otherwise justiciable controversy to obtain judicial resolution of that controversy."[41] For example, the pedestrian's walking companion cannot sue for damages claiming that he has been permanently affected by a fear of walking under trees (*subarboraphobia*). However, if the companion is the pedestrian's husband or wife, then he or she has standing to sue for loss of income, services, and companionship. Even so, if the husband is the tree surgeon and accidentally drops the limb on his wife, in most states she cannot sue for damages because of the doctrine of interspousal immunity.

Once the complaint is filed, the defendant's attorney files an **answer** or files a **cross complaint,** to which the plaintiff may file a **reply.** The contents of all of these documents are called the **pleadings.** Both sides may then make pretrial motions for **summary judgment** or **summary dismissal** of some or all of the complaints or cross complaints, based on the pleadings before the court. The attorneys can make motions for summary judgment at any time

[41] *Black's Law Dictionary,* p. 1260.

before the judge or jury delivers a verdict. Pretrial hearings can also be held at any time, but especially after **discovery,** which is another pretrial procedure that allows each side to examine (depose) the other side's experts and witnesses, compelling them to answer questions put to them, and to inspect many of the other side's documents or physical evidence as well.

Most Americans have an appreciation for trial-court procedures gained from watching courtroom dramas on television. Some trial rules are specific to criminal procedures, and we consider them in the next section. However, two procedural rules deserve special attention. The first is the doctrine of ***res judicata,*** which holds that once a cause of action has been litigated, it cannot be litigated again. For example, if the plaintiff-pedestrian loses his case, he can appeal the decision to a higher court on legal grounds, but he cannot ask the same trial court or another court at the same level to hear the case over again on a question of fact that the original court has already decided. A retrial could only be ordered for cause by a higher court. Otherwise, the matter is finished. It is *res judicata,* a thing adjudicated.

The second doctrine is **collateral estoppel,** which requires that a particular *fact* decided in one trial cannot be relitigated by one of the parties in that trial during some subsequent cause of action. For example, suppose that during the trial of his case against the tree surgeon, the pedestrian admitted that he was stumbling drunk and did not see the signs warning of "men in trees." Following his first trial, he might bring an action against the sign company, charging that its signs are too unspecific or too small for pedestrians to see. But because of his uncontested admission of inebriation in the previous trial he is collaterally estopped from asserting in the trial against the sign company that he was cold sober when the accident occurred.

Judicial procedures and judges' incentives. Most rules of judicial procedure, like most rules governing decisions in common-law cases, are judge-made rules. Today many procedural rules have been fashioned by legislatures, especially where federal courts are concerned. However, long-standing doctrines for the guiding of procedure and the deciding of cases—precedent, *stare decisis,* rules of jurisdiction and standing, *res judicata,* collateral estoppel, and others—were all formed by the decisions of judges themselves.

The major conclusion drawn from an examination of these rules and doctrines is that they encourage the parties to a controversy to settle out of court. Clear precedent leads to a realistic assessment of the probability that each party will win; as we show earlier, an agreement on that probability leads to settlement rather than suit. *Stare decisis,* the adherence to precedent, reinforces this agreement on the probability of winning. Rules of jurisdiction and standing do not serve to invite people to litigate their differences. Rather, they limit frivolous actions and direct those who insist on litigating to the most appropriate forum (court), where judges are most likely to know and adhere to the correct precedents. *Res judicata* and collateral estoppel are plainly doctrines of judicial economy. They are even viewed as limiting the parties' expenditures on litigation to an efficient level.[42] Therefore, perhaps such doctrines themselves emerged because of the litigants' interests and decisions, much as other common-law rules did.

The limiting nature of these rules and doctrines is also consistent with our view of judges' incentives. Judges are not interested in maximizing case load; they would prefer to spend their time building reputations for fairness and legal skills. These preferences would lead them to adhere to precedent and carefully inspect issues of jurisdiction and standing. Even when a higher court prods them to increase output, most judges respond with the temporary expedient of taking cases "out of line" that they can dispose of quickly, thus giving the appearance of increasing output.

The Common Law as Government

Our introduction to law and judicial decision making has raised an alternative we did not contemplate in Chapter 3 when we listed reasons for preferring the outcomes of public choice to those of private choice and vice versa. There, our reference to the kind of public-choice method contemplated was more or less indefinite. In Chapters 4 through 11 we have taken this method to be the use of an elected government—president and Congress—with appointed bureaucrats. Now, we must contemplate a second method, public choice by judiciary, for that method has many properties that make it appear attractive.

Safety regulation. Chapter 11 reports the effects of FDA regulation of drug safety on the development of new chemical entities. Those effects are believed to be largely negative, and many scholars now agree that by keeping some good drugs off the market and preventing the development of others, FDA regulations are killing more people than they are saving. As Chapter 11 points out, such regulations are understandably chosen by bureaucrats and supported by elected officials who ignore undetectable errors (for example, the stifling of discovery) and minimize the probability of making detectable ones (for example, approving a drug with fatal side effects).

How would a judge at common law handle the drug safety problem? First, notice that a regulator makes decisions about the safety of particular drugs before they are sold, and therefore he is responsible for the quality of those decisions. By contrast, in the absence of a specific statute requiring him to act, a judge at common law would probably not give standing to a litigant who

---

[42] *Res judicata* has been justified on efficiency grounds: "The cost of relitigation is positive, while the benefit in reducing error costs is in general zero since there is no way to determine which outcomes in a series of inconsistent outcomes . . . are the correct ones. Whenever the chain is broken, there is no reason for thinking the last decision more probably correct than a prior inconsistent decision." Posner, *Economic Analysis of Law,* 2nd ed., p. 454.

argued that someone other than himself will be harmed in the future by ingesting a particular drug. Rather, a judge at common law would make decisions about the safety of a particular drug after it is sold.[43] That is, a litigant would appear with a specific complaint, which the judge or jury would then decide.

Actual litigation of cases involving alleged injury from particular drugs has recently been carried out under a rule of strict liability rather than negligence. In other words, the drug companies have been held liable for injury even though they have not been shown to be negligent in their development, testing, or production activities. Suppose that in the absence of regulation, courts adopt a strict liability rule governing payment for injuries caused by legal drug use, and suppose that judges and juries are not biased. They may err, but not systematically one way or the other. Finally, suppose that all injured parties who were not informed of and did not contractually agree to accept the probability of nonfrivolous injuries when they bought the drug go to trial. If all of these assumptions hold, then the drug companies will take an efficient level of care in developing and testing their drugs, for they will experience the full impact of any unexpected or uncontracted costs their activities impose on others.[44] Therefore, under common-law rules of liability, the entire *regulatory* (as distinct from information-gathering) function of the FDA would be superfluous and costly. By extension, the same can be said for the regulatory functions of OSHA, CPSC, and NHTSA.

Pollution control. Before the creation of the EPA in 1970, there were substantial limits on citing injuries or damages from pollution as a cause of action. Some legislation was passed in the late 1950s, but common-law rules concerning property rights and torts had not developed to the point where they could alleviate complex environmental problems that arise with multiple-source air and water pollution. Serious problems of standing occurred because litigants often could prove only trivial damages. Trespass actions were difficult because courts were unwilling to view pollution as a physical invasion of a plaintiff's property, which would be required to prove a trespass. The class action had not developed to the point where it could overcome the very real free-rider problems of paying for a lawsuit against a polluter. Nuisance actions were equally difficult to litigate. Finally, it was almost impossible to pinpoint blame when dozens of polluters' emissions were chemically combining and recombining to form dangerous secondary pollutants.

---

[43] Donald Wittman, "Prior Regulation versus Post Liability: The Choice Between Input and Output Monitoring," *Journal of Legal Studies,* 6 (January 1977), pp. 193–211. See also Posner, *Economic Analysis of Law,* 2nd ed., pp. 276–278.

[44] There are serious incentive problems associated with applying a standard of strict liability to pharmaceutical company activities, and a standard of negligence may be more appropriate. However, these are unsettled questions, and we assume strict liability here simply for purposes of illustration.

The members of Congress responded before the courts did so, and therefore we cannot say whether more efficient common-law rules of liability might have been fashioned. Probably, given the vast number of potential litigants and the underdeveloped condition of case law in this area, subsequent judicial action in the absence of statutory and administrative law would have resolved the problems of pollution only imperfectly, at least in the short run. The EPA has hardly provided a model of efficient rule making, however. Rather, its personnel have proceeded in almost perfect compliance with the bureaucrats' operational code, taking almost every opportunity to enlarge their budget, the size of their workforce, and the extent of their jurisdiction.[45]

In terms of rule making and enforcement, the members of Congress and their EPA agents have adopted the most time-consuming and costly method of pollution abatement imaginable. They have imposed air and water quality standards on various regions of the country and have placed limits on the emissions of individual polluters. Economists are nearly of one mind that the use of nationally imposed standards is an extremely inefficient method of pollution control. Standards do not allow for individual variations in preferences, nor do they give polluters incentives to find new technologies of pollution control. Emissions standards are also anticompetitive because they impose equal costs on producers no matter how large their output is. For example, the development of antipollution equipment is as expensive for General Motors as it is for Chrysler. Accordingly, Chrysler pays more for each car it produces than does GM, which explains some of Chrysler's financial problems.[46] EPA personnel prefer standards because they require a huge staff to create, administer, and enforce.

The most efficient approach to pollution control is the use of an **emission charge,** sometimes called an effluent charge or a Pigouvian tax.[47] This charge is placed on each polluting firm and is calculated according to the level of the firm's pollution emissions. As output increases, so do pollution levels, so the charge is levied per unit of output. Economists prefer the effluent charge because it is efficient. It balances the damages caused by pollution with the value of each firm's output. It is simple and inexpensive to administer, although it is not entirely free of problems. EPA personnel oppose effluent charges because they would create a "license to pollute." Actually, EPA officials issue such licenses daily in other forms. The real reason why they

---

[45] Paul B. Downing and Gordon L. Brady, "Constrained Self-Interest and the Formation of Public Policy," *Public Choice,* 34 (1979), pp. 15–28, and Paul Sabatier, "Social Movements and Regulatory Agencies: Toward a More Adequate—and Less Pessimistic—Theory of 'Clientele Capture,'" *Policy Sciences,* 6 (September 1975), pp. 301–342.

[46] Kenneth W. Clarkson, Charles W. Kadlec, and Arthur B. Laffer, "Regulating Chrysler Out of Business?" *Regulation,* 3 (September/October 1979), pp. 44–49.

[47] For an analysis of the theory behind the emission-charge policy, see Peter H. Aranson, Terry A. Ferrar, and Peter G. Sassone, "Pigouvian Policies in Closed Behavioral Systems," *Public Choice,* 33 (1978), pp. 5–26.

oppose effluent charges is that implementation of such charges would probably require an EPA less than one-half the size of the present one.

Judges at common law have no incentive to increase the size of their staffs, as we showed earlier. More to the point, the effluent charge turns out to be a close analogue of "the imposition of strict liability in tort."[48] Damages are calculated as in a tort action, but the victims do not collect for their injuries, since all monies go to the public treasury. Furthermore, effluent charges have no anticompetitive effect, though they give polluters an incentive to develop and adopt efficient pollution-control technology—technology whose cost is less than the cost of the amount of damage abated.

It may be too much to expect that judges could have the administrative and fact-gathering capabilities of bureaucrats or that bureaucrats would have the incentives of and make decisions like judges. However, the inefficient development of environmental policy by administrative law leads us to ask whether an updated environmental tort law, administered by the courts, would produce a better result.

Contractual relations. The field of transportation provides a head-to-head comparison of a marketplace controlled by the adversarial system of common law and one regulated by a congressionally mandated commission. In *Hadley v. Baxendale,* the court held that the defendants were not responsible for damages that they had no reason to expect to occur. A lesson derived from this case, but one that is less often drawn, is that those who want a particular service, such as speedy and timely delivery of an industrial part or of their household furnishings, must take the responsibility of explicitly contracting for the desired performance. In essence, the court was really encouraging the voluntary, market provision of private goods and services, based on explicitly formulated contracts.

During the development of the ICC, the trucking industry gained control of the commission and used it to impose contracts with uniform provisions. Truckers and their customers could not bargain for contract provisions that departed from the requirements of ICC regulations. For instance, customers trying to move their home furnishings could not demand service on a particular date at a particular time, nor did a customer have recourse to legal relief if the trucker complied with ICC regulations. The ICC's creation of a trucking industry cartel also outlawed competitive bidding on most aspects of interstate trucking services, including price. Economists agree that the ICC's regulation of trucking was inefficient and inferior in all respects to a voluntary contract system controlled by common-law rules such as are laid down in *Hadley v. Baxendale.* Since trucking has now been partially deregulated, we shall have a test of the economists' judgment. Plainly, the different incentives of judges and bureaucrats should make some difference in the rules under which interstate trucking services are bought and sold.

---

[48] Posner, *Economic Analysis of Law,* 2nd ed., p. 280.

In sum, judges at common law are probably incapable of raising armies, of building interstate highway systems, or even of running entire school districts. However, they are now responsible for defining and enforcing property rights, reducing the production of certain external costs associated with torts and crimes, and ruling on performance under contracts. Their suitability to do more must be explicitly contemplated in considering the larger questions of public choice.

CRIMINAL LAW

Our earlier description of varieties of law points out that criminal law is likely to be statutory law, that the plaintiff at trial is "the state" or "the United States" as represented by a state or federal prosecutor, and that the judgment of the court following a conviction will ordinarily be designed to make the commission of the crime cost more than it was worth. These differences only begin to separate criminal law from civil law, and these and other differences are sufficiently great to treat criminal law apart from the common law and other forms of statutory law.

Crimes as Public Bads

Formally, a **crime** is "A positive or negative act in violation of penal law; an offense against the State or the United States."[49] That is, a crime is an activity that statutory law categorizes as a crime. Yet, most people understand that a crime means (or should mean) something more than merely the violation of a particular statute. In particular, "A crime may be defined to be an act done in violation of those duties which an individual owes to the community, and for the breach of which the law has provided that the offender shall make satisfaction to the public."[50]

This second definition of a crime points out some important differences between criminal law and civil law, including common law and equity. For example, in a common-law case such as a tort action or a contract dispute, a general or specific obligation or duty that one person owes another person in their capacities as private persons is usually at issue. But in a criminal action, a duty owed "to the community" is at issue. That is, "the community" now has standing.[51]

Why should "the community" have standing? It is not sufficient for us to argue that "the community's laws have been broken," or that the "public

---

[49] *Black's Law Dictionary,* p. 334.

[50] *Black's Law Dictionary,* p. 334.

[51] The existence of a criminal action does not eliminate a private plaintiff's standing to proceed in a parallel civil case arising from the crime. For example, if A murders B, B's family can sue A for B's "wrongful death."

interest" has been injured by the alleged felon. For as many earlier chapters of this book point out, law may be the result of an incoherent public-choice process or it may reflect the private interests of a limited number of persons.

What appears to distinguish criminal violations from, say, tortious activities or breaches of contracts is the level of external diseconomies each imposes on people other than the specific civil-law plaintiff or criminal-law victim. For instance, when the tree surgeon caused the limb to fall on the pedestrian, few persons unconnected with either party were affected by the accident. Conceivably, one or two especially sensitive souls might have taken to avoiding walks down shady lanes, but without fear of drawing an interpersonal comparison of utilities, it is fair to say that all such external damage was extremely limited, which is one reason that courts seldom give standing to vicarious plaintiffs.[52]

By contrast, with crimes such as murder or rape, far more severe levels of external diseconomies may occur. These external diseconomies rest on two different sorts of calculations. First, each time such a crime occurs, people act *as if* they recalculate the probability that they might be victims in the future. Fear is one result of these calculations, and anticipatory attempts to avoid being a future victim are another result. Second, the absence of sanctions beyond damages to the victim would not create a sufficient cost for the felon, for he would not bear the full costs his actions impose on others. Since these costs are widespread, the jobs of defining crimes, prosecuting criminals, and making them bear the full costs of their activities by punishing them is vested in "the community."

The private cost–public bads distinction between civil wrongs and criminal wrongs is obviously one of degree. For example, private suits against polluters are allowed, even though others in the community besides the plaintiff bear the cost of pollution. On the other hand, prostitutes may be convicted and fined or imprisoned even though their "victimless crime" creates relatively low levels of external costs. Nevertheless, for most crimes, the placement of the job of prosecution upon a public official as well as the public assumption of the cost of prosecution follow naturally from the external costs and free-rider problems involved.

Criminal Justice Procedure

Figure 12.2 reproduces a flow chart of the criminal justice system, prepared by the President's Commission on Law Enforcement and Administration of Justice. The chart shows the similarity between the procedure

---

[52] Another reason is the extensive number of suits that would result if standing were granted to vicariously damaged plaintiffs.

followed in criminal cases and the one followed in civil cases (Figure 12.1) and emphasizes the decisions participants make at each stage in the process.

The process begins when the police directly observe a crime or when someone, perhaps the victim, reports the crime to them. The police, the victims, and other participants or bystanders enjoy substantial discretion in deciding whether to report a crime or not. Victims may refrain from reporting a crime because they fear retribution, because they do not regard the crime as substantial, because they have no faith that the perpetrators will be brought to justice, or because they are unaware that the damage inflicted on them was the result of criminal activity. The police may do nothing about a crime because they know the district attorney is not interested in prosecuting that particular kind of crime, because they have been bribed to "look the other way" (which sometimes happens when organized crime is involved), or because they decide to allocate their scarce resources to investigating more serious crimes. Bystanders sometimes fail to report crimes because they do not believe the observed activity should be a crime or because they do not want to pay the cost of becoming a witness, of "getting involved."

Once someone reports a crime and the police arrest a suspect, however, the case goes to the prosecutor, who is in a position analogous to the plaintiff's attorney in a civil suit. The prosecutor must decide whether or not the case is substantial enough to proceed to trial or whether some or all of the charges should be dropped. The prosecutor's office (the office of the district attorney, state's attorney, attorney general, or United States attorney) also faces a budget constraint, and therefore those in charge must decide which cases to prosecute and which to let go. Those cases the prosecutor decides to pursue are presented to a **grand jury,** which is the kind of jury used to issue **indictments,** or, depending on local law and the severity of the alleged crime, the prosecutor may indict the defendant directly. (Indictments for felonies are usually by grand jury, while indictments for misdemeanors are usually by the use of a public officaial's complaint, sometimes called indictment by **information.)**

If the defendant is indicted, he or she appears at an **arraignment** to enter a plea and to choose a jury trial or a trial before a judge. Then, the trial takes place. At any time before the verdict is rendered, the prosecution and defense have an opportunity to make a **plea bargain,** which is the criminal-law equivalent of a settlement out of court in a civil suit. Ordinarily, plea bargains occur before trials begin, because the defendant at that time can offer the prosecution the possibility of "sparing the taxpayer" the expense of a trial and the certainty of a conviction on a lesser offense rather than the risk of an acquittal on the more severe offense for which the defendant has been charged.

If the defendant is convicted at trial, he or she must decide whether to appeal and the court must decide on an appropriate sentence. If the convict is sentenced to prison, the sentencing decision is reiterated at each hearing for parole (release from prison).

This chart seeks to present a simple yet comprehensive view of the movement of cases through the criminal justice system. Procedures in individual jurisdictions may vary from the pattern shown here. The differings weights of line indicate the relative volumes of cases disposed of at various points in the system, but this is only suggestive since no nationwide data of this sort exists.

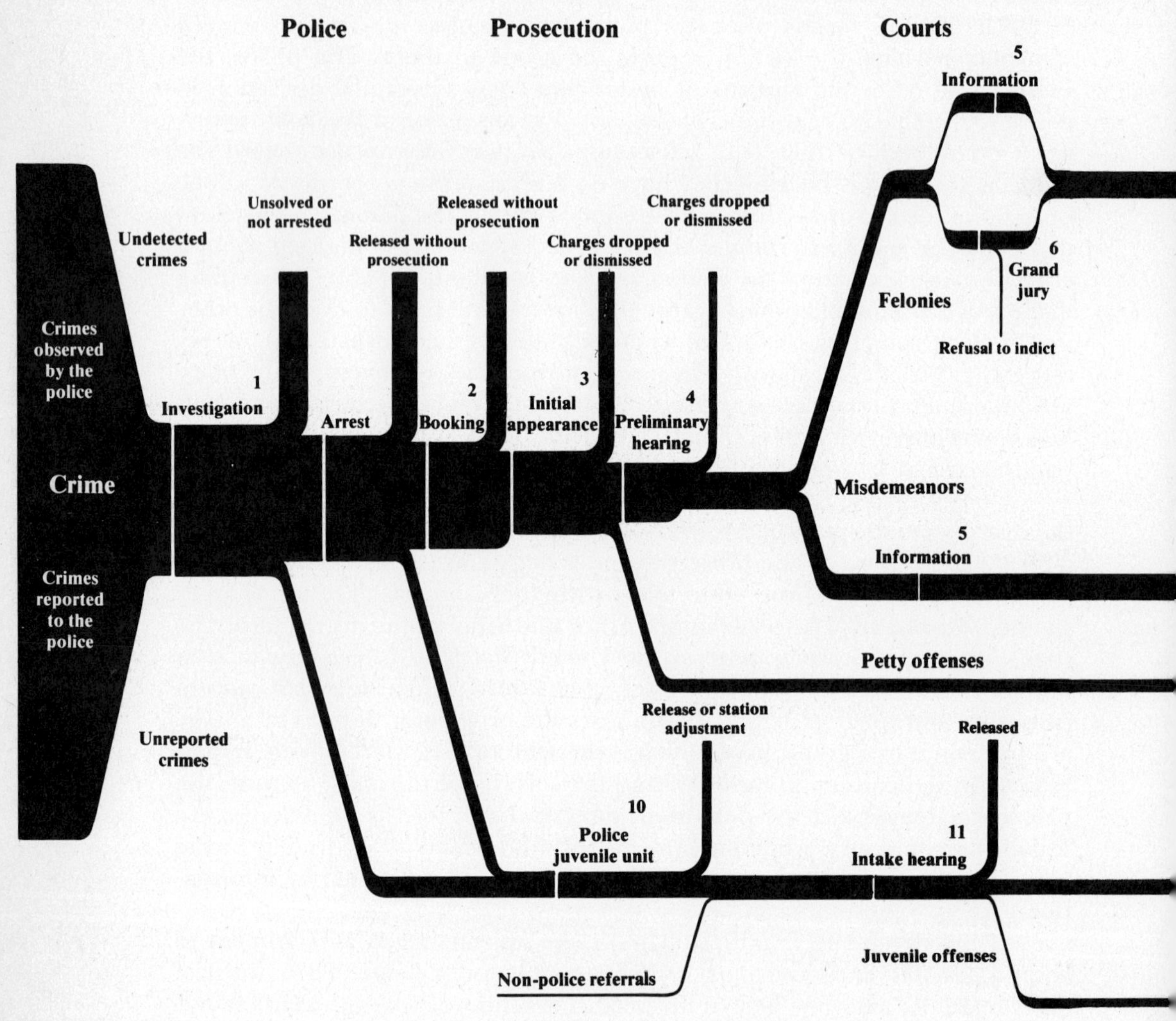

1 May continue until trial.

2 Administrative record of arrest. First step at which temporary release on bail may be available.

3 Before magistrate, commissioner, or justice of peace. Formal notice of charge, advice of rights. Bail set. Summary trials for petty offenses usually conducted here without further processing.

4 Preliminary testing of evidence against defendant. Charge may be reduced. No separate preliminary hearing for misdemeanors in some systems.

5 Charge filed by prosecutor on basis of information submitted by police or citizens. Alternative to grand jury indictment; often used in felonies, almost always in misdemeanors.

6 Reviews whether government evidence sufficient to justify trial. Some states have no grand jury system; others seldom use it.

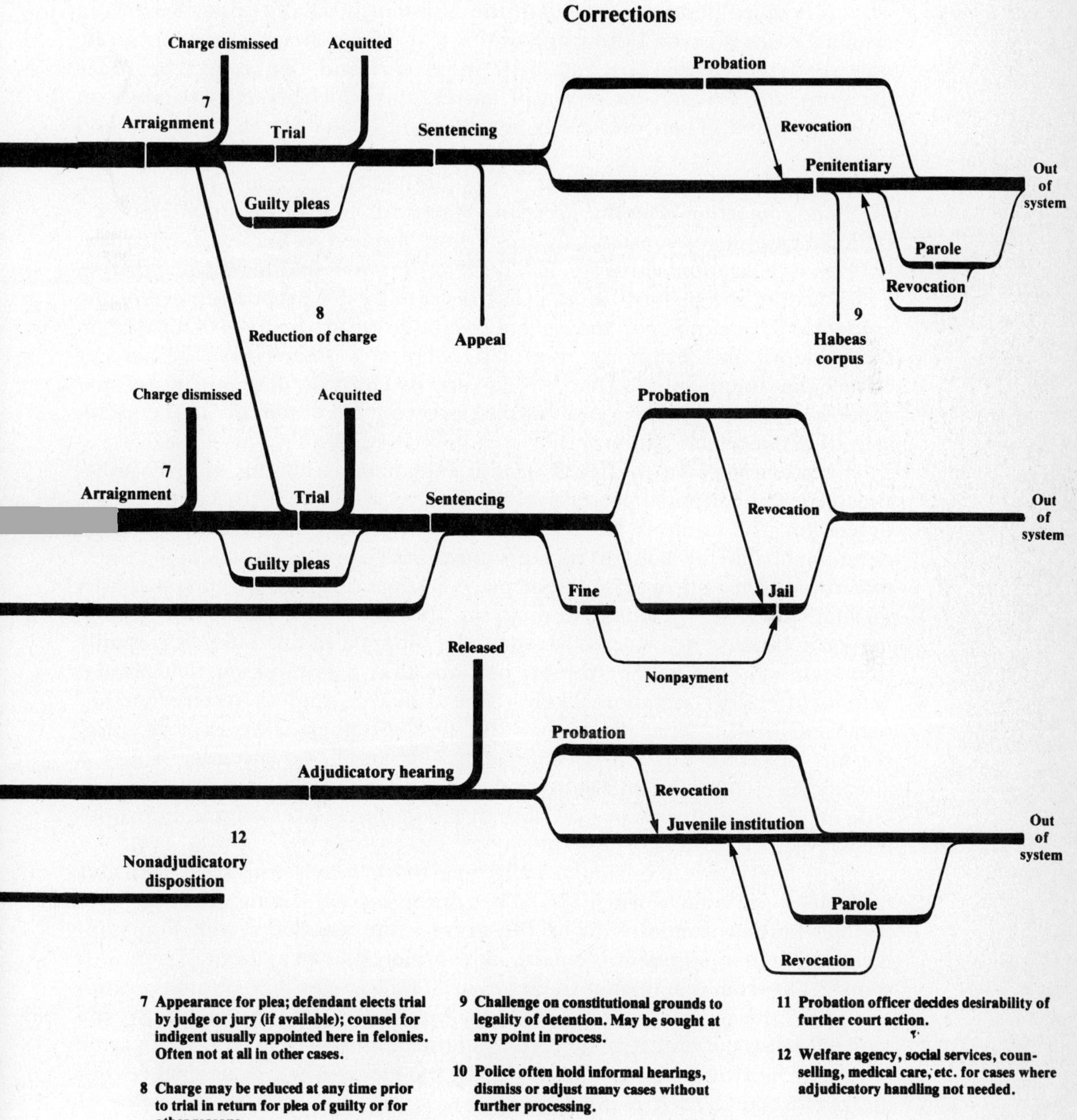

Figure 12.2 Criminal justice process in the United States.

Source: President's Commission on Law Enforcement and Administration of Justice, *The Challenge of Crime in a Free Society* (Washington, D.C.: U.S. Government Printing Office, 1967), pp. 8–9.

Decision Making in Criminal Cases

A detailed description of all of the decisions by all of the participants in criminal cases is beyond the scope of this text. Here, though, we concentrate on two decisions that are especially important and that reflect on other decisions: the decision to convict or acquit, and which sentence to place on those convicted. Then, we briefly consider the related decisions of bail and parole.

The conviction-acquittal decision. Standards for convicting a felon in a criminal case differ substantially from those applied to finding a defendant liable in a civil action. To assign liability (for example, find for the plaintiff) in a civil action, the plaintiff must prove his case by the **preponderance of the evidence.** This expression means that the judge or jury believes that based on the evidence and testimony presented, there is a greater than 50 percent chance that the plaintiff's charge is correct. By contrast, in criminal cases the prosecution must prove its case **beyond a reasonable doubt,** or "to the exclusion of a reasonable doubt."

Legal writers have offered several explanations for this difference between civil and criminal procedure, the most common being that convicting a defendant of a crime is far more serious for the defendant than finding a defendant liable for damages in a tort or contract dispute. Most people believe that conviction and imprisonment place a stigma on the defendant that is qualitatively different from a finding, say, that a plumber is liable for damaging a rug because he incorrectly repaired a plugged drain. There is certainly some truth in this belief. Indeed, perhaps that is one reason that alleged second offenders are more likely to be convicted and to receive harsher penalties for the same crime than are first offenders. (We explore other reasons in our discussion of sentencing.) After all, an offender who has already been convicted and sentenced to prison for a previous felony receives little or no additional stigma because of his second conviction and imprisonment.

An alternative explanation, and one more nearly consistent with our rational-choice framework, finds the key difference explaining the divergence in fault-finding standards to be the great waste associated with imprisonment.[53] When a judgment is entered at common law, an amount of money is transferred from one litigant to the other. The transfer may be in error, but except for the possibility of allocating money to a less highly valued use, the money itself is not lost. If an incorrect judgment is entered in equity, the value of specific performance may be less than the value of nonperformance, but the performance itself is not lost. However, in criminal cases, the value of work that is lost when a person is sentenced to prison is not transferred to anyone else. It is simply lost.

---

[53] Posner, *Economic Analysis of Law,* 2nd ed., pp. 433–434.

We can rephrase this analysis in a more familiar framework. Consider Table 12.1, which illustrates the judge's or jury's conviction-acquittal decision problem. The decision as described in this table is analogous to the president's decision to hold fire or to launch a counterattack when confronted with evidence of a Soviet nuclear first strike (see Table 10.1). The goal of a trial, if such can be said to exist, is to convict the guilty and acquit the innocent. However, error can occur. The defendant may be factually guilty but the judge or jury may acquit him, in which case the judge or jury has falsely rejected the hypothesis that the defendant is factually guilty. Or, the defendant may be factually innocent but the judge or jury may nevertheless convict him, in which case the judge or jury has falsely rejected the hypothesis that the defendant is innocent.

Criminal law in the United States requires that the hypothesis of innocence be rejected "beyond a reasonable doubt." Such a requirement makes it far more likely that a judge or jury will commit Error II than Error I. The justification for this bias against convicting innocent defendants has always been couched in moral and humanistic terms. Undoubtedly, Western values are extremely important in forming such a preference in the trade-off between the probabilities of making these two errors.

Our previous observations provide a simpler explanation for the same preference, however. Indeed, a moral aversion to convicting a factually innocent person may be incorporated as a cost of Error I. With Error I, we wrongly forgo the value of the factually innocent party's product. With Error II, we wrongly forgo the deterrent effect associated with convicting and imprisoning a factually guilty defendant. Notice that in criminal cases, the cost of each Error II committed is probably quite a bit smaller than the cost of each Error I. That is, the resources that are lost when a defendant is erroneously found guilty and imprisoned are quite a bit larger than the resources that are lost when a factually guilty defendant is incorrectly declared innocent. Of course, in civil cases, error does not impose these forgone costs. Therefore, the standard for conviction on the testimony and evidence in criminal cases is far more stringent than standards for fixing liability in civil cases.

Jury size and decision rules. A jury empaneled to try a case is called a **petit jury.** The law traditionally requires a unanimous verdict of a twelve-

Table 12.1 Conviction-Acquittal Decision Problem

Judge or Jury's Strategies	*States of Nature* factual innocence	factual guilt
find defendant innocent	Correct decision	Error II
find defendant guilty	Error I	Correct decision

person petit jury to convict in criminal cases. Acquittal also requires unanimity, and a jury whose members cannot reach unanimity one way or the other is called a **hung jury.** As a practical matter, cases with only one or two jurors opposing conviction are usually retried, depending on the seriousness of the alleged offense. But cases with only one or two jurors opposing acquittal are usually dropped. A jury's failure to reach a unanimous verdict results in a **mistrial.**

In recent years, there has been considerable experimentation with jury size and jury decision rules in different states. Statute law in nearly all states continues to require the unanimity of a twelve-person jury to convict in criminal cases. However, some states empanel juries of as few as six members in criminal cases, and other states have departed to a greater or lesser extent from the requirement of unanimity. Generally, civil actions require a majority vote of a jury to find for the plaintiff, but sometimes a greater percentage of the votes is required.

The Supreme Court has been active in setting standards of constitutionality concerning jury size and decision rules.[54] In the decade of the 1970s, it approved the use of six-member juries for trying both state felony cases and federal civil cases.[55] It also accepted the constitutionality of less-than-unanimous decisions, even in criminal cases.[56] But it found the use of juries with fewer than six members for trying serious criminal offenses to be unconstitutional.[57]

Theoretical and empirical studies of the effects of varying jury size and jury decision rules are numerous, and in a few of its recent decisions the Supreme Court has cited many of them.[58] Some theoretical concepts from these studies place certain problems of jury size and jury decision rules in focus. The first concepts concern jury size and individual juror competence to vote correctly.

Suppose the defendant is factually innocent, that each juror is as likely to render a correct decision as is any other juror, and that the decision rule

---

[54] For a review of the Court's reasoning in the cases involved, see Bernard Grofman, "Jury Decision Making Models and the Supreme Court: The Jury Cases from *Williams v. Florida* to *Ballew v. Georgia*," *Policy Studies Journal,* 8 (Spring 1980), pp. 749–772.

[55] *Williams v. Florida* 398 U.S. 78 (1970), and *Colegrove v. Battin,* 413 U.S. 419 (1973).

[56] *Johnson v. Louisiana,* 406 U.S. 356 (1972), and *Apodaca v. Oregon,* 406 U.S. 404 (1972).

[57] *Ballew v. Georgia,* 435 U.S. 233 (1978).

[58] The classic general work on juries is Harry Kalven, Jr. and Hans Zeisel, *The American Jury* (Chicago: University of Chicago Press, 1966). Reviews of recent works are provided in Bernard Grofman, "Jury Decision-Making Models," in Stuart S. Nagel, ed., *Modeling the Criminal Justice System* (Beverly Hills, Calif.: Sage, 1977), pp. 191–203, and in Stuart S. Nagel and Marion G. Neef, *Decision Theory and the Legal Process* (Lexington, Mass.: Heath, 1979), pp. 187–215.

requires unanimity to convict. Under these conditions, the probability that the jury unanimously votes for an incorrect judgment—commits Error I—declines as the number of jurors increases. The mathematical calculation underlying this finding is straightforward. Suppose each juror has a 60 percent (0.6) chance of being right, which also means he or she has a 40 percent (0.4) chance of being wrong. A one-person jury is incorrect 40 percent of the time, a two-person jury 16 percent of the time, a three-person jury 6.4 percent of the time, and a four person jury 2.56 percent of the time. (The calculation of the jury's probability of convicting a factually innocent person involves simply raising each juror's probability of deciding incorrectly to the *n*th power, where *n* is the number of jurors.)

Table 12.2 reports these probabilities of jury error for alternative jury sizes and probabilities that each juror decides incorrectly. Two results are readily apparent. First, as the competence of each juror—that is, the probability that he or she votes correctly—increases, the probability that the entire jury commits Error I very quickly declines. Accordingly, suppose that we set some arbitrary maximum probability of an incorrect conviction that we would accept, and suppose that we are also interested in minimizing the size of the jury consistent with that probability for the purpose of saving court costs. Under these conditions, the more competent we expected each juror to be, the smaller the size of jury we would require. For instance, Table 12.2 places in boxes the entries at which the Error I probability first falls to or below 1.0 percent. Where this number falls is a function of jury size. If we thought each juror would vote wrong 50 percent of the time, then we would require a seven-person jury. For individual juror error of 60 percent, the jury would have to hold nine members, and so forth.

Similarly, juror competence to avoid error may be related to the simplicity of the case and the clarity of the evidence at hand. If so, then we would probably require a smaller jury to try less complex litigation or litigation that achieved a high degree of evidentiary clarity. Our notions of minimum standards for jury error might also reflect the seriousness of the case the jury is to decide. For example, we might be concerned not merely with the trade-off between Error I and Error II, but also with the absolute size of each error. As the cost of Error I increases, the maximum probability of jury error we would allow should decrease, in which case we would require a larger jury.

These findings rest on the simplifying assumptions that unanimity is required and that all jurors share an equal probability of being right. However, we can relax both of these assumptions (although the mathematics become quite involved). Generally, most of the findings deduced when these assumptions are relaxed tend to support the conclusions reached in the simplest case, however.

The second set of concepts we review here is already familiar. Recall from Chapter 4 that the choice of a decision rule is based on considerations of external costs and decision costs. That discussion of decision rules suggested that juries trying capital cases (those involving the possibility of a death

Table 12.2 Probability of Incorrect Conviction as a Function of Jury Size and Juror's Probability of Voting Correctly (Juror Competence)

Each Juror's Probability of Voting Correctly (Juror Competence)	*Jury Size* 1	2	3	4	5	6	7	8	9	10	11	12
1.0	.00	0.00	0.00	0.00	0.00	0.00	0.00	0.00	0.00	0.00	0.00	0.00
0.9	.100	.010	.001	*	*	*	*	*	*	*	*	*
0.8	.200	.040	.008	.002	*	*	*	*	*	*	*	*
0.7	.300	.090	.027	.008	.002	*	*	*	*	*	*	*
0.6	.400	.160	.064	.026	.010	.004	.002	*	*	*	*	*
0.5	.500	.250	.125	.063	.031	.016	.008	.004	.002	.001	*	*
0.4	.600	.360	.216	.130	.078	.047	.028	.017	.010	.006	.004	.002
0.3	.700	.490	.343	.240	.168	.118	.082	.058	.040	.028	.020	.014
0.2	.800	.640	.512	.410	.328	.262	.210	.168	.134	.107	.086	.069
0.1	.900	.810	.729	.656	.590	.531	.478	.430	.387	.349	.314	.182
0.0	1.00	1.00	1.00	1.00	1.00	1.00	1.00	1.00	1.00	1.00	1.00	1.00

* Less than .001, all entries rounded off to three places.

penalty) would probably operate under a decision rule of unanimity because the external cost involved is large. The preceding discussion of the waste created by imprisonment for criminal offenses as compared with the transfer of resources in civil cases (but not their waste) explains why juries in criminal cases are usually required to operate under a decision rule of unanimity while juries in civil cases usually operate under a decision rule of majority rule. The external costs of error are greater in criminal cases than in civil actions. But there is no reason to believe decision costs differ. Hence, this central observation about resource waste versus resource transfer explains not merely the jury decision requirements of "a preponderance of the evidence" in civil cases and being "beyond a reasonable doubt" in criminal cases, but also the differences in the size of the juries required to reach a decision for the plaintiff.

Sentencing. After a verdict for the plaintiff is rendered in a civil action, the judge or jury must fix damages. If the defendant has acted "outrageously" or willfully, maliciously, or fraudulently, a judge at common law may award the plaintiff exemplary or punitive damages above the actual damage he or she sustained. But in most civil suits the purpose of damages is "to make the plaintiff whole." That is, civil damages are designed to compensate the plaintiff for the injury he or she has suffered, no more and no less. This rule is so well embedded in the common law that judges will refuse to enforce penalty clauses for non-performance in written contracts. For instance, a contract may contain a "liquidated damages" clause, which states the amount one party will pay the other upon non-performance. However, if this payment is referred to as a penalty, which raises the interpretation that it was meant to deter the parties from breaching the contract, then judges will not enforce it. (A liquidated damages provision must also reflect actual damages; otherwise, it is unenforceable.)

By contrast, when a judge or jury renders a verdict of *guilty* in a criminal action, one or the other must also decide on a sentence. The typical criminal sentence can be a monetary fine, a term of specified length to be served in the penitentiary with or without probation, and in certain instances the disqualification from serving in public office or enjoying the right to vote. Fixing damages in a civil action may be difficult, especially when pain and suffering or the value of a human life (in wrongful death actions) are involved. However, fixing an appropriate penalty in a criminal action taxes the wisdom of even the best judge, because the goals of sentencing are not as apparent as the goals of awarding damages and also because the idea of efficiency is difficult to translate into an optimal sentence.

Despite a growing tendency in some states to impose **determinate sentences,** those absolutely fixed by law, statutory law in most jurisdictions continues to grant judges extensive discretion in sentencing. Sometimes, criminal codes distinguish among different classes of felonies or misdemeanors and define mitigating or aggravating circumstances that should respectively shorten or lengthen a prescribed sentence. Criminal codes also dictate particular ranges of sentences for various classes of felonies and misdemeanors, allowing even more discretion where there are mitigating circumstances or where the offense was aggravated.

There are six commonly acknowledged goals that prison sentences are supposed to accomplish. They are: **retribution, victim compensation, rehabilitation, special deterrence, general deterrence,** and **incapacitation.** When passing sentence, a particular judge may have one or more of these goals in mind, yet believe that some of them are inappropriate. However, at one time or another each of these goals has provided a justification for imprisonment.

Sentencing to achieve retribution follows from the idea that the convict "has committed a wrong . . . [and] must suffer in return. The State . . . is entitled if not morally obligated to hurt the individual who has broken the criminal law, since a crime is by definition a wrong committed against the State. Imprisonment should be punishment, not only by depriving the individual of his liberty, but also by imposing painful conditions under which the person must live within the walls."[59] In considering retribution, we must remove all other goals of sentencing to find the core concept that remains. Retribution is not punishment for deterrence, nor is it rehabilitation or incapacitation. Retribution can only be considered the *reaffirmation of the moral authority of the State.* As such, retribution rests on an organic fallacy. However, if a sentencing judge believes in the *State* or *society* as an organic entity, which itself has rights and authority, then he or she might impose a sentence consistent with achieving retribution.

Sentencing may also be a way of compensating the criminal's victim. In this view, the victim receives a form of payment as the result of the punishment inflicted on the felon. Sentencing to achieve a compensatory payment for victims may accomplish a more utilitarian purpose than is immediately apparent, for it replaces personal retribution with retribution in the name of the *State.* Therefore, a victim or his sympathizer may forgo vengeance if the state is already taking its pound of flesh, and further violence may be avoided.

Rehabilitation as a goal of sentencing raises the expectation of a change in the convict's personality, financial capabilities, or decision making. The method of rehabilitation can range from psychoanalysis and behavior modification to formal education and job training. Scholars on either side dispute the ethical premises of certain forms of behavior modification as well as the economic efficiency of job training. Convicts apparently learn what evidence parole-board members use to measure the extent of rehabilitation. Convicts then provide the appropriate evidence to maximize their probability of parole. Once outside prison walls, they revert to participating in criminal activity. The overall success rate of attempts to rehabilitate is unknown.

---

[59] *The Society of Captives: A Study of a Maximum Security Prison* by Gresham Sykes (© 1958 by Princeton University Press; Princeton paperback, 1971), p. 9. Reprinted by permission of Princeton University Press.

Prison sentences to achieve the goal of special deterrence are designed to make the felon think twice before he or she commits another crime. Those who sentence to achieve special deterrence believe "that for those who have been imprisoned the experience is (or should be) sufficiently distasteful to convince them that crime had best be avoided in the future. This decision to forgo crime is not expected to come from a change in the attitudes and values concerning the wrongness of crime. Rather, it supposedly flows from a sharpened awareness of the penalties attached to wrongdoing."[60] Special deterrence relies on learning. The convict finds out just how unpleasant imprisonment can be, and this knowledge leads him to reassess the cost of imprisonment so that when confronted with the opportunity to commit a crime in the future, he will decide that the expected costs outweigh the expected benefits. The interesting aspect of special deterrence is that those who believe that imprisonment can achieve it *ceteris paribus* must necessarily also prefer shorter prison sentences than do those who believe that imprisonment has no special deterrent effect on the convict. For, if a convicted murderer is not deterred from future murders by having been in prison, who would dare let him loose on the streets?

General deterrence as a sentencing goal refers to the belief that punishing an actual criminal deters a potential one. By this view, "imprisonment is important as a deterrent not for the individual who has committed a crime and who has been placed in a prison but for the great mass of citizens who totter on the edge. The image of prison is supposed to check errant impulses, and . . . it is fear rather than morality which is expected to guide the individual in his action."[61]

Scholars disagree sharply about whether sentencing A to prison has a deterrent effect on B. Even more acute is the debate over capital punishment as a general deterrent to murder. One study, based on sophisticated econometric techniques, finds that on the average, each execution of a convicted murderer prevents between seven and eight future murders.[62] This finding has been subject to concerted attack.[63] However, a judgment on the merits of the claim that capital punishment has a greater deterrent effect than impris-

---

[60] Sykes, *The Society of Captives,* p. 10.

[61] Sykes, *The Society of Captives,* p. 10.

[62] Isaac Ehrlich, "The Deterrent Effect of Capital Punishment: A Question of Life and Death," *American Economic Review,* 65 (June 1975), pp. 397–417, and Ehrlich, "Capital Punishment and Deterrence: Some Further Thoughts and Additional Evidence," *Journal of Political Economy,* 85 (August 1977), pp. 741–788.

[63] Alfred Blumstein, Jacqueline Cohen, and Daniel Nagin, *Report of the Panel on Research on Deterrent and Incapacitative Effects; Deterrence and Incapacitation: Estimating the Effects of Criminal Sanctions on Crime Rates* (Washington, D.C.: National Academy of Science, 1978), and Susan O. White and Samuel Krislov, eds., *Understanding Crime—An Evaluation of the National Institute of Law Enforcement and Criminal Justice* (Washington, D.C.: National Academy of Science, 1977). But see Isaac Ehrlich in cooperation with Randall Mark, "Fear of Deterrence: A Critical Evaluation of the 'Report of the Panel on Research on Deterrent and Incapacitation Effects,' " *Journal of Legal Studies,* 6 (June

onment requires a knowledge of econometric theory beyond the scope of this text.

For many people it matters little whether executing A deters B from murdering C, for they believe it is morally wrong for the *State* to take a life for any reason under any conditions. Others believe that execution should be mandatory whether or not it deters potential murderers. This is the retribution view of capital punishment.

Compared with general deterrence, there is little debate about incapacitation, the "warehouse" function of prison sentences. Escapes and prison violence aside, an inmate cannot easily commit a crime against someone who is not in prison. Therefore, there are computable benefits from and costs of incarceration aimed at incapacitation, and these benefits and costs can form the basis of a judge's sentencing decisions.

A simple example shows how a judge might arrive at a sentence based solely on incapacitation.[64] Suppose incapacitation is the judge's only goal in sentencing and that the convicted felon's only imaginable crime now or in the future is stealing television sets worth $100 each. The judge also believes that if the felon remains free, as an effect of growing older he will slowly substitute legal activities for illegal ones so that he will steal fewer and fewer television sets as the years pass. Suppose the judge believes that the felon will steal ten sets in the first year after conviction, then nine, then eight, then seven, and so forth, so that the judge believes over the next ten years the thief will steal fifty-five television sets (10 + 9 + 8 + 7 + 6 + 5 + 4 + 3 + 2 + 1) for a loss to potential victims of $5500. If the judge sentences the felon to an immediate term of a year in jail, then the felon will steal no television sets in the first year because he will be incapacitated, but thereafter will steal forty-five sets (9 + 8 + 7 + 6 + 5 + 4 + 3 + 2+ 1) for a loss to potential victims of $4500. We shall call the costs of stolen television sets a nonincarceration cost, *NC*.

However, incarceration carries a clear cost at least equal to the maintenance of the felon in prison. Suppose this cost is $500 a year. Figure 12.3 shows the added (marginal) costs of incarceration, *MIC,* and of non-incarceration, *MNC.* Notice that the marginal non-incarceration costs form a step function. If the felon is not imprisoned, then he steals $1000 the first year, $900 the second, $800 the third, and so forth. *MIC* is a straight line because the costs of maintaining the felon in prison do not change from year to year. Accordingly, to calculate a total cost of incarceration, *IC,* we simply multiply $500 times the number of years the sentence will run.

Figure 12.4 illustrates the total cost of incarceration plus non-incarceration, *NC* + *IC,* as a function of the sentence imposed. A minimum

---

1977), pp. 293–316. For a more recent discussion, see Stephen A. Hoenack and William C. Weiler, "A Structural Model of Murder Behavior and the Criminal Justice System," *American Economic Review,* 70 (June 1980), pp. 327–341.

[64] This example is drawn from Peter H. Aranson, "The Simple Analytics of Sentencing," in Gordon Tullock and Richard E. Wagner, eds., *Policy Analysis and Deductive Reasoning* (Lexington, Mass.: Heath, 1978), pp. 33–45.

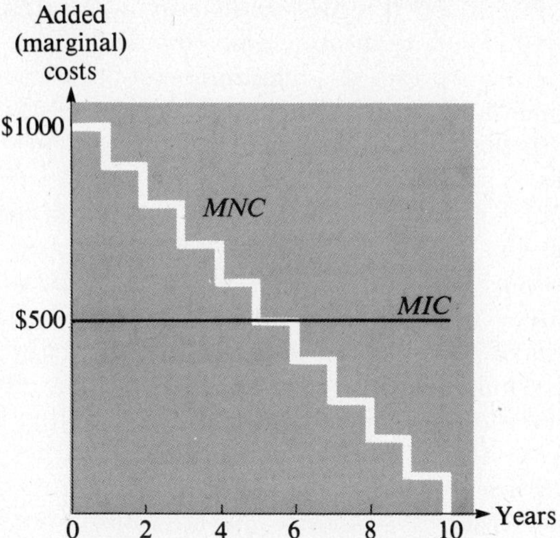

Figure 12.3 Marginal costs of incarceration (*MIC*) and non-incarceration (*MNC*).

Source: Peter H. Aranson, "The Simple Analytics of Sentencing," reprinted by permission of the publisher, from *Policy Analysis and Deductive Reasoning,* edited by Gordon Tullock and Richard E. Wagner (Lexington, Mass.: Lexington Books, D. C. Heath and Co., © 1978, D. C. Heath and Company), p. 35.

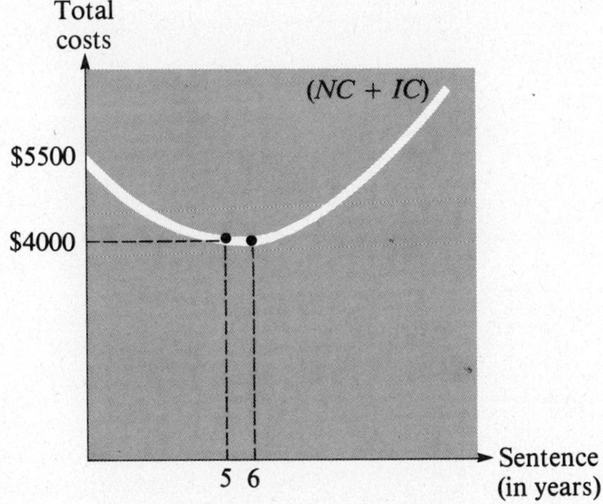

Figure 12.4 Total cost of a sentence of varying length.

Source: Peter H. Aranson, "The Simple Analytics of Sentencing," reprinted by permission of the publisher, from *Policy Analysis and Deductive Reasoning,* edited by Gordon Tullock and Richard E. Wagner (Lexington, Mass.: Lexington Books, D. C. Heath and Co., © 1978, D. C. Heath and Company), p. 35.

occurs for a sentence of between five and six years. For such a sentence, others will have to pay $4000 in both incarceration costs and non-incarceration costs. Also, notice that in Figure 12.3 this minimum cost occurs where the marginal non-incarceration cost curve, *MNC,* intersects the marginal incarceration cost curve, *MIC.* This property is useful for illustrating reasons underlying variations in sentences.

Now consider Figure 12.5, which shows a common marginal incarceration cost curve but three different, "smoothed out" marginal non-incarceration cost curves for three different felons, A, B, and C. A is a young high-school graduate who was unfortunate enough to be caught shoplifting an expensive item of jewelry. The judge believes that after a two-year sentence, A's future criminal activity each year will not be sufficiently damaging to others to exceed the cost of imprisonment. On the other hand, B has been before the judge to be tried and sentenced for an earlier offense, and the judge recalculates upward his or her estimate of the probability that B will steal again. Finally, C is a professional thief who has never shown an interest in any other manner of earning a livelihood. The judge is tired of finding C in court and therefore sentences C to a period of eight years in the penitentiary.

Figure 12.6 shows a different variation in sentencing. There, two convicted felons present the judge with the same marginal non-incarceration cost but with different marginal incarceration costs. A is a mother of several

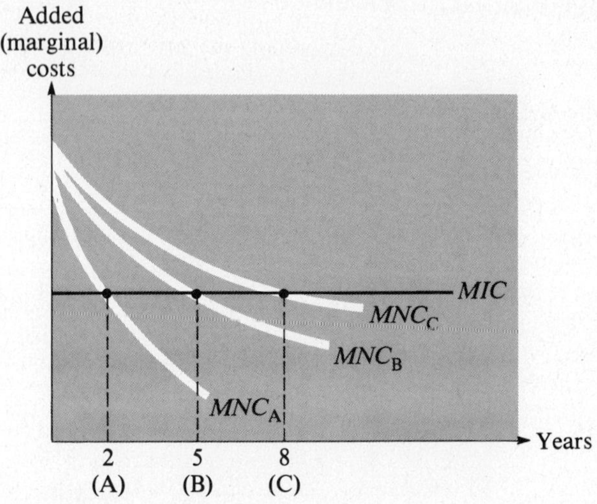

Figure 12.5 Varying marginal costs of non-incarceration based on judge's expectations about felon.

Source: Peter H. Aranson, "The Simple Analytics of Sentencing," reprinted by permission of the publisher, from *Policy Analysis and Deductive Reasoning,* edited by Gordon Tullock and Richard E. Wagner (Lexington, Mass.: Lexington Books, D. C. Heath and Co., © 1978, D. C. Heath and Company), p. 37.

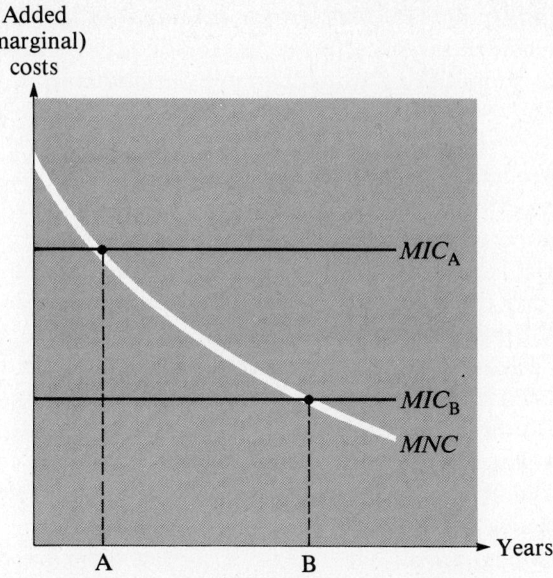

Figure 12.6 Varying marginal costs of incarceration based on judge's expectations about felon.

Source: Peter H. Aranson, "The Simple Analytics of Sentencing," reprinted by permission of the publisher, from *Policy Analysis and Deductive Reasoning,* edited by Gordon Tullock and Richard E. Wagner (Lexington, Mass.: Lexington Books, D. C. Heath and Co., © 1978, D. C. Heath and Company), p. 39.

children, who would have to be placed in foster homes at taxpayers' expense if she were imprisoned. B is a single woman who has committed the same crime. The longer sentence for B, on whom no one relies for nurturing or support, follows logically.

This discussion explains judges' sentencing decisions if they act as if our assumptions approximate their beliefs. However, sentencing practices have been attacked not only because of disagreements over goals and over the likelihood of achieving them, but also because of sentencing differences that have emerged in statistical studies of real sentencing. For example, a belief that white judges are disproportionately harsh in sentencing black convicts and that judges are sometimes arbitrary and capricious in their sentencing decisions in other ways forms the basis for many criticisms of sentencing in the United States.[65] However, most studies of sentencing fail to control statisti-

[65] Donald L. Barlett and James B. Steele, "Crime and Injustice," *The Philadelphia Inquirer,* 1973; Edward Green, "Inter- and Intra-Racial Crime Relative to Sentencing," *Journal of Criminal Law, Criminology, and Police Science,* 55 (September 1964), pp. 348–358; and Marvin E. Frankel, *Criminal Sentences: Law Without Order* (New York: Hill and Wang, 1972).

cally for variations in judges' goals, or for statutory requirements, or even for recidivism. Therefore, at present we are inadequately informed as to the degree of racial prejudice or unexplainable variations in judges' sentencing decisions.

Bail and probation. A person charged with a crime may be released on his personal recognizance, may be released on bail, or may be held without bail or for failure to make bail. The decision to release with or without bail—the pre-trial release decision—has been analyzed with many of the same tools used to study the conviction-acquittal decision and the sentencing decision, for many of the same questions are involved.[66] The person who sets the conditions for release faces the prospect, on the one hand, of incorrectly setting free an accused person who will not appear for trial or who will commit another crime, and on the other hand, of incorrectly holding without bail an accused person who would subsequently obey the law and faithfully appear for his or her trial. The parallels with the decision problem depicted in Table 12.1 are apparent.

The decision to parole—to release a convict from prison before his or her full sentence has ended—also recapitulates the sentencing decision. However, the parole decision raises two considerations not present at sentencing. First, imprisonment may have somehow affected (positively or negatively) the probability that the felon will again commit crimes. Second, prison officials may have used the possibility of parole as an incentive for the inmate to abide peaceably by prison regulations: "time off for good behavior." Its use may be an efficient expedient within the entire criminal justice process.

Constitutional Protection in Criminal Cases

In its hypothetical discussion of presidential decision making during a suspected nuclear attack, Chapter 10 pointed out that most legislators want the president to be able to launch a counterstrike on his own initiative. However, because of the extreme costs associated with error in such a decision, legislators also have sought to structure the president's decision in advance by passing laws improving the accuracy of his information and by inquiring about contingency plans if the president cannot act. For instance, the Armed Services Committees of the House and Senate meet in secret sessions to learn how accurate our DEW-line protection systems really are, and congressional investigators probe witnesses from the Department of Defense and the White House to find out how the president would or should react to this, that, or the other contingency. They are also interested in whether NATO field commanders have the authority to launch a nuclear counterstrike or not.

---

[66] Stuart Nagel, Marian Neef, and Sarah Slavin Schramm, "Decision Theory and Pre-Trial Release: Decision Theory in Criminal Cases," *University of Miami Law Review,* 31 (November 1977), pp. 1433–1491.

A similar process of qualification and decision structuring has occurred in the criminal law. Our present procedural system for trying criminal cases minimally requires a judge, usually a jury, a prosecutor, a defendant, and a statutory or common-law definition of a particular crime. Nevertheless, in the hands of a judge or jury, the decisions to convict or acquit and to impose sanctions can wrongly impose terrible costs. Furthermore, the opportunity for abuse is great. Therefore, constitution writers and judges who interpret the Constitution have embroidered criminal-justice procedures with extensive and elaborate safeguards. Whether participants in such procedures have followed the rules laid down in the Constitution and in subsequent judicial decisions or not is also a matter that is constantly before the courts for review. Here, we describe some of the more important safeguards in criminal procedures as they appear in the Constitution and in subsequent Supreme Court cases that interpret it.

Habeas corpus. Article 1, Section 9 requires that "The Privilege of the Writ of Habeas Corpus shall not be suspended, unless when in Cases of Rebellion or Invasion the public Safety may require it." *Habeas corpus* means "you have the body," and a **writ of *habeas corpus*** requires that the body be produced. A judge may issue such a writ to release someone from imprisonment when the judge believes that the imprisonment is unlawful. The writ of *habeas corpus* can also applied if the trial court did not have *in personam* jurisdiction. For example, during the Civil War, Lambdin P. Milligan, a resident of Indiana who had never been in the armed forces, was charged with several offenses, including inciting insurrection and giving aid to the Confederates. A military commission tried, convicted, and sentenced him to death by hanging. Milligan petitioned the circuit court for a writ of *habeas corpus,* but that court, unable to decide what to do, sent the case to the Supreme Court. Mr. Justice Davis delivered the opinion of the Court, that when civil courts are not in operation as a result of military actions or foreign invasion or civil war, then military authority may govern. But "if this government is continued *after* the courts are reinstated, it is a gross usurpation of power. Martial law can never exist where the courts are open, and in the proper and unobstructed exercise of their jurisdiction."[67] Milligan was therefore released on a writ of *habeas corpus.*

The writ of *habeas corpus* has been used by federal courts to remove prisoners from the jurisdiction of state authorities when in the opinion of the federal court the prisoners may have been deprived of constitutional rights.[68] The writ of *habeas corpus* cannot substitute for a proper appeal, but over the years its use has been extended beyond narrow questions of proper jurisdiction and unlawful imprisonment to include challenges to convictions in state courts based on alleged violations of nearly any constitutionally guaranteed right.

---

[67] *Ex Parte Milligan,* 4 Wall. 2, 18 L.Ed. 281 (1866).

[68] *Fay v. Noia,* 372 U.S. 391 (1963).

Bills of attainder. Article 1, Section 9 also states that "No Bill of Attainder or ex post facto Law shall be passed." Section 10 of the same Article similarly restricts the states: "No State shall . . . pass any Bill of Attainder, [or] ex post facto Law. . . ." A **bill of attainder** is a legislative act that names a particular person for execution or other punishment. Such an act is designed to punish specific persons. Of course, a particular legislative act does not have to be called a bill of attainder to be one. For example, a 1943 appropriations act stated that no government funds "shall be used, after November 15, 1943, to pay any part of the salary . . . of Goodwin B. Watson, William E. Dodd, Junior, and Robert Morss Lovett," three government officials, unless they were renominated by the president and approved by the advice and consent of the Senate before the cutoff date. These people had been accused of being associated with Communist organizations in the United States. In *U.S. v. Lovett,* the Supreme Court found this law to be a bill of attainder and therefore declared it unconstitutional.[69]

Ex post facto legislation. An **ex post facto law** is retroactive legislation, a law that imposes a penalty or increases the penalty for an action already completed. For example, suppose that the members of Congress pass a law tomorrow making it a crime for any American citizen to join the armed forces of another nation, and declaring that any citizens who are found to have been members of the armed forces of other nations before tomorrow are guilty of violating this law. Such a law would be ex post facto legislation. Most of the Supreme Court's earlier attention to ex post facto legislation has been concerned with laws that canceled debts owed by the government to former government employees who have been convicted of particular crimes.

Jury trial and venue. Article 3, Section 3 of the Constitution states that "The trial of all Crimes, except in Cases of Impeachment, shall be by Jury; and such Trial shall be held in the State where the said Crimes shall have been committed; but when not committed within any State, the Trial shall be at such a Place or Places as the Congress may by Law have directed." The Sixth Amendment (whose other provisions we will discuss momentarily) also holds that "In all criminal prosecutions, the accused shall enjoy the right to a . . . trial . . . by . . . jury of the State and district wherein the crime shall have been committed, which district shall have been previously ascertained by law. . . ." These provisions guarantee three rights. The first is the right of a trial, the second is the right of a jury trial, and the third is the right to have the trial in the state where the alleged offense occurred.

In most cases, the right to a trial and the right to a trial by jury have been combined to require the right of a trial by jury. Earlier, we briefly review the Supreme Court's position on jury size and jury decision rules. Challenges brought against convictions by juries of fewer than twelve or by juries using a

---

[69] 328 U.S. 303 (1946).

decision rule requiring less than unanimity assert that these variations do not meet the Sixth Amendment's guarantee of a trial by jury.

The Supreme Court has also been interested in limitations on the right to trial by jury. For example, in *McKeiver v. Pennsylvania,* the Court refused to extend the right of a jury trial to certain aspects of juvenile delinquency proceedings.[70] However, the Court has also addressed more obvious limits on the right to a jury trial. For example, in the conviction appealed in *Duncan v. Louisiana,* a judge found the defendant guilty of simple battery, which in Louisiana is a misdemeanor carrying a maximum prison term of two years and a maximum fine of $300.[71] The judge sentenced Duncan to sixty days and a fine of $150. Louisiana law provides for jury trials in criminal cases only if capital punishment or hard labor is a potential sentence. The Supreme Court found for Duncan: "In the case before us the Legislature of Louisiana has made simple battery a criminal offense punishable by imprisonment for two years and a fine. The question, then, is whether a crime carrying such a penalty is an offense which Louisiana may insist on trying without a jury. We think not. . . ." Accordingly, the Court reversed the denial of appeal by the Supreme Court of Louisiana and remanded the case for a proceeding "not inconsistent with this opinion."

Search and seizure. In the course of their investigations of crimes, law enforcement officials sometimes try to acquire evidence bearing on the determination of guilt or innocence. The Fourth Amendment holds that "The right of the people to be secure in their persons, houses, papers and effects, against unreasonable searches and seizures, shall not be violated, and no Warrants shall issue, but upon probable cause, supported by Oath or affirmation, and particularly describing the place to be searched, and the persons or things to be seized." Like other constitutional safeguards in criminal-justice procedures guaranteed by the Bill of Rights, the guarantee provided in the Fourth Amendment has produced an extensive amount of litigation and a large number of Supreme Court opinions.

Modern developments have complicated the application of the Fourth Amendment. For example, can a telephone booth be considered an extension of a person's home? Does the placement of electronic bugging devices constitute a search? Are metal detectors located in airport concourses and in other public buildings, and used to reveal the presence of concealed weapons, a form of unreasonable search? Courts have had to address all of these questions. In *Katz v. United States,* for example, the Supreme Court reviewed the conviction of a bookie who was charged with sending wagering information by telephone from Los Angeles to Miami and Boston, which constituted a federal offense.[72] During the trial, the United States Attorney introduced evidence

---

[70] 403 U.S. 528 (1971).

[71] 391 U.S. 145 (1968).

[72] 389 U.S. 347 (1967).

gained by FBI agents, who overheard the bookie by using an electronic listening device attached to the outside of a public telephone booth. The Court overturned the conviction even though the search and seizure were outside the bookie's home. The Court held that safeguards against unreasonable searches and seizures "do not vanish when the search in question is transferred from the setting of a home, an office, or a hotel room to that of a telephone booth. Wherever a man may be, he is entitled to know that he will remain free from unreasonable searches and seizures."[73]

Raising the Fourth Amendment's probable-cause requirement, the Court has also had to address the problems involved with seizures associated with arrests and "stop-and-frisk" actions. In *Terry v. Ohio,* the Court agreed that "a police officer may in appropriate circumstances and in an appropriate manner approach a person for purposes of investigating possibly criminal behavior even though there is no probable cause to make an arrest."[74] However, the justices have had to go into great detail to define what they mean by "probable cause," "appropriate circumstances," and "in an appropriate manner."[75]

Double jeopardy. The most extensive constitutional guarantees of rights to defendants and potential defendants appear in the Fifth Amendment: "No person shall be held to answer for a capital, or otherwise infamous crime, unless on presentment or indictment of a Grand Jury, except in cases arising in the land or naval forces or in the Militia, when in actual service in time of War, or public danger; nor shall any person be subject to the same offence to be twice put in jeopardy of life or limb; nor shall be compelled in any criminal case to be a witness against himself, nor be deprived of life, liberty, or property, without due process of law; nor shall private property be taken for public use, without just compensation."

The Fifth Amendment's prohibition of **double jeopardy** is the criminal law's version of *res judicata.* A person cannot be tried twice for the same offense, but there are exceptions to this basic doctrine. First, in the case of a mistrial caused by the prosecution's error, the trial judge must balance the interests of the parties to decide whether a retrial on the same offense would constitute double jeopardy or not.[76] (Rarely do they decide that a retrial would be double jeopardy.) Naturally, the trial judge's decision may be reviewed by a higher court. A mistrial caused by a hung jury does not preclude another trial, however.

Second, in some instances a single act violates both state and federal law.

---

[73] More generally, "The Government's activities in electronically listening to and recording the petitioner's words violated the privacy upon which he justifiably relied while using the telephone booth and thus constituted a 'search and seizure' within the meaning of the Fourth Amendment." *Katz v. U.S.,* 389 U.S. 347 (1967).

[74] 392 U.S. 1 (1968), as reported in *Adams v. Williams,* 407 U.S. 143 (1972).

[75] See, for example, *U.S. v. Robinson,* 414 U.S. 218 (1973).

[76] *U.S. v. Jorn,* 400 U.S. 470 (1971).

For example, a defendant may have stolen money from a state-chartered bank insured by a federal agency. Then, the defendant may first be acquitted in state court of the charges brought under the state's robbery statute. Subsequently, he might be convicted in federal court of holding up a federally insured bank. The Supreme Court has not overturned such convictions.[77]

Third, many people believe that the Fifth Amendment's prohibition against double jeopardy prohibits a second trial when a person successfully overturns a previous conviction on appeal. However, the successful appeal only signifies that the previous conviction was in some sense defective. It does not mean that the defendant is immune from further criminal actions.[78]

Self-incrimination. The "right to remain silent" is the most widely known Fifth Amendment guarantee. Generally, a defendant does not have to testify at his trial. Nor, by extension, does the defendant, even before being charged with a crime, have to answer the questions of a police interrogator. Indeed, any information the police gather from interrogating a subsequently accused or tried person is not admissible as evidence at the trial unless that person has been informed of his right to remain silent.[79]

The prohibition against enforced **self-incrimination** has extended into many areas. For example, ordinarily the members of Congress cannot compel a witness to offer self-incriminating testimony at congressional hearings. However, at the request of prosecutors or congressional committee members, a federal judge may grant immunity from prosecution if the interrogators so desire. If immunity is granted, then any information gained cannot be used for subsequent prosecution.[80] This is called **use immunity** and is distinct from **prosecution immunity,** which bars further criminal actions on specified charges.

The Supreme Court has combined certain Bill of Rights guarantees to form stronger requirements for the conduct of criminal-justice activities. The case of *Mapp v. Ohio* provides a good example of such a combination.[81] On May 23, 1957, three Cleveland police officers broke into Dollree Mapp's home, abused her, barred her attorney from entering, and allegedly proceeded to search both for someone wanted for questioning in a recent bombing case and for hidden gambling paraphernalia. A thorough search turned up only a trunk containing "lewd and lascivious books and pictures," and Mapp was subsequently convicted in Ohio courts for possession of obscene material. No search warrant was ever produced at trial, although the police

[77] A single action "denounced as a crime by both national and state sovereignties is an offense against the peace and dignity of both, and may be punished by each. . . ." *U.S. v. Lanza,* 260 U.S. 377 (1922). See also *Bartkus v. Illinois,* 359 U.S. 121 (1959).

[78] *Trono v. U.S.,* 199 U.S. 521 (1905).

[79] *Miranda v. Arizona,* 384 U.S. 436 (1966).

[80] *Kastigar v. U.S.,* 406 U.S. 441 (1972).

[81] 367 U.S. 643 (1961).

Coral Gables Police Department

2801 Salzedo Street
P. O. Box 340608
Coral Gables, Fla. 33134

CONSTITUTIONAL RIGHTS WARNING
PRIOR TO CUSTODIAL INTERROGATION

1. You have a right to remain silent. The Constitution requires that I so inform you of this right and you need not talk to me if you do not wish to do so. You do not have to answer any of my questions. Do you understand?

   YES NO

   ______ (Initial) ______ (Initial)

2. Should you talk to me, anything which you might say in answer to my questions can and will be introduced into evidence in court against you. Do you understand?

   YES NO

   ______ (Initial) ______ (Initial)

3. If you want an attorney to be present at this time or at any time hereafter, you are entitled to such counsel. If you cannot afford to pay counsel, we will furnish you with counsel, if you so desire. Do you understand?

   YES NO

   ______ (Initial) ______ (Initial)

4. Do you wish to have an attorney at this time?

   YES NO

   ______ (Initial) ______ (Initial)

5. Knowing your rights as I have just related them to you, are you now willing to answer my questions without having an attorney present?

   YES NO

   ______ (Initial) ______ (Initial)

____
WITNESS Date

____
SIGNATURE OF SUBJECT

____
WITNESS Date

Police forces have created forms such as this to document that a person taken into custody for questioning in the investigation of a crime has been informed of his or her constitutional rights including "the right to remain silent."

claimed to have had one at the time of the search. However, in the words of the Court, "there is, in the record, considerable doubt as to whether there ever was any warrant for the search of defendant's home." Mr. Justice Clark delivered the opinion of the Court that "the freedom from unconscionable invasions of privacy and the freedom from convictions based upon coerced confessions do enjoy an 'intimate relation' in their perpetuation of 'principles of humanity and [liberty].' " Mr. Justice Black concurred, for "when the Fourth Amendment's ban against unreasonable searches and seizures is considered together with the Fifth Amendment's ban against compelled self-incrimination, a constitutional basis emerges which not only justifies but actually requires the exclusionary rule."

This rule, first enunciated in *Boyd v. U.S.*, combines the Fourth and Fifth Amendments to form the doctrine that material illegally seized from the defendant, or material gathered in an unreasonable search or a warrantless search, when brought into court as evidence against a defendant, constitutes a form of self-incrimination.[82] In sum, the prosecution cannot use illegally seized evidence, for it is the "fruit of the poisonous tree."[83]

Speedy trial. Besides the right to a jury trial in the state where the crime was committed, the Sixth Amendment also guarantees certain procedural rights in criminal actions. "In all criminal prosecutions, the accused shall enjoy the right to a speedy and public trial by an impartial jury . . . and to be informed of the nature and cause of the accusation; to be confronted with witnesses against him; to have a compulsory process for obtaining witnesses in his favor, and to have the Assistance of Counsel for his defense."

There are at least four good reasons for requiring speedy trials. First, the absence of a speedy trial requirement raises the possibility of serious abuse. For example, a defendant who has earned the displeasure of the prosecutor could be charged with a crime and held without bail until his trial began ten years later. Second, witnesses may die, move out of the jurisdiction, or lose a clear recollection of the events they will testify about if a long time period elapses between the commission of the crime and the trial. Third, the requirement of a speedy trial gives prosecutors an incentive to act expeditiously and to select with care the cases they intend to pursue. Fourth, all parties whose future welfare depends on a trial's outcome have a strong interest in the speedy initiation and completion of proceedings. Of course, delay has often been used strategically in legal actions.

Both the Supreme Court and the members of Congress have been busy defining what the guarantee of a speedy trial means. In *Barker v. Wingo,* Mr. Justice Powell, speaking for the Court, proposed a balancing test—one that would compare the prosecution's interest in a fully developed case with the

---

[82] 116 U.S. 616 (1886).

[83] See *Wong Sun v. U.S.,* 371 U.S. 471 (1963), and *Silverthorne Lumber Co. v. U.S.,* 251 U.S. 385 (1920).

defendant's interest in disposing of the charges against him. But, "A balancing test necessarily compels courts to approach speedy trial cases on an *ad hoc* basis. We can do little more than identify some of the factors which courts should assess in determining whether a particular defendant has been deprived of his right. Though some might express them in different ways, we identify four such factors: Length of delay, the reason for the delay, the defendant's assertion of his right, and prejudice to the defendant."[84]

Many members of Congress were unsatisfied with this formulation, because "The task of balancing these factors and arriving at a conclusion which is fair in all cases is a difficult task. It provides no guidance to either the defendant or the criminal justice system. It is, in effect, a neutral test which reinforces the legitimacy of delay."[85] Accordingly, to place firm time limits on the initiation of trials, the members of Congress passed the Speedy Trial Act of 1974.[86] This act, to be phased in over five years, set a schedule of maximum allowable time spans between arrest and indictment, indictment and arraignment, and arraignment and trial. However, the Speedy Trial Act applies only to the federal courts, not to the states (many of which have their own speedy trial laws).

Public trials. While the Constitution guarantees the right to a public trial, most of the litigation concerning that right has been undertaken by members of the press seeking to cover criminal trials. The right to have access to a trial and other judicial proceedings has been widely disputed in recent years.

The interests of a defendant in having an open trial or a closed trial seem clear. First, the defendant might wish an open trial to focus publicity on the proceedings. He may be a popular figure with a popular cause, and therefore the presence of reporters and members of the public in the courtroom might put pressure on the judge and jury to favor him. Second, public inspection helps to insure that the innocence of the factually innocent defendant is widely known. Third, if the defendant expects the prosecution to act in an offensive manner, he might well want public attention on the trial.

Similarly, the defendant might have good reason to want the trial closed. He may not wish to be held up for public disgrace. He may not wish to expose his family to the sordidness of a public trial. He may have acted in a manner contrary to notions of decency, which will be brought out at the trial even though those actions do not bear directly on the trial's outcome. The defendant may also believe that he cannot have a fair trial if either the trial itself or other portions of the proceedings are open to the public. For example, in *Gannett Co. v. DePasquale,* the Court found that barring the public from

---

[84] 407 U.S. 514 (1972).

[85] House Judiciary Committee, as quoted in Harold W. Chase and Craig R. Ducat, *1975 Supplement to Constitutional Interpretation* (St. Paul, Minn.: West, 1975), p. 211.

[86] 88 Stat. 2076.

preliminary hearings was acceptable because those hearings were over a motion to suppress evidence prejudicial to the defendant.[87] Had the evidence been reported in the press, potential jurors might have learned about it, making it most unlikely that a fair trial could have been possible.

The prosecution also may share an interest in either an open or a closed trial. For example, the prosecution may prefer an open trial to embarrass the defendant, or the prosecutor may be using the trial of a notorious case as a stepping-stone to higher public office. Alternatively, both the prosecution and the defense may have reasons to prefer that the trial be open or closed. For instance, in an open trial, with the public present, witnesses for one side or the other might be better able to coordinate their testimony. They need not be present in the courtroom to do so, for others can report to them the nature of what was said under oath. This possibility might affect the credibility of either side's case. Exposing a trial to public view also increases the likelihood that false statements will more easily be detected than if the trial had been closed. Again, this effect of open trials may be an advantage or disadvantage to either side.

The public is also said to have an interest in open trials. In *Richmond Newspapers, Inc. v. Virginia,* Chief Justice Burger noted that "The early history of open trials in part reflects the widespread acknowledgement that public trials had significant community therapeutic value. People sense that, especially in the administration of criminal justice, the means used to achieve justice must have the support derived from public acceptance of both the process and its result."[88] In particular, "When a shocking crime occurs, a community reaction of outrage and public protest often follows. Thereafter, the open processes of justice serve an important prophylactic purpose, providing an outlet for community concern, hostility, and emotion."[89]

The members of the press understandably concentrate on the possible violation of First Amendment freedoms when appealing decisions to close trials to the public. Despite protestations that they are performing a public service, the interests of the members of the press quite frankly are to write good stories and sell newspapers, or to increase television audience ratings.

Because of the many conflicting interests involved, the large number of separate and distinguishable proceedings in which the issue may arise, and the conflicting constitutional guarantees invoked, the Supreme Court has had difficulty in formulating rules to govern the requirements for public trials. In *Gannet Co. v. DePasquale,* a majority of the members of the Court held that a hearing on pre-trial motions to suppress evidence was not constitutionally required to be open.[90] But one year later, in *Richmond Newspapers, Inc. v. Virginia,* a majority voted for an open trial in a criminal case where there were

[87] 443 U.S. 368 (1979).

[88] 48 L.W. 5012 (1980).

[89] 48 L.W. 5012 (1980).

[90] 443 U.S. 368 (1979).

no findings sufficient to overcome a presumption that the trial should be open.[91] However, the justices' individual reasons for this decision differed considerably.

Impartial jury. The Sixth Amendment's guarantee of an impartial jury is probably the most difficult constitutional safeguard to put into practice, since there is no reasonable way to test jurors' sincerity when they swear to decide a case impartially. Partiality toward the prosecution or defense can arise from several sources. First, a juror may be of the same race, religion, ethnic group, or social standing as the defendant or the prosecutor and may have a natural affinity toward one side and a dislike for the other even before the trial begins. Second, pre-trial publicity may have helped a juror form an opinion about the guilt or innocence of the defendant, and therefore he may be biased. Third, the prosecution may commit procedural errors during the course of the trial that might destroy the juror's impartiality. For example, the defendant's previous criminal record is germane for the sentencing decision but not for determining his guilt or innocence. If the prosecution mentions the defendant's past criminal record, the judge might instruct the jury to disregard the prosecutor's remarks, and on the motion of the defense attorney the court may even declare a mistrial. However, the defense attorney cannot attack his client's character or take other actions prejudicial to the defendant's cause and then expect the judge to declare a mistrial. If there has been substantial pre-trial publicity, and if the defendant believes that a fair trial is impossible, he may ask the court for a change of venue. If pre-trial publicity is severe, a conviction can be overturned on appeal.[92] And, if the Supreme Court believes that publicity might have affected jurors during the trial, a conviction again can be overturned.[93]

Procedures, restrictions, and prejudicial tendencies affecting juror selection are also important for jury impartiality. As long ago as 1880, the Supreme Court overturned the murder conviction of a black man because state law excluded blacks from juries.[94] The soundness of such a ruling cannot be doubted. However, where race or other identifying characteristics are concerned, the official notice of the presence or absence of members of the appropriate group on the jury raises a practical problem and a logical one. The practical problem is that including such a person may make a conviction or a unanimous acquittal impossible. For example, a defense attorney may very much fear that in trials of white defendants for crimes against black victims, the presence of black jurors may make conviction more likely. That presumption appeared to form the basis for the selection of jurors in the Florida trial of police officers immediately preceding the Miami race riots of

---

[91] 48 L.W. 5012 (1980).

[92] *Rideau v. Louisiana,* 373 U.S. 723 (1963).

[93] *Sheppard v. Maxwell,* 384 U.S. 338 (1966).

[94] *Strauder v. West Virginia,* 100 U.S. 303 (1880).

1980. The trial of officers accused in the beating death of black insurance agent Arthur McDuffie was moved from Miami to Tampa on a motion for change of venue. The defense successfully challenged all potential black jurors, and the resulting six-person all-white jury found the defendants innocent of all charges. The trial that same year of Miami's black superintendent of schools, Dr. Johnny Jones, on theft charges resulted in a conviction by a jury from which prosecution challenges had similarly excluded all blacks. Plainly, the kinds of practical problems raised by these cases are not easily solved.

The logical problem created by lack of impartiality associated with discriminatory jury selection is a pure delight. In 1979, a male defendant found guilty of murder by a Missouri court asked the Supreme Court to overturn his conviction because Missouri jury selection procedures tended to discourage women from sitting as jurors.[95] The Supreme Court agreed to hear the case, and during oral argument an attorney for a women's rights organization, speaking as an **intervenor** (a third party who enters a suit to protect his or her own interest), argued that there was an onerous and illogical discrimination in the jury selection process and therefore the defendant's conviction should be overturned. One Supreme Court justice wanted to know why, if men and women were equal, it made one whit of difference who sat on the jury. The attorney responded somewhat hesitatingly that there was a difference, but one that she could not describe.

The right to be informed of the nature and cause of the accusation. The Sixth Amendment requirement that a defendant "be informed of the nature and cause of the accusation" against him rests on several grounds. First, one cannot construct an adequate defense without such information. Second, if he does not know the charges against him, a defendant could put himself in jeopardy whenever he spoke to police, for there is always the possibility that his words would be self-incriminating with regard to the offense with which he is charged or with regard to other offenses. Similarly, the constitutional sufficiency of a charge cannot be assessed unless it is made plain and communicated. Hence, the statutes under which a defendant is charged must also be clear. A statute's vagueness is sufficient ground for challenging an indictment or conviction brought under it.

The defendant's right to be confronted with witnesses against him. The right to confront one's accusers or witnesses for the prosecution is a fundamental rule of fairness in criminal trials. It also implies the right of cross-examination and the right to require the prosecution to produce its evidence. The prosecution must cooperate with the defense in pre-trial discovery. Provided that both sides have had the opportunity to cross-examine an un-

[95] *Duren v. Missouri,* 47 L.W. 4089 (1979).

available witness, that witness need not appear at a judicial hearing to have his or her testimony weighed.[96]

The defendant's right to compulsory process for obtaining witnesses. **Compulsory process** is, "Process to compel the attendance in court of a person wanted there as a witness or otherwise; including not only the ordinary subpoena, but also a warrant of arrest or attachment if needed."[97] It is one right that a defendant can easily abuse. For example, upon being charged with a criminal offense, the defendant might have his attorney issue subpoenas to all of the prosecutor's friends and relatives as well as to the family members and acquaintances of the prosecution's principal witnesses. Of course, judges may try to prevent this abuse, and on appeal the Supreme Court will ordinarily support their decisions to quash subpoenas when relevance cannot be shown.[98]

The right to have assistance of counsel. The right to counsel has been fully expanded upon and incorporated into criminal procedures at every level. Before 1963, the defendant's ability to enjoy counsel depended upon his financial status or ability to convince an attorney (perhaps a public defender) to supply legal services at no cost or at reduced cost. The Supreme Court held that in special circumstances an attorney must be made available to the defendant. These circumstances depended upon the intellectual ability of the accused to defend himself, the seriousness of the offense, and the presence or absence of public hostility. However, in 1963 the Court ruled in *Gideon v. Wainwright* that the right to counsel was guaranteed under the Sixth Amendment (as extended to the states by the Fourteenth Amendment) for every person accused of having committed a serious crime.[99] In *Argersinger v. Hamlin* the Supreme Court decided that a defendant could not be imprisoned for conviction of a misdemeanor unless he had had the aid of counsel or had waived his right to counsel.[100] By 1980, the Court extended the right to counsel to considerations of sentencing. The defendant *Baldasar* had been convicted of theft in an Illinois court for the second time and received a sentence of from one to three years. In his first conviction for theft, he had not had aid of counsel. If the second conviction had been his first, he would have received a sentence of just under a year in length. The Court held that he could not be sentenced as a second offender, because he did not have the benefit of counsel in his first trial.[101]

The right to counsel combines easily and naturally with other constitu-

---

[96] *Barber v. Page,* 390 U.S. 722 (1968).

[97] *Black's Law Dictionary,* p. 261.

[98] *Wagner v. U.S.* 397 U.S. 923 (1970), *cert. denied.*

[99] 372 U.S. 335 (1963).

[100] 407 U.S. 25 (1972).

[101] *Baldasar v. Illinois,* 48 L.W. 4481 (1980).

tional guarantees. For example, the Fifth Amendment prohibition of compelled self-incrimination would often be vacuous without the right to counsel. This was essentially the position of the Court in *Escobedo v. Illinois* and in *Miranda v. Arizona.*[102] When they are first detained, many suspects in criminal cases are not able to fathom the importance of their interrogators' questions. Others are simply unable or unwilling to remain silent unless an attorney is present to recommend that course forcefully. The right to have an attorney present at interrogations—indeed, the right to refuse to speak with the police at all—obviously diminishes the widespread effectiveness of "third-degree" interrogation techniques.

Excessive bail and cruel and unusual punishment. The Eighth Amendment holds that "Excessive bail shall not be required, nor excessive fines imposed, nor cruel and unusual punishments inflicted." This chapter has briefly outlined decision-making considerations in bail and sentencing decisions. Ordinarily, appellate courts will not review bail or sentencing decisions. The Supreme Court has not been overly active in either area. However, those few cases in which it has spoken have sometimes achieved a degree of notoriety. The Court has held that excessive bail is an amount greater than that necessary to require the defendant to appear for trial, and that the pre-trial freedom of the defendant is desirable so that he might aid in the preparation of his defense.[103]

Sentencing decisions, especially where the death penalty is possible, have attracted substantial public attention. In the notorious case of *Louisiana ex rel. Francis v. Resweber,* the Supreme Court was asked to declare a second electrocution to be a violation of the Eighth Amendment's prohibition of cruel and unusual punishment. The condemned man had been placed in the electric chair, but it had failed to electrocute him because of its state of disrepair.[104] The Court denied the request, and a second electric chair worked more efficiently.

More recently, in *Furman v. Georgia,* the members of the Court stated their beliefs in separate opinions that the death penalty was *perhaps* unconstitutional because it is "uncivilized and inhuman punishment" (Mr. Justice Brennan) and *certainly* because it is "so wantonly and so freakishly imposed" (Mr. Justice Stewart). The Court's ***per curiam* order** (an unsigned announcement that states the Court's decision but sometimes not the reasons for it) held that under state law as it was then constituted, "the imposition and carrying out of the death penalty in these cases constitutes cruel and unusual punishment in violation of the Eighth and Fourteenth Amendments."[105] Six years

---

[102] 378 U.S. 478 (1964), and 384 U.S. 436 (1966).

[103] *Stack v. Boyle,* 342 U.S. 1 (1951).

[104] 329 U.S. 459 (1947).

[105] 408 U.S. 258 (1972).

later, in *Gregg v. Georgia,* the Supreme Court was asked whether or not it regarded capital punishment as cruel and unusual punishment per se.[106] The Court said no, and upheld the Georgia death sentence in the case before it. In an opinion filed by Mr. Justice Stewart, the new Georgia statute qualifying the use of the death sentence passed muster because it was neither arbitrary nor capricious.

> Georgia's new sentencing procedures require as a prerequisite to the imposition of the death penalty, specific jury findings as to the circumstances of the crime or the character of the defendant. Moreover to guard further against a situation comparable to that presented in *Furman,* the Supreme Court of Georgia compares each death sentence with the sentences imposed on similarly situated defendants to ensure that the sentence of death in a particular case is not disproportionate. On their face these procedures seem to satisfy the concerns of *Furman.* No longer should there be "no meaningful basis for distinguishing the few cases in which [the death penalty] is imposed from the many cases in which it is not. . . ."

In a few other Eighth Amendment cases, the Supreme Court has tried its hand in a limited way at rationalizing the severity and use of criminal-justice sanctions. For example, in *Trop v. Dulles,* the Court said that the Immigration and Nationality Act of 1940 unconstitutionally imposed the cruel and unusual punishment of depriving naturalized citizens of their citizenship for desertion in time of war.[107] In *Robinson v. California,* the Court struck down a state statute that made "the status" of narcotic addiction a criminal offense.[108] Following Robinson, many lower courts extended the doctrine to strike down convictions for public drunkenness. However, in *Powell v. Texas,* the Court reversed this trend, arguing that narcotic addiction is itself not an act, while public drunkenness is an act.[109] And in 1980, the Supreme Court refused to strike down a Texas statute calling for life imprisonment for habitual offenders.[110]

THE FEDERAL JUDICIARY

Judges at common law decide concrete cases and controversies between real litigants. Their task is to resolve actual, ongoing disputes, but in judging those disputes and in stating the reasons for their decisions in written opinions, they also make law. Our review of constitutional guarantees in criminal-justice procedures shows that federal judges in general and Supreme Court

[106] 428 U.S. 153 (1976).

[107] 356 U.S. 86 (1958).

[108] 370 U.S. 660 (1962).

[109] 329 U.S. 514 (1968).

[110] *Adams v. Texas,* 48 L.W. 4869 (1980).

justices in particular also make law. For example, the Constitution does not specifically guarantee indigent persons the assistance of counsel in criminal cases. However, in *Gideon v. Wainwright,* the Court interpreted the Constitution to require that result. That was lawmaking, just as Congress makes a law when it does its constitutional duty "to provide for the common defense" by appropriating $20 billion for a new weapons system. However, we shall find that lawmaking or rule making by federal courts differs in a few key respects from rule making by common-law courts.

Constitutional Provisions and Authority

The structure of the judiciary. Article 3, Section 1 of the Constitution holds that "The judicial Power of the United States, shall be vested in one supreme Court and in such inferior Courts as the Congress may from time to time ordain and establish." Courts created under this provision are called **Article 3 courts**; they are distinguished by the uniform provision that their members "shall hold their Offices during good Behaviour. . . ." The members of Congress may also establish **Article 1 courts,** such as military courts of justice or administrative law courts, under the "necessary and proper" clause of Article 1, Section 8.

The members of Congress and the president set the size of the Supreme Court and the salaries of its members and of the members of other federal courts ("which shall not be diminished during their Continuance in Office"), and establish any other kinds of federal courts below the Supreme Court that they deem appropriate. The Supreme Court has varied in size from six at its initiation to ten in 1863. It arrived at its present size of nine in 1869. The number and structure of inferior courts (federal courts below the Supreme Court) have also varied. Originally, there were thirteen district courts and three circuit courts of appeals. The members of the Supreme Court would aid in the deliberations of the circuit courts by "riding circuit," which meant that they were assigned to these courts and from time to time attended them to hear cases.

In 1891, an act of Congress divided the country into nine circuits and established a federal court of appeals in each circuit. The pre-existing circuit courts remained in operation until 1912. Today, there are eleven federal judicial circuits, as indicated in Figure 12.7, with a total of 132 circuit court judgeships. The first circuit, made up of four New England states, is the smallest, with four circuit court judgeships; the fifth circuit, made up of the southeastern states and Texas, is the largest, with twenty-six judgeships. (The fifth circuit is scheduled to be divided into two circuits in the fall of 1981.) The District of Columbia circuit has eleven circuit court judgeships. Each federal judicial circuit also has district courts below the circuit courts of appeals. Every state has at least one district judgeship (New York, the largest in this regard, has forty-three).

The real number of sitting judges may be larger than the number

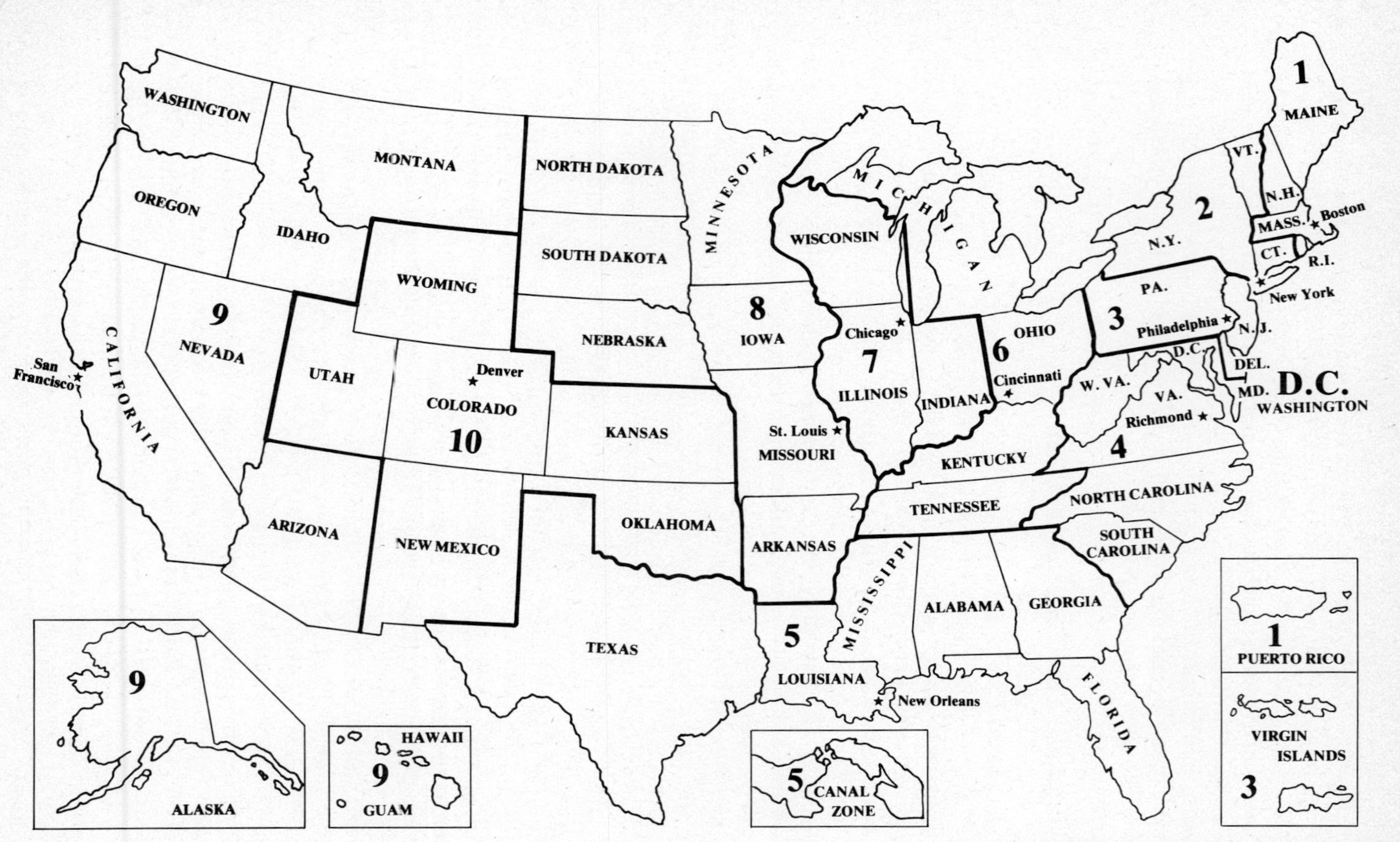

Figure 12.7 The eleven federal judicial circuits.
Source: Federal Reporter, 2nd series (St. Paul, Minn.: West, 1979).

provided for by law because some judges take **senior status,** a judicial equivalent of retirement, but nevertheless continue to hear cases. (Of course, it is theoretically possible that the number of sitting judges will fall below the number provided for by law because of vacancies.) The actual structuring of the federal judiciary below the Supreme Court, as well as the structuring of the Supreme Court itself (but not its existence), is basically in the hands of the president and the members of Congress.

Jurisdiction. Article 3, Section 2 of the Constitution reads in part:

> The judicial Power shall extend to all Cases in Law and Equity, arising under this Constitution, the Laws of the United States, and Treaties made, or which shall be made under their Authority;—to all Cases affecting Ambassadors, other public Ministers and Consuls;—to all Cases of Admiralty and maritime Jurisdiction;—to Controversies to which the United States shall be a Party;—to Controversies between two or more States;—between a State and Citizens of another State;—between Citizens of different States;—between Citizens of the same State claiming Lands under the Grants of different States, and between a State or the Citizens thereof, and foreign States, Citizens or Subjects.
>
> In all Cases affecting Ambassadors, other public Ministers and Consuls, and those in which a State shall be a Party, the supreme Court shall have original jurisdiction. In all the other Cases before mentioned, the supreme Court shall have appellate Jurisdiction, both as to Law and Fact with such Exceptions, and under such Regulations as the Congress shall make.

A court may have original jurisdiction or appellate jurisdiction. **Original jurisdiction** means that it hears a case for the first time. **Appellate jurisdiction** means that it hears the case on appeal from the decision of some other court. Figure 12.8 illustrates the structure of original and appellate jurisdiction in the federal judiciary. Article 3 gives the Supreme Court original jurisdiction in cases in which a state, ambassador, public minister, or consul is a party. For example, if a river or stream departs from its historical course, a legal dispute may arise between two states concerning the location of the border between them. In such cases, the Supreme Court has original jurisdiction. Ordinarily, the Court would appoint an expert, called a *special master,* to hear the case. His decision would then be reviewed and approved by the Court.

The Eleventh Amendment limits the federal judiciary's jurisdiction over cases between a state and the citizens of another state: "The Judicial power of the United States shall not be construed to extend to any suit in law or equity, commenced or prosecuted against one of the United States by Citizens of another State, or by Citizens or Subjects of any foreign State." This amendment was adopted after the Supreme Court decided *Chisholm v. Georgia,* in which it overturned a federal district court's ruling that a South Carolina

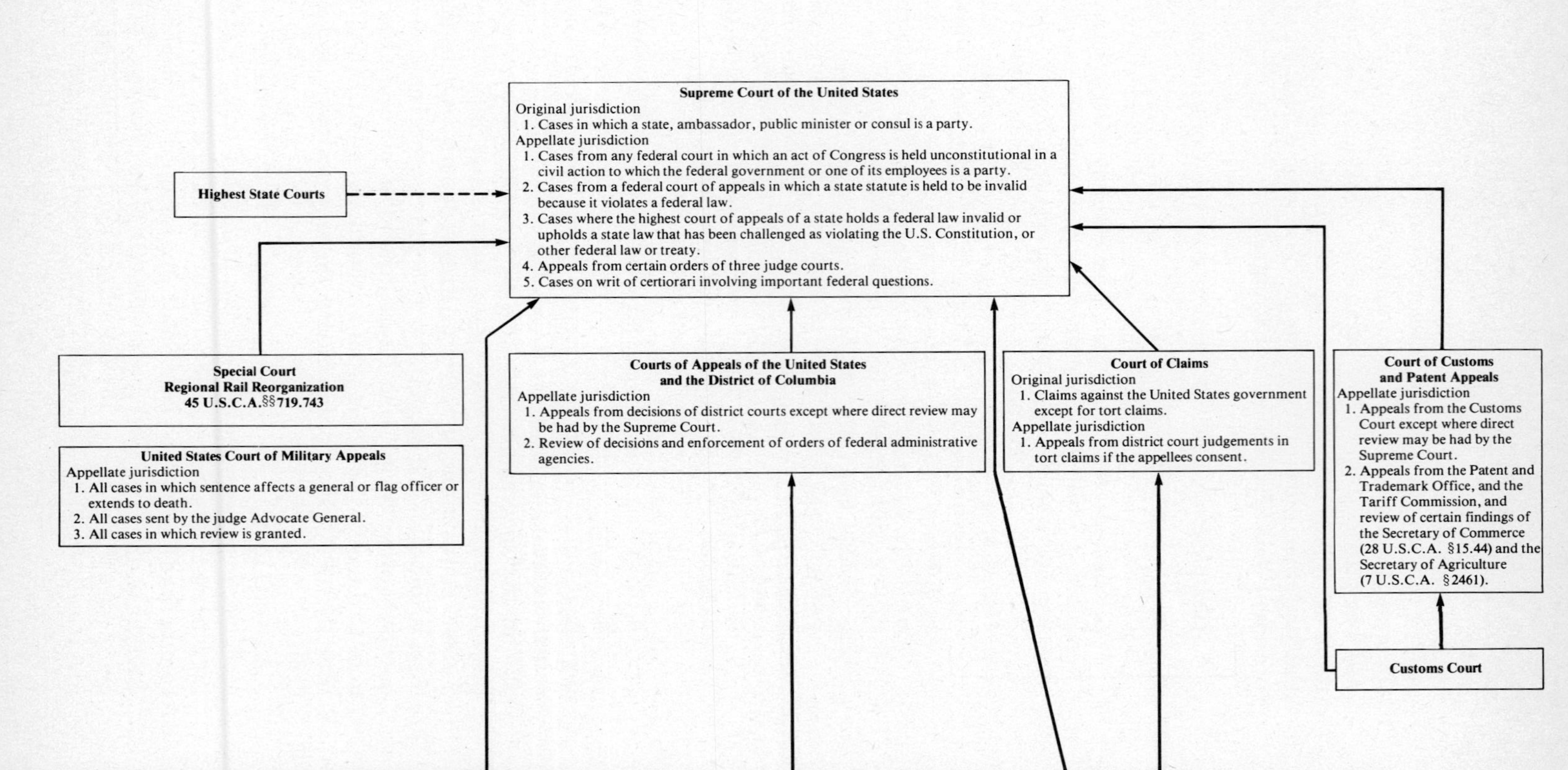
Supreme Court of the United States
Original jurisdiction
1. Cases in which a state, ambassador, public minister or consul is a party.
Appellate jurisdiction
1. Cases from any federal court in which an act of Congress is held unconstitutional in a civil action to which the federal government or one of its employees is a party.
2. Cases from a federal court of appeals in which a state statute is held to be invalid because it violates a federal law.
3. Cases where the highest court of appeals of a state holds a federal law invalid or upholds a state law that has been challenged as violating the U.S. Constitution, or other federal law or treaty.
4. Appeals from certain orders of three judge courts.
5. Cases on writ of certiorari involving important federal questions.
Highest State Courts
Special Court
Regional Rail Reorganization
45 U.S.C.A.§§719.743
United States Court of Military Appeals
Appellate jurisdiction
1. All cases in which sentence affects a general or flag officer or extends to death.
2. All cases sent by the judge Advocate General.
3. All cases in which review is granted.
Courts of Appeals of the United States and the District of Columbia
Appellate jurisdiction
1. Appeals from decisions of district courts except where direct review may be had by the Supreme Court.
2. Review of decisions and enforcement of orders of federal administrative agencies.
Court of Claims
Original jurisdiction
1. Claims against the United States government except for tort claims.
Appellate jurisdiction
1. Appeals from district court judgements in tort claims if the appellees consent.
Court of Customs and Patent Appeals
Appellate jurisdiction
1. Appeals from the Customs Court except where direct review may be had by the Supreme Court.
2. Appeals from the Patent and Trademark Office, and the Tariff Commission, and review of certain findings of the Secretary of Commerce (28 U.S.C.A. §15.44) and the Secretary of Agriculture (7 U.S.C.A. §2461).
Customs Court

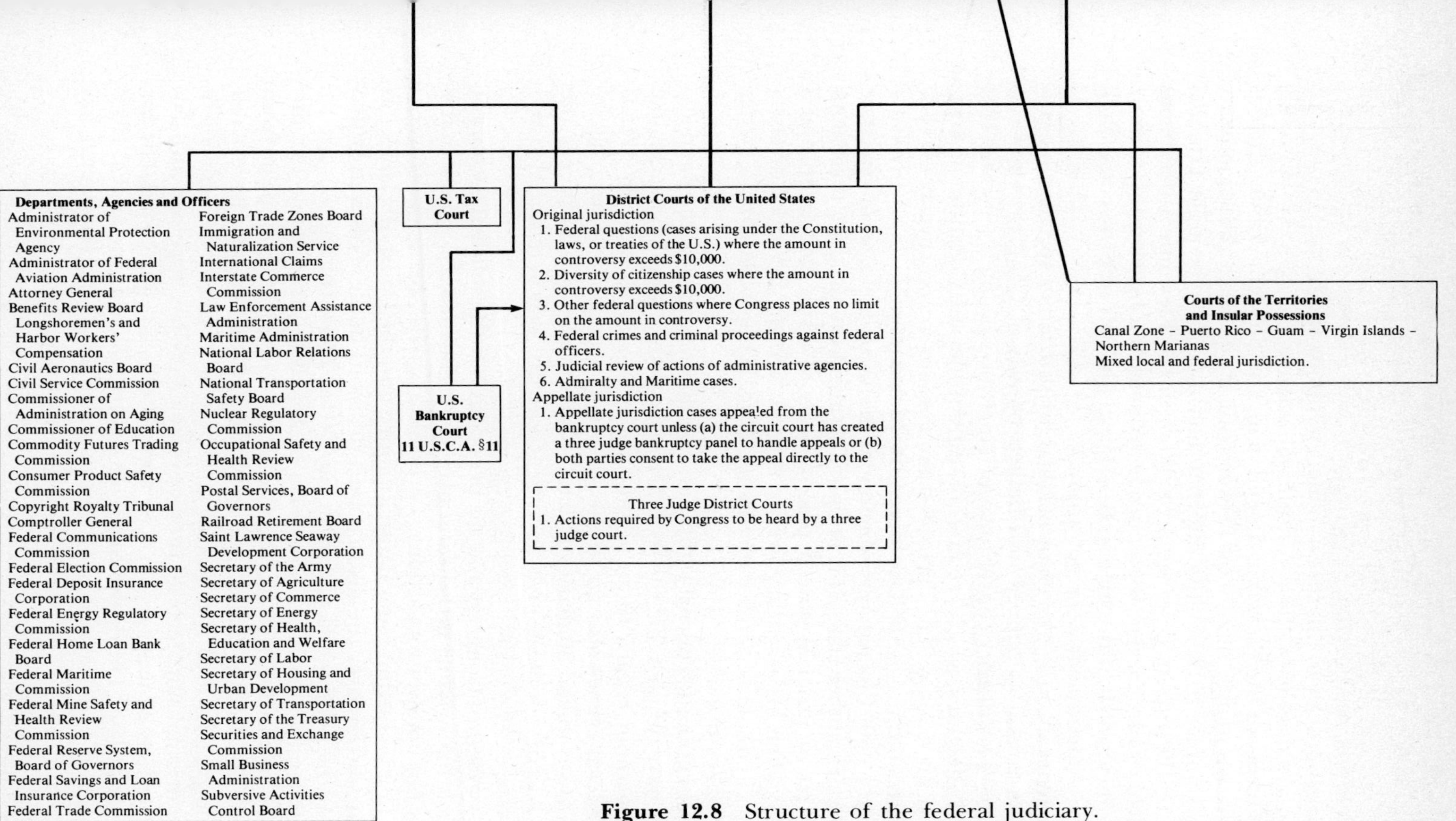

Figure 12.8 Structure of the federal judiciary.

Source: Kenneth W. Clarkson, Roger LeRoy Miller, and Bonnie Blaire, *West's Business Law: Text and Cases* (St. Paul, Minn.: West, 1980), p. 15.

resident could not sue the state of Georgia.[111] Officeholders in various states responded very quickly to this threat to their positions and helped to overturn the decision in *Chisholm* by the constitutional amendment process. However, despite the terms of the Eleventh Amendment, the Supreme Court still has original jurisdiction over many suits between one state and citizens of another state. For example, if the state's attorney had originally brought criminal action against the citizen, then the prohibition in the Eleventh Amendment has been held not to prevent the Supreme Court from hearing the citizen's appeal. In other words, if the state is the original plaintiff or prosecutor, then the Eleventh Amendment does not apply.

Other federal courts also enjoy original jurisdiction as specified in Article 3, Section 2, and as defined and limited by acts of Congress known as judiciary acts. The district courts have original jurisdiction over cases that raise **federal questions,** which are cases brought under the Constitution, laws, or treaties of the United States provided the amount in controversy exceeds $10,000. District courts also have **diversity jurisdiction** in cases involving more than $10,000. Diversity jurisdiction occurs when a citizen of one state sues a citizen of another state. It is designed to avoid the problem that might occur if judges or juries in state A place a party to a suit from state B at a disadvantage when his adversary lives in state A. But the future of diversity jurisdiction is in doubt because of increasing federal court case loads, a matter Chapter 13 takes up.

In other cases, such as civil rights and civil liberties actions, the members of Congress have decided that the federal district courts should have original jurisdiction without regard to an amount of money in controversy. Trials involving federal crimes also go to the district courts, which have original jurisdiction over them. Similarly, federal courts hear cases involving the judicial review of administrative agency actions as well as admiralty and maritime cases.

The members of Congress and the president have established a Court of Claims, which has original jurisdiction over claims against the United States government but not over tort actions. Tort claims against the federal government must first be filed in federal district court, and the Court of Claims has appellate jurisdiction over the district court decisions in these cases provided the appellee (the petitioner's opponent) in district court consents.

Most federal courts have some form of appellate jurisdiction. The Supreme Court hears appeals in five kinds of cases. First, it takes appeals from federal court decisions in civil cases in which an act of Congress is declared unconstitutional, provided the federal government or one of its agents is a party to the original suit. Second, the Supreme Court has appellate jurisdiction over decisions of federal courts of appeals that invalidate state law for violating federal law. Third, the Supreme Court will hear on appeal cases from the highest appellate court of any state, provided the state court has

[111] 2 Dall. 419 (1793).

found a federal law invalid or has upheld a state law but the petitioner claims the state law violates the United States Constitution, federal law, or treaties. Fourth, the Supreme Court has appellate jurisdiction over certain decisions of three-judge federal courts. Finally, the Court will hear other cases on appeal involving "important federal questions." The Supreme Court is especially interested in hearing cases on appeal if different federal circuit courts of appeals have arrived at contradictory decisions.

The federal circuit courts of appeals have appellate jurisdiction over federal district court decisions, unless a hearing by a court of appeals is circumvented because the case goes directly from federal district court to the Supreme Court. Depending upon the dictates of the Congress, district courts or the courts of appeals, and especially the court of appeals in Washington, D.C., exercise appellate jurisdiction to review the decisions of federal regulatory agencies and other bureaus.

Methods of appeal. Beyond cases of original jurisdiction, which go on the Court's **Original Docket,** petitioners may ask the Supreme Court for a **writ of *certiorari*.** Using this procedure, the petitioner tells the Court why it should be interested in the case and why the case falls within the Court's appellate jurisdiction. A writ of *certiorari* literally requires the lower court whose decision the petitioner is appealing to send a certified record of the case to the higher court. Disputes brought to the Court requesting a writ of *certiorari* go on its **Appellate Docket.** The Court may refuse to issue a writ of *certiorari*—deny *certiorari*—without explanation, for it has discretion over which of these cases it hears. The Court also receives petitions ***in forma pauperis***. These are usually filed by poor people (mostly prison inmates) who do not have the aid of an attorney. These go on the Court's **Miscellaneous Docket.**

Finally, the Court receives cases on **writ of appeal,** which also go on its Appellate Docket. By statutory law, the Court must consider these cases and either take them or explain its reasons for not doing so. Cases asking for a writ of appeal include those in which a state's highest appellate court finds a federal law (including treaties) unconstitutional or otherwise upholds a state law or state constitutional provision against the claim that it contradicts federal law or the Constitution. If a federal court of appeals finds that a state law or some part of a state's constitution violates the federal Constitution, or if the same court finds a federal law unconstitutional and the United States is a party to the suit, then again a writ of appeal may be used. If the case comes from a federal district court, the United States is a party, and a federal law is held unconstitutional, it also comes to the Court on writ of appeal. The same holds true for district court cases in which the United States is a party in a civil suit concerning federal antitrust laws, interstate commerce, or communication laws. Special three-judge district court panels are required to hear certain cases, which may be taken to the Supreme Court on a writ of appeal if the three-judge panel issues or fails to issue an injunction and the losing party

UNITED STATES DISTRICT COURT
SOUTHERN DISTRICT OF NEW YORK

-------------------------------- x

REPUBLICAN NATIONAL COMMITTEE, THE RIPON SOCIETY OF NEW YORK, INC., PAUL C. CARDAMONE, JOHN A. SCHMID, Plaintiffs, v. FEDERAL ELECTION COMMISSION, JOAN D. AIKENS, ROBERT O. TIERNAN, VERNON W. THOMPSON, NEIL STAEBLER, WILLIAM L. SPRINGER, THOMAS E. HARRIS, EDMUND L. HENSHAW, JR., STANLEY J. KIMMET, GRIFFIN B. BELL, W. MICHAEL BLUMENTHAL, Defendants.	CIVIL ACTION NO. COMPLAINT FOR DECLARATORY AND INJUNCTIVE RELIEF

-------------------------------- x

Plaintiffs, by their attorneys, Lord, Day & Lord, as and for their complaint herein, based upon information and belief, allege as follows:

INTRODUCTION

1. This action challenges the constitutionality of those provisions of federal law which compel presidential candidates to comply with limits on campaign expenditures in order to receive federal campaign funding and forbid them from raising and spending small contributions to communicate with voters. It alleges that the presidential candidate supported by plaintiffs in 1980 must, as a result of a combination of legal and practical factors, accept federal campaign funding and that the provisions as to expenditure limits are an unconstitutional condition on the

receipt of such funds. One effect of such a condition is to restrict and inhibit political communication among and between candidates, their supporters and the voters. Another is to restrict and inhibit "grass roots" participation in presidential campaigns. Expenditure limits, moreover, severely disadvantage candidates challenging incumbent Presidents, because incumbents, by the very nature of holding office, engage in activities which influence the outcome of the election but which are not affected by limits on expenditures. Finally, the amounts raised and spent by labor organizations on a variety of partisan political activities are completely unlimited. Because these activities can be an integral part of the campaign of a presidential candidate with substantial union support, and cannot as a practical matter be efficiently engaged in by any other group, all other groups and candidates are severely disadvantaged in presidential campaigns and the political process generally. As a result of these effects, conditioning federal campaign funding on compliance with limits on expenditures by presidential candidates is unconstitutional. This complaint does not challenge the legal limits on contributions and does not seek to limit the political activities of incumbent presidents or labor organizations. Rather, it seeks only to allow presidential candidates to raise and spend small contributions in order to increase the information available to voters, to allow citizens to participate in "grass roots" political activities in presidential campaigns, and to eliminate the unfair advantages expenditure limits give incumbent presidents and candidates supported by a substantial number of labor organizations.

This complaint was filed June 16, 1978, in Federal Court on behalf of certain Republican organizations who challenged the constitutionality of certain federal election laws. This form for complaints is one commonly used. The case raised a federal question.

wishes to appeal. Any time a federal court declares a federal law unconstitutional, the case can similarly go directly to the Supreme Court on a writ of appeal.[112]

The Court need not reach the merits of cases brought to it on writ of appeal, but it must state its reasons for refusal. (Furthermore, its action—unlike the denial of *certiorari*—technically may itself create a precedent.) Indeed, the Court can state its reasons for denying any case brought to it. For example, it may refuse the case "for want of a substantial federal question." A controversy presented to the Court may also pose a **political question,** which the Court is loathe to address. As Chapter 4 points out, the Court took this position in *Colgrove v. Green,* an early reapportionment case, and in *O'Brien v. Brown,* a case involving delegate selection methods (PR vs. SMD) for the 1972 Democratic National Convention.[113] The Court may also believe that it does not have appellate jurisdiction, or the controversy may not be "ripe" for appeal because the petitioner still has legal remedies available. However, the Court will hear any case if four justices so request. This is known as the **rule of four.**

Appointments to the federal judiciary. As Chapters 9 and 10 point out, the president "shall nominate, and by and with the Advice and Consent of the Senate, shall appoint . . . Judges of the supreme Court, and all other Officers of the United States, whose Appointments are not herein otherwise provided for, and which shall be established by law. . . ." This means that the president also appoints the members of federal district courts and circuit courts of appeal, with the advice and consent of the Senate.

The appointment process for federal judges has been described in some detail.[114] All appointments to the federal judiciary are political decisions for both the president and the members of the Senate. Nor do the members of the Supreme Court stay their hand from trying to affect the outcome of these decisions. For example, Chief Justice Taft, a former president, was constantly involved in advising his successors in the White House about appointments to the Supreme Court, and apparently other judges have also mixed in.[115] Party identification and ideology obviously are important in the appointments of federal judges at all levels. Presidents are anxious to use judicial appointments as patronage and to see that their public policy views are perpetuated in law. Senate members are no less interested in both aspects of the appointment process.

---

[112] This summary of writs of appeal relies on Rohde and Spaeth, *Supreme Court Decision Making,* pp. 118–119.

[113] 328 U.S. 549 (1946), and 92 S.Ct. 2718 (1972).

[114] Harold W. Chase, *Federal Judges: The Appointment Process* (Minneapolis: University of Minnesota Press, 1972). See also Stuart Teger, "Presidential Strategy for the Appointment of Supreme Court Justices," *Public Choice,* 31 (Fall 1977), pp. 1–22.

[115] Walter F. Murphy, *Elements of Judicial Strategy* (Chicago: University of Chicago Press, 1964), pp. 73–78.

Table 12.3 illustrates the nature of ideological voting on Supreme Court nominations. From 1968 to 1971, members of the Senate had the opportunity to vote on four presidential nominations to the Court, those of Abe Fortas to be chief justice and Clement Haynsworth, Harold Carswell, and William Rehnquist to be associate justices. The Fortas nomination was supported by Senate liberals, although a vote of cloture (the vote calculated in Table 12.3) did not carry, and therefore Fortas's nomination was withdrawn. President Nixon unsuccessfully nominated Haynsworth and Carswell, two southern judges, but his nomination of Rehnquist was successful.

Table 12.3 divides the members of the Senate who voted on all four motions into five groups. Those who voted for cloture of debate on the Fortas nomination and against the nominations of Haynsworth, Carswell, and Rehnquist are labeled Liberal-4; those who defected from one of these votes are labeled Liberal-3; those who voted only one half the time with the liberal position are labeled Split; those senators who defected in three out of four votes from the liberal position are labeled Conservative-3; and those senators

Table 12.3 Comparison of Average ACA Ratings, 1968–1971, and Senators' Positions in Votes on Fortas, Haynsworth, Carswell, and Rehnquist Nominations to the Supreme Court

ACA Rating	Liberal-4	Liberal-3	Split	Conservative-3	Conservative-4
95.1-100					
90.1-95					2
85.1-90					5
80.1-85				3	2
75.1-80					6
70.1-75					2
65.1-70			1		2
60.1-65					1
55.1-60				2	2
50.1-55			1		2
45.1-50			1	1	1
40.1-45			1	1	1
35.1-40					
30.1-35	1*	1	1		
25.1-30		3		1	
20.1-25	3	2			
15.1-20	3	2			
10.1-15	2	2			
5.1-10	3				
0.0- 5	8				

Source: Adapted from Wayne Sulfridge, "Ideology as a Factor in Senate Consideration of Supreme Court Nominations," *Journal of Politics,* 42 (May 1980), p. 565.

* Entries are numbers of senators in each category.

who voted against the motion for cloture of debate on the Fortas nomination and for the nominations of Haynsworth, Carswell, and Rehnquist are labeled Conservative-4. Table 12.3 shows that as the Americans for Constitutional Action (ACA) ratings of senators increase (that is, as senators are recorded as more conservative on overall roll-call votes), the senators are more and more likely to adopt a conservative position when voting on Supreme Court nominations.

There have been a number of efforts to make the appointment of federal judges less political and more concerned with the qualifications and character of the people nominated. Of course, satisfying political preferences and having competent and honest judges are not necessarily contradictory goals, although it is pure happenstance if the best-qualified candidate also turns out to be the one most politically suitable for a judgeship. The American Bar Association's Committee on the Federal Judiciary regularly reviews proposed appointments of judges. Chapter 9 points out the importance of senatorial courtesy in the appointment of district court judges. With the cooperation of the administration and the Justice Department, senators in several states have appointed merit-selection panels to help them in choosing federal judges, and the president is now required by law to promulgate voluntary merit-selection standards for senators and their panels to follow. About one-half of the states now have such panels, but it is not yet clear whether they are effective in choosing the best-qualified candidates or whether their advice will be heeded.

Decision Making in the Supreme Court

When judges decide cases at common law or in equity, they apply or interpret old rules or create new ones. The body of precedent they use is almost entirely made up of case law. Federal judges will apply case law in controversies tried under their diversity jurisdiction if the litigants live in different states, more than $10,000 is at issue, and one or both of them want a federal court trial. In such cases, the federal judges will apply either the statutory law or the case law of the state in which the tort, breach of contract, or trespass, say, is believed to have occurred. Occasionally the district judges may also have to interpret the state statutory law or case law, but if there has been an interpretation of that law by the state judiciary, then the federal district court must abide by that interpretation.

In most other cases, members of the federal judiciary are involved in deciding the meaning of federal laws and the Constitution and in ruling on the appropriateness of peoples' activities that are controlled by federal statutes or by the Constitution, and on the constitutional appropriateness of statutes and decisions of federal administrative agencies and bureaus. Deciding what a statute, an act of Congress, means is called **statutory construction.** Passing on the constitutionality of acts of Congress or of other agencies of the federal government is called **judicial review.**

Judicial review. The Constitution does not give the members of the Supreme Court an explicit right to judge the constitutionality of acts of Congress. However, Supreme Court justices are rational decision makers who (not surprisingly) look for opportunities to expand their jurisdictions and thereby to affect public policy. In pursuit of these goals, the justices constantly face other decision makers in and out of the national government, who have their own preferences, which sometimes conflict with the preferences of the justices. Therefore, the justices may sometimes have to restrict and carefully define their jurisdiction to avoid open confrontations. More importantly, the justices are constantly in gaming situations where conjectural variation is widespread.

The development of the Court's right of judicial review highlights many of the strategic aspects of judicial decision making. While a few writings and an occasional court decision supported judicial review in colonial times, the doctrine was neither formally stated nor firmly entrenched until the Court decided the famous case of *Marbury v. Madison.*[116] This case began with an oversight during a change of administrations. President John Adams, a Federalist, lost the election of 1800 but served until the inauguration of Thomas Jefferson, a Republican, who was inaugurated on March 4, 1801. (Jefferson's Republican party eventually became the modern Democratic party.) In the election of 1800, control of the Congress also changed hands. But in their lame-duck period between the election and the inauguration, the president and members of Congress decided to staff the judiciary with as many good Federalists as possible. Accordingly, the Judiciary Act of 1801 provided for several new federal judgeships and required that the president not fill the next vacancy on the Supreme Court, thus depriving President-elect Jefferson of the opportunity to name one Supreme Court justice.

The lame-duck Congress also gave President Adams the right to appoint several new justices of the peace for the District of Columbia. Adams did not sign some of these commissions until the night before Jefferson's inauguration. The commissions were then delivered to John Marshall, Adams's secretary of state. But Jefferson was inaugurated before the commissions were delivered to the appointees, and on Jefferson's orders James Madison, the newly appointed secretary of state, refused to deliver them. William Marbury, one of the would-be justices of the peace who was denied his commission, along with others, petitioned the Supreme Court for a **writ of *mandamus*,** asking the Court to order Madison to deliver their commissions.[117]

Marbury presented the Court, and especially its chief justice, John Marshall (who had simultaneously served as Adams's secretary of state), with a terrible dilemma.[118] If the Court issued a writ of *mandamus* to Secretary of

---

[116] 1 Cranch 137 (1803).

[117] A writ of *mandamus* is a command given by a higher court to a lower court or to a government official requiring that a particular act be done.

[118] Robert G. McClosky, *The American Supreme Court* (Chicago: University of Chicago Press, 1960), p. 41.

State Madison, he would surely ignore it, thus diminishing the prestige of the Court and its ability to affect the structure and policy of the national government. But if *Marbury* was denied, then the Federalist cause would be damaged, and President Jefferson's claims that the Federalists' "midnight appointments" were improper would be upheld. Underlying these conflicting goals was the ever-present confrontation between Republican and Federalist philosophies. The Republicans, no friends of the Court, viewed the federal judiciary with democratic suspicion. By contrast, the Federalists saw the judiciary as a nationalizing force, one that could help to weld a nation out of the former independent colonies.

Marbury came to the Court under the terms of Section 13 of the Judiciary Act of 1789, which read in part: "The Supreme Court shall . . . have power to issue . . . writs of *mandamus,* in cases warranted by the principles and usages of law, to any courts appointed, or persons holding office, under the authority of the United States."[119] In the Court's long-term struggle to fashion the right of judicial review, Chief Justice Marshall's opinion stands out for its brilliance. He agreed with Marbury that his commission should be delivered: "When a commission has been signed by the president, the appointment is made; and the commission is complete when the seal of the United States has been affixed to it by the secretary of state." Marshall also agreed that a writ of *mandamus* was appropriate. "This, then, is a plain case for a *mandamus,* either to deliver the commission, or a copy of it from the record. . . ." But Marshall then pointed out that the section of the Judiciary Act under which Marbury brought his plea gave the Court *original jurisdiction* to issue writs of *mandamus.* However, the Constitution, in Article 3, did not grant the Court original jurisdiction over such matters. Therefore, the members of Congress had expanded the Court's original jurisdiction beyond the provisions of the Constitution. Could they do so? Marshall said no, but he did not leave the matter there. He proceeded to drive huge spikes into the coffin of unlimited congressional discretion to step beyond the Constitution, and in doing so he built a strong foundation for judicial review. His words in *Marbury v. Madison* are worth quoting at length.

> If an act of the legislature, repugnant to the constitution, is void, does it, notwithstanding its invalidity, bind the courts, and oblige them to give it effect? Or, in other words, though it be not law, does it constitute a rule as operative as if it was a law? This would be to overthrow, in fact, what was established in theory; and would seem, at first view, an absurdity too gross to be insisted on. It shall, however, receive a more attentive consideration.
>
> It is, emphatically, the province and duty of the judicial department, to say what the law is. Those who apply the rules to particular cases, must of necessity expound and interpret the rules. If two laws conflict with each other, the courts must decide on the operation of each.

---

[119] 1 Stat. 73.

> So, if a law be in opposition to the constitution; if both the law and the constitution apply to a particular case, so that the court must either decide that case conformable to the law, disregarding the constitution; or conformable to the constitution, disregarding the law; the court must determine which of these conflicting rules governs the case: *this is of the very essence of judicial duty.* [emphasis added]

Marshall concluded, "If then, the courts are to regard the constitution, and the constitution is superior to any ordinary act of the legislature, the constitution, a not such ordinary act, must govern the case to which they both apply." Marbury was due his commission, but he had gone to the wrong court, one that Marshall ruled lacked the original jurisdiction the Congress had unconstitutionally granted it.

In much of its early development of case law, the Supreme Court extended and refined the concept of judicial review. But few opinions can match the brilliance of Chief Justice Marshall's in *Marbury*, for it satisfied the Republicans about the appointments while at the same time enunciating and fertilizing a doctrine that the Federalists supported and the Republicans viewed as a usurpation of democratic rights. Members of the Court since Marshall have combined a mixture of parries, thrusts, and strategic retreats to maintain their position in the national government and to have their views create an impact on public policy.

Supreme Court justices' ideologies and goals. When adhering to precedent or when creating a new precedent by trying to make sense out of conflicting claims, judges at common law or in equity tend to adopt rules that create efficient outcomes in the world they govern. Our model of the common-law judge does not require that he or she have any special knowledge of economics or of other social sciences to make sense out of the cases argued. For, the interests of the litigants tend to leave efficient rules untouched but create the conditions under which inefficient rules are constantly relitigated. Even so, nothing in the decision making of the common-law judge militates against efficiency, and those judges who really understand the nature of the case law they apply might actually come directly to grips with efficiency questions.

With Supreme Court decision making, our entire frame of reference must change, however. Certain rules promulgated by the Supreme Court do make sense in terms of efficiency. For example, before *Gideon v. Wainwright,* the Court had created an elaborate structure of conditions under which the defendant was guaranteed aid of counsel. Those rules were sufficiently complex that the Court had to review lower court decisions time and time again. In *Gideon,* the Court finally cast aside all of these conditions and simply made it a matter of law that a defendant is entitled to the aid of counsel in criminal proceedings. The judicial economy achieved was great, not only from the savings in costs of appeals, but also in savings for the trial courts and prosecutors involved. The Supreme Court has also been invited to use efficiency criteria in its decisions in several recent cases in which either the appellants or appellees themselves, or other persons and groups submitting briefs ***amicus curiae*** (as a friend of the court) have stated their positions explicitly in terms of economic efficiency.[120]

But criteria of efficiency or Pareto optimality very often can neither directly nor indirectly help Supreme Court justices make decisions in the cases they review. For example, what would be the efficient or Pareto optimal decision in *Brown v. Board of Education,* the public-school desegregation case whose effects have not yet been fully realized?[121] Certainly, for those who supported or opposed school desegregation, the matter was and continues to be a zero-sum game, in which all outcomes are Pareto optimal. Just as certainly, the effects of the decision in *Brown,* which were once thought to be highly beneficial, have now been seriously questioned, especially as they have been implemented in later decisions concerning the use of busing to achieve desegregation.[122]

In *Brown,* the members of the Supreme Court did what they thought the Constitution required, and that is exactly the point. While judges have considerable latitude in interpreting the Constitution as they see fit, their beliefs about what that document requires need not point to decisions that are efficient or Pareto preferred. How, then, do Supreme Court justices make decisions? The best answer we can provide is that they come to the Court much as voters come to the voting booth, with a set of attitudes. These attitudes concern issue dimensions, just as in an election. Each justice acts as if he has a most-preferred position on each issue, and with the exception of certain strategic problems we discuss momentarily, the justices vote according to their public policy preferences and state those preferences in their opinions.

One extensive study of Supreme Court decision making that uses this view has successfully predicted how the justices would vote in particular cases.[123] The study began with the assumption that the justices' votes in past cases would reveal their issue positions, and that their votes in future cases would depend on those revealed preferences. The study constructed issue dimensions, called scales, for a large number of different issues. Then, these scales were statistically reduced and combined into three basic issue dimensions. The first basic issue dimension concerns civil liberties and was constructed from the justices' votes in cases involving defendants in criminal proceedings, persons alleged to be national security risks, or persons litigating other guarantees of the Bill of Rights. This basic issue dimension is called the

---

[120] See, for example, *Moorman Mfg. Co. v. Bair,* 437 U.S. 267 (1978), and *American Petroleum Institute v. Marshall,* 48 L.W. 5022 (1980).

[121] 347 U.S. 483 (1954).

[122] *Keyes v. School District,* 413 U.S. 189 (1973), and *Dayton Board of Education v. Brinkman,* 97 S.Ct. 2766 (1977).

[123] Rohde and Spaeth, *Supreme Court Decision Making.* The following discussion reports the results in chapter 7.

Freedom Issue. A second basic issue dimension concerns various forms of discrimination based on politics, socio-economic status, or race. The justices' votes in the associated cases are combined into the Equality Issue. Finally, a number of cases form a basic issue dimension concerning government regulation of the economy and related aspects of government economic activity. This basic issue dimension is called the New Dealism issue.

Each basic issue dimension is statistically "normalized" so that it runs from −1.00 to +1.00. For example, a justice located at +1.00 on the Freedom Issue dimension would probably have voted in appeals of criminal cases to support most of the claims of petitioners that they had been denied Bill of Rights guarantees. On the other hand, justices located at −1.00 on the New Dealism Issue dimension would probably have voted against the government in all cases arising from disputed government regulations. Table 12.4 shows the average scale scores of the justices in cases decided between 1958 and 1973. The justices are arrayed from more "liberal" at the top of the table to more "conservative" at the bottom.

Suppose the judges evaluate each petitioner's claim according to how close it falls to their own most-preferred issue position. Through the application of various statistical techniques, we can then predict the justices' decisions in all cases in which they voted. Table 12.5 shows these predictions of the justices' votes for cases occurring from the spring of 1970 through the end of

Table 12.4 Supreme Court Justices' Positions on Basic Issues, 1958–1973

	Scale Score (Issue Position)		
Justice	**Freedom**	**Equality**	**New Dealism**
Douglas	.75	.79	.79
Warren (through 1968)	.65	.61	.43
Fortas (1965–1968)	.63	.64	.24
Brennan	.38	.50	.61
Goldberg (1962–1964)	.63	.63	.18
Marshall (from 1967)	.52	.54	.34
Black (through 1970)	.56	−.44	.56
Stewart	.08	−.12	−.13
White (from 1962)	−.30	−.08	.16
Clark (through 1966)	−.51	−.20	.25
Blackmun (from 1970)	−.33	−.43	−.29
Powell (from 1971)	−.32	−.38	−.48
Whittaker (through 1961)	−.38	−.67*	−.06
Harlan (through 1970)	−.33	−.37	−.42
Frankfurter (through 1961)	−.12	−.81*	−.36
Burger (from 1969)	−.46	−.60	−.47
Rehnquist (from 1971)	−.59	−.77	−.43

Source: From *Supreme Court Decision Making* by David W. Rohde and Harold J. Spaeth. San Francisco: W. H. Freeman and Company. Copyright © 1976, p. 143.

* Based on a smaller number of cases.

Table 12.5 Predicted Votes of Justices

	Total			*1972–1973 Terms Only*		
Justice	**Right**	**Wrong**	**% Right**	**Right**	**Wrong**	**% Right**
Rehnquist	35	3	92.1	29	3	90.6
Powell	32	3	91.4	27	2	93.1
Blackmun	51	5	91.1	32	0	100.0
Douglas	50	6	89.3	30	3	90.9
Brennan	51	7	87.9	28	5	84.8
Burger	48	9	84.2	32	1	97.0
Marshall	47	9	83.9	27	6	81.8
Black	14	3	82.4	—	—	—
White	46	11	80.7	28	4	87.5
Stewart	46	11	80.7	28	4	87.5
Harlan	13	4	76.5	—	—	—
Totals	433	71	85.9	261	29	90.00

Source: From *Supreme Court Decision Making* by David W. Rohde and Harold J. Spaeth. San Francisco: W. H. Freeman and Company. Copyright © 1976, p. 147.

the 1973 Court term. The underlying statistical model has obviously reached a high degree of predictive success. One implication of this finding is that judges are reasonably consistent in the values they bring to decide cases before them.

Coalition formation. The statistical model's inability to explain all of the justices' votes may partially result from other strategic considerations in their decision-making processes. In particular, the judges face a constant problem of constructing winning coalitions for each case they decide to consider. There are two kinds of coalitions involved with each case. The first is a **decision coalition.**[124] This coalition is made up of the justices in the majority who decide to vote for or against the petitioner solely on the merits and without regard to agreement among themselves on the reasons for the decision. By contrast, the members of an **opinion coalition** have agreed to support a single opinion, called the **opinion of the Court,** which explains the reasons for their decision. If a majority of the members voting agree on an opinion, forming an opinion coalition, then the Court's statement on the points of law in dispute becomes the law of the land. Stated differently, opinion coalitions make precedents, rules, which control the decisions of all lower courts as well as the activities of other members of the government and the citizenry.

If the chief justice is a member of the decision coalition (the majority),

[124] Rohde and Spaeth, *Supreme Court Decision Making,* p. 196. See also Rohde, "Policy Goals and Opinion Coalitions in the Supreme Court," *Midwest Journal of Political Science,* 16 (May 1972), pp. 208–224.

then following a vote on the merits, he assigns either himself or some other member of that coalition to try to write an opinion of the Court. When the chief justice is not a member of the decision coalition, the senior associate justice in the decision coalition—the one who has been on the court the longest—assigns himself or one of the other justices in the decision coalition to write the opinion of the Court. However it has been reported that Chief Justice Burger has broken with this tradition by assigning opinions on at least one occasion in which he was in the minority.[125] Not surprisingly, in important cases the opinion-assigner will often take the job of writing the opinion himself or will turn it over to a justice close to him on the issue dimension involved.[126]

Opinion-assignment decisions themselves have many strategic aspects that make them more complex than this description suggests. In particular,

> An astute Chief Justice can also utilize his opinion-assigning power to increase his influence on the Court. When in agreement with the majority, the Chief Justice can assign the opinion to the most moderate member, hoping that his mild statement of the doctrine might prevent defections or even gain adherence. The Chief may even assign the opinion to a wavering justice, hoping that this task—if not further reflection and research—will strengthen the Justice's resolve and perhaps sway the minority. Alternatively, the Chief Justice may use the opinion-assigning power to reward his coalition within the Court. He can assign the opinions in interesting and important cases to those Justices who tend to vote with him, leaving the dregs for those who vote against him on issues he thinks important. This authority may also be used as a means of encouraging an elderly or failing colleague to retire. Chief Justice Fuller withheld opinions from old Justice Field to help nudge him off the bench, and Taft tried the same tactic with McKenna.[127]

Research has borne out the validity of most of these observations.[128] Undoubtedly, the most important aspect of opinion assignment concerns its effects on the Court's subsequent ability to create an opinion coalition.

When it decides most cases, the Supreme Court is not usually faced with a threat to its jurisdiction or to its place in the national government. In these situations, the activity of the Court constitutes a game being played among the

---

[125] Nina Totenberg, "Behind the Marble, beneath the Robes," *New York Times Magazine* (March 16, 1975), p. 15, *passim.*

[126] Rohde and Spaeth, *Supreme Court Decision Making,* chapter 8. See also David W. Rohde, "Strategy and Ideology: The Assignment of Majority Opinions in the United States Supreme Court" (unpublished Ph.D. dissertation, University of Rochester, 1971).

[127] Reprinted from *Elements of Judicial Strategy* by Walter F. Murphy, by permission of The University of Chicago Press, p. 84. © 1964 by the University of Chicago. All rights reserved.

[128] Rohde and Spaeth, *Supreme Court Decision Making,* chapter 8.

justices. This game is an n-person game, such that n (usually nine) is the number of justices taking part in the case. Therefore, the job of building an opinion takes place within the framework of an n-person game.

The opinion writer will want the opinion of the Court to reflect his public policy preferences exactly. That is the goal we assume that Supreme Court justices and other judges pursue. But the four other justices who must concur (if all nine justices are sitting) will surely occupy different positions on the issue dimension involved in the case. How, then, should the opinion writer proceed?

> The opinion writer can apply some sort of marginal analysis to the alternatives he confronts. His minimum need—his essential need—is for four additional votes if he is to speak with the institutional authority of the Court. Thus, given the high value of these first four votes, he should rationally be willing to pay a relatively high price in accommodation to secure them. Once majority acquiescence has been obtained, the marginal value of any additional vote declines perceptively, as would the price which an opinion writer should be willing to pay. However, the marginal value of another vote is never zero, though the asking price may exceed its real value and may have to be rejected.[129]

Especially important is the pivotal voter, the last justice who enters into the coalition. That justice can and sometimes does impose severe costs on the opinion writer and on the other members of the opinion coalition. Those costs are measured in concessions that they must make in the opinion's content and rulings to keep the pivotal justice in the coalition. One report of a communication between justices during the opinion-coalition formation process shows the pressure that the pivotal justice can bring to bear on the opinion writer. In the 1889 proceedings of the Court, Mr. Justice Gray wrote Mr. Justice Miller this note:

> After a careful reading of your opinion in *Shotwell v. Moore,* I am very sorry to be compelled to say that the first part of it (especially in the passage which I have marked in the margin) is so contrary to my convictions, that I fear, unless it can be a good deal tempered, I shall have to deliver a separate opinion on the lines of the enclosed memorandum.
>
> I am particularly troubled about this, because, if my scruples are not removed, and Justices Field, Bradley and Lamar adhere to their dissent, your opinion will represent only four judges, half of those who took part in the case.[130]

Understandably, justices who are assigned opinions in cases in which there is no threat to the Court will tend to fashion those opinions in such a way

---

[129] Murphy, *Elements of Judicial Strategy,* pp. 64–65.

[130] Quoted in Charles Fairman, *Mr. Justice Miller and the Supreme Court 1862–1890* (Cambridge, Mass.: Harvard University Press, 1939), p. 320, as quoted in Murphy, *Elements of Judicial Strategy,* pp. 57–58.

that minimum winning coalitions will form, so in these situations a large number of five-to-four votes should occur. In the absence of an external threat, the members of the Court are basically playing a constant-sum game, because only a fixed number of concessions can be made concerning the grounds on which an opinion of the Court is written. Constant-sum games are played just like zero-sum games, and therefore, on the basis of the size principle, we expect minimum winning coalitions to form in a large number of cases.[131]

In other cases, the Court must make a decision that will antagonize people not on the Court and might even lead certain members of Congress to change the statutes controlling the Court's appellate jurisdiction. A number of cases come to mind in which the Court faced external threats. These include *Brown v. Board of Education* and *U.S. v. Nixon* (the famous White House tapes case).[132] In these situations, the Court is playing a game not merely among its own members but against those who might be hostile to its opinion. In such cases, we expect the justices to gain more utility from protecting the Court than from dividing among themselves. So, in the presence of an external threat, they commonly unite behind a unanimous opinion.

Indeed, as Figure 12.9 shows, that is precisely what happens. When the Court is in a threat situation, the justices form eight- and nine-member opinion coalitions more often and five-member opinion coalitions less often than when the Court is in a non-threat situation. Furthermore, when the justices join a grand opinion coalition, they sometimes harshly abandon their positions on the issues involved for the sake of unity. This observation explains at least some of the incorrect predictions in Table 12.5.

---

[131] Larger opinion coalitions may form if it is difficult to get some justice *not* to agree. There is an alternative coalition formation hypothesis, one that argues that coalitions should be "connected" in the sense that they include members who are adjacent to each other on the issue dimension. For example, justices A, B, C, D, and E may be arrayed in that order on an issue dimension. A connected coalition would have all five as members; an unconnected one would have, say, A, B, D, E, and F. Unconnected coalitions are less stable because their members are more dispersed on the issue dimension. Similarly, smaller connected coalitions are more stable than larger ones because larger ones are again ideologically more dispersed. See Robert Axelrod, *Conflict of Interest: A Theory of Divergent Goals with Applications to Politics* (Chicago: Markham, 1970). This hypothesis is originally applied to the Court's opinion-coalition formation process in Rohde, "Policy Goals and Opinion Coalitions in the Supreme Court." We use the size principle rather than the connected-coalition hypothesis because the two make the same predictions about coalition size and because the connected-coalition hypothesis is internally inconsistent. For example, if a coalition of A, B, C, D, and E forms and issues an opinion close to the opinion writer, A, then C can drop out, thus forcing A to add F to the coalition, bringing the opinion closer to C. Hence, by its logic, the connected-coalition hypothesis would lead us to predict coalitions that become unconnected.

[132] 41 L.Ed. 2d 1039 (1974). See also Steven J. Brams and Douglas Muzzio, "Unanimity in the Superior Court: A Game Theoretic Explanation of the Decision in the White House Tapes Case," *Public Choice,* 32 (Winter 1977), pp. 67–83.

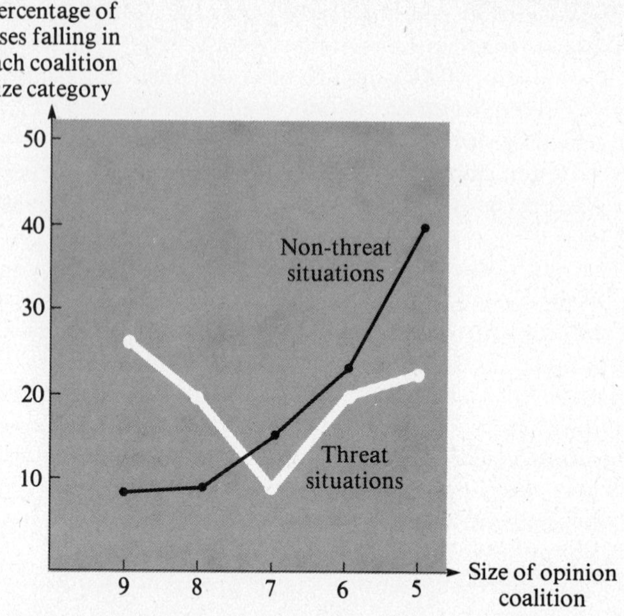

Figure 12.9 The size of Supreme Court opinion coalitions in threat and non-threat situations.

Source: David W. Rohde, "Policy Goals and Opinion Coalitions in the Supreme Court," *Midwest Journal of Political Science,* 16 (May 1972), p. 219.

JUDICIAL ACTIVISM AND JUDICIAL RESTRAINT

One student of the Court has pointed out that in the period between 1954 and 1978, the Supreme Court was a major public policy maker in five areas: desegregation, reapportionment, criminal-justice procedures, obscenity laws, and abortion.[133] Reviewing the progress of Supreme Court decisions in this period, another commentator has argued that the Court went too far. Some of its earlier decisions were desirable, but, "We may debate whether we have a better society or commonwealth or a worse one as a result. I believe we have a considerably worse one, because a free people feels itself increasingly under the arbitrary rule of unreachable authorities. . . . It is now time for the Court to act with the prudence that must in a free society be the more regular accompaniment of its actions."[134]

These observations are part of an ongoing debate concerning **judicial**

[133] Martin Shapiro, "The Supreme Court: From Warren to Burger," in Anthony King, ed., *The New American Political System* (Washington, D.C.: American Enterprise Institute, 1978), p. 179.

[134] Nathan Glazer, "Toward an Imperial Judiciary?" *The Public Interest,* 41 (Fall 1975), pp. 122–123.

activism and **judicial restraint.** These terms take on vastly different meanings depending upon who is using them. First, they can refer to the way in which the Court makes its decisions. If its opinions move slowly from one case to the next, deciding disputes on narrow grounds of technicalities rather than on constitutional principles, and if it appeals to the authority of *stare decisis* and precedent, then the Court is believed to be exercising judicial restraint. On the other hand, if the Court leaps into new territory by enunciating the widest decision possible in a particular case, even though the case could be decided on narrower grounds, then it is said to be indulging in judicial activism.

Another set of meanings of judicial activism and judicial restraint concerns the Court's relationship with other branches of the national government. If the Supreme Court refuses to accept anything that smacks of a political question, or if it defers regularly to the other branches of government, claiming that a petitioner either has not exhausted his remedies or must go to the legislature for relief, then some people will call that judicial restraint. On the other hand, if the Court becomes a principal legislator in the governmental process, and if its decisions pronounce it fit to assume this role, then others will call that judicial activism.

Attitudes toward judicial activism and judicial restraint depend on values concerning the appropriateness of judicial activity in general. People have attachments to the consistent rule of law and the use of orderly procedures, and these attachments are based on personal values as well as on a disutility for risk. More often, though, attitudes toward judicial activism and restraint depend on the actual decisions of the Court at the time. During Chief Justice Warren's tenure on the Court, for example, many people were horrified by what they regarded as the Court's dangerous social engineering. They framed their disagreement with the Court not merely in terms of the specific decisions involved and the particular public policies adopted, but also in terms of a theory that the Court ought to exercise judicial restraint. But when Chief Justice Burger and three other conservative justices came to the Court, the defenders of judicial restraint suddenly became advocates of judicial activism, for they urged the Court to overturn precipitously the precedents that had been generated during the Warren era. Similarly, those who had applauded the judicial activism of the Warren Court now suddenly found merit in judicial restraint when considering the Burger Court's decisions. Of course, earlier chapters have reported debates about procedures when the outcomes of the procedures were really at issue (for example, consider the argument over delegate selection rules in the 1972 Democratic National Convention, as reported in Chapter 4).

However, beyond these different meanings of judicial activism and judicial restraint, and aside from specific considerations of public policy, a core question remains about the appropriateness of members of the federal judiciary acting or refusing to act as makers of law rather than as interpreters of law or as umpires. We have indicated some satisfaction with judicial rule making in cases at common law or in equity. However, like the justices themselves, we find it difficult to accept standards for making decisions, such as judicial activism or judicial restraint. For, in the absence of public policies that are clearly Pareto-preferred or efficient, no general public policy standards except the Constitution itself apply. Therefore, we cannot say in advance whether the Court should be bold or timid, or whether its members should do more or less rule making relative to the other branches of the federal government. Hence, in considering this last institution of the American national government, we come full circle to address questions about procedure that can only be answered by an appeal to personal values.

QUESTIONS FOR DISCUSSION AND REVIEW

1. Would you approve of judges at common law and in equity who adopted rules that consistently held for the poorer litigant and against the wealthier one? Why? Why not? What would be the effect of such rules on those whose relationships they govern?
2. If judges replaced FDA commissioners as those in charge of initially *approving* drugs for human use, would they make their decisions any differently than do the commissioners? What differences might emerge? Why?
3. Should litigants have to pay for *full* court costs? What would be the effect of such a policy? Can you explain the present policy of not making litigants pay the full costs of governmentally provided court services?
4. Are courts democratic or dictatorial? Is this a strength or a weakness?
5. Can you suggest a standard judges might use in deciding constitutional law cases that would be similar to one used for deciding cases at common law? Is there any way to make opinions in constitutional law cases promulgate efficient or Pareto-preferred rules?
6. What would be the effects of leaving the appointment of judges entirely up to judges? Would you approve of such a change in appointment procedures? Why? Why not?
7. Do you believe the judiciary is the "least dangerous branch?" Why? Why not?

NEW CONCEPTS AND TERMS

administrative law
amicus curiae
answer
appellate courts

Appellate Docket
appellate jurisdiction
arraignment
Article 1 courts
Article 3 courts
beyond a reasonable doubt
bill of attainder
civil law
class action
collateral estoppel
common law
complaint
compulsory process
constitutional law
contract
crime
criminal law
cross complaint
damages
decision coalition
determinate sentences
discovery
diversity jurisdiction
double jeopardy
efficiency
emission charge
equity
ex post facto law
federal question
felony
general deterrence
grand jury
hung jury
in forma pauperis
information
in personam jurisdiction
incapacitation
indictment
injunction
injunctive relief
intentional tort
intervenor
judicial activism
judicial restraint
judicial review
Miscellaneous Docket
misdemeanor
mistrial
negligence
opinion coalition
opinion of the Court
organic law
Original Docket
original jurisdiction
per curiam order
petit jury
plea bargain
pleadings
political question
precedent
preponderance of the evidence
property law
prosecution immunity
rehabilitation
reply
res judicata
retribution
rule of four
self-incrimination
senior status
special deterrence
specific performance
standing to sue
stare decisis
statutory construction
statutory law
strict liability
subject-matter jurisdiction
summary dismissal
summary judgment
tort
use immunity
victim compensation
writ of appeal
writ of *certiorari*
writ of *habeas corpus*
writ of *mandamus*

Part IV

The Coming Agenda

Chapter 13: Change and Reform

Most people who seek change or reform of our political processes and governmental institutions do so because they want some particular public policy adopted. For example, at the beginning of the Kennedy administration many people called for the weakening of the House Rules Committee because a majority of its members were blocking bills granting federal aid to education. Similarly, during the Vietnam War, many Americans advocated laws to limit the president's activities as commander-in-chief because they opposed the administration's continued participation in widening (or not ending) the war. Here, we pay little attention to such issue-specific proposals for procedural or institutional reform. Issues change daily, and lasting reforms that address particular public policy issues will have consequences beyond the issues involved. Furthermore, an analysis of how reforms affect the particular public policy issues they are designed to resolve will not be of enduring interest.

Chapter 13 therefore concerns how procedural or institutional reforms might affect the three central problems this book identifies: the incoherence of social choice, the pursuit of private welfare through public means, and the political actions of intense minorities. These are long-standing problems of any representative democracy, and proposals for change must address each of them. Chapter 13 begins by describing these problems anew and then turns to piecemeal change and reform. By "piecemeal," we mean those changes that would directly affect only one political procedure or governmental institution.

Campaign finance laws and congressional committee system restructuring are two examples of piecemeal change and reform. Next, we investigate systemic reforms, by which we mean changes designed to affect all procedures and institutions of American politics and government. Constitutional tax and spending limits are examples of systemic reforms. Finally, Chapter 13 concludes with a note on the consequences of change and reform.

13

Change and Reform

Throughout this book we have only briefly mentioned various problems of reforming politics and government and changing public policy in the United States. The reason for largely ignoring these problems of change and reform is a belief that discussing them would be premature until we understood the theory and practice of public choice in the United States. The preceding chapters provide the groundwork for that understanding, and therefore a discussion of change and reform should now be productive.

PROBLEMS OF PUBLIC CHOICE IN THE UNITED STATES

Earlier chapters have identified three central problems of public choice in the United States and in other representative democracies. Each problem grows out of the public-policy-making process. Sometimes these problems afflict decisions taken at every stage of that process. More often, they arise out of decisions made in one or two institutions, yet their existence also reflects the inability of institutions (presently) not afflicted by them to correct those problems in the institutions in which they are found. But, wherever and whenever it arises, each problem shows itself in the perceived inadequacies of public policies that follow in its wake. This chapter first describes these three problems. Then, proposals for piecemeal and systemic reform are considered.

Cyclical Majorities

The first problem arises out of the failure of pure strategy equilibria to exist in elections and legislatures.[1] As a consequence of this failure, though one public policy is eventually adopted, many others were equally likely to have been adopted; the final outcome is the result of chance or cunning. The public policy chosen thus seems arbitrary, unpredictable, and incoherent. Preference distributions that can destroy pure strategy equilibria also give candidates and lawmakers incentives to use strategies of ambiguity and agenda control respectively. Candidates adopt a strategy of ambiguity because, as Chapters 2 and 7 demonstrate, with cyclical majorities, any pure electoral strategy taken can be defeated by some other strategy. To avoid being pinned down to a clear stand on the issues, candidates offer voters lotteries over public policy positions or withdraw altogether from public policy discussions. Legislators adopt a strategy of agenda control because, as Chapters 8 and 9 point out, they can thereby secure the passage of those public policies that they most prefer.[2]

The public choices that emerge from electoral and legislative processes in which the paradox of voting is a possibility seem entirely uncompelling. Surely, no ethical quality attaches to one outcome rather than another. Just as certainly, those political and governmental processes that are susceptible to these problems may appear to be shams. The democratic mystique holds that representative government is capable of expressing "the will of the people" in law and public policy. But this mystique is seriously damaged by an understanding of how fragile, malleable, and unstable public policy might become.[3]

Candidates' and lawmakers' inability to find undominated pure strategy equilibria can also lead to decidedly inefficient results. For instance, consider the problem of designing an optimal structure of property rights, which Chapter 3 offers as one reason for collective action. Beyond the obvious protections of titles to real estate, other examples of the agents of government constructing property rights include patents and copyrights, FCC frequency

---

[1] This problem is referred to throughout this book in various forms, such as the *paradox of voting, Arrow's paradox,* and *cyclical majorities.* All of these forms follow from the absence of pure strategy equilibria in elections or legislative voting or both. The terms are used here interchangeably, although they sometimes label distinguishable problems and processes.

[2] See the discussion of the Powell Amendment in Chapter 9 and later in this chapter.

[3] Public policy instability is a direct consequence of group decision making in general and democratic decision making in particular. Dictators—those who govern alone—have no such problem as long as they try to maximize their own self-interest, narrowly defined. (Of course, if they tried to maximize their subjects' welfare, then policy instability could reemerge, since they would be trying to duplicate in their own minds something like a democratic process.) Policy ambiguity and agenda manipulation are inevitable costs of living in a (representative) democracy—which observation, incidentally, is not an endorsement of dictatorship.

allocations to broadcasters, CAB and ICC route and entry regulations, and, most important, enforcement of contracts and protection against theft.

Chapter 2 describes a property-rights problem in which a rancher's cattle stray onto a farmer's land, destroying some crops.[4] In the presence of such external diseconomies, it does not matter whether the farmer has a property right to keep his fields untouched, which he can legally defend against the rancher, or whether the rancher has a property right for his cattle to roam, which he can legally defend against the farmer. In either case, use of the land will flow to the person willing to pay the most for it. For instance, if the law protects the rancher instead of the farmer, then the farmer can pay the rancher to restrain his cattle. The result is economically efficient no matter who has the right. However, it matters crucially whether the agents of government, be they legislators, bureaucrats, or judges, *have* established *some* form of property right. Without such rights, the result is unpredictable and potentially violent. Certainly, there will be an optimal level of neither ranching nor farming.

Voting on a structure of property rights can become extraordinarily complex. Bills might contain several different sections, and these could substantially alter the structure of pre-existing rights. However, as motions grow more complex, the probability of a voting cycle grows.[5] Cyclical majorities in this case would make the outcomes of future legislative decisions on property rights uncertain. People would not know how long they could continue to use resources to which they now have rights, since the outcomes of the political process would be unpredictable, perhaps even random. But as rights to use a resource grow uncertain, the "net present value," or flow of future expected utility, from owning property, declines. People react by reducing their investments in those resources whose net present values decline. As a consequence, the uncertainty created by a lack of pure strategy equilibria in elections or the lawmaking process results in an underinvestment in productive resources, including human capital: education, training, and maintenance of personal physical well-being.

As the example of the farmer and rancher shows, however, *ceteris paribus* a *certain* assignment of property rights would be more efficient than an uncertain one. A lack of pure strategy equilibria generates ambiguity, manipulation, and therefore uncertainty among members of the electorate. Their subsequent downward adjustments of investments lead to inefficient results compared to those that might prevail if pure strategy equilibria were present. Since nearly every change in public policy also changes property rights, this

---

[4] Ronald Coase, "The Problem of Social Cost," *Journal of Law and Economics*, 3 (October 1960), pp. 1–44.

[5] Bruce D. Bowen, "Toward an Estimation of the Frequency of Occurrence of the Voting Paradox in U.S. Senate Roll Call Votes," and Herbert F. Weisberg and Richard G. Niemi, "Probability Calculations for Cyclical Majorities in Congressional Voting," in Niemi and Weisberg, eds., *Probability Models of Collective Decision Making* (Columbus, Ohio: Merrill, 1972), pp. 181–231.

problem is fully general. As Chapter 12 points out, an efficient policy or structure of property rights will also be prospectively Pareto optimal—if people do not know what position they will hold under that structure (for example, if they do not know whether they will be ranchers or farmers). Naturally, people prefer certainty to both uncertainty and risk. The uncertainty generated by the possibility that equilibria do not exist thus also renders American political and governmental processes Pareto inferior compared to a hypothetically more stable, predictable (but perhaps unattainable) world.

Private Wants–Public Means

The second problem concerns the pervasive tendency to legislate and to deliver private benefits at collective cost through the bureaucratic process.[6] We first identified this problem in Chapter 3 by suggesting that people use government to extract goods and services of value only to themselves but at everyone else's expense. The problem reemerges in Chapter 6, which points out that the incentives of interest-group leaders and members induce them to lobby legislators for private goods rather than public goods. The actual private goods sought are also sometimes likely to cost more than they are worth. Chapter 7 shows that the incentives of election candidates often overlay those of interest-group leaders and members; for, promises to deliver private goods to their constituents are superior electoral strategies compared to promises to deliver collective goods. Chapter 9 describes legislators' electoral connections, congressional rules and procedures, and the structure of committees and the deference accorded to them. These all combine to produce logrolled bills, which have something for everyone individually but little collectively except for higher direct (tax) or indirect (regulatory) costs. Chapter 10 shows that presidents are susceptible to the same problems as are legislators, and Chapter 11 identifies federal bureaucrats as major dispensers of these private benefits.

Today, this problem seems partially understood even in the conventional wisdom of the press. The *iron triangles,* made up of interest groups, interested bureaus, and concerned congressional committees, are said to dominate the legislative process. The relationships among the members of these triangles, when placed in the electoral environments of House and Senate members, are believed to create and reinforce a *Washington Establishment.* House and Senate members gain benefits from these relationships in the form of an enhanced probability of reelection, and bureaucrats in the form of more secure and expanding budgets and jurisdictions.

The demand for the collective provision of private benefits carries with it certain very serious problems. First, making the provision of these benefits a

---

[6] This section's title is taken from Gordon Tullock, *Private Wants, Public Means: An Economic Analysis of the Desirable Scope of Government* (New York: Basic Books, 1970).

public-choice problem diverts attention from areas in which the public sector appears to have a comparative advantage, namely, in the production of real public goods and the suppression of significant public bads. For example, a particular senator's demand for a new air base in his state detracts from the ability of other senators or DOD officials to plan a balanced, optimal national defense strategy. As Chapter 11 suggests, decisions about the production of public goods such as national defense are extremely difficult anyway. When those decisions become further confused by a scramble for private benefits, the real, originally contemplated purpose of a particular form of collective action is forgotten, and at best the eventual result seems randomly chosen. Too, the overactive search for private benefits in one area, such as national defense, becomes time-consuming and detracts from legislators' abilities to consider other important areas, such as pollution control and the reduction of inflation and unemployment.

The collective supply of private goods creates a second problem, which Chapter 6 isolates. People ordinarily would not buy many of these goods in the private sector because it would be inefficient to do so: the costs exceed the benefits. In private-sector purchases, buyers prefer goods to the money they exchange for them. Otherwise, the purchase (exchange) would be inefficient and would not be consummated. However, if the purchase price can be spread out over the entire population—which is possible for private goods collectively supplied—then the efficiency of a transaction no longer remains relevant. To take the previous example, suppose the air base adds $25 million to the economy of the senator's state, but locating it in that state adds $26 million to its cost compared to an alternative site in another state. If citizens in the senator's state had to pay the full $26 million, they might not want the base. However, such costs are spread out over taxpayers everywhere, and therefore the senator will probably try to get the base located in his state.

Indeed, since purchases made in the private sector are likely to be efficient, people will often prevail upon public-sector decision makers to carry out inefficient ones. Consequently, various collectively supplied private goods are not worth their cost. That this problem creates Pareto-inferior programs seems evident. Chapter 6 points out that with such programs as the air base, a direct cash transfer will often give program recipients a preferred benefit at lower cost to the taxpayer. (In the case of the air base, the cost of such a transfer to the taxpayers would be $25 million, $1 million less than the additional $26 million the base costs.) Examples of Pareto-inferior outcomes resulting from the public provision of private goods abound, but two come to mind: poverty programs and mass transit systems.

Poverty programs. At one time, poverty programs in the United States were principally the function of charitable organizations. However, during the Great Depression, private charities could not easily cope with the growing demand for their services. At the same time, private giving shrank with the decline of economic activity. Public poverty programs in various forms expanded greatly in the 1930s and again during the administration of Lyndon B. Johnson.

As Chapter 3 observes, a public poverty program is a collective redistribution of wealth or income. One public-goods aspect of poverty programs, among others, grows out of the interdependence of people's utilities. For example, a child's failure to get enough to eat diminishes the utility of most adults who find out about it. Government bureaus are used to identify such children (and others) and to coordinate efforts to relieve their suffering. If all goes well, recipients of aid will eventually become self-sufficient.

There are two methods for aiding poor people. The first gives money directly to recipients. They can then adjust their purchases to reflect their own preferences. This method is direct; its administrative costs are the lowest possible for poverty programs; and a recipient's utility is highest with simple grants of money. For, welfare administrators who try to select specific goods and services for poor people could never replicate the different market-basket combinations that recipients themselves would choose and therefore prefer.[7]

The second method is to give **benefits in kind** to recipients. These include free or subsidized medical care, food stamps, Head Start programs for young children, school lunch programs, job training, symphony orchestra passes, special rates on public transportation, subsidized (sometimes public) housing, and lower property taxes for the widowed or elderly. An "energy stamps" program, another benefit in kind, is sometimes proposed to ease the burden of rising fuel costs. Table 13.1 shows that benefits in kind make up about 58 percent of the monetary value of federal support given to the poor. The percentage for state and local programs is probably much higher. These programs have grown enormously costly to administer. Some estimates now suggest that nearly one-half of every welfare dollar goes for administration. By giving money instead of in-kind benefits, administrative costs could be reduced. The monetary value of benefits flowing to recipients from various poverty programs could then be substantially increased at no added cost. Alternatively, if most of the administrative costs were returned to the taxpayers, while recipients received their benefits entirely in money rather than in kind, both recipients and taxpayers would be better off.

The failure of representative democracy as reflected in benefits-in-kind poverty programs is very real. Poor people are not receiving benefits at anywhere near the level that is theoretically achievable, and some would argue

[7] An argument against simple cash transfers raises the problem of what recipients might actually do with the money. Scholars of public finance sometimes speak of **merit goods,** whose consumption, some argue, should be encouraged by collective action. The notion behind merit goods is that people may be unable to choose wisely for themselves and that the poor might use some money given to them to buy less meritorious goods, such as heroin, alcohol, and lottery tickets. However, many benefits in kind can be converted into money. Furthermore, "That provision for merit goods is frequently directed at the poor suggests paternalism as an explanation." Richard A. Musgrave and Peggy B. Musgrave, *Public Finance in Theory and Practice* (New York: McGraw-Hill, 1973), p. 81.

Table 13.1 Federal Outlays Benefiting the Poor, Selected Fiscal Years

	1964	1966	1969	1973
Federal outlays (in billions)				
Cash payments	$6.4	$7.1	$8.2	$11.1
Food and housing transfers	0.3	0.3	0.7	3.5
Education	0.1	0.6	1.2	1.9
Health	0.7	0.8	3.5	5.4
Manpower	0.2	0.9	1.4	2.5
Other	0.2	0.5	0.9	1.9
Total	$7.9	$10.3	$15.9	$26.2
Total federal cash transfers (in billions)	$6.4	$7.1	$8.2	$11.1
Total federal in-kind transfers (in billions)	$1.5	$3.2	$7.7	$15.1
Federal transfer per poor person	$219	$361	$660	$1139
Federal cash transfer per poor person	$177	$249	$340	$482
Federal in-kind transfer per poor person	$42	$112	$320	$657

Source: Edgar K. Browning, "How Much More Equality Can We Afford?" Reprinted with permission from: *The Public Interest,* No. 43 (Spring 1976), p. 91. © 1976 by National Affairs, Inc. Data compiled from United States Department of Health, Education, and Welfare, Office of the Assistant Secretary for Planning and Evaluation, Office of Program Systems, "Federal Outlays Benefiting the Poor—Summary Tables" (March 1974), Table 1.

that taxpayers are paying much more than is necessary to achieve the same level of benefits that recipients now enjoy. The cause of this failure seems evident. The announcement of a "war on poverty" is an invitation for the members of several interest groups to find ways to benefit from supplying the troops. Even if interest-group leaders are unimaginative, political entrepreneurs seldom long remain so. Thus, grocers and farmers and food processors get behind the food-stamp program because food stamps substantially diminish welfare recipients' costs of purchasing food, which vastly increases the demand for what the program's supporters sell *and for nothing else!*[8]

[8] This increased demand makes the price of the subsidized commodity rise, which represents a hidden program cost for those whose purchases of the commodity are not subsidized. This effect is enhanced even further because benefits in kind such as food stamps lead recipients to over-consume food compared to their pattern of spending if they were just given the monetary equivalent of the food stamps. For another example of the same phenomenon, the Medicare and Medicaid programs are one major reason for recent rapid increases in medical care costs. See Keith B. Leffler, "Explanations in Search of Facts: A Critique of A Study of Physicians' Fees," (Miami: Law and Economics Center Occasional Paper, 1978).

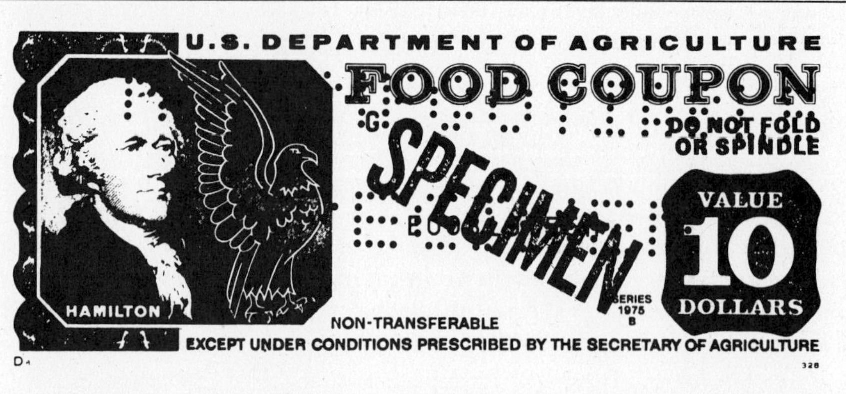

The food stamp program is a benefit-in-kind resource redistribution, because the stamps are officially exchangeable for food only. However, the stamps are easily traded on the black market, which is why the Department of Agriculture official insists (and the law requires) that only stamps marked "specimen" could be reproduced here. The food stamp program is administered by state governments. The detailed application form reprinted on the right covers five pages and itemizes the applicant's income, wealth, and expenses.

STATE OF FLORIDA
DEPARTMENT OF HEALTH AND REHABILITATIVE SERVICES

For Office Use Only

Case number ______

Date received ______

Application for Food Stamps–Part 1

Step 1. Complete Page 1

To begin to apply for food stamps, you can complete this first page, tear it off and give it to us. We are required to take action on your application within 30 days from the date you give us this first page. So, the sooner you give us the first page, the quicker you will know whether you will receive food stamps. Now go to Step 2.

Step 2. Complete Pages 2-5

Pages 2-5 must be completed before we can see if you're eligible for food stamps. You can return pages 2-5 to us along with the first page or at the time of the interview we will schedule for you. Try to fill out as much as possible now. Your case worker will help you with the rest during the interview.

Your name | Telephone number where you can be reached

Mailing Address | City | State | Zip Code

If you don't have a street address, tell us how to get to your home.

Sign here | Today's date

If You Need Food Stamps Right Away

If your household (you and the people who live and eat with you) has little or no income right now, you may be able to receive food stamps within a few days. Answer the following questions only if your household has little or no income and needs food stamps right away.

Has anyone in your household received any income so far this month?

☐ Yes ☐ No If yes, how much? $

Did your household's only income recently stop?

☐ Yes ☐ No

Does anyone in your household expect to receive income later this month?

☐ Yes ☐ No ☐ Don't know If yes, how much? $ When?

How many people live in your home and eat with you? (Include yourself)

Is anyone in your household 60 years or older?

☐ Yes ☐ No

How much do the members of your household have in cash and savings? (Give your best estimate of the total.)

$

HRS—SES FORM 3000, May 79 (Replaces March 79 edition which may be used; obsoletes earlier editions & DFS-FS-351)

Symphony orchestra administrators, employees, and patrons point out how nice it would be if the poor were exposed to "culture." Naturally, they would be more than willing to sell tickets for otherwise empty balcony seats to the poverty agency at half price. College and university administrators facing financial adversity do everything they can to develop government-supported, specialized education programs for the poor and unemployed. Enrollments expand, and the intellectual community's support and enthusiasm for teaching recent American literature sometimes to those who can hardly read or write suddenly blossom.

Members of the huge welfare bureaus at the federal, state, and local level would much rather distribute benefits in kind than cash payments, for their bureaus can only grow in size and jurisdiction by administering such large and difficult projects. Each benefit in kind will require a different set of eligibility standards and caseworkers to impose it, a different purchasing system and purchasing office, and a different monitoring team. Each benefit in kind will also make allies for the bureau among those from whom it purchases the benefits to be distributed. Chapter 11 raises the possibility that poverty-agency bureaucrats might even share a perverse incentive to keep people on welfare for the purpose of maximizing the number of clients.

The more complicated the poverty-alleviation system is, the more likely its employees are to make mistakes. House and Senate members will then enjoy ever-expanding opportunities to be ombudsmen for their respective states and districts. The more involved the purchases and the more complicated the transactions are, the more likely it is that serious fraud and corruption will occur in such bureaus. Thus, members of Congress, who themselves enacted many of these programs, can gain further electoral advantage by posing as outraged defenders of the taxpayer's dollars.

Perhaps poverty programs might not be enacted without a coalition of multiple interests, and the programs' principal purpose—to redistribute resources to the poor—would go unfulfilled. Indeed, there is evidence to confirm this view. Income support programs giving money benefits have been proposed, most notably by former Senator George S. McGovern (D-S.D.) in his 1972 presidential race, and later by Presidents Nixon, Ford, and Carter. The legislative failure of many of these programs stems from the incentives of House and Senate members, bureau staffs, and various interest groups to preserve the *status quo* of in-kind benefit programs. Therefore, the argument of political infeasibility of cash grant programs rings true.

But that is precisely the problem. Under present arrangements, a public policy failure emerges. Caused by the demand for the collective provision of private benefits, this failure seriously undermines the ability to pursue what many regard as an important goal: the elimination of poverty. This failure occurs even though Americans today are probably spending enough money on welfare and poverty programs to raise everyone in the United States well above the poverty level. The final blow comes when welfare recipients are themselves blamed for both specific and general failures of poverty programs.

Mass transit systems. One of the greatest disappointments of public policy in the last two decades is the failure of federal, state, and local governments to develop efficient mass transit systems for large cities. The public-goods aspects of these systems depend upon economies of scale in fuel consumption, air pollution, and *potential* fixed and operating costs. As fuel costs continue to rise, public mass transit will grow more attractive and the political demand for greater federal spending on public mass transit systems will become more insistent. However, the record has been disappointing. From 1950 to 1973, passengers riding mass transit systems fell from about fourteen million to about five million, the number of passengers per system employee fell from 58,000 to 38,000, and operating expenses as a percentage of operating revenues increased from 89 percent to 131 percent.[9] Large cost overruns and delays in creating new systems seem all too apparent.

The problem with publicly supplied mass transit systems is the same problem afflicting current poverty programs: namely, that decisions about private goods, divisible benefits, fashion the ultimate form these systems take. For example, routes are not laid out along heavily populated corridors, where they could serve the largest numbers of people. Instead, they are chosen to reflect the interests of those whose approval must be secured for the system to be built. Major terminals are placed beneath or adjacent to large downtown department stores, in exchange for which the system is supported and endorsed by members of the central city's chamber of commerce. The streets torn up to accommodate the system are usually lined with smaller businesses in competition with and enjoying fewer organized political resources than the larger downtown establishments.[10]

If the approval of adjacent suburban cities or counties is required for the system to be constructed, then decisions about routing through these districts reflect the preferences of suburban officeholders. Land speculation in contemplation of selling rights of way at inflated prices proceeds unabated. Businesses ask for route variations to improve their financial positions. Construction firms in the metropolitan area view the project as a great source of income. And, construction workers also support the program because under

---

[9] B. Bruce-Briggs, "Mass Transportation and Minority Transportation," *The Public Interest,* 40 (Summer 1975), p. 62.

[10] Larger businesses confront a reduced level of free-rider problems in pursuing collective action by lobbying and other political activities. They usually capture most of the benefits of such activities. So, politics produces for them private rather than collective goods. By contrast, as the argument reviewed in Chapter 6 would suggest, small businesses do confront free-rider problems. This explains the difference between large and small businesses in their respective levels of organized political resources. But successful political entrepreneurs sometimes can overcome these differences. However, as Chapter 11 comments, the same differences emerge in the willingness and ability of businesses to litigate against regulatory agencies. See Mancur Olson, Jr., *The Logic of Collective Action: Public Goods and the Theory of Groups,* rev. ed. (New York: Schocken, 1971).

the terms of the Davis-Bacon Act they will probably be paid more than the going wage rate for working on it.

Transit workers and transit union officials also welcome the new system as an endless source of benefits. As public employees, transit workers can extract far greater concessions from city government than they would from a smaller, private transit system operator. After all, they vote, and they can also tie up the entire city with a transit strike, especially if many people come to rely on the system. The inconvenience of a strike would be politically unacceptable, and therefore mayors, city managers, and city councilors usually acquiesce in the workers' demands. This acquiescence partially explains why transit workers' salaries, controlling for inflation, nearly doubled between 1950 and 1973 and average worker pay per passenger during that time, again controlling for inflation, increased from 8 cents to 23 cents.[11] In sum, the overall interests of the system's riders and others who face fuel shortages, increasing air pollution, and escalating transportation costs are often lost in the ensuing demands for private benefits.

Debates and discussions about poverty programs, mass transit systems, and other public policies are usually carried on in total disregard of the political and governmental realities that ultimately shape them. Publicly stated justifications for such programs refer principally to their public-goods aspects. In the broadest forums, citizens are urged to support candidates who promise as officeholders to enact public policies in the purest, most beneficial forms. But, the privately acknowledged reasons for each policy, which really shape its final form, often seem to have nothing to do with the efficient supply of an optimal level of some public good.

Intense Minorities

The third central problem occurs when those with intensely held preferences enter politics to achieve their goals. Those with intense preferences on a particular issue see little else except that issue when judging election candidates or various public policies.[12] Citizens who hold intense preferences are usually called "single-issue voters."

Intense preferences are not confined to the public sector. Most of us know someone who seems to be monomaniacal about achieving a particular goal. People form intense preferences to enter certain professions, to marry particular persons, or to take trips to faraway places about which they constantly fantasize. In the private sector, we take little notice of a success or failure to satisfy intense preferences. Of course, a success can be the source of

---

[11] Bruce-Briggs, "Mass Transportation and Minority Transportation," p. 62.

[12] The problems of intense minorities and intense preferences are analyzed and described in Chapter 7, in the text accompanying Table 7.5. The intense-minority problem bears a strong resemblance to the cyclical majority and private wants–public means problems. See Chapter 7, footnote 15, and Chapter 9, footnote 17. Here, though, these three problems are treated separately.

great happiness, and a failure can have tragic consequences. However, unless public policy is involved (for example, government regulations artificially limit places in professional schools, or prohibit miscegenation, or bar travel to particular countries), then beyond the personal and family level, we seldom react to the success or failure of another to satisfy an intense preference.

When citizens with intense preferences engage the political process, however, public goods and public bads immediately become involved. Especially if two groups of such people oppose each other, the simultaneous satisfaction of the members of both groups by public-sector action becomes an impossibility. Public policy concerning abortion, which has found such frequent mention in these pages, is the best example of the problem. A public policy banning abortion would represent a collective good that displays a negative externality for those who would *legalize* abortion, whereas a public policy of doing nothing—allowing abortion—would represent a collective good that displays a negative externality for those who *oppose* it. In such cases, the political process will systematically fail to satisfy some fraction of those with conflicting intense preferences.

One cannot judge by scientific criteria such as Pareto optimality whether those with intense preferences should be satisfied.[13] To make such a judgment would require an interpersonal comparison of utilities. However, as Chapter 7 points out, the political party out of office in a two-party system can bring up issues that actuate minorities with intensely held preferences. They do so not because party members share those preferences, but because they want to form a coalition of minorities to topple the incumbents in the governing party.

This strategy can lead to Pareto-inferior results. How so? Suppose we are asked if *electoral* public choice, *ceteris paribus,* should be made by majority rule. A priori, the answer must be "yes." With no knowledge of actual issues, a reasonable person choosing a public-choice procedure expects to be in the majority more often than in the minority. Hence, that person would prefer majority rule.[14] It follows that everyone would prefer a system in which coalitions of intense minorities did not affect the results. For, such coalitions can lead to the rejection of incumbents who enjoy a majority on issues about which minority preferences have not been actuated. Even if the party out of office succeeded in taking control of the White House or the Congress, there is no evidence that its members would treat intense minorities any differently. Since the majority is worse off and the minority is unaffected by the change of party in control, the result is Pareto inferior. Similarly, the possibility that

[13] The problem of reconciling preferences held by intense minorities with conflicting preferences held by not-so-intense majorities is a central concern of democratic political philosophy. See Willmoore Kendall and George W. Carey, "The 'Intensity' Problem and Democratic Theory," *American Political Science Review,* 62 (March 1968), pp. 5–24. Here, though, only the Pareto-inferior results from the political participation of intense minorities are considered, along with effects various proposals for reform might have on the problem's resolution.

[14] For a proof of this proposition, see Chapter 4, footnote 3.

coalitions of minorities might form leads to campaign obfuscation and strategic ambiguity. Candidates offer voters lotteries over policies, if they offer anything at all, even though most voters would prefer a certainty. Politics and government in the United States simply do not handle the intense minorities problem very well.

Subsidiary Problems

The three major problems just identified include a host of subsidiary, sometimes more familiar problems that derive from them. For example, many believe that elections and officeholders should not be "bought," and they view the potential for the abuse of political money as a serious problem. However, as Chapter 6 observes, campaign contributions often represent an exchange for political favors, public policies enacted. But people will seldom contribute large amounts of money to election campaigns unless they expect private, divisible benefits in return. The buying of candidates and officeholders thus becomes part of the larger problem of private wants-public means. For another example, during the 1950s, many citizens were unhappy because the federal government failed to provide aid for school construction. As Chapter 9 points out, the legislative failure of school aid bills resulted from agenda manipulation. This parliamentary strategy was made possible by the larger problem of an induced cyclical majority in Congress. For a third example, those who hold intense preferences about such public policies as abortion, gun control, women's rights, or gay rights resent the unwillingness of elected officeholders to take unambiguous positions on these issues. But officeholders are only trying to avoid the formation of a coalition of minorities against them.

Not every political or governmental problem grows out of one of our three central problems. Sometimes they are the results of ordinary decision-making errors. For example, Jefferson's embargo of trade with Europe backfired because he failed to understand the nature of economic development. (Or, perhaps Jefferson was himself an intense minority on the subject of "foreign entanglements.") For another example, many people viewed the Carter administration as particularly error-ridden and inept in its handling of both domestic and foreign policy. Nor can we easily find that the apparent crimes—errors—of the Nixon administration are the result of one of these three central problems. However, many problems seem to derive from one of these three central problems. Earlier chapters point out the contributions each process or institution makes toward creating them.

PIECEMEAL CHANGE AND REFORM

It now proves useful to consider various proposals for change and reform of American politics and government in the light of how the occurrence of these problems might be affected. What, if anything, can or should be done about these problems? Here, some proposed reforms are examined. Each is chosen with an eye to how it might help solve or fail to solve a central problem. This section considers **piecemeal reforms,** those affecting only one or two major political procedures or government institutions. The next section considers **systemic reforms,** those that try to change the entire environment or results of public policy decision making.

Election Reforms

Compulsory voting. Proposals to compel people to vote (usually by fining them for abstaining) arise periodically, and especially when off-year elections attract few citizens to the polls. Advocates of compulsory voting justify this reform by elevating the act of voting to a civic virtue, which they are willing to force others to share.[15] However, our concern is not with the ethical properties of the reform, but with its effects on the three central problems.

First, the effect that compulsory voting might have on the absence of pure strategy electoral equilibria is a matter of pure speculation. If the voters added by compulsory voting are like all other voters in their preferences, the existence or nonexistence of equilibria might not be affected by compulsion. But the new voters might hold preferences on some issues that have not yet been addressed in elections. If that is so, the election grows more complicated, and the probability of a voting cycle increases.[16]

Second, compulsory voting might ameliorate the private wants–public means problem, but that is doubtful. Bringing everyone to the polls would induce current abstainers to vote, and these people may be less likely than others to be presently receiving private benefits from government.[17] Perhaps they would vote against candidates who promise to become delegates for narrow constituency interests. But this seems unlikely. A more reasonable expectation is that political entrepreneurs, candidates, would redouble their efforts to find new private, divisible benefits to induce these former abstainers to cast their ballots for them. Hence, compulsory voting might only make the private wants–public means problem worse.

Third, what affect might compulsory voting have on the intense-minority problem? Recall from Chapter 7 that if electoral competition occurs over only one issue dimension, or over many dimensions but preferences are distributed symmetrically about some median position, then in the absence of

---

[15] One suspects that compulsory-voting advocates sometimes expect the increased turnout to favor the party or candidates they support.

[16] See footnote 5.

[17] Recall from Chapter 5 that income and turnout are positively correlated. Poor citizens vote less often than middle-income citizens. They also pay practically no income taxes. Thus, they do not receive private benefits in the form of tax loopholes, unless one counts their exemption from paying income taxes a loophole. Yet, welfare programs may provide them with private benefits.

abstention the candidates must converge. Therefore, compulsory voting will produce candidates who are indistinguishable in the public policies they advocate.

Suppose abstention is allowed, however. If preferences are distributed bimodally, severe abstention from alienation will pull candidates apart. As a result, those citizens with preferences lying at one of the two modes but at some distance to the left or right of the median position will occasionally find satisfaction in the candidacies variously of, say, a Barry Goldwater or a George McGovern. However, with compulsory voting and candidates converged, a thirst for like-minded, off-center candidates will go unslaked. If voters at some distance from the median hold their preferences intensely, they will find issues around which to form political movements and parties. But these issues are usually at hand, for citizens at some distance from the median often hold intense preferences about particular issues. For example, under the control of such citizens (activists) the 1980 Republican platform came out opposed to abortions, gun control, and the Equal Rights Amendment. Under compulsory voting, with major-party candidates converged to the center of the issue dimension, these movements and parties will oppose the major-party candidates. Thus, compulsory voting is likely to exacerbate the intense-minorities problem by mobilizing intense minorities more rapidly.

Approval voting. Some political scientists are now advocating the adoption of **approval voting** to solve several problems they find in the electoral process.[18] Using this system, citizens would be able to vote for any of the candidates running against each other. For example, if three candidates ran for a Senate seat, a voter could cast a ballot for all three, for any two, or for just one of them. Approval voting, it is argued, would "increase voter turnout . . . , increase the likelihood of a majority winner in plurality contests and thereby both obviate the need for runoff elections and reinforce the legitimacy of first-ballot outcomes, and . . . help centrist candidates, without at the same time denying voters the opportunity to express their support for more extremist candidates."[19]

Approval voting is said to reduce the likelihood that people will vote not for their first-choice candidate but instead for their second choice to reduce the probability that their third choice will win. As Chapter 5 points out, this practice sometimes occurs in three-candidate elections if someone's most-preferred candidate has little or no chance of winning. People vote for their second choice merely to avoid throwing their votes away and allowing their last choice to win. Under approval voting, citizens could vote for both their first and second choices, thus avoiding the problem.

---

[18] For a theoretical overview of approval voting, see Steven J. Brams and Peter C. Fishburn, "Approval Voting," *American Political Science Review,* 72 (September 1978), pp. 831–847.

[19] Brams and Fishburn, "Approval Voting," p. 831.

Approval voting is also said to avoid the possibility that two candidates will split the votes between them, thus allowing the third candidate to win. For example, under the current system, a left-wing candidate, say, could enter an election and draw votes away from the Democratic party's major candidate. Left-wing (or right-wing) candidates might threaten to use this strategy simply to extract concessions from the Democrat (or Republican). Alternatively, "single-issue" candidates might threaten to use the same strategy against either party. For example, if many Catholic voters live in a district and if most of them are Democrats, a potential anti-abortion candidate might threaten to run unless the Democratic candidate fully embraces the anti-abortion stand.

Approval voting is expected to make this strategy less profitable, which would simultaneously reduce the severity of the intense minority problem. Furthermore, candidates who run with no chance of winning are really trying to manipulate elections by altering citizens' agendas. That is, they are trying to induce implicit cycles based on their understanding of voters' preferences. In this sense, approval voting is also claimed to be *strategy-proof,* which ameliorates the effects of the cyclical majority problem.

Approval voting is now under consideration in a few states for use in presidential primary elections. Generally, many candidates run in these elections, and therefore the outcomes often seem ambiguous. Approval voting might help to clarify the meaning of outcomes in such elections. However, while approval voting has been claimed to be a useful electoral reform, the underlying problems of cyclical majorities and intense minorities have not disappeared. Approval voting merely manipulates the rules governing elections, and in so doing helps to clarify the meaning of an election outcome *if a meaning really exists.* A change in voting systems by itself cannot create coherence where there is none. Arrow's impossibility theorem remains fully general, and it covers elections using approval voting as well as more conventional rules.

Government funding of campaigns. Government funding of campaigns along with the abolition of all private campaign contributions is advocated as one way of severing the connection between interest groups and elected officeholders. This reform strategy is direct, and parts of it have already been adopted, though on a quasi-voluntary basis, for presidential campaigns. Bills to provide for federal funding of congressional campaigns now appear annually. The reform's directness makes it extremely attractive. When it is adopted, many argue, no longer will officeholders extract resources from organized groups in the population in exchange for a hostage public policy. No longer will political entrepreneurs be able to provide "the best public policy that money can buy." And, no longer will interest groups try to buy it. However, this reform carries with it certain problems.

First, the connection between interest groups and elected officeholders will not be completely severed. The coin of payment will change but not the fact of payment. Political entrepreneurs now exchange public policy for money, plurality, and the labor required to produce an electoral plurality. If money in the form of campaign contributions cannot be exchanged, then more emphasis will be placed on the ability of interest groups to produce plurality and the labor that creates plurality, and in the process new demands for the public supply of private benefits will emerge.

If candidates increasingly heed voters instead of dollars, will democracy be better served? Not necessarily, for as Chapter 6 points out, the voters who will be heeded most are organized in interest groups, and they will continue to demand the public supply of private benefits. Without private campaign contributions, officeholders will probably listen more closely to the demands of larger groups than they did when money contributions were allowed. However, there is no guarantee that candidates will listen to larger *numbers* of voters, only that they will pay more attention to those *voters* who are better organized in larger groups. Officeholders will thus pay closer attention to those groups whose members have solved the free-rider problems of formation and maintenance. But as Chapter 6 also points out, political entrepreneurs are largely responsible for solving these free-rider problems. Hence, those entrepreneurs—the elected officeholders—will search out new ways to organize new groups for political action. This action will take the form of mobilizing votes or campaign labor rather than financial contributions.

The principal way this has been done in the past is for House and Senate members to pass laws creating private benefits in the form of monopolistic conditions, along with bars to entry in various trades, professions, and industries. These arrangements are decidedly Pareto inferior. Therefore, a reform that prevents direct money contributions might well leave unchanged or even exacerbate the problem it was intended to solve—the demand for the collective provision of private, divisible benefits.

This first problem of a persistent, though altered, connection between interest groups and election candidates creates another problem, the problem of illegal payments or bribes to officeholders.[20] Labor-intensive organizations, such as trade unions, will be able to promise campaign workers and large blocks of votes to candidates. As a consequence, they will probably do relatively better under a prohibition of monetary contributions than would otherwise be true. On the other hand, organizations with smaller memberships will probably suffer. To redress this shift in advantage, money will flow from small groups to officeholders through *sub rosa* channels, and therefore graft and corruption can be expected to become more common.

The third problem with government funding of election campaigns is that incumbent officeholders themselves constitute an interest group, with each member sharing the goal of reelection by large margins at little personal expense. From an incumbent's perspective, the satisfaction of this goal represents a private benefit. Therefore, since incumbents do the drafting, cam-

---

[20] The shifting allocations accompanying complete government financing of campaigns are predicted in Sam Kazman, "The Economics of the 1974 Federal Election Campaign Act Amendments," *Buffalo Law Review*, 25 (Winter 1976), pp. 519–543.

paign finance laws will probably be drafted with incumbents in mind. As Chapter 6 reports, past campaign contribution legislation has a distinctly pro-incumbent bias. Incumbents will undoubtedly continue to pass laws maintaining their advantages. Campaigns will probably be slightly underfunded so that *unknown* challengers will be unable to wage earnest campaigns. Regulations concerning who is eligible to receive campaign funds will also probably be stringent. Third-party candidates, except by sheer chance, will probably be eliminated from the political process, for they will not qualify for public support.

If elected officeholders are to be responsive and not merely monopoly purveyors of private benefits at collective cost, there is something to be said for maintaining or expanding the competitiveness of elections. Government funding of campaigns with a concomitant restriction on contributions might be counterproductive for maintaining this competitiveness. Alternatively, Chapter 6 points out that present contribution limits and disclosure requirements already strongly favor incumbents. Perhaps, then, full government funding cannot produce further advantages for incumbents. This conclusion is subject to revision with changes in economic conditions, however.

Referenda. A **referendum** is a direct election in which citizens choose public policy without the immediate intervention of elected officeholders. Its use has often been proposed to overcome the perceived failings of legislatures, and the private wants–public means problem in particular. Several nations, states, and cities use referenda for various purposes.[21] Referenda can recall elected officeholders and make them face another election. They have also been used to decide on bonded indebtedness, state constitutional amendments, affirming (or denying) the legal rights of homosexuals, prohibiting smoking in public facilities, rescinding legislatively imposed bilingualism, and reducing taxes and spending.

Two forms of referenda are especially intriguing. The first is a negative referendum, which can overturn the acts of a legislative body. This system is used in Switzerland. If enough voters are opposed to new public policies enacted by the legislature, then referendum voting on those policies may eliminate them. This system might be used to reduce the frequency with which more blatant private-benefits legislation becomes law.

A second form of referendum is used in the city of Atlanta and in other municipalities. The city is prohibited from deficit spending in its annual operating budget. However, if the voters approve it in a referendum, the City Council can incur long-term debt for capital projects by issuing municipal bonds. Two kinds of motions usually appear on the ballot in these bond referenda. The first would establish bonded indebtedness to pay for public programs that really create private benefits for particular, identifiable neighborhoods or groups in the city. The second would create bonded indebted-

[21] See David Butler and Austin Ranney, *Referendums: A Comparative Study of Practice and Theory* (Washington, D.C.: American Enterprise Institute, 1978).

ness to finance programs more clearly akin to real public goods, including projects such as the construction of a new central library or a complete repaving of *all* roads. In these elections, members of each group that is pursuing a private benefit show up at the polls to vote *for* their respective proposals. While at the polls, and having paid the cost of voting, they proceed to vote *against* all of the other groups' private-benefit proposals. As a result, all or nearly all private-benefit programs are defeated. Voters then proceed to judge the public-goods programs on their merits. Some pass; others do not.

This referendum arrangement appears to have had some success in limiting the private wants–public means problem. However, it remains susceptible to manipulation, which was accomplished in the referendum establishing MARTA, Atlanta's rapid transit system. That program created a swamp full of private benefits, and the discussion of rapid transit systems earlier in this chapter accurately describes the system as adopted in Atlanta. MARTA supporters merely put enough private benefits together in the same referendum vote to have the program approved. Since the federal government pays for a substantial part of the program, its overall economic desirability was seldom questioned in *Atlanta.*

Direct elections have been scorned since the days of the Greek philosophers, and nearly every major political thinker in Western history who has considered the matter has judged direct democracy to be inherently flawed. The theoretical reason for this disdain seems apparent. Legislatures do enjoy obvious comparative advantages of knowledge and expertise in lawmaking. However, do-it-yourself democracy (lawmaking) has an inherent logic. This logic is best explained by supposing that there is some underlying issue dimension, which measures the proportion of public policy decisions made directly by voters or, conversely, by elected officeholders. Citizens and constitution writers might prefer and choose some equilibrium proportion along this dimension, from zero to 100 percent direct decisions. Wherever this equilibrium falls, an increase (or decrease) in legislators' abilities efficiently to carry out theoretical functions such as creating optimal levels of public goods, would result in an increase (or decrease) in the proportion of public choices made indirectly—by legislatures.

An increased demand for the use of referenda, in this view, could be attributed to a decline in elected officeholders' lawmaking abilities. Such a decline might be the result of their taking on a decidedly narrowly focused delegate role of producing private benefits rather than a broadly focused trustee role of producing public goods. In other words, referenda might be sought to correct the Pareto-inferior allocations resulting from the private wants–public means problem.

Nevertheless, referenda are susceptible to manipulation. Someone must administer a referendum, which provides this opportunity for manipulation, as Chapter 11 points out in its discussion of how bureaucrats set agendas for referendum votes. Furthermore, to call for a special referendum election or to put a referendum issue on the ballot in a regularly scheduled election, its backers must secure a number of signatures of registered voters, as determined by law. If the required number of signatures is low, referenda can be used capriciously by those with intense preferences who time and again call for referendum elections to decide on impossible motions. Access to the referendum process at low cost thus forces others to pay for yet another expensive election. But if threshold requirements for calling a referendum are too high, use of referenda becomes rare, and at some point their advantages might be lost.

Other reforms. This discussion does not exhaust the universe of possible election reforms. For example, each year House and Senate members consider the approval of a constitutional amendment abolishing the electoral college. Chapter 9 points out that this change could make a pure strategy public policy equilibrium in the electoral college irrelevant where none existed in the undifferentiated electorate. Or, a new pure strategy equilibrium in the undifferentiated electorate might arise where none existed in the electoral college. Even if such an equilibrium did exist before *and* after the change, the direct election of the president might shift it in any direction. The only definitive conclusion one might reach is a modest one. We do not know what effects the direct election of the president would have on public policy as a consequence of the (new) presence or absence of equilibria or of a change in the location of equilibria induced by abolishing the electoral college.

Nor do we know how the central problems of intense minorities and private wants–public means might become manifest if presidents were elected directly. If the members of an intense minority or of an interest group seeking the collective supply of private benefits were strategically located in a single state, and if that state suddenly became crucial for an electoral college victory, then the minority or interest group might expect to have its demands satisfied. However, under direct voting for the president, the effect of being concentrated in one state would be washed out, and a group could not expect success unless its numbers were large and its organization robust. Such predictions have a decided *ad hoc* quality, however. Therefore, they are not terribly satisfying.

Institutional Reforms

Proposals to reform various government institutions—the Congress, the presidency, the bureaucracy, and the courts—are commonplace, and they often entail procedural changes in two or more of these institutions at the same time. Reforms of institutional procedures by constitutional amendments have been relatively infrequent. The Twelfth Amendment, ratified in 1804, changed the method of electing the president. The Seventeenth Amendment, ratified in 1913, provided for direct election of senators. The Twentieth Amendment, ratified in 1933, shortened the period during which presidents would be lame ducks and more carefully defined congressional rights and procedures in the event that the president-elect or the vice-president-elect should die or otherwise be unable to serve. The Twenty-second Amendment, ratified in 1951, limited the president to two terms. The Twenty-fifth Amendment, ratified in 1967, specified procedures for making the vice-president acting president if the president became disabled. It also provided for filling vacancies in the office of vice-president. Beyond these procedural amendments, the first ten amendments restrict congressional rights to pass certain forms of legislation. However, most past institutional reforms have resulted from decisions directly taken by elected officeholders. Similarly, most but not all proposed reforms that have yet to be enacted appear to be taking a legislative rather than a constitutional amendment route.

Congressional reforms. Three broad groups of congressional reforms are chosen for discussion here. The first group concerns House and Senate members' terms of office. As Chapter 10 reports, there is some support for the view that these terms should be increased from two to four years for House members, reduced from six to four years for senators, and that House, Senate, and presidential elections should occur simultaneously.[22] Lengthened House terms would at least partially diminish the close attention representatives now give their districts. As a consequence, House members should be able to act a bit more like trustees and a bit less like delegates. A minor reduction in the private wants–public means problem could follow, since representatives might inspect various proposals for the collective supply of private goods with a bit more care. However, representatives' reduced attention to their districts might serve merely to raise the price of those private benefits they do decide to supply in the future. After terms are lengthened, access to House members might shift to relatively better-organized groups, which can afford to pay such costs. Ombudsman activities also might suffer. Of course, the effects of shortening Senate terms would be in the opposite direction.

The real intent of proposed reforms to coordinate presidential and congressional elections is to place House and Senate members under firmer presidential leadership while at the same time reducing the public policy disparities said to result from the election of presidents and House members at different times with different constituencies holding different preferences. Simultaneous terms and elections are predicted to create firmer presidential leadership and something closer to the British system, in which parties, rather than candidates, are elected to govern. Accordingly, this reform contemplates the emergence of coherent party platforms, which would give each party its public policy direction. Electing the president and House and Senate members at the same time might reduce the dispersion of public policy positions held by members of the majority party. Members of Congress from the president's party (usually the congressional majority) are more likely to be

---

[22] Louis W. Koenig, "More Power to the President (Not Less)," *New York Times Magazine,* January 3, 1965, p. 7.

elected pledged to the president's program than presently holds true. In sum, the adoption of this reform is expected to "produce a President and two houses of Congress in better harmony on policy and outlook than the present fragmented elections permit."[23]

This reform proposal might have more appeal in a political order in which the election agenda consists entirely of broad public policy questions—exclusively public goods—than in one with a highly fragmented electorate whose agenda consists principally of proposals to enact private benefits at collective cost. The hypothesis underlying this proposal—that somehow presidents respond less than House members to appeals of diverse interests—is naive. As Chapter 10 suggests, presidents face coalitions of minorities among members of the House and Senate and in the electorate. Presidents seem as susceptible as legislators to the private wants–public means problem, even though the stakes they play with are usually higher because access to them is more difficult.

Since voters in presidential and congressional elections are drawn from the same constituency, differently divided, we cannot say what might happen if all of their elections occurred simultaneously. Perhaps this might create coinciding pure strategy equilibria for presidents and for the House and Senate taken together; perhaps not. However, endowing presidents with election coattails would probably give a special advantage to the majority of the moment at the beginning of the four-year term. But over that period, the congressional and electoral majority might increasingly become dominated by a coalition of minorities, particularly because the president would not have the benefit of political information from the results of an off-year election. Thus, the incumbent president might fail to adjust his policies to a changing preference distribution and so be defeated. The new president might then be chosen by a coalition of minorities. Therefore, the public-policy-making process again may become fragmented at the outset.

A second set of congressional reform proposals would restructure the committee system.[24] First, committees would be consolidated so that each committee oversees a single public policy area. Second, the Appropriations, Ways and Means, and Budget Committees in the House and the Appropriations, Finance, and Budget Committees in the Senate would be merged in each chamber to form a single policy committee on taxing and spending. Third, committee chairmanships and memberships would be rotated among House members at regular intervals.

The proposal to combine committees so that each exercises comprehensive control over a single subject matter grows out of the belief that a fragmen-

---

[23] Koenig, "More Power to the President (Not Less)," p. 7.

[24] These reforms, among others, are suggested in Donald M. Fraser and Iric Nathanson, "Rebuilding the House of Representatives," in Norman S. Ornstein, ed., *Congress in Change: Evolution and Reform* (New York: Praeger, 1975), pp. 288–294. But they are not identical to the Fraser-Nathanson reforms, especially with regard to merging the Appropriations and Ways and Means committees.

tation of committee jurisdictions creates inferior public policies. For example, Table 13.2 shows that in the first five months of the Ninety-fifth Congress (January–June 1977), various energy bills were submitted in eighteen different House committees and various health bills in sixteen. The earlier discussions in Chapter 9 about committee decision making and in Chapter 11 about iron triangles and the position of congressional committees in those triangles provides evidence that fragmented committee jurisdictions allow the members of each committee to create private benefits at collective cost in every public policy area.

Proposals to consolidate committees over single subject areas seek to address the problems of policy fragmentation and lack of direction rather than the demonstrable Pareto inferiority of the resulting public policies. However, committee consolidation might reduce the effects of the private wants–public means problem. Combining the Appropriations, Ways and Means (or Senate Finance), and Budget committees would also force members to confront directly the costs of the various programs for which they now separately raise, authorize, and appropriate funds. In sum, budget constraints might constrain even a bit more.

Committee consolidation is certainly worth trying, and in recent years legislators have accomplished limited parts of it, especially in the Senate. However, this reform runs the risk of merely increasing the private-goods stakes but certainly not the fact of private-goods production. For example, under present arrangements, a community hospital in some small town might succeed in extracting private benefits in the form of a bill giving it and a few other small hospitals a special subsidy. The hospital is likely to receive some benefits because it has so many points of access into congressional decision making. But if all health expenditures were consolidated under a single committee, its leadership might become relatively less responsive to demands from small organizations or individual firms but relatively more responsive to the demands of larger organizations with greater resources. Such consolidations immediately contract the available points of access to the Congress. Smaller hospitals thus might become relatively more disadvantaged by laws enacted under consolidation, and larger hospitals might find greater advantages in them. Of course, larger organizations do extract private benefits under current committee arrangements, but their ability to do so might increase, and the ability of smaller organizations might decline, under a consolidated committee system.

This same pattern should hold true for most persons, groups, and firms. The free-rider problem of political organization will only make it worse. For example, a large medical center or a consortium of such centers can far more easily solve their own organization (free-rider) problems than can widely scattered small hospitals and clinics. In competing for access to a single consolidated health committee in Congress, the smaller hospitals and clinics will do less well than they do presently under a widely dispersed, congressional committee subject-matter jurisdiction.

Table 13.2 Energy and Health Bills Referred to House Committees in the First Five Months of the Ninty-fifth Congress *(in percentages)*

Committee Referred to	**Energy Bills**	**Health Bills**
Agriculture	4	2
Appropriations	1	1
Armed Services	1	1
Banking, Finance, and Urban Affairs	9	1
Education and Labor	3	–
Government Operations	3	10
House Administration	1	1
Interior and Insular Affairs	10	1
International Relations	8	1
Interstate and Foreign Commerce	27	45
Judiciary	4	3
Merchant Marine and Fisheries	5	1
Post Office and Civil Service	1	2
Public Works and Transportation	9	1
Rules	1	1
Science and Technology	9	–
Small Business	3	–
Veterans Affairs	–	2
Ways and Means	2	28
Total	101*	101*

Source: Adapted from U.S. Congress, House, Commission on Administrative Review, *Administrative Reorganization and Legislative Management,* vol. 2, H. Doc. 95–232, 95th Cong., 1st sess., 1977, p. 33. As appearing in Samuel C. Patterson, "The Semi-Sovereign Congress," in Anthony King, ed., *The New American Political System,* © 1978 by American Enterprise Institute for Public Policy Research, Washington, D.C., p. 162.

*Does not add to 100 because of rounding errors.

Advocates of rotating committee memberships and chairmanships on a regular basis note that committees often "become . . . either 'graveyards' or 'unrestrained promotional agencies' for their jurisdictional matters."[25] Rotation might reduce the private wants–public means problem. Then again, it might not. Representatives' electoral connections remain untouched by this reform. Therefore, the importance of universalism and inter-committee reciprocity might increase because of it. Nothing then will have been accomplished except to put inexperienced people on committees about whose subject matter they have little knowledge. These naïfs will then become easier

[25] Fraser and Nathanson, "Rebuilding the House of Representatives," p. 293.

marks for bureaucrats and executive-branch members with superior knowledge and expertise about the relevant public policy area.

The final set of proposals for congressional reform considered here involve congressional control of the executive branch and the bureaucracy. House and Senate members show a growing tendency to pass laws enabling the president to take certain actions that either will require subsequent congressional approval or can be overturned by a majority vote of a quorum in one or both chambers. Similarly, recent proposals to reform the regulatory process argue for a legislative veto with which House and Senate members could overturn the actions of a bureau or regulatory commission. These reforms are intended to suppress the "lawmaking" capacities of the executive branch and the independent regulatory commissions, and to bring the "rules" and actions promulgated by appointed officeholders into greater conformity with policies enunciated in the legislative branch.

Clearly, these reforms would not in any sense reduce the intense minority problem, the cyclical majority problem, or the private wants–public means problem. House and Senate members would still make their legislative decisions in a political environment in which these problems continue to exist. These reforms also overlook the obvious: bureaucratic decisions today are probably pretty much the way House and Senate members want them, so it is not clear what further congressional controls might accomplish.

Nevertheless, there is some possibility that the more outlandish regulations growing out of bureaucratic processes might become susceptible to control by a legislative veto, although such a veto could be used to overcome Pareto-preferred bureaucratic decisions as well as Pareto-inferior ones. When House and Senate members reach a season of especially heightened concern for interest-group demands—election time—they might try to overrule any bureau decisions that would shut off or reduce the flow of private benefits to particular groups. In sum, a congressional veto of executive branch and bureaucratic decisions would probably only serve to ensure that the private goods that executive-branch members and bureaucrats dispense are more nearly in line with the wishes of House and Senate members.

Presidential reforms. While proposals to reform the presidency are as varied as those aimed at the Congress, they enjoy a higher salience than do congressional reforms because of the president's preeminence. Most proposals concern the president's relations with the Congress. Recall from Chapter 10 that such proposals are very much conditioned by public policy conflicts. For example, when reform advocates agree with the president but disagree with the congressional lawmaking equilibrium, their reforms seek to increase the president's control over the Congress. The opposite preference for reform happens when reform advocates side with the Congress against the administration. However, certain reform proposals are more nearly general because they would affect and be affected by our three central problems.

First, former President Jimmy Carter and others have recommended that the president be limited to a single six-year term. Analyzing this reform's effects is difficult because since the ratification of the Twenty-second Amendment in 1951, we have had precious little experience with second-term presidents, those who knew they could not serve another term. Eisenhower made it through two terms, but Kennedy was assassinated with more than a year of his first term left. Johnson was entitled to run for another term but (perhaps judiciously) decided against it. Less than a year after Nixon began his second term, he was desperate for public support, and not long thereafter he resigned. Ford was never elected to a full term. Nor did Carter win a second term. Thus, since the ratification of the Twenty-second Amendment, no president except Eisenhower has served out a term during which he knew he was legally barred from running again. Consequently, we have little or no historical experience of how presidents act who are not running for reelection—who have no palpable electoral connection.

A problem of conjectural variation arises. On the one hand, as Chapter 7 observes in theory and Chapter 10 in practice, presidents confront coalition-of-minorities challenges in the Congress and in the electorate. This problem may even have grown more severe in recent years than it once was. Presidents already enjoy a relatively short period during which their public and congressional support allows them to propose legislation without serious opposition. Lengthening the president's term by 50 percent might allow the coalition of minorities against him to consolidate and grow even larger. In recent years, presidential popularity in the electorate and support in the Congress have reached such low levels at term's end that further erosion could make presidential leadership impossible.

On the other hand, as noted in Chapter 7 and earlier in this chapter, sometimes opposition-party members actuate the formation of a coalition of minorities even though they share no intense preferences with its members. Their intention is to topple the incumbent party or officeholder, not to change public policy to satisfy the intense minority. However, if presidents were limited to a single six-year term, there would be no reason to try to undermine their chances of reelection. Hence, there would be one less incentive for using a coalition-of-minorities strategy. Other reasons for using it might remain, however. For example, opposition-party members might try to undermine the president's public support simply to reduce the positive effects of his coattails and endorsements in the two congressional elections during his term, and to shatter public and congressional support for his current legislative programs. One cannot estimate in advance how important these considerations might become in providing incentives for using a coalition-of-minorities strategy. However, they would probably remain important, and therefore presidents might find themselves running a caretaker government in the last two years of their six-year term.

What of the private wants–public means problem? A single six-year term might allow presidents to take a devil-may-care attitude toward reelection considerations. Presidents, it is argued, would then be able to lead the government without worrying about various interest groups or demands for private benefits. But if the president must consult the Congress to pass legislation, he probably could not overcome congressional incentives to pass private-goods legislation. Indeed, interest-group leaders no longer would worry about the president's reelection chances; they would have to contribute to a presidential campaign only once every six years, and their financial resources would become otherwise meaningless to the president. Yet, they might raise their bids for congressional action.[26] Demands for private benefits would shift almost entirely to the Congress. Even if the president vetoed the resulting legislation, a two-thirds vote overturning his veto would be easier to accomplish by increasing universalism and spreading collectively supplied private benefits far and wide.

A second set of proposals for presidential reform contemplates making the president more like the British prime minister. These reforms include provisions for holding a congressional vote of no confidence, after which a new presidential election would be called, and for allowing cabinet officers to sit as members of the House or Senate or drawing cabinet officers from the Congress. These reforms are proposed variously to create greater presidential accountability to the Congress, greater agreement between the legislative and executive branches on matters of public policy, and the possibility of presidents either reconfirming or terminating their electoral mandates. Such sweeping changes are difficult to assess, especially since most proposals fail to adopt the entire British system. For example, it has not yet been seriously suggested that House and Senate members should choose the president, as members of Parliament now choose the prime minister. Nor can the president and his cabinet resign under these proposals and thus compel a new congressional election.

Even so, the British system has not escaped the private wants–public means problem. If anything, this difficulty has grown worse in Great Britain than in the United States because parliamentary votes of no confidence, which can topple a government, make the electoral connection between legislators and interest groups even more secure. The cyclical majorities problem will remain in any legislative body. But, public policy disagreements between the legislative and executive branches might be reduced by making the president directly responsible to House and Senate members and vice versa.

Bureaucratic reform. In the last few years, the president and members of Congress have considered various proposals for reforming the bureaucracy. Some have been adopted. Many have not. Three sets of proposals have been advanced. The first set invokes internal structural reforms, which seek to make bureaucrats act more efficiently by changing internal procedures. One such proposal would have bureaus adopt advanced data processing methods and management techniques to modernize and streamline operations. An-

---

[26] A similar shift of giving to congressional campaigns occurred following public funding of presidential elections in the early 1970s.

other, already partially implemented, would have agencies prepare benefit-cost or benefit-risk analyses of major rules changes and proposed projects. A third proposal, also partially implemented, would exempt high-level bureaucrats from the protection of civil service regulations so that they might be more easily hired and fired.

Making internal operations more efficient always seems desirable, but it avoids the more important and prior question of "efficiency for what purpose?" Those who believe that a particular bureau should not exist or that its job should not be performed in the public sector (and perhaps not be performed at all) do not want the bureau to be more efficient. For example, pacifists are less than indifferent to the efficiency of the DOD. And, most sensible industrialists would prefer to have both the Justice Department's Antitrust Division and the FTC's Bureau of Competition staffed by bunglers rather than by competent attorneys. This ambivalence about the internal efficiency of bureaus merely reflects the ambiguity about and disagreement over the goals that the leaders of such organizations are supposed to pursue. Bureaucrats will probably act efficiently only to the extent that efficiency finds some reinforcement in their operational code.

The degree of technical operating efficiency achieved by various bureaus is also largely a function of presidential and congressional preferences and demands. The IRS is probably the most efficient tax-collecting organization in the world. But IRS efficiency is closely related to the incentives of presidents and members of Congress. They prefer a bureau that extracts as much money from the population as possible in as painless a manner as possible. They have no comparable incentive to see that HHS is run efficiently. Indeed, their incentives sometimes run in the opposite direction.

Bureau operating efficiency bears little or no relationship to the three central problems except that inefficient bureau operations allow legislators to perform ombudsmen services for their constituents. As Chapters 9 and 11 observe, these services result in the creation of distinctly private goods for individual voters. House and Senate members would thus be ambivalent about enormous improvements in the efficiency of bureau operations.[27]

A second set of proposals would try to solve many problems of federal bureaus by reducing their independence and placing more intensive control and oversight in the hands of the president and members of Congress. One such reform calls for **sunset legislation,** which would require each bureau to

---

[27] We should also point out that achieving efficiency of internal operations is itself costly. Therefore, perfect efficiency may be neither possible nor desirable. For example, a Social Security Administration with flawless internal efficiency would see to it that all recipients received their monthly payments and that such payments always arrived on time. A less efficient administration might see to it that 99.9 percent of recipients received their payments within two days of the date payment is due. However, the more efficient administration could pay only 90 percent of what the less efficient one could afford on the same budget. After all, efficiency costs money. Most recipients would prefer the slightly more risky payments by the less efficient administration.

undergo periodic review. Unless the president and members of Congress acted positively by passing a law, the agency would go out of business. Another reform would allow the president and members of Congress to order the reconsideration of particular agency decisions. A third reform would require different agencies to coordinate their activities. For instance, the DOE could not undertake policies that seriously undermine environmental quality, while the EPA could not adopt regulations that substantially reduce automobile fuel economy.

The central weakness of these proposals is that they ignore the acquiescence and sometimes active cooperation of the president and members of Congress in the present state of affairs. An act of Congress could have implemented any of these proposals at an earlier date. These proposals place the burden of reforming federal bureaus squarely on the shoulders of the president and members of Congress, who bear a substantial responsibility for the problems under consideration. Moreover, any residual desires among bureaucrats to produce optimal levels of public goods efficiently might seriously be jeopardized by placing bureaus under the control of House and Senate members and *their* electoral connections. Insofar as interest groups demand the public supply of private benefits or coalitions of intense minorities threaten both the president and members of Congress, increased presidential and congressional control of the bureaus might also increase bureaucrats' sensitivity to demands for private benefits and coalition-of-minorities problems.

A final set of reform proposals, reflected in the recent deregulation activities of the CAB and ICC, rests on the belief that most problems of bureaucratic action are inherent in any bureaucracy, probably as a result of unclear measures of public-goods production. As long as bureaus continue to perform various public services, these problems will remain. Therefore, an appropriate strategy might be to reduce the citizenry's reliance on bureaus for the production of various goods and services. As an alternative, federal agencies might try to contract more activities out to the private sector. For example, the VA could become simply an insurance agency, compensating veterans for stays in private-sector hospitals. All VA hospitals could then be closed or sold off. Alternatively, many present bureau activities could be carried on entirely in the private sector, with little or no public-sector control. The United States Post Office provides a likely target for this reform.

The immediate problem with these reforms, as with so many others discussed earlier, is that they are not politically acceptable. Neither the VA nor the Post Office is staffed with apathetic or politically inept people. They vote. They understand the nature of the public policies that affect them. And, they are well connected through various interest groups to different members of Congress. In very specialized instances, such as with airline regulation, the benefits to consumers of deregulation become so large that a real electoral advantage went to the officeholders who supported it and electoral punishment to those who did not. However, for most forms of regulation and other bureaucratic activities, the costs imposed on the public, while chronic and large in the aggregate, are not individually great enough to become election issues. Hence, reforms such as airline deregulation are certain to be rare. They may also be only temporary, since the underlying political forces that created the regulations—the demands for private benefits at collective cost—have not been removed.

Another problem with this set of reforms is that they cannot be accomplished by parts. For example, if VA hospitals were closed and veterans were directly subsidized only for their health care, this would still be an inefficient program: the veteran-recipient would prefer a cash transfer of an equivalent amount of money. Similarly, private hospitals would suddenly become extremely interested in VA policies, and especially those concerning hospital eligibility standards for taking care of veterans. These problems pervade most agencies that contract services out to the private sector. Suppliers of services and other goods quickly become another set of agency clients. The preferences of these new clients soon are reflected in the legislative and regulatory processes.

Judicial reform. Many proposals to reform the judicial process, especially at the federal level, are really issue-specific attempts to limit the Supreme Court's appellate jurisdiction over particular public policy areas. For example, in the wake of various Supreme Court decisions requiring school busing to achieve racial integration, prohibiting prayers and other religious observances in the public schools, and reversing state anti-abortion statutes, various members of Congress who opposed these decisions submitted bills to deprive the Court of future appellate jurisdiction in the relevant policy areas. Most such bills were buried in committee, and thus House and Senate procedures afforded some protection to the Court's continuing jurisdiction over these matters. Concerning our three central problems, little can be said about proposals to limit the Court's jurisdiction except to point out that they usually arise in the presence of intense minorities.

Other proposals for judicial reform are not so policy-specific. For example, one set of proposed reforms seeks to reduce the extensive case loads now faced by most courts in the United States. Proposed reforms include computerizing control of case flows, expanding the number of judges, eliminating the diversity jurisdiction of federal courts, establishing a national court of appeals to screen cases for Supreme Court consideration, and increasing the use of private arbitration procedures.[28] In earlier attempts to reduce case loads, state and local district attorneys developed the practice of plea bargaining, which has become highly controversial.

That the case loads of the courts have substantially increased in recent

[28] See, for example, *Federal Judicial Center Report of the Study Group on the Case Load of the Supreme Court* (Washington, D.C.: Administrative Office of U.S. Courts, 1973).

years cannot be doubted. Table 13.3 shows the remarkable increase in federal district and appeals court case loads between 1962 and 1979. This increase is far larger than the increase in population over the same period. One prediction suggests that "if the growth rate of federal appeals remains constant, by the year 2010 there will be 1 million appeals decided each year, requiring 5,000 [appeals court] judges. . . . With appeals running at 10% of the total cases initiated . . . the [district] courts would be hit with 10 million cases annually. Long before then, of course, the system would have collapsed."[29]

In most civil cases, the proposed reforms to diminish case loads would probably be ineffective and perhaps even counterproductive. As Chapter 12 points out, overwhelming case loads do not evolve from the judiciary's inefficient operation, nor are they necessarily the product of empaneling too few judges. Furthermore, judges themselves already have an incentive to try to reduce case loads. Even if all of these proposed reforms were adopted, it is doubtful that case loads would substantially decline. Indeed, they might even grow.

An understanding of the case load problem begins with the realization that it is really a private wants–public means problem. When plaintiffs in ordinary civil suits and defendants in criminal trials refuse to settle out of court or plea bargain, respectively, they turn to the court for the provision of a private benefit: damages, specific performance, or a verdict of *not guilty.* But the use of the courts is heavily subsidized. Plaintiffs and defendants in civil cases need not fully pay for the use of the physical facility or the time of courtroom personnel. Hence, the amount of courtroom services demanded is greater than it would be if litigants had to bear the full cost. A "correct" price would ration the supply of courtroom services so that there would be no delays because of shortages. (Delays might still occur because of litigation strategies.) The present system rations courtroom services by waiting. In other words, the extensive case load facing each judge is analogous to the line of automobiles waiting to fill up at gas stations during shortages. However, unlike gasoline shortages, in litigation, "justice delayed is justice denied." If the number of judges were substantially increased, the cost of using the judicial process (as measured by the cost of delays) would decline. More people would then file suits, for they could expect their cases to be resolved more quickly. Dockets would soon fill up again, and there would probably be no net gain.

While the public-goods aspects of legal precedents are fully acknowledged in Chapter 12, most *individual* litigants nevertheless view the judicial process as a private good. Part of the cost of supplying that good is borne by taxpayers generally. Thus, a potential litigant need not be completely concerned about whether the legal action contemplated will produce expected benefits in excess of *full* expected costs, just as the potential polluter need not

---

[29] Professor John Barton of Stanford University, quoted in *Business Week,* June 6, 1977, pp. 58–64, as cited in William H. Adams, III, "Would We Rather Fight than Settle?" *Florida Bar Journal,* 51 (October 1977), p. 498.

Table 13.3 Federal Court Case Loads, 1962–1979

Fiscal Year	*District Courts** Filed	Terminated	Pending June 30	Fiscal Year	*Appeals Courts* Filed	Appeals Terminated	Pending	Increase in appeals pending
1962	61,836	57,996	67,968	1962	4,823	4,167	3,031	656
1963	63,630	62,379	69,219	1963	5,437	5,011	3,457	426
1964	66,930	63,954	72,195	1964	6,023	5,700	3,780	323
1965	67,678	65,478	74,395	1965	6,766	5,771	4,775	995
1966	70,906	66,184	79,117	1966	7,183	6,571	5,387	612
1967	70,961	70,172	79,906	1967	7,903	7,527	5,763	376
1968	71,449	68,873	82,482	1968	9,116	8,264	6,615	852
1969	77,193	73,354	86,321	1969	10,248	9,014	7,849	1,234
1970	87,321	80,435	93,207	1970	11,662	10,699	8,812	963
1971	93,396	86,563	100,040	1971	12,788	12,368	9,232	420
1972	96,173	95,181	101,032	1972	14,535	13,828	9,939	707
1973	98,560	98,259	101,333	1973	15,629	15,112	10,456	517
1974	103,530	97,633	107,230	1974	16,436	15,422	11,470	1,014
1975	117,320	104,783	119,767	1975	16,658	16,000	12,128	658
1976	130,597	110,175	140,189	1976	18,408	16,426	14,110	1,982
1977	130,567	117,150	153,606	1977	19,118	17,784	15,444	1,334
1978	138,770	125,914	166,462	1978	18,918	17,714	16,648	1,204
1979	154,666	143,323	177,805	1979	20,219	18,928	17,939	1,291
% increase				% change				
1979				1979				
over 1962	150.1	147.1	161.6	over 1962	319.2	354.2	491.9	–
over 1978	11.5	13.8	6.8	over 1978	6.9	6.9	7.8	–

Source: Administrative Office of the United States Courts, *1979 Annual Report,* as appearing in *Congressional Quarterly Weekly Report,* 38 (February 16, 1980), p. 401.

* Civil cases only.

be concerned with the costs that his use of the ambient air as a "sink" imposes on others. Hence, there is too much litigation and too much pollution.[30] Various reform proposals do little to get at this central problem.

Here, one confronts a clear quandary. On the one hand, "justice delayed is justice denied." On the other, justice with an explicit price tag has not yet been accepted. Of course, people do pay for justice and for the associated court services. They also pay somewhat higher attorneys' fees because of a greater demand for attorneys' services consequent to the increased litigation. However, an overuse of the courts remains.

An increase in the cost of court services would help to eliminate backlogs. Most court filing fees were set years ago; they have not been increased to reflect inflation; and, they only partially cover the cost of filing suit itself. Even a modest increase in these fees would probably substantially reduce current case loads. The public defender's office or an individual judge could be empowered to waive such fees for indigent litigants.

Attempts to limit jurisdictions, especially appellate jurisdictions, of various courts pose another problem, however. The analysis in Chapter 12 reveals that the amount of litigation increases when disputants cannot agree on the probability that each will win in court. This failure of their probability estimates to coincide in turn results from a lack of clear precedent governing their case or from a known capriciousness on the part of particular judges in applying clear precedent. If precedent is absent or unclear, then *more,* not less, litigation is desirable. Without such litigation, efficient rules will have fewer opportunities to evolve. Stifling litigation could thus be counterproductive.

Clearly, the present partial bearing of litigation costs by the public sector can be explained by the public-goods production associated with making (efficient) precedents. Unfortunately, legal scholars have not yet discovered a constitutionally permissible way to subsidize precedent-creating cases through their entire course of litigation and appeal while charging litigants in cases governed by clear precedent the full cost of court services.[31]

SYSTEMIC REFORMS

The Founding Fathers created a structure of checks and balances with interlocking control of and responsibility for public policy. If something went wrong in one institution, then the members of another were expected to correct it. For example, senators and representatives can override the president's veto, accept or reject the treaties he negotiates, confirm or fail to confirm his appointments, direct him to execute certain laws in a specified manner, and impeach and convict him if that should become necessary. On

---

[30] Adams, "Would We Rather Fight than Settle?" p. 498, footnote 1.

[31] William M. Landes and Richard A. Posner, "Adjudication as a Private Good," *Journal of Legal Studies,* 7 (March 1979), pp. 235–284.

the other hand, the president can veto acts of Congress, call Congress into session, and lecture its members at will. Supreme Court members are nominated by the president and confirmed by the Senate, but they can declare presidential decrees and acts of Congress unconstitutional.

Given the nature of these checks and balances, citizens seldom contemplate thoroughgoing reforms of the entire political and governmental structure in the United States. Most people believe that if something is amiss in one branch of government it will soon be corrected in another. Hence, piecemeal reform has usually been the order of the day.

The Founding Fathers surely did not contemplate the central problems described throughout this book.[32] More important, these problems afflict decisions taken at every stage of the public-policy-making process in the United States. For example, a coalition of minorities can arise in the electorate, be reflected in the preferences and decisions of House and Senate members, affect the president's popular support and chances of reelection, become entrenched in bureaucratic decision making, and find voice in the most intractable cases brought before the Supreme Court. Cyclical majorities and the closely related problem of Arrow's impossibility theorem are embedded in any voting system. The private wants–public means problem similarly afflicts public policy decision making at every stage. Because checks and balances might not work when the same problems affect every part of government and politics, proposals for systemic reform are becoming more common.

Tax and Spending Limits

One proposed systemic reform would place limits on taxing and government spending. These would fix taxes or tax rates at some preestablished level, which government expenditures could not exceed except in times of emergency. (A constitutional amendment for this purpose is reprinted at the end of Appendix B.) In sum, government would be limited as to how much it could tax, and spending could not exceed tax revenues. Some tax and spending-limit proposals would only affect taxes; others would only affect spending, and a few would limit both. However, all of these proposals would affect the three central problems described here.

First, a strict spending limit would mean that no new private-benefit programs could be created unless either older programs were deleted or tax revenue (but not tax rates) expanded to reflect an expanding economy. Tax and spending limit reforms thus would appear partially to solve the private wants–public means problem. However, that appearance must be seriously

[32] There is one exception: Madison certainly understood the problems of intense minorities and private wants–public means. He saw these as derived from the evils of "faction." But Madison believed that the Constitution overcame the problem of factions. He seems to have been in error. See James Madison, *Federalist Paper No. 10,* in Paul L. Ford, ed., *The Federalist* (New York: Holt, 1898).

qualified, for various programs now in existence display varying degrees of "publicness" (nondivisibility) and "privateness" (divisibility). The winners in the newly constrained legislative appropriations process would be those best organized for political action. But as Chapter 6 points out, superior organization goes hand in hand with the ability to deal in private benefits. Programs with relatively greater levels of "privateness" thus would more likely be retained or adopted than those with relatively greater levels of "publicness." In other words, a spending limit might begin a competitive process in Congress, which would tend to eliminate those programs that are more nearly "public" than "private."

Second, the legislative and electoral processes will continue to be afflicted by a lack of pure strategy equilibria. This raises the possibilities not only of ambiguity and agenda control but also of a collective inability to choose the "correct" tax and spending levels. It will not be known in advance whether the tax and spending levels chosen will in any sense be better than those arrived at in the present, albeit fragmented, political process.

Third, since taxing and spending represent important political resources for all government personnel, when these become limited, other resources will be sought, although these will probably be less valued. One such resource is regulation. As Chapter 11 points out, taxation by regulation—the enforced private-sector transfer of money or services between two or more persons or firms—is often carried out by regulatory decree. The regulatory process creates benefits for some and costs for others. James Madison identified the political problem of private-goods redistribution by regulation: "Every new regulation concerning commerce or revenue, or in any manner affecting the value of the different species of property, presents a new harvest to those who watch the change, and trace its consequences; a harvest, reaped not by themselves, but by the toils and cares of the great body of their fellow-citizens. This is a state of things in which it may be said with some truth that laws are made for the *few,* not for the many."[33]

An inability to tax and spend directly will probably lead the agents of government to find indirect methods of producing private, divisible benefits. Hence, a new flow of regulations might follow the imposition of tax and spending limits. Regulations, which are really indirect taxes, seem especially useful for satisfying the demands of intense minorities, for those with intensely held preferences very often seem more interested in regulating the actions of others than in monetary appropriations. Of course, if those with intense preferences find political satisfaction cheaper to come by, they will demand more of it.

In spite of these problems, tax and spending limits may be attractive because they directly assail the public bad involved in the private wants–public means problem. The size of government itself, including the level of direct and indirect taxes, is set not by conscious consideration but by thousands of

---

[33] James Madison, *Federalist Paper No. 62,* as cited in Ford, *The Federalist.*

smaller decisions, many of which produce private goods at collective costs. Tax and spending limits put a direct monetary ceiling on the size of government, and by doing so, they tend to force a recognition of how much the component parts of government actually cost (directly). In this sense, tax and spending limits bear a strong resemblance to pollution-control laws that impose air quality standards on large geographical areas. Both pollution and taxes are by-products of other activities. Agents in the public sector try to control the polluting activities of those in the private sector, but up until now no one has discovered a way for those in the private sector to control the tax and spending activities of those in the public sector. Tax and spending limits provide a new but largely untested control mechanism.

Decentralization

A second systemic reform proposal would not directly limit the level of public-sector activity, but would shift the decision-making locus to smaller units of government. Chapter 1 describes the increasing centralization of government activities in the United States. There may be good reasons for accomplishing certain tasks under the direction of a more centralized government. For example, economies of scale may be present. However, centralizing political decision making sometimes effectively cancels competition among jurisdictions. By maintaining government activities over smaller geographical areas and populations, it becomes possible to generate competition. Even a modest proliferation of government units also can offer citizens a degree of choice that is not available to them in a more nearly centralized system.

Reform by decentralization can ameliorate the intense minority problem merely by allowing people to move. For example, if those opposed to abortion do not wish to live in a community where it is allowed, they can move to one where it is not. Alternatively, those who do not wish to have the agents of government interfere with their right to have an abortion can move to a community where abortion is legal. Certainly, not everyone who shares an intense preference is going to move. However, the possibility of moving to a competing city or state limits the cost that can be imposed on any one person. It also provides for a closer reflection of citizens' preferences than might be possible in a relatively more centralized regime. Intense minorities can certainly arise in smaller political jurisdictions. But, the availability of another place to live reduces the extent to which the members of intense minorities can impose their preferences on others (and vice versa) unless "interstate warfare" breaks out.

Decentralization is not likely to solve the cyclical majorities problem unless it leads people with the same preferences to congregate in the same jurisdictions. Nor would decentralization necessarily ameliorate the private wants–public means problem. Certainly, claims for private benefits would be reduced in smaller areas, and their blatantness might become more apparent.

However, smaller nations, such as Great Britain, have not been more successful in avoiding this problem than have larger ones, such as the United States.

Still, jurisdictions that succeed relative to others in finding partial solutions to the private wants–public means and the cyclical majority problems would probably attract more citizens. *Ceteris paribus,* those who move to such jurisdictions are those who expect to do better under the political arrangements adopted in them. Those already living in such areas will find their wealth increased by the newcomers' demands for property and established services, thus creating an added incentive to find solutions. These two problems lead to Pareto-inferior results, and jurisdictions that solve them will improve the lot of their citizens.

Chapter 1 also notes that direct or indirect interpolity competition partially resolves the problems of setting correct prices and outputs for public goods.[34] While externalities continue to be a natural consequence of public price and output decisions, people will be able to live in jurisdictions where these problems are more nearly resolved to their satisfaction. Problems of economies of scale remain, and decentralization may become too expensive because of the economies of scale forgone. Even so, the scale economy problem may be overcome by a voluntary and creative intermingling of programs at various levels of government.

FINAL THOUGHTS ON CHANGE AND REFORM

All proposals for public-sector reform share two important characteristics. First, the full consequences of each reform are almost never fully anticipated. For example, the reforms discussed in this chapter have been analyzed in terms of their ability to increase or diminish the effects of three central problems. But there are certainly other criteria by which reforms might be judged. And, because of the complexity of the subjects under study, it is not even clear that the effects on these three central problems have been correctly anticipated. Thus, reforms should be made with great care. This is neither a counsel of despair nor an admonition not to change the way things are. However, it is a clear warning of a great human capacity to make things worse with the best of intentions.

The second characteristic of reform helps to avoid some unanticipated consequences. Among all known proposals for reform, all costless changes have already been made. TANSTAAFL. That is, any reform not yet adopted is probably going to impose costs on some people. Often, those citizens' protests will indicate where certain unanticipated consequences of reform might lie. But these consequences are very real and should not be overlooked or discounted.

---

[34] See Charles M. Tiebout, "A Pure Theory of Local Expenditures," *Journal of Political Economy,* 64 (October 1956), pp. 416–424.

QUESTIONS FOR DISCUSSION AND REVIEW

1. As a general rule, are piecemeal reforms superior to systemic reforms? Why? Why not? Are different levels of reform better for some problems than others? Which problems? Which reforms?
2. Do domestic and foreign policy differ in how they are affected by the three central problems? In what manner? How would each of these two public policy areas be affected by various reforms described in this chapter?
3. Which central problems do you regard as most and least serious? Why? Are there other problems that are more serious? Why? Could any of these be regarded as a derivative of one of the three central problems? Why? Why not?
4. Considering the reasons for collective action described in Chapter 3, how well do you think public choice in the United States is working? Would any of the reforms listed in this chapter make it work better or worse?
5. Do you believe individual human beings are responsible for or can do anything about the three central problems? Why? If so, who?
6. In terms of public policy, does it make much difference who the members of Congress, the administration, the bureaucracy, or the courts are? Why? Why not?
7. If solving one or more of the three central problems would make people better off, why do entrepreneurs fail to come forward to solve them?

NEW CONCEPTS AND TERMS

approval voting
benefits in kind
merit goods
piecemeal reforms
referendum
sunset legislation
systemic reforms

Appendix A

Glossary

This glossary contains a brief definition or description of all *New Concepts and Terms* listed at the end of each chapter and appearing in the appropriate chapter in boldface. The chapter in which the text first discusses the concept or term is noted in parentheses. Italicized words are concepts or terms discussed elsewhere in the glossary. Entries in quotation marks followed by an asterisk (*) are from *Black's Law Dictionary,* 5th ed. (St. Paul, Minn.: West, 1979).

Abstention from alienation (5). Abstention that can occur if the *citizen's* preferred candidate is not close enough to his own most preferred issue position (*bliss point*). See *abstention from indifference; calculus of voting.*

Abstention from indifference (5). Abstention that can occur if the *citizen* does not perceive a sufficiently large utility difference between the election of the two candidates, that is, if $B = U_d - U_r$ or $U_r - U_d$ is not great enough. See *abstention from alienation; calculus of voting.*

Active-negative president (10). One who devotes a great amount of energy to the job of being president and who believes that he must fend off threats from a hostile political and governmental environment to defend himself and the nation against misfortune. See *active-positive president; passive-negative president; passive-positive president.*

Active-positive president (10). One who devotes a great amount of energy to the job of being president and who believes that his political and governmental environment is to be manipulated for positive purposes. See *active-negative president; passive-negative president; passive-positive president.*

Activist (6). Participant in politics who does "more" than simply vote but "less" than run for office. See *amateur activist; professional activist.*

Administrative law (12). The body of law controlling the procedures of various government bureaus, agencies, commissions, and administrations. See *civil law; common law; constitutional law; criminal law; organic law; property law; statutory law.*

Advertising (9). Activities of elected representatives to "package" themselves and give themselves public recognition, much like brand-name recognition. See *credit claiming; position taking.*

Advice and consent (9). The constitutionally granted right of members of the Senate to approve or withhold approval of treaties and certain presidential appointments.

Allocation strategy (7). In *election* campaigns, the candidate's *strategy* in devoting nonspatial resources of money, time, and labor to various uses and in different parts of his constituency. See *attribute strategy; coalition strategy; issue ambiguity strategy; issue position strategy; issue salience strategy.*

Alternative (2). The action a decision maker chooses (from among other alternatives) in *decision making under conditions of risk* or *decision making under conditions of certainty.* See *strategy.*

Amateur activist (6). One whose regular source of income is not politics. See *activist; professional activist.*

Amicus curiae (12). A "friend of the court." A person or group that submits a brief *amicus curiae* stating its position in a case before the court, with the supposed intention of helping the court reach a decision. See *intervenor.*

Answer (12). In a lawsuit, the defendant's response to the *complaint.* See *cross complaint; pleadings; reply; standing to sue.*

Appellate court (12). A court to which litigants appeal for a review of a lower court ruling. See *appellate jurisdiction; original jurisdiction.*

Appellate Docket (12). Disputes brought to the Supreme Court requesting a *writ of certiorari* or on *writ of appeal* go on its Appellate Docket. See *Miscellaneous Docket; Original Docket.*

Appellate jurisdiction (12). The jurisdiction of a court to hear cases on appeal from the decisions of other courts. See *appellate court; original jurisdiction.*

Approval voting (13). A system of voting proposed for use in primaries and in other *elections* in which a voter can cast votes for any or all of the candidates he approves of. Approval voting is proposed to end the problem of a citizen's voting for his second choice to avoid throwing his vote away on a first choice not likely to win the election.

Arraignment (12). A legal proceeding at which a defendant appears to enter a plea and to choose a jury trial or a trial before a judge.

Arrow's paradox (3). There cannot exist a decision mechanism that produces a connected and transitive group decision and simultaneously satisfies all five of Arrow's conditions. See *citizens' sovereignty; complete preference ordering; cyclical majority; independence from irrelevant alternatives; non-dictatorship; non-perversity (positive association of individual and social values); transitive preference ordering; universal admissibility of individual orderings.*

Article 1 courts (12). Courts such as military courts of justice or administrative law courts established by Congress under the "necessary and proper" clause of Article 1, Section 8 of the Constitution. See *Article 3 courts.*

Article 3 courts (12). Courts established by Congress under Article 3 of the Constitution. They are distinguished by the provision that their members "shall hold their Offices during good Behaviour." See *Article 1 courts.*

***As if* provision** (1). In scientific theories, a metaphor that need not hold true. For example, decision theory holds that people act *as if* they choose their actions and *as if* they choose to pursue their goals efficiently. But the *as if* provision eliminates the requirement of a conscious choice for the theory to hold true.

Attribute strategy (7). In *election* campaigns, a candidate's varying of the emphasis (salience) he places on different personal attributes. See *allocation strategy; coalition strategy; issue ambiguity strategy; issue position strategy; issue salience; issue salience strategy.*

Axiom of connectedness (1). A decision maker holds a preference or indifference relation over all pairs of *outcomes.* See *axiom of transitivity; complete preference ordering; preference ordering.*

Axiom of transitivity (1). If a decision maker prefers outcome X to outcome Y (or is indifferent as between them), and if he prefers outcome Y to outcome Z (or is indifferent as between them), then he prefers outcome X to outcome Z (or is indifferent as between them). See *axiom of connectedness; complete preference ordering; preference ordering; transitive preference ordering.*

Benefits in kind (13). Welfare benefits or other forms of government *resource redistributions* that are given in specific commodities or services rather than in money. For example, food stamps, housing allowances, and medical care for the poor are examples of benefits in kind, but simple money transfers are not benefits in kind. See *merit goods.*

Beyond a reasonable doubt (12). The standard used by judges or juries for convicting a defendant in a criminal case. See *preponderance of the evidence.*

Bicameralism (9). The constitutional provision for a legislature of two houses. See *unicameralism.*

Bill of attainder (12). A legislative act that names a particular person for execution or other punishment, or an act designed to punish specific persons. Prohibited by Article 1, Section 9 of the Constitution.

Bimodal preference distribution (5). A *preference distribution* with two *modes.* See *symmetric preference distribution; unimodal preference distribution.*

Blanket primary (4). One in which each voter can vote in one party's primary for one office and another party's primary for another office. See *challenge primary; closed primary; nomination by primary; open primary.*

Bliss point (5). The citizen's point of greatest *utility,* or most preferred position, on an *issue.*

Borda count (3). A public choice mechanism (*election*) that gives points to each *alternative* depending on where the alternative stands in each decision maker's *preference ordering* (for example, "one" point for first choice, "two" points for second choice, and so forth). The points for each alternative are then summed and the alternative with the lowest number of points is declared the winner. Borda counts do not exhibit *independence from irrelevant alternatives.*

Bureau (11). A nonjudicial organization within a government whose personnel (bureaucrats) are unelected. See *bureaucracy.*

Bureaucracy (11). A collection of bureaus at some level of government. See *bureau.*

Cabinet (10). An extraconstitutional organization, made up of the heads (secretaries) of the *executive departments* of the federal government and other people of the president's choosing.

Calculus of voting (5). $R = PB + D - C$. The sum of the *private consequences of voting* and *the collective consequences of voting;* the *expected utility* from voting minus the expected utility from abstaining.

Capture hypothesis (11). The hypothesis that *independent regulatory commissions* are taken over by the industries they are supposed to regulate. See *life cycle; revolving door.*

Challenge primary (4). One in which a would-be candidate challenges the place on the general *election* ballot of a candidate nominated by a convention; challenge primaries will occur if allowed by law and if called for by petitions with an adequate number of signatures. See *blanket primary; closed primary; nomination by primary; open primary.*

Chicken (2). A two-person *nonzero-sum game* modeled on the contest between adolescent drivers who propel their cars at each other, the first one to swerve being called "chicken." Useful for analyzing certain international relations problems.

Chief diplomat (10). The president's constitutionally derived right to be manager and major policy maker of the foreign policy and diplomatic activities of the United States. See *chief executive; chief legislator; chief of state; commander-in-chief.*

Chief executive (10). The president's constitutionally derived right to be head of the executive branch of government, including most of the federal *bureaucracy.* See *chief diplomat; chief legislator; chief of state; commander-in-chief.*

Chief legislator (10). The president's constitutionally derived right to influence the legislative process by initiation of legislation, veto, and recommendation and through other means derived from these rights. See *chief diplomat; chief executive; chief of state; commander-in-chief.*

Chief of party (10). The president's historically derived right to lead his political party, which is supported by his patronage appointments to federal positions, his right to appoint the chairman of his party's national organization, and his ability to funnel federal resources to the constituents of elected officeholders of his party. See *manager of prosperity; protector of the peace; voice of the people; world leader.*

Chief of state (10). The right of the president, indirectly derived from the Constitution, to act as the nation's major ceremonial figure. See *chief diplomat; chief executive; chief legislator; commander-in-chief.*

Citizen (4). A person legally entitled to vote. See *voter.*

Citizens' sovereignty (3). One of the five conditions of Arrow's impossibility theorem; there must be some configuration of individual preferences that produces each alternative among those under consideration as the collective choice. See *Arrow's paradox; independence from irrelevant alternatives; non-dictatorship; non-perversity (positive association of individual and social values); universal admissibility of individual orderings.*

Civil law (12). Civil law has two meanings. First, the term denotes law that is not *criminal law.* Second, the term denotes law that is not derived from the *common law.* Many European nations do not let judges "make" law but instead confine them to applying complicated statutes covering every imaginable contingency to specific cases. The body of such statutes is also called the civil law. Civil law in this sense is of Roman origin, as compared to the common law, which is of Anglo-Saxon origin. See *administrative law; constitutional law; organic law; property law; statutory law.*

Class action (12). A suit brought by one or a few people on behalf of a "class" of people, all of whom could claim a cause of action against the same defendant for the same activities.

Classificatory group (5). A group of people who share some very general characteristic such as age, sex, race, or income. See *primary group; secondary group.*

Closed primary (4). One in which *voters* must indicate their party identification beforehand, usually by registration, and in which they can only vote in the primary *election* of their party. See *blanket primary; challenge primary; nomination by primary; open primary.*

Closed rule (9). Bills reaching the floor of the House of Representatives for consideration with a closed rule cannot be amended. A closed rule is granted by members of the House Rules Committee. See *open rule.*

Cloture (9). A mechanism for ending a filibuster or for otherwise stopping debate on a bill. Cloture in the Senate requires an affirmative vote from sixty percent of all senators. See *discharge petition; suspension of the rules.*

Coalition (2). A number of people who join together, explicitly or implicitly, to coordinate strategies and thus to achieve some goal they hold in common.

Coalition strategy (7). In *election* campaigns, a candidate's *strategy* in adding, joining, or excluding organizations of *activists* in his electoral coalition. See *allocation strategy; attribute strategy; coalition; issue ambiguity strategy; issue position strategy; issue salience strategy.*

Collateral estoppel (12). A particular question of fact decided in one trial cannot be relitigated by one of the parties in that trial during some subsequent trial. See *res judicata.*

Collective action (1). Action that occurs with force or the threat of force; "force" means physical coercion. See *private action; private choice; public choice.*

Collective consequences of voting (5). The effects a vote is expected to have on the *election* outcome; usually stated in *expected utility* and listed in the *calculus of voting* as *PB.* See *private consequences of voting.*

Collective (public) good (3). *Good* exhibiting either *jointness of consumption* or *jointness of supply* or both. See *free-rider problem; private good; public bad.*

Collectivity (1). A number of individual human beings who share some characteristic or who make some decisions by *public choice.*

Commander-in-chief (10). The president's constitutionally derived right to be commander of the armed forces of the United States and to direct its national defense policy. See *chief diplomat; chief executive; chief legislator; chief of state.*

Common law (12). Judge-made law first developed in England following the Norman conquest of 1066. Judges appointed by the kings of England applied local customs to the cases they heard and eventually adopted uniform principles, or legal rules, for deciding cases. The common law had a parallel development in the United States. Today, much of the common law is codified in statutes such as the uniform commercial code. See *administrative law; civil law; constitutional law; criminal law; equity; organic law; property law; statutory law.*

Complaint (12). In a lawsuit, the plaintiff's statement of why he has *standing to sue,* why the court in which he is filing the complaint has jurisdiction over the case, and the nature of the injury he has suffered or is about to suffer. See *answer; cross complaint; pleadings; reply.*

Complete preference ordering (1). One that is both connected and transitive over all *outcomes.* See *axiom of connectedness; axiom of transitivity; preference ordering; transitive preference ordering.*

Complex election (6). An *election* with *activists.* See *simple election.*

Complexity (1). A characteristic of decision makers that they can hold several *goals* simultaneously. See *conflict; methodological individualism; ordering; scarcity; subjectiveness; variety.*

Compulsory process (12). "Process to compel the attendance in court of a person wanted there as a witness or otherwise; including not only the ordinary subpoena, but also a warrant of arrest or attachment if needed."* Compulsory process is guaranteed to defendants by the Sixth Amendment to the Constitution. See *discovery.*

Conflict (1). A characteristic of decision situations that if one person can achieve his *goal* sometimes another person cannot. See *complexity; methodological individualism; ordering; scarcity; subjectiveness; variety.*

Consent Calendar (9). The agenda, or calendar in the House of Representatives on which limited bills without controversial substance are placed. Bills on the Consent Calendar are privileged. See *Discharge Calendar; Private Calendar; privileged bill.*

Conservative Coalition (9). A coalition of Republicans and southern Democrats who joined together in the Congress to prevent the passage of many laws concerning civil rights and government intervention in economic matters. The Conservative Coalition was an important force in the Congress until the administration of Lyndon B. Johnson.

Constant-sum game (2). One in which the payoffs to the players sum to a constant number for all possible *strategies* chosen. In two-person constant-sum games, the payoffs sum to the same constant for all possible pairs of *strategies* chosen. See *nonzero-sum game; zero-sum game.*

Constitutional law (12). The body of law including the Constitution and all subsequent court opinions that interpret it or refer to it for authority in finding another law or action constitutional or unconstitutional. Much of constitutional law is case law, but it is also *statutory law,* for the members of Congress sometimes enact statutes to fulfill specific, constitutionally prescribed purposes. See *administrative law; civil law; criminal law; organic law; property law.*

Contract (12). "An agreement between two or more persons which creates an obligation to do or not to do a particular thing. Its essentials are competent parties, subject matter, a legal consideration, mutuality of agreement, and mutuality of obligation."*

Cooperative game (2). A game in which the players can communicate. See *non-cooperative game.*

Credit claiming (8). Activities by elected representatives to take credit for legislation beneficial to their constituents or members of particular *interest groups.* See *advertising; position taking.*

Crime (12). "A positive or negative act in violation of penal law; an offense against the State or the United States."* "A crime may be defined to be an act done in violation of those duties which an individual owes to the community, to and for the breach of which the law has provided that the offender shall make satisfaction to the public."* See *criminal law.*

Criminal law (12). Distinguished by three properties. First, it is defined by *statutory law.* Second, the government (federal or state) is usually named as the plaintiff (prosecution). Third, upon conviction of a *crime,* defendants may ordinarily receive penalties that are intended to deprive them of more utility than they gain by committing the crime in the first place. See *administrative law; civil law; common law; constitutional law; felony; misdemeanor; organic law; property law.*

Cross complaint (12). In a lawsuit, a *complaint* by the defendant against the original plaintiff. See *answer; pleadings; reply; standing to sue.*

Cross-filing (4). The practice of candidates running in the primary *elections* of more than one party. See *nomination by primary.*

Cumulative voting (4). A system of voting in certain *elections* in which *citizens* have more than one vote; they can use all of their votes for just one candidate or spread their votes around among the candidates in any manner they choose; in such elections, there are usually more than two candidates. See *proportional representation system; single-member district system.*

Cyclical majority (3). An intransitive group decision created by a majority-vote *public choice* mechanism. See *Arrow's paradox; axiom of transitivity; transitive preference ordering.*

Damages (12). "A pecuniary compensation or indemnity, which may be recovered in the courts by any person who has suffered loss, detriment, or injury, whether to his person, property, or rights, through the unlawful act of omission or negligence of another. A sum of money awarded to a person injured by the *tort* of another."*

Decision coalition (12). The *coalition* made up of the justices of the Supreme Court in the majority who decide to vote for or against the petitioner solely on the merits of the case and without regard to agreement among themselves on the reasons for the decision. See *opinion coalition; opinion of the Court.*

Decision cost (4). The payments one person must make to others to get them to agree to a desired action or policy in a *public choice* procedure such as an *election* or in market exchange. Decision costs vary directly with the number of people required by the *decision rule* to make a public choice. See *external cost.*

Decision making under conditions of certainty (2). Decision making when for each *alternative* chosen, the prevailing *state of nature* is known with certainty. See *decision making under conditions of risk; decision making under conditions of uncertainty.*

Decision making under conditions of risk (2). Decision making when for each *alternative* chosen, the decision maker believes each possible *state of nature* will occur with a known probability. See *decision making under conditions of certainty; decision making under conditions of uncertainty.*

Decision making under conditions of uncertainty (2). Decision making when for each *strategy* chosen, the decision maker believes either that the prevailing *state of nature* is unknown or that the probability that particular states of nature will occur cannot be estimated. See *decision making under conditions of certainty; decision making under conditions of risk.*

Decision rule (4). In an *election,* the rule that states how many votes must be cast for a *motion* for it to be adopted. Decision rules may be stated in absolute numbers of votes or in percentages of the votes cast. See *decision cost; external cost.*

Decision theory (1). The theory of human action and decision making based on the assumption of *rational choice.* See *economic science; political science.*

Delegate (8). An elected representative who seeks to enact his constituents' preferences and to serve their interest as they define it, not as he does. See *fiduciary; politico; representational focus; representational style; trustee.*

Determinate sentences (12). Sentences in criminal cases that are fixed by law and that allow the judge no latitude or discretion.

Determinism (5). The theory that conditioning or group membership leads people to vote as they do.

Diminishing marginal utility (2). A property of *utility* that as each unit of value is added, the corresponding increase in utility grows smaller.

Direct election (4). One such as a *referendum,* in which the *motions* for which *citizens* vote are *public policy outcomes* themselves rather than candidates or representatives. See *direct (pure) democracy (democracy); indirect election; indirect (representative) democracy (republic).*

Direct (pure) democracy (democracy) (4). An *election* system that principally uses *direct elections* rather than *indirect elections* to make *public policy* decisions. See *indirect (representative) democracy (republic).*

Discharge Calendar (9). In the House of Representatives, a bill removed from a committee's jurisdiction by a *discharge petition* goes on the Discharge Calendar, where it remains for at least seven days, after which House members may consider it. See *Consent Calender; Private Calendar.*

Discharge petition (9). A method House members may use to take a bill away from a committee and turn it over to full House consideration; requires the signatures of more than one half of the members of the House. See *cloture; Discharge Calendar; suspension of the rules.*

Discovery (12). A pretrial procedure that allows each side to examine (depose) the other side's experts and witnesses, compelling them to answer questions put to them, and to inspect many of the other side's documents or physical evidence as well. See *compulsory process.*

Diversity jurisdiction (12). The jurisdiction of federal district courts to hear disputes between citizens of different states.

Division of the question (8). The practice in legislatures of breaking a complex motion down into the simplest possible separate motions.

Doctrine of responsible party government (7). A set of beliefs first stated by American academics around the turn of the century, that *political parties* and their candidates should offer *citizens* clear and distinct *public policy* positions in *elections* and that parties should also hold themselves accountable to carry out their promises if they win office.

Double jeopardy (12). Prohibited by the Fifth Amendment, double jeopardy occurs if a person is tried a second time for an offense for which he has already been found not guilty. See *res judicata.*

Economic science (1). The body of knowledge arising from the application of *decision theory* to *private choice;* see *political science, rational choice.*

Efficiency (12). Efficiency has two different meanings when used by economists and political scientists. The first meaning is *Pareto optimality.* The second meaning is that output is maximized for a fixed level of input or input is minimized for a fixed level of output.

Election (4). A *collective action* decision procedure consisting of at least two *motions,* and a rule that aggregates the vote(s) into a collective choice.

Electoral college (4). An institution used to elect the president of the United States. *Voters* in each state cast their votes for one of the presidential candidates; except in Maine, the candidate who receives a plurality of votes has his electors from that state (made up of its number of senators—two—plus representatives) become members of the electoral college. The votes in the electoral college for each candidate are then added up and a winner declared, or, if there is no majority winner, then the *election* goes into the House of Representatives.

Emission charge (12). A pollution control technique, sometimes called an effluent charge or a Pigouvian tax, which charges each firm a fee, or tax, based on its level of pollution emissions.

Equilibrium strategy (2). The strategy that works best for a player in a game if his opponent is also at his equilibrium strategy. See *equilibrium strategy pair.*

Equilibrium strategy pair (2). In *two-person games* the pair of strategies that find each player in equilibrium; the pair of strategies from which neither player has an incentive unilaterally to depart. See *equilibrium strategy.*

Equity (12). Equity emerged as a body of law in England to overcome the perceived limits of the *common law* in cases where it did not provide an adequate remedy. The law of equity is now often considered a part of common law, for the two had a parallel development and in England the chancery courts, which handled suits in equity, and the common law courts were combined in the 1870s. Equity and the common law are both judge-made law. See *administrative law; civil law; constitutional law; criminal law; injunction; injunctive relief; organic law; property law; specific performance; statutory law.*

Exclusive committee (9). A member of the House of Representatives may belong to no other House committee if he is a member of an exclusive committee.

Executive agreement (10). An agreement between the president of the United States and the leader of another nation concerning some aspect of relations between the two countries. An executive agreement is the law of the land and has the legal status of a treaty, but it does not require the *advice and consent* of the Senate.

Executive department (10). The departments of the federal government whose heads (secretaries) are members of the president's *cabinet.*

Expected utility (2). A measure of the payoff from choosing an *alternative* in *decision making under conditions of risk.* $U(O_i)$, the decision maker's *utility* for each *outcome* that might occur if he chooses a particular alternative a_j, is multiplied by P_{ij}, the probability that the outcome will occur if that alternative is chosen. Then, all multiplied terms are added $[P_{1j}U(O_1) + \ldots + P_{ij}U(O_i) + \ldots + P_{nj}U(O_n)]$ to calculate each alternative's expected utility. See *expected value; value.*

Expected value (2). A measure of the payoff from choosing an *alternative* in *decision making under conditions of risk.* O_i, the value of each *outcome* that might occur if the decision maker chooses a particular *alternative* a_j, is multiplied by P_{ij}, the probability that the outcome will occur if that alternative is chosen. Then, all multiplied terms are added $[P_1O_1 + \ldots + P_{ij}O_i + \ldots + P_{nj}O_n]$ to calculate each alternative's expected value. See *expected utility; utility; value.*

Ex post facto law (12). Retroactive legislation; a law that imposes a penalty or increases a penalty for an action already completed but not illegal when completed. Prohibited by Article 1, Section 9 of the Constitution.

External cost (3). One that varies inversely with the number of people required to consent to a decision in a decision procedure such as an *election. Externality.* See *decision cost; decision rule; negative externality.*

External economy (3). See *positive externality.*

Externality (3). The change in *utility* created by the production of a public good or *public bad.* See *external cost; external economy; free-rider problem; positive externality.*

Federal question (12). The dispute at issue in cases brought under the Constitution, laws, or treaties of the United States; federal district courts have original jurisdiction over such questions.

Felony (12). A serious *crime.* Federal *criminal law* and criminal law in most states categorize as felonies those crimes for which a convict may be executed or sentenced to prison for more than one year. See *misdemeanor.*

Fiduciary (8). In politics and government, the obligation of an elected representative to place his constituents' interests above his own. In law, "A person having a duty, created by his undertaking, to act primarily for another's benefit in matters connected with such undertaking."* See *delegate; politico; representational focus; representational style; trustee.*

Filibuster (9). In the Senate, a device for stalling a bill by carrying on a continual debate, until the desire to turn to other matters leads the bill's sponsors to drop its consideration. See *cloture.*

Fiscal illusion (7). Created by public officials and others whose purpose is to lead voters to underestimate the costs of public programs and to overestimate their benefits.

Fraud (2). Entering into a bargain when performance is known to be infeasible.

Free-rider problem (3). The problem of getting people to contribute to the supply of a *collective good* that displays a *positive externality* (public good). A problem associated with supplying non-divisible (jointly consumed) goods. See *jointness of consumption.*

Game theory (2). That part of *decision theory* that explains and predicts *decision making under conditions of uncertainty* in the presence of two or more decision makers (one of whom may be nature). See *decision making under conditions of certainty; decision making under conditions of risk; games of strategy; strategy.*

Games of strategy (2). *Decision making under conditions of uncertainty* when two or more players (opponents) choose each other's *state of nature.* See *game theory.*

General deterrence (12). The goal of imposing sentences on criminals to deter all others from committing the same *crimes.* See *incapacitation; rehabilitation; retribution; special deterrence; victim compensation.*

Gerrymander (4). The practice of constructing districts in *single member district systems* to maximize the number of districts the candidates of one party might win.

Goal (1). An *outcome* that a decision maker prefers to some other outcome; that which decision makers pursue by *rational choice.* See *complexity; conflict; methodological individualism; ordering; scarcity; subjectiveness; variety.*

Good (3). Anything that produces a change in at least one person's *utility* with a change in the amount of it produced or consumed. See *collective (public) good; private good; public bad.*

Graft (6). The illegal payment of money to government officials in exchange for government contracts or other benefits.

Grand coalition (2). A *coalition* of the whole. A coalition of all players.

Grand jury (12). The jury used to issue *indictments* for serious *crimes.* See *felony; information; misdemeanor; petit jury.*

Group theory (6). A theory of the political process that holds that groups form spontaneously in response to their members' mutually perceived threats or opportunities. See *free-rider problem; Marxist theory; pluralist theory; power elite theory.*

Hung jury (12). One unable to reach a unanimous verdict.

Ideology (3). The pattern of *utilities, externalities,* a person gets from the presence or absence of various collectively supplied public and *private goods.*

Impeachment (9). The right of members of the House of Representatives to indict a federal officeholder for some offense ("Treason, Bribery, or other high Crimes and Misdemeanors"); impeachment is not equivalent to conviction, which must be judged by members of the Senate.

Incapacitation (12). The goal of imprisoning criminals so that they will not be able to commit crimes during their sentence. See *general deterrence; rehabilitation; retribution; special deterrence; victim compensation.*

Independence from irrelevant alternatives (3). One of the five conditions of Arrow's impossibility theorem; the paired rankings between two *alternatives* produced by a public or private choice mechanism should not be affected by the location of some third (irrelevant) alternative. See *Arrow's paradox; Borda count; citizen's sovereignty; non-dictatorship; non-perversity (positive association of individual and social values); universal admissibility of individual orderings.*

Independent regulatory commission (11). Agency created by an act of Congress and directed by commissioners appointed by the president, with the *advice and consent* of the Senate, to legislatively determined, staggered terms; supposedly independent of presidential, congressional, or political influence and control. See *capture hypothesis; life cycle; revolving door.*

Indictment (12). An accusation issued by a *grand jury* stating that a person is charged with a *crime.* See *information.*

Indifference contours (7). In a two-dimensional issue space, a line showing combinations of positions on the two *issues* from which a *citizen* receives the same *utility.*

Indifference point (2). In calculating *utility,* the point at which the decision maker is indifferent as between an intermediately preferred *outcome* and a lottery involving some probability of receiving his most and least preferred outcomes.

Indirect election (4). One in which *voters* vote for candidates to represent them rather than for *public policy motions.* See *direct election; direct (pure) democracy (democracy); indirect (representative) democracy (republic).*

Indirect (representative) democracy (republic) (4). A nation in which *citizens* more often vote for representatives who then choose *public policies* than for direct public policy *motions* themselves. See *direct election; direct (pure) democracy (democracy); indirect election.*

In forma pauperis (12). Petitions *in forma pauperis* are usually filed in courts by indigent persons (mostly prison inmates) who do not have the aid of an attorney and cannot afford filing fees.

Information (12). A method of indicting a defendant for a *misdemeanor,* usually in the form of a complaint by a public official. See *indictment.*

Information closure (10). The tendency of presidents and other executive decision makers to filter out most information except what they want to hear. See *information overload.*

Information overload (10). The tendency for presidents or other executive decision makers to be burdened by too much information, without a reliable means for separating accurate from inaccurate information or important from unimportant information. See *information closure.*

Injunction (12). An order by a court that a party to a judicial process act or cease acting in a certain manner. For example, in a suit in *equity,* the court demands performance by issuing an injunction ordering a defendant to comply with the terms of the contract. See *injunctive relief; specific performance.*

Injunctive relief (12). A plaintiff receives injunctive relief when a court issues an *injunction* to a defendant. See *equity.*

***In personam* jurisdiction** (12). A court's jurisdiction over actions brought by or against persons belonging to particular classes. For example, a military court ordinarily lacks *in personam* jurisdiction over civilians. See *standing to sue; subject matter jurisdiction.*

Instrumental issue (5). An issue in an *election* campaign in which a candidate's position on the *issue* will affect the outcome of some *primary issue* or the achievement of some prime *goal.*

Intense minority (7). A group of persons numbering less than a majority, all of whom prefer a particular position on some *issue* such that an *election* candidate who satisfies their preference on that issue will defeat one who does not, no matter what positions the candidates take on all other issues.

Intentional tort (12). Intentional *torts* include defamation (slander if spoken, libel if written), trespass, conversion (theft), assault, battery, and fraud. Distinguished from torts arising because of accidents caused by *negligence* or accidents in the case of *strict liability.*

Interest group (6). An organization whose members seek private and collective benefits in the electoral and governmental processes but who do not directly offer candidates for nomination and *election.* See *activist; political party.*

Interpersonal comparison of utilities (2). A comparison of the *utilities* two persons have for the same or different *outcomes.* A comparison not warranted by *decision theory.* See *subjectiveness.*

Intervenor (12). A person or group that has a stake in the outcome of a lawsuit and that enters the proceedings with the permission of the court. See *amicus curiae.*

Intransitive preference ordering (1). A *preference ordering* that is not transitive. For example, a decision maker who prefers *X* to *Y*, *Y* to *Z*, and *Z* to *X* has an intransitive preference ordering. See *Arrow's paradox; complete preference ordering; cyclical majority; transitive preference ordering.*

Investigation (9). The right of (and activity by) House and Senate members to study problems (usually by committee hearings) before, during, or even after the consideration of bills. See *oversight.*

Iron law of oligarchy (6). A hypothesis in *political science* holding that no matter how democratic their avowed purpose, successful political organizations must be tightly controlled and dictatorially directed oligarchies.

Iron triangle (11). The hypothesized relationship among an *interest group,* the *bureau* that dispenses benefits to the interest group's members, and the congressional committee or subcommittee whose members oversee the bureau and have the interest group's members as part of their constituency and electoral *coalition.* This coalition is often seen as opposed to actions that would harm any of its members.

Issue (5). A measurement of some aspect of an actual or potential *collective action* or the result of some *collective action.* See *issue position strategy.*

Issue ambiguity strategy (7). In *election* campaigns the candidate's *strategy* of offering *citizens* different positions on the same *issue* with varying probabilities, or of ignoring certain issues altogether. See *allocation strategy; attribute strategy; coalition strategy; issue position strategy; issue salience strategy.*

Issue position strategy (7). In *election* campaigns, the candidate's *strategy* in taking positions on *public policy issues.* See *allocation strategy; attribute strategy; coalition strategy; issue ambiguity strategy; issue salience strategy.*

Issue salience (5). The relative importance a *citizen* attaches to an *issue.* See *issue salience strategy.*

Issue salience strategy (7). In *election* campaigns, the candidate's *strategy* associated with varying the emphasis placed on each campaign *issue.* See *allocation strategy; attribute strategy; coalition strategy; issue ambiguity strategy; issue position strategy; issue salience.*

Jointness of consumption (3). Jointly consumed *goods* are non-divisible; they cannot be withheld from those who do not pay for them. See *collective* *(public) good; externality; free-rider problem; jointness of supply; private good; public bad.*

Jointness of supply (3). The supply of jointly supplied goods does not diminish with the addition of more users or consumers. See *collective (public) good; externality; jointness of consumption; private good.*

Judicial activism (12). The tendency of *appellate courts* to leap into new territory by enunciating the broadest decisions in particular cases and by ignoring or overturning *precedent,* even though such cases could be decided on narrower grounds. Also, the tendency of appellate courts to become principal legislators in the governmental process. See *judicial restraint.*

Judicial restraint (12). The tendency of *appellate courts* to move solely from one case to the next, to decide disputes on narrow grounds of technicalities rather than on constitutional principles, and to appeal to the authority of *precedent.* Also, the tendency of appellate courts to refuse to accept anything that smacks of a *political question* and to defer regularly to the other branches of government, claiming that petitioners either have not exhausted their remedies or must go to the legislature for relief. See *judicial activism.*

Judicial review (12). The action of the Supreme Court in passing on the constitutionality of acts of Congress or of other agencies of the federal government. See *statutory construction.*

Life cycle (11). A hypothesis concerning the natural history of *independent regulatory commissions.* Agencies are born in congressional deliberations, supposedly with weak mandates but with the best of intentions; the agencies then enjoy an activist youth, trying to control those whom they were designed to regulate; but in maturity and old age they become the protectors of the regulated to protect themselves against competition. See *capture hypothesis; revolving door.*

Logrolling (9). Vote trading by elected representatives in support of each other's bills. See *pork-barrel legislation.*

Malapportionment (4). The division of a state or nation into *election* districts with greatly varying numbers of people in each district.

Manager of prosperity (10). The president's legislatively and historically derived right to control various aspects of the economy through direct policy intervention and through indirect intervention by the appointment of the members of the principal economic *independent regulatory commissions* and boards. See *chief of party; protector of the peace; voice of the people; world leader.*

Marxist theory (6). An interpretation of the political process resting on the belief that political events reflect the clash of economic classes. See *free-rider problem; group theory; pluralist theory; power elite theory.*

Maximin strategy (2). The *strategy* that guarantees a player the greatest minimum payoff. See *minimax strategy; security level.*

Mean (5). The average position in a distribution. See *median; mode; preference distribution.*

Median (5). The position in a distribution for which there are as many observations above it as below it. For example, the median position in a *preference distribution* has as many *citizens* preferring positions above the median as preferring positions below it. See *mean; mode.*

Merit goods (13). Those granted by *resource redistribution* programs in which the recipient's preferred consumption patterns are intentionally ignored to give the recipient a collection of *goods* and services that the donor or the donor's representative deems more appropriate. For example, *benefits in kind* such as medical care and food stamps for the poor are merit-good substitutes for payments of money, which the recipient might spend to purchase goods not meeting the approval of the donor or the donor's agent.

Methodological individualism (1). An approach to social science that holds that the actions of individual human beings must be the fundamental unit of analysis. See *collectivity; organic concept of politics; organic fallacy; subjectivity.*

Minimax strategy (2). The *strategy* that guarantees a player the smallest maximum loss. See *maximin strategy; security level.*

Minimum winning coalition (2). A *coalition* that would not win if one member were deleted. See *size principle.*

Miscellaneous Docket (12). Petitions received by the Supreme Court *in forma pauperis* go on its Miscellaneous Docket. See *Appellate Docket; Original Docket.*

Misdemeanor (12). A *crime* not as serious as a *felony,* for which judges may impose short prison terms or monetary fines.

Mistrial (12). One during which a legal error is made; one a judge ends before it is completed because of some error or event that renders it legally imperfect. A jury's failure to reach a unanimous verdict results in a mistrial.

Mixed strategies (2). A set of two or more strategies that a player in a game chooses to play, each with some known probability. See *issue ambiguity strategy; pure strategy.*

Mode (5). A position in a distribution that has a higher value than have the positions to either side of it. For example, in a *unimodal preference distribution,* more *citizens* prefer the position at the mode than prefer positions to either side of the mode. See *bimodal preference distribution; mean; median.*

Monopoly (3). A public or private firm that alone produces a *good* or service for which there are no close substitutes. See *welfare loss.*

Motion (4). In an *election,* the object of the *citizen's* vote. See *direct election; indirect election; referendum.*

Negative externality (3). The loss in utility created by the production of a *public bad.* See *external cost; externality.*

Negligence (12). A *tort* arising because of negligence occurs as the result of an "omission to do something which a reasonable man, guided by those ordinary considerations which ordinarily regulate human affairs, would do, or the doing of something which a reasonable and prudent man would not do."* See *intentional tort; strict liability.*

Nomination by caucus (4). At one time a method of nominating candidates for elected offices in which a caucus of officeholders and political *activists* would gather informally to dictate the party's choice. Today, a regularized *election* procedure at the local level to choose representatives to a district-wide, state-wide, or other form of nominating convention. See *nomination by convention; nomination by petition; nomination by primary; nomination by request.*

Nomination by convention (4). A system of nomination for presidential and vice-presidential *election* candidates, as well as for other major elected offices, used today by both major parties; delegates are chosen at the state and local level by various means. See *nomination by caucus; nomination by petition; nomination by primary; nomination by request.*

Nomination by petition (4). A nomination method used in *elections* in which a specified number or proportion of *citizens* must sign a petition for a candidate if his or her name is to appear on the ballot. See *challenge primary; nomination by caucus; nomination by convention; nomination by primary; nomination by request.*

Nomination by primary (4). A popular *election* to choose a party's candidates in a general election. See *blanket primary; challenge primary; closed primary; nomination by caucus; nomination by convention; nomination by petition; nomination by request; open primary.*

Nomination by request (4). A nomination method used in small organizations in which names are placed on a ballot by request of the nominee. See *nomination by caucus; nomination by convention; nomination by petition; nomination by primary.*

Non-cooperative game (2). One in which the players cannot communicate. See *cooperative game.*

Non-dictatorship (3). One of the five conditions of Arrow's impossibility theorem; there must be no person whose preferred *outcome* is the social choice no matter what all other persons' preferred outcomes might be. See *Arrow's paradox; citizens' sovereignty; independence from irrelevant alter-*

natives; non-perversity (positive association of individual and social values); universal admissibility of individual orderings.

Non-perversity (positive association of individual and social values) (3). One of the five conditions of Arrow's impossibility theorem; if a participant in a public or private choice procedure raises an *alternative* in his *preference ordering,* then the alternative should not fall (be lowered) in the social preference ordering. See *Arrow's paradox; citizen's sovereignty; independence from irrelevant alternatives; non-dictatorship; universal admissibility of individual orderings.*

Nonzero-sum game (2). One whose payoffs for each set of *strategies* chosen sum to some number other than zero. See *constant-sum game; zero-sum game.*

***N*-person game** (2). A game with three or more players. See *two-person game.*

Open primary (4). A primary *election* in which *voters* do not have to declare their party identification but choose in the voting booth the ballot of the *political party* in whose primary contest they want to vote. See *blanket primary; challenge primary; closed primary; nomination by primary.*

Open rule (9). Bills reaching the floor of the House of Representatives with an open rule may be amended. The open rule is decided upon by the members of the House Rules Committee. See *closed rule.*

Operational code of the bureaucrat (11). A set of decision rules that bureaucrats are believed to use when they are choosing to develop and implement various *public policies.*

Opinion coalition (12). A *coalition* made up of the Supreme Court justices in the majority who have agreed to support a single opinion in a particular case. See *decision coalition; opinion of the Court.*

Opinion of the Court (12). A single opinion issued by at least a majority of the justices (*opinion coalition*) of the Supreme Court. Such an opinion becomes the law of the land, and it is binding on all lower courts in subsequent cases. See *decision coalition.*

Ordering (1). A decision maker's ability to state a preference as between (or among) two (or more) *outcomes.* See *complexity; conflict; methodological individualism; preference ordering; scarcity; subjectiveness; variety.*

Organic concept of politics (1). An approach to social science that holds that the actions of *collectivities* must be the fundamental unit of analysis. See *methodological individualism; organic fallacy.*

Organic fallacy (1). The attribution of individual human qualities to *collectivities.* See *methodological individualism; organic concept of politics.*

Organic law (12). The law that states the fundamental rules by which a government is established and under which its agents operate. *Constitutional law* is organic law. See *administrative law; civil law; common law; criminal law; property law; statutory law.*

Original Docket (12). Cases of *original jurisdiction* go on the Supreme Court's Original Docket. See *Appellate Docket; Miscellaneous Docket.*

Original jurisdiction (12). The jurisdiction of a court to hear a case before it has been heard by any other court. See *appellate jurisdiction.*

Outcome (1). The result of an event, such as a decision. All *goals* are outcomes, but not all outcomes are goals. A *good,* service, or state of the world is an outcome if someone's decision (action) might affect the probability that it occurs. See *alternative; state of nature; strategy.*

Oversight (9). The right of (and activity by) House and Senate members to examine (usually through committee hearings) the workings of the laws and agencies they have created. See *investigation.*

Pareto optimality (2). The property of an *outcome* such that there exists no other outcome that the players or bargainers jointly prefer; or, there exists no other outcome that makes at least one person better off without making anyone else worse off. See *efficiency; Pareto preferred.*

Pareto preferred (2). One *outcome* is Pareto preferred to another if it would be *Pareto optimal* if these were the only two outcomes under consideration. All Pareto optimal outcomes are Pareto preferred, but not all Pareto preferred outcomes are Pareto optimal. See *efficiency.*

Passive-negative president (10). One who devotes little energy to the job of being president and who believes that he and the nation are threatened by a hostile political and governmental environment. See *active-negative president; active-positive president; passive-positive president.*

Passive-positive president (10). One who devotes little energy to the job of being president and who believes that his political and governmental environment is benign. See *active-negative president; active-positive president; passive-negative president.*

Patronage (6). The exchange of money (for example, campaign contributions or endorsements) for appointment to government office. See *graft.*

***Per curiam* order** (12). An unsigned announcement of the Supreme Court's decision that states the decision on the merits of the case but sometimes not the reasons for it.

Petit jury (12). The jury empaneled to try a case. See *grand jury.*

Piecemeal reforms (13). Those reforms affecting only one or two major political procedures or governmental institutions. See *systematic reforms.*

Plea bargain (12). The *criminal-law* equivalent of a settlement out of court in a civil suit. An agreement between a defendant and the prosecutor that the defendant will plead guilty to a lesser offense than the one with which he could be charged in exchange for which the prosecutor will not prosecute him on the more serious offense and thus avoid the expense of a trial and the risk of a "not guilty" verdict.

Pleadings (12). The initial documents in a lawsuit, made up of the *complaint* and *answer,* and sometimes also including a *cross complaint* and *reply.*

Pluralist theory (6). An interpretation of the political process resting on the belief that different groups dominate political and governmental decision making in each group's area of interest, but that this domination is not cumulative so that the domination of one area does not aid in dominating another. See *free-rider problem; group theory; Marxist theory; power elite theory.*

Plurality equilibrium principle (7). In two-candidate, single-member district *elections,* a party's candidates for a particular office in the long run adopt pure plurality equilibrium *strategies* if these strategies exist.

Pocket veto (9). The practice of withholding the president's constitutionally required approval of a bill. The president exercises a pocket veto if he fails to sign a bill within ten days after he receives it for consideration from the Congress provided that the Congress has adjourned before ten days have elapsed. Such a bill cannot become law. See *veto.*

Political entrepreneur (6). One who arranges and executes the exchange of votes, payments, endorsements, labor, and *public policy* in the electoral and legislative processes.

Political party (6). An organization whose members actually nominate candidates for elective office. See *activist; interest group.*

Political question (12). A controversy brought to the Supreme Court, which it may refuse to address because in the judgment of the justices it presents a controversy that could also and perhaps better be settled in the political institutions of the government, such as in the Congress.

Political science (1). The body of knowledge arising from the application of *decision theory* to *public choice.* See *economic science; rational choice.*

Politico (8). An elected representative who combines the properties of a *delegate* and *trustee.* See *fiduciary; representational focus; representational style.*

Pork-barrel legislation (9). Legislation designed to benefit particular legislative districts rather than the nation as a whole. See *logrolling.*

Position taking (9). A legislative activity by elected representatives analogous to taking *issue position strategies* in *elections.* See *advertising; credit claiming.*

Positive externality (3). *External economy.* The positive utility associated with the production of a *public good.* See *externality; free-rider problem.*

Power elite theory (6). An interpretation of the political process resting on the belief that the nation is governed by a small "power elite," whose members are ordinarily unelected and unappointed. See *free-rider problem; group theory; Marxist theory; pluralist theory.*

Precedent (12). "An adjudged case or decision of a court considered as furnishing an example or authority for an identical or similar case afterwards arising or a similar question of law."* See *stare decisis.*

Preference distribution (5). The location of citizens' *bliss points* on a *public policy* issue. The figure or graph showing the relative frequencies with which citizens' *bliss points* fall at various positions on an *issue* dimension.

Preference ordering (1). A decision maker's preference or indifference relation over a set of *outcomes.* See *axiom of connectedness; axiom of transitivity; complete preference ordering.*

Preponderance of the evidence (12). The standard used by judges or juries in finding for the plaintiff in a civil (noncriminal) action. The preponderance of the evidence standard requires that the plaintiff's complaint has a greater than 50–50 chance of being true. See *beyond a reasonable doubt.*

Primary group (5). Small, closely-knit groups such as families and small churches. See *classificatory group; secondary group.*

Primary issue (5). An underlying issue in an *election* campaign directly measuring some aspect of *goal* achievement. See *instrumental issue.*

Prisoners' dilemma (2). A *nonzero-sum game,* which when played in its noncooperative form leads the players to a pair of *outcomes* that they jointly less prefer to another pair of outcomes. The prisoners' dilemma also exists in *n*-person form.

Private action (1). Action that occurs without force or the threat of force; "force" means physical coercion. See *collective action; private choice; public choice.*

Private bill (9). One submitted to aid a particular person rather than classes of *citizens* or all of the citizens considered together. For example, the members of the Congress might pass a private bill to circumvent immigration laws for a particular alien trying to gain entry into the United States. Private bills are privileged. See *Private Calendar; privileged bills.*

Private Calendar (9). The calendar, or agenda, on which *private bills* are placed in the House of Representatives. See *Consent Calendar; Discharge Calendar.*

Private choice (1). Decision making that occurs in the absence of force. See *collective action; private action; public choice.*

Private consequences of voting (5). The costs and benefits a *citizen* receives from voting that do not depend on the *election outcome.* In the *calculus of voting,* these are denoted by D (sense of civic duty) and C (cost of voting). See *collective consequences of voting.*

Private good (3). One that exhibits neither *jointness of supply* nor *jointness of consumption.* As distinguished from a *collective (public) good;* one that is divisible.

Privileged bill (9). One that goes directly to the members of the House of Representatives for consideration. Bills without privilege must go through the Rules Committee. See *private bill; Private Calendar.*

Professional activist (6). One whose regular source of income is politics. See *activist; amateur activist.*

Progressive ambition (8). The desire among officeholders to win *election* to a higher office than they now hold. See *static ambition.*

Property law (12). The body of law that addresses an entire range of problems concerning more or less compatible uses of land and other resources as well as problems of title, trespass, and nuisance. See *administrative law; civil law; common law; constitutional law; criminal law; equity; organic law; statutory law.*

Property right (3). The legal ability to own title to a particular resource and the conditions under which the resource can be used and its title transferred (sold) to others.

Proportional representation system (4). An *election* system in which *voters* vote for a slate of candidates and in which a party wins a proportion of the seats in the representative assembly according to the proportion of votes its slate wins in the election. See *cumulative voting; single member district system.*

Prosecution immunity (12). An immunity against prosecution granted for testimony given, which bars further criminal actions on specified charges. See *use immunity.*

Protector of the peace (10). The president's legislatively and historically derived right to act in national emergencies and disasters such as natural disasters, strikes, riots, financial crises, or military attacks. See *chief of party; manager of prosperity; voice of the people; world leader.*

Public bad (3). A *collective good* that displays a *negative externality.* See *external cost; externality.*

Public choice (1). Decision making that occurs in the presence of force or the threat of force. See *collective action; private action; private choice.*

Public policy (1). The pattern of *collective action* in a nation. See *ideology.*

Pure strategy (2). In a game, a single *strategy* that a player chooses with 100 percent probability. See *mixed strategy.*

Rational choice (1). The postulate that people efficiently pursue their *goals;* purposive choice. See *decision theory; economic science; political science.*

Reciprocity (9). The practice by members of particular legislative committees or subcommittees to support or at least not interfere with decisions of members of other committees or subcommittees. See *universalism.*

Referendum (13). A *direct election* in which *citizens* choose a *public policy* without the immediate intervention of elected officeholders. See *direct (pure) democracy (democracy); indirect (representative) democracy (republic).*

Rehabilitation (12). The goal of sentencing criminals to programs that raise the expectation of a change in their personality, financial capabilities, or decision making. Methods of rehabilitation can range from psychoanalysis and behavior modification to formal education and job training. See *general deterrence; incapacitation; retribution; special deterrence; victim compensation.*

Reply (12). In a lawsuit, the plaintiff's response to the defendant's *cross complaint.* See *answer; complaint; pleadings; standing to sue.*

Representational focus (8). The manner in which an elected representative defines his constituency. For example, his focus may be his district, his state, his region, or the nation. See *delegate; fiduciary; politico; representational style; trustee.*

Representational style (8). The manner in which an elected representative defines his task of representation; he may be a *delegate,* who seeks to enact his constituents' stated preferences directly into law, or a *trustee,* who tries to enact his constituents' interests into law as *he* defines those interests, not as they define them; or, he may combine the delegate and trustee styles, in which case he is called a *politico.* See *fiduciary; representational focus.*

Res judicata (12). Once a cause of action has been litigated, it cannot be litigated again on a question of fact that the court has already decided. See *collateral estoppel; double jeopardy.*

Resource redistribution (3). An increase in one person's wealth, income, or *utility* at the expense of another person's wealth, income, or (sometimes) utility. Resource redistributions may occur as the result of both *private* and *public choice.*

Retribution (12). The goal of sentencing criminals to inflict harm on them in proportion to the harm they have done. Punishment for its own sake, not for *rehabilitation,* or other goals. See *general deterrence; incapacitation; special deterrence; victim compensation.*

Retrospective voting (5). A voting decision based on an assessment of the party's or candidates' past records in office.

Revolving door (11). The movement of private sector managers from their firms to the *independent regulatory commissions* that are supposed to regulate their firms and back again to the private sector. Sometimes the revolving door begins with the agency and then moves to the public sector. More recently, a revolving door has developed between certain regulatory agencies, such as the Environmental Protection Agency, and public interest groups concerned with problems the agencies regulate. See *capture hypothesis; life cycle.*

Rider amendment (9). An amendment to a Senate bill presently under consideration by the full Senate, which need not be germane to the subject of the original bill. A rider amendment can place an entirely new question before the full Senate for consideration.

Rule of four (12). An informal Supreme Court rule that the justices will hear any case if four justices so request.

Scarcity (1). A characteristic of decision makers that they must sometimes trade off the achievement of one *goal* for the achievement of another. See *complexity; conflict; methodological individualism; ordering; subjectiveness; variety.*

Secondary group (5). Organizations such as professional groups, labor unions, and large clubs. See *classificatory group; primary group.*

Security level (2). The lowest possible payoff a player can receive from choosing a particular strategy. See *maximin strategy; minimax strategy.*

Self-incrimination (12). The Fifth Amendment "right to remain silent" prevents involuntary self-incrimination. A defendant does not have to testify at his trial nor must he answer a police interrogator's questions before a trial or *indictment.*

Senatorial courtesy (9). If a federal officer will serve in a particular state, and if the president and at least one senator of that state are of the same party, then the president must clear a nomination for that office with the senator.

Seniority (9). The number of uninterrupted terms an elected official has been in office. Seniority in the House and Senate correlates with desirable committee appointments and holding important committee chairmanships.

Senior status (12). The judicial equivalent of retirement. However, federal judges with senior status often continue to hear cases.

Simple election (6). An election without *activists.* See *complex election.*

Single-member district system (4). An *election* system in which the state, nation, or other political unit is divided into districts, or jurisdictions; an election is then held in each district to send a single member to the legislature. See *cumulative voting; proportional representation system.*

Size principle (2). For certain classes of *n*-person *zero-sum games,* only *minimum winning coalitions* form.

Spatial theory (7). A theory of the electoral process using the concept of *issue* spaces, or issue dimensions, over which citizens' preferences are distributed and on which candidates adopt *issue position strategies* to win.

Special deterrence (12). The goal of sentencing criminals to teach them how unpleasant imprisonment can be, leading them to reassess the costs of imprisonment so that when confronted with the opportunity to commit a *crime* in the future, they will decide that the expected costs outweigh the expected benefits. See *general deterrence; incapacitation; rehabilitation; retribution; victim compensation.*

Specific performance (12). In a suit at *equity,* the judge's order that the losing party perform under the terms of the *contract* that has been breached. See *common law; injunction; injunctive relief.*

Standing to sue (12). "That a party has sufficient stake in an otherwise justiciable controversy to obtain judicial resolution of that controversy."* See *answer; complaint; cross complaint; pleadings; reply.*

Stare decisis (12). "The policy of courts to stand by *precedent* and not to disturb settled point."*

State of nature (2). The event connecting *alternatives* and *outcomes.* The prevailing condition in some decision situation if a particular alternative or *strategy* is chosen. The decision of an opponent in a *game of strategy.*

Static ambition (8). The desire among officeholders to win reelection to the same office they now hold. See *progressive ambition.*

Statutory construction (12). The action of a court in deciding what a statute, an act of Congress, means. See *judicial review.*

Statutory law (12). Law created by the members of a legislature, for example, law enacted by the members of Congress. Statutory law also includes treaties and executive agreements. See *administrative law; civil law; common law; constitutional law; criminal law; equity; organic law; property law.*

Strategy (2). The action a decision maker chooses (from among other strategies) in *decision making under conditions of uncertainty* (as in *games of strategy*). See *alternative.*

Strict liability (12). A *tort* arising under strict liability, liability without fault, holds a person liable for injury caused to others even if the defendant acted as a "reasonable man" would act. Judges usually impose strict liability when the activity causing the injury is inherently an "abnormally" dangerous one. See *intentional tort; negligence.*

Subjectiveness (1). *Goals* are personal; no scientific basis exists for claiming that one person's goals are better than another's. See *complexity; conflict; interpersonal comparison of utility; methodological individualism; ordering; scarcity; variety.*

Subject-matter jurisdiction (12). The jurisdiction of a court to try cases involving particular kinds of complaints. For example, a tax court lacks subject-matter jurisdiction over a trial on the charge of murder. See *in personam jurisdiction.*

Summary dismissal (12). Following the *pleadings* in a lawsuit, and upon a motion for summary dismissal, the judge may decide that a *complaint* or *cross complaint* is without merit and grant the motion for summary dismissal made respectively by the defendant or plaintiff. See *summary judgment.*

Summary judgment (12). Following a motion for summary judgment, the court may decide the issues raised in the *complaint* and *cross complaint,* based on the *pleadings* before the court. See *summary dismissal.*

Sunset legislation (13). A law requiring a set of *bureaus* to undergo periodic review, which might result in the bureaus' or their programs' being abolished.

Suspension of the rules (9). Any rule of the House of Representatives (and of many other legislative bodies) may be suspended by a vote of at least two-thirds of a quorum. Suspension of the rules in the House is sometimes used to bypass committee consideration of a particular bill. See *cloture; discharge petition.*

Symmetric preference distribution (5). One that has the same number of people preferring positions on either side and equidistant from the *median.* See *bimodal preference distribution; mean; mode; unimodal preference distribution.*

Systemic reforms (13). Those reforms that try to change the entire environment or results of public policy decision making. See *piecemeal reforms.*

TANSTAAFL (1). "There ain't no such thing as a free lunch." See *complexity; conflict; scarcity; variety.*

Tort (12). "A private or civil wrong or injury, other than a breach of contract, for which the court will provide a remedy in the form of an action for damages."* All tort actions must have three elements: "Existence of legal duty from defendant to plaintiff, breach of duty, and damage as a proximate result."* See *intentional tort; negligence; strict liability.*

Transitive preference ordering (1). A decision maker has such a *preference ordering* if he prefers *X* to *Z* (or is indifferent as between them) when he prefers *X* to *Y* (or is indifferent as between them) and *Y* to *Z* (or is indifferent as between them) for all possible *X*'s, *Y*'s, and *Z*'s. See *axiom of transitivity; complete preference ordering; intransitive preference ordering; ordering.*

Trustee (8). A representative who seeks to represent his constituents by enacting laws in their interest as *he* defines their interest, not as they do. See *delegate; fiduciary; politico; representational focus; representational style.*

Two-person game (2). A game with two players. See *n-person game.*

Unicameralism (9). The constitutional provision for a legislative body of only one house. See *bicameralism.*

Unimodal preference distribution (5). A *preference distribution* that has at most one *mode.* See *bimodal preference distribution.*

Universal admissibility of individual orderings (3). The first condition of Arrow's impossibility theorem; all possible individual *preference orderings* of *alternatives* under consideration must themselves be considered in a public- or private-choice procedure. See *Arrow's paradox; citizens' sovereignty; independence from irrelevant alternatives; non-dictatorship; non-perversity (positive association of individual and social values).*

Universalism (9). A practice by members of congressional committees, which leads them to include benefits in their legislation for as many members of the entire House or Senate as possible. See *reciprocity.*

Use immunity (12). A person has use immunity if he gives evidence to a court or congressional hearing in exchange for an agreement that the information he gives will not be used against him in subsequent legal actions. See *prosecution immunity.*

Utile (2). A unit of *utility.*

Utility (2). A decision maker's personal, comparative evaluation of different outcomes. See *expected utility; expected value; utile; value.*

Value (2). An external, objective standard that counts (enumerates) the number of units in an outcome. See *expected value; utility.*

Variety (1). The characteristic of decision situations that different decision makers hold different *goals;* that decision makers hold different *preference orderings* over *outcomes.* See *complexity; conflict; methodological individualism; ordering; scarcity; subjectiveness.*

Veto (9). The president's withholding of constitutionally required approval of a bill passed by the House and Senate. When the president vetoes a bill, he sends it back to the chamber in which it originated, stating his reasons for disapproval. See *pocket veto.*

Victim compensation (12). The goal of sentencing criminals to compensate the victim, the form of payment being punishment inflicted on the felon. Compensatory payment of this nature replaces personal *retribution* with retribution in the name of the "State." See *general deterrence; incapacitation; rehabilitation; special deterrence.*

Voice of the people (10). The president's historically derived right to be "the leading formulator and expounder of public opinion in the United States." The president's ability to preempt public opinion by stating a clear view of what *public policy* should be or by stating the existing public policy consensus as he sees it. See *chief of party; manager of prosperity; protector of the peace; world leader.*

Voluntary action (2). *Private action.* See *collective action.*

Voter (4). In an *election,* a *citizen* who decides to cast a ballot.

Welfare loss (11). The hypothetical economic loss brought about by the presence of a *monopoly,* usually defined by the added price a monopolistic firm charges above the competitive price and the lower output of the monopoly as compared with the output of a competitive firm.

World leader (10). The president's historically derived right to participate in and lead the international *coalitions* of which the United States is a member; this right grows out of the military and economic preeminence of the United States. See *chief of party; manager of prosperity; protector of the peace; voice of the people.*

Writ of appeal (12). A petition to the Supreme Court concerning a case that by statutory law the court must consider and either take or explain its reasons for not doing so. Cases also included are those in which: a state's highest appellate court finds a federal law (including treaties) unconstitutional or otherwise upholds a state law or state constitutional provision against the claim that it contradicts federal law or the Constitution; a federal court of appeals finds that a state law or some part of a state's constitution violates the Federal Constitution, or the same court finds a federal law unconstitutional and the United States is a party to the suit; a federal district court proceeding has been held, the United States is a party, and a federal law has been held unconstitutional; The United States is a party in a civil suit concerning federal antitrust laws, interstate commerce, or communication laws. A special three-judge district court panel has been required to sit and appeal is being taken if the three-judge panel issues or fails to issue an injunction and the losing party wishes to appeal; a federal court has declared a federal law unconstitutional. Such cases go on the Court's *Appellate Docket.*

Writ of *certiorari* (12). Using this procedure, a petitioner tells the Supreme Court why it should be interested in a case and why the case falls within the Court's *appellate jurisdiction.* This writ literally requires the lower court whose decision the petitioner is appealing to send a certified record of the case to the Supreme Court.

Writ of *habeas corpus* (12). A writ issued by a judge requiring that a person be released from imprisonment when the judge believes that the imprisonment is unlawful. For example, a writ of *habeas corpus* can be applied if the trial court sentencing the imprisoned person did not have *in personam jurisdiction.*

Writ of *mandamus* (12). A litigant petitions a court for a writ of *mandamus* when he asks the court to order a government officer to act in a particular manner. A writ of *mandamus* is a command given by a court to a lower court or government official requiring him to do or to cease doing a particular act.

Zero-sum game (2). A game for which the payoffs to the players sum to zero for all possible *strategies* chosen. In a two-person zero-sum game the payoffs sum to zero for each pair of strategies chosen. See *constant-sum game; nonzero-sum game.*

Appendix B

The Constitution of the United States

We the People of the United States, in Order to form a more perfect Union, establish Justice, insure domestic Tranquility, provide for the common defence, promote the general Welfare, and secure the Blessings of Liberty to ourselves and our Posterity, do ordain and establish this Constitution for the United States of America.

Article I

SECTION 1. All legislative Powers herein granted shall be vested in a Congress of the United States, which shall consist of a Senate and House of Representatives.

SECTION 2. The House of Representatives shall be composed of Members chosen every second Year by the People of the several States, and the Electors in each State shall have the Qualifications requisite for Electors of the most numerous Branch of the State Legislature.

No Person shall be a Representative who shall not have attained to the age of twenty five Years, and been seven Years a Citizen of the United States, and who shall not, when elected, be an Inhabitant of that State in which he shall be chosen.

Representatives and direct Taxes shall be apportioned among the several States which may be included within this Union, according to their respective Numbers, *which shall be determined by adding to the whole Number of free Persons, including those bound to Service for a Term of Years,* and excluding Indians not taxed, *three fifths of all other persons.*[1] The actual Enumeration shall be made within three Years after the first Meeting of the Congress of the United States, and within every subsequent Term of ten Years, in such Manner as they shall by Law direct. The Number of Representatives shall not exceed one for every thirty Thousand, but each State shall have at Least one Representative; and until such enumeration shall be made, the State of New Hampshire shall be entitled to chuse three, Massachusetts eight, Rhode-Island and Providence Plantations one, Connecticut five, New-York six, New Jersey four, Pennsylvania eight, Delaware one, Maryland six, Virginia ten, North Carolina five, South Carolina five, and Georgia three.

---

1. Throughout, italics are used to indicate passages altered by subsequent amendments. In this instance, for example, see Fourteenth Amendment.

When vacancies happen in the Representation from any State, the Executive Authority thereof shall issue Writs of Election to fill such Vacancies.

The House of Representatives shall chuse their Speaker and other Officers; and shall have the sole Power of Impeachment.

SECTION 3. The Senate of the United States shall be composed of two Senators from each State, *chosen by the Legislature thereof,*[2] for six Years; and each Senator shall have one Vote.

Immediately after they shall be assembled in Consequence of the first Election, they shall be divided as equally as may be into three Classes. The Seats of the Senators of the first Class shall be vacated at the Expiration of the second Year, of the second Class at the Expiration of the fourth Year, and of the third Class at the Expiration of the sixth Year, so that one third may be chosen every second Year; *and if Vacancies happen by Resignation, or otherwise, during the Recess of the Legislature of any State, the Executive thereof may make temporary Appointments until the next Meeting of the Legislature, which shall then fill such Vacancies.*[3]

No Person shall be a Senator who shall not have attained to the Age of thirty Years, and been nine Years a Citizen of the United States, and who shall not, when elected, be an Inhabitant of the State for which he shall be chosen.

The Vice President of the United States shall be President of the Senate, but shall have no Vote, unless they be equally divided.

The Senate shall chuse their other Officers, and also a President pro tempore, in the Absence of the Vice President, or when he shall exercise the Office of President of the United States.

The Senate shall have the sole Power to try all Impeachments. When sitting for that Purpose, they shall be on Oath or Affirmation. When the President of the United States is tried, the Chief Justice shall preside: And no Person shall be convicted without the Concurrence of two thirds of the Members present.

Judgment in Cases of Impeachment shall not extend further than to removal from Office, and disqualification to hold and enjoy any Office of honor, Trust or Profit under the United States: but the Party convicted shall nevertheless be liable and subject to Indictment, Trial, Judgment and Punishment, according to Law.

SECTION 4. The Times, Places and Manner of holding Elections for Senators and Representatives, shall be prescribed in each State by the Legislature thereof; but the Congress may at any time by Law make or alter such Regulations, except as to the Places of chusing Senators.

The Congress shall assemble at least once in every Year, and such Meeting shall be on the first Monday in December, unless they shall by Law appoint a different Day.[4]

SECTION 5. Each House shall be the Judge of the Elections, Returns and Qualifications of its own Members, and a Majority of each shall constitute a Quorum to do Business; but a smaller Number may adjourn from day to day, and

---

2. See Seventeenth Amendment.
3. See Seventeenth Amendment.
4. See Twentieth Amendment.

may be authorized to compel the Attendance of absent Members, in such Manner, and under such Penalties as each House may provide.

Each House may determine the Rules of its Proceedings, punish its Members for disorderly Behaviour, and, with the Concurrence of two thirds, expel a Member.

Each House shall keep a Journal of its Proceedings, and from time to time publish the same, excepting such Parts as may in their Judgment require Secrecy; and the Yeas and Nays of the Members of either House on any question shall, at the Desire of one fifth of those Present, be entered on the Journal.

Neither House, during the Session of Congress, shall, without the Consent of the other, adjourn for more than three days, nor to any other Place than that in which the two Houses shall be sitting.

SECTION 6. The Senators and Representatives shall receive a Compensation for their Services, to be ascertained by Law, and paid out of the Treasury of the United States. They shall in all Cases, except Treason, Felony and Breach of the Peace, be privileged from Arrest during their Attendance at the Session of their respective Houses, and in going to and returning from the same; and for any Speech or Debate in either House, they shall not be questioned in any other Place.

No Senator or Representative shall, during the Time for which he was elected, be appointed to any civil Office under the Authority of the United States, which shall have been created, or the Emoluments whereof shall have been encreased during such time; and no Person holding any Office under the United States, shall be a Member of either House during his Continuance in Office.

SECTION 7. All bills for raising Revenue shall originate in the house of Representatives; but the Senate may propose or concur with Amendments as on other Bills.

Every Bill which shall have passed the House of Representatives and the Senate, shall, before it become a Law, be presented to the President of the United States; if he approve he shall sign it, but if not he shall return it, with his Objections to that House in which it shall have originated, who shall enter the Objections at large on their Journal, and proceed to reconsider it. If after such Reconsideration two thirds of that House shall agree to pass the Bill, it shall be sent, together with the Objections, to the other House, by which it shall likewise be reconsidered, and if approved by two thirds of that House, it shall become a Law. But in all such Cases the Votes of both Houses shall be determined by Yeas and Nays, and the Names of the Persons voting for and against the Bill shall be entered on the Journal of each House respectively. If any Bill shall not be returned by the President within ten Days (Sundays excepted) after it shall have been presented to him, the Same shall be a Law, in like Manner as if he had signed it, unless the Congress by their Adjournment prevent its Return, in which Case it shall not be a Law.

Every Order, Resolution, or Vote to which the Concurrence of the Senate and House of Representatives may be necessary (except on a question of Adjournment) shall be presented to the President of the United States; and before the Same shall take Effect, shall be approved by him, or being disapproved by him, shall be repassed by two thirds of the Senate and House of

Representatives, according to the Rules and Limitations prescribed in the Case of a Bill.

SECTION 8. The Congress shall have Power To lay and collect Taxes, Duties, Imposts and Excises, to pay the Debts and provide for the common Defence and general Welfare of the United States; but all Duties, Imposts and Excises shall be uniform throughout the United States;

To borrow Money on the credit of the United States;

To regulate Commerce with foreign Nations, and among the several States, and with the Indian Tribes;

To establish an uniform Rule of Naturalization, and uniform Laws on the subject of Bankruptcies throughout the United States;

To coin Money, regulate the Value thereof, and of foreign Coin, and fix the Standard of Weights and Measures;

To provide for the Punishment of counterfeiting the Securities and current Coin of the United States;

To establish Post Offices and post Roads;

To promote the Progress of Science and useful Arts, by securing for limited Times to Authors and Inventors the exclusive Right to their respective Writings and Discoveries;

To constitute Tribunals inferior to the Supreme Court;

To define and punish Piracies and Felonies committed on the high Seas, and Offences against the Law of Nations;

To declare War, grant Letters of Marque and Reprisal, and make Rules concerning Captures on Land and Water;

To raise and support Armies, but no Appropriation of Money to that Use shall be for a longer Term than two Years;

To provide and maintain a Navy;

To make Rules for the Government and Regulation of the land and naval Forces;

To provide for calling forth the Militia to execute the Laws of the Union, suppress Insurrections and repel Invasions;

To provide for organizing, arming, and disciplining, the Militia, and for governing such Part of them as may be employed in the Service of the United States, reserving to the States respectively, the Appointment of the Officers, and the Authority of training the Militia according to the discipline prescribed by Congress;

To exercise exclusive Legislation in all Cases whatsoever, over such District (not exceeding ten Miles square) as may, by Cession of particular States, and the Acceptance of Congress, become the Seat of the Government of the United States, and to exercise like Authority over all Places purchased by the Consent of the Legislature of the State in which the Same shall be, for the Erection of Forts, Magazines, Arsenals, dock-Yards, and other needful Buildings;—And

To make all Laws which shall be necessary and proper for carrying into Execution the foregoing Powers, and all other Powers vested by this Constitution in the Government of the United States, or in any Department or Officer thereof.

SECTION 9. The Migration or Importation of such Persons as any of the States now existing shall think proper to admit, shall not be prohibited by the Congress prior to the Year one thousand eight hundred and eight, but a Tax or duty may be imposed on such Importation, not exceeding ten dollars for each Person.

The Privilege of the Writ of Habeas Corpus shall not be suspended, unless when in Cases of Rebellion or Invasion the public Safety may require it.

No Bill of Attainder or ex post facto Law shall be passed.

No Capitation, or other direct, Tax shall be laid, unless in Proportion to the Census or Enumeration herein before directed to be taken.

No Tax or Duty shall be laid on Articles exported from any State.

No Preference shall be given by any Regulation of Commerce or Revenue to the Ports of one State over those of another: nor shall Vessels bound to, or from, one State, be obliged to enter, clear, or pay Duties in another.

No Money shall be drawn from the Treasury, but in Consequence of Appropriations made by Law; and a regular Statement and Account of the Receipts and Expenditures of all public Money shall be published from time to time.

No title of Nobility shall be granted by the United States: And no Person holding any Office of Profit or Trust under them, shall, without the Consent of the Congress, accept any present, Emolument, Office, or Title, of any kind whatever, from any King, Prince, or foreign State.

SECTION 10. No State shall enter into any Treaty, Alliance, or Confederation; grant Letters of Marque and Reprisal; coin Money; emit Bills of Credit; make any Thing but gold and silver Coin a Tender in Payment of Debts; pass any Bill of Attainder, ex post facto Law, or Law impairing the Obligation of Contracts, or Grant any Title of Nobility.

No State shall, without the Consent of the Congress, lay any Imposts or Duties on Imports or Exports, except what may be absolutely necessary for executing its inspection Laws: and the net Produce of all Duties and Imposts, laid by any State on Imports or Exports shall be for the Use of the Treasury of the United States; and all such Laws shall be subject to the Revision and Control of the Congress.

No State shall, without the Consent of Congress, lay any Duty of Tonnage, keep Troops, or Ships of War in time of Peace, enter into any Agreement or Compact with another State, or with a foreign Power, or engage in War, unless actually invaded, or in such imminent Danger as will not admit of delay.

Article II

SECTION 1. The executive Power shall be vested in a President of the United States of America. He shall hold his Office during the Term of four Years, and, together with the Vice President, chosen for the same Term be elected as follows:

Each State shall appoint, in such Manner as the Legislature thereof may direct, a Number of Electors, equal to the whole Number of Senators and Representatives to which the State may be entitled in the Congress but no Senator or Representative, or Person holding an Office of Trust or Profit under the United States, shall be appointed an Elector.

The Electors shall meet in their respective States, and vote by Ballot for two Persons, of whom one at least shall not be an Inhabitant of the same State with themselves. And they shall make a List of all the Persons voted for, and of the Number of Votes for each; which List they shall sign and certify, and transmit sealed to the Seat of the Government of the United States, directed to the President of the Senate. The President of the Senate shall, in the Presence of the Senate and House of Representatives, open all the Certificates, and the Votes shall then be counted. The Person having the greatest Number of Votes shall be the President, if such Number be a Majority of the whole Number of Electors appointed; and if there be more than one who have such Majority, and have an equal Number of Votes, then the House of Representatives shall immediately chuse by Ballot one of them for President; and if no Person have a Majority, then from the five highest on the List the said House shall in like Manner chuse the President. But in chusing the President, the Votes shall be taken by States, the Representation from each State having one Vote; A quorum for this purpose shall consist of a Member or Members from two thirds of the States, and a Majority of all the States shall be necessary to a Choice. In every Case, after the Choice of the President, the Person having the greatest Number of Votes of the Electors shall be the Vice President. But if there should remain two or more who have equal Votes, the Senate shall chuse from them by Ballot the Vice President.[5]

The Congress may determine the Time of chusing the Electors, and the Day on which they shall give their Votes; which Day shall be the same throughout the United States.

No Person except a natural born Citizen, or a Citizen of the United States, at the time of the Adoption of this Constitution, shall be eligible to the Office of President; neither shall any Person be eligible to that Office who shall not have attained to the Age of thirty five Years, and been fourteen Years a Resident within the United States.

In Case of the Removal of the President from Office, or of his Death, Resignation, or Inability to discharge the Powers and Duties of the said Office, the Same shall devolve on the Vice President, and the Congress may by Law provide for the Case of Removal, Death, Resignation or Inability, both of the President and Vice President, declaring what Officer shall then act as President, and such Officer shall act accordingly, until the Disability be removed, or a President shall be elected.[6]

The President shall, at stated Times, receive for his Services, a Compensation which shall neither be encreased nor diminished during the Period for which he shall have been elected, and he shall not receive within that Period any other Emolument from the United States, or any of them.

Before he enter on the Execution of his Office, he shall take the following Oath or Affirmation:—"I do solemnly swear (or affirm) that I will faithfully execute the Office of President of the United States, and will to the best of my Ability, preserve, protect and defend the Constitution of the United States."

SECTION 2. The President shall be Commander in Chief of the Army and Navy of the United States, and of the Militia of the several States, when called into

---

5. Superseded by the Twelfth Amendment.
6. See Twenty-fifth Amendment.

the actual service of the United States; he may require the Opinion, in writing, of the principal Officer in each of the executive Departments, upon any Subject relating to the Duties of their respective Offices, and he shall have Power to grant Reprieves and Pardons for Offences against the United States, except in Cases of Impeachment.

He shall have Power, by and with the Advice and Consent of the Senate, to make Treaties, provided two thirds of the Senators present concur; and he shall nominate, and by and with the Advice and Consent of the Senate, shall appoint Ambassadors, and other public Ministers and Consuls, Judges of the supreme Court, and all other Officers of the United States, whose Appointments are not herein otherwise provided for, and which shall be established by Law: but the Congress may by Law vest the Appointment of such inferior Officers, as they think proper, in the President alone, in the Courts of Law, or in the Heads of Departments.

The President shall have Power to fill up all Vacancies that may happen during the Recess of the Senate, by granting Commissions which shall expire at the End of their next Session.

SECTION 3. He shall from time to time give to the Congress Information of the State of the Union, and recommend to their Consideration such Measures as he shall judge necessary and expedient; he may, on extraordinary Occasions, convene both Houses, or either of them, and in Case of Disagreement between them, with Respect to the Time of Adjournment, he may adjourn them to such Time as he shall think proper; he shall receive Ambassadors and other public Ministers, he shall take Care that the Laws be faithfully executed, and shall Commission all the Officers of the United States.

SECTION 4. The President, Vice President, and all civil Officers of the United States, shall be removed from Office on Impeachment for, and Conviction of Treason, Bribery, or other high Crimes and Misdemeanors.

Article III

SECTION 1. The judicial Power of the United States, shall be vested in one supreme Court and in such inferior Courts as the Congress may from time to time ordain and establish. The Judges, both of the supreme and inferior Courts, shall hold their Offices during good Behaviour, and shall, at stated Times, receive for their Services, a Compensation, which shall not be diminished during their Continuance in Office.

SECTION 2. The judicial Power shall extend to all Cases, in Law and Equity, arising under this Constitution, the Laws of the United States, and Treaties made, or which shall be made, under the Authority;—to all Cases affecting Ambassadors, other public Ministers and Consuls;—to all Cases of admiralty and maritime Jurisdiction;—to Controversies to which the United States shall be a Party—to Controversies between two or more States;—*between a State and Citizens of another State*[7]—between Citizens of different States;—between Citizens of the same State claiming Lands under Grants of different States, *and between a State or the Citizens thereof, and foreign States, Citizens, or Subjects.*[8]

7. See Eleventh Amendment.
8. See Eleventh Amendment.

In all cases affecting Ambassadors, other public Ministers and Consuls, and those in which a State shall be Party, the supreme Court shall have original Jurisdiction. In all the other Cases before mentioned, the supreme Court shall have appellate Jurisdiction, both as to Law and Fact, with such exceptions, and under such Regulations as the Congress shall make.

The Trial of all Crimes, except in Cases of Impeachment, shall be by Jury; and such Trial shall be held in the State where the said Crimes shall have been committed; but when not committed within any State, the Trial shall be at such Place or Places as the Congress may by Law have directed. SECTION 3. Treason against the United States, shall consist only in levying War against them, or in adhering to their Enemies, giving them Aid and Comfort. No Person shall be convicted of Treason unless on the Testimony of two Witnesses to the same overt Act, or on Confession in open Court.

The Congress shall have Power to declare the Punishment of Treason, but no Attainder of Treason shall work Corruption of Blood, or Forfeiture except during the Life of the Person attained.

Article IV

SECTION 1. Full Faith and Credit shall be given in each State to the public Acts, Records, and judicial Proceedings of every other State. And the Congress may by general Laws prescribe the Manner in which such Acts, Records, and Proceedings shall be proved, and the Effect thereof.

SECTION 2. The Citizens of each State shall be entitled to all Privileges and Immunities of Citizens in the several States.

A Person charged in any State with Treason, Felony, or other Crime, who shall flee from Justice, and be found in another State, shall on Demand of the executive Authority of the State from which he fled, be delivered up, to be removed to the State having Jurisdiction of the Crime.

No Person held to Service or Labour in one State, under the Laws thereof, escaping into another, shall, in Consequence of any Law or Regulation therein, be discharged from such Service or Labour, but shall be delivered up on Claim of the Party to whom such Service or Labour may be due.[9]

SECTION 3. New States may be admitted by the Congress into this Union; but no new State shall be formed or erected within the Jurisdiction of any other State; nor any State be formed by the Junction of two or more States, or Parts of States, without the Consent of the Legislatures of the States concerned as well as of the Congress.

The Congress shall have Power to dispose of and make all needful Rules and Regulations respecting the Territory or other Property belonging to the United States; and nothing in this Constitution shall be so construed as to Prejudice any claims of the United States, or of any particular State.

SECTION 4. The United States shall guarantee to every State in this Union a Republican Form of Government, and shall protect each of them against Invasion; and on Application of the Legislature, or of the Executive (when the Legislature cannot be convened) against domestic Violence.

---

9. See Thirteenth Amendment.

Article V

The Congress, whenever two thirds of both Houses shall deem it necessary, shall propose Amendments to this Constitution, or, on the Application of the Legislatures of two thirds of the several States, shall call a Convention for proposing Amendments, which, in either Case, shall be valid to all Intents and Purposes, as Part of this Constitution, when ratified by the Legislatures of three fourths of the several States, or by Conventions in three fourths thereof, as the one or the other Mode of Ratification may be proposed by the Congress; Provided that no Amendment which may be made prior to the Year One thousand eight hundred and eight shall in any Manner affect the first and fourth Clauses in the Ninth Section of the first Article; and that no State, without its Consent, shall be deprived of its equal Suffrage in the Senate.

Article VI

All Debts contracted and Engagements entered into, before the Adoption of this Constitution, shall be as valid against the United States under this Constitution, as under the Confederation.

This Constitution, and the Laws of the United States which shall be made in Pursuance thereof; and all Treaties made, or which shall be made, under the Authority of the United States, shall be the supreme Law of the Land; and the Judges in every State shall be bound thereby, any Thing in the Constitution or Laws of any State to the Contrary notwithstanding.

The Senators and Representatives before mentioned, and the Members of the several State Legislatures, and all executive and judicial Officers, both of the United States and of the several States, shall be bound by Oath or Affirmation, to support this Constitution; but no religious Test shall ever be required as a Qualification to any Office or public Trust under the United States.

Article VII

The Ratification of the Conventions of nine States, shall be sufficient for the Establishment of this Constitution between the States so ratifying the Same.

Done in Convention by the Unanimous Consent of the States present the Seventeenth Day of September in the Year of our Lord one thousand seven hundred and eighty seven and of the Independence of the United States of America the twelfth. In witness whereof We have hereunto subscribed our Names.

ARTICLES IN ADDITION TO, AND AMENDMENT OF, THE CONSTITUTION OF THE UNITED STATES OF AMERICA, PROPOSED BY CONGRESS, AND RATIFIED BY THE LEGISLATURES OF THE SEVERAL STATES, PURSUANT TO THE FIFTH ARTICLE OF THE ORIGINAL CONSTITUTION.

Amendment I

[Ratification of the first ten amendments was completed December 15, 1791.]

Congress shall make no law respecting an establishment of religion, or prohibiting the free exercise thereof; or abridging the freedom of speech, or of the press; or the right of the people peaceably to assemble, and to petition the Government for a redress of grievances.

Amendment II

A well regulated Militia, being necessary to the security of a free State, the right of the people to keep and bear Arms, shall not be infringed.

Amendment III

No Soldier shall, in time of peace be quartered in any house, without the consent of the Owner, nor in time of war, but in a manner to be prescribed by law.

Amendment IV

The right of the people to be secure in their persons, houses, papers, and effects, against unreasonable searches and seizures, shall not be violated, and no Warrants shall issue, but upon probable cause, supported by Oath or affirmation, and particularly describing the place to be searched, and the persons or things to be seized.

Amendment V

No person shall be held to answer for a capital, or otherwise infamous crime, unless on a presentment or indictment of a Grand Jury, except in cases arising in the land or naval forces, or in the Militia, when in actual service in time of War or public danger; nor shall any person be subject for the same offence to be twice put in jeopardy of life or limb; nor shall be compelled in any criminal case to be witness against himself, nor be deprived of life, liberty, or property, without due process of law; nor shall private property be taken for public use, without just compensation.

Amendment VI

In all criminal prosecutions, the accused shall enjoy the right to a speedy and public trial, by an impartial jury of the State and district wherein the crime shall have been committed, which district shall have been previously ascertained by law, and to be informed of the nature and cause of the accusation; to be confronted with the witnesses against him; to have compulsory process for obtaining witnesses in his favor, and to have the Assistance of Counsel for his defence.

Amendment VII

In Suits at common law, where the value in controversy shall exceed twenty dollars, the right of trial by jury shall be preserved, and no fact tried by a jury, shall be otherwise reexamined in any Court of the United States, than according to the rules of the common law.

Amendment VIII

Excessive bail shall not be required, nor excessive fines imposed, nor cruel and unusual punishments inflicted.

Amendment IX

The enumeration in the Constitution, of certain rights, shall not be construed to deny or disparage others retained by the people.

Amendment X

The powers not delegated to the United States by the Constitution, nor prohibited by it to the States, are reserved to the States respectively, or to the people.

Amendment XI

[January 8, 1798]

The Judicial power of the United States shall not be construed to extend to any suit in law or equity, commenced or prosecuted against one of the United States by Citizens of another State, or by Citizens or Subjects of any Foreign State.

Amendment XII

[September 25, 1804]

The Electors shall meet in their respective states and vote by ballot for President and Vice President, one of whom, at least, shall not be an inhabitant of the same state with themselves; they shall name in their ballots the person voted for as President, and in distinct ballots the person voted for as Vice President, and they shall make distinct lists of all persons voted for as President, and of all persons voted for as Vice President, and of the number of votes for each, which lists they shall sign and certify, and transmit sealed to the seat of the government of the United States, directed to the President of the Senate;–The President of the Senate shall, in the presence of the Senate and House of Representatives, open all the certificates and the votes shall then be counted;–The person having the greatest number of votes for President, shall be the President, if such number be a majority of the whole number of Electors appointed; and if no person have such majority, then from the persons having the highest numbers not exceeding three on the list of those voted for as President, the House of Representatives shall choose immediately, by ballot, the President. But in choosing the President, the votes shall be taken by states, the representation from each state having one vote; a quorum for this purpose shall consist of a member or members from two thirds of the states, and a majority of all the states shall be necessary to a choice. And if the House of Representatives shall not choose a President whenever the right of choice shall devolve upon them, *before the fourth day of March next following,*[10] then the Vice President shall act as President, as in the case of the death or other constitutional disability of the President.—The person having the greatest number of votes as Vice President shall be the Vice President, if such number be a majority of the whole number of Electors appointed, and if no person have a majority, then from the two highest numbers on the list, the Senate shall choose the Vice President; a quorum for the purpose shall consist of two-thirds of the whole number of Senators, and a majority of the whole number shall be necessary to a choice. But no person constitutionally ineligible to the office of President shall be eligible to that of Vice President of the United States.

Amendment XIII

[December 18, 1865]

SECTION 1. Neither slavery nor involuntary servitude, except as a punishment for crime whereof the party shall have been duly convicted, shall exist within the United States, or any place subject to their jurisdiction.

SECTION 2. Congress shall have power to enforce this article by appropriate legislation.

Amendment XIV

[July 28, 1869]

SECTION 1. All persons born or naturalized in the United States, and subject to the jurisdiction thereof, are citizens of the United States and of the State wherein they reside. No State shall make or enforce any law which shall abridge the privileges or immunities of citizens of the United States; nor shall any State deprive any person of life, liberty or property, without due process of law; nor deny to any person within its jurisdiction the equal protection of the laws.

SECTION 2. Representatives shall be apportioned among the several States according to their respective numbers, counting the whole number of persons in each State, excluding Indians not taxed. But when the right to vote at any election for the choice of electors for President and Vice President of the United States, Representatives in Congress, the Executive and Judicial officers of a State, or the members of the Legislature thereof, is denied to any of the male inhabitants of such State, being twenty-one years of age, and citizens of the United States, or in any way abridged, except for participation in rebellion, or other crime, the basis of representation therein shall be reduced in the proportion which the number of such male citizens shall bear to the whole number of male citizens twenty-one years of age in such State.

SECTION 3. No person shall be a Senator or Representative in Congress, or elector of President or Vice President, or hold any office, civil or military, under the United States, or under any State, who, having previously taken an oath, as a member of Congress, or as an officer of the United States, or as a member of any State legislature, or as an executive or judicial officer of any State, to support the Constitution of the United States, shall have engaged in insurrection or rebellion against the same, or given aid or comfort to the

10. Altered by the Twentieth Amendment.

enemies thereof. But Congress may by a vote of two thirds of each House, remove such disability.

SECTION 4. The validity of the public debt of the United States, authorized by law, including debts incurred for payment of pensions and bounties for services in suppressing insurrection or rebellion, shall not be questioned. But neither the United States nor any State shall assume or pay any debt or obligation incurred in aid of insurrection or rebellion against the United States, or any claim for the loss or emancipation of any slave; but all such debts, obligations, and claims shall be held illegal and void.

SECTION 5. The Congress shall have power to enforce, by appropriate legislation, the provisions of this article.

Amendment XV

[March 30, 1870]

SECTION 1. The right of citizens of the United States to vote shall not be denied or abridged by the United States or by any State on account of race, color, or previous condition of servitude.

SECTION 2. The Congress shall have power to enforce this article by appropriate legislation.

Amendment XVI

[February 25, 1913]

The Congress shall have power to lay and collect taxes on incomes, from whatever source derived, without apportionment among the several States, and without regard to any census or enumeration.

Amendment XVII

[May 31, 1913]

The Senate of the United States shall be composed of two Senators from each State, elected by the people thereof, for six years; and each Senator shall have one vote. The electors in each State shall have the qualifications requisite for electors of the most numerous branch of the State legislatures.

When vacancies happen in the representation of any State in the Senate, the executive authority of such State shall issue writs of election to fill such vacancies: *Provided,* That the legislature of any State may empower the executive thereof to make temporary appointments until the people fill the vacancies by election as the legislature may direct.

This amendment shall not be so construed as to affect the election or term of any Senator chosen before it becomes valid as part of the Constitution.

Amendment XVIII

[January 29, 1919]

SECTION 1. *After one year from the ratification of this article the manufacture, sale, or transportation of intoxicating liquors within, the importation thereof*

into, or the exportation thereof from the United States and all territory subject to the jurisdiction thereof for beverage purposes is hereby prohibited.
SECTION 2. *The Congress and the several States shall have concurrent power to enforce this article by appropriate legislation.*
SECTION 3. *This article shall be inoperative unless it shall have been ratified as an amendment to the Constitution by the legislatures of the several States, as provided in the Constitution, within seven years from the date of the submission hereof to the States by the Congress.*[11]

Amendment XIX

[August 26, 1920]

The right of citizens of the United States to vote shall not be denied or abridged by the United States or by any State on account of sex.

Congress shall have power to enforce this article by appropriate legislation.

Amendment XX

[February 6, 1933]

SECTION 1. The terms of the President and Vice President shall end at noon on the 20th day of January, and the terms of Senators and Representatives at noon on the 3rd day of January, of the years in which such terms would have ended if this article had not been ratified; and the terms of their successors shall then begin.
SECTION 2. The Congress shall assemble at least once in every year, and such meeting shall begin at noon on the 3rd day of January, unless they shall by law appoint a different day.
SECTION 3. If, at the time fixed for the beginning of the term of the President, the President elect shall have died, the Vice President elect shall become President. If a President shall not have been chosen before the time fixed for the beginning of his term, or if the President elect shall have failed to qualify, then the Vice President elect shall act as President until a President shall have qualified; and the Congress may by law provide for the case wherein neither a President elect nor a Vice President elect shall have qualified, declaring who shall then act as President, or the manner in which one who is to act shall be selected, and such person shall act accordingly until a President or Vice President shall have qualified.
SECTION 4. The Congress may by law provide for the case of the death of any of the persons from whom the House of Representatives may choose a President whenever the right of choice shall devolve upon them, and for the case of the death of any of the persons from whom the Senate may choose a Vice President whenever the right of choice shall have devolved upon them.
SECTION 5. Sections 1 and 2 shall take effect on the 15th day of October following the ratification of this article.
SECTION 6. This article shall be inoperative unless it shall have been ratified as

11. Repealed by the Twenty-first Amendment.

an amendment to the Constitution by the legislatures of three fourths of the several States within seven years from the date of its submission.

Amendment XXI

[December 5, 1933]

SECTION 1. The eighteenth article of amendment to the Constitution of the United States is hereby repealed.

SECTION 2. The transportation or importation into any State, Territory, or possession of the United States for delivery or use therein of intoxicating liquors, in violation of the laws thereof, is hereby prohibited.

SECTION 3. This article shall be inoperative unless it shall have been ratified as an amendment to the Constitution by conventions in the several States, as provided in the Constitution, within seven years from the date of the submission hereof to the States by the Congress.

Amendment XXII

[February 26, 1951]

SECTION 1. No person shall be elected to the office of the President more than twice, and no person who has held the office of President, or acted as President, for more than two years of a term to which some other person was elected President shall be elected to the office of President more than once. But this Article shall not apply to any person holding the office of President when this Article was proposed by the Congress, and shall not prevent any person who may be holding the office of President, or acting as President, during the term within which this Article becomes operative from holding the office of President or acting as President during the remainder of such term.

SECTION 2. This article shall be inoperative unless it shall have been ratified as an amendment to the Constitution by the legislatures of three fourths of the several States within seven years from the date of its submission to the States by the Congress.

Amendment XXIII

[March 29, 1961]

SECTION 1. The District constituting the seat of Government of the United States shall appoint in such manner as the Congress may direct:

A number of electors of President and Vice President equal to the whole number of Senators and Representatives in Congress to which the District would be entitled if it were a State, but in no event more than the least populous State; they shall be in addition to those appointed by the States, but they shall be considered, for the purposes of the election of President and Vice President, to be electors appointed by a State; and they shall meet in the district and perform such duties as provided by the twelfth article of amendment.

SECTION 2. The Congress shall have power to enforce this article by appropriate legislation.

Amendment XXIV

[January 23, 1964]

SECTION 1. The right of citizens of the United States to vote in any primary or other election for President or Vice President, for electors for President or Vice President, or for Senator or representative in Congress, shall not be denied or abridged by the United States or any state by reason of failure to pay any poll tax or other tax.

SECTION 2. The Congress shall have the power to enforce this article by appropriate legislation.

Amendment XXV

[February 19, 1967]

SECTION 1. In case of the removal of the President from office or of his death or resignation, the Vice President shall become President.

SECTION 2. Whenever there is a vacancy in the office of the Vice President, the President shall nominate a Vice President who shall take office upon confirmation by a majority vote of both Houses of Congress.

SECTION 3. Whenever the President transmits to the President pro tempore of the Senate and the Speaker of the House of Representatives his written declaration that he is unable to discharge the powers and duties of his office, and until he transmits to them a written declaration to the contrary, such powers and duties shall be discharged by the Vice President as Acting President.

SECTION 4. Whenever the Vice President and a majority of either the principal officers of the executive departments or of such other body as Congress may by law provide, transmit to the President pro tempore of the Senate and the Speaker of the House of Representatives their written declaration that the President is unable to discharge the powers and duties of his office, the Vice President shall immediately assume the powers and duties of the office as Acting President.

Thereafter, when the President transmits to the President pro tempore of the Senate and the Speaker of the House of Representatives his written declaration that no inability exists, he shall resume the powers and duties of his office unless the Vice President and a majority of either the principal officers of the executive departments or of such other body as Congress may by law provide, transmit within four days to the President pro tempore of the Senate and the Speaker of the House of Representatives their written declaration that the President is unable to discharge the powers and duties of his office. Thereupon Congress shall decide the issue, assembling within forty-eight hours for that purpose if not in session. If the Congress, within twenty-one days after receipt of the latter written declaration, or, if Congress is not in session, within twenty-one days after Congress is required to assemble, determines by two thirds vote of both Houses that the President is unable to discharge the powers and duties of his office, the Vice President shall continue to discharge the same as Acting President; otherwise, the President shall resume the powers and duties of his office.

Amendment XXVI

[June 30, 1971]

SECTION 1. The right of citizens of the United States, who are eighteen years of age or older, to vote shall not be denied or abridged by the United States or any State on account of age.

SECTION 2. The Congress shall have the power to enforce this article by appropriate legislation.

Proposed Constitutional Amendment[12]

SECTION 1. Equality of rights under the law shall not be denied or abridged by the United States or by any State on account of sex.

SECTION 2. The Congress shall have power to enforce, by appropriate legislation, the provisions of this article.

SECTION 3. This amendment shall take effect two years after date of ratification.

Proposed Constitutional Amendment[13]

SECTION 1. For purposes of representation in the Congress, election of the President and Vice President, and article V of this Constitution, the District constituting the seat of government of the United States shall be treated as though it were a State.

SECTION 2. The exercise of the rights and powers conferred under this article shall be by the people of the District constituting the seat of government, and as shall be provided by the Congress.

SECTION 3. The twenty-third article of amendment to the Constitution of the United States is hereby repealed.

SECTION 4. This article shall be inoperative, unless it shall have been ratified as an amendment to the Constitution by the legislatures of three-fourths of the several States within seven years from the date of its submission.

Proposed Constitutional Amendment[14]

SECTION 1. Total government outlays in any fiscal year shall not exceed the spending limit. The spending limit is equal to the average of total budget receipts in the three most recent fiscal years.

SECTION 2. Total government outlays include all budget and off-budget expenditures plus the present value of commitments for future outlays.

---

12. The Equal Rights Amendment was proposed by Congress and submitted to the states for ratification in March, 1972. In July, 1978, Congress extended the deadline on ratification to June, 1982.

13. Congress submitted this proposed amendment to the states for ratification in August, 1978.

14. Drafted by Professor Allan H. Meltzer, Carnegie-Mellon University; now under discussion in the Congress.

SECTION 3. The rate of growth of total budget receipts in any fiscal year shall not exceed the average rate of growth of an appropriate index in the most recently completed calendar year. The index shall be chosen by Congress and may be changed by ⅔ vote of each house.

SECTION 4. In the event that an emergency is declared by the President, the Congress may by ⅔ vote of each house authorize outlays for that fiscal year in excess of the spending limit.

SECTION 5. Congress shall enact all necessary legislation to implement the amendment.

Table of Cases

Names Index

Subject Index